Coercion to Compromise

NEW TITLES IN THE SERIES

Revolution and the Making of the Contemporary Legal Profession: England, France, and the United States
Michael Burrage

Regulating Commercial Gambling: Past, Present, and Future
David Miers

Law as a Social System
Niklas Luhmann; translated by Klaus A. Ziegert
Edited by Fatima Kastner, Richard Nobles, David Schiff, and Rosamund Ziegert

English Lawyers between Market and State: The Politics of Professionalism
Richard Abel

Coercion to

Compromise

Plea Bargaining, the Courts and the
Making of Political Authority

MARY E. VOGEL

UNIVERSITY PRESS

2007

OXFORD
UNIVERSITY PRESS

Oxford University Press, Inc., publishes works that further
Oxford University's objective of excellence
in research, scholarship, and education.

Oxford   New York
Auckland   Cape Town   Dar es Salaam   Hong Kong   Karachi
Kuala Lumpur   Madrid   Melbourne   Mexico City   Nairobi
New Delhi   Shanghai   Taipei   Toronto

With offices in
Argentina   Austria   Brazil   Chile   Czech Republic   France   Greece
Guatemala   Hungary   Italy   Japan   Poland   Portugal   Singapore
South Korea   Switzerland   Thailand   Turkey   Ukraine   Vietnam

Copyright © 2007 by Mary E. Vogel

Published by Oxford University Press, Inc.
198 Madison Avenue, New York, New York 10016

www.oup.com

Oxford is a registered trademark of Oxford University Press

Library of Congress Cataloging-in-Publication Data
Vogel, Mary E.
Coercion to compromise : plea bargaining, the courts, and the making of political
authority / Mary E. Vogel.
p. cm. — (Oxford socio-legal studies)
Includes bibliographical references and index.
ISBN 978-0-19-510174-4; 978-0-19-510175-1 (pbk.)
1. Plea bargaining—Social aspects—United States—History—19th century.
2. Plea bargaining—Massachusetts—Boston—History—19th century.
3. Social classes—Massachusetts—Boston—History—19th century.
I. Title.   II. Series.

KF9654.V64 2000
345.73'052—dc21   00-022944
                       Rev.

9 8 7 6 5 4 3 2 1

Printed in the United States of America
on acid-free paper

for
Tony Long
ami, inspirateur, compagnon, amour
with all my love

Preface

To many an observer, plea bargaining appears profoundly unjust. Perhaps most troubling about this practice, which has profoundly shaped American criminal law, is its seeming tendency to reward the underserving. Critics also see in the practice a certain coerciveness—especially when the granting of leniency is made contingent on the specific content of testimony or other act desired by a prosecutor. As one consequence, plea bargaining has sparked the popular imagination and generated enduring controversy. Yet, despite this interest, its origins remain surprisingly obscure.

Plea bargaining has been the subject of many important sociological and historical works such as Lawrence Friedman and Robert Percival's pathbreaking historical account of the practice in *The Roots of Justice: Crime and Punishment in Alameda County, California, 1870–1940* and Allen Steinberg's insightful analysis of its links to private prosecution in late-nineteenth-century Philadelphia. Although several scholars have persuasively argued that plea bargaining originated in the nineteenth century, none has claimed generalizability for any of the explanations previously advanced. My own work attempts to shed new light on circumstances, as yet unnoticed, surrounding the earliest instances of plea bargaining known to exist.

This book examines the important, but neglected, subject of how plea bargaining began by exploring the events attending its appearance in the city of Boston, Massachusetts, during the first half of the nineteenth century. In doing so, it contextualizes the rise of this controversial practice, considering in particular the political needs of the elite that led to its establishment. In the aftermath of the American Revolution, shipping and trade in foreign markets created a quite cohesive and stable social class of merchants and financiers. Out of this class emerged an elite which shaped the ideology of republicanism and, as a consequence, the imaginative construction of legal ideas in Boston during the 1830s and 1840s—a period that, significantly, was also the formative era of American law. It is this elite, its political strategies, and its adaptation of republicanism within the arena of the city's political and legal relationships that is the subject of the book. While the class consciousness of elites often proves weaker and less unitary in practice than initially suspected, such was not the case here where a sense of class interests and the actions that would foster them was strong.

While the focus of this study is on Boston's political elite and its response to the challenges facing it, no such group can be discussed apart from the context of the society and culture that produce it and that it tries to shape or lead to its own advantage. Hence, this work also treats other social groups and classes, especially in examining both the social conflict that gave rise to plea bargaining and the transformation of the practice that occurred once it was set in place and institutionalized. Amidst tumult, crime, and unrest during the 1830s, the courts stepped forward as agents of the state to promote political stability in ways that bolstered the legitimation of fledgling institutions of self-rule. One consequence of their innovation was the rise of plea bargaining.

Change in the practice first occurred after the Civil War when growth of the laboring classes, segmentation of labor markets along ethnic lines, and articulation of a politics of residence acted together to produce new and distinct patterns of political coalition. What emerged was a politics with an identity rooted in ethnicity and it spawned new political forms—an urban politics first of patronage and then reform—that influenced sentencing policy. Even as labor unions mobilized, workers participated in strikes and boycotts, and the Knights of Labor voiced their considerable demands, one finds that the power of unionism as a basis of combination was gradually limited. This occurred through court action, social divisions within the laboring ranks, and the rise of powerful employers' associations at the same time that social mobility and patronage in jobs and contracts for nonunion workers undercut labor cohesion. In Boston concern over safeguarding one's job and wages among prior waves of early immigrants propelled nationalism and exclusionary nativism, rather than labor brotherhood, to prominence as a source of solidarity and a basis for interpreting what it meant to "be American" in an ever more heterogeneous society. As the struggle of those lower down the social scale for power after mid-century met resistance from more affluent members of society in Boston, struggle for control of the city's institutions—especially the courts—moved to the forefront of the contest.

As the nineteenth century drew to a close, plea bargaining underwent a second change. Administrative bureaucratization and the creation of large-scale public institutions advanced to serve the needs of growing cities. In some areas this accompanied the rise of a middle class with an ambitious commitment to "progressive" reform though, in Boston, this was preceded by the consolidation of a strong affluent and autonomous ethnic urban leadership that persisted far later into the twentieth century than in other cities. While trade unionism had reaped gains in Europe for workers that led to their incorporation as a major constituency in the new social democratic coalitions sprouting up in many countries, court action to restrict labor in the United States, coupled with other conditions described above, meant that no comparable move by the middle class to strike a political accommodation with organized labor was necessary. Progressivism, thus, found its support on a solidly middle-class footing. Emphasizing moral education and the socializing role of society's caretaking institutions, reformers sought to supersede patronage and to gain power to use public institutions to inculcate a sense of individual responsibility for moral conduct. In their quest, these middle-class reformers channeled the efforts of institutions including family, school, and courts alike to produce both sound early childhood socialization and rehabilitative human development.

In large part, scholarly reticence on the origins of plea bargaining can be attributed to the difficulty of detecting and measuring the practice. Since plea bargaining was rarely noted explicitly in the dockets of the courts, its historical contours and dynamics must be charted by means of inference. Because bargaining is multifaceted and can occur in many forms and at various stages as a case moves through the courts, the process of induction involved in analyzing the dockets is subtle and complex; it had proved a stumbling block to scholars for many years. As a result, most scholars have previously relied on the partial, though explicit, information provided by the records of the appellate courts. My own book is an effort to enhance our understanding of this important legal practice by taking a new methodological approach.

To address these questions and others, I have drawn on a wide variety of source materials. Archives at the Boston Municipal Court; the Boston Public Library; the Social Law Library; the Colonial Records Project; the records of the Massachusetts Superior Court; the records of the Supreme Judicial Court; the Federal Census Repository in Waltham, Massachusetts; and the Commonwealth of Massachusetts archive at Columbia Point have provided rich wellsprings of primary data for this project. This work has also drawn on published and unpublished materials—including the papers, speeches, memoirs, and diaries of Boston judges, lawyers, politicians, and other officials from the Massachusetts Historical Society; Langdell Library of Harvard Law School and Widener Library of Harvard University.

In any research, there are countless people who do much to nurture the project along the way. In my work on this book, I have been fortunate indeed to benefit from the help and support of many colleagues and friends. My research has been advanced at crucial points by grants from the Mark de Wolfe Howe Fund of Harvard Law School, the Nuala McGann Drescher Fund, the American Philosophical Society, and the Curley Family Fund. A Fellowship from the Mary Ingraham Bunting Institute at Radcliffe College of Harvard University during 1992–1993 and stays as a Visiting Scholar at the American Bar Foundation during autumn 1996; Visiting Assistant Professor at Northwestern University during 1996–1997; John Adams Fellow at the University of London in 1998; and Visiting Scholar at the Centre for Socio-Legal Studies and Visiting Fellow at Wolfson College of Oxford University in 1999 afforded time for critical rethinking and, most of all, sustained writing. Opportunities to talk there with Florence Ladd, Morton Horwitz, Ann Thomas, Zipporah Wiseman, Terry Fisher, Aldon Morris, Chris Tomlins, John Zvesper, Lawrence Lustgarten, Chris McCrudden, Keith Hawkins, Doreen McBarnet, Peter Bartrip, Spencer Zifcak, Sharon Witherspoon, Caroline Sawyer, Mavis McLean and Bryant Garth greatly stimulated my thinking on this manuscript. My debt is especially great to Jack R. Pole, whose work along with that of Bernard Bailyn, first sparked my interest in the English roots of American legal practices and who welcomed me for discussions over tea that lasted to dusk on many a cold, wintry afternoon in Oxford.

At various points, this work has been strengthened by the thoughtful commentary of scholars at professional meetings or lively discussion in other forums. Surely no one has had a more profound formative influence on my scholarship, generally, and this book, in particular, than Orlando Patterson. The privilege of learning from his creativity, intellect, humor and kindness is a source of constant inspiration. My treasured colleague, John H. Gagnon has been a continuing source of most special friendship, wit and revitalizing intellectual challenge. His encouragement and support have lent strength to continue on and to see this study to fruition. Members of the Center for the Study of Social Transformation at the University of Michigan, where I taught as Visiting Assistant Professor in the Sociology Department in 1997–1998, provided continual stimulation. At Northwestern, the Sociology Department, especially Aldon Morris, Carol Heimer, Arthur Stinchcombe, Charles Ragin and Marika Lindholm demonstrated what a lively intellectual community can be at its best. At the University of California at Santa Barbara, more recently, my colleagues

Dan Linz, Gayle Binion, Bill Felstiner, Erhard Blankenburg, Bill Bielby, John Mohr, and the Institutions Seminar provided a lively setting in which to revise the text. Finally, in England the Institute for Advanced Legal Studies at the University of London and the kind generosity of its Director Dr. Barry A. K. Rider and his Assistant Christine Murray provided that most precious of gifts—a stimulating genial place to copy edit this book and send it to press. Finally, at King's College London, Alan Norrie's warm encouragement affirmed that, having completed corrections to the page proofs, it was time to let the work go to the printer. Catherine Calder superbly helped me do so. Mac Runyan, Judy Tanur, Mark Granovetter, David Halle, Michael Schwartz, Steve Rytina, Kitty Calavita, David Greenberg, Allen Steinberg, Wilbur Miller, Alessandro Pizzorno, Jonathan Levy, Yu Xie, Jonathan Simon, Susan Silbey, Dick Howard, Trond Peterson, Rick Lempert and Carroll Seron have all, through their comments, contributed greatly to the production of this work and any merits it may possess. Its limitations remain, of course, my own.

At an early stage, Rob Pirro, Sylvia Contreras, Andy Opel, and, especially, Lynn Itagaki provided invaluable research assistance as did John Callahan, Joanna Bott, Rachel Duncan, Jeff Hunter, Cian Murphy, and Tammy Morgan later on. The anonymous reviewers for Oxford University Press offered many insightful suggestions that importantly clarified the arguments advanced in this book. Francis Shiels, Clerk of what is now the Boston Municipal Court, and his office staff, especially Ann Marie Wren, were unflagging in their cordiality and assistance in providing access to key court records. David deLorenzo at Special Collections in Langdell Library of Harvard Law School gave generously of his vast knowledge of nineteenth-century legal materials. Dedi Felman, my editor at Oxford University Press, has been the deeply intelligent, humorous, engaging and patient guide most authors can only hope for. I am profoundly grateful for her faith in this work and for giving it space and time to develop. Keith Hawkins of Oriel College, Oxford University, kindly welcomed this work into his distinguished Oxford Socio-Legal Studies series. Finally, the warm hospitality and friendship of Kenneth "Andy" Andrews and Marne Meredith, Janet Wilson, Dalma Flanders, Rosalind King, Paul Collett, and also of David Vogel, Clare O'Keefe, Conrad, Derek, Nick and Riley during the final stages of production bolstered my energies and renewed my spirits on innumerable frosty winter evenings. My heartfelt thanks to each of them.

At every stage, my family has been a nourishing source of encouragement and support. My mother, Virginia Vogel McLeod, and my stepfather, the late Thomas Donald McLeod, have been steadfast in their belief in me and this project and in their spirited commitment to doing all humanly possible to help in practical ways that it might be completed. Words cannot convey the measure of my love and thanks. Much earlier, my father Robert J. Vogel, Jr., my grand-parents Vera McHale Kloss and Charles Kloss and my grandfather Robert J. Vogel, Sr., all of beloved memory, laid a groundwork of loving encouragement and belief in women's work on which this project, like so much of my life, builds. My sisters have played a special role indeed. Christine Vogel has been there at every dark moment with sage counsel, unshakable faith, unfathomable generosity, and the most moving warmth and care. Gina Vogel, in her won-derful cards, "care packages," and holiday parties, has fostered family ties that are a constant source of grounding and support. My brothers and our vast family of in-laws, step-siblings, and a youthful clan of children, especially Jes-sica and Caitlin Vogel, have brought wise advice and good cheer on many crucial occasions. More than anyone, Tony Long, my partner in love and life, has participated in the creation of this book with me. His affection, humor and support nurture and sustain all I do. In his capacity to see and make moving beauty in the simplest of ways lies much of the inspiration for this work. My loving thanks, Tony, for the golden thread you bring to the tapestry of my life.

Contents

A photo gallery appears after page 146

Coercion to Compromise

I

Plea Bargaining

A Distinctively American Practice

Under a legal system where it has been said that "law is what the courts do," one striking feature of the American criminal courts is the widespread and well-established system of plea bargaining that has arisen. Though highly controversial and much debated, its beginnings are surprisingly obscure. Now, in this book, my desire is to shed light on them. While often imagined to be either an innovation or a corruption of the courts after World War II, the practice proves, actually, to have much deeper and more extensive historical roots. With guilty pleas accounting, presently, for approximately 90 percent of all convictions, understanding how plea bargaining, a major contributor to those guilty pleas, developed is tantamount to knowing what the law, in fact, is.

Some revolutions are ushered in with bloodshed, death, and political upheaval. Other political shifts tiptoe in more quietly so that only afterward does the recognition dawn that an enormous change has taken place. Plea bargaining, as it first appeared, involved a remaking of the second kind. In bits and pieces, a step at a time, a profound local transformation occurred in the American courts during the early nineteenth century that would fundamentally change the nature of American criminal justice. It would also have lasting consequences, though, as yet, still unforeseen, for the contours of the state and the process of its formation. My study explores the social origins of plea bargaining and the adaptations of it that took place as the practice rose to prominence.

My purpose is to explain how plea bargaining began in an effort to learn why it arose when and where it did and why it took the cultural form it did. What one finds is that the social forces that gave rise to plea bargaining are very different from those to which it has traditionally been attributed. Understanding the first stirrings and life course of this curious practice also lends unique insight into the problems that the practice presents today. As one delves beneath the surface to the deeper workings of contemporary plea bargaining, those difficulties are found to stem from three things: the changed social context in which the common law now operates; heavy reliance today on formal institutions for punishment at the expense of earlier more informal community-based approaches to social control; and a democratic politics fundamentally riven by tension between "law rule," on the one hand, and "self rule," on the other.

These discoveries are significant because, by the late nineteenth century and continuing to this day, most cases in the lower criminal courts have been resolved through plea bargaining. Although our popular image of justice is of a jury trial with defendants presumed innocent until proven guilty, a very different process has been the mainstay of the American courts.

In thinking about order, we often tend to think in terms of social structures and institutions and to downplay human agency. Our inquiries frequently center on the economy or on the nation state more so than individual lives (Arendt, 1959; Somers, 1996). In our quest for what is generalizable, we also often emphasize what is common rather than the human choices that produce local variation and change (Katznelson and Zolberg, 1988; Moore, 1967; and Bendix, 2001). As one example, state action from the top down has, until lately, preoccupied more writers than have local initiatives shaping politics from the bottom up (Andrews, 1997; Somers).[1] Only recently have stories of local voluntarism and contestation, along with their effects on state formation, become more widely told (Sewell, 1980; Andrews; Skocpol, 1992). In these pages, I examine one pathbreaking local transformation in the American courts, namely the rise of plea bargaining, that profoundly changed the nature of criminal justice. In exploring such a controversial practice, this book examines causal forces and processes of varied temporal rhythms and highlights the transformative power of events at crucial moments in history (Sewell; Gramsci, 1971). Focusing on such social reconstruction, this work presents a layered dynamic account of how plea bargaining came into being. Theoretically, it enriches our understanding of the nature and extent of the relative institutional autonomy of the courts. By focusing on change as a complement to the social reproduction that is emphasized in the *new institutionalism,* it also deepens our knowledge about how institutions and culture adapt to contestation and disruptive events in a process of constitutive social change (Vogel, 1988, 1999, 2001).

The Paradox of Plea Bargaining

To explain how plea bargaining emerged, I focus on its beginnings in antebellum Boston—the first sustained instance of the practice known, thus far, to exist. Boston was a national center of legal innovation from which new ideas and practices spread to other cities through diffusion. Plea bargaining appears to have been one such distributed legal innovation. Once it began in this city, it spread quickly to others. An urban political elite, seeking to maintain its position of power, played a key role in its establishment. This privileged group, responding to political challenge in a specific social and temporal context, shaped much of the imaginative construction of American legal ideas during this formative era. It was this elite's perception of crisis and threat, along with its effort to preserve social order, the legitimacy of self-rule, and its own dominance, which shaped the practice of plea bargaining in a single locale that would then become a national and, eventually, international phenomenon.

When one hears that a plea bargain has been struck, the words bring many different images to mind. In this study, one can take it to refer to the entry of a guilty plea by a defendant in anticipation of leniency from a prosecutor or judge—a process that may be either implicit or explicit. Concessions may take the form of charge reductions but in antebellum Boston leniency in sentencing appears far more common, at least in the lower courts, in the earliest workings of the practice.[2] Perhaps most troubling to many observers is why a practice might be adopted that provides its reward of leniency precisely to those who acknowledge their culpability and, thus, would seem not to merit it—in fact to be least deserving of it. In this book, I attempt to illuminate this paradox by showing that plea bargaining must be understood by focusing, not only on the courtroom itself and attributes of individual cases, but also at the macrosocial level on the context of both local politics and the American state in terms of the dilemmas of democratization, the demands of partisan contest as the nation made its transition to a second and then third party system, and the process of incorporating new immigrants (Meyer et al., 1979). The rise of plea bargaining, as one line of response, can be seen as a product of two sets of beliefs received from the English common law legal heritage and from Christianity, respectively, amidst the historic tensions of the day.

Another reason why plea bargaining sometimes seems especially paradoxical is that it represented a shift by the American courts away from the articulation of guilt or innocence in a case and toward compromise at just the moment when immigrant groups from diverse cultures, many unfamiliar with the common law, began to flood the cities of the urban Northeast. Social conflict attendant to industrialization also began, at this point, to be voiced. Viewed in this light, the ability of the courts to educate the public by affirming social norms and legal rules might seem to have been abandoned precisely when its socializing influence was most needed. However, this turns out not to be the case. As we shall see, the process of incorporating immigrants in antebellum Boston focused its discourses and instruments on creating practical relationships, webs of social control, and images of membership, a task to which courtroom leniency was especially well suited.

The story of plea bargaining involves both continuity and change. The continuity was that of republican ideology, already contested by Democrats nationally with the election of Andrew Jackson as president. Republicanism espoused a vision of political rule by an elite community of civic-spirited citizens who were guided by an holistic sense of society's interests. They saw themselves linked to those less advantaged through deference.[3] Republicanism, in this sense, became the ideological underpinning for governance in the form of a well-regulated society in which the courts were active partners in the United States during the early to mid-nineteenth century (Novak, 1996). Within this continuity, however, crucial conditions, dynamics, and events brought change. Plea bargaining, as part of a changing stance of the criminal courts, arose in response to widespread conflict, crime, and a sense of crisis that called for a capable state response under very new social constraints.

The antebellum years in Boston were a time of passage between two political cultures. The old Federalist framework of politics remained in place in the city into the 1830s but splintering had already begun in both it and the political elite supporting it. In 1834, Democrats mounted a successful electoral challenge and, in a startling victory, Theodore Lyman was elected Boston's first Democratic mayor. This partisan opposition, emerging just as the franchise was extended more fully in the mid-1830s, weakened elite control and challenged its domination of local electoral politics through the Federalist, National Republican and, later, Whig Parties. It is in this context that plea bargaining arose. Though the Federalist Party as a political vehicle would eventually disintegrate, Boston's sturdy elite resurfaced time and again, phoenix-like, ultimately joining forces after mid-century with like minded partisans at the state level to forge the Commonwealth's Republican party—albeit with a much-changed agenda and new political strategies.

Beginnings in Partisan Contest and Political Stabilization

During the early nineteenth century, concern abounded in Boston about widespread crime and unrest. In the 1820s and 1830s, social conflict grew rife there as in much of the urban Northeast. Although confidence in the new market-based society of the day was robust, concern was palpable about what the recent democratic turn in politics would mean, practically speaking, for social life. Construction of mills and factories changed the organization of work and the class structure. Growth of cities brought contact between strangers in local neighborhoods. The start of massive European immigration brought flood tides of persons seeking asylum or simply a better life. All combined to create a sense of massive change, crisis, and social transformation. The public, already apprehensive about the viability of self-rule, grew more vexed as political foment waxed in Europe and the revolutionary year of 1848 approached. A sense of the fragility of self-rule and its potential instability mounted. When the franchise was extended "universally" just then, it required that whatever solution to this situation might be devised should not jeopardize popular political support.

The Constitution was still relatively new, urban political institutions were spare and fragmentary,[4] and local political parties were virtually nonexistent.[5] City officials, extremely conscious of the rioting and protest afoot in Europe, feared what the future might hold for American attempts at self-rule. Faced with these problems, the key task of social ordering fell largely to the courts. They, who, along with the tax collectors, were one of the few local public institutions yet in place, stepped forward as agents of the fledgling state to reclaim order and to mold a practical working relationship with its citizens (Skowronek, 1982). In so doing, the courts drew on a time-honored tradition of episodic leniency—that is, frequent but irregular pardons and grants of clemency— from the British common law and adapted it into the practice of plea bargaining. In England, episodic leniency dispensed by the state had, as we shall see, operated along with some privately negotiated leniency. It traditionally nurtured order as well as easing tensions among social groups (Hay et al., 1975; King, 2003). Responding to this dilemma, the courts stepped in and tapped the common law tradition of leniency. This was done as one thrust of a much broader campaign to cultivate order and stability.

To understand why plea bargaining arose in this way, one must consider the nature and timing of the crisis, the contours of the nascent state, and the distinctive common law legal culture that provided a unique repertoire on which to draw.

In telling the story of plea bargaining, explanation is found in three inter-locking themes. First, relations of deference and dependence receded, albeit incompletely, as crime, rioting, and unrest surged. Second, state response to these events transformed traditional legal mechanisms as court action shifted from a presumption of innocence to a form of compromise known as plea bargaining. Third, simultaneously, the courts became institutions of policy-making while the political elite in Boston adjusted to a new more-inclusive electorate to remain at the summit of partisan power in their "well-regulated society" long after their brethren had been eclipsed in other cities (Novak, 1996).

Origins of Plea Bargaining: Controversial Beginnings

This work owes a debt to previous early research on plea bargaining's history by Albert Alschuler (1968, 1995a, 1975b), John Langbein (1978b), Albert Reiss (1975), Lawrence Friedman (1973), Raymond Moley (1929), Milton Heumann (1975), Malcolm Feeley (1973, 1979a, 1979b), Charles Clark and Harry Shul-man (1937), and others, but then departs in terms of the point in time at which we understand plea bargaining to begin. Contrary to popular perception, I find that plea bargaining emerged in the American criminal courts during the 1830s and 1840s. Correctly dating the first stirrings of the practice allows one to see clearly its origins as part of a process of dynamic contestation. It was one where an elite worked to promote social order and political stability and to reconso-lidate its partisan power during the Age of Jackson.[6]

Previous explanations of plea bargaining, both contemporary and histori-cal, have mainly adopted an institutional perspective. In recent decades, many authors have explored the provocative and controversial practice from this standpoint.[7] Crime commissions acknowledged the existence of plea bargain-ing as early as the 1920s and 1930s (Missouri Association for Criminal Justice Survey Committee, 1926; New York State Crime Commission, 1927). More contemporary studies have primarily probed three facets of bargaining practice: the consequences of plea bargaining,[8] the types of cases that tend to be bar-gained,[9] and explanations as to why plea bargaining occurs.[10]

Despite the extent of this research, the results of these previous studies present a most unusual and interesting pattern. Although a number of clearly articulated and intuitively appealing hypotheses were proposed, several so-phisticated methodologies employed, and some quite solid data used, the find-ings of this work—particularly regarding the consequences of the practice—have been remarkably indeterminate or inconclusive. Most significant, in light of this research, are the limits of the spate of explanations as to why such bargaining occurs. Most, who focus on plea negotiations today, point to the inherent gains and cost savings to be had by competing parties who engage in cooperation. Where those models fall short is that, as they are specified, comparable gains would accrue through bargaining under virtually any justice system in the Western world. If the cooperation argument were correct, one would expect to have seen plea bargaining worldwide and throughout time. Yet, when one looks historically at the origins of plea bargaining, it appears that, while discretion certainly has been widely exercised both publicly and privately, no system comparable to plea bargaining had arisen either on the European continent or even in England, which shared the common law system, prior to its appearance in the United States (Friedman, 1981; Langbein, 1979; Feeley, 1979a).

By the late 1970s, several very interesting works had appeared that advanced our understanding by probing early instances of plea bargaining. These authors suggested that the practice dated back to some point in the late nineteenth century and probably not before. My own work owes a special debt to much of that very recent research by Lawrence Friedman (1979, 1981 and 1993); Lawrence Friedman and Robert Percival (1981); Albert Alschuler (1979), John Langbein (1979), Malcolm Feeley (1982), Albert Reiss (1975), Allen Steinberg (1984 and 1989), and William McDonald (1979 and 1985), among others. My account, however, diverges to push backward in time the origin of plea bargaining and, then, to rethink the causes which gave rise to it. These latest studies, which primarily analyzed appellate decisions suggested various historical explanations for the emergence of plea bargaining. Some authors have linked its rise to the expanding role of the public prosecutor and to prosecutorial discretion (Reiss, 1975; Ferdinand, 1992; Fisher, 2000). Others have intimated that the practice stemmed from the establishment of a professional police force or from the old corrupt police practice of compounding a felony (Alschuler, 1979; Friedman, 1979). A third line of thinking has pointed to the growing complexity of the criminal trial and to caseload pressure (Alschuler, 1979; Feeley, 1982; Rothman, 1980). Still a fourth argument has contended that, by shifting the burden of decision making from the courtroom and juries to lawyers and professionals, plea bargaining was part of a movement to rationalize and professionalize criminal justice (Friedman, 1993; Friedman and Percival, 1981).

Few of these authors had examined the dockets and history of a particular locale to test their hypotheses about the origins of the process. While each of the arguments sketches an important piece of the story, each, on historical grounds, also presents some problems. The office of the prosecutor in New

York long predated what we now know from McConville and Mirsky (1999) to be the initial striking rise of guilty pleas there during the 1840s, undercutting a causal argument about the rise of the prosecutor's power (Reiss, 1975; Moley, 1929). Conversely, as we shall see, establishment of public prosecutors in the lower criminal court in Boston lagged the rise of plea bargaining there, creating another problem of timing, although prosecutors do play a role later.

One effort to show that plea bargaining began in regulatory cases involving liquor law violations in Boston's mid-tier courts, where prosecutors were active during the early 19th century, bases its case on the creaky limb of just *nine* instances over nearly fifty years of what are termed *clear plea bargains* (Fisher, 2000). These are defined as written evidence of a charge reduction upon entry of a plea of nolo contendere (Fisher, 2000). While arguing persuasively that charges were thus reduced in such a case every five years or so, Fisher bypasses the more pertinent question of whether those defendants were treated more leniently than the average liquor violator of comparable type. Given the British regulatory tradition of foregoing a formal charge altogether if a violation is corrected, there is reason to think that these cases may have involved particularly serious or habitual offenders open to relatively severe penalties. Such a plea of nolo contendere, under prevailing habitual offender laws, may have been a step of intermediate severity, short of conviction, in more serious cases. A similar point could be made for the high guilty plea rate that emerges in those offenses (Fisher, 2000; Ferdinand, 1992).

Apart from whether this evidence suffices to establish a pattern of plea bargaining, Fisher's account raises historiographical and empirical issues too. Fisher contends that such "deals" were the "product of a nearly instantaneous reaction of two chemical ingredients—the existence of a public prosecutor and that prosecutor's power to bargain by means of the charge decision [due to enactment of mandatory sentencing laws]" (p. 889). Yet he does not attempt to explain why earlier prosecutors, who, as Michael Tonry (1992) has shown, faced similar mandatory penalty schemes, appear not to have negotiated then. Nor does Fisher suggest why judges, who held wide power to bargain in the absence of mandatory sentencing laws, had not chosen to do so nor why prosecutors had not used their capacity to control imposition of costs to bargain earlier. Each of these points suggests that there was something about the moment that caused plea bargaining to emerge then and not before. Yet Fisher explicitly rejects any causal role for social context as an unnecessary complication. Pointing simply to the enactment of a mandatory sentencing law during this period, Fisher states: "My own explanation . . . is . . . brief: Prosecutors . . . bargained . . . because they could" (p. 904).

One immediate problem that his surprising repudiation of social context creates is that Fisher (2000) ignores the shift occurring in pleas of nolo contendere for all types of offenses during that period toward the forging of more contractual and contingent agreements. Fisher, in his own explanation, accepts Tonry's earlier finding that mandatory penalties shift power to the prosecutor. However, Fisher then challenges Tonry's empirical finding that mandatory sentencing laws *reduce* plea bargaining overall because defendants contest their cases more vigorously and claims, instead, that such laws not only favored but actually produced plea bargaining (Tonry, 1992). It is this which makes it crucial to distinguish whether Fisher's "bargainers" are being treated leniently or harshly relative to others committing the same crime—a question Fisher does not, and perhaps cannot, answer.

The compounding of felonies, cited as an explanation by a second group of authors, dates back to precolonial England, predates the establishment of a professional police force in the United States, and was practiced primarily by police detectives who descended from the venerable constabulary, which had existed for more than a century before plea bargaining arose (Radzinowicz, 1956, 313–318). Again, the sequencing was problematic. Peter King (2003) points to private compounding and payment of satisfaction in late eighteenth century England but these cases were often left open in the docket and differed in form and legal implication from the guilty plea bargain which closed the case with a conviction.

The third line of argument, attributing causality to the rise of a professional police force, founders on the fact that the police existed in London prior to the United States. If it alone were the key causal factor, the practice should have arisen first in Britain, which it did not. Further, a full-time paid police force was not established in Boston until after plea bargaining had begun. Though the police do eventually begin to present some evidence in the lower court, newspaper stories and other vignettes do not suggest a major role for them in the courtroom during the early years of the practice (Gil, 1837; Fenner, 1856).

For its part, caseload pressure had been decried as a problem in the American courts since colonial days so that it, too, long predated nineteenth-century plea bargaining—weakening claims for its status as a proximate cause. Heumann has shown that even present-day caseload and complexity do not automatically lead new prosecutors to bargain; instead, socialization by peers into the process is required (Heumann, 1981; Dimond, 1975).[11] Finally, complexity was a relative latecomer to the lower criminal courts (McConville and Mirsky, 1999). Criminal trials there during the 1830s and 1840s were expeditious affairs that usually involved only the defendant and a judge, without attorneys for prosecution or defense (Vogel, 1999, 2001; McConville and Mirsky, 1999). Only after mid-century did trials become the more-complex events that Feeley (1982) describes but, by then, plea bargaining was already in place. Historical analysis, thus, showed each prior explanation to encounter stumbling blocks in terms either of temporal sequence or empirical evidence of bargaining.

In contrast, Friedman's argument about rationalization and the rise of professionalism in the late nineteenth century coincides timewise with some of the earliest instances of plea bargaining previously documented—in 1880 in California (Friedman and Percival, 1981) and in 1870 in Philadelphia (Steinberg, 1984). Coupled with Friedman's (1993) observation that the practice "certainly existed" in the late nineteenth century "and perhaps even earlier," Friedman and Percival presented an important and persuasive part of the picture of plea bargaining in the late nineteenth century and pointed the way for the probability that it began much earlier.

The sense that there lay an important story still untold here was affirmed by a landmark special issue of *Law and Society Review* on plea bargaining some years ago. It concluded that, in the scholarly search to understand the practice, there are as yet "no definitive answers" (Feeley, 1979a, p. 204). Much the same claim could still be made today. Similarly, Samuel Walker (1980), in his classic history of criminal justice, comments that "the historical origins of plea bargaining remain obscure" (p. 112). In his book on plea bargaining titled *The Process Is the Punishment,* Malcolm Feeley (1979b) mused that "the way we are framing the question may need to be reformulated" (p. 148).

Despite the limitations of that previous work, many scholars have been loathe to move beyond those accounts to ask what other causes, including structures, processes and events beyond the courtroom, may have produced this practice. With notable exceptions such as Friedman and Percival (1981), McConville and Mirsky (1999), and Steinberg (1984), court efficiency, work group cooperation, the prosecutor, the police, trial complexity, and crowding in the courts still dominate much of the research on plea bargaining.

By contrast, philosophers and, increasingly, sociologists of law and legal historians have emphasized both the intimate relationship of law to politics and society and the influence of political and social forces on actors in the courts (Friedman, 1993; Garland, 1990; Skrentny, 1993; Simon, 1993; Novak, 1996; and Forbath, 1991). Their theorizing about law has highlighted its implications for processes of social ordering and for the role of the state. Among the earliest to emphasize these relationships were E. P. Thompson and scholars working in collaboration or dialogue with him (e.g., Hay et al., 1975; Hobsbawm, 1972; Brewer and Styles, 1980; and Stone, 1981). Thompson (1975) focused specifically on the role law plays in elaborating relations of power and political authority. He argued that law cannot be meaningfully understood apart from its social context, which shapes beliefs, incentives and interests to which those in a legal forum respond. This paper starts with that presumption of the societal embeddedness of the courts (Granovetter, 1985).

Thus, early explanations of plea bargaining were notable for their lack of attention to two key things: first, its origination as an American phenomenon despite roots in the "old world" and, second, how its emergence may have been causally shaped by changes in social context, events, and culture that shaped how those in the courtroom perceived and pursued their interests. This study focuses on those prior omissions and explores how judges drew on a unique element of common law legal culture, "episode leniency," as they responded to a perceived crisis of social order. Social relationships, institutions, and discourse were transformed in ways that produced a rescripting of legal practice, plea bargaining as part of an effort to secure both stability and a new postrevolutionary conception of political authority.

Historically what had been distinctive about the common law tradition of leniency was its capacity, through practices such as pardons, character witnesses, and surety, to strengthen informal social ties between elites and those of lower rank (Hay et al., 1975). This helped preserve and reproduce the existing structure of social rank with the inequalities it contained. By the late seventeenth century, ruling elites within England had moved beyond the age of monarchial absolutism and were confronted with the problem of maintaining control over a populace of which they were only a small minority (Hay et al., 1975). As one part of its response, England enacted a series of extremely harsh laws (Hay et al., 1975; Cottu, 1822). Paradoxically, though, they often were not fully enforced. Instead, the cultural tradition of "episodic leniency" consolidated and was applied—a custom whereby the state frequently, but irregularly, granted pardons or decided not to prosecute or not to convict (Hay et al., 1975). The sporadic quality meant that receipt of leniency could not be counted on.

In political terms, the combination of severe legal codes coupled with leniency had powerful effects. It contributed to incentives among the lower classes to value, conserve or even nurture bonds of reciprocity, loyal employment, and clientelism as a sort of broad protective canopy with members of the elite and the middling ranks (Hay et al., 1975). This fostered a generalized store of political good will that might, among other things, assist one in causing a prosecution to be foregone or to produce a powerful advocate to plead for mercy on one's behalf if one ran afoul of the law (Hay et al., 1975).[12] The result, as E. P. Thompson (1975) has noted, was a system of justice that helped support continuity of the existing structure of social class through the loose ties of mutuality it promoted. In a sense, this was an early social bond approach to social control and order. Yet, despite its reliance on social capital and networks of relationships, it sidestepped appearances of particularism through procedural consistency and constancy in the laws substantively applied. Thus, legal mechanisms of episodic leniency had the consequence of helping to legitimate the political system of self-rule, despite material inequality, by conveying a message of universality and formal equality before the law.

Clearly, Hay et al. (1975) were describing a period of agricultural oligarchy in England almost a century before the era on which this work focuses. However, legal developments in early nineteenth century America show episodic leniency again to be at work—though having been adapted in a new and quite different way and serving some additional purposes. Plea bargaining emerged as a widespread new mechanism when judges adapted the idiom of leniency from common law legal culture for the American context of mass politics. Leniency, once more, would be used to cultivate order and stability by fostering not only hierarchical social ties but also processes of social classification in an urbanizing "nation of strangers" and new relationships between citizens and the state.

As politics became a popular phenomenon, it grew impossible for the law to uphold order by force alone.[13] It became vital for a regime to win popular consent to its governance. If won, the regime's chances of stabilizing political life and maintaining power were greatly enhanced.[14] If not, a period of political reaction or instability could ensue—in the extreme case, a change of government might follow. Historically, regimes seeking to cultivate support have created ideologies to legitimate their power.[15] In virtually every society, the language of law has played a key role in such imagery by helping to bolster political legitimacy. By drawing conflicts into court, legal remedies also preempt extralegal and political solutions to conflict (Hindus, 1980). The universality and formal equality of law reinforce a regime's claims to represent the interests of all (Thompson, 1975).

The story of plea bargaining suggests that construction of political authority as a basis of popular support relies not only on legal codes per se but in practical social arrangements for interpreting them that create connections between citizens and state, shape action and thinking in ways that solidify popular support, and promote acceptance of governance and rules as binding.[16] How episodic leniency, reworked into plea bargaining, helped to construct such acceptance and what social dynamics shaped this metamorphosis are the focus of what follows.

Given what prior arguments had left untouched, my own book focuses on a single city, Boston, and analyzes criminal cases whose records were sampled systematically from the nineteenth-century court docketbooks, searching them for first evidence of concessions accorded when guilty pleas were entered. This study advances a fresh explanation based on contextualized analysis of those historical documents (Lijphart, 1971). Patterns of bargaining, measured as guilty pleas accompanied by concessions, were then examined for their relation to changes in social, political and cultural context as well as events hypothesized to be causal. My aim is to create a longitudinal account of changes in social structural, processual and decisional features as well as more contingent conjunctural and volitional happenings believed to have given rise to plea bargaining relative to their theorized effects on court action. The destination of my analytic journey is to enable inferences about what incentives, interests, and cultural codes participants responded to as they began to consummate "bargains." By reconstructing the social world of the Boston courts, a wealth of new insights into a legal practice that, it appears, may be distinctively American in origin were unearthed.

Constitutive Structural Change and Human Agency

In setting out to explore the process by means of which plea bargaining arose, we approach an empty canvas and, like the artist, begin to assemble the tools with which to work. To study social change, historical sociologist Philip Abrams (1982) directs our attention to the relation between social structure and human agency as a basis for conceptualizing that process. Abrams noted that the problem of historical analysis is to find a way of depicting the human experience which recognizes both that "history and society are made by constant and more or less purposeful individual action . . . [and that this] individual action . . . is [at the same time] made by society and history" (p. xiv). Here the interplay of the purposive activity of humans as agents with the social and material conditions of life in a temporal process of structuring provides a starting point. As humans respond to the incentives their social world presents, they act and forge new patterns of interaction that may be said to be constitutive of social structural change (Ollman, 1976).

As it changes, social structure, in turn, presents new dilemmas, alternatives, and rewards that condition subsequent action. Hence, the humans whose lived experience are the stuff of history operate as both subjects and objects in the flow of change. Marx and Engels (1970) noted this reciprocity of human agency and social structure when they observed that "circumstances make men just as much as men make [their] circumstances" (p. 59). Weber (1978) advances a similar claim when he argues that human agency responded to both

the structure of economic conditions and the ideational constructs of Calvin-
ism to give rise, albeit unintentionally, to capitalism. This occurred as new
ways of acting forged new structural relationships. Subsequently, those structures proceeded to reshape human needs and motivations again as the supplanting of religious spirit by a utilitarian rationality and bureaucracy transformed production and exchange relations—this time to an "iron cage" that
threatened to mute human voluntarism.

Beyond this reciprocity, focus on what Abrams (1982) refers to as structuring—that is, "the processes mediating structure and practice"—provides an
approach for conceptualizing this interplay of social structure with human
choices and action. Abrams also urges attention to the sequencing of social
events in time as a product of this reciprocity and to the social origins and
consequences of these events.[17] In conceptualizing social change, then, the
reciprocity of social context and human action with respect to it assumes an
indeterminate and contingent quality. Social relationships and the sequencing
of events are contingent not only on the immediate structural setting of action
but also on the imaginative constructions that humans produce to understand,
deliberate, and dissent over events that are unfolding. While social theory accepts that patterns in the relation between human action and social structure
can be explained, it is also generally acknowledged that an element of openness
exists in social life that makes way for that interpretive process. Society, rather
than consisting of a play of determinate material and social forces, emerges
as, at least partly, socially constructed or as a human creation.[18]

Viewed in this light, the lives of ordinary men and women achieve a certain
degree of freedom from determinate constraint by their social context and
regain "dynamic qualities of unruliness and unpredictability."[19] At the same
time, the human tendency to theorize social experience elevates to a position
of critical importance the paradigmatic discourses and shared meanings that
are embodied in culture. Bear with me now as we consider with what, at first,
may seem undue attention, the nature of these discourses.

Law as "Modality of Rule": The Making of Political Authority

In reflecting on the origins of plea bargaining, it pays to remember that the
political discourse that prevailed in the early nineteenth century in the United
States was permeated and dominated by law.[20] Perhaps the clearest indication
of this new authority of law was the articulation of an ideology of "the rule of
law." The central premise of this ideology was that political power should be

exercised according to rules embodied in a body of law and system of rights that are made known in advance, are characterized by fairness, and constrain the weak and powerful alike. That is to say, law is held to exhibit two crucial qualities—first, universality, or the applicability of law to all, and second, formal equality under the law or the requirement that the law treat all persons coming before the court equally without regard for social standing.[21] Increasingly, during the latter half of the eighteenth century, law moved to center stage, from what had previously been a marginal position of some disrepute, as one of several competing discourses through which worldviews that gave meaning to social action and reproduced social relations were shared. Initially limited in influence, law rose to a position of "supreme imaginative authority" that by 1800 had lent it virtually "unbounded influence" (Tomlins, 1993, p. 21).

This change was marked by thoroughgoing shifts in the nature and standing of the legal project and of those who propounded it. Most fundamental was change in law's intellectual organization and scope from a bevy of discrete local discourses about particular parochial concerns to a single translocal "holistic, 'scientific,' anglocentric," and systematized discourse (Tomlins, 1993, pp. 21–22). At the same time, the status and stance of its proponents shifted markedly from a sort of "shabby notoriety" and "unself-conscious disorganization" to the "social authority" and "professional self-awareness" of an intellectual elite (pp. 21–22).

Certainly, this new prominence was not accorded to law without contest. Antilegalism, as part of a broader antistatism, persisted as a theme in American political culture (Horwitz, 1977, pp. 561–66; Klare, 1982, pp. 133–34). Insofar as the Founding Fathers had committed the new republic to uphold "life, liberty, and the pursuit of happiness," some argued that the rule of law was a dubious choice for accomplishing it. Constitutionalism in America, following the tradition of British common law of the eighteenth century, did not rely heavily on government to promote social and economic justice because citizens felt they must constantly be on the watch after excesses in the state's exercise of power (Reid, 1987a and 1978; Mill, 1975; Tomlins, 1993, p. 23). In short, citizens believed that they could not unreservedly trust government, and one fundamental dilemma of liberty in a world of self-rule, as they saw it, was how to safeguard their rights against the intrusions of the state.[22] To use law as a cornerstone of political discourse, then, it would be necessary either to transform the British common law constitutional tradition or to revise the stated commitments of the Founders. Modulation of some of those commitments to safeguard order and property did occur (Nedelsky, 1990). However, an oppositional Constitutionalism, initially propounded during the revolutionary era, resurged in the 1820s as Democratic-Republicans moved to contest Federalist power. Their challenge was rooted in a republican conception of civic virtue (Katz, 1987, pp. 22–37; Wood, 1991; Friedman and Scheiber, 1988, pp. 217–51).

Despite the rise of law to prominence as a paradigmatic political discourse, during the late 18th century, the common law traditions that were loosely knit together under the canopy of an ideology of the "rule of law" existed in competition with other influential discourses—specifically, those of republicanism, evangelical Christianity, commerce or political economy, and "police" (Tomlins, 1993, p. 24).[23] As the Enlightenment's visions of the power of human reason spread, great interest stirred about the relation of human beings to their social world, and theorizing began about the means by which that relation might be managed. This occurred first in the realm of religion and science and, later, through politics and the economy (Tomlins, 1993, p. 24).[24]

Each of these competing modes of discourse offered a conception of the relation of human action to its [social] context and put forward a unique view of how human action should be moderated and how this capacity to temper human behavior should be organized (Tomlins, 1993). Classical republicanism advocated moderation of action by "a secular civic-minded virtue, sustained by propertied independence"; evangelical Christianity proposed moderation by the individual's "redemptive commitment to a transcendent Christian morality—'enthusiasm'—sustained by strict new codes of self conduct"; political economy envisioned moderation by the "pursuit of individual self-interest, sustained by the equilibrating effects of the market" in a "well-regulated society"; and policing urged moderation by the "pursuit of safety and happiness—individual and communal welfare—sustained (in America) by the promise of 'free' governments embodying the sovereignty of the people" (Tomlins, p. 25; Novak, 1996).

These discourses also embodied a conception of social transformation. As social change accelerated during the creation of the new republic, these languages of narrative grew interconnected until finally giving way during the latter part of the nineteenth century to the new imaginative construction of liberalism that retheorized liberty into the language of rights and eventually, also the relation of human action to the new market society into individualized terms.[25] But first there was a period of several decades when the ideology of a "rule of law" held sway (Reid, 1978; Novak, 1996; Wood, 1991; Forbath, 1991). As the institutions and political culture of the new republic took form during the late eighteenth and early nineteenth centuries, thinking about law moved to a position of prominence; it played a new and vital role (Hutchinson and Monahan, 1987, p. 104–105; Wood, 1991, p. 323). One might go so far as to contend that appeal to "the rule of law . . . [emerged as] the integral, though far from the only, constituting element of the society" and that it exerted a powerful formative influence "in molding . . . [a] civic consciousness" (Tomlins, 1993, pp. 26–27).

In these crucial years, law, thus, advanced beyond its customary tasks of providing a language and institutional means of social control. It began to provide a basis for collective self-understanding and for orienting action both individually and as a society. Through its language and precepts, the common law profoundly influenced the new order. Key facets of the course charted under the influence of law as a mode of rule included: the restriction of legislative and state administrative power as potentially intrusive on individual liberty; movement toward particular meanings of concepts such as democracy, sovereignty, and citizenship; and, especially, a preeminent role in the polity for both judicial review and the language and institutions of the common law (Tomlins, 1993, p. 28; Vogel, 1999; Skowronek, 1982; Reid, 1978 and 1987a).

William Forbath (1991) points, in particular, to the rise of the formidable power of the American judiciary to review the constitutionality of legislation, in contrast to the more limited powers of the judiciary in England, as central to the enhanced role of law in America during the antebellum years—a power enabled, at least in part, by Madisonian federalism, the separation of powers, and the absence of a strong central administrative state. This statement is echoed by Gordon S. Wood (1969 and 1991), who points to the articulation during the 1780s and 1790s of " 'an exclusive sphere of activity for the judiciary' as 'the most dramatic institutional transformation of the early Republic'—the high point of a 'remarkable process by which the judiciary in America suddenly emerged out of its colossal insignificance to become by 1800 the principal means by which popular legislatures were controlled and limited' " (p. 323). In Frank Michelman's (1988) terms, the country had become culturally and institutionally "Law's Republic" (p. 1493). From the common law would be derived a structure of relationships and means for modulating social conflict that profoundly shaped the new nation.

As relations of deference weakened and pressures for popular rule through the legislatures of representative democracy mounted, the fact that "the people" who governed were not the same as "the people" who were ruled brought renewed fears for liberty (Mill, 1975). Republicanism had valued liberty, upheld by law, as a means of assuring the conditions that fostered free expression by elite citizens as they deliberated with the holistic interests of the entire community in mind. Liberty in a context of self-rule was now, through the rise of liberalism, initially as an oppositional discourse, to demarcate not only the acceptable scope of individual action but also protection for citizens against excesses by the government they had chosen in its exercise of power (Mill,

1975, pp. 7–8). As liberalism emerged, Democratic partisans struggled to adapt the discourse of law and, especially, that of rights to reflect their own interests and orientations.

What was remarkable here, then, is that as discourse changed and elicited novel kinds of action, a web of social relationships was forming. Just as ideology in the form of beliefs inherited by American colonists from the English Opposition with their emphasis on the rights of "freeborn Englishmen" had shaped the American Revolution, legal ideas provided both a discourse and a framework of relationships for organizing the new republic (Bailyn, 1967; Wood, 1991; Reid, 1978; Skowronek, 1982; Tomlins, 1993). In a new political context of self-rule, not only did a regime have to be formed but a justification of it was needed to win popular support for it. In seeking to justify the new order that was being established and to gain acceptance for it, appeals to the traditional authority of royalty or to the charismatic sway of Revolutionary heroes were not enough. Instead, it was crucial that rules be enacted and offices designated in law to endow them with a special status in the project of structuring the relationship between reasoning individuals and their state. In short, what was being established were images and ways of acting that were constitutive of a new form of modern political authority whose basis of legitimation lay in legality.

Formation of a Limited Early State of Courts and Parties

The nascent web of a new political authority notwithstanding, the challenge of promoting social order was made especially difficult in America by two features of political life in the early republic: the structure of the state and the fact that the United States was a state before becoming a nation. In the history of European nation-states, a centralized administrative capacity and the cultural power of nationality have traditionally proved to be important assets in maintaining social order and in legitimating the use of coercion when it is invoked. Absence of both features in the United States opened the way for a rise of the courts to prominence as part of an effort to maintain social order, promote political stability, and, later, incorporate immigrants into the American way of life.

Amidst the flow of cultural and historical change, each epoch has its distinctive character. For the United States, the nineteenth century was a period of state building. With the great absolutist monarchies having faded and France and America having experienced tumultuous revolutions, the early nineteenth century saw intensive activity to organize self-government and to create insti-tutions to translate visions of self-rule into a reality.

In the early years of the republic, the American state, constructed on the model of Madisonian federalism, was so weak that it led some scholars to argue that there was, for all practical purposes, no state at all.[26] Absent a strong central administrative bureaucracy, they argued, relatively extensive judicial power also curbed the prerogatives of both legislatures and political executives. Judges' powers, it was observed, stood in tension with widely embraced ideologies of democracy and popular sovereignty and created a tension between "law rule" and "self-rule" in American politics that persists to this day (Michelman, 1988, pp. 1500–1502). Philosopher George Friedrich Hegel was among those who challenged the very existence of an American state because the country lacked the formal institutional arrangements common to the great European states (*Philosophy of History*, 1956, pp. 84–87; cited in Skowronek, 1982, p. 7).[27]

Countering such a view, Stephen Skowronek (1982) has argued quite com-pellingly that, from the outset, America maintained "an integrated organization of institutions and procedures whose purpose [at a minimum] was to control the use of coercion" throughout the nation (Skowronek, 1982, p. 5).[28] Richard John (1998) has pointed to the rise of the U.S. postal service in the 1830s as another sign of state activity during this period. Rejecting arguments that no state per se existed in early nineteenth-century America, Skowronek urges, instead, that the political institutions that did exist be treated as a particular kind of state (Skowronek, p. 5). He acknowledges, however, that, among the many unusual features of life in early America, one finds a state that, besides being extremely limited, "failed to evoke any sense of a state" (p. 5).

This notion of the unique, or "exceptional," quality of the American state and its politics has recently been challenged by Katznelson and Zolberg (1988), among others, who argue that all states vary along a continuum in terms of administrative capacity and that weakness in this area is not solely a quality of the early American republic. Skowronek finds support, however, for his con-tention that post-Revolutionary political institutions in the United States were highly distinctive relative to other societies of the day. He correctly points out that several leading European commentators, such as Alexis de Tocqueville, remarked precisely on the absence, not of any state at all, but of a sense of one among the people. According to Tocqueville (1997), lack of a history of aris-tocratic rule and of opposition to it in America coupled with early development of self-rule and a spirit of popular sovereignty precluded any sense of separa-tion between its citizens and the state. In his view, this caused state and civil society to blend into one in America and government to function like an "invisible machine," while its people experienced only a muted awareness of the state (Tocqueville, 1997, pp. 72–75).

Similarly, for Marx, the United States was "the most perfect example of the (subtle power of the) modern state" and represented "the most advanced class yet to come to political power" (Marx and Engels, 1970, p. 80). Marx, like Tocqueville, attributed the lack of a sense of the state in America to "its political democracy" and "principles of political equality" that conveyed, in his view, the appearance of mediating social conflicts though, in fact, the bases of contest persisted (Skowronek, 1982, p. 7). In the absence of fixed social divisions and in light of the early establishment of self-rule, Marx saw "a 'fictive state' . . . —a state 'trying to realize itself as pure society' " (p. 7).

Skowronek (1982) draws on but differs from both Tocqueville and Marx in concluding that what made the American state "the great anomaly . . . [in the] Wes[t]" was the fact that it was possessed of a "highly developed democratic politics . . . [well before] a concentrated [centralized] governing capacity [was developed]" (p. 8). That is, he argues that America was remarkable in terms of "the peculiar way power was organized" (p. 8).[29] As William Novak (1996) shows, the situation in the early republic in no way should be understood as having produced a vacuum of state power. To the contrary, government regulation was widespread in public order and safety, political economy, public property, morality, and public health throughout the nineteenth century (Novak, 1996). In fact, it increasingly appears that free market liberalism was preceded by an extended period of "well-regulated" social life that lasted far longer than previously thought, with liberalism and laissez-faire market activity becoming predominant only after the Civil War (Vogel, 1999; Novak, 1996).

As a consequence of the uncommon nature of its state, the task of state-building in the United States posed a distinctive challenge. Eventually, it occurred in two waves: the first after the American Revolution and the second during the late nineteenth and early twentieth centuries. The task of state formation in the latter phase after the Civil War became one of renegotiating the relation between state and civil society in the presence of a well-developed democratic politics that had been set in place during the antebellum years (Skowronek, 1982). As the nineteenth century drew to a close and issues such as "the rise of . . . [cities on a large scale and] the accentuation of class tensions" claimed civic attention, new national institutional capacities were needed that required a different and more centralized mode of governance than formerly existed (p. 9). In *The Search for Order*, Robert Wiebe (1996) has demonstrated that a comparable pressure existed at the local level which led to the creation of large-scale urban public institutions at the local level during this same period. To make this change, however, established means of wielding power had to be challenged to set in place "new national administrative institutions . . . free from the clutches of party domination, direct court supervision and localistic orientations" (p. 15). In a word, "governmental authority had to be concentrated . . . and . . . [its] offices insulated from the people at large" (p. 9). To establish these new capacities "the . . . [existing] state organization[s] ultimately had to be thrown into [a period of] internal disarray" (p. 9).

Apart from the notable qualities of the American state, one must confront inevitably the deeper thorny problem of what is meant by the state as it existed in the nineteenth century to understand the challenges that its formation posed. Scholars have recently emphasized power and the multiplicity of forms that it takes; solidarity and duties as part of power; state power as "symbolic violence;" and the processes whereby state power is reproduced (Foucault, 1995; Ewald, 1986 and 2005; Soysal, 1995; Bourdieu, 1991; Donzelot, 1997 and 1984).[30] Especially since the appearance of the new institutionalism, cultural forms of power and their preservation have been highlighted. Originally advanced as a complement to theories of state autonomy and state culture, to Marxian and class conflict theories, and to theories of the relative autonomy of the state, institutionalist perspectives have had some unintended effects. Primary among them was to deemphasize human agency and contestation; human development and consciousness as a shaper of a contingent voluntarism; material bases of power; social conflict; and processes of transformation and change. As the focus of analysis has turned to power, both authority and legitimation have been downplayed—partly because these theories accord scant attention to human choice. My own work acknowledges the many vital contributions of institutionalist theorizing but focuses too on change and the role of personal agency in generating it.[31]

Max Weber (1978) offers the classic observation that the state is "that agency within society which possesses the monopoly of legitimate violence" (p. 65). This legitimacy, typically rooted in the specification of state offices and functions in law, extends to political leaders and constitutes the basis of political authority in most democratic nations. Charles Tilly (1975) in his book *The Formation of the Nation States of Modern Europe* works from Joseph Strayer's (1970) elaboration on and refinement of Weber's scheme. Strayer defines the state as a "political . . . [unit] persisting in time and fixed in space, the development of permanent, impersonal institutions, agreement on the need for authority that can give final judgments, and acceptance of the idea that this authority should receive the basic loyalty of its subjects" (p. 10; cited in Tilly, 1975, p. 26). Thus, Strayer explicitly incorporates facets of authority and legitimation directly into his conception of the state.

Strayer (1970), then, fleshes out his concept of the state very much in the Weberian spirit emphasizing permanence, bureaucratic administration, and legitimate authority. It lends an emphasis that is very much an institutional one even as it highlights voluntarism in compliance with state commands. It stands in contrast to what is probably the main alternative conception of the state prevalent in political theory, that is, the formation of a more informal polity, whose members share a common political tradition and mode of governance, as used by Louis Hartz (1955) in his opus *The Liberal Tradition in America*.[32] Here it seems that the view of the state advanced by Hartz seems in its informality and emphasis on cultural tradition to commingle key facets of the concept of nation with that of the state. Thus, in my own work, it is, following Strayer rather than Hartz, that the authority, institutions, and coercive capacity of the state are emphasized.[33] In contrast to the concept of government which traditionally excludes the legislative branch, I rely for my analysis on that of the state which includes executive, legislature, and judiciary (Nettl, 1969, pp. 570–71).

As we shall see, it is because the United States embarked on its process of state building, both in the context of democracy and along the lines of the relatively weak decentralized Madisonian model, that the courts assumed a uniquely expansive role in state formation during the antebellum years. For purposes of this study, the significance of the distinctive form, namely that of a state of "courts and parties," that developed in America lies in the crucial role it accorded to the judiciary in structuring conflict and providing a dominant political discourse—a role that had vital consequences for the way interactions of citizens would be shaped and modulated (Forbath, 1991, pp. 25–27).

State before Nation: Articulating a Relational Political Identity

In the life of the nineteenth-century nation-state, the experience of nationality typically preceded the emergence of a state.[34] When we speak of a nation, usually we are referring to persons imbued with the same culture and recognizing each other as sharing membership in a bounded group (Gellner, 1983). Usually this membership implies mutual rights and duties (Gellner). In the United States, this customary pattern of political development was reversed. This occurred because the vast immigration to America precluded the cultural or ethnic homogeneity on which nationhood normally rests.

While the early American republic was inhabited mostly by descendants of the colonists and by recent émigrés of Anglo-Saxon descent, migration had, by the 1830s and 1840s, begun to draw heavily from Ireland and, to a lesser extent, from other corners of Europe as well. After the failed Revolution of 1848, the ranks of German labor, particularly political activists fleeing their homeland, were well represented on ships reaching American ports. By century's end, eastern and south-central Europeans from Italy and Russia, among other countries, comprised the bulk of new arrivals. Asians, engaged to work on the construction of the railroads, settled in great numbers west of the Mississippi River. Incorporation of this flood of new arrivals was, however, far from simple as the power of the nativist movement throughout the nineteenth century attests.[35]

The immediate consequence of this unusual pattern of political development in the United States was that nationality, which was relied on to provide a kind of customary support and informal solidarity that undergirded state building in much of Europe, was not available as Americans tackled that challenge. To the contrary, cultural homogeneity, which had been a fundamental presumption of early republicanism, declined markedly after 1840.

What this meant is that, in the United States, political identity could anchor itself neither in cultural affinity nor in consanguinity (Gellner, 1983; Brubaker, 1992). Instead, commonality was achieved intellectually through a shared commitment to liberty. For its emotional fuel, nationality drew on the nativist and patriotic movements of the nineteenth century and on racial exclusion. Thus, for immigrants, political identity as an American was achieved only through an arduous process of socialization. In this context, identity was primarily a relational matter. The question of what it meant to be "American" found a response in the only way available—what one believed and, more importantly, what one did, who one interacted with, and the social groupings to which one belonged. Political discourse of the day was rife with imagery of the process of "becoming American" even as the potent forces of nativism produced resistance to further extension of the ranks of citizens. To a significant degree, being "American" came in this prenational state to mean the membership achieved as a consequence of entering the web of duties and responsibilities associated with citizenship.

Forging Citizens in the Context of an Extended Franchise

In the American republic of the early nineteenth century, with its absence of a strong centralized administrative state, challenges to social order were of considerable concern. Along with rioting and crime, artisanal discontent over the degradation of craft was strong (Katznelson and Zolberg, 1988). Although labor sentiment did not coalesce into a unified class position until after the

Civil War, the early years of the century saw the mobilization of Workingmen's parties during the 1820s and 1830s in some cities, which represented the beginnings of a response by "producers" to the changes wrought by industrialization (Wilentz, 1984; Katznelson and Zolberg, 1988). Subsequently, the nativist movement of the mid-1830s and 1840s critiqued and "interpreted" this tumultuous change afoot in ethnic, cultural, and religious terms (Katznelson and Zolberg, p. 26). It was a period of militancy and strikes by labor movements to obtain "a shorter workday, free public schooling, and democratic political reforms" (Katznelson and Zolberg). After the Civil War these diverse political initiatives congealed into a set of class-based dispositions and institutions. Tensions between the interests, standpoints, and behavioral dispositions of workers and their employers precipitated conflicts after mid-century that, at times, threatened class warfare (Montgomery, 1979 and 1981).

Beyond the organization of state power, what also distinguished American politics during the latter part of the nineteenth century was the division that arose, as Shefter puts it, "between the politics of work and off-work" (Katznelson and Zolberg, 1988, p. 26). Interests in the workplace were pursued through what was, despite the quasi-socialist leanings of the Knights of Labor, ultimately, by the early twentieth century, a reformist and generally procapitalist trade union movement. The labor movement mobilized quite independently of the politics of residential community that arose and centered, after mid-century, on the provision of services by primarily ethnic, urban, and cross-class political machines (p. 25). Whether as a consequence of the reach of judicial review and court use of injunctions to limit labor protest or because of the rise of powerful associations of employers to combat the organizing power of labor, American trade unions gradually desisted from their most vigorous strategies and tactics such as boycotts, sympathy strikes, and national political mobilization (Forbath, 1991; Hattam, 1993; Voss, 1994). Thus, in a phenomenon known as "American exceptionalism," labor played a lesser and weaker role in partisan electoral politics than did trade union movements in other countries. No labor-based political party, comparable to the Socialist parties of Europe, emerged in the United States (Forbath; Katznelson and Zolberg, p. 26). Nor did the kind of coalition between labor and the middle class congeal to give rise to social democracy as it did in Scandinavia and Germany at the dawn of this century (Esping-Anderson, 1988). In contrast, ethnic politicians mobilized support on the basis of neighborhood ties, ethnic identity, demand for city services, and contracts for city projects that often employed vast numbers of local unskilled, nonunion laborers (Katznelson and Zolberg, p. 26). Downplaying social class interests and associated conflict, the politics of residence emphasized patronage and the distribution of goods, services, work, and help in times of need (Bridges, 1984).

Prior to mid-century, despite much social conflict, local political institutions, like national ones, were new, fragmentary, and relatively weak (Lane, 1971). It was, as yet, uncertain whether the republic would prevail and how liberty and self-rule would endure in the face of mounting material inequality (Lane, 1971). Skowronek (1982) points out that, at the local level, only two major institutions—the courts and the tax collector—were yet in place to intervene in shaping the relation of the populace to the nascent state.

Extension of the franchise widened the circle of those claiming full citizenship and participating in electoral politics and, in so doing, changed it— particularly as immigration radically reconstituted the population of the cities such as Boston.[36] Foremost among Enlightenment ideas was the perfectibility of human nature and the vital role played by education in socializing and enhancing the moral capacities of the individual. T. H. Marshall notes that "It was increasingly recognized, as the nineteenth century wore on, that political . . . [self-rule required] an educated electorate, . . . [just as] scientific manufacture needed educated workers and technicians" (1964, p. 90; see also Soysal, 1995). As a consequence, education came to be seen not just as a social advantage but as an essential crucible of citizenship (Soysal). In this educational project, the courts, along with the schools, played a key role.

This view of education as a training ground for the habits of mind and character that would produce responsible and productive citizens found one of its first eloquent public expressions in America in the words of Horace Mann on behalf of the Common Schooling movement, the forerunner of public education, in the 1830s and 1840s. "It may be an easy thing to make a Republic," Mann wrote, "but . . . a very laborious thing to make Republicans" (*Twelfth School Report*, p. 78; cited in Cremin, 1982, p. 14). Mann continued to state that however moral may be the characteristics of a people, the populace must, "if [they be] citizens of a Republic, understand something of the true nature and functions of the government under which they live" (p. 14). Over the course of the nineteenth century, the nature of the education that reformers sought to provide shifted increasingly to an emphasis on such personal traits as "effective self-direction" but emphasis on the importance of education as a training ground for citizenship in a world of self-rule continued into the era of progressive politics and philosophical pragmatism that marked the dawn of the twentieth century (Dewey, 1997a and 1997b).

The Common Schooling movement was not alone in the quest to inculcate citizenship. Absent strong centralized national political institutions and given the weak and fragmentary nature of local governance, what we shall see as this work unfolds is that the courts stepped to the fore as a powerful educative force. The mission of the courts was to modulate social conflict, to promote political stabilization, and, initially, to reconsolidate weakening Federalist political dominance. Ultimately, that elite control of electoral politics gave way to democratization. This book shows that as the nineteenth century progressed, the role of the courts was transformed. This happened, first, with the rise of ethnic politics as the courts became intertwined with the rise of patronage and, then again, at the turn of the century, with the emergence of courts as large-scale urban institutions and their use, in place of more informal community-based procedures, to address the problem of maintaining social order. While much headway has been made in recent years in exploring the process of state formation, it is widely acknowledged that the role of the judiciary in these processes has been largely overlooked (Tilly, 1975, p. 6). This question of the role of law and the courts, in general, and plea bargaining, in particular, in state formation is among the primary themes explored in this book.

Comparatively Informed Historical Analysis

Before exploring this tapestry of causal influences, we must examine the earliest contours of plea bargaining to clearly specify the socio-legal outcome that is being explained. First, though, a word about methodological approach. This book builds on critical analysis of prior explanations to develop a fresh interpretive account. To probe the rise of plea bargaining as a legal innovation, this study employs sociological methods of comparatively informed historical research to explore both patterns of bargaining and the configuration of social influences that caused it to emerge in the time and place it did and to be transformed over the course of the nineteenth century.[37] Although primarily a causal analysis of one society, this work is comparatively informed. Contrasts to England, also a common law country, are prevalent throughout. Specific paired comparisons to other societies on individual analytic points are also drawn.

By focusing on the dockets, on the lives and criminal careers of actual defendants, and by examining primarily the activity of the lower or popular court, this work tells the story of the changing complexion of law in the early nineteenth-century United States from the "bottom up" in the style of the "new" social history and historical sociology. Analytically, this study of legal change involved two major challenges: first, establishing the outcome, that is, the pattern of pleas and concessions constitutive of plea bargaining that are found to exist; and, second, accounting for the emergence of this practice in terms of the structures, conjunctural conditions, strategies, events, and cultural images that shaped it.[38]

A comparative historical approach was chosen because it enables one to structure analysis where the instances of a phenomenon are relatively few while, at the same time, making the strongest possible use of the available data in building a causal argument.[39] This approach seeks to explain a well-defined pattern of events in history by constructing causal configurations or patterns of necessary social forces to account for those outcomes (Skocpol, 1984, p. 375). Thus, a constant set of social features is examined systematically over time, although the particular form each takes and the way it operates may vary. Features examined are primarily five: social structure, regime form, political ideology, legal culture, and contours of the state apparatus.

Because plea bargaining typically was not explicitly noted in the nineteenth-century dockets, its measurement and description has, with a few notable exceptions, long stymied most scholars. In this study, a method has been devised to enable the detection and systematic study of the practice. Rates of plea bargaining are delineated by analyzing, and this is extremely important, both guilty plea rates *and* attendant charge or sentencing concessions at ten-year intervals from 1830 to 1920. Next, the patterns of bargaining that were identified are explained in terms of their relation to key social, political, and cultural changes hypothesized to be causal. While not fully comparative in the sense of drawing systematic contrasts to the entire legal systems of one or more other societies, the argument is comparatively informed, that is, informed by specific limited comparisons on individual points. Comparisons to England, which shares the common law legal heritage with the United States, are particularly prevalent throughout.

To create variation in the outcome of this study against which to test the capacity of competing theoretical accounts to explain, this study does not simply establish that plea bargaining has occurred. Instead, it specifies five crucial features of the practice, each of which would be illuminated by an adequate theoretical explanation. The five crucial features of bargaining patterns that I analyze and explain in what follows include: first, the emergence of plea bargaining, that is, the initial appearance of significant guilty plea rates accompanied by attendant concessions; second, differences in the frequency of bargaining across various types of criminal offenses; third, variability in the relation of guilty pleas to concessions once the practice is established; fourth, the precise cultural form that leniency took when it assumed the guise of the plea bargain; and fifth, the initial appearance of plea bargaining in the courts of the United States and not in those of other countries.

Methodologically, this book employs both interpretation of contrasting variations and work toward limited, contextualized generalizations through causal analysis. Britain and the United States are contrasted in their uses of episodic leniency. This forms a basis for probing why plea bargaining arose in America but not in England, from which the United States inherited much of the early foundation of its legal culture. Causal analysis specifies the constellation of factors that historically gave rise to plea bargaining as a new form of leniency in the United States. Methods of difference and of concomitant variation are used to test ideas about structural, conjunctural, and volitional causes and the transformative power of events at work.[40] The method of difference is employed to explore why plea bargaining emerged when it did, the types of cases bargained, why it took the cultural form it did, and why it originated in the United States rather than in Britain. Concomitant variation plays a part in probing how the practice varied over time.[41]

Because plea bargaining received little scholarly attention as it arose in the nineteenth century and was a pragmatic, customary, and often implicit practice, relatively little documentary material, except appellate decisions, exists from that period to describe this practice as it occurred. Thus, my work takes a new tack. Plea bargaining is detected inferentially by assessing quantitatively the extent to which those defendants who plead guilty fare better in terms of disposition and sentencing than those who do not.

Events unfold in this study between 1830 and 1920. Previous studies (Alschuler, 1979; Langbein, 1978a, 1979) show that, before this, guilty pleas were quite rare both in the American colonies and in Britain. By 1920, plea bargaining was widespread and institutionalized in much the form it exhibits to this day. This study of plea bargaining, beginning in the 1830s, depicts three distinct phases in the historical establishment and transformation of the process—1830–1860, 1860–1900, and 1900–1920.[42] Each period possesses an inner unity with transition from one to the next marked by watershed events (Stalnaker, 1967). Each exhibits a change in the texture of the configuration of causal forces being examined so that if, in fact, those forces do play a formative role in shaping plea bargaining as is argued here, significant transformations in the contours of plea bargaining should be evident too.

The city of Boston was chosen as the site for this historical study. Although explanation unfolds here at the level of society, the nature of the social forces shaping the interplay of law and politics in the lower courts requires empirical observation at the level of local government.[43] Boston was one of the relatively few lower court districts that combined high-quality continuous records for the nineteenth century and a well-documented political history. It also provided a good basis for later comparison to other locales. In antebellum Boston, the lower court, the Boston Police Court, was founded in 1821. In 1866, as the result of a court reorganization, the Boston Police Court was abolished and replaced by a court of comparable jurisdiction, the Boston Municipal Court. The Police Court and, later, Municipal Court, which are the equivalent of a county district court, are the arena we primarily study here (Dimond, 1975). The lower court was chosen because, in sheer numbers of cases, it was the primary experience that most citizens had of courts and the law. In making this selection, the records of the higher courts were also examined. The Supreme Judicial Court, the highest court, was not chosen due to its unique nature and the small number of cases it heard annually. The Court of Judicature in Suffolk County (later renamed the Superior Court), the mid-tier court, was bypassed because available primary data are limited to the partial record of Minute Books and to a small systematic sample of case files saved when the vast majority were recently destroyed. Thus, one would be forced to rely on a precoded data tape of selected variables for all cases made before the files were destroyed. Examination revealed the tape to employ quite general coding schemes unsuitable for this study.

Analytically, the study employs both quantitative and qualitative means of interpreting historical evidence. Data were analyzed for, approximately 1,000 randomly sampled cases from the complete court docket. Using computer-generated lists of random numbers, cases were selected 100 each at ten-year intervals between 1830 and 1920 to create a representative picture of the composition of the court's caseload (see table 1.1). That simple random sample was supplemented with another stratified random sample of approximately 2,000 additional cases, again selected at ten-year intervals, involving five selected offenses: larceny, assault and battery, common drunkard, drunkenness, and nightwalking.[44] Again, lists of random numbers were used, and case selection was balanced by plea to ensure cell sizes as adequate as possible for robust statistical analysis.[45] These offenses were chosen because in most years they jointly comprised over 60 percent of the caseload in the docket and provided a good mix of offenses against property, personal security, and the moral order for study. Guilty plea rates are constructed using both the simple random sample and, for 1830, 1840, and 1850, as well as for 1831 (i.e., shoulder year) and 1835 (i.e., mid-decade), complete counts of all pleas in the docket. Concessions are profiled using the stratified sample. Support for a clear trend of growth in the centrality of guilty pleas over, what is, historically speaking, a short time span is also marshaled from others (Ferdinand, 1992; Moley, 1929; McConville and Mirsky, 1999; Fisher, 2000). I then use qualitative analysis of archival and secondary sources to interpret and contextualize these findings. These patterns of plea bargaining are explained on the basis of social relationships,

TABLE 1.1. Caseload Composition of the Boston Police Court, 1830–1860 (Simple Random Sample)

	1830	1840	1850	1860
Personal Safety				
Assault and battery (A&B)	32	24	17	19
A&B with glass tumbler	—	—	1	—
Assault	1	—	—	—
Assault with a knife	1	—	1	—
Threats and assault	1	—	—	1
Forcibly stealing	1	—	—	—
Threats	—	2	—	1
Assault/intent to rape	—	—	1	1
Attempt rescue prisoner	—	—	1	—
A&B on officer	—	—	2	—
False imprisonment	—	—	—	1
Common railer/brawler	—	—	—	1
A&B with an instrument	—	—	2	—
Property				
Forgery	—	—	1	1
Trespass	2	1	—	—
Emptying a vault	—	—	1	—
Larceny	9	16	16	19
Defamation	1	—	—	—
Breaks shop windows	1	—	1	4
Rescuing cows legally held	—	1	—	—
Embezzlement	—	—	—	1
Breaking and entering and stealing	—	2	—	4
Goods/false pretenses	—	1	—	—
Obtains stolen goods	—	—	1	—
Robbery	—	—	1	—
B&E/felony intent	—	—	3	1
Defacing building	—	—	—	1
Stealing/putting in fear	1	—	—	—
Setting fire to dwelling	—	1	—	—
Pilferer	1	—	—	—
Moral Order, Chastity, Decency				
Wanton and lascivious	1	1	—	—
Lewd and lascivious	7	2	—	—
Drunkenness	1	6	21	14
Common drunkard	18	21	11	15
Nightwalker	1	1	—	—
Common nightwalker	—	—	—	2
Vagrant and Disorderly				
Vagabond	4	2	—	—
Dangerous and disorderly	3	—	—	—
Contempt	1	—	—	—
Idle and dissolute	—	—	—	1
Idle and disorderly	—	—	—	1
Disturber of the peace	—	5	1	—

	1830	1840	1850	1860
Brandy to prisoner	—	—	—	1
Nuisance	—	1	—	—
Vagrant	1	—	—	—
Ordinances/Regulatory				
Remaining open past 10 p.m.	—	1	—	—
Selling spirits w/o license	1	1	—	—
Removing house offal against by-laws	—	3	4	1
Humming tunes	—	1	—	—
Keeping swine in street	—	—	1	—
Rubbish on street 1 hr.	—	—	1	—
Retailing spirits on Sunday	1	—	—	—
Driving horse to left of center	1	—	—	—
Throwing straw in street	1	—	—	—
Cutting clothesline	1	—	—	—
Selling glass of gin w/o license	1	—	—	—
Keeping dog w/o license	1	—	—	—
Keeping gaming implements	—	1	—	—
Baggage wagon in street more than 1 hr.	—	1	—	—
Obstructing horse cars on metropolitan railroad	—	—	—	1
Knowingly selling corrupted meat	—	1	—	—
Horse at large	—	—	—	1
Keeping house of ill fame	—	—	1	—
Using wagon w/o license	—	—	1	—
Sidewalk iced more than 6 hrs.	—	—	1	—
Lighted cigar in street	—	—	1	—
Cellar door open more than 5 hrs.	—	—	1	—
Disobedient and stubborn child	1	—	—	—
Malicious mischief	—	—	1	—
Internal Police				
Secular business on Lord's Day	1	—	—	4
Insanity	1	4	5	2
Totals	98	100	102	98

institutions, laws, cultural ways of acting and thinking, events, and discourse hypothesized to be causal. Quantitative analysis of the docket of the lower court is combined with interpretive study of case decisions, papers and diaries of lawyers and judges, public documents, and newspapers as well as secondary sources.

To strengthen the results of the comparatively informed historical analysis, a second explanatory strand of the study explores, on just a limited basis, the incidence of concessions granted by the court to various social and economic groups—using here only the most basic techniques of statistical analysis. This part of the study relies on the collection of information on the class, race, gender, and ethnicity of a subset of the defendants, who had been sampled from the dockets, through use of socio-economic data noted in the docket and jail records along with the difficult and time-consuming process of linking (or matching) the defendants with their entries in the 100 percent coverage manuscript U.S. Census Schedules.[46]

As we turn now to examine the insights that this research produced, the second chapter builds on efforts in this introductory one to contextualize law and the courts amidst the politics of the day. The chapter delves in more detail into the historical specifics of the structural and imaginative world of the courts of nineteenth-century Boston. Republicanism, the rise of a "rule of law," tension that emerged between "law rule" and "self rule," and the emergence of popular democracy to challenge elite dominance are examined as aspects of social and political life that fundamentally shaped the role and functioning of the courts. The third chapter provides theoretical perspective on court activity in the early republic, in general, and on plea bargaining, in particular. Strengths and weaknesses of alternative theoretical perspectives on law are examined, and competing models are then formulated and the problematics to which each sensitizes us highlighted.

In the fourth chapter, attention turns to the rich empirical detail of this study as early patterns of plea bargaining are, for the first time, fully described on the basis of empirical analysis of cases sampled from a complete docket. Here we begin to examine competing theoretical accounts in light of the patterns of bargaining exhibited by the data. The fifth chapter explores the cultural tradition of episodic leniency among the imaginative constructions of the common law and probes its increasingly prominent use by the courts for purposes of social control during the early nineteenth century. Developments in the legal cultural tradition of leniency and the influences that shaped them are highlighted.

The next three chapters, six through eight, weave the tapestry that explains the emergence of plea bargaining, its role in political stabilization and social ordering, and the creation of post-Revolutionary political authority. The ninth chapter explores the transformation of plea bargaining after mid-century with the rise of ethnic politics and then the emergence of large-scale bureaucratic urban institutions for social control and individualization of treatment as the middle class reformers acceded to power under the mantle of Progressivism.

A conclusion reflects back over the rich pattern of legal change analyzed and considers what it tells us about the origins of plea bargaining, the sensitivity and contingency of law and the efficacy of the courts with respect to their social context, and the role of law and legal institutions in the distinctive process of the American experience of state building. It also offers poignant insights into some of the possible causes of the many pitfalls that beset plea bargaining in the American courts today.

2

Liberty and the Republican Citizen

Rise of the Rule of Law

As the United States moved beyond the years of the American Revolution and embarked on its project of popular rule, the task of implementing self-governance was shaped by a distinctive form of ideology—namely, that of republicanism. It was the republican vision with its focus on civic participation, commitment to the holistic interests of society, and a grounding in a framework of law that supported court initiatives to promote social and political stability and to articulate relations of legitimate political authority. Yet the republican vision was a rich and subtle one with many variants colored by the differing viewpoints of those embracing it. As John Adams succinctly put it, "there is not a single more unintelligible word in the English language than republicanism" (Adams; cited in Kerber, 1988, p. 1652). In the meanings of republicanism in all its facets, we find much of the political texture of the day. It helps us to understand how the Framers of the Constitution could, in the aftermath of the American Revolution, forge a political community that limited the role of the propertyless and in which only a portion of citizens could vote (Kerber, p. 1653).

As is so often the case, republicanism as an ideology was elaborated in different forms and shades of meaning by the elite than by the laboring classes. Its power was consolidated by the rise to prominence of the cultural image of the "rule of law" and the molding of a law-abiding people structured, at least initially, by relations of deference. Because local political institutions were still only skeletally formed and political parties at that level had not yet been established, the judiciary assumed a unique importance in interpreting social rules, elaborating social policies instrumental to the "common good," and crafting the protections and responsibilities of citizenship.

Republican ideology, as it developed, also illuminates the local political contest and sense of crisis that emerged during the 1830s and 1840s in Boston as the Federalist political elite struggled to remain at the acme of power long after the influence of their partisan brethren had been eclipsed in other cities. One indication of the restiveness of the popular democratic spirit and the con-testation of elite power that it generated at this point lies in that, during this period, judicial reliance on the common law was challenged, and popular sup-port surged for statutory law enacted by the more representative legislative assemblies (Horwitz, 1977). Developing conceptions of republican self-rule meant that officials began to experience pressures to adapt law rule to accom-modate the growing demands of popular sovereignty. At the same time, the courts struggled to promote a "well-regulated society" and to favor common law precedent over legislative expressions of the people (Hall, 1989). Judges moved increasingly to attempt to reconcile "law rule" with "popular sover-eignty" by crafting case decisions to promote the "good" of the community and by viewing themselves as representatives of the popular will who were adapting law to the changing needs of the times (Horwitz). As part of that project and of the consequent rise of a social policy orientation on the part of judges, legal discretion began to be used in new ways and through new mechanisms in criminal cases.

Republicanism in the Historical Imagination

In recent years, the prevailing assumption that America had been born "free, rich and modern" has come under challenge (Appleby, 1992, p. 15). In its stead, there has come a recognition that colonists arrived in the Americas with a far richer and more extensive set of beliefs, traditions, and predispositions than previously supposed. Articulation of the imaginative structures, or culture, cre-ated out of them has challenged the heretofore widely held view that Lockean liberalism dominated the worldview of colonial Americans.

For many generations, the history of the United States, prior to and just after its revolutionary break with England, had been conveyed as a tale of progress (Appleby, p. 4). In that tale, illiberal and discordant elements, such as Puritan intolerance, Loyalist opposition to the American Revolution and anti-Federalist sentiment, gradually were shunted aside (Miller, 1970). Aristocratic ideals such as honor, deference, and the graceful passage of leisure were treated as vestigial remnants (Appleby, p. 5). In this first Whig American historiography, the American Revolution was portrayed as ushering in democratic politics amidst a society of plenty that erased traditional distinctions of status and virtue. In their creation of free institutions and an ethos of egalitarianism, Americans, in this view, were said to be advancing the frontiers of civilization. Perhaps the greatest power of this historiography was the values it promoted and the contours of power it helped to craft, for it implicitly suggested an attack on dependency and difference (Appleby, p. 7).

As the notion of "progress" and human perfectibility grasped the popular imagination in the wake of the Enlightenment, its power encouraged those who embraced it during the nineteenth century to believe that others before them had espoused it as well; and so intellectual lineages for American politics were constructed by some that harked back to Francis Bacon, John Locke, Isaac Newton, and Adam Smith for what was said to be their inspiration to early American liberalism. In the emphasis on progress, the free citizens of civil society were presumed by others to share an identity of ultimate interests or sense of the common good—a condition said to have been recognized and embraced by Thomas Jefferson as being of none other than divine origin. Rather than acknowledge that the rise of human reason had helped define individual interests and had ushered in an era of aggressive and acquisitive action, such behavior was simply dismissed as deviant or atavistic (Appleby, 1992). Conceptions of the American people and their origins that were elaborated during these years were thought to comprise a kind of civil religion, which, along with American Protestantism, was a source of normative doctrinal prescription and consensus. By the early twentieth century, the lightning swift advance of industry and development of economic prosperity during the nineteenth century reinforced and strengthened the hand of historians who tended to interpret the Revolution and the decades following it, retroactively, in liberal terms.

Then, countering this historiographic celebration of liberalism, Progressive historians in the early twentieth century began to challenge the concept of the American Revolution as the patriotic response of an undifferentiated people. Beginning with the work of Charles Beard, the Progressives argued that the American colonists had been importantly divided by class and region. Highlighting interest-based conflicts, the Progressives now depicted the American Revolution as a product of the opposition of two pairs of forces—on the one hand, the elite capitalist ruling classes in England pit against those in America and, on the other, the merchant princes "cum" landed elite against the laboring masses (Appleby, 1992, p. 13). In this view, the Constitution reflected the dominant conflict of the day between farmers and proto-capitalists, a conflict seen by the Progressives as motivating politics throughout the nineteenth century. Deconstructing the concept of a unified "American people" struggling to establish institutions of self-rule, the Progressives pointed to the importance of occupation and income groups. However, as research moved into areas previously neglected by the Whigs, the fundamental economic determinism of the Progressives hit on intransigent elements that spurred rethinking once again. In particular, attitudes and sensibilities at times displaced or overrode such interests in ways that could not be immediately explained in economic terms—particularly among the lower classes (Pole, 1961 and 1957).

Confronted with the intractability of post-Revolutionary political life to purely economic explanation, historians soon discovered that colonial Americans of the Revolutionary era were far less oriented to capitalism and a profit motive than previously thought (Brown, 1955). They also learned that a greater share of white males than had been suspected enjoyed the vote (Brown, 1955). Without the elements of contest over economic interest and disenfranchisement, the claim that class conflict motivated post-Revolutionary America flagged. Once these points were established, postcolonial America began to be reimagined as a democracy centered on a consensual middle class but in short order attention still again refocused, this time on the ideology of republicanism (Appleby, 1992, pp. 14–23, 320–39). One crucial seedbed of this reformulation was Bernard Bailyn's (1967) pathbreaking analysis of the American Revolution, which touted the vital role played in it by ideology and oppositional political consciousness. The other was J. G. A. Pocock's (1975) fresh and innovative analysis of the tradition of Atlantic republicanism.

Among the most puzzling features of colonial politics for Progressive historians had been the propensity of enfranchised men of the middling ranks to vote for their social betters for political office and to abstain from candidacy themselves (Pole, 1961, p. 642; Appleby, 1992, p. 14). Particularly after it was discovered that the franchise in the early republic was more widely held than previously thought, the frequency with which elite members of society were chosen for elected office raised questions about the nature of self-rule in post-Revolutionary America (Brown, 1955, pp. 401–8; Pole, p. 641). One important signpost pointing the way to a new formulation came when analysis of the role of this deference in postcolonial society revealed the pivotal significance of prevailing consciousness and beliefs to the politics of the day (Pole, p. 642).

As the focus on progress and then on the dominance of economic influences and solely interest-based conflict abated, historians and sociologists began to undertake concrete contextualized efforts to reconstruct colonial society in its own terms. What came forward clearly was the power of the traditions that settlers brought from their homelands and their desire to preserve those outlooks and to establish them anew in America (Appleby, 1992, p. 15). Appleby points out correctly that this tendency was often strongest among the poorest segments of society and that these efforts to preserve traditions and familiar customs were indeed successful (p. 15).

Among the elite of colonial society, what Jack Greene (1969) has termed the "mimetic impulse" had produced on the part of a provincial American gentry a conscious imitation of the styles and behavior of the metropolitan elites of their European homelands (cited in Appleby, 1992, p. 16). Based on the marked persistence of patriarchal authority among colonial households, their resistance to geographic mobility, and their later responsiveness to religious revivals after the Revolution, it increasingly appears that those Americans accommodated social change even more slowly than did their British forebearers (Appleby, p. 15). Such acknowledgment of the prevalence of hierarchy was also, as we shall see, prominent in the workings of the courts. As Appleby points out, acknowledgment of the mediating role of such beliefs and their capacity, in some contexts, to override rational self-interest pointed up the powerful significance of culture.

Contours of Republican Ideology

In light of accumulating evidence of the power of beliefs, historical inquiry into the origins of the American Revolution turned to focus on the workings of ideology, knowledge, and culture. Its goal was to articulate how beliefs mediated the relation between individual behavior and society as rebellion stirred.

The term "ideology" was first used by the French philosopher Destutt de Tracey at the end of the eighteenth century to refer to the science of achieving truth by "purifying ideas of their distortions" (Bell, 1962). While the meaning of "ideology" has undergone many transformations since that time, a key facet of the concept, as we know it today, is still distortion—but now that which ideas themselves introduce into perception. Most often today, ideology is used to refer to "a pattern of beliefs and concepts (both factual and normative) which [claims] to explain social phenomena with a view to directing and simplifying the socio-political choices facing individuals and groups" (Johnson, 1969, p. 23).

In practice, ideology is most closely associated with the work of Karl Marx, which argues that the structure of capitalism has historically given rise to a distinctive pattern of class relations and to struggle between classes. In the

Marxian view, ideas and beliefs reflect underlying economic power. The dominant ideas of an historical period, according to Marx, are those of a ruling class, and, as these ideas permeate society, they help ruling class[es] consolidate a position of dominance. While this tradition has recently been elaborated by neo-Marxian sociologists, among others, historians have more often turned to Max Weber in their treatment of ideology and, especially, as filtered through the writings of anthropologist Clifford Geertz.

Weber, one may recall, explicitly challenged Marx for espousing a too one-sided materialist focus on social life that Weber felt underestimated the role of ideas in shaping history. In Weber's view, articulated in his well-known essay "The Social Psychology of the World Religions," culture and ideas act in interplay with interests to shape the path of human affairs. More specifically, Weber likened the role of culture and ideas to that of the railway "switchman," as being to determine the track along which material and ideal interests play themselves out (Gerth and Mills, 1946). Arguing that beliefs arise out of our need to grasp lived experience in a meaningful sense in order to devise orientations to action and as a basis for commitments, Weber contended that such ideas form as men and women act with respect to the values that they hold. Commonly held beliefs are, in Weber's view, elaborated into systems of meaning and may achieve permanence as culture. They also serve to define the boundaries of community or, in Weber's (1949) terms, of a cultural nation rather than a social class.

In the hands of Clifford Geertz (1973), these shared beliefs or "webs of significance" are seen as supplying coherence to the legal, political, economic, and other activity of society (p. 9). As Appleby (1992) notes, ideology differs from knowledge in that "its concern [is] with that structuring of consciousness which shapes identity and channels emotions" (p. 19). In Geertz's terms "ideology is ornate, vivid, deliberately suggestive: by objectifying moral sentiment through the same devices that science shuns, it seeks to motivate action" (p. 219). As for its origins, Geertz points to "strain" within a society, arguing that "It is a loss of orientation that most directly gives rise to ideological activity" (p. 219). In the context of ideology, reason operates "within a given construction of reality" (Appleby, 1992, p. 20). Renewed emphasis on culture and, specifically, republican ideology in post-Revolutionary America prompted "the abandonment of liberalism's conceptually lean, rational, autonomous, self-improving individual in favor of a social creature given to passion, responsive to symbols, animated by moral imperatives, and bonded to others by shared world views" (Appleby, p. 20).

Among the early works to challenge both the Whig and, later, Progressive interpretation of history was Perry Miller's landmark analysis of Puritanism in colonial New England (1970). Rejecting the Whig historians' interpretation of the Puritans as forerunners of democracy and early advocates of individual freedom, Miller reconstructed a portrait that showed the Puritans to exhibit disdain for the self-interest that is so central to liberalism.[1] Inspired by the new focus on ideology and by Miller's magisterial work, Bernard Bailyn (1967) and later Gordon Wood (1991) reexamined the American Revolution and the subsequent framing of the Constitution. Scrutinizing the writings of the colonists, Bailyn and Wood found references, not to liberal democracy, but to classical models of politics from the ancient world to which Englishmen had turned after their Civil War (Appleby, 1992). Central to these models was the concept of republicanism.

The republican model of politics envisioned an elite community of citizens, possessed of civic virtue and engaged in deliberation with the interest of the entire community in mind. In its emphasis on the good of the whole, republicanism stands in stark contrast to the pluralist politics of liberalism that sees good politics as "a market-like medium through which variously interested and motivated individuals and groups seek to maximize their own particular preferences" (A. Bentley, 1949; cited in Michelman, 1988, p. 1508). In the republic, civic virtue stood as the fundamental guarantee of both political stability and the social order that ensured liberty (Pocock, 1975). Kerber (1988) points out, however, that, while supportive of social order in general, classical republicanism "stands in a skeptical relationship to commerce and capitalism" (p. 1663). Sunstein (1988) characterizes the defining commitments of republicanism as: (1) deliberation, (2) political equality, (3) agreement as a regulative ideal, and (4) citizenship. Freedom, in this view, is seen as participation in the process of collective self-determination (Sunstein, p. 1539). However, if white males came to their "full humanity" through political participation, the vision was also "an exclusive one that favored the propertied few" (Kerber, p. 1664). Those not so privileged by reason of race or gender were denied access to such participation.

Among the distinctive features of republicanism is the "normative role" it accords to politics. Because agreement is presumed to be reached through deliberation, republicanism relies heavily on "the independence of mind . . . , the authenticity of voice, and . . . the diversity . . . of views that citizens bring to 'the debate of the commonwealth'" (Michelman, 1988, p. 1504). As a consequence of its focus on this key role of debate in the process of collective self-determination, republicanism has highlighted the importance of setting in place social and economic conditions that promote "an informed and active citizenry that would not permit its government either to exploit or dominate one part of society or to become its instrument" (Horwitz, 1977, pp. 71–72).

Michelman points out the crucial "dependence of such conditions . . . on the legal order" (p. 1505). Primary among the most valued protections were those of speech and of property (Kerber, 1988, p. 1665).

While such attention to law might seem contradictory in light of the republican focus on virtue, Sunstein (1988) points to Pocock's (1981) observation that "citizenship [even] in the Italian republics was for the most part defined in jurisdictional and jurisprudential terms . . . An Italian commune was a juristic entity, inhabited by persons subject to rights and obligations . . ." He goes on to say that "to define these and to define the authority that protected them was to define the citizen and his city, and the practice as opposed to the principles of citizenship was overwhelmingly conducted in this language" (pp. 357, 360; cited in Michelman, 1988, p. 1505).

Arising in England in the aftermath of the British civil war in the latter half of the seventeenth century, republicanism exhibited a dramatic awareness of the historicity of the nation as an enterprise and of its susceptibility to the degenerative processes of time (Appleby, 1992). This sensitivity appears due to both the coloring of Florentine political thought by the rise and fall of the Roman Empire and to the appearance of republicanism in the British political arena at a crucial transformative juncture, a "Machiavellian moment," that would reshape that nation's history (Pocock, 1975). Out of this awareness of the vulnerability of nations to decay, republicanism embodied an intent concern about encroaching corruption. In Appleby's words, "civil society was treated like a fragile vase . . . [requiring] exquisite care" (p. 21).

In England, republicanism was "a language of nostalgia pitting the [gentry of the] Country against the [moneyed men of commerce whose wealth enhanced the] Court . . . [In short, it pit] the rural against the commercial" (Kerber, 1988, p. 1664). This Renaissance ideology was essentially "hostile to change," and it viewed the "remarkable innovations [of the eighteenth century] . . . as an alien intrusion" (Appleby, 1992, p. 22). Thus, republican writings expressing fears of "luxury, degeneration, loss of virtue, decaying standards, and . . . enslavement" can be understood, not only as commentaries on citizenship, but as "reactions to the economic developments which were rendering the [political] models of antiquity . . . irrelevant to modern Europe" (Appleby, p. 22). Unlike the Whig historians who depicted the leaders of the American Revolution as possessed of rational self-interest and touting progress, the republican vision conveys unease about change. In Appleby's words, "Like Miller's Puritans [before hand], Bailyn's patriots and Wood's Founding Fathers were nostalgic about the past . . . [and were bent in the American Constitutional project on saving] what was best from a social transformation beyond their control and beneath their civilized standards" (p. 23).

Citizenship in the Republic

In the deliberative focus of republicanism, citizenship, as just mentioned, played a crucial role. Sunstein (1988) points out that republicanism "emphasized the role of the polis as the locus for achieving freedom through [political participation as a form of] active citizenship" (p. 1547). Under this rubric, citizens were required to "subordinate their private interests to the public good through . . . [involvement] in an ongoing process of collective self-determination" (Sunstein, pp. 1547–48). Michelman (1988) goes further to argue that in the republican view, "citizenship—participation as an equal in public affairs in pursuit of a common good—appears as a primary, indeed constitutive interest of the person" and political engagement is considered "a positive human good because the self is understood as partially constituted by, or as coming to itself through, such engagement" (p. 1503). While politics in the republic is seen as motivated through civic virtue, the articulation of a citizen's rights and responsibilities, as Michelman noted following Pocock, is nonetheless accomplished through the legal order.

In the republic, the scope of citizenship was drawn narrowly and encompassed only a political elite. Noncitizens, including, but not limited to, women, children, and African-Americans, were reduced to dependency on the humanism of that circle. In Michelman's (1988) words, "classical republicanism . . . [excluded] from the political community all those whose voices would by reason of supposed defect of understanding, foreignness of outlook, subservience of position, or corruption of interest—threaten disruption of a community's normative unity" (p. 1495). In practical terms, this acclaimed "homogeneity" of outlook and interest enabled construction in the United States of a " 'well-regulated society' that claimed a commitment to the people's welfare" (Novak, 1996). It was a society in which the courts, as will be shown, played a key role in its processes of socialization and social ordering.

Republicanism in the Language of Labor

While the commitments and attitudes of political elites in the early republic have received considerable attention, less is known about the lives and ideological stance of the ordinary laboring men and women whose efforts powered the striking social change of the day. Increasingly, it is evident that, while citizens of colonial America may have been but loosely linked to the profit motive, economic and social life had been sufficiently transformed by the mid-nineteenth century that industrialization was well under way and that labor had, by the heyday of the Knights of Labor during the 1870s, elaborated a class-based consciousness (Forbath, 1991). As an ideological basis of this outlook, workingmen had elaborated their own interpretation of the traditional ideas of republicanism (Forbath).

The stance of American labor during the early nineteenth century has always presented an interpretive puzzle in that the labor laws that were established in the United States during the decades after the American Revolution afforded workers "far fewer protections against exploitation, injury, illness and unemployment than the laws of the dozen other leading Western industrial nations" and exclude a far greater number of workers from their coverage (Forbath, 1991). Above we saw that American labor history has been called "exceptional" for the absence of a sustained labor-based political party committed to social reform and economic redistribution. While it increasingly appears that specific features of American life, such as a broad power of judicial review and the rise of a politics of residence, explain some of the more limited reforms that labor ultimately sought, it is also clear that, until the 1870s, American artisans and workers did possess an assertive consciousness of their class interests and pressed vigorously for both gains in the workplace and broader social change (Katznelson and Zolberg, 1988; Voss, 1994; Forbath). The imaginative construction that organized emotions, oriented action, and served as a basis for forging commitments was labor's distinctive variant of the ideology of republicanism.

In its initial premises, labor's viewpoint echoed that of the political elite regarding a virtuous and independent citizenry committed to a common good. Where organized labor's position diverged was in its claim that "citizens' political and economic independence were intertwined—both requiring a measure of equality" (Forbath, 1991). In the eyes of the laboring classes, law's primary task was to "preserv[e] the social conditions necessary for a self-governing citizenry," primary among which was "the use of government power to quell the tyranny of [capitalists and especially] of the corporations . . ." (Forbath). Labor's republicanism, while decidedly more skeptical of capitalism, was not more antistatist than that of society as a whole. Some argue that "this lack of anti-statism . . . has often been mistaken for an absence of radicalism" (Forbath). In fact, gains sought by labor after mid-century were far reaching and included such dramatic proposals as "hours laws[,] . . . abolition of private banking, public funding for worker owned industry and nationalization of monopolies" (Forbath).

It may, then, not be the absence of a class-based political consciousness that needs explaining in America but rather the subsequent reconstitution of such a consciousness into "voluntarist and individualist unionism pure and simple" (Forbath, 1991). The proximate cause of this change, Forbath contends, was the rise of a uniquely weighty power of judicial review and "a sustained . . . attack [by the courts at century's end] on the right of workers to organize collectively and to strike—especially in the form of sweeping boycotts and general sympathy strikes" (Forbath). Other accounts have emphasized mobilization by employers who organized to counter union power (Hattam, 1993; Voss, 1994). By the last decades of the nineteenth century, the judiciary had communicated its readiness to support union efforts to bargain collectively only if boycotts and sympathy strikes were abandoned. Broad class-based reforms were also stricken from the agenda. Faced with such options, Forbath argues, labor "moved away from the . . . [radical republicanism] of the old Knights of Labor to the more rights-based and individualist political language of liberalism—a language which, . . . [combined] with political choices, . . . radically narrow[ed] the agenda of labor" (Forbath, 1991). Although the activity of the judiciary was proximate, other factors at work, in addition to the aforementioned strength and organization of American employers and a politics of "residence," included the decentralized structure of the American state with its separation of powers, which allotted the courts their considerable power to quell a popular movement, socio-economic mobility and the emergence of a growing middle class which weakened labor's class identity, allotment of patronage on a strictly non-union basis and ethnic divisions that could be exploited to weaken labor (Forbath; Hattam, 1993; Voss, 1994). Amidst elite fears that economic inequality might produce political unrest or a challenge to property itself, Forbath argues that "the rules of the game in terms of market, property and class relations had been . . . [placed partially beyond] legislative control" (Forbath).

The fragility of the Framers' vision was that it rested on "an assumption of a republican politics of deference," and as the democratic spirit stirred during the 1820s and 1830s, that assumption came into question (Appleby, 1992). As pressures for democratic self-rule mounted, "the role of the state apparatus was thrown into upheaval . . . [and] the influence of mass political parties" came into its own (Forbath, 1992). As a result, there emerged in the United States what Stephen Skowronek has termed a "state of courts and parties." During the antebellum years, it accorded significant power to the courts and judicial review at the expense of the legislative and executive branches. Later, it privileged ethnically distinct patronage-based political parties with which a mass-oriented labor party found it difficult to compete. Despite these differences, as we shall see in a later chapter, the model of American citizenship that evolved after mid-century bore, along with its fundamentally liberal character, far more resemblence to the corporatist approach embraced by many European societies, albeit often mediated in the United States by ethnic groups and sometimes voluntary associations, rather than organized labor, than has previously been thought.

"Popular Sovereignty" and the "Rule of Law"

In its reliance on law to establish the conditions under which deliberative self-determination could flower, republicanism created a scheme that would reveal a basic contradiction as changes afoot in civil society unfolded. The tension lay in that Americans, like many in the modern West, understood political freedom to imply two key dimensions: "first, that . . . [a] people are politically free insomuch as they . . . gover[n] themselves collectively, and, second, that . . . [they] are . . . free insomuch as they are governed by laws and not men" (Michelman, 1988, pp. 1499–1500).

According to the first principle, Americans are bound by a political tradition of common self-determination through representative democracy. In light of the second, citizens are assured of a framework of laws that establish the conditions under which interests may be pursued and the expressive deliberation that is so vital to self-rule accomplished. This latter principle refers particularly to the legal guarantees, most importantly rights, that are embedded in the Constitution. It implies that they are not subject to elimination or revision in response to the changing preferences of the populace at a moment in time. Although it is clear that laws are made, among other things, to protect citizens from both state excess and powerful neighbors, the claim of law to stand apart from the sway of prevailing opinion is less transparent. On closer inspection, some tension becomes apparent, particularly in the American case, between what may be termed "law rule" and "self rule." As Michelman (1988), observes, "law . . . [stands generally] in a circular relation with politics as both outcome and input, both product and prior condition" (p. 1501). English constitutionalism, a fundamental series of enduring precedents, enables both adaptation of laws over time through interpretation and replacement by a new act of Parliament (Jowell, 1994). The tension is heightened in the United States, however, with its written Constitution specifying high hurdles for amendment that make it particularly hard to change. Given the primacy of law as a "modality of rule" in the United States, the dependence of republican self-governance on a legal order to ensure the conditions required for deliberative self-determination, and the viscosity of its Constitution in terms of change, this tension emerged with special significance in America.

After the American Revolution, the common law was formally "received" and accepted in most newly established states. Many believed that the customary quality of the common law gave its provisions a known and trustworthy status. However, by the turn of the century, conflicts between preeminence of law and the principle of "popular sovereignty" produced, as we shall see, efforts to reconcile them. Judges came increasingly to view themselves as agents of the will of the people. As they did, the judiciary moved toward a more activist stand and began, by the 1830s, to consider the policy consequences of their decisions beyond the individual cases at hand in light of their implications for what they envisioned as the common good (Horwitz, 1977). Yet, these gestures notwithstanding, the underlying tension remained.

The Rise of Liberalism

Ultimately, commerce and the social and technological changes of the eighteenth century created pressure to construct a new discourse that could encompass them. When they did, it produced "a language totally unassimilable to the social grammar of civic humanism" or republicanism (Appleby, 1992, p. 334). Classical republicanism had presumed "the predominance of politics" over all other social institutions that were seen as subordinate (Appleby, p. 334). Economy, in this view, served only the personal needs of private households (Appleby, pp. 334–35). In Joyce Appleby's words, even "time [itself] existed within the polity [whereas] . . . outside churned a meaningless sequence of events ruled by fortune" (Appleby, p. 335).

No language existed in the republican ideology for depicting a system of exchange that was dominated by economic institutions and transcended the politically "well-regulated society" of national boundaries. The sense of commercial relations that defined a social order and the path of progress was new (Appleby, 1992, p. 335). Efforts to understand and grapple with both market trade and the economic transformation under way in society eventually gave rise in America after mid-century, to a liberal administrative state. Earlier, however, it elicited, in the hands of Jacksonian Democrats, an oppositional discourse of liberalism that bespoke new assumptions about the human personality and behavior that were more individual and self interested than before (Appleby, 1992, p. 335).

Throughout the seventeenth and eighteenth centuries, there had emerged in intellectual circles "an abstract model of the market" and, most important, "ideas about how regularities, [growth, and progress] emerged from the apparently random behavior of market bargainers" (Appleby, 1992, p. 335). Gradually, a framework of liberal free-market thought emerged that moved beyond classical republicanism's lament of commerce (p. 335). It flowered first in Adam Smith's trenchant analysis of the working of an "Invisible Hand" in economic life in . . . *The Wealth of Nations*, published in 1776. Yet the political power of liberalism flowered as Americans drew, not on the Scottish moralists, but on Cesare Beccaria and, especially, John Stuart Mill. Jacksonian Democrats adapted the concept of freedom, as we shall see, and also that of citizenship to produce a rights orientation that better reflected the interests and experiences of the less-privileged. It may be due to this development of liberalism as a discourse of counterpoint, rather than dominance in the United States, that the social hierarchies of status and privilege so characteristic of the early re-public persisted strongly well into the nineteenth century even as liberal Dem-ocratic discourse gained sway. As the century unfolded, "the [image of the] individual with [his or her] wide-ranging needs and abstract rights appeared to challenge the [virtuous] citizen with concrete . . . [responsibilities] and pre-scribed privileges" (Appleby, p. 336). Freedom, in this new vision, was no longer participation in collective self-determination. It pointed instead to the ability of individuals, possessed of rights, to identify and pursue their own interests and goals.

What is perhaps most striking about the life history of liberalism in Amer-ica is that once these ideas achieved majoritarian prominence after the mid-nineteenth century, they were rarely questioned or even acknowledged as a theory or spoken of as such (Appleby, 1992). Instead, they melded into the intellectual fabric of American life and asserted themselves as the seemingly natural order of things as if they had always prevailed (Appleby, p. 10). Amer-ican liberalism, partly due to these origins, was a curious blend of "materialism and morality" (p. 4). The utilitarian liberalism of Jeremy Bentham, which, with its focus on the good of the "greatest number," seemed in some ways a natural successor to republicanism, found little favor among liberals in America. In-stead, it was the good of the individual that American liberals aspired to pro-mote (p. 4). Appleby notes that this was reinforced by the fact that evangelical Protestantism was beginning to articulate "an individual Christian message," which also emphasized ideas of natural rights (p. 4).

Liberalism, as it emerged in the United States, then, emphasized, at least initially, the freedom of the human individual, the capacity of humans to reason and to act on the basis of their own interests, the universal tendency of humans to seek personal freedom, the value of free choice and rights rooted in the order of nature, the reliance of self-government on individual self-restraint, and the binding power of the "rule of law," as long as it respected "life, liberty and property" (Appleby, 1992, p. 1). Gradually a vision emerged of an economy that produced order in society, not through the social regulation of the republic, but without significant direct political intervention by the state to coerce or compel. Later, this liberal vision would rise to dominance and, eventually, be complemented, late in the century, by the emergence of the liberal state and its institutions (Novak, 1996).

3

Law, Social Order, and the State in Social Theory

To say that "law is what the courts do" à la Holmes conveys much of the essence of legal practice under the common law tradition. It focuses attention on the growing body of decisions that judges hand down, which stand as precedents for later choices, and on the social forces that shape them. To stop there, however, is to fail to attend to law's greatest strength and its broadest intellectual significance. That potency lies in law's inherent role in articulating relations of power and political authority and also in the nature of law as an imaginative structure of major formative consequence. In practical terms, what law does is to establish the scope and limitations of state power, to specify a framework and rules of the game within which action transpires, and to consolidate relations of citizenship (Thomas and Meyer, 1987; Katzenstein, 1998 and 1987). Equally important is the power of law as a mode of discourse to open up interpretations of human affairs that may orient beliefs in particular ways, shape forms of social organizing, and influence the decisions men and women make and the lines of action that they create.

Law and Political Power: A Macrosocial Approach

The centrality of law to the rich tapestry of politics and social life is a theme that has preoccupied philosophers of law and classical social and political theorists alike. Oddly, contemporary sociologists of

law have focused relatively little attention on this fundamental macrosocial
linkage of law to politics. Instead, much scholarship throughout the 1960s and
1970s tended to explore law in relative isolation and to highlight "internal"
theories of law, that is, perspectives that focus on the structures, rules, and
dynamics inside the courts from the vantage point of an institutional perspective.[1] Despite the limitations of previous studies, many scholars have been loath
to move beyond those accounts and others focusing on gains in efficiency and
cost savings, which can virtually always be had through cooperation, to ask
what other causes, such as the social and cultural context of the courts and key
events, may have produced plea bargaining. With notable exceptions such as
Friedman and Percival (1981), McConville and Mirsky (1999), and Steinberg
(1984), court efficiency, work group cooperation, the prosecutor, the police,
trial complexity, and crowding in the courts still dominate much of the research
on plea bargaining. As shown in the first chapter, comparative analysis and
examination of historical sequencing reveal that these elements alone fail in
logical terms to explain why plea bargaining appeared first in America and why
at the time and in the form that it did. In part, this may be because telling the
story of plea bargaining in terms solely of courts and policing is a bit like
examining an American Presidency in light only of events in and about the
White House and other governmental institutions without regard for social
context or world affairs.

In this study, linkages of law to social life outside the courts are restored
both to focus key institutional dynamics more clearly and to probe the interplay
between social structural, cultural and political changes, on the one hand, and
a particular set of innovative legal developments, on the other, that culminated
in the appearance of plea bargaining. As one explores the rise of plea bargaining, one sees that, while the practice exhibited an appearance of "market"
exchange before judges and was shaped to some extent by incentives and constraints faced by the court bureaucracy and by the professional life of lawyers,
the more significant causes lie beyond the walls of the courthouse. Thus, this
study moves beyond an institutional analysis solely of activity in the courts to
one that analyzes the courts in the societal context of one major American
city—namely, Boston, Massachusetts. My intent in this work is to explore the
dramatic shifts in social relationships and politics that changed both the incentives and the imaginative structures for interpreting their world that both
court officials and litigants faced in America during the antebellum years. My
task is to examine how the life of the courts was reshaped as men and women
acted on the basis of their interests and their changing interpretations of the
world.

Law and the Nature, Capacities, and Limits of the State

Historically, philosophers and, increasingly, sociologists of law and legal historians have emphasized the intimate relationship of law to politics and society (Friedman, 1993; Garland, 1990; Skrentny, 1993; Simon, 1993; Novak, 1996; Forbath, 1991). Their theorizing about law has typically unfolded in the context of broader theoretical inquiries into the nature of politics. What has been of greatest interest in their work has been its implications for the nature, capacities, and limitations of the state. From the Athenians of ancient Greece in the fifth century b.c. to the great Roman jurists, to medieval Scholasticism, to the Renaissance, to the Enlightenment, and on through the nineteenth and early twentieth centuries, there are both strong continuities but also vivid changes in conceptions of the nature and consequences of law.

First and foremost, virtually all these theories pose the thorny question, "What is law?" Of equal interest ever since Plato first reflected on this subject in the *Minos* is the question of the source of law, specifically, whether law exists as a product of nature or as a social convention. In Plato we find the beginning of a fundamental distinction, which has remained at the center of this dialog— that between natural law, which is inherent in nature and tends to be seen as manifest in reason, on the one hand, and positive, or statutory and enacted laws, on the other. Other enduring themes include the relation of law to justice, an issue originally raised in Aristotle's *Nichomachean Ethics,* as well as the virtually universal interest in the linkages of law to freedom. More concrete, but still perennial, concerns include the nature of property and contract and the rationale for criminal penalties as means toward goals of expiation, retribution, deterrence, or rehabilitation, among others.

In theorizing about law since the Enlightenment, one can distinguish, in a loose sense, three intellectual traditions in thinking about the nature of law and its relation to the state. Despite much diversity within each line of thought, one can confidently discern contours of a tradition of primarily British liberalism with natural rights, utilitarian, and republican variants[2]; a second French communitarian tradition[3]; and a third rich and diverse series of arguments, defined more by the process of their development than by a shared substantive content, which, for want of a better term, I shall call German idealism and dialectical response with Kantian,[4] Hegelian,[5] Marxian,[6] and Weberian[7] variants.

Oddly, historians appear to have moved earlier to emphasize the linkage of law to politics than have contemporary sociologists of law. Scholars of an historical bent who have worked in close harmony with the traditions of Western political philosophy include pathbreaking writers such as Friedman and Percival (1981), Friedman (1993), Horwitz (1977, 1992), Tomlins (1993), Forbath (1991), Thompson (1975), Hay et al. (1975), and Stone (1981) to name just a few. Their work has highlighted the implications of law for processes of social ordering and for the role of the state. Among the earliest to emphasize these relationships were E. P. Thompson and scholars working in collaboration or dialog with him (e.g., Hay et al., 1975; Hobsbawm, 1972; Brewer and Styles, 1980; Stone, 1981). Others soon joined them in exploring how law articulates and sustains relations of power and authority. In their writings, one can construe an implicit argument that law cannot be studied apart from its societal context that shapes so many incentives and interests to which actors in court respond. This book starts with that presumption of the societal "embeddedness" of the courts (Granovetter, 1985).

Law and Social Order in Historical Sociology

In their writings, both Thompson (1963, 1975) and Hay et al. (1975) explore the social forces shaping political authority in early modern Britain. Throughout the work, their purpose remains consistent—to explore how law is viewed by various social groups and to probe how the provisions of the law, as actually implemented, affect the contours of a political system that importantly influences both social action and access to resources for diverse segments of British society. By examining the action to which law gives rise and also the social response that it elicits, Thompson and his colleagues hoped to show how law helps hew both processes of class formation and the rise of political resistance and movements for social or political change. Thompson (1975) takes as one laboratory events surrounding passage and attempts to enforce the Waltham Black Act of 1723. Enacted during the ascendancy of the Whig oligarchy under Robert Walpole, this act "at one blow created fifty new capital offenses, all . . . [involving] threats to property" (Stone, 1981, p. 195). From that starting point, Thompson probes a rich sweep of the legal and social history of early modern England. Based on his analysis, he concludes that law is a "selective instrument for class justice"—a claim challenged for its narrowness by other authors.

More subtle and nuanced is Thompson's broader treatment of the common law legal culture of Britain. Historically, what distinguished the common law, both he and Hay et al. (1975) argue, was its tradition of episodic leniency with its capacity, through the use of practices such as pardons, testimony by character witnesses, and surety, to encourage informal social ties between members of elites and persons of lower rank. This, according to both authors, helped preserve and reproduce the existing social structure with the hierarchies and inequalities that it contained. By the late seventeenth century, having moved beyond the age of monarchial absolutism, ruling elites within England found themselves confronted with the problem of maintaining control over a population of which they comprised only a small minority.[8] The solution arrived at was "a mixture of terror tempered by mercy . . . and an awesome display of the majesty of the law" (Stone, 1981, p. 192).

While royal pardons and grants of mercy have ancient historical roots, Thompson (1975) points out that, in responding to this political dilemma, new emphasis was placed on mechanisms of leniency. Specifically, England enacted during the early eighteenth century a series of exceedingly harsh laws. Paradoxically, though, they often were not fully enforced. Instead, there rose up alongside these laws a customary tradition of "episodic leniency"—that is, of frequently, but irregularly, granting pardons or deciding not to prosecute or not to convict (Hay et al., 1975; Thompson, 1975). The sporadic quality meant that leniency could not be counted on. In political terms, the combination of severe legal codes coupled with leniency had powerful effects. It nurtured an inclination among the lower "classes" to forge and preserve bonds of reciprocity, loyal employment, and clientelism with members of the elite and the middling ranks (Hay et al). This ensured a store of political good will that might, among other things, help cause a prosecution to be foregone if evidence were weak or that, perhaps, could produce a powerful advocate to plead for mercy on one's behalf if one ran afoul of the law (Hay et al.).

The result, as Thompson (1975) has noted, was a political system whose "flexible power reinforced the whole social system of deference and dependence" (Stone, 1981, p. 193). This situation combined with the much-noted, more overt countervailing tendency of judges to give the benefit of doubt and technicality to defendants and the periodic refusal of juries to convict when such an outcome ran counter to their sense of natural justice to produce a system of justice that strongly supported the existing social order, including its hierarchies of social difference. In large part, this was because it conveyed a strong message of universality (i.e., applicability of law to all) and equality (i.e., treatment of all defendants according to the same procedures) before the law. Of course, the dependency fostered by episodic leniency was only one way in which the existing social order was reinforced. Thompson has argued in detail in his analysis of the Black Act how the ruling strata in England, like the privileged throughout time, "created new laws . . . as well as adapting old legal forms in order to [bolster and] legitimize its own property and status" (Thompson, p. 260).

Countering this view, Lawrence Stone (1981) has raised a number of questions about the conclusions Thompson and his colleagues reach. Stone contends primarily that, in those authors' overemphasis on processes of class conflict in eighteenth-century British society, they display three lapses of historiographical judgment: first, failing to highlight "the extreme precariousness of the balance between the forces of law and order and those of anarchy in 18th century England"; second, misestimations of the structure of rank and privilege during the eighteenth century and of major changes underway within it; and third, an erroneous singlemindedness in depicting seventeenth- and eighteenth-century British law in large part "as an instrument of class oppression."[9]

On the first count, Stone sides with J. H. Plumb (1977), one of the deans of British scholarship on the Whig era, in asserting that historians have overemphasized class struggle and revolution with the result that too little attention has been paid to the ways society affirms social order and counters anarchy. Subsequent scholarship has, however, recast much of what Stone terms anarchy as the contention of an emergent democratic spirit. However, early extension of the franchise more broadly than first imagined in postcolonial America and the philanthropic movements of the 1820s appear to illustrate such quests for order.

Second, Stone (1981) claims that Thompson's depiction of eighteenth-century social life as a struggle between patricians and plebians, between "great predators" and lesser predators, and as ultimately constituting " 'class war without class [as we know it today]' . . . in a culture of paternalist reciprocity" is oversimplified (p. 190). He asserts that this depiction of the class structure misses the key structural change of the period, which is the

> remarkable, and probably unique, rise in numbers, wealth, leisure
> and education of the "middling sort," minor gentlemen, tenant
> farmers, small professional men, business men, monied men, small
> merchants, shopkeepers, clerks, apothecaries, scriveners, surveyors,
> auditors, artists, engravers, and so on. (p. 196)

Stone continues that it was these

> law abiding people of property whose demands for equal justice for
> all, due legal process, and participation in the political system led to
> the enormously popular Wilkite movement [in England] in the late
> 18th century, and ultimately to the first Reform Bill of 1832. (p. 196)

Thus, Stone points out that it was largely these middling ranks, largely omitted from Thompson's narrative, who were the main impetus of radical protest and movements for social and political change during the late eighteenth and early nineteenth centuries.[10] Much subsequent research has highlighted the role of artisans in these movements for change (Thompson, 1963; Sewell, 1980; Katznelson and Zolberg, 1988). The middling ranks appear, as we shall see, to have played a part in movements, such as those mentioned a moment ago, to extend political rights and to initiate social reform.

Stone's (1981) third criticism is that Thompson places excessive emphasis on the use of law in the service of class oppression. Here he focuses on the notion that Thompson labors unfairly to make his claims "plausible" by "narrowing the focus [of his study]" (p. 197). Stone argues that, by excluding the civil law and heightening attention to the criminal law, Thompson fails to recognize that England was "a profoundly legalistic society . . . [in which] patricians were as bound by the rules of the common law as were the middling sort or the plebeians" (p. 197). Yet, other legal historians, most notably Morton Horwitz (1987 and 1977), contend that inequality was pervasive in the development of the civil law as well.

Stone (1981) concludes his critique with the argument that, by freeing historical sociology and social history from these misconceptions, scholars will be freer to explore the interplay between an "increasingly complex," changing social structure and prevailing political arrangements—in particular, to explore the paradoxical juxtaposition during this period of "ideas about property, authority and deference, on the one hand, and ideas about equality before the law, freedom and natural justice, on the other" (p. 198). Informed by both Thompson and Stone as well as others, it is such rich and contextualized analysis of the innovative legal behavior to which these structural changes and shifting "webs of significance" gave rise that this study attempts.

What Thompson (1963, 1975), Hay et al. (1975), Brewer and Styles (1980), and Stone (1981) have succeeded admirably in doing, both despite and, in part, because of their differences is to contribute mightily to crafting basic contours of an historically oriented and theoretically informed macrosocial sociology of law. Clearly Hay et al. were describing a period of agricultural oligarchy in England almost a century before the era on which my own work focuses. While these earlier works all explore British law, they serve, nonetheless, as an excellent launching pad for examining nineteenth-century American law, generally, because of the rich insights that they offer about the interplay of law, politics, and social structure, and, particularly, because of their ability to illuminate the operation of common law traditions of leniency. As we shall see, legal developments in early nineteenth-century America show episodic leniency, once again, to be at work though having been adapted in a new way. Plea bargaining emerged as a widely used new legal mechanism when judges adapted the idiom of leniency from the common law legal culture for the American context of mass politics.

The Autonomy of the State and Popular Consent

In the dialog or, at least, dialectical exchange between Thompson and Stone, their differences point to an intriguing historical and theoretical problem—the varieties of state response to social conflict and its consequences for the processes of state formation and social change.

Increasingly, since the 1960s, the case has been persuasively argued that, within the context of a structural analysis of historical change, a certain relative autonomy accrues to the modern state that allows, among other things, variability in responding to crisis (Poulantzas, 1978a, 1975, 1980; Skocpol, 1979). However, with the exception of works such as Skocpol's *States and Social Revolutions* and Novak's *The People's Welfare*, the texture of that autonomy, though recognized in principle, has all too rarely been portrayed in rich detail (Foucault, 1986, 1995).

Ultimately, in the exchange between Stone and Thompson, the competing, and ostensibly conflicting, interpretations that they offer reveal some important compatibilities. Stone critiques Thompson for failing to recognize law's role in maintaining order to stem anarchy during the eighteenth century. Remember that he also charges that Thompson errs in depicting law as "a selective instrument" of "class oppression" and emphasizes that the upper classes too were rule bound by the law. Yet, in what signals a key compatibility in these authors' positions, one crucial historical effect of law is highlighted—namely, that in maintaining order and upholding existing social arrangements, legal rules and the courts inherently strengthen prevailing inequalities and relations of power as well. In an economic and social system characterized by competing interests and increasingly unequal distributions of wealth, circumstances do not favor everyone equally. Thus, behind the rule-boundedness of society, which sustains social order, these scholars see a powerful guarantor of the inequalities of resources and power that coexisted with the assurances of fairness, universality, and equality provided by a "rule of law."

What both authors also illuminate is that, as the ages of religious and then monarchial absolutism were left behind and politics gradually emerged in the West as a popular and, at least, quasi-electoral phenomenon, law too was transformed in new ways. As politics became popularized, it grew impossible for law to uphold order by force alone. Instead, it became vital for a regime to win consent of the populace to its governance. If won, the regime's chances of stabilizing political life and maintaining power were greatly enhanced.[11] If not, a period of political reaction or instability could ensue—in the extreme case, a change of government might follow. It is in this project of nurturing popular support that the imaginative structures, so importantly highlighted by scholars such as Weber (1978), Lukacs (1971), Benjamin (1969), Gramsci (1971), Bourdieu (1991 and 1993), and Foucault (1980 and 1982), assume a vital role.

Historically, regimes seeking to cultivate support have created and highlighted ideologies to legitimate their power. As Patterson (1982) has succinctly put it "all power strives for authority" (p. 35). In Weber's (1978) terms, a regime attempts to inculcate among a populace the sense of its legitimation—that is, a belief in its "right to command" and in their "duty to obey" (p. 943). In virtually every modern society, the language of law and the discourse to which it gives rise has played a key role in such imagery by bolstering political legitimacy. By drawing conflicts into court, legal remedies also preempt extralegal and political solutions to conflict (Hindus, 1980). The universality and formal equality of law reinforce a regime's claims to represent the interests of all.

If the exercise of power in modern society is not simply to be a politically expensive show of naked force, then an approach is needed for stabilizing, or limiting, social conflict and a rhetoric showing that things are as they should be must be articulated. Law has historically played a key role in accomplishing both these purposes. Weber (1978) highlights the centrality of legitimation to the persistence of political authority. Antonio Gramsci (1971) has distinguished two bases of political rule in modern society: coercion or rule by force, on the one hand, and hegemony, which refers to the role of ideology in cultivating and sustaining the consent of the governed, on the other. He points to the strength and durability of political regimes that succeed in establishing such acceptance.

Thompson and Hay et al. have argued that, in eighteenth-century England, harsh laws were combined with discretionary grants of leniency in ways that promoted relations of reciprocity between members of local elites and the artisanal and laboring classes. According to their account, law, thus, contributed to the achievement of a dynamic political balance. Perhaps most challenging, however, these applications of law had to be widely accepted if popular consent were to be won. Here the rule-boundedness of the elite by the same body of laws that were accepted by the masses appears to have been a key factor. Hay et al. (1975) point to the occurrence of highly publicized executions of gentlemen or nobility from time to time as constituting a symbolic reminder to the masses of the universality of the legal codes. In this belief in the universality and evenhandedness of the law lay one key to its acceptance.[12] To sustain a legitimating ideology, then, real benefits in some sense must accrue to the populace—and typically they do.

How episodic leniency, reworked into plea bargaining, helped to construct political authority that was widely viewed as binding[13] and what social forces fostered it are explored in what follows.

Law and State Formation: Challenge to "Liberal Myth"

Although it has become commonplace to associate a "rule of law" with democracy, our knowledge about the role played by law in the process of forming democratic states is still limited. In recent years, a number of compelling scholarly works, among them William Novak's *The People's Welfare*, have challenged much prevailing wisdom about the role of law in antebellum American society. In place of a "liberal mythology" of law, a vision of a "well-regulated society" committed to the "people's welfare" and rooted in common law adjudication has been advanced (Novak, 1996).

Throughout this past century, it has been common to interpret nineteenth-century political and legal history through the prism of the rise of liberalism (Novak, 1996). Now what Novak has termed that "modern liberal mythology" has been problematized.[14] In its most prominent form, that mythology appeared as liberal American constitutionalism, which portrayed an independent judiciary that safeguarded private property and individual rights from legislative incursion. As Novak points out, its roots lay in "limiting doctrines" of due process, vested rights, and judicial review (Corwin, 1911, 1929, and 1948; Novak).

In contrast with this view of a "protective naysaying judiciary," a second variant, known as "legal instrumentalism," portrayed a more "proactive vision" of law in creating conditions for economic growth and market expansion (Novak, 1996; Horwitz, 1977). Casting law as "reflexive" and a "mirror" of social processes, instrumentalists contended that law was transformed in the decades before the Civil War to promote conditions that were healthy economically for an industrializing society (Gordon, 1984; Novak; Kloppenberg, 1993). Although a powerful corrective to liberal constitutionalism, instrumentalism, in its pure form, was in turn attacked both for its "materialist reductionism" and for ignoring what Novak has termed law's "constitutive" and "constructive" capabilities (Novak).

As dust settled after the critique of instrumentalism, Novak has shown that an initial interpretive parry produced an uneasy amalgam of the prior two views (Novak, 1996). This "reformed constitutionalist" paradigm viewed the courts as both protecting property by limiting unreasonable state intervention and moving in private law to constrain antidevelopmental facets of common law (Novak). The resulting commitment to "dynamic individual rights" over a "common good," however conceived, was seen as consonant with both liberalism and a growing market economy (p. 23). In this view, judicial decisions in both private and constitutional law together facilitated capitalist expansion.

Now the theoretical landscape on law and American state formation has again been revolutionized (Novak, 1996; Orren, 1991). New research has challenged all prior visions, including the "reformed constitutionalist" one that highlights rights as "trumps" that bolster active capitalist interests, with another quite different model of a "well-regulated society" (Novak, 1996). According to this view, society is latticed with social hierarchy, rather than rife with competitors and is committed to pursuing the "people's welfare" or a common good (Novak). Resonant, as Novak shows, with the republican political traditions touted by historians J. G. A. Pocock and Gordon Wood, this new approach treats the politically powerful legal paradigm of the day as a customary cultural development rooted in common law. To Novak's mind, this viewpoint was originally a natural outgrowth of a dynamic, common law-based conception of the "rule of law."

Central to this new theoretical sensibility on law were four interrelated components drawn from the common law and antithetical to liberalism: (1) a focus on man as a social being in society rather than as an atomized and isolated individual; (2) a "relative and relational" theory of individual rights; (3) a pragmatic, "dynamic pre-Enlightenment conception" of the rule of common law; and (4) an overall concern with "the people's welfare," which was seen as obtainable in a "well-regulated" society (Novak, 1996). Concurring with Tomlins' earlier observation that law was the primary American "mode of governance" and the "paradigmatic discourse" for explaining American life during the early nineteenth century, Novak charges that past scholarship has wrongly imputed to the antebellum years many facets of our contemporary liberal worldview. He seeks to restore a sense of the "public prerogatives" and of the "privileges and duties" that were central to the nineteenth-century American "rule of law."

My own work responds to this important argument by contending that the rise of market society and the persistence of hierarchy were not mutually exclusive in the United States during the antebellum years. To the contrary, the workings of the markets reinforced both social hierarchy and Whig market-based economic power. Distinctive conceptions of freedom, practical efforts to instill it, emergent notions of political authority, financial regulations, and comprehensive pricing structures all powerfully leveraged the workings of exchange in markets that were formally "free."

My work also retrieves liberalism and shows how its rise was not entirely precluded by social regulation during these antebellum years. The discourse of this "well-regulated society" was not a single unitary one. Instead, discourse, as I will show, emerged as a ground of contestation. Capacities of language to shape and construct social reality led Jacksonian Democrats to struggle to re-work the Whig vision of liberty into a new, more rights-based one that was consonant with their own experiences and interests.

During the antebellum years, the imagery of a well-regulated society served as the conceptual canopy in a project of constructing post-Revolutionary polit-ical authority and in reimagining the political subject in a way suited to a world of self-rule. Much of the work of consolidating that authority and of articulating a sense of the duties and rights of political membership was, as we shall see, undertaken by the courts. Ultimately the conception of the citizen that emerged was one of a person formally free but with liberty to choose among options whose contours and terms of trade were, in fact, extremely limited. That dis-tinctive vision of freedom reflected commitment to a "regulated" society and a particular notion of the "people's welfare" that fostered growth while explicitly tolerating, and even reinforcing, existing contours of economic and political power. Both in formal judicial decisions and in practical discretionary arrange-ments for resolving cases before the courts, a vision of political subjectivity was elaborated and inculcated.

As courts and community leaders worked to shape that conception of post-Revolutionary authority and of the political subject, however, twin issues of "What order?" and "Whose welfare?" began to be raised. As market forces differentiated economic interests and geographic mobility uprooted commun-ity ties, the relational, "well-regulated" world envisioned by legal scholars such as Joseph Story increasingly came under strain. Traditional social hierarchies ultimately were threatened by the rise of free markets though they initially proved resilient (Orren, 1991). I will show that, as the democratic spirit stirred during the Age of Jackson, struggle surfaced, both within and among social ranks, to appropriate and transform the language and imagery of liberty and social membership. Courts, workplaces, churches, and schools all provided key institutional arenas in which this contest unfolded. In response, judges, like employers, ministers, educators, and philanthropists, worked to ensure the "embeddedness," or to reconnect, persons of all ranks in the powerful network of informal social control afforded by the web of membership of everyday life. That is to say, they sought to reassert the social, relational, and ordered nature of their society as they or, more accurately, the Whigs envisioned it.

As this emphasis on social hierarchy and informal control heightened the power of employers and patriarchs, some among the "producing" ranks began to press for freedoms such as the ability to sever an employment relation, the abolition of slavery, and protections against what had traditionally been the intrusive supervisory powers of the state over the personal lives of defendants in criminal cases. As they did, they found inspiration in post-Enlightenment liberal ideas from France, England, and Germany as translated, among other things, through Unitarianism and then transcendentalism (Sellers, 1991). Despite these stirrings of contestation, it was the post-Federalist Whig conception of a well-regulated hierarchical society committed to the "common good" and grounded in common law that, despite many changes ushered in by the American Revolution, dominated legal discourse well into the nineteenth century (Wood, 1991; Novak, 1996). The pervasiveness and coherence of this struggle is evidenced, in part, by strong parallels and interplay between developments in labor law and those in the criminal courts.

My work, then, while accepting the power of the legal discourse of a "well-regulated society" committed to the popular welfare, challenges any conception of it as a universal and monolithic one—highlighting contestation in the arenas of language, cultural practices, and institutional arrangements as part of a process of constituting the disparate realities of competing social groups.

As we turn now to focus in closer detail on the role of plea bargaining in this drama, the story that unfolds suggests that construction of political authority as a basis of popular order relies, not only on legal codes per se, but in practical social arrangements for interpreting them that create relationships between citizen and state, shape action and thinking in ways that solidify popular support, and promote acceptance of authority as binding.[15] How episodic leniency, reworked into plea bargaining, helped to construct such acceptance and what social forces shaped this metamorphosis are the focus of the pages of this book that follow.

Early Sociological Perspectives on Law: Weber and Marx

Much of today's theorizing about the state and law as well as the factors shaping them has its earliest roots in the writings of Karl Marx and Max Weber. Historically, some of the most compelling arguments put forward to account for the ascendancy of the influence of a common law-based "rule of law" during this period have tended in the direction of economic "instrumentalism" that depicted legal developments of the day as responding to the needs of a nation embarked on a project of economic growth and development (Friedman, 1973;

Hurst, 2001; and Tomlins, 1993, p. 28). In this view, law's heightened importance in the modern era stems from the fact that prodigious market activity and production "requires legal improvements that increase the certainty and predictability of exchange relationships" (Gordon, 1984, pp. 78–81). Enhanced productivity, according to this view, enables the owners of capital to flourish and fosters the well-being of an elite united by shared class interests. While most persuasively and consistently argued by Friedman (1973, 1977, 1979, 1981, and 1993) and Horwitz (1977), this view finds what may be its pithiest statement in Hall's (1989) claim that "Personal and group interests have always ordered the course of legal development; instrumentalism has been the way of the law" (p. 353). In its emphasis on human interests, social class, and the tendency of law to reflect prevailing material and social conditions, this outlook owes much to sensitizing concepts borrowed from the works of Karl Marx.

In the Marxian view, laws are part of the political ideology of a society—just as, for him, religion and philosophy are ideologies as well. As ideology, law, like all cultural elements, is portrayed as mirroring social arrangements rooted in the structure of the economy. The defining feature of that economy for Marx is what he terms a mode of production or the structured set of social relations in terms of which the productive activity of a society is organized, with capitalism being, in Marx's estimate, the most powerful yet to arise in human history. According to Marx, such productive arrangements—be they ancient, feudal, or capitalist—give rise to a class structure that is differentiated into social groups whose members possess common interests as a result of their shared orientation toward the organization and ownership of the means of production. While Marx acknowledges the existence of transitional and intermediate classes in his political writings, he emphasizes the paramount role of the wage laboring and capitalist classes, to which he sees all other classes tending to reduce, in the industrializing economy of his day. Thompson (1975) has noted the heavy dependence of capitalism on the legal order because law defines the relationships such as property, contract, and sale that are constitutive of that form of production.

For Marx, ultimately, property emerges as the area of law that is of greatest consequence. Property, in his view, is an inherently social phenomenon—only as a member of society can a person meaningfully claim ownership. The significance of this for capitalism is that private property is the sine qua non of the exclusive ownership of the tools and materials for production that defines the capitalist class. It is this exclusivity which compels those who do not own them to work for others for a wage. Thus, it is private property that, paradoxically, both sustains capitalism and lays the groundwork for the conflict that imperils it. Absent this institution of ownership, capitalist production and exchange would founder.[16]

While law for Marx is primarily an ideology that historically has upheld private property and articulated the productive arrangements of capitalism, he also accords legal institutions several other very specific roles (Cain and Hunt, 1979). First, the power that arises from economic inequality is obscured and criticism quelled because law conveys a message of applicability to all and of equal treatment, despite the fact that class-based inequality remains unchanged. It, thus, supports state claims to represent the interests of all citizens. As a result, according to Marx, the potential for political movements seeking change may be diminished. Second, by upholding social order, law reinforces the existing social order and, with it, the inequality it contains. Third, law in the Marxian view provides a framework for resolving disputes among members of the ruling elite which may further stabilize elite dominance.

Despite the strong linkages Marx presumes between law and ruling class interests, he is often interpreted to hold that law develops according to an at least partially autonomous logic that reflects some degree of freedom of the state from economic influences (Cain and Hunt, 1979).[17] Where such independence exists, law and politics may operate and develop, to some extent, according to their own inner logics. Fred Block (1977), for example, argues that public officials, by responding to the demands of their constituents in their quest for reelection, tend to promote a healthy business climate that, consequently, bolsters the position of the owners of capital. Yet, whatever the relative autonomy that accrues to legal discourse and logic, this does not diminish for Marx the role of the economy as a pivotal formative influence in law as in every other area of social life.

In terms of social change, law for Marx can neither constrain nor initiate social transformation (Cain and Hunt, 1979). He sees law as incapable of forestalling transition if a restructuring of economic conditions is taking place—though the path and pace of change may be susceptible to influence. Thus, for example, legislation in England that was proposed to safeguard the customary privileges of villagers by preventing the enclosure of common grazing lands as private property was ultimately defeated as the bourgeoisie came to power.

While law tends, in Marx's view, to promote ruling class interests, it is rarely used for short-term gain though, in principle, it could be. The long-run interests of an elite generally preclude such a step since such action would focus popular awareness on the consonance of law with the interests of that elite. For its part, labor may, on occasion, enter into alliances with segments of the bourgeoisie, such as where workers exchange their political support for desired legislative changes. The laboring classes may, in the Marxian view, also draw on law to exploit conflicts that emerge within the ranks of the ruling elite. Despite such departures, forms of law are ultimately linked for Marx with economic conditions and, thus, political or legal reform alone cannot produce enduring social transformation.

In contrast, Max Weber (1978) depicts an emerging role for law in the modern day as a "modality of rule" and a basis for the legitimation of a state's political authority. As an advocate of parliamentary democracy, Weber's interest in authority lies in the fact that it elicits a people's acknowledgment both of a ruler's right to command and of their own concomitant duty to obey. As a consequence, citizens tend to subjectively accept the commands and to comply with them. Such voluntary compliance is crucial to a democratically elected government seeking to avoid delegitimating resort to force.

Among the forms of political authority that Weber distinguishes—traditional, charismatic, and rational-legal—it is the latter that he contends prevails in the West in the modern day. Rational-legal authority is distinguished by the fact that its basis of legitimation lies in the specification of the rules by which it operates and the offices of those who administer it in law (Weber, 1978). In contrast to traditional and charismatic forms of authority, the hallmark of rational-legal authority is rationality in its logic and its implementation by means of bureaucracy—the organizational manifestation of rationality. At the level of the state, Cotterrell (1981) has shown that this form of authority tends to produce "a political association with a . . . written constitution, rationally ordained law, and an administration bound to rational rules or laws, administered by trained officials" (pp. 76–77; cited in Tomlins, 1993, p. 30). Tomlins notes that "In the early republic, . . . [establishing] the rule of law . . . [meant] creating 'a country founded upon an explicit constitution and bills of rights, and governed by statute'; in other words, the track which Weber held out to be characteristic of . . . [rational legal authority]" (p. 23). He goes on to argue that Americans located domination in institutions and ideas that represented a "track of formal [procedural] rationality and[, as the nineteenth century wore on,] bureaucracy" (p. 23). These elements co-existed alongside the basic substantive rationality of the common law. Interestingly, Weber (1978) also recognizes that even in highly rational bureaucracies, discretion persists and he notes that judges and political officials tend to do everything in their power to preserve and amplify that prerogative.

Legal innovation or change, in Weber's (1978) view, is initiated when the existing legal repertoire proves insufficient to meet the needs of a significant status group. Initially, he argues, new lines of action are devised that over time become habits. These habits eventually acquire the status of custom, then achieve normative power, and, finally, emerge as law. Thus, in contrast to Marx's view of law as fostering elite interests, Weber depicts law as arising out of what is often relatively consensual custom and as initiated by status groups rather than by social classes.

The importance of rationality to modern political authority is very much in keeping with Weber's view that the advance of rationalization constitutes the crucial motor force of history in modernity. In law, that rationality has many facets—a major distinction, in his view, being the contrast between substantively and formally rational legal systems. The former focuses on arriving at a "just" outcome, taking into account the many mitigating factors of a case, whereas the latter implies the application of systematized procedures, often coupled with highly codified laws and rules, to cases. While used broadly by Weber to characterize legal development in the West, rationalization clearly has advanced more fully in some Western systems of law than others. The term applies particularly well to the German Rechtstaadt and to the French Napoleonic code but less well to the British common law and to American law during the earliest decades of the nineteenth century. Weber recognized seemingly irrational aspects in both British and early American law—both in the considerable discretion exercised by judges and in the variability in procedure that inevitably arose under the primarily substantive rationality of the common law. Interestingly, one can infer from Weber's work that rationality in law is not necessary for either either economic rationalization or prosperity. England, where economic rationalization outpaced all Europe, was far less formally rational legally than many economically less-developed countries of the European continent.

In terms of the rationality of British and American common law, David Sugarman (1983) argues that, "although in formal Weberian terms the [common law-based] legal system . . . [has much that is] genuinely nonrational, it was, in addition to its substantive rationality in decision-making and increasing formal rationality in its procedures and institutions, considered on its own terms, 'functionally and rationally successful'" (pp. 44–46; cited in Tomlins, 1993, p. 31). That is, Sugarman contends "that [elements of apparent] irrationality may have a [de facto] rationale . . . [in] that it may also constitute a structure for securing wealth, power and status—a system whereby certain groups maintain and legitimate themselves" (pp. 43, 41; cited in Tomlins, 1993, p. 31). Thus, rather than referring only to a particular logic and set of institutions of rule, establishment of rational-legal domination, or authority, may also be better understood as "the creation of a new context for action through the empowerment of a particular form of 'creative imaginary activity'—legal discourse—

as the modality of rule in a society . . . intimately related to [and existing in mutual interplay with] its other structures of wealth, power, and status" (p. 32).

In the next several chapters, these alternate theoretical visions and the factors they highlight regarding the forces that shape the laws and legal practices that modulate relations of human actors to their social settings are considered in terms of their ability to explain the rise of plea bargaining in the American courts. Broadly speaking, the Marxian-inspired views see law as shaped by interests committed to promoting economic development, protecting property and disciplining labor. Alternately Weberian and neo-Weberian views suggest that law, generally, and plea bargaining, specifically, are the consequence of advancing rationalization that produces law as a modality of rule and basis of legitimation for political authority that is administered bureaucratically, even as officials work to safeguard their discretion. These approaches have been the starting point for virtually all contemporary theorizing about the state—both in specific theories of the state, per se, and in broader macrosocial theorizing which explores the state in societal context such as Foucault, Bourdieu, Habermas, and Gramsci. To assess the relative power of these competing approaches, the patterns of earliest plea bargaining must be identified and described. It is to this task that I turn in the next chapter. But first let us explore how contemporary theorists have elaborated on the visions that Marx and Weber outlined and the causal factors and interpretive themes which their competing views suggest.

Statist, Conflict and Contingent Theoretical Traditions of State and Law

As the linkages between law and social policy, on the one hand, and between legal institutions and the state, on the other, have increasingly been recognized in recent years, how one thinks about politics and the state has become important in shaping how one thinks about law.[18] Marx's and Weber's writings can now be seen as cornerstones of a dialogue among three main strands of scholarship that focuses specifically on law and the state—namely, statist theory, which explores the state apparatus as an agent in institutional terms; conflict theory, which probes the patterns of interest impinging on and shaping state action; and a third view wherein state and society forge social policy together in mutually contingent interaction.

In thinking about nineteenth-century law in the West, the attention of social theorists has typically tended to turn to the celebrated debate that we have just been examining between Marx and Weber about the nature of the state and law. This debate centered, as we have seen, on twin questions. The first was whether law and the state emanate from society as a whole and reflect its inequalities or whether law and the state, acting in interplay with various other spheres of social life, are constituted through more or less autonomous institution building that can pattern social life and change. The second question was whether law, as Marx argued, primarily plays a role in disciplining the laboring classes or whether, per Weber, modern law signals a primary historical movement of rationalization that is constitutive of purposive action, systematic economic activity, efficiency, and bureaucratization.

While Marx and Weber, individually, have been perennial favorites in the study of law, social welfare, and state formation, it is important to point out that each now is also seminal to a broad approach to the theory of the state—for Marx it is society-based class conflict theory and, for Weber, it is statist theory. To these classic basic approaches, we can add a third blended theory of mutually contingent partnership between state managers and civil society in crafting state activity.

It is the writings of German philosopher Georg Hegel that mark the true beginning of "statist" theorizing but it is important to realize that his work was preceded by a series of primarily prescriptive approaches, ranging from Machiavelli's practical political counsel to cameralism which paved the way for his approach (Steinmetz, 1993, p. 21). In contrast to the former who outlined strategies for use by a ruler in maintaining princely power, cameralism, as an updated form of police science in the mid-seventeenth century, reinvigorated an approach to governance, begun with Aristotle, that depicted "a 'positive' state orientation toward change . . . [along with] growth and assurance of the public good . . ." (Steinmetz, p. 21; Small, 1909; Foucault, 1984; Steinmetz, p. 121; Axtmann, 1997).[19]

Cameralism is the science of benevolent bureaucratic administration using means of finance, economics and policing (Small, 1909). The concept of Commonwealth on which it centers emerged out of the Italian Rennaissance and envisions a sovereign nation state . . . dedicated to the prosperity and improvement, both materially and spiritually, of its people through scientific and technological progress (Spannaus, 2002, p. 1). Under the "enlightened absolutist rule" envisioned by the cameralist project, the state "was to encourage work discipline, trade, and economic growth (the 'common welfare'), with the ultimate purpose of strengthening the state's own finances;" it also included "primitive forms of social policy . . . , [poor] relief . . . [and] punishment for idleness . . ." (Sommers, 1930, p. 158; cited in Steinmetz, p. 21).

Central to cameralism was the belief that the prosperity of a state depended on its ability to craft and implement such policies (Spannaus, 2002, p. 2).[20]

Originating in the Council of Florence in 1439, this political philosophy spread to Germany-Austria, France, England and America (Small, 1909).[21] Surfacing in England and the United States as the "commonwealth movement," cameralism appears to have greatly interested both Alexander Hamilton, through the influence of Louis XIV's French Controller General Jean-Baptiste Colbert, and also America's frequent envoy to France, Benjamin Franklin (Spannaus and White, 1996). More favorable to industrial progress than the more pastoral sentiments of early Democratic-Republicanism, these ideas envisioned a key role for social policy and for regulation in social and economic life to promote the "people's welfare" (Spannaus and White, 1996). As part of its pursuit of the "people's welfare," cameralism envisioned a strong and active role for the state in social welfare, through regulation as well as largesse, in addition to manufacturing and economic development.

In France, cameralism gave rise primarily to a theory of national economic development espoused, first, by Jean Bodin and, later, by Jean-Baptiste Colbert, who promoted mercantilism in the interest of bolstering the productive power of France (Spannaus, 2002, p. 4). Cameralists in Germany-Austria emphasized policies promoting social welfare as well as prosperity and highlighted the importance of education to that project. Writing in the sixteenth century, Melchior von Osse advised a ruler who sought a prosperous state: "maintain . . . [the people] in good prosperous circumstances, . . . [ensure that they] live virtuously, and . . . [see that] some among them are promoted to learning, and to good arts, and many wise and learned people are in their numbers . . ." (Spannaus, 2002, p. 4). He urged state policies of: "caring for widows and orphans, of controlling prices for necessities if they went out of reach, and of curing abuses in prisons and courts" (Spannaus, 2002, p. 5). Veit von Seckendorff, later, added demands for government health care and for "clean water, treatment of sewage, good education, abolition of usury, suppressing parasites (such as gamblers), and providing means by which everyone could make a decent living" (Spannaus, 2002, p. 5). The quest to promote "general welfare" was the goal of such policies (Spannaus, 2002, p. 5). In their pursuit of the "common welfare," Germano-Austrian cameralists were inspired by a belief in the interdependence of society's parts.[22] In their vision of a state which cares for and promotes the life chances of each citizen, the cameralists presented a powerful theoretical alternative to early Hobbesian British liberalism and also to later Scottish moralism.

Cameralism blossomed, perhaps most fully, during the late seventeenth century in the writings of the philosopher Gottfried Wilhelm Leibniz whose views offer almost "an antithesis of free market economics" ("Society and Economy," cited in Spannaus, 2002, p. 6). "Is not," Leibniz asks, "the entire purpose of Society to release the artisan from his misery?" ("Society and Economy," cited in Spannaus, 2002, p. 6). He argues that proper policy enables a society to "eliminate a deep-seated drawback within many republics, which consists in allowing each and all to sustain themselves as they please, allowing one individual to become rich at the expense of a hundred others, or allowing him to collapse, dragging down with him the hundreds who have put themselves under his care" ("Society and Economy," cited in Spannaus, 2002, p. 6).[23]

By the late eighteenth century, Austrian cameralist Johann von Justi had channelled attention beyond social welfare, pure and simple, to societal infrastructure. Governmental activities of a state, he argued, "must be so ordered that by means of them happiness of the state . . . [can] be promoted" (von Justi, *Staatswirtschaft;* cited in Spannaus, 2002, p. 10). Such happiness, he argued, requires freedom, protection of property and strong industry which the state must have the wealth to provide (Spannaus, 2002, p. 10). Going beyond von Osse's emphasis on food, medicine and sanitation for the population, von Justi urged the importance of "regulat[ing] trade, . . . [providing] good infrastructure, [in the form of] . . . harbors, roads, rivers, canals and a postal system." Joseph von Sonnenfels, the last great cameralist, underscored the importance of infrastructure by re-emphasizing its importance to the development of manufacturing.

By the early nineteenth century, cameralism was giving way in Germany and Austria to admiration for free market exchange. Though the United States had no bureaucratic administrative capacity on a scale even remotely comparable to that of Germany and Austria to rely on, recognition of the power of social policy did take hold.[24]

By the latter part of the eighteenth century in Germany, Joseph von Sonnenfels and others began to pare back, though not entirely eliminate, the focus of "police" to a more-restricted project of social order and safety and to downplay its attention to "public welfare" (Small, 1909). At just this time, although "moralists" of the Scottish enlightenment were arguing for the limitation of state intervention to international security, infrastructure, and the administration of justice, Jeremy Bentham and, later, the British utilitarians were supplanting Hobbesian liberalism with another one advocating a state committed to pursuit of "the greatest good of the greatest number" (Mill, 1975). The Atlantic Republican tradition, as we have seen, had already introduced in America ideas of civic virtue, political participation and a commitment to the "people's welfare"—though motivated in a way intriguingly different from either the cameralist or Benthamite vision. Thus, prior to the rise of statist theorizing per se, from three quite different normative perspectives, practical political conceptions of the "common good" and the state role in fostering it were being imagined.

In the early writings of Georg Hegel, perhaps the first modern theoretical statist thinker, he depicts the state as "a creature of property" and often speaks of "the state" broadly and extends the term to what he later would call "civil society," the realm of "atomized subjectivity, needs and markets" (Steinmetz, 1993, p. 21; Avineri, 1970).[25] By the 1820s, however, Hegel clearly distinguished between the two and touts the autonomy of the state bureaucracy as a "universal class" while pointing to the state itself as a source of moral purpose (Hegel, 1967, par. 205). Nonetheless, he maintains a causal linkage between state and society when, for instance, he attributes the rise of a state welfare function to the uprooting of ties of kinship that resulted from modernization and the supplantation of the role of family by the state—an argument echoed, later, by Habermas (Sugarman, 1983; Hegel, 1967). Conservative thinkers subsequently drew on Hegel's early notion of the hold of the propertied on the state but argued that it was conditioned by class structure and tended to occur primarily under republican or other representative forms of government where the interests of the middle class predominate as against an ostensibly more "interest blind" monarchial rule (Steinmetz, 1993).

Writing at the dawn of the twentieth century, Max Weber and Otto Hintze articulated much of the basis of contemporary state-centered theories that tout the autonomy of the state from civil society and the crucial role of bureaucracy within it. Hintze emphasized the "primacy of the political" and described a "growing 'subordination of the economy to the requirements of government'" (Hintze, 1975; Steinmetz, 1993). Weber too envisioned a relatively autonomous state bureaucracy, which, though efficient, weakened democratic accountability, and foresaw increasing domination by that state apparatus. Though a committed liberal politically, he feared that prospects for reform to overcome these tendencies were limited (Weber, "Bureaucracy" and "Politics as a Vocation" in Gerth and Mills, 1946). Wary of the potential that society might be transformed into an "iron cage" due to the advance of instrumental rationality and the decline of both voluntarism and critical judgment, Weber challenged paternalistic state welfare initiatives that might foster personal dependency but, in keeping with his liberal beliefs, supported broad rights for workers to organize, boycott and strike (Weber, 1978, pp. 1390–91; Mommsen, 1984, p. 120; Steinmetz, 1993).

More recently, developments in state-centered theory have highlighted three things: the autonomy of state managers, state capacities and institutions, and the consequences of state activity (Steinmetz, 1993). Theorizing about state autonomy increasingly has focused on the diversity of views and interests of state managers that may shape their decisions and policy-making irrespective of powerful interests in civil society (Nordlinger, 1981; Steinmetz, 1993, p. 23). Such dynamics have led some theorists to portray the state as "potentially autonomous" in contrast with some neo-Marxian views that depict the state and politics as more simply reflective of patterns of economic interests in society (Skocpol, 1979, 1995). Institutionalists highlight the capacities of the state in terms of structure, staff, resources, and legally endowed powers as well as its cultural practices (Soysal, 1995; Skocpol, 1979; Esping-Anderson, 1988; Thomas, et al., 1987). Authors such as Skocpol, Soysal, and Thomas, et al. point to the formative influence of both international and transnational politics and culture in shaping state action. Those focusing on consequences of state action argue that states establish enabling frameworks that may prompt new action, enable the raising of certain issues while impeding others and leverage choices made (Dobbin, 1994). Thus, Dobbin examined new patterns of railroad ownership and strategic behavior that developed in response to federal antitrust legislation of the late 1890s. Similarly, Skocpol observes, "state . . . [structure and] activity . . . encourage formation of some groups and collective . . . action (but not others) and make possible the raising of certain . . . issues but not others" (Skocpol, 1984, pp. 3–43).

A second set of explanations of state formation and action, in contrast to statist theories, focus, not on the preferences of managers or the capacities and resources of the state and its institutions, but on society itself and on conflicts and norms within it that shape state action. This tradition has strong roots in Marxian theorizing, which, as we saw, depicts the state as reflecting underlying economic relations (Kennedy, 1979; Kelman, 1987; Klare, 1982; Horwitz, 1977). One can find several variants of this society-based argument. The first, and most direct is an instrumentalist claim that the state is a mechanism with which powerful classes defend their interests (Marx and Engels, 1970; Horwitz, 1977). Here, connections are drawn clearly between purposes of particular groups of capitalists and state activity. A second line of argument contends that the state, while frequently out of step with the needs of individual capitalists, in fact, upholds the long-term interests of capitalists as a class and that its form varies historically in response to those needs (Steinmetz, 1993). Such is the tack taken by much of social democratic theory, which attributed the rise of a state social welfare function in Germany and Sweden to state efforts to counter a socialist threat from restive labor (Esping-Anderson, 1988; Lindholm, 1991). Piven and Cloward have made a similar argument about state response to social movements more generally (Piven and Cloward, 1979).

A third set of neo-Marxist theories explain state action in terms of structurally based "constraints and pressures" on the state, rooted in the structure of capitalism, which influence state action (Steinmetz, 1993, p. 28). Among the pressures that these arguments highlight is the need on the part of the state to sustain the legitimacy of its authority in the eyes of the populace—one consequence of which is state efforts to ameliorate the harshest deprivations experienced by the laboring classes under capitalism (Offe, 1984 and 1985).

Increasingly there is recognition that issues of race and gender have pervaded the project of state building across the board. In fact, Higham's (1964) work hints that exclusions along such lines may have been emotional fuels for nationalism and solidarity in the United States where citizens, many of whom were recent immigrants, did not share a common language, culture or ethnicity. Catherine MacKinnon (1983), in her pioneering work on gender inequality in the law, argues that the norms embodied by the state throughout its institutions are male norms that disadvantage women. Evidentiary, jurisdictional and other legal hurdles for prosecuting crimes such as rape, along with differentials in sentencing, are used by her to provide a classic, illustration of her argument (MacKinnon, 1983; Genovese, 1976; Reidy, 1995). Evidence marshalled by critical race theorists and other scholars abounds to support a parallel argument that the norms are also "white" norms (Higham, 1964; Haney-Lopez, 1999; Ignatiev, 1996). In a related argument about the legal bases of inequality, Linda Kerber, Norma Basch and Carole Pateman, among others, show that citizenship itself traditionally presumed property ownership and sometimes literacy from which women and non-"whites" were largely excluded in many states (Kerber, 1980; Basch, 1986 and 1982; Pateman, 1975). In addition to the many exclusions and disadvantages under which women labored, laws and social policy also did much to communicate cognitive images of inferiority and dependency. Nancy Fraser shows that some social policy programs involving primarily males, such as social insurance and veterans' pensions, are depicted as meriting entitlement while programs involving females, such as social welfare assistance, are presented as implying dependency (Fraser, 1992). Beyond the nature of the benefits it provides, social policy, such as that in criminal justice, constructs and reinforces norms of acceptable behavior, especially sexual mores, for both men and women. Weir et al. (1988) suggest the term "gender regime" to depict these normative schemes of gender relations.

Finally, several theorists see state response to capital as a possible relation, though a contingent and mutually constructed rather than a necessary one, depicting state and society as partners in shaping social policy (Offe, 1984). Works of Fred Block advance claims of this sort, contending that capitalism can influence policy even when the primary objectives of state managers are quite autonomous (Tilly, 1990, p. 887; Block, 1977). For instance, Block shows that politicians depend on having adequate tax revenues to implement their policy initiatives—revenues that require conditions conducive to business investment and a healthy economy to fill the state coffers—a state of affairs that also benefits capitalists.

From each of these three groups of statist theories, society-based conflict theories and theories of mutually contingent partnership between state and society, we can draw insights about the primary forces shaping both state formation and state action, especially law. The society-based conflict theories direct our attention to the nature and strength of the process of economic growth and development underway in a society (or what Moore (1967) called the "bourgeois impulse"); the contours of the structure of social classes; and elites and their relation to each other and to the state. This approach prompts that law be explored in terms of its relation to ruling interests and, especially, labor discipline and the reinforcement of existing inequalities.

Statist theories focus us on: the extent of the autonomy or political accountability of state officials and the incentives they face (including links of law to politics and the extent of access to and use of the franchise); the structure of the state; the capacity and cultural practices of state institutions; consequences of state action; the nature of political authority; and the content and purposes of social policy. Here we are directed to the extent to which forces of rationalization, especially bureaucratization, are at work informing the state and shaping its action and also what role culture and ideas as well as material interests play.

Finally, theories of mutuality encourage us to probe unintended consequences and the confluence of resultant action with patterns of interest. Study in this vein centers on the contingency of action and, often, the import of key events.

Specific Existing Theories about State and Law in Society

Against the backdrop of broad theoretical traditions exploring the forces shaping the state, per se, and its actions in law, another series of theories, most strongly anchored in analysis of civil society, offer specific unified sensitizing visions of the role that laws play in modern democratic society. These works emphasize the relation of the state to civil society; point to additional factors that shape state laws, policies and decision making; and probe the relation of the state to other forms of power and social control. During recent decades, scholarship on the state, law, and social policy has been dominated, first, by the "statist" theorists and then, lately, by another smaller group of "civil society" thinkers advancing comprehensive theories of society in which a vision of the role of law and the state is embedded (Steinmetz, 1993, p. 18; Skocpol, 1984, 1992). Now we examine the thinking of Michel Foucault, Pierre Bourdieu, Jurgen Habermas, and Antonio Gramsci, each of whom provides unique insight into some aspect of the problem of plea bargaining's development.

Foucault, in his emphasis on society's middle level institutions as a source of power, highlights the role of law and the Courts as mechanisms of social classification and also institutional bases of non-legal power such as families, schools, hospitals, workplaces, and social welfare organizations. Bourdieu pinpoints how social and cultural as well as economic capital give rise to differential life chances and how critical awareness of inequality is overcome by structural processes that reproduce social inequality. Bourdieu also recognizes culture as a source of symbolic power and violence. Habermas reasserts the role of economic inequality as a source of conflict and highlights the roles of legitimation and social welfare in stabilizing that tension in a democratic society. Antonio Gramsci looks at the underside of even democratic politics and ideology as hegemonic and sustaining of inequality. He centers our attention on the power of such ideologies to slow change through the generation of identification on the part of the privileged and hope among the disadvantaged.

Most recently, scholars such as Michel Foucault and Pierre Bourdieu have turned attention to the decentralization and multiplicity of forms of power as well as how power is acquired, exercised, and reproduced. Besides probing the ways power and domination operate and shape modes of social classification and patterns of social mobility, both authors also highlight a shift in the manifestation of coercion from physical brutality to "gentle" or symbolic violence (Steinmetz, 1993, p. 35; Foucault, 1984, p. 254; Bourdieu, 1977, p. 193).

Best known for imagining power in a way that limits the pivotal role of the state, Foucault emphasized its many forms and locales. Critiquing Marx for viewing power as too economically determined and too concentrated in the formal mechanisms of the state, Foucault explores the diversity of modes of power and seeks to show its decentralized institutional and cultural forms. Though critical of the project of law during the early years of his career as a form of power that is negative and restrictive, Foucault moved later to an intense interest in law, governing and social regulation. Foucault sees law as a form of power, specifically state coercion, and locates it as part of society's broader venture of social control. As modernity has brought heightened attention to governance, law's importance has grown and it has become, according to Foucault, a key instrument in the state's repertoire of power.

In his analysis of social control, Foucault (1980) emphasized knowledge and, especially, the middle-level socializing institutions of society as sites for the exercise of power. Though sometimes alleged to have rejected any role for the state due to his contention that "power isn't localized in the state apparatus," Foucault explicitly countered such a view, saying that "relations of power . . . [simply] extend beyond the limitations of the state" (p. 122). Overemphasis on the state as the locus of power tends, Foucault argued, to lead to a conceptualization of power as "juridical and negative" (Steinmetz, 1993, p. 37; Foucault, 1980, p. 121). Yet Foucault acknowledges that the phenomenon of "governmentality," whereby a state characterizes social problems and, thus, designates a target population for action and a range of possible solutions can play a highly influential formative social role. In his analysis, Foucault actually replaces sovereignty with the more fluid image of a mobile field of force relations (Hunt and Wickham, 1994). Foucault also rejected the state-civil society dichotomy as tending to over-idealize society as a "good, lively, and warm ensemble" (Foucault, 1983, p. 50).

For Foucault, society exercises perhaps its most extensive power through its role in the project of classification and, through it, social control. Here his primary focus was on disciplines, practices and institutions of control that operate outside or parallel to the formal framework of law, which Foucault saw as in tension, but also interplay, with law (Hunt and Wickham, 1994). These disciplinary mechanisms, which constitute a sort of underside of the law, exert their power by classifying, sorting, and socializing. Institutions of carceral control such as asylums, hospitals, and prisons are classic examples. Relying on techniques of surveillance and information gathering, these institutions and their practices "naturalize" the process of control. As the disciplinary apparatus has grown in power, one sees, according to Foucault, the appearance of processes of normalization, or socialization based on norms, complementing and, sometimes, somewhat displacing the role of law and the juridical system. The subject of the disciplines must not just avoid breaking rules but must embrace prescribed standards which they internalize and use as a guide for their behavior.

Foucault proposed that state action per se, as a specific form of power, could be analyzed in terms of its deployment of positive techniques and strategies of power, which he refers to as "governmentality" or the constituting of problems as targets for specific types of government action ("Cameralism and Police Science" in Rabinow, 1984). One intriguing facet of Foucault's portrait of the state is his vision of historical transitions in approaches to "governmentality." Sketching four phases, Foucault pointed to: pastoralism; the early monarchic state; the "police" state; and the modern legal welfare state (Foucault,

1984, p. 227). Individualizing in its focus, pastorship was based on the partic-ular knowledge by a "shepherd" of each one's "sheep" and stood in contrast to the subsequent "centralised and centralising" power of the modern state from the Renaissance onward over its people (Foucault, p. 227; Steinmetz, 1993).

During the second phase, that of the monarchic state, power was both "individualizing and totalizing" (Foucault, 1982, p. 208; Steinmetz, 1993, p. 38). By the mid-seventeenth century, as monarchial absolutism drew to a close, Foucault observed a shift in concern on the part of the early state away from the "divinity" of the prince and the cultivation of princely power to a focus on how to introduce "economy" and prosperity through processes of social "ordering" to everyday life ("Cameralism and Police Science" in Rabinow, 1984; Steinmetz, p. 38). Foucault is focusing historically here on the years from the emergence of cameralist use of social regulation to promote state social policy goals of prosperity to the rise of the professional expert in a context of large scale institutions—approximately the mid-seventeenth to the late nine-teenth centuries. In contrast with the pastor, then, who fostered the lives of individual subjects and the early state that was focused on princely power, the late modern state emphasized social ordering through social regulation. It re-lied increasingly on processes of "normalization," which impinged on the body and worked largely through schemes of classification, that, particularly later, included those of law (Steinmetz, p. 38). With the rise of the welfare state, we see a return to some of the states's earliest characteristics for it is both a "uni-versalizing legal-juridical form of sovereignty . . . as well as 'pastoral power wielded over . . . individuals'" (Foucault, 1984, pp. 235, 237, 254; Foucault, 1988, 1980; Steinmetz, p. 38). Thus, the state today for Foucault provides a combination of "security" and "discipline" (Steinmetz, p. 38).

Despite Foucault's many criticisms of Marx, his use of discipline, as a state concern, represents a continuity with Marxian analysis, though Foucault left ambiguous his sense of the precise nature of the relation of state activity to capitalism and to markets. Transition from one phase of governmentality to the next also remains an open question, with Foucault relying on his traditional vision of ruptures and social discontinuities punctuating historical change. In part, this ambiguity necessarily stems from Foucault's vagueness on the nature and extent of human agency. Despite hinting at human resistance in the face of power, Foucault does little to articulate a social psychology of the human subject or to elaborate positive agentic strategies or lines of action. Perhaps most interesting of all, Foucault almost completely sidesteps the rise to pre-eminence of democracy as a form of governance.

Among those who worked with Foucault, Jacques Donzelot and Francois Ewald continue to focus on the socializing influences of middle-level institutions. In particular, they contend that, where social policy emerges as a state concern, a new sphere of life which they refer to as the "social," is constructed that is characterized by "solidarity," "bonds of social reciprocity between social classes," and the "socialization . . . of risk . . . [through] social insurance" (Donzelot, 1984, pp. 108–10, 175; Ewald, 1986, pp. 10, 327; Steinmetz, 1993, p. 39). Focused primarily on legal text rather than on juridical practice, their vision of "la société assurantielle" downplays rights in favor of duties or responsibilities and largely bypasses matters of conflict to showcase a focus on the mutuality to which these developments give rise. Thus, for this study, Foucault asks how the social classifications that shape life chances are made and what role state "governmentality" and society's mid-level institutions play in that process.

In Pierre Bourdieu, one finds, as in Foucault, a similar focus on the forces of coherence in social life but a richer treatment of human agency and choice and of the processes creating social distinction. Bourdieu highlights cultural practices as a site of power and basis of social reproduction. He attempts to debunk what he sees as a false contrast between subjective and objective by showing how the so-called objective aspects of social life depend on what we traditionally think of as subjective understandings that are often unstated and that the "subjective" is conversely shaped by the seemingly objective circumstances amidst which it arises (Calhoun et al., 1994).[26] Positing the roots of objectivity, then, in the subjective, Bourdieu seeks to use this approach to develop a new theory of knowledge (or epistemology).[27]

Proposing a theory of cultural practice, Bourdieu highlights the crucial role of quasi-rules which regulate patterns of ongoing behavior that are constitutive of social structure and institutions. It is these practices and routines that give life, in his view, much of its continuity (Calhoun et al., 1994). Hewing a path between views of women and men as constituting social life and constituted by it, Bourdieu treats social life as a "mutually constituting interplay of structures, dispositions and actions in which structures and knowledge produce orientations to action and [the resulting patterned acts] . . . are constitutive of social structure" (Calhoun et al.).[28] Practice, however, does not simply reflect orientations shaped by social structure; instead it reveals "improvisation" that draws on culture, personal trajectory and ability to "play the game" of interaction (Calhoun et al.).

The capacity for structured improvisation is conditioned by what Bourdieu calls the "habitus," a repertoire of "generative schemes" for action that are both durably inscribed in the "social construction of self" and transposable across "fields" or areas of life (Calhoun et al., 1994).[29] Some speak of the habitus as the "site of the person in action" where structure and action meet and interplay (Calhoun et al.).[30]

If Bourdieu sought to provide a more nuanced view than Marx or Foucault of human agency amidst structured patterns of actions and relationships, he also offered a different conception of power and a subtler view of culture. For Bourdieu, as for Marx, the source of power lay primarily in capital. Whereas, for Marx, capital was an inherently economic concept, however, Bourdieu expands it to include social and cultural advantages as well. Society is structured, according to Bourdieu, by the uneven allotment of this capital.[31] One's capacity to accumulate capital within the context of these distributions defines one's trajectory or life chances.

Social and cultural capital, the first two of his three types, are forms of what Bourdieu calls "symbolic capital" and, consequently, a basis of symbolic power which mask economic domination by "essentializing" it—a theme developed earlier and more fully by Antonio Gramsci, as we shall see in a moment (Calhoun et al., 1994).[32] In this way symbolic capital contributes to the maintenance and legitimation of class relations through "misrecognition" (Calhoun et al.). In agreement with Marx, Bourdieu depicts economic capital, his third sort, as primary because it is most easily transformed into the other forms of capital. Given this primacy of the economic form, it is not surprising that Bourdieu places social class, which is a product of one's relation to economic capital, at the center of his analysis.[33]

Eschewing a Marxian teleological philosophy of history along with the reflection theory of culture, Bourdieu undertakes "relational" analysis of cultural practices within a field.[34] One's standing is the product of the interplay between activity repertoires of the habitus and one's place at any given point in a field of positions shaped by distributions of capital that change historically over time (Calhoun et al.). Each field is embedded in a structured set of societal class relations and institutions where struggle is ongoing both for power and to define the field (Calhoun et al.). Social practices take form as improvising individuals draw in their actions on class habitus and capital within the logic of a field.[35]

Bourdieu helps us to understand, finally, how the habitus and cultural practices of dominated groups veil the bases of their subordination (Calhoun et al., 1994). Growing reliance by the poor on security, in the sense of social welfare as a state function that abates the recognition of inequality, is highlighted. Social control, we also see, occurs through the use of state power to specify a range of tolerable deviation in behavior and to punish acts that exceed that range (Calhoun et al.). Failure to safeguard liberty, for Bourdieu, does not, as for Habermas, jeopardize legitimation but is rather folly in the exercise of power, quite simply bad government, and can be remedied by a change of regime.

In sum, Bourdieu highlights the potential for regulated "improvisation" within the context of "habitus" as well as the enabling power and constraints imposed on action by various forms of "capital" and location within a particular symbolic "field" (Bourdieu, 1977, pp. 72, 79; 1984, pp. 170–71; 1985). Perhaps most widely known, then, is Bourdieu's analysis of social reproduction whereby social groups, specified in terms of their distinctive forms of capital, replenish their ranks and ensure continuity of the structured patterns of relationships that bolster their prospects and life chances. Although Bourdieu attends more fully than Foucault to social conflict by drawing on notions of "habitus," "field," and struggles over distinction in ways quite compatible with neo-Marxist theory of a partially autonomous state, his work, practically speaking, tends to be used most often to account for the perpetuation of social reproduction rather than for conflict, rupture, and discontinuity. Focusing, as he did, on culture and its capacity to foster coherence and continuity while dampening struggle and change, Bourdieu's work is often applied in ways that depart considerably from his belief in the primacy of economic capital to present a macrosocially grounded institutional analysis.

Turning to the state, Bourdieu depicts a "partially autonomous" bureaucratic field and sketches the means on which it relies and the strategies that it employs (Bourdieu, 1989, p. 538). The state, for Bourdieu, emerges as an institutional mechanism for reproducing the power of social groups (p. 538). As Bourdieu sees it, the state also has a certain "magical power" to "ratify the value and even the very existence of relations and events such as marriages, births, accidents or illnesses" and to accord them "a veritable ontological promotion, a transmutation, a change of nature or essence" (p. 538; Steinmetz, 1993, p. 36).

Social policy formation by state managers, for Bourdieu, is a form of "symbolic violence" that conceals the overt coercion of the economic field and better enables elites to reproduce their power (Bourdieu, 1977, p. 196). Strategies for concealment, in his view, include "legitimacy-giving . . . [initiatives], public . . . [policies and philanthropy]" (p. 196). Bourdieu, like Habermas, was explicit about depicting a clearer link between capitalism, politics, and social policy than did Foucault. If Bourdieu also offered a more complex and nuanced account of human subjectivity and greater clarity in his account of the linkages of politics and social policy to capitalism than did his fellow Parisian, his account left much unsaid on questions of social conflict, democratic governance, and, especially, social change. These problems are, as we shall see, precisely those which had been taken up so powerfully by Jurgen Habermas. As we shall also see, they, along with culture, were central to the writings of Antonio Gramsci as well. Thus, Pierre Bourdieu leads us to ask what role various forms of capital play in shaping life chances, what processes of social reproduction are at work and what sorts of misrecognition and specific cultural practices play a role in recreating and sustaining inequality.

Unlike Foucault and Bourdieu, who challenged a too statist conception of power, Jurgen Habermas highlights the role of the state and argues that Marx had, to the contrary, been too limited in his vision of the impact of state power. In fact, Habermas suggests that the state has played a vital transformative part in the transition from traditional society that was organized along lines of kinship to a capitalist one that is re-oriented to markets and other economic institutions. Without the state, he contends, the security, order, and predictability needed for those markets to function would not have existed.[36]

Despite this key role for the state, it probably oversteps to attribute to Habermas a statist view of politics. Habermas (1985) sees economically based class structures, domination, and conflict, along with social movements mobilizing from the life world as against the colonizing tendencies of the modern day, as primary dynamics of social change. Throughout much of the twentieth century, the scope of state activity expanded with the rise of social welfare as a state function—though this role has come under challenge since the late 1970s. But, earlier, with the appearance of democracy, ideology, and, especially, law in the hands of the state emerged as vital in maintaining social order—a role that continues strongly into the present day (Habermas, 1998). However, political legitimation, to which, Habermas (1975) argues, ideologies contribute, has weakened and created dilemmas of justification and motivation.

Though Habermas emphasizes processes of social transformation, he also was deeply engaged in exploring continuities such as the capacity of modern man to sustain an ongoing normative basis for social life. Like many of the Frankfurt School, Habermas lamented the lack of a moral or ethical dimension to Marxian theory and sought in his work to reconnect politics and law to ethics and morality. This was especially important, in his view, with the emergence of democracy whose distinctive form of political authority, the rational-legal, relies heavily on law and places new burdens on it.

Since Aristotle, politics has, as Habermas (1991) shows, gradually become detached from morality or ethics and, subsequently, thought of in a sequence of new ways.[37] By the time of Macchiavelli, politics had become a means for achieving and maintaining social order. Law was dissociated from the attainment of virtue and became simply a means of organizing society. Next, in the hands of Hobbes, politics became a science or, as Habermas (1991) puts it, law was positivized. Law became rationalized as a means for ordering human affairs. In form, laws became formal rules that humans impose on each other by contract. Justice meant only the validity and implementation of these contracts. With the appearance of democracy, politics entered, yet again, a new phase for now it became necessary to achieve social order through compliance that is, at least to some extent, voluntary. That is to say that democratic governance relies heavily on political authority, rather than coercion, for social ordering because the need to resort to force undercuts its claim to represent the popular will. As Max Weber has shown, authority in a democracy tends to be of a sort that he calls rational-legal which bases its claim to legitimation on the fact that it governs according to rules enacted in law and functions under the leadership of officials whose positions are specified in law. This has the very significant consequence that anything that weakens law jeopardizes not just order but authority itself. With modern advances in science, technocratic control may extend its reach in its place.

The problem, as Habermas sees it, is that if we seek politically active citizens, control of society, whether it be political or technocratic, is not enough. For, as we have seen, a democracy must evoke some degree of subjective acceptance lest it seem to float free of its moorings in the popular will. Especially in light of persisting class struggle and the breakdown of traditional bases of legitimation, state motives for acting need to be justified. Yet, Habermas argues, since the late 19th century, the state has distanced itself from issues of legitimation which, together with media exploitation and degradation of symbols has created a crisis of legitimation.[38] This has been accompanied by a decline in genuine political dialogue and emergence of a passive consumerist approach to politics. Both of these developments unfold concomitant with what Foucault sees historically as the expansion of the disciplines and the rise of the expert though Habermas still envisions a more statist, rather than decentralized, concentration of power.

In terms of the modern state, the great danger, according to Habermas, is that political authority in a democracy tends to be of what Max Weber terms the rational-legal type. This means that claims on the obedience of citizens are legitimated by the fact that governance is according to rules enacted in law and by officials whose offices are specified in law. The fear for Habermas is that rational-legal authority becomes a means for legitimating state action that is entirely procedural—enhancing a tendency of the state to become severed or drift apart from healthy reciprocal communication between state and citizen to bring norms and law together. This has resulted in what Habermas terms legitimation crisis.[39] As this happened, the state, always eager to act on the basis of its own expertise and free from the constraint of public accountability, moved, according to Habermas, to an increased reliance on control, surveillance, and policing. The divergence of norms and laws reinforces public apathy and the sense that one's vote matters little and that big money talks which further dampens already declining political participation. Weakening of legitimation can often be compensated by the state through financial incentives such as social welfare payments but the fiscal crisis of the 1970s has currently ruled that option out as too expensive today. Failures to protect liberty through legal safeguards, for Habermas in contrast with Bourdieu, entails more than flawed governance that may lead to regime change but rather a crisis in a nation's system of democratic governance itself.

Habermas advances, then, a more developed view of the state than Foucault and, in particular, highlights the advance of democracy and the unique challenges of a mode of governance based, not on tradition but, instead, on the free choices of reasoning citizens. In his focus on the "colonizing" tendencies of rationalization and its resistance through activity generated in the solidarities and play of interests in the "life sphere," Habermas anticipated much of the democratisation achieved by new social movements from civil society in eastern Europe in recent decades.

In Habermas's work, one finds fellowship with the Frankfurt School tradition that knowledge leading to mastery inevitably emerges as a form of domination. Alternatively, questioning, challenge through authentic dialogue, the disruption of established patterns of unconscious association through film, disequilibrating images and persuasion through art, and the experience of critical awareness through the solidarities and resistance of the lifeworld safeguard the capacity to create and imagine afresh the new without succumbing to what Kant, as early as the late eighteenth century, referred to as the "heteronomous" influences of society. This capacity for what Emerson, inspired by Kantian legacy, termed "self-reliance" pervaded the American experience of constitution making as well as early approaches to thinking about good governance.[40]

Habermas has done much in recent years to modulate his early universalist Kantian metaphysics by tempering his work with a social psychology grounded in Meadian symbolic interactionism and Piercian pragmatism. Much still remains to be done, however, in articulating a view of the role of culture and non-statist forms of power as well as in elaborating a thoroughgoing social psychology. These problems ranked high among those taken up by Antonio Gramsci. Habermas, then, leads us to ask about the role of the state in forging and sustaining political authority, the transformative capacity of the state in social and political development, the stabilizing role of social welfare when legitimation is weak and the part played by knowledge in domination.

Antonio Gramsci, like Foucault and Bourdieu, sought to broaden our understanding of power beyond the statist conception of his day though he approached his quest quite differently. While, in some ways, this created affinities with Marxian-inspired society-centered theories of the state, Gramsci, spurred by his interest in patterns of state formation in the modern west, extended his inquiry into the realms of culture, language, and consciousness. Though familiar with the work of Georg Lukacs on class consciousness, Gramsci rejected the seamless unity of the "totality" of subject and object envisioned by Lukacs' realism and opted instead for a more perspectival modernist approach (Holub, 1992, p. 7).[41] In contrast to Lukacs' "realistic, denotative depiction of reality," Gramsci posits a "meaning-producing" view of humanity (p. 9).[42]

It is in his concern with the modernization of the "life world," which introduced new forms of what Habermas would call "colonizing" rationality as monopoly capitalism arose during the late nineteenth century, that Gramsci finds common ground with critical modernists, including those of the Frankfurt School.[43] This affinity is most noticeably evident in his essay on "Americanism and Fordism" (Gramsci, 1971). Thus, he, too, critically examines "the effects of rationalization on culture, society, the individual, values and knowledge, focusing, in particular, on resultant problems of domination, alienation and reification" in what Habermas would term the "life world" (Holub, 1992, pp. 12–13).[44] Originally dismissing cinema as "a . . . [cultural product] designed hegemonically to manipulate and control the . . . [mobilization] of desire," he later explored, in ways quite similar to those of Walter Benjamin, its potential for disrupting standard patterns of association in the mind of the viewer and for producing "meanings capable of challenging the status quo" (p. 16). Perhaps the most significant divergence between Gramsci and the Frankfurt School is the former's interest in the "micro-conditions for the production of meaning in communicative processes" and in "the structure of language" (p. 17).[45]

In Gramsci's early work we find a focus on "ideas and the power of the state," while later he highlights the "production of hegemony, . . . systems of signification and communication, and . . . the materiality of language" (Holub, 1992, p. 17). Ultimately, voluntarism, for Gramsci, entails freedom and is imagistic and enunciative (p. 21). It means living amidst conditions that allow one to produce, rather than simply consume, meaning (p. 17). In this sense, Gramsci has much in common with Kant's wariness of the capacity of the heteronomous influence of culture to promote passive conformity (Kant, 1959). His thinking also shares much with Habermas' critique of culture consumption and growing civic passivity in politics. At a macrosocial level, Gramsci is exploring the conditions for the possibility of mobilization for democratic change.

For Gramsci, power, then, extends beyond the apparatus of the state to the micro-conditions for and processes of communication whereby meaning is produced. It is through this communicative action, in Gramsci's view, that ideas are formed and that culture and ideology are elaborated. For Gramsci, as for Foucault and Bourdieu, power inhabits a multiplicity of forms. Central to Gramsci's analysis of power is his concept of hegemony, or ideological control, which he distinguished from coercion or the overt use of force. Hegemony, for Gramsci, entails the permeation through civil society (e.g., schools, trade unions, and churches) of a system of values, beliefs, attitudes, and morality that are, in one way or another, supportive of the established order and of the class interests that dominate it (Gramsci, 1971; Sassoon, 1987). To the extent that such ideology is internalized by the populace, Gramsci argues, it assumes a kind of commonsense quality as elites influence it in ways that depict their dominance as part of the natural order of things to which common consent is given (Gramsci; Sassoon).

In part because of this crucial role of ideology and culture in his analysis, Gramsci situates power both in the state as well as in civil society and its institutions, often tending to elide the boundary between the two (Anderson, 1976–77). Among the means by which the state wields its power are the making of laws and social policy as well as their interpretation. This necessarily sparks a competition for legislative dominance as part of a broader struggle to control society's norm-creating positions. Influence in lawmaking is an essential lynchpin since Gramsci believed strongly in the need to engage the masses in the political project, not only intellectually but emotionally as well. Failing that, Gramsci, writing in Italy of the 1930s under the shadow of fascism, fears, in ways similar to Habermas, a turn by the state to an excessive reliance on coercive control and surveillance resulting possibly in the rise of authoritarian or fascist rule.

Hegemony, then, involves both ideological and political domination. Where both exist, it tends to stabilize prevailing relations of power and to inhibit change. In Gramsci's view, an elite typically seeks to sustain an "historical bloc," a relatively stable social formation, which it dominates. Law plays a role in the creation of both political and ideological hegemony, both by unifying elites (e.g., consolidation of common viewpoints and norms) and by promoting mass conformity. As an educative instrument, law can be used both persuasively and coercively. In the former sense, it creates a cultural tradition, cultural repertoires and pressure both to act in certain ways and to conform. In the latter, law shapes the outcomes of court cases and the contours of regimes of enforcement.

For Gramsci, one fundamental role of law is an educative one: of establishing a normative order that supports prevailing ruling class hegemony. However, social change, in his view, is possible and can be won through strategic political action. In contrast to Bourdieu's emphasis on the continuity of social reproduction, Gramsci envisions change unfolding through a process of contestation with greatest potential for generative breakthroughs and transformations at key "conjunctural" moments when economic and political conditions are ripe to yield to the new. Contestation, if it is to be successful, Gramsci argues, must move actively beyond resistance of the sort envisioned by Foucault to posit an alternate competing social vision to which it wins the consent of the masses. Oppositional groups, he believes, may use law as they work to establish this "counter-hegemony" and, with it, begin the formation of a new historical block. Struggle to control lawmaking, interpretation and enforcement and, with them, norm creating positions, is, for Gramsci, a primary task of opposition politics.

Change, then, as Gramsci sees it, emanates from both social structural tension and political mobilization. Moving beyond Foucault's "resistance" and even Bourdieu's "improvisation," Gramsci, like Habermas, offers a "generative" vision of politics. He also offers a conception of critique and the democratic formulation of alternative visions of the future through "anticipatory consciousness" or what Ernst Bloch terms the consciousness of hope through contest (including that over language and imagery as shown in his work on regional Italian theater under fascism) as well as on both constitutive and discontinuous social change.

Pointing to fundamental differences in processes of communication and meaning creation among different social groups, Gramsci argues that there is an inherent tendency among those privileged by a social order to read and arrive at relatively homogeneous interpretations of a text (Holub, 1992). Though Gramsci states and observes this as an empirical regularity without explanation, there is the suggestion that perhaps identification with the order at hand impinges on perceptual and cognitive processes. Here Gramsci proffers one hypothetical account for the historically alleged complacency and distrust of dissent on the part of the middle and upper middle classes. Among the ranks of those who are less privileged, however, Gramsci argues for the existence of an anticipatory mental framework that is generative of critique, dissent and alternative social visions—a consciousness thirsting for freedom and imbued with the principle of hope.

Continuity and Change: A Generative Sociology

In moving to reflect and build on Marx and Weber, then, several authors painted in rich tones views that contested or elaborated aspects of those authors' earlier emphasis on labor discipline and rationalization. Bourdieu and

Gramsci explored the dynamics of social reproduction and cultural forces shaping political preferences and resisting egalitarian social change. Habermas built on Weber's vision of authority, bureaucracy and the state to probe the dynamics of their development and change. He focuses, especially, on the possibilities for averting Weber's spectre of the "iron cage" and colonizing rationality as well as the social movements to which the life world gives rise amidst encroaching culture consumption and legitimation crisis. Foucault, while rejecting explicit bases in either Marx or Weber uses them as a springboard to launch an alternate vision of institutional control.

As we turn to our empirical analysis, each of these thinkers suggests certain sensitizing concepts and more or less explicit hypotheses. Bourdieu directs our attention to social and cultural capital as forms of power and to how processes of social reproduction that maintain labor discipline and foster social continuity while modulating change. Gramsci highlights culture and partisan political activity focusing on how hegemonic ideologies can shape preferences and sustain existing social arrangements while economic forces can create conjunctural moments that open the way for political activism to usher in change.

Foucault pinpoints forms of power and control exercised not only by the state but through the disciplines and society's middle level institutions. He underscores the import of language and processes of classification, or social sorting, as sources of inequality. Historically, Foucault, in contrast to other theorists, points us to ruptures and discontinuities as sources of change and observes the rise of the expert and knowledge in the late nineteenth century as a particular basis of power.

Habermas focuses us on the continuing importance of economic power, social class and conflict despite the rise of the state in the modern day as a transformative source of power. Within this context he points to the changing nature of state power beginning in the late nineteenth century as declining political dialogue and the rise of culture consumption produced weakened political participation; divergence of laws from norms symptomizing legitimation problems; and a shift to increasing reliance on state control, surveillance and policing. What Habermas sees that others seem largely to miss is the significance of movements for democracy and their stirrings in the life world which gives voice to them.

4

Contours of Early Plea Bargaining

Patterns of Pleas and Concessions

For a citizen in Massachusetts, social life changed dramatically over the course of the nineteenth century and brought much that was new. As manufacturers and craft workshops multiplied and cities began to flourish, so the daily activities of the courts changed markedly too. As decisions for this period show, some courts at the beginning of the century expressed reluctance in accepting guilty pleas under any circumstances (Alschuler, 1979; Langbein, 1979).[1] Yet over the course of the nineteenth century, the daily operations of both the lower- and middle-tier courts were transformed until by 1880, approximately 90 percent of the cases in the lower court were resolved by a plea of guilty. Plea bargaining had by then also become common in the middle-tier Superior Courts. This metamorphosis extended beyond the frequency with which guilty pleas were entered to influence their form, meaning, and consequences.

Since plea bargaining is defined for this study, to mean a defendant's entry of a guilty plea in anticipation of concessions from the prosecutor or judge, my work began by examining patterns in the disposition and sentencing of cases to see whether leniency was, in fact, granted and, if so, at what point historically it first appeared. This was done to establish what the outcome, the historical pattern of plea bargaining that would be explained, actually looked like. It was one of the greatest challenges faced in conducting this study. Where pleas were explicitly negotiated or bargained, a terse written notation outlining the terms of the agreement could sometimes be found in the dockets, Record Books or case files for the court. More often, indirect clues existed such as notations of a change in plea accompanied by a reduction in the sentence or the charge shown in the docket.[2] In most instances, however, the negotiations, at least in the lower court, proved to be implicit and left no literary trace. As a result, a first basic hurdle was to conceptualize plea bargaining in such a way that it could be measured and studied. What signs, I asked, do you look for to know whether plea bargaining is operating?

Building on my definition of plea bargaining as the entry of a guilty plea in anticipation of concessions, I sought indirect evidence that the practice was occurring by studying two of its constitutive elements—namely, guilty pleas, on the one hand, *and* concessions, on the other. In probing for change in the contours of plea bargaining once established, I examined both movement in guilty plea rates and shifts in disposition and sentencing with respect to plea over time. Using an inferential approach, I view entry of guilty pleas, on the one hand, and leniency attending such a plea, on the other, as the two building blocks that analytically comprise plea bargaining. Where both are present together in large numbers of cases, plea bargaining, by definition, can be understood to occur. Leniency need not, however, be granted every time a guilty plea is entered. Guilty plea rates are computed using the cases randomly sampled from the Boston docket, for each decade from 1830 through 1920. Concessions were then explored both by analyzing explicit notations in court documents and by undertaking quantitative analysis with the stratified random sample of systematic variation in case outcomes by plea.

Prior to 1830, it has long been argued, guilty pleas were rare in common law cases, and had not been frequent any earlier in American colonial or British history (Alschuler, 1979; Langbein, 1979). Recently Fisher (2000) has challenged that received wisdom arguing that data from the Middlesex County middle-tier courts in Massachusetts suggest that such pleas as early as the late eighteenth century may have been somewhat higher than Alschuler and Langbein would indicate—though not shown to have been routinely accompanied by concessions. However, Fisher's method of combining pleas of nolo contendere, which were increasing, with guilty pleas and treating them as equivalent while simultaneously stipulating their differences raises at least as many questions as it answers. Nor can the study reliably estimate the relation of plea to leniency since its use of averages for aggregates of cases prevents incorporation of repeat offending into the analysis. My study shows that plea bargaining existed by the 1830s and, by 1860, had been solidly established and institutionalized; it was spreading by diffusion to other cities.

The Emergence of Plea Bargaining

When did plea bargaining begin? Contrary to popular perception, experience of the lower court in Boston strikingly demonstrates that plea bargaining emerged there during the 1830s and 1840s—much earlier than formerly supposed—and concentrated in offenses against property and security of the person. In contrast to Fisher's claim that plea bargaining in Middlesex County began in cases of liquor regulation, *none* of the five cases of that type in the lower Court in Boston in our random samples for 1830 and 1840 exhibit a guilty plea (or plea of nolo contendere). Instead, two defendants entered pleas of not guilty and the other three were, in traditional fashion, left blank presumably to remain so contingent on future good behavior.[3] Patterns of guilty pleas and concessions in Boston show that by 1840 in this court, the practice of plea bargaining, involving both entry of guilty pleas *and* the granting of attendant concessions, was set in place and continued into the twentieth century.

Prior to the 1830s, guilty pleas of any sort—apart from evidence that they produced concessions—have been argued by several scholars to have been rare (Alschuler, 1979; Langbein, 1975). Instead, the courts have been depicted as encouraging defendants to exercise their right to a presumption of innocence (Alschuler; Langbein, 1978).[4] Friedman (1981) and Alschuler (1979) estimate that guilty pleas, whether bargained or not, accounted for only 10 to 15 percent or less of all convictions in the United States prior to the 1830s. Plea bargaining is also argued by them not to have existed previously in England or any other country outside the United States (Langbein; Alschuler). In fact, they note that official reports suggest that defendants rarely pled guilty altogether either in England or elsewhere outside the United States until the last quarter of the nineteenth century (Langbein; Alschuler).

Concessions, which in addition to the guilty plea comprise the second key element of a plea bargain, historically were also not granted with the entry of such a plea on a widespread and regular basis in the United States, England, or any other country prior to the nineteenth century (Alschuler, 1979; Langbein, 1979). Although leniency in the form of pardons and grants of clemency had a long history, they were quite different from the plea bargain. They were granted after disposition, did not involve direct exchange and never achieved the widespread routine use that, as we shall see, plea bargaining did. In Boston's early nineteenth-century Municipal Court, the mid-level equivalent of what later became the criminal side of the state Superior Court, pleas of nolo contendere, negotiated by lawyers for clients, were increasingly used as part of a growing deployment of leniency in those years. However, this was usually an explicitly contractual process negotiated by an attorney that differed from plea bargaining, as chapter 5 will show.

Three isolated instances of concessions granted explicitly with the entry of a guilty plea have been reported in early British history. First, Langbein (1979) has discovered a single statute of 1485 authorizing a justice of the peace to convict a defendant of a summary offense if he confessed his crime but authorizing the justice to bind the defendant over for prosecution as a felon should he deny his guilt. Second, Cockburn (1975; cited in Alschuler, 1979) found that, quite suddenly for a period lasting two to three years, defendants in approximately half the cases before the Home Circuit assizes confessed to the offenses charged in their indictments and were sentenced immediately, with the charges confessed to having been reduced in some cases. However, both the altered indictments and the high rate of confessions of guilt disappear abruptly within a few years. For the next three decades, the frequency of guilty pleas entered before the Home Circuit was sharply reduced (Alschuler, 1979).

Finally, French jurist, Charles Cottu, reports an isolated instance in early nineteenth-century England where a prosecutor queried in open court whether a defendant would plead guilty to the lesser of two counts charged and, with his so doing, declined to offer evidence on the more serious of the pair of offenses—a step that resulted in acquittal of the defendant by the jury (Alschuler, 1979). While these are only occasional instances of informal negotiation, they highlight the existence of long-standing incentives to cooperate through exchange between prosecution and defense. However, in each case, the patterns of actual exchange were isolated or short-lived prior to the emergence of plea bargaining in the United States during the early- to mid-nineteenth century.

Despite occasional instances of compromise, there is no evidence that anything approaching the pervasive and highly routinized practice of plea bargaining common to the United States had developed elsewhere before the late nineteenth century.[5] Pardons and grants of clemency, which tended to occur after sentencing, involved, prior to the 1830s, no element of the direct, albeit often implicit, exchange inherent in plea bargaining.

Popularization of Guilty Pleas

In Boston, beginning in the 1830s, however, judges' reticence in accepting guilty pleas was replaced by the beginnings of plea bargaining (Vogel, 1988,

1999; Ferdinand, 1992). Guilty pleas, the first element of bargaining, began to be entered in more significant numbers in common law–based cases during the late 1830s.[6] By the 1840s, guilty pleas were regularly accepted for virtually every sort of offense, a pattern that continued into the twentieth century (see figure 4.1).[7] According to complete counts of *all* cases in the Police Court docket made for this study, guilty pleas surged from less than 15 percent of all pleas entered in the docket in 1830 to 28.6 percent in 1840. Guilty pleas then rose to 52 percent of all pleas in 1850, to 55.6 percent in 1860, and to a high of 88 percent in 1880. (See tables 4.1 and 4.2 for supplementary data supporting a growth trend.)[8] Thereafter, guilty pleas declined somewhat in frequency during the era of Progressive reform.[9]

While overall guilty plea rates are interesting, disaggregated figures are much more telling. Defendants' tendency to plead guilty varied among different types of offenses. (See table 4.3 for these offense-specific rates and tables 4.4 and 4.5 for supplementary offense-specific trend data.)[10] Because changes in the composition of caseload (e.g., presence of more offenses of types likely to elicit guilty pleas) can effect the overall pattern of pleas, the random sample was analyzed to see if the general rise in guilty pleas was evident for all categories of offenses. Changes in the composition of the court caseload over the period studied were explored, and disaggregated guilty plea rates were computed separately for each type of offense.

Analysis revealed a substantial concentration in the sorts of offending charged in the docket. Of the approximately 1,000 randomly sampled cases, fully 36 percent involved charges of drunkenness. Larceny, assault and battery, and common drunkard accounted for another 25 percent. Together, these four offenses accounted for 62 percent of the cases in the sample. Since these offenses have the analytically useful feature of representing both offenses against property and offenses against morals, they were chosen to use, together with nightwalking (or prostitution), for a disaggregated analysis of individual offenses. While plentiful in the docket across the entire study period, each type of offense varied in specific frequency over time.

Drunkenness cases increased heavily from a low of 3 percent of the cases sampled in 1840 to a high of 78 percent of cases sampled in 1900. Assault and battery cases tapered off in the lower court docket and common drunkard cases disappeared entirely after 1870—it appears that both these offenses increasingly found original jurisdiction in the higher court. Larceny cases remained more or less constant in its frequency in the docket over these years, registering a slight decline after the mid-nineteenth century. What makes the composition of the caseload particularly important is that different kinds of offenses show markedly different guilty plea rates.

Guilty plea rates for each specific offense, computed from the random sample for this study, show a more than doubling for most offenses between the early 1830s and 1860.[11] Recent descriptions of the same Police Court docket by Ferdinand (1992) reveal offense-specific patterns of plea that are, for the most part, closely comparable to my own figures shown in table 4.3. As one looks at differentials in guilty plea rates computed from my sample across offenses, one can see readily that the mounting combined guilty plea rate for all offenses was partly a function of the changing mix of cases in the docket— especially, after 1840, large numbers of drunkenness cases with their high guilty plea rates (refer back to table 4.3). As table 4.3 shows, drunkenness consistently exhibited one of the highest guilty plea rates of any offense in the sample, while those for larceny, assault and battery, and common drunkard

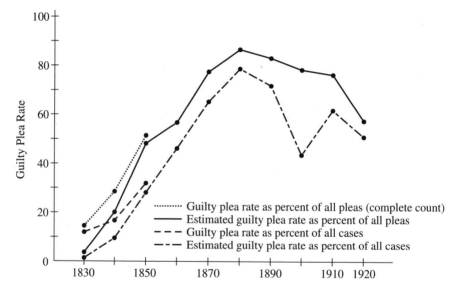

FIGURE 4.1. Guilty plea rates, Boston Police Court, 1822–1866, and Boston Municipal Court, 1866 to present.

Note: Guilty plea rates for 1830, 1840, and 1850 were constructed from complete counts of *all* pleas entered in the Boston Police Court docket. Estimated guilty plea rates from the simple random sample for those years are also presented to illustrate the relation of the sample estimates to the population. Rates for 1860–1920 were estimated solely from the data in the same simple random sample constructed for this study. In each case, guilty plea rates are presented as a percentage of *both* total number of pleas and total number of cases—two of the most common ways of constructing such rates. Constructing guilty plea rates as a percentage of all convictions, a third option, is often bureaucratically easier but tends to inflate the rates since those not convicted almost universally plead not guilty.

TABLE 4.1. Aggregate Guilty Plea Rates for All Offenses, Boston Police Court, 1830–1860

| | Complete Count of Docket | | | | | | Sample (Estimates) | |
	Guilty Pleas as % of All Cases (1)	Guilty Pleas as % of All Pleas (2)	Ratio of Not Guilty to Guilty Pleas (3)	Total Guilty Pleas (4)	Total Not Guilty Pleas (5)	Total Cases (6)	% of All Cases (7)	% of All Pleas (8)
1830	10.2	14.9	5.7:1	189	1,075	1,855	2.0	3.1
1840	16.8	28.6	2.5:1	400	1,001	2,383	9.9	18.2
1850	33.0	52.0	0.9:1	674	621	2,042	29.0	49.2
1860	N.A.	N.A.	0.8:1	45	36	99	45.5	55.5

Note: Data for cols. (1)–(6) for 1830, 1840, and 1850 are based on counts of all (for 1850 approximately half of) the cases in the Boston Police Court docket. Total cases in the docket in 1850 was 4,811. Rates in col. (2), which are computed by taking guilty pleas as a percentage of all cases in which a plea of any kind is entered, are those used in this study. Figures in cols. (7) and (8) plus material in all columns for the year 1860 are estimates, unlike the earlier years' complete counts, and are based on the simple random sample drawn for this study.

TABLE 4.2. Guilty Plea Rates: All Offenses, Boston Police Court, 1870–1920[a]

	% of Total Cases		% of Total Pleas		Rates of NG/G Pleas		Sample Size
	%	N	%	N	Ratio	N	
1870	66.0	66/100	78.6	66/84	0.30:1	18/66	100
1880	80.0	84/105	88.0	84/95	0.13:1	11/84	105
1890	73.7	76/103	84.4	76/90	0.18:1	14/76	103
1900	44.1	45/102	78.9	45/57	0.26:1	12/45	102
1910	63.8	67/105	77.0	67/87	0.30:1	20/67	105
1920	50.5	52/103	57.1	52/91	0.80:1	39/52	103

[a] Simple random sample; supplement to figure 1 and table 4.1.

cases were far more variable. The steadily growing share of these drunkenness cases in the docket served to boost and to smooth an already rapidly increasing guilty plea rate for other offenses. In terms of the frequency of guilty pleas, perhaps the most dramatic shift is evident in 1880 when the guilty plea rate plummeted for nearly all offenses, dropping completely to zero for some, except for drunkenness, where 99 percent of the cases indicated that a guilty plea was entered. Interestingly, this occurred just five years before the quest of ethnic immigrants for political power in Boston culminated in the election of the first Irish mayor—a pattern interpreted later. Thus, the pattern of offense-specific guilty plea rates had two crucial facets: an extremely high guilty plea rate for drunkenness, particularly after mid-century, and a slightly lower and variable, though very substantial, one for larceny and assault and battery. However, somewhat surprisingly, high guilty plea rates varied in terms of whether they entailed leniency.

In terms of establishing exactly when guilty pleas increased in Boston and what patterns were evident as they began to be entered in large numbers on a continuing basis, the data also reveal a clear pattern. In Boston's lower court, the data show a remarkable upturn in total guilty pleas for all offenses combined from a rate consistently less than 15 percent to a rate of nearly 30 percent between 1830 and 1840, establishing the presence of guilty pleas on a significant basis. Once the rise started, guilty pleas did not drop off but continued to appear prominently in the dockets well into the twentieth century. Most important, entry of a guilty plea came to be associated on a regular basis with the second constitutive element of bargaining—namely, leniency or concessions.

TABLE 4.3. Offense-Specific Guilty Plea Rates, Boston Police Court, 1830–1860

	Complete Count of Docket						Sample (Estimates)
	Guilty Pleas as % of All Cases (1)	Guilty Pleas as % of All Pleas (2)	Ratio of Docket Not Guilty to Guilty Pleas (3)	Guilty Pleas (N) (4)	Not Guilty Pleas (N) (5)	Total Cases (N) (6)	Guilty Pleas as % of All Pleas (7)
Larceny							
1830	13.7	19.1	4.2:1	34	144	249	0.0
1840	12.6	27.5	2.6:1	38	100	302	20.0
1850	21.4	39.2	1.6:1	67	104	313	14.3
1860	47.4	50.0	1.0:1	9	9	19	50.0
Assault and battery							
1830	6.7	10.6	8.5:1	31	262	293	0.0
1840	7.3	15.0	5.7:1	27	153	368	0.0
1850	15.5	35.3	1.8:1	53	97	343	12.5
1860	36.8	41.2	1.4:1	7	10	19	41.2
Common drunkard							
1830	8.1	9.2	9.9:1	29	286	359	0.0
1840	13.6	15.3	5.6:1	67	372	491	0.0
1850	45.2	47.8	1.1:1	100	109	221	63.6
1860	53.3	53.3	0.9:1	8	7	15	53.3
Drunkenness							
1830	9.1	75.0	3.0:1	1	3	11	N.A.
1840	49.7	58.3	0.7:1	80	57	161	100.0*
1850	56.8	57.6	0.7:1	166	122	292	61.9
1860	85.7	85.7	0.2:1	12	2	14	85.7

(continued)

TABLE 4.3. Continued

	Complete Count of Docket						Sample (Estimates)
	Guilty Pleas as % of All Cases	Guilty Pleas as % of All Pleas	Ratio of Docket Not Guilty to Guilty Pleas	Guilty Pleas (N)	Not Guilty Pleas (N)	Total Cases (N)	Guilty Pleas as % of All Pleas
	(1)	(2)	(3)	(4)	(5)	(6)	(7)
Nightwalking							
1830	25.0	26.7	2.8:1	4	11	16	0.0
1840	10.0	10.0	9.0:1	2	18	20	N.A.
1850	45.7	45.7	1.2:1	16	19	35	N.A.
1860	50.0	50.0	1.0:1	1	1	2	50.0

Data Sources: Data for 1830, 1840, and 1850, except in col. (7), are based on counts of all cases in the docket of the Boston Police Court. Figures for col. (7) and all of 1860 are estimates based on data from the simple random sample drawn from that docket for this study.

*Due to the considerable difference between the guilty plea rates generated from the sample estimate and the complete count of all cases in the docket for 1840, figures were reverified. It appears this is one instance where a finite sample produced an estimate markedly different from the underlying population based on chance alone.

TABLE 4.4. Guilty Plea Rates: Supplementary Trend Data Showing Growth in Guilty Pleas

	Larceny		Assault and Battery		Public Drunkenness		Prostitution	
	% of Total Cases	Ratio NG/G	% of Total Cases	Ratio NG/G	% of Total Cases	Ratio NG/G	% of Total Cases	Ratio NG/G
1832	7.3	8:1	4.2	14:1	7.1	12:1	4.2	19.5:1
1834	5.4	6:1	3.3	19:1	8.7	9:1	20.2	4:1
1836	14.1	3:1	7.8	8:1	8.7	9:1	22.8	3:1
1838	14.9	3:1	11.9	5:1	21.7	3:1	10.5	8:1
1840	13.8	3:1	7.0	8:1	23.3	3:1	27.2	2:1
1842	23.3	1.5:1	10.7	6:1	36.2	1.7:1	25.2	2:1
1844	19.2	1.5:1	11.8	3:1	46.0	0.9:1	21.0	2:1
1846	18.6	2:1	13.8	4:1	48.7	0.9:1	33.3	1.6:1
1848	21.0	1.7:1	7.3	4:1	51.8	0.9:1	55.9	0.8:1
1850	22.2	1.5:1	6.4	3:1	51.3	0.9:1	48.4	0.7:1

Note: By computing guilty plea rates by taking guilty pleas as a percentage of total cases, Ferdinand shows high rates for public drunkenness. This is partly a function of the fact that, in contrast with other types of cases, ordinary drunkenness cases are very rarely transferred to higher court unless a prior record exists. This boosts the guilty plea rate for drunkenness because few such cases are absent a plea and the base for comput-ing the guilty plea rate contains only guilty and not guilty pleas but no transfers to swell the base and pull the rate down. Comparing ratios of not guilty to guilty pleas reveals that, during the late 1830s (when plea bargain-ing began), guilty pleas for larceny have a presence equal to or even more substantial than such pleas for drunkenness cases, which were relatively rare during those years.

Source: Ferdinand 1992.

TABLE 4.5. Mid-Decade Data Showing Continuity of Growth in Guilty Pleas[a]

	% of All Cases	% of All Pleas	Ratio of NG/G Pleas	Guilty Pleas (N)	Not Guilty Pleas (N)	Total Cases (N)
Larceny						
1831	11.2	16.2	93/18	18	93	161
1835	7.8	20.8	95/25	25	95	321
Assault and Battery						
1831	6.3	10.6	178/21	21	178	334
1835	6.1	11.4	240/31	31	240	505
Common Drunkard						
1831	8.9	10.2	167/19	19	167	212
1835	9.0	11.9	207/28	28	207	299
Drunkeness						
1831	0.0	0.0	1/0	0	1	1
1835	0.0	0.0	0/0	0	0	0
Nightwalking						
1831	0.0	0.0	0/0	0	0	0
1835	27.3	27.3	16/6	6	16	22

Note: Data for this table are based on a complete count of all cases in the docket of the Police Court in 1831 (i.e., a shoulder year of 1830 which opens the decade when plea bargaining began) and 1835 (i.e., a midpoint in that decade). These data add robustness and ensure that the end points of this crucial decade are not aberrations.

[a] Offense-Specific Guilty Plea Rates: Shoulder Year and Mid-Decade, Boston Police Court, 1831 and 1835.

Multiplicity of the Forms of Concessions

What others tend to ignore, as they emphasize plea rates, is the concessions that together with guilty pleas constitute a plea bargain. Turning now to that leniency, it is clear that it took many forms and that it was initially evident only for certain kinds of cases. To describe this densely patterned fabric of concessions, a nested probability model, described in what follows, has been used to estimate the effect of plea on the likelihood of leniency in disposition and sentencing (refer back to figure 4.2 for an illustrative schematic application of that model to larceny cases in the year 1850).[12] Probabilities were computed to assess the effects of

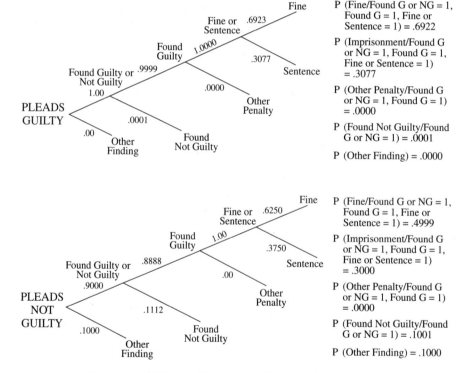

FIGURE 4.2. Nested probability model—effects of plea on the probabilities of various intermediate and reduced form final outcomes. (Stratified sample for larceny offenses, 1850)

Reduced form probabilities of five final outcomes (i.e., other than G or NG, acquittal, other penalty, fine, or sentence) shown in the right margin are computed as the multiplicative product of all intermediate probabilities along the branch leading to that final disposition or sentence.

plea on the ultimate chances of various final outcomes in a case, including likelihood of transfer to Municipal Court, chance of acquittal, and type of sentence imposed (see table 4.6). Using the stratified sample, probabilities were tabulated both for the aggregate of all offenses and, separately, for each of the five offenses singled out for study—larceny, assault and battery, common drunkard, drunkenness, and nightwalking (i.e., prostitution).[13] To take into account the possible effect of a prior criminal career, these probabilities were recomputed, controlling for existence of a previous conviction.

Separate linear regression models were then used to estimate, in cases where a sentence had been imposed, the effect of plea on the magnitude of that sentence (see tables 4.7 and 4.8). Finally, consequences of plea for the court costs one paid and for one's chances of winning special explicit post-sentencing concessions (e.g., probation, early discharge, and suspension of sentence)[14] as well as for one's risk of confinement for nonpayment of a fine were also tallied.[15] This diverse array of interrelated forms of concession were then brought together with offense-specific guilty plea rates to construct a composite picture of the early contours of plea bargaining. In operational terms, the question asked was simply whether those who pled guilty fared better. Guilty pleas that have no consequence for sentencing or, for some offenses, systematically exact a premium, do not constitute a plea bargain.[16] This panoramic view of plea bargaining as a whole demonstrates the rich texture of the practice during the early decades of its history.

Concessions in the Magnitude of Sentences

In exploring concessions, this analysis turned first to sentencing magnitude. The effects of plea on amount of fine or duration of a term of imprisonment were estimated (see table 4.7). In operational terms, the question was whether those pleading guilty fared better. To measure the influence of plea on sentencing magnitude, coefficients for the effect of plea on the amount of fine or duration of the term of imprisonment were estimated using an ordinary least-squares linear regression model.[17] Average fines and terms of imprisonment produced by "guilty" and "not guilty" pleas were also computed (see table 4.8). Bearing in mind that a record of past criminal offenses might produce a more severe sentence, the coefficients were then reestimated controlling for a criminal career in the form of a prior conviction or of multiple counts or associated cases pending against the defendant (see table 4.9). A Report of the Inspector of Prisons on the Suffolk County House of Corrections shows the importance of prior convictions due to their prevalence with 75 of 219 male inmates and

TABLE 4.6. Probabilities for Final Case Dispositions (Stratified Random Sample)

	Larceny		Assault & Battery		Drunkenness		Common Drunkard		Nightwalking	
	Guilty	Not Guilty	Guilty	Not Guilty	Guilty	Not Guilty	Guilty	Not Guilty	Guilty	Not Guilty
1830										
Other than G/NG	⊕ .6666	.5000	○ .1112	.2000	No Cases		⊕ .3334	.0000	⊕ .4000	.0833
Not Guilty	⊖ .00003	.0833	⊖ .1112	.2000			○ .0000	.0000	○ .0000	.0000
Other than fine/imprisonment	⊖ .1666	.2499	○ .0000	.0000			○ .0000	.0000	⊖ .0001	.0834
Fine	○ .0833	.0833	⊕ .8887	.6666			○ .0000	.0000	○ .0000	.0000
Imprisonment	○ .0833	.0833	○ .0000	.0000			⊖ .6666	1.0000	⊖ .5999	.8932
1840										
Other than G/NG	⊖ .0000	.1250	⊕ .3187	.0556	⊕ .2631	.0000	⊕ .3334	.0000	⊕ 1.0000	.0000
Not guilty	⊖ .0000	.1190	⊖ .0002	.1667	○ .0000	.0000	○ .0000	.0000	○ .0000	.0000
Other than fine/imprisonment	⊖ .0000	.1250	○ .0000	.0000	○ .0000	.0000	○ .0000	.0000	○ .0000	.0000
Fine	⊕ .2000	.1875	⊖ .6812	.7221	⊖ .7369	1.0000	○ .0000	.0000	○ .0000	.0000
Imprisonment	⊕ .8000	.4374	⊖ .0001	.0556	○ .0000	.0000	⊖ .6666	1.0000	⊖ .0000	1.0000
1850										
Other than G/NG	⊖ .0000	.1000	○ .0000	.0000	○ .0000	.0000	○ .0000	.0000	○ .0000	.0000
Not guilty	⊖ .0001	.1001	⊖ .0000	.2174	○ .0000	.0000	⊖ .0001	.0834	⊖ .0000	.1000
Other than fine/imprisonment	○ .0000	.0000	⊕ .1000	.0435	⊕ .0500	.0000	⊖ .0001	.0834	○ .0000	.0000
Fine	⊕ .6922	.4999	⊕ .8000	.6086	⊖ .9000	1.0000	⊖ .0000	.0833	⊖ .0556	.1999
Imprisonment	⊕ .3077	.3000	⊖ .0999	.1304	⊕ .0500	.0000	⊕ .9998	.7498	⊕ .9444	.7000

	Larceny		Assault & Battery		Drunkenness		Common Drunkard		Nightwalking	
	Guilty	Not Guilty	Guilty	Not Guilty	Guilty	Not Guilty	Guilty	Not Guilty	Guilty	Not Guilty
1860										
Other than G/NG	⊕ .0769	.0000	⊕ .0770	.0953	○ .0000	.0000	○ .0000	.0000	○ .0000	.0000
Not guilty	⊖ .0770	.2778	⊖ .0001	.2381	○ .0000	.0000	○ .0000	.0000	○ .0000	.0000
Other than fine/ imprisonment	○ .0000	.0000	⊕ .0769	.0000	○ .0000	.0000	○ .0000	.0000	○ .0000	.0000
Fine	⊕ .5383	.4444	⊕ .7690	.5713	⊖ .9167	1.0000	⊕ .0667	.0001	○ .0000	.0000
Imprisonment	⊕ .3078	.2778	⊖ .0770	.0953	⊕ .0833	.0000	⊖ .9333	.9999	○ 1.0000	1.0000

Note: These estimates are final reduced-form probabilities of five major case dispositions: other outcome (mainly transfer to Municipal/higher court); acquittal; other penalty (not fine or imprisonment); fine; and a term of imprisonment. (These are the probabilities presented down the right-hand margin in Figure 4.22.)

TABLE 4.7. Effects of Plea on Duration of Imprisonment and Amount of Fine

	Imprisonment					Fines				
	Larceny	Assault & Battery	Drunkenness	Common Drunkard	Nightwalking	Larceny	Assault & Battery	Drunkenness	Common Drunkard	Nightwalking
1840										
Constant	3.6250	Terms	All fines	4.4666	All pled	4.4545	3.5384	2.3333	All pled	All terms of
Plea	−.0795	constant		.6242	not guilty	−1.0259	−.1748	.2380	not guilty	imprisonment
N	27	3		26		18	24	23		
1850										
Constant	2.3846	All fines	Terms	2.2500	3.1428	5.5000	4.1428	2.0769	All pled	11.5000
Plea	.0598		constant	2.1500***	.5042	.0454	.5630	−.1324	not guilty	−6.5000
N	22			13	24	17	31	31	3	3
1860										
Constant	2.4000	3.5000	Terms	4.2272	3.3333	9.5000	4.9166	3.0000	Fines are	All terms of
Plea	1.6000	−1.5000	constant	.0941*	2.023**	−5.3571	2.4833	.0909	constant	imprisonment
N	6	3		50	23	15	22	32		

Note: Coefficients were computed using primarily the stratified random sample. For 1840 and 1850, because the larceny and assault and battery cases are, as we shall see, integral to my argument, data from the simple random sample and the stratified random sample—both randomly selected offense-specific samples—were pooled for more robust estimates and small targeted but randomly drawn samples were added to the pool. These included: 32 larceny cases for 1840 (8 NG/Fine, 8 G/Fine, 8 NG/Imprisonment, and 8 G/Imprisonment); 20 larceny cases for 1850 leading to imprisonment (10 plead guilty, 10 plead not guilty); and all assault and battery cases for 1850 that led to imprisonment (none existed of simple assault and battery—only two cases of assault on an officer in discharge of his duty, which is a much more serious offense).

$* = p < .10$, $** = p < .05$, $*** = p < .01$.

TABLE 4.8. Average Fines and Terms of Imprisonment

	Larceny		Assault & Battery		Drunkenness		Common Drunkard		Nightwalking	
	Guilty	Not Guilty	Guilty	Not Guilty	Guilty	Not Guilty	Guilty	Not Guilty	Guilty	Not Guilty
Fine ($)										
1840	⊖ 3.6666	4.5833	⊖ 3.364	3.5238	⊕ 2.571	2.333	○ No cases	1.6667	Imprisonment only	
1850	⊖ 6.2500	6.3333	⊕ 4.7058	3.6250	⊖ 1.9445	2.0769	○ 1.000	1.000	⊖ 5.000	11.5000
1860	⊖ 4.6666	9.7142	⊕ 6.2000	4.4615	⊕ 3.0909	3.0000	○ No cases	2.667	Imprisonment only	
Imprisonment (months)										
1840	⊖ 3.5454	4.0000	○ No cases	6.0000	Fines only		⊕ 5.0908	4.4666	○ No cases	4.643
1850	⊖ 2.4444	2.5000	Fines only		○ 2.000	No cases	⊕ 4.4000	2.5000	⊕ 3.647	3.1428
1860	⊕ 4.0000	2.5000	⊖ 2.000	3.500	○ 2.000	2.000	⊕ 4.3213	4.2272	⊕ 5.356	3.333

Note: Averages were computed using the data described in the note to table 4.7.

TABLE 4.9. Effects of Plea on Imprisonment and Fine Controlling for Criminal Career (Stratified Sample)

	Imprisonment					Fines				
	Larceny	Assault and Battery	Drunkenness	Common Drunkard	Nightwalking	Larceny	Assault and Battery	Drunkenness	Common Drunkard	Nightwalking
1840[a]										
Guilty pleas	−.1723	No cases with careers	No cases with careers	.6454***	All pled not guilty	.5454	No cases with careers	No cases with careers	No cases with careers	Imprisonment only
Significance	(.7496)			(.0006)		(.8657)				
Career	2.0405***			.6454	2.0833***	5.0000				
Significance	(.0007)			(.1608)	(.0025)	(.3406)				
R^2	.0063			.4335		.1324				
N	9			26	14	14				
1850[b]										
Guilty Pleas	No cases with careers	No cases with careers	Terms are constant	No cases with careers	.4196	No cases with careers	No cases with careers	.1327	No cases with careers	No cases with careers
Significance					(.4215)			(.1693)		
Career					1.4375			−.0114		
Significance					(.2306)			(.9521)		
R^2					.1068			.0663		
N					24			31		
1860										
Guilty pleas	No cases with careers	No cases with careers	Terms are constant	No cases with careers	1.6428**	No cases with careers	No cases with careers	−1.057***	No cases with careers	Imprisonment only
Significance					(.0139)			(0.0000)		
Career					−1.7142			2.0000***		
Significance					(.1199)			(0.0000)		
R^2					.4381			1.0000		
N					23			32		

Note: Entry of prior record or other signs of a criminal career into the equation renders the effect of a guilty plea for drunkenness in 1850 positive and that for 1860 negative—the only reversals of sign, despite numerous changes in the magnitude of coefficients, created by that variable.

[a] Data were supplemented with a targeted sample of 32 randomly selected larceny cases balanced by plea and sentence to boost sample size for robust estimates.

[b] Data from the stratified sample were pooled with that from the simple random sample and with small targeted randomly drawn samples of 20 larceny cases (10 pled guilty, 10 pled not guilty) and of all assault cases in the docket for that year that led to imprisonment.

* = $p < .10$. ** = $p < .05$. *** = $p < .01$.

70 of 140 females being repeat offenders. Of these, 23 males (or 10.5 percent) and 27 females (or 19.3 percent) had been imprisoned five or more times (Boston City Documents, No. 23, 1837, p. 21). (See table 4.10.) In our random sample 1% of defendants in 1830 and 9.9% in 1840 have prior convictions. In addition, 4% of defendants in 1830 were charged with multiple counts in the same case and 2% in 1840 were charged with another case in that year's docket. (See tables 4.11 and 4.12.)

By the 1830s, the Commonwealth of Massachusetts had passed an habitual offender statute mandating more severe sentencing for recidivists. Being a "career" offender unerringly was a powerful shaper of sentencing severity— sometimes by making a term of imprisonment more likely or, alternately, by boosting the size of a fine or length of confinement. Most often, though, as we shall see, a prior conviction meant transfer up to the middle tier Municipal Court. This diversity of impacts of a criminal career underscores the import of detailed analysis of individual cases, rather than aggregated data, so that such factors can be taken into account.[18]

Data from the Boston court revealed effects of plea on sentencing magnitude to be quite widespread and consistent between 1830 and 1920 with substantial concessions for certain types of offenses and, interestingly, appar-

TABLE 4.10. Prior Commitments to the Suffolk County House of Corrections of Current Inmates in 1837

	Number of Times Committed	
	Male	Female
First Time	144	70
Second Time	23	24
Third Time	16	17
Fourth Time	13	2
Fifth Time	6	5
Sixth Time	5	2
Seventh Time	3	0
Eighth Time	4	5
Ninth Time	1	3
Ten or More Times	4	12
Total	219	140

Source: Report of the Inspector of Prisons on the Suffolk County House of Corrections. *Boston City Documents,* No. 23, 1837, p. 21.

TABLE 4.II. Former Convictions[a]

	1830 (N = 100)	1840 (N = 101)	1850 (N = 100)	1860 (N = 99)
Former Conviction(s)	1% (1)	9.9% (10)	0	1% (1)

Source: Random samples drawn for this study from the dockets of the Boston Police Court for 1830, 1840, 1850 and 1860.

TABLE 4.I2. Associated Cases[a]

	1830 (N = 100)	1840 (N = 101)	1850 (N = 100)	1860 (N = 99)
Currently charged in other cases	0	2% (2)	1% (1)	2% (2)

Source: Random samples drawn for this study from the dockets of the Boston Police Court for 1830, 1840, 1850 and 1860.

[a]Calculated as a percent of all cases in sample.

ent premiums, despite what were sometimes high guilty plea rates, for others. Concessions varied in form in this lower court during the late 19th and early 20th centuries—appearing primarily as sentencing leniency in individual cases during the antebellum years, then as changes in the sentencing structure during the years of ethnic conflict lasting into the 1890s and finally as more open-ended supervisory practices that could avert conviction altogether during the years of the Progressive Era. As we shall see, however, Progressivism looked much different in Boston than in other American cities. Prior to the Civil War, pleading guilty tended to reduce the size of sentences of imprisonment and fines primarily for the offenses of larceny and assault and battery, especially in 1840. In common drunkard and, to a lesser extent, drunkenness and nightwalking cases, it had the reverse effect, exacting a premium instead. (Tables 4.7 and 4.8 show the coefficient of the plea effect on amount of fine and duration of imprisonment for the five selected offenses.)[19] The data for 1830 to 1860 show that for larceny and for assault and battery cases, where pleading guilty was at that time most likely to produce leniency, reductions in cases where fines were imposed range from $0.17 to $5.35, although in one unusual year, guilty pleas exacted a premium of $2.48 in the fines levied. For cases resulting in imprisonment, guilty pleas might produce a reduction of as much as one-and-a-half months for some types of offenses but exact premiums for others.

In exploring the effect of plea on sentencing magnitude, the primary question of interest was whether pleading "guilty" is consistently associated with a shorter term of imprisonment or a lower fine. Since the data being analyzed are individual-level data, which are technically less likely than the more commonly used aggregated data to produce regression coefficients that are significant at the .001 or .01 levels, and since the number of cases in any one analytic subsample here is limited, a large number of significant coefficients was not expected. Nonetheless, significant coefficients were found. However, significance was also assessed using the "sign test," a simple binomial probability test, in terms of the overall pattern of coefficients for the five selected offenses as a whole. When we want to know whether one treatment or condition gives better results (or, in this case, more-positive or lenient (reduced sentences) than another, the "sign test" provides a standard technique for deciding (Mosteller, Fienberg, and Rourke, 1994, pp. 475–77). In using this test, one replaces differences between measurements or other comparisons by plus (+) or minus (−) signs.[20]

It was hypothesized that, were there no significant relation between plea and duration of imprisonment or amount of fine, the coefficients for the effect of plea would be equally likely to exhibit positive and negative signs—that is, positive and negative effects would occur with equal frequency. Specifically, absent any effect of plea, the simple probability of any particular sign being positive or negative would be .50. Thus, a simple binomial probability was estimated for each of two batches of cases disaggregated by offense—those that resulted in fines and those that produced sentences. This represents the probability that the resultant pattern of coefficients would be produced if, in fact, there were no relation between the type of plea entered and duration of imprisonment or amount of fine.[21]

Based on this test, the probability that the pattern of effects that we observed for pleading guilty on duration of imprisonment stem from chance alone is .0900 (or 9 in 100) across all offense-specific coefficients.[22] While the larceny and assault and battery cases (two out of four negative coefficients showing reduced variation) varied over time, offenses against the moral order (five out of five positive coefficients show longer sentences for guilty pleas showed clearly that concessions were not being granted there. In fact, in morals and vice cases, a premium seems to be exacted in these years where a guilty plea is entered. Combining both groups of offenses, the signs of seven of the nine coefficients are in the hypothesized direction. With a probability of only .0900 (again 9 in 100) of occurring by chance, this is approximately equivalent to significance of the effect on duration of imprisonment at a .10 level of confidence.

In contrast, the effect of plea on amount of fine across all offenses shows less systematic effect. The probability that the pattern of fines for larceny and assault and battery (three out of six negative coefficients) would occur by chance is .6560 and that for the offenses against moral order (two of four coefficients showing a premium exacted) is .6880. Thus, we find fairly strong evidence that plea shapes magnitude of sentence, at least in terms of duration of imprisonment imposed, though not obviously from these results, for fines. That said, the probability of all three coefficients for larceny and for assault and battery in the crucial transition year of 1840 being negative due to chance alone is only .1250, again approaching significance at the .10 level of confidence.[23] Thus, we found evidence that guilty pleas resulted in concessions in the form of reductions in the length of imprisonment and, in a more-specialized way, in amount of fine, particularly for cases involving the offense of larceny against property.

When these coefficients were reestimated, controlling for the effect of a criminal career, two findings were striking (see table 4.9). First, the almost complete absence of cases involving defendants with prior criminal careers among those reaching disposition in the Police Court stands in sharp contrast with the many cases that showed prior convictions, other cases pending, or multiple counts listed among those initially charged. Table 4.9 shows that the reason for this was that cases involving offenders with criminal careers were usually transferred to the Municipal (middle-tier) Court. Second, when dispositions were reached in such cases, a criminal career, though frequently affecting the magnitude of an effect of plea alone, overtook and reversed the sign of the coefficient for plea in only three instances: those of larceny for 1840 and of drunkenness for 1850 and 1860. In the former two instances, the effect of plea shifted from a discount to a premium, while the reverse was true for drunkenness in 1860.

Type of Sentence Imposed

Beyond the effect of plea on magnitude of sentence, a guilty plea tended to produce even more substantial concessions by affecting the "type" of sentence imposed. Generally speaking, such a plea may enhance the probability that a fine (or other moderate sentence) rather than a harsher term of imprisonment is imposed. Thus, I next explored the effect of choice of plea on case disposition, especially on type of sentence. Because disposition is a complex process with many branches, the nested probability model, previously mentioned, was used. (See figure 4.2 for a sample diagram of the decision tree.)[24] Visually, this model can be thought of as a family of decision trees, each showing the probability for one year, given a plea of "guilty" versus "not guilty," that a defendant incurs each of a sequence of intermediate disposition and sentencing outcomes (i.e., nodes along the branches of a tree) as well as each of five final outcomes (i.e., the end points on the tree) as the case moves through the justice system. Probabilities were computed for each study year and type of offense.

In this analysis, the five final outcomes (along the right margin) are the primary concern: the ultimate probabilities of fine, imprisonment, other sentence, acquittal, and other outcome (i.e., outcome other than guilty or not guilty).[25] The intermediate outcomes (or branches) decompose those final outcomes to show, given a plea, what each step in the disposition and sentencing process contributed to producing the different end results. Consequences of pleading guilty for imposition of a fine relative to a harsher term of imprisonment, on the one hand, and for transfer to Municipal Court, on the other, are the crucial points here.[26] Thus, those steps in the process of disposition are broken out for special consideration.

Starting with a subsample of all those defendants who entered a plea of either guilty or not guilty in a particular study year, simple linear probability models were used to estimate the effect of plea at each decision point (or node) on the probability of a case moving forward along each of two possible paths open to it.[27] What is of greatest interest here, of course, is whether pleading guilty substantially reduces one's risk of being imprisoned while increasing the chance of receiving the more limited punishment of a fine.

As to whether pleading guilty increases one's chances of a more lenient disposition, especially a fine instead of imprisonment, figures for the aggregate of all offenses indicate that it does, both in intermediate and final outcomes. (See table 4.13 and table 4.6 respectively.)[28]

Aggregates can, however, be misleading because they are shaped in part by the mix of cases they incorporate and by changes in that mix.[29] Offense-specific analysis, then, is crucial for decomposing the aggregate pattern into its meaningful components. My analysis reveals that concessions in terms of type of sentence imposed varied from one type of offense to another. As table 4.13 shows, from 1840 on, for larceny and for assault and battery cases, those entering guilty pleas were consistently more likely to receive lenient treatment. Between 1840 and 1860, such defendants had a greater chance, given that a fine or imprisonment was imposed, of receiving the less-severe fine. The exception was 1840 when defendants in larceny cases pleading "guilty" were less likely to receive a fine and more likely to receive imprisonment than those pleading "not guilty." Even that can be interpreted as an underlying concession, however, since terms of imprisonment in that year are more prevalent than previously for guilty pleas due to transfer of an unusually large number of the

TABLE 4.13. Conditional Probabilities of Intermediate Outcomes of Fine or Imprisonment, Given That a Fine or Sentence Was Imposed (Stratified Sample)

	Larceny[a]		Assault & Battery[a]		Drunkenness		Common Drunkard		Nightwalking	
	Guilty	Not Guilty	Guilty	Not Guilty	Guilty	Not Guilty	Guilty	Not Guilty	Guilty	Not Guilty
1830										
Fine	○ .5000	.5000	○ 1.0000	1.0000	No Cases		○ .0000	.0000	○ .0000	.0000
Imprisonment	○ .5000	.5000	○ .0000	.0000			○ 1.0000	1.0000	○ 1.0000	1.0000
1840										
Fine	⊖ .2000	.3000	⊕ .9999	.9285	○ 1.0000	1.0000	○ .0000	.0000	○ .0000	.0000
Imprisonment	⊕ .8000	.7000	⊖ .0001	.0715	○ .0000	.0000	○ 1.0000	1.0000	○ 1.0000	1.0000
1850										
Fine	⊕ .6923	.6250	⊕ .8889	.8235	⊖ .9474	1.0000	⊖ .0000	.1000	⊖ .0556	.2222
Imprisonment	⊖ .3077	.3750	⊖ .1111	.1765	⊕ .0526	.0000	⊕ 1.0000	.9000	⊕ .9444	.7778
1860										
Fine	⊕ .6362	.6153	⊕ .9090	.8571	⊖ .9167	1.0000	⊕ .0667	.0001	○ .0000	.0000
Imprisonment	⊖ .3638	.3847	⊖ .0910	.1429	⊕ .0833	.0000	⊖ .9333	.9999	○ 1.0000	1.0000

[a]Stratified random sample with pooling of stratified random sample and simple random sample for larceny and assault and battery in 1850. In addition, small targeted random samples of larceny cases in 1840 and of larceny and assault and battery cases in 1850 were added per note in Table 4.7.

relatively serious larceny cases involving pleas of "not guilty" to Municipal Court—a far more serious and expensive affair than Police Court. (See "Other than G/NG" in table 4.6.) Previously, in 1830, those pleading guilty to larceny were far more likely to be transferred than those pleading "not guilty." Thus, one major facet of the leniency attending guilty pleas that emerged after 1830 was a reduced risk of transfer to the middle tier court. Thus, while a larger share of guilty plea cases in the lower court in 1840 result in imprisonment, this, when examined fully, turns out to reflect concessionary leniency.

The probability that entry of a guilty plea would result in a fine rather than a term of imprisonment was greatest during the first half of the nineteenth century. Concessions in the form of imposition of the more-lenient fine tended to be most strong for offenses related to property and personal security, which emerged as a central concern in both criminal and civil law during this period (Nedelsky, 1990; Nelson, 1967). This finding supplements the evidence of leniency in the magnitude of sentences imposed on entry of a guilty plea for offenses against property that was previously noted.

For common drunkard, drunkenness, and nightwalking cases, no direct effect on intermediate outcomes, either positive or negative, of plea on sentence type was evident in 1840 (see table 4.13). In focusing on all final results, however, we find systemic evidence of an actual premium exacted when defendants pled guilty to these offenses in the more-frequent transfer of the cases to Municipal Court than in those where pleas of "not guilty" were entered. Referring to table 4.6, we find that, in 1840, all those transferred for these morals offenses had pled guilty while, for larceny, those pleading guilty were less likely to be transferred. (See "Other than G/NG" in table 4.6.) In drunkenness cases, pleading "guilty" was initially even riskier since it increased both one's chances of transfer to Municipal Court and one's risk of a term of imprisonment if the case stayed in the Police Court. By 1850, the risk of transfer in morals cases generally was considerably reduced. However, the tendency to exact a premium for guilty pleas in these cases continued (see tables 4.6 and 4.13). In stead of a guilty plea producing greater likelihood of a fine and reducing the chance of a term of imprisonment in Police Court, the reverse was true. Probabilities of final dispositions show that those pleading "guilty" to drunkenness, common drunkard, and nightwalking were more likely ultimately to face terms of confinement in prison than fines (see table 4.6). In 1850, intermediate probabilities of fine relative to imprisonment, given that a sentence is imposed, provide further evidence that premiums were being exacted in those cases when a guilty plea was entered by imposition of terms of incarceration (see table 4.13).

Concessions may have been absent initially for drunkenness, common drunkard, and nightwalking cases and premiums exacted upon the entry of guilty pleas in part because links to traditional morality restricted compromise. It is also true that such cases held fewer tangible consequences for the "people's welfare" that was then being shaped by economic growth.[30] These breaches of moral order, especially nightwalking, require some subtlety to interpret since many of the cases involved habitual offenders and were transferred to Municipal Court.[31] Provisions for recidivists in these vice cases have already been discussed. In addition, many lengthy sentences in Police Court were initially suspended for twenty-four hours—inviting defendants, sometimes explicitly, to leave town. Equally important, many of the drunkenness, common drunkard, and nightwalking cases involved women. Females raised a trenchant issue. In this "well-regulated society," in which markets and capitalism were expanding apace, women were imagined to be of two sorts: those living under "household governance" (i.e., indicated by "wife of . . .") and those unattached living independently. In a society still oriented to hierarchy that regarded every household as a "little commonwealth" and a training ground for governance, it was those living on their own who were thought to pose the greatest threat and who tended to be penalized for an infraction with particular severity. This is reflected in the social characteristics of defendants transferred, among the most dangerous offenders, to middle tier Municipal Court in 1830. After controlling for features such as plea and criminal career, which exerted a powerful influence, women, including a large number of single women, spinsters, and widows, appear to have abounded among those defendants whose cases were sent

TABLE 4.14. Social Determinants of Transfer to Municipal (Superior) Court: All Offenses, 1830 (Stratified Sample)[a]

Criminal career	.4185*
Guilty plea	.3192*
Value stolen	.1063**
Sex of defendant	1.1843***
Constant	−.3968

$R^2 = .7948$, $N = 12$

Significance of F-test $= .0148$

* $= p < .10$. ** $= p < .05$. *** $= p < .01$.

[a]Because regression analysis was conducted using listwise deletion, inclusion of the powerful explanatory variable, "value stolen," focuses this analysis on larceny cases. Experimentation with various functional forms showed this one to produce strongest results.

TABLE 4.15. Effects of Plea and Social
Determinants on Duration of
Imprisonment in Larceny Cases

Minor	−1.0708*
Sex of defendant	1.1599*
Guilty plea	−.4738
Value stolen	.0101
Career	2.1039***
Constant	2.5800
$R^2 = .7815, N = 16$	
Significance of F-test = .0043	

* = $p < .15$. ** = $p < .05$. *** = $p < .01$.

to the higher court, just as they appear to have been among those being sentenced more harshly (see tables 4.14 and 4.15).[32]

Leniency, by shaping type of sentence, then, was most common for the property-related offense of larceny and for assault and battery. Both were worrisome as threats to the security and predictability in daily affairs that was vital to healthy markets and growth (Horwitz, 1977; Nedelsky, 1990; Nelson, 1981). Perhaps due to their secular nature, no lingering religious proscription appears to have inhibited bargaining here. Significance, now of a plea's effect on type of sentence, was again assessed by applying the "sign test" to the probabilities presented in tables 4.6 and 4.13. For larceny and assault and battery, the likelihood that the series of effects of plea on the simple intermediate probability of a fine instead of imprisonment (five out of six reduced probabilities of imprisonment when pleading "guilty") could occur by chance alone is .1093. The comparable probability for offenses against the moral order (four out of five greater probabilities of imprisonment when pleading "guilty") is .1880. Combining these analyses, the probability that nine of eleven coefficients would exhibit the expected sign by chance alone is .0330—the functional equivalent of statistical significance at the .03 level of confidence.

Turning to the reduced form final (or summary) outcomes, the systemic effects of plea on type of sentence where one is ultimately imposed are less clear. The probability that the series of effects of plea (i.e., three of six negative effects) on final probability of imprisonment for the larceny and for assault and battery cases in 1840, 1850, and 1860 could occur by chance is .6560. For offenses against the moral order, the comparable probability of a reduced chance of a harsher term of imprisonment (i.e., four of seven positive effects) is approximately .5000—not discernably different from chance. Combining these analyses, the probability of seven out of thirteen effects of plea in the predicted direction is again .5000—the equivalent of chance pure and simple which indicates absence of a systematic effect from this angle. In part because of the interplay between chance of transfer to Municipal Court and probability of imprisonment (i.e., reduced chance of transfer to the middle tier court produces greater imprisonment, which, on the face of it, can appear harsh), the effects of plea here are somewhat subtle. However, as was the case for magnitude of sentence, evidence here suggests that plea leverages case disposition and type of sentence, primarily by shaping the intermediate probability of fine or imprisonment, given that a sentence of some type was imposed, and also by systematically shaping a defendant's chances of transfer to Municipal Court. Once again, leniency was concentrated on offenses against property and personal security.

Chances of Acquittal

If defendants are to benefit from pleading guilty, concessions must overcome the initial disadvantage that pleading guilty virtually eliminates one's chances of being acquitted or found "not guilty." Since the plea of guilty is, by definition, an admission of culpability, one would expect a guilty plea to produce a near certainty of conviction such that, if one thinks in expected value terms, the weight of a sentence would be greatly increased by the high probability of its being imposed.

The data, not surprisingly, show that the probability of acquittal was reduced virtually to zero by a guilty plea (see table 4.6). It does turn out, however, that where pleas of guilty are entered, outcomes other than "guilty" or "not guilty," such as "released" or "placed [open] on file," were occasionally arrived at in the Police Court, offsetting the reduced chances of acquittal somewhat. This was particularly true during the era of Progressive reform when, under an increasingly Irish bench, the Court granted repeated continuances apparently as a sort of court supervised recognizance to allow the judge to assess a defendant's behavior. If satisfactory, a defendant was often released or the case filed to be reactivated only upon receipt of a new complaint in an adaptation of probation that left no record of conviction. The meliorative effect of these alternatives in countering reductions in acquittal brought about by entry of a guilty plea is incorporated in the reduced form final outcomes; where the ultimate probability variously of receiving a fine or term of imprisonment relative to some other disposition is thus abated despite the reduced chances of acquittal.

Table 4.6 shows the aggregate and offense-specific acquittal rates resulting from a plea of "not guilty." These rates reveal that for the combined group of all offenses and for larceny and assault and battery, the probability of acquittal encountered by those going to trial was quite substantial in some years, ranging to a high of .278 in Police Court during the antebellum years, although that was rare. For the common drunkard and drunkenness cases, chances of acquittal were virtually nil across the entire period studied until 1920. These relatively low acquittal rates may have been an important contributor to the high guilty plea rates for drunkenness after 1850 relative to the somewhat lower ones for larceny and assault and battery.

Other Concessions

Beyond what has been mentioned—namely, reductions in sentencing magnitude, effects on the type of sentence imposed, and alternative dispositions— several other types of concessions played a role in the nineteenth-century "bargaining" process. Primary among them were: savings in court costs to the defendant, special explicit concessions (e.g., early discharge), a reduced probability of recognizance being required, and diminished probability of confinement for nonpayment of a fine. Of these, court costs and explicit concessions had especially powerful financial repercussions for a defendant.

Court costs, which fell when a defendant pled guilty, sometimes totaled as much as two or three times the amount of a fine during the nineteenth century (Handlin and Handlin, 1969). Explicit concessions, such as probation or expedited release from jail or prison, restored the capacity to work and with it earnings otherwise lost. Given the prevailing wage for a male laborer of approximately $1.00 per day, early release could easily swamp both reduced fine and costs in value—a vital concern for families living at the margin of subsistence without savings.

Composite Analysis of the Building Blocks of Bargaining

As study of bargaining's contours progressed, it became apparent that the process was rich with many adjustable elements. It was a massive and highly differentiated process that worked in different ways at different times. To summarize the variety of the process, composite charts show the types of concessions made (see tables 4.16 and 4.17).[33] Concessions, we see, that are stage specific were somewhat more abundant in 1840 and 1860, whereas systemic concessions were slightly more frequent in 1850. The frequent concessions for

TABLE 4.16. Composite Chart of Concessions Accompanying Guilty Pleas: Boston
Police Court

	Larceny	Assault and Battery	Common Drunkard	Drunkenness	Nightwalking
1840	PMC−, $−, T−, E−	PF/FS−, PI/FS−, $−	PI/FS−	None	None
1850	PMC−	PF/FS+, PI/FS−, T−	None	$−	$−
1860	$−, C−	PMC−, PF/FS+, PI/FS−, T−	None	C−	None

Legend:

PF/FS = conditional probability of fine as intermediate outcome (given that a fine or term of imprison-
        ment is imposed)
PI/FS = conditional probability of imprisonment as intermediate outcome (given that a fine or term of
        imprisonment is imposed)
PMC = probability of transfer to Municipal (higher) Court
$ = amount of fine
T   = duration of time of imprisonment
C   = costs
E   = explicit concessions (e.g., early discharge from House of Correction)
+   = greater for a plea of guilty than of not guilty
−   = less for a plea of guilty

TABLE 4.17. Systemic Probabilities of Concessions as Final Outcomes
Accompanying Guilty Pleas, Boston Police Court (Compiled from Table 4.6)

	Larceny	Assault and Battery	Common Drunkard	Drunkenness	Nightwalking
1840	PMC−	SPF+, SBI−	None	None	None
1850	PMC−, SPF+, SPI−	SPF+, SPI−	None	SPF+, SPI−	None
1860	SPF+, SPI−	SPF+, SPI− PMC−	None	None	None

Legend:

PMC = probability of transfer to Municipal (higher) Court
SPF = system's probability of fine (reduced form) as final outcome
SPI = final probability of imprisonment (reduced form) as final outcome
+   = greater for a plea of guilty than not guilty
−   = less for a plea of guilty

crimes against property and the person and, only later, for crimes against the moral order, are also evident from these charts.

Total concessions, like guilty pleas, are most evident, during the antebellum years, for crimes against property and the person—offenses central to social and economic stability. The two constitutive elements of plea bargaining, a combination of guilty pleas and concessions, were less evident until mid-century and after for offenses against the moral order, such as drunkenness that had closer links to traditional moral and religiously based proscriptions which may have produced resistance to overt compromise. During the first half of the nineteenth century, drunkenness cases, which disproportionately involved Irish defendants (perhaps due to selective law enforcement or, alternately, to drinking in public houses rather than at home) show fewest concessions. The primary concessions evident for drunkenness during this extended period of Yankee political control took the form of cost savings. Only in 1860 did widespread concessions begin to appear in drunkenness cases, and they accelerated during the years 1870 and 1880. Given the extraordinary coincidence in timing, it is worth noting that these were the decades of the rise of ethnic politicians to power in the ward of Boston.

One final interesting subtlety of the bargaining process was the role of costs. As we shall see, it appears that for the years 1860 through 1880, concessions in general frequently took the form of cost differentials. These were politically "safer" since they could be rationalized in relatively apolitical terms as accruing from improved administrative efficiency while still dispensing enormous gains. Explicit concessions also became increasingly important toward the end of the nineteenth century as part of a broad movement toward new, more institutionally supervised and professionally crafted, but still discretionary, practices consonant with the rubric of individualized treatment and heightened public discourse about the social welfare of the poor.

Does Caseload Pressure Play a Part?

Interestingly, while delay was a constant criticism in the higher courts, all signs are that cases moved quickly through the lower court, almost always reaching trial before a judge within one day in the early part of the century (Gil, 1837).

Continuances were rare (see tables 4.18 and 4.19 for the pattern of continuances and days to disposition). As shown in table 4.18, no case in the random samples drawn from the dockets for 1830, 1840, or 1850 for which a date of disposition was recorded received more than one continuance. In 1830, 96.7 percent of all cases show no continuance while the figures for 1840 and 1850

TABLE 4.18. Cases Receiving Continuances

	1830		1840		1850		1860	
	N	%	N	%	N	%	N	%
No Continuances	89	96.7	81	95.3	89	95.7	85	90.4
One	3	3.3	4	4.7	4	4.3	8	8.5
Two	0	0	0	0	0	0	1	1.1
Not Applicable	8	NA	16	NA	7	NA	5	NA
	100	100.0	101	100.0	100	100.0	99	100.0

Data Source: Random Samples drawn for this study from the dockets of the Boston Police Court for 1830, 1840, 1850 and 1860.

are 95.2 percent and 95.6 percent, respectively. A single continuance was granted in 3.2 percent of cases in 1830, 4.7 percent in 1840 and 4.3 percent in 1850. Thus, there does not appear to be a significant shift over this 20 year period. Not until 1860 does the share of cases receiving no continuance fall to 90.4 percent as shown in table 4.19.

Rapid dispositions were the rule. As shown in table 4.19, data on the duration (or days to disposition) of the cases reveal that 91.3 percent of cases in 1830, 88.2 percent in 1840 and 86.8 percent in 1850 reached disposition

TABLE 4.19. Duration of Disposition from Time of Examination

	1830		1840		1850	
	N	%	N	%	N	%
Same Day	84	91.3	75	88.2	79	86.8
Two	2	2.2	2	2.4	3	3.2
Three	2	2.2	1	1.2	2	2.2
Four	1	1.1	2	2.4	0	0
Five	1	1.1	1	1.2	1	1.1
Six	1	1.1	1	1.2	1	1.1
Seven	1	1.1	1	1.2	0	0
Nine	0	0	1	1.2	1	1.1
Ten					1	1.1
Thirteen	0	0	1	1.2	1	1.1
Fifteen					1	1.1
Forty-one					1	1.1
Not Applicable	8	NA	16	NA	9	NA
	100	100.1	101	100.2	100	99.9

TABLE 4.20. Caseload of the Boston Police
Court 1823–1840 (Numbers of Cases Handled)

Year	Total Cases Listed in Docket
1823	2349
1824	2279
1825	1964
1826	1895
1827	1769
1828	1907
1829	1917
1830	1855
1831	1598
1832	1904
1833	2197
:	:
1840	2382

Sources: "Plain Facts Addressed to the Inhabitants of Boston on
the City Expenses for the Support of Pauperism, Vice and
Crime." Published by the Council of the Massachusetts Temperance Society. Boston: Ford and Damrell, May 1834, p. 15; Attorney General's Annual Report, Commonwealth of Massachusetts,
Senate Document No. 15, 1841, Part II, p. 21.

the same day that examination was conducted and a plea entered. For those
cases *not* concluded the same day, average duration was 4 days in 1830 and 5.5
days in 1840 before surging to 9.25 days in 1850.

The picture of plea bargaining that emerges from my data raises questions
about the intuitively popular view that mounting caseload pressure in the
courts may have given rise to plea bargaining. Findings of this analysis, however, suggest that the surge of guilty pleas that heralded the rise of plea bargaining in the Police Court during the 1830s and 1840s occurred during a time
of modestly fluctuating caseload. Plea bargaining thus appears to have preceded rather than followed the marked increase in caseload seen after 1840.
(See table 4.20 which shows actual numbers of cases handled by the Police
Court and figure 4.3, which shows trends in rates of increase in guilty pleas
as one indicator of bargaining relative to rates of increase in caseload.) Though
number of cases (or caseload) handled by the Police Court increased by 28.4
percent between 1830 and 1840, that is considerably less than the growth of
211 percent (189 to 400) in raw numbers of guilty pleas, 91.9 percent (14.9 to
28.6 percent) in guilty pleas as a percent of all pleas, and 63.7 percent (10.2 to

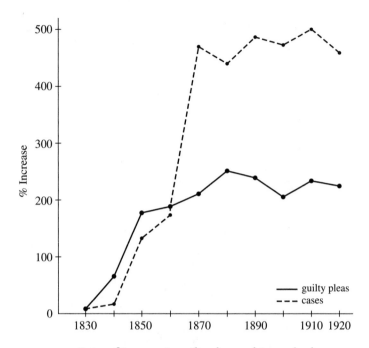

FIGURE 4.3. Rates of increase in guilty pleas and in caseload pressure

16.8 percent) of guilty pleas as a percent of all cases. It is also a lower rate of growth than that of the city population as a whole, estimated at between 52 and 65 percent (*Statistics of the United States. Seventh U.S. Census Compendium. Table CCXVI*, 1850, p. 192). Boston grew from 61,392 to between 93,385 and 101,385 from 1830 to 1840.

More importantly, comparison of total caseload in the Boston Police Court shows that while caseload rises 28.4 percent from 1855 cases in 1830 to 2383 cases in 1840, it is vital in interpreting these figures to set them in context. Without that care, one's conclusions could be misleading. If one looks at annual figures on caseload for the Police Court from its inception in 1822, one finds that the number of cases handled in 1840 was almost identical to that in 1823—the first full year of operations. The Police Court's docket shows 2,349 cases in 1823 and 2,383 in 1840. (See table 4.20). Thus, the caseload in this Court actually declines during the mid- to late 1820s. It rises briefly to a lower peak from 1828 to 1830, and then slumps again before resuming 1823 to 1824 levels in 1840. Thus, plea bargaining emerges in the Police Court perceptibly between 1834 and 1836 at a time when caseload is neither particularly high for this Court nor growing especially rapidly.

Thus, in terms of the origins of the practice, this temporal sequence provides little support for a caseload pressure argument though it warrants further study. Nor do guilty plea rates vary with changes in caseload once the practice of plea bargaining is established. While caseload increased steadily over the last half of the nineteenth century, guilty plea rates and concessions attendant to bargaining fluctuated. For instance, rates of increase in guilty pleas decline between 1880 and 1900 while rates of increase in caseload continue to grow. When coupled with the fact that crowding had been a source of complaint about the Courts generally in Massachusetts since the colonial period, this lack of systematic covariation further challenges the relevance of caseload as a cause of plea bargaining. This supplements Church's (1976) prior finding, previously discussed, that sudden increase in caseload does not necessarily boost rates of plea bargaining. It also dovetails with Heumann's (1981) finding from Chicago that new prosecutors, even in busy courts, do not naturally bargain but must learn to do so.

Pleas and Concessions: The Institutionalization Process

Although patterns of plea and concession demonstrate plea bargaining's emergence during the 1830s and 1840s, one wonders how aware of it people were at the time. Here two points are of interest. First, fluctuations in concessions are mirrored for some offenses by parallel shifts in the tendency to plead guilty. While the data show only an association and not a causal link, there is little reason, on logical grounds, to imagine that greater numbers of guilty pleas would evoke more extensive concessions. Among the cases sampled for this study, when concessions offered them were substantial, defendants more often pled "guilty" (see table 4.21). This mirroring tells us that, not only was a "bargaining" process in place by 1840, but also that institutionalization appears to have been underway whereby a public, aware of concessions sometimes being granted, varied the frequency with which they individually pled guilty.[34]

Second, while inference is powerful, it is compelling to find some indication that the people of the day recognized the practice of plea bargaining explicitly and had some language for talking about it as well as acting "as if" they did. The historical origins of the term "plea bargaining," detailed later indicate that the public was probably acutely aware. In general there is surprisingly little reference to these discretionary practices of leniency in the diaries and papers of the day—perhaps because they arose so gradually and naturally out of practices already so widely accepted in common law custom. An anecdote, however, is telling: In 1837, Thomas Gil, court reporter for the *Boston Morning Post*, published his court vignettes. While not making too much

TABLE 4.21. Guilty Pleas and Concessions: The Process of Institutionalization (Stratified Sample)

	Larceny		Assault and Battery	
	Concessions	Guilty Plea Rate	Concessions	Guilty Plea Rate
1840	PMC−, T−, $−, E−	.20	PF/FS−, PI/FS−, $−	.00
1850	PMC−	.14	PF/FS+, PI/FS−, T−	.12
1860	$−, C−	.50	PMC−, PF/FS+, PI/FS−, T−	.41

Legend: See list for Table 4.16.

of it, he used the term "bargain" to describe this practice (Gil, 1837). As we shall see, the name "bargain," derived probably from Henry Clay's "corrupt bargain," with which the public dubbed this practice provides some clues about the public skepticism that may have initially greeted the practice as it does in many quarters today.

Thus, in terms of our first two key outcomes, the emergence of plea bargaining and the types of offenses in which it occurred, we see that bargaining emerged in the 1830s and 1840s and that in this Court it appeared first primarily as sentence bargaining in offenses against property and security. It remains now to explain why plea bargaining should operate this way initially. It also remains to explain why the relation between guilty pleas and concessions in individual cases varied over time, why plea bargaining took the particular cultural form that it did, and why it seems to have originated, as a routine and widespread practice, in the United States.

Responses to Marx and Weber: Hypothetical Explanations

Contemplating two key features of plea bargaining—its emergence and the types of offenses where it occurred—we see that bargaining emerged in the 1830s to 1840s and that it centered on offenses against property and security of the person. It appears that Court staff and litigants familiar with the workings of the court (and probably the public too) were aware that leniency was likely to be granted if a guilty plea were entered and had a language for talking about the practice as a "bargain" as well. Let us now consider what these findings may imply.

Earlier in this work, we examined first theoretical ideas advanced by Karl Marx and by Max Weber on law, politics, and their interplay with society. We then went on to consider the thinking of Michel Foucault, Pierre Bourdieu, Jurgen Habermas and Antonio Gramsci on these subjects. Harking back for a moment, one may recall that the Marxian perspective pointed to labor discipline and maintenance of social order that furthered the interests of a ruling elite as possible explanations for patterns of court activity such as plea bargaining. Weber's thinking on law, in contrast, centers attention on increasing rationalization of the law, both in logical style and in the bureaucratic form of its administration, and to plea bargaining as a potential innovative element of that advancing rationality.

While Marx and Weber each provide certain insights that establish a fruitful starting point, neither is entirely persuasive in accounting for the rise of plea bargaining in the United States. A Marxian view highlights the importance of industrialization, which was getting under way in the United States in the 1830s, and of the role of law and political ideology during this period. Marx also accurately directs our attention to the protection of property and personal security as one means of contributing to the predictability congenial to economic growth. Finally, Marx emphasizes the role of economic conditions in giving rise to the relative deprivation that may breed discontent with a political order and also the historical role of law in strengthening elite power in the face of dissent. Thompson (1975) has argued, following Marx, that leniency has historically tended to be accorded to protesters and rioters under the common law up to the point at which state authority is seriously challenged—at which point the mobilization is met with the full force of the law.

What the Marxian view is less able to explain is why, if industrialization and the rise of commercial capitalism prompts the emergence of plea bargaining (among other forms of leniency) due to needs for predictability, security, and enhanced elite influence, plea bargaining did not arise first in England where those economic developments had occurred earlier. Nor can Marx account for the fact that the social world of the 1830s and 1840s in which plea bargaining arose was one where relations of deference were still strong, at least in New England, and class conflict as an organized struggle of labor and capital was still relatively undeveloped, even though the Workingmen's Party had begun to stir. Finally, Marx proffers no ready explanation either for the form plea bargaining took or for its precipitous rise in drunkenness cases later than others and only as ethnic immigrants moved to begin to consolidate their political power after mid-century.

In Weberian terms, the 1830s and 1840s, pinpointed by my study as the decades when plea bargaining emerged, were also years during which the courts saw popular mobilization, on the one hand, and official moves, on the other, for greater rationality in both the logical structure of law and its administration. Mobilization primarily took the form of the codification movement which presented a popular challenge to precedent-based common law and urged a turn to statutory enactments by legislatures. It may also be significant that the mid- to late-1840s, which were years early in the life of plea bargaining, was a period when new emphasis on rational and efficient management led the Commonwealth of Massachusetts to collect its first data on case outcomes and conviction rates from district attorneys. Since neither District Attorneys nor public prosecutors of any other type argued cases in the Police Court during the 1830s when plea bargaining began, this does not seem likely to have caused plea bargaining. This atmosphere may, however, have helped encourage subsequent adoption of the practice in higher courts where prosecutors were active. It is such interconnections with processes of advancing rationalization that Friedman (1993) points to as fostering the adoption of plea bargaining in Alameda County, California, although his focus is the latter half of the century.

But codification ultimately failed, and Weber emphasizes the contrasts between the common law on which early American law was based with its significant irrationalities and substantial discretion, and the Roman Law of the European continent with its structured codes anchored in formal procedural rationality. If rationality held the key to the rise of plea bargaining, one might have expected to see it appear first in the context of the legal rationality of the European continent—that is, unless the peculiar nature of the substantive rationality and discretion of the common law may provide a partial answer.

While Marx and Weber do not provide ready-made complete answers to the question of why plea bargaining arose, they do provide an important start and sensitize us to certain issues as I turn to build on the insights they have provided to construct an alternative, more-limited, historically and culturally specific account of the rise of plea bargaining. As I do, my work draws on the broader conceptions of the multiplicity of power, complexity of human agency, and efficacy of gradual transformative change that emerges from scholars such as Foucault, Bourdieu, Habermas, and Gramsci, who built on or responded to those earlier works. As such, my study is embarked on a project of generating hypotheses to stimulate richly contextualized middle range theorizing both about the socially embedded institutional forces giving rise to plea bargaining and legal innovation, in particular, and more generally about the role of law in the process of state making and the construction of political authority.

Marx and Weber both focus attention, on who were the initiators of the legal change that came to be known as plea bargaining. Weber's vision challenges Marx's emphasis on social class and signals instead the key role of status groups. Both highlight the crucial importance, either positively or negatively, of the imaginative structures—the discourses and language, ideologies, and legal culture—that constitute the repertoire of unifying symbols and orientations that inform human choices and nudge action in certain directions more readily than in others. Both also emphasize the power of the economic institutions of a society. Yet, whereas Marx highlights both the reflexivity of culture and politics along with economically generated conflict, Weber emphasizes the historical contingency of class relations and points to status groups as more significant than social class in relatively stable times. Weber also reminds us that ethnicity may operate as a crucial stratifying force. Ethnicity may define a status community or, when underscored by racial difference, a relatively permanent grouping that is nearly a caste, at least for a time. Finally, the contours of the state apparatus are a vital concern to Marx and Weber and their progeny as they struggle to interpret not only the relation between ruler and ruled but also the role of law amidst popular rule. Weber, of course, centers on political authority and the role of law as a basis for legitimation of that authority. But one man's legitimation is another man's hegemony, and Marx highlights the consequences for social inequality of an increasingly competitive economic order and the tendency of ideology and legal culture to sustain that project.

Our finding of plea bargaining's emergence during the mid-1830s points, in Marxian terms, to a period of conflict and change that began in the 1820s. As we shall see, it is one of rising crime, especially violence; rioting and unease over quality of life. These years mark the period of greatest increase in inequality in the United States of the entire nineteenth century. That the practice centers on offenses against property and personal security suggests a possible role in sustaining that institutional lynchpin of capitalist economic growth. Yet what exactly is the practice doing and why?

That plea bargaining began during the 1830s and 1840s also suggests in Weberian terms, it may have been linked to the quests for cognoscibility and rationality in law and legal administration of the day. Premiums exacted for guilty pleas in offenses against the moral order also indicate that religious belief may somehow be conditioning the practice. Yet who, per Weber's query, were the bearers of the practice and might there be customary roots discernible out of which the practice arose?

It remains now to build on these ideas to explain why plea bargaining arose at the point in time that it did, why it concentrated on particular types of offenses, and how those accused responded to the concessions offered. It also remains to explain why plea bargaining took the particular cultural form that it did and why it originated in the United States. To account for each of these features of plea bargaining, we now turn to analyze the conditions that gave rise to it.

As we explore these questions, Foucault, Bourdieu, Habermas and Gramsci offer four quite different theoretical models to guide our study. Foucault proposes a model of law and its related disciplines as noneconomic forms of institutional and linguistic power. Bourdieu offers a view of law and its institutions as cultural practices that shape the distributions of capital and processes of social reproduction. Habermas provides a model of law as an instrument of the state for economic transformation and basis of modern democratic political authority. Gramsci's model presents law as educative and hegemonic.

In some ways these models are mutually exclusive and others complementary. Each affords a unique touchstone against which to pit my data. Specifically, I will explore changes in the layered temporalities of structures, institutions, strategies, and transformative events that gave rise to plea bargaining and shaped it. In this venture, my focus is on: the timing of dynamics of and parties to the emergence of plea bargaining, the distinctive imaginative constructions of the common law and of Puritanism that offered a unique cultural repertoire on which to draw, and the contours and strength of the state.

5

Episodic Leniency in Britain and America

In the courts of urbanizing Boston, the reticent acceptance of guilty pleas that had been the norm in the Police Court during the 1820s gave way to plea negotiation. The dockets show that plea bargaining emerged and was established, not as a fluke or isolated recurrence, but as a continuing practice during the 1830s and 1840s. In light of the fact that this curious practice is, at least until the latter half of the nineteenth century, a distinctively American one, we now explore why plea negotiation arose and why it emerged in the particular time and place that it did.

The activity of the Boston court suggests that plea bargaining began during the 1830s as part of an effort to stabilize both social unrest and partisan contest and to do so in a language consonant with nascent political institutions of popular rule. The courts appear to have assumed this role largely out of necessity, since they were, amidst what Skowronek (1982) has termed an American state of "courts and [political] parties," the primary local experience citizens had of the state until organized political parties rose to prominence in the cities later in the antebellum years. As urbanizing Boston grew, inequality increased and the class structure began to change. As social and political tensions of burgeoning city life mounted, elite Bostonians appear to have drawn on time-honored legal and cultural traditions of the common law and used them in new ways to promote stability and to foster consent of the populace to both the new and still-fragile political arrangements of the republic and their own beleaguered partisan dominance. Abetted by the close linkage of law and politics in American life, this turn yielded, among other things, a new legal formation, plea bargaining, that would eventually, itself, be transformed as the nineteenth century unfolded.

Social Conflict and Popular Rule: Recrafting Leniency

Fundamental to plea bargaining, we have found, in addition to a guilty plea, were the granting of leniency on a frequent basis and the exercise of discretion by a judge (or later a prosecutor) in determining how a case was to be handled and under what circumstances concessions might be accorded. As shown previously, guilty pleas, whether attended by concessions or not, were quite rare in the Police Court prior to the 1830s. Episodic leniency and judicial discretion had long histories, however, in both the well-established British common law and the newer American legal tradition, which was changing rapidly in its "formative era" during this dynamic period.

Among the few historical studies of plea bargaining that have been conducted, many authors emphasize prosecutors' discretion regarding charge, the decision to prosecute and sentencing as a crucial precondition for the practice (Alschuler, 1979; Friedman, 1981; Steinberg, 1984). What has, until now, been largely ignored by them is that cases in the lower courts during these years were usually heard solely by a judge without a prosecutor or defense attorney being present. This is not to deny that the prosecutorial discretion to which scholars point is widespread and has a long history both in American law and in the British common law tradition on which it drew. This common law based tradition of discretion, so evocatively portrayed by Weber, presents a marked contrast to the highly codified and procedurally rationalized law of the European continent.[1] It appears to stem from the substantive, as opposed to formal, orientation to justice that characterizes the common law. Historically, this common law focus on a just or equitable outcome, as opposed to the procedural fairness of the Roman Law, has allowed judges and, later, prosecutors broad latitude to consider a wide range of mitigating factors in determining the outcome of a case (Weber, 1978).

What is intriguing, on the face of it, is why plea bargaining never arose in England where these common law traditions might have provided fertile ground for a discretionary practice of this sort. What did arise in England, however, was an extensive and highly developed system of episodic leniency that took many and varied forms. As social changes in Massachusetts during the nineteenth century gave rise to new political groupings that sought expression, legal discourse moved to an authoritative position of imaginative or cultural supremacy. As it provided the language in which new needs were articulated and old privileges defended, each group moved to interpret legal culture in ways meaningful to its needs. As we shall see, law, during this period, increasingly was seen as reflecting popular will, and judges emerged as architects of social policy and of the path of change. In this setting, one notable legal innovation developed as men and women drew on the language and forms of the time-honored tradition of episodic leniency and reforged it, along with indigenous elements of the Puritan religious practice of admonition, to produce a new discretionary form—namely, that of plea bargaining.

Among the dominant elements of British political culture under the common law, then, one finds a long and distinct tradition of episodic grants of leniency.[2] As noted previously, Hay et al. (1975) have attempted to show the centrality of this tradition to the process of social control in early modern England. Central to it were the long-established practice of the pardon, which is highlighted by Hay et al., and the vestiges of the medieval practice of the "prayer of benefit of the clergy." Beginning during the colonial period and increasingly over the course of the late eighteenth and early nineteenth centuries, case decisions in the Massachusetts courts reveal the operation of both these and several other forms of episodic leniency. What was wholly new in the United States during the nineteenth century was the way these practices were drawn on and the new forms of discretionary leniency that were created to bolster social control in a society where both order and elite dominance were under challenge, a social control that drew extensively on themes from the language of a politics of popular consent.

The Cultural Repertoire of Leniency in the Common Law

The cultural repertoire provided by the traditions of the common law played a key role in determining why plea bargaining emerged and took the form it did. It also importantly influenced how plea bargaining worked once it was established. Among the common law elements received and adapted from the British, the American courts inherited the time-honored traditions of discretion in judicial decision making and the episodic granting of leniency. By the 1830s, it is clear that legal discretion, as a political prerogative, was hotly contested by the masses but nonetheless operative—though changing in form. At this time, various forms of episodic leniency other than plea bargaining began to be used in purposive ways that demonstrate an increasing tendency to consider decisions made in the criminal courts explicitly as an instrument of social policy.

This adaptation of relatively explicit court mechanisms of leniency to serve policy purposes provided a foundation on which the more implicit practice of plea bargaining drew.

The British tradition of episodic leniency, described so eloquently by Hay et al. (1975), was received in America during the colonial and Early National periods as part of the broader legacy of common law. Key vehicles of leniency received from the British included primarily the pardon, the plea of "nolo contendere," the granting of immunity in exchange for testimony, and the "nolle prosequi."[3] Another British practice of medieval origin, that of "benefit of the clergy," had only a short-lived history in the United States, in general, and in Massachusetts, in particular.[4] During the early nineteenth century, indications are abundant that these practices were beginning to be used in new ways, namely, in a more-explicit and purposive fashion to deter future misbehavior among offenders by crafting conditional sentences and concomitantly increasing state oversight over their lives (Horwitz, 1977). Drawing on liberal ideas of the human capacity for progress from the Enlightenment, these initial changes undertook to deter future unsavory behavior.[5] The use of these explicit and increasingly conditional vehicles of leniency to promote deterrence began during the 1820s and 1830s as the role of policy considerations in judicial decision making became more prevalent. The structuring of decisions in the higher courts to promote the "people's welfare" (or common good) was quite well accepted by the 1840s as will be shown—and the new uses of discretionary forms of episodic leniency were one manifestation of this change. Plea bargaining built on and moved beyond these explicit agreements, as it offered a more implicit and customary form of leniency that reduced state oversight and seems to have substituted a more community-based control instead. As a form of leniency, it retained considerable discretion for judges and consequently enhanced state ability to interpret law with policy concerns in mind. While less likely than explicit forms of leniency to require specific behaviors, the plea bargain was, as we shall see, used to convey a sense of moderation on the part of the state and to articulate and imbue an understanding of citizenship. It may also have encouraged ties of loyalty and deference toward employers and other social "betters."

Despite many important similarities, plea bargaining differed from the other new forms of leniency in three significant ways. First, entry of a guilty plea contrasted with most earlier forms of leniency by closing the case, eliminating opportunities for continued formal supervision by the state. Second, relative to the widely used practice of pardon, leniency was moved up from a postjudgment to a prejudgment event—making it part of the trial process itself and introducing new rules for arriving at a disposition.[6] Third, it was simple in form and could be undertaken by defendants themselves without the costly advice of counsel. Thus, even though discretion was maintained, this more-discrete, accessible, and less-costly practice was more acceptable to the masses. Let us consider first the new uses of leniency that had been developed.

In the British tradition, pardon tended to arise as a possibility primarily after conviction, and it entailed a grant of leniency by the Crown. Hay et al. (1975) have shown that pardons were extensively granted, and that ability to obtain them was an important elite prerogative.[7] Similarly, Langbein (1978a) has shown that "in the eighteenth century, royal review of judicial recommendations for pardon and commutation became a regular and systematic part of ordinary criminal procedure" (p. 297). However, pardons were typically granted after a defendant had been convicted, and in no case was a plea of guilty involved, either as a sign of repentance or for any other reason.

Langbein reports the following case, which suggests the general reluctance of the courts to accept guilty pleas in cases involving a request for a pardon during this period:

> Stephen Wright . . . , caught robbing a physician in his surgery at gunpoint, told the court he wanted to admit his guilt in order to spare the court trouble. He hoped he might "be recommended to his Majesty's mercy by the Court and the Jury" (a reference to the system of royal review and occasional commutation of capital sentences on the advice of trial judges). The court "informed him, if there were any favorable Circumstances in his Case, if he pleaded guilty, the Court could not take any notice of them; and that the Jury cannot report any favorable Circumstances, because the Circumstances do not appear to them; Upon which he agreed to take his Trial." (p. 278)[8]

Thus, pleas of guilty appear to have been discouraged where a request for pardon was contemplated, just as they were in other cases.

Full pardons, as case decisions show, remit any punishment and blot out of existence the guilt turning a new man out into society to begin afresh by the grace of the state. However, though it restores rights to one "civilly dead," it does not restore his estate where it has become vested in his heirs or others by attainder (*In re Deming*, 10 Johns, 232, 483 (NY 1813); *Whitcomb v. State*, 14 Ohio 282 (1846); *Ex parte Garland*, 71 US (4 Wall) 333, 18 L Ed 366 (1866)).

What was distinctive about the tradition of pardon, as described by Hay et al., is that the tradition, in its own informal way, induced not just observance of the laws, when granted conditionally, but appears also to have presented positive initiatives among the populace to nurture community membership

and social ties with powerful members of the local elite or employers, ministers, family or other stalwart citizens who could intervene on one's behalf in
requesting clemency or commutation should one come before the court. It was
the frequency of formal complaint and court appearance that lent this incentive
power. Thus, as has been shown by Hay et al. (1975) and Stone (1981) the
system of pardon presented incentives to forge communal ties, and especially
cross-class ones, that actively reinforced the existing system of class and status
relations along with the many privileges and the relations of deference that it
supported.

Clearly, the tradition of pardon received wide use in the American colonies.
As they grew more common in the United States, however, pardons grew much
more politically controversial than they had been in England. Kuntz (1988)
found frequent pardons a source of much exasperation to law enforcers, in
Boston, New York, and Philadelphia alike between 1830 and 1880. Hindus
(1980) estimates that in Massachusetts at mid-nineteenth century approximately 12 percent of all convictions were eventually pardoned.

Initially an end in itself, the pardon had by 1803 begun to be used conditionally in Massachusetts as a way of ensuring continued good behavior (*Acts
and Resolves*, 1803, no. 117). Thus, an act of 1803 authorized that "the governor
. . . may, by and with the advice of the council, . . . grant a pardon upon such
conditions, with such restrictions, and under such limitation, as he may think
proper" (*Revised Statutes*, Part IV, ch. 142, sec. 12). By the early 1800s, then,
the pardon was increasingly being used as a means of ongoing control and
supervision over some convicted offenders—a practice that would be extended
and formalized in cases involving suspended sentences and probation later in
the century in Massachusetts. Although pardons were increasingly used as a
means of oversight, this was a practice that in the notoriety it attracted, had
the disadvantage of being politically volatile and the object of much severe
public criticism.

During this same period, pleas of "nolo contendere" and promises of immunity in return for testimony as a state's witness also began to be used in
new ways. Such cases were fairly rare, however, relative to another more numerous group of cases that were dropped or left open on file or simply blank.
The change was that instead of a plea being accepted and the case closed, pleas,
mainly in the higher court, began to be negotiated but then were continued
"open" without resolution for a time as an element of insurance to compel a
change in ways on the part of the accused.[9] The deterrent effect of leaving a
case "open" was reinforced in Massachusetts by that state's habitual offender
statutes, which prescribed additional penalties for the defendant should the

case be reopened later due to another complaint. This negotiated use of pleas appears to represent a sort of turning point, though, in that these relatively explicit negotiations reveal it, in contrast to the pardon, to be a sort of direct request for leniency while the case is in process. This feature can also be seen, subsequently, in the plea bargain.

An inquiry by the Massachusetts legislature in 1845 into charges of malpractice leveled against Ashael Huntington, county attorney for Essex County, provides a striking example of this sort of negotiation attending a plea of nolo contendere and of the legislature's clear approval of them.[10] Huntington, who would later go on to become state Attorney General, was charged with delay in turning over various fees that he had collected to the Treasurer and with "taking less than might have been required on the discharge of indictments found and not tried" (*House Report*, Jan. 1845, p. 7). Huntington replied that he had on certain occasions, when he thought it in the public interest, discharged persons accused of selling liquor without a license "on receiving less than might have been demanded . . ." (p. 7). He then stated:

> Whenever a number of penalties had been demanded in different counts of the same indictment, and the defendant came forward and proposed an adjustment, (his) . . . usual course has been: 1st To require the party to enter a plea of nolo contendere, 2nd To enter into an agreement to abstain from future sales of liquor without a license, 3rd To pay at least one penalty to the Commonwealth and all the costs which had then accrued, and 4th That the indictment should then stand continued as security that the defendant would fulfill his agreement, and to be further prosecuted in case the defendant still continued in his course of a willful violation of the laws. (pp. 7–8)

The House Report notes that it was:

> very distinctively in evidence, that this course was taken openly and publicly by the respondent, and impartially applied to all; that it was known to the Courts, the Bar, the County Commissioners, and all other persons who occasion to take any interest in the administration of this department of the law. And it was also clearly proved, that this course was not only known but much and justly approved as tending more than any other course in the class of cases to which it was applied; to attain the just end of all punishment, the prevention of the offense, the reformation of the offender. (p. 8)

Once closed, the plea of nolo contendere had the advantage for the defendant that he could not be retried for that offense, nor could his plea be construed as an admission of guilt in a situation where civil proceedings as well as criminal ones were to be initiated. What is interesting, and offers insight into the rise in popularity of the guilty plea, is that, although guilty pleas are mentioned quite often in case decisions during the nineteenth century, they appear to be infrequently challenged relative to cases involving negotiated pleas of nolo contendere. This may be because the latter tended more often to be negotiated explicitly so that the terms of the agreement were more accessible to contention.

Grants of immunity in exchange for testimony as a state's witness also changed during this period. Such grants became more accessible and certain as evidenced by the decision of the federal court in *United States v. Lee* in 1846, which formalized the court's obligation to informants.[11] That such immunity must be granted through a pledge—and is not automatic simply upon confession or testimony that implicates the accused along with any accomplices—is evident from several decisions in both federal court and the Massachusetts courts.[12] However, two Massachusetts decisions clearly indicate that the pledge may be either "express or implied," drawing it a step closer to the often implicit plea bargain than to the explicitly negotiated plea of nolo contendere.[13] Usually the prosecutor's pledge of immunity resulted in his entry of a nolle prosequi in the case, which meant that the case could be reinstated again at a later date. Another approach in some states was that the cases were continued to allow time for a pardon to be applied for and received.

The nolle prosequi or decision by the prosecutor not to pursue a case was the final discretionary element of the legal culture of leniency that was received and transformed during these years. Available evidence indicates that by the late 1830s, it (like the plea of nolo contendere) was being used to negotiate agreements that would deter future offenses and ensure the defendant's continued good behavior. As with grants of immunity, the "insurance" stemmed from the fact that prosecution could be reinitiated where a nolle prosequi had been entered.

A vignette from Thomas Gil's (1837) court reports provides a glimpse of this insurance element at work in the Boston Police Court during the 1830s. The case was one brought by Mrs. Julia Bench against her husband, Harold Bench, on grounds of bigamy.[14] Says Thomas,

> Mrs. Bench applied to the court through a relative, and obtained a warrant for his arrest; and, thus, before she was well aware of the effect of the movement, in the heat of natural resentment, she had

booked him for the State Prison, where, as she afterwards learned, he could be of no use either to herself or any of the other Julias.

After breakfast (next day) as the Gods would have it the unhappy pair unexpectedly met in one passage of the courthouse . . . Early feelings gushed forth in the bosoms of both; he was all penitence, she was all forgiveness. The lawyers on both sides were sent for . . . The learned practitioners caught the contagious romance of the scene; and laying aside their quirks and quibbles, set their wits to work, like Christians and gentlemen, to perfect the work of reconciliation. They all returned to the judge's private room, and in precisely one hour and a half, the complainant came out, paid the costs of court which had accrued, and consented to a nolle prosequi. This arrangement leaves everything exactly as it stood prior to the issuing of the warrant—in statu quo—and all parties are still free to prosecute, or not prosecute, as seemeth good unto them. (pp. 113–15)

In sum, what we see in the new uses of these traditional discretionary practices of the pardon, Ashael Huntington's use of the plea of nolo contendere, the granting of immunity based on a pledge, and the allowance that prosecution might be reinstated where a nolle prosequi had been entered is the channeling of discretion into more-explicit and formally structured, although open-ended, agreements involving both clearer behavioral requirements and more specific guarantees to the defendant. For the most part, these agreements were designed to deter future misdeeds and compel some desired behavior by means of state supervision as the practice of recognizance had previously done after judgment and that of leaving cases "open" or blank had done before.[15] To this end, judges took the insurance for good behavior required at sentencing by recognizance and moved it up to the stage of plea, providing new ground rules for disposition and sentencing, and, sometimes, adjustments to the charge entered as well. This step may well have responded to the situation of defendants in the lower court during this period, who, as members of a marginal class, had neither the resources nor social ties to enable them to pay surety. This stood in contrast to the sense during the highly litigious colonial period that defendants were simply normal members of society who had erred.

Thus, negotiation at the plea stage had begun before plea bargaining appeared. What plea bargaining changed was the form of the agreement. Here, in ways resonant of Perry Miller's (1970) depiction of the angular and relatively intolerant tone of Puritanism, the plea bargain appears to have drawn on the cultural template of the Puritan practice of "admonition" as a model. Influenced perhaps by the evangelical revivalism of the day, which sought to reignite religious fervor, and by a resistance to the encroachment of commercial capitalism, which had eroded traditional patterns of deference, plea bargaining in cultural terms harkened to symbolism from the world of religious tradition to restore virtuous behavior as well as punishing wrongs. Plea bargaining resembled a secular form of admonition, wherein a judge voiced the disapprobation of and subsequent reconciliation with the community, but in which the initiative must be taken by the defendant.

Religious Practice of Admonition: A Cultural Template

Even as common law traditions ensconced the use of leniency as a mechanism for stabilizing social conflict, an indigenous discretionary practice had also entered the courts. This was the practice of "admonition," and it originated in the religious courts that long operated side by side with them in New England.[16] Notations in the secular docket indicate that this practice, which in the religious courts involved a conciliatory grant of leniency by a congregation after hearing a confession of guilt, had emerged as a symbolically powerful practice in the lower court (Nelson, 1981). Admonition was a process whereby an accused offender appeared before his or her religious congregation to confess publicly and be rebuked by a congregation collectively expressing, often shouting, their admonition. After this, the community typically extended leniency to the accused as a sign of forgiveness, reconciliation and reception back into its midst (Nelson, 1981).

While admonition originated as a feature of the Puritan congregations and religious courts during the colonial period, its interpenetration with the secular legal sphere by the 1830s can be seen in several ways.[17] First is one of the 100 cases in my random sample from the docket of the Boston Police Court for 1830. This is the case of Sarah Barker, widow, who is recorded as living in Temple Street with Zebediah Glover, carpenter.[18] According to the docket "some citizens found the defendant in the street in a state of beastly intoxication, carried her to the watch house at the Gaol and she is brought into court." According to the notes in the docket, as no one appeared to prosecute, "she is discharged with admonition." It is important to note that no entry indicating "admonition" appears in any of the 900 cases sampled in 1840 or after once plea bargaining had begun. However, as late as 1837, several court vignettes published by Thomas Gil of the *Boston Morning Post* employ this term. One report describes a case involving an adulterous husband and his mistress charged with lewd and lascivious behavior who were dismissed with "admonition to go and sin no more" (p. 14).

As popular sovereignty increasingly captured the imagination of the masses during the early- to mid-nineteenth century, concern grew among republican citizens about the potential challenge the romanticism of the popular will presented to the notion of "law rule"—particularly as the franchise was extended "universally during the mid-1830s. Specifically, apprehension mounted that the people, possessed of a sense of their own omnipotence and acknowledging no limits to the power of popular opinion, would, in the words of Justice Theophilus Parsons (1835), come "to suppose that they, the people, cannot err" (p. 18). Parsons, in his Phi Beta Kappa lecture to the graduates of Harvard University, continued:

> Let there be established within a republic, the doctrine, that whatever a majority may be led to agree upon, that majority, on no other evidence, and for no other reason, may regard, and assert, and enforce, as right; ... establish this doctrine in the lives, in the practices, in the hearts of the people, and the foundations of the moral and the social, no less than of the political world, are broken up. ...
> (pp. 21–22)

Parsons goes on to argue that with such untempered enthusiasm for the powers of the popular will that:

> Every new appeal to the people will call upon lower motives, and baser feelings, than were aroused before, and at length the cup of degradation will be full, and the people will declare, by every act, that they have lost all relish for Liberty, unless it be corrupted into license. (p. 22)

Exhorting his audience to resist such tendencies, Parsons warned of the danger of raising the popular will above the law and, especially, of failing to seek the consonance of popular will with Divine Will and the standards of natural law. Parsons (1835) states:

> But let the opposite sentiment ... prevail; invigorate the body politic with the principle that right is not their creation, and depends not on their will, but on His will who made them free, only that they might the more freely seek and find it in His will—and you will send your country forward upon a career which cannot but be forever onward and upward. (p. 22)

Pointing to the advance of secularization and to widespread fears about corruption, decay, and the decline of virtue on the part of republican citizens increasingly unnerved by the prospects of popular rule, Parsons stated, "The true assailants of the law and of the peace of society are not now the indigent; . . . But they whom we have now to resist, are the poor in all that constitutes wealth of character . . ." (p. 27). In his call to virtue and to recognition of a higher, eternal standard above the popular will, Parsons bespeaks the angst of republican fear about corruption and nostalgia for the past in a commercializing world.

Confronted with popular concern about morality and the potential of the "political power of this country . . . [to now attack] the property of the country," the adoption of admonition by the secular courts assumes particular significance (Parsons, 1835, p. 14). In moral and educative terms, it is a call to virtue restored and to acknowledgment of the limits of popular rule. Yet, in the secular courts, admonition required no confession. In the plea bargain, the acknowledgment of culpability by the defendant draws the practice one step nearer to the reconciliation implied by the religious practice. That the acknowledgment of guilt was humbling for the penitent is shown by Nelson's (1981) anecdote about a Harvard president who adamantly refused to confess and be admonished. However, in that very recognition of the power of the community lies a crucial reason as to why leniency took the form of the plea bargain. In it lay an acceptance of the republican social order, which, increasingly finding itself under challenge, reaffirmed not only virtue but the community membership and relations of deference so essential to its makeup as well.

Admonition, like the pardon, initially involved leniency episodically granted by grace of the congregation or state, respectively, when guilt had been established. However, the leniency was an end in itself with no element of exchange involved. Because leniency was awarded after the facts had been presented and a determination, though not necessarily a sentence, arrived at, the court still affirmed the content and universality of social rules. In contrast, the changes in the use of pardon, plea of "nolo contendere," "nolle prosse," and grants of immunity during the early 1800s involve a shift to explicit compromise and exchange moved up prior to judgment. Across the board, more formally structured agreements were used in these cases to promote desired behavior. To defendants the cost was more-extensive state supervision—an element that the populace strongly protested and that paved the way, along with weakening notions of deference, for a relatively tolerant reception for plea bargaining by the populace once it began.

Stirrings of Direct Compromise in the Civil Sphere

Changes in leniency examined thus far have centered primarily on shifts in the ways leniency was granted in the context of case decisions in the criminal courts. In addition, a few occasional instances have been found of statutes that promulgated direct compromise unrelated to these forms of leniency in civil cases. In Massachusetts, practices that involved "compromise" or settlement, as it is known today, arose in the civil courts from the colonial period onward prior to comparable developments in the criminal sphere. Actual "compromise" or settlement of civil cases appears in federal case law in 1842, indicating a practice in place prior to that year.[19] The "referencing" of disputes, a practice in civil law akin to arbitration, also dates back to the colonial period (Moglen, 1983, p. 138). Although legally binding, the decisions of referees could be appealed through normal court channels.

Occasional Cases of Direct Compromise in Criminal Courts

In the criminal sphere, such early instances of direct compromise appeared later than they did in civil cases. A quartet of indigenous discretionary legal practices made their way to the criminal law courts during the late colonial and early National periods. These practices included: compromise of debt foreclosures authorized by a "confessional act" of 1782, payment of satisfaction, reduced penalties for confessions to fornication where a woman had become pregnant, and growing acceptance of the long-standing practice of compounding a felony (Handlin and Handlin, 1969). Introducing a new element of informality and overt exchange into court proceedings, these practices created a precedent for the parties to litigation to resolve cases out of court upon restitution being made.

An isolated but intriguing "confessional act" was enacted in 1782 in the aftermath of Shays Rebellion and recurring protest over court costs accruing from widespread debt foreclosure. This act allowed debtors to plead guilty and resolve their cases at reduced court costs (Handlin and Handlin, p. 33). Even more interesting, however, is a practice that appears to have newly emerged in the Massachusetts criminal courts during the 1830s. This was a provision in the *Revised Statutes of 1835* allowing that certain criminal prosecutions may be stayed upon payment of reparation to the injured party.[20] In its focus on cases that also had civil remedies, this provision appears to represent an extension of the civil notion of reparation into the criminal sphere—a shift that may have reflected not only liberal utilitarian sentiments of reimbursement but also the preference of lawyers for the practice of civil law. What is important to note is that once plea bargaining begins a sustained rise in Boston's lower court during the 1830s, it is in these same offenses of assault and property-related crimes where they predominate, while the practice is less evident in cases of drunkenness or offenses against the moral order despite high guilty plea rates for those offenses.[21]

Another isolated formal instance of concessions or reduced penalty attendant to a plea of guilty is found in a fee schedule from the late 1700s showing a lower penalty for fornication upon confession of guilt. Arising at a point when advancing secularization meant that the hold of Puritanism had waned, this statute appears to reflect the declining moral significance attached to such victimless religious offenses. Further, since such cases generally arose only when pregnancy resulted and the prospect of state support for the child and mother loomed large, acknowledgment of guilt appears likely to have established paternity even more effectively than a finding of guilt at trial. Thus, a policy purpose was served and the lower penalty may have constituted an incentive to elicit it. What is peculiar about this statute is that, as already noted, once plea bargaining begins its serious rise, it is substantially less predominant in these sorts of morals offenses.

Finally, the time-honored and strictly illegal practice of compounding a felony appears to have occurred with some frequency and to have attracted a fair amount of publicity during the middle decades of the nineteenth century.[22] Roger Lane (1971) recounts numerous, well-publicized instances of police detectives solving robberies and thefts by means of promises of immunity, though primarily for information or testimony as a state's witness in crimes where the individual in question was not personally involved, rather than direct dealing with a culprit in a case, though that too did sometimes occur. Although the 1819 decision of the Massachusetts courts in *Commonwealth v. Pease* indicates that some such cases were, in fact, ultimately prosecuted, Lane depicts enforcement as exceedingly lax by mid-century. He notes that during the 1869 hearings on whether to shift control of the Boston Police from the city to the metropolitan level, Judge Foster of the Superior Court testified that it was "difficult to show at what point it (i.e., compounding) was illegal, if recovery was not specifically made a condition of failure to prosecute" (Lane, pp. 153–54). City Solicitor C. H. Hill argued that in cases like the Concord Bank burglary in 1867 where "the whole community had a stake in the recovery . . . it was often difficult to show that compounding was not in the public interest" (p. 154). Responding to concerns of morality and justice, Hill cited the argument of utilitarian legal reformers that "reimbursement was more important than punishment, following Bentham's dictum that 'everything which can be repaired is nothing'" (p. 154).

The forms of leniency just described, along with the practice of admonition, constituted a crucial component of the cultural repertoire on which plea bargaining drew. In analyzing the role of ideas in social change, Weber has reminded us that although it is "not ideas, but material and ideal interests, [that] directly govern men's conduct," it is "very frequently the 'world images' that have been created by 'ideas' [which] have, like switchmen, determined the tracks along which action has been pushed by the dynamic of interest" (Weber; cited in Gerth and Mills, 1946, p. 280). In responding to the political challenges of the 1830s and 1840s, it will be shown that the common law tradition of episodic leniency and the religious practice of admonition played a powerful role in shaping both the lines of action taken and the cultural form of the solution produced. Mechanisms of leniency, as an element of political and legal culture, thus emerged strongly in American law. In part as a result of the burgeoning activist stance of the judiciary and its publicly acknowledged policy stance, judges busily hammered out new adaptations of leniency for limited use in promoting behaviors believed to serve the interests of the community. What was distinctive about plea bargaining was the way it drew on this established tradition to produce a new and innovative cultural form, one entailing entry of a guilty plea, a firmer and more predictable link to concessions, and the rise of a quid pro quo.

Beacon Hill and Site of the Future Statehouse: "Beacon Hill from Derne Street," 1811, from original watercolor by John Ruebens Smith (Boston Public Library)

Josiah Quincy, Mayor of Boston. Engraving by Stuart, 1830s (Boston Public Library)

Contrast with the World of Elites: "The Old Feather Store," ca. 1855–1860 (courtesy of the Bostonian Society/Old Statehouse)

Harrison Gray Otis, Mayor of Boston. Engraving by Kilburn, 1840s (Boston Public Library)

Beacon Hill in the 1840s, "The Streets of Boston, Tremont Street, No. III., lithograph by Phillip Harry. Published by Bouve and Sharpe, 1843 (Boston Public Library)

"New Map of Boston" (Boston Public Library)

Former president John Quincy Adams, ca. 1840 (Boston Public Library)

Abolitionist "William Lloyd Garrison," artist and date unknown (Boston Public Library)

African Meeting House, Smith Court (Society for the Preservation of New England Antiquities)

"View of the West End Toward the Charles Street Jail," 1858, Southworth and Hawes (Boston Public Library)

Cultural Life in Elite Boston at Mid-Century: "Entrance to the New Boston Theatre, Washington Street," 1850, artist unknown (Boston Public Library)

The Intensity of Winter: "Sleighing in Haymarket Square, Boston," 1859, Winslow Homer, artist (Boston Public Library)

Dress and Sociability in Downtown Boston: "Boston Evening Scene at Corner of Court and Brattle Streets," 1857, Winslow Homer, artist (Boston Public Library)

Burning of the Old Statehouse, Boston, November 1832, 1858, artist unknown (The Bostonian Society)

Typical Market Scene at Mid-century: "Corner of Washington and Boylston Streets, Boston—The Old Boylston Market," date and artist unknown (Boston Public Library)

Portrait of a Nineteenth-century Prisoner, Boston: "Committed to State Prison, Charlestown, when only 17 years old. He went to jail September 7, 1876. Thirty-seven years was in solitary confinement," written in pencil on the back of the photo. Creator Leslie Jones (Boston Public Library)

Police Station No. 4, Lagrange Street, ca. 1880 (Boston Public Library)

Horse-drawn Van for Prisoner Transport, early 1900s, artist unknown (Boston Public Library)

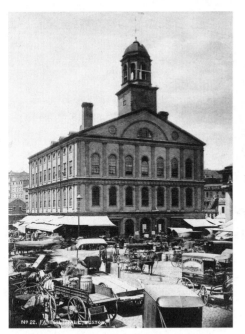

"Fanueil Hall Market" (near the wharves), 1880–1910, artist unknown (courtesy of the Bostonian Society/Old Statehouse)

First Irish Mayor: "Hugh O'Brien, Mayor of Boston, 1885–1888," ca. 1888, John Angel James Wilcox, artist (Boston Public Library)

(*right*) "Boston, Scene of the Great Fire, Efforts to Save Old South Church," 1872 (Boston Public Library)

(*below*) "West End Adult Evening Class," 1890, photographer unknown (Boston Public Library)

"Lower State Street Toward the Ferry Terminal and Waterfront," 1908 by Thomas E. Marr (Boston Public Library)

"Grove and Baker Sewing Machines, 1147–1195 Washington Street, ca. 1860–1875 (Boston Public Library)

"Court Street," ca. 1860–1870 (courtesy of the Bostonian Society/Old Statehouse)

"Attorney William H. Lewis Defends Henry Spellman and Cecil Brown," 1910 by Edmunds E. Bond, artist (Boston Public Library).

1747–1745 Washington Street, South End, ca. 1860 by Josiah T. Hawes (Boston Public Library).

"North Square," ca. 1895 (courtesy of the Bostonian Society/Old Statehouse)

Street Scene at the Turn of the Century: "Old Corner Bookstore, Washington and School Streets, 1900," artist unknown. Published by Halliday Co. (Boston Public Library)

(*above*) "Boston Public Library Façade and Flowers, Copley Square," ca. 1910, by Thomas E. Marr (Boston Public Library)

(*left*) Late Nineteenth-century Mayor "Josiah Quincy, Jr., Mayor of Boston," photomechanical print, ca. 1890s, artist unknown (Boston Public Library)

"Washington Street Looking North from Temple Place," 1908 by Thomas E. Marr (Boston Public Library)

"S.S. *Carmania* Docking in Boston," date and photographer unknown (Boston Public Library)

"Women and Children in Morton Street," ca. 1900 (courtesy of the Bostonian Society/Old Statehouse)

POLICE CLEARING THE DIAMOND.

"Police Clearing the Diamond, 1903 World Series" (Fenway Park) (Boston Public Library)

Symbol of Irish Presence in Boston: "Rally for Irish Independence at Fenway Park," early 1900s, artist unknown (Boston Public Library)

Anti-capitalist Spirit: "Sacco Plays Capitalists in Fiery Speech in Court, 1921," Norman Dedham, artist (Boston Public Library)

6

The Emergence of
Plea Bargaining

Improvization in Law

In the years of the ascendancy of the judiciary in America, many
scholars have portrayed in rich detail the power that accrued to the
courts through judicial review (Forbath, 1991; Ely, 2000; Burt,
1992). This capacity, won through the separation of powers, enabled
the courts to review the constitutionality of enactments by the legislatures and ultimately elevated "law rule" above the primary vehicle
of "popular" or "self-rule." It has long been accepted that the might
of the American judiciary partly drew its strength from the relatively
weak and decentralized state that was constructed in the United
States, one crafted on the model of Madisonian federalism. Another
contributor to the ascendancy of judicial power was the prominence
of a discourse rooted in law as a legitimating language of politics.
Finally, the activist stance of judges, who decided cases with an eye
for their policy consequences beyond the case at hand, has also long
been emphasized (Horwitz, 1977). In exploring the many uses to
which leniency was put by the courts in efforts to elicit behavior
beneficial to society we can see in some detail the fabric of that judicial activism and growing power of the courts in concrete terms.
Having examined the symbolic repertoire of the common law tradition of leniency, we must now ask what circumstances combined to
cause leniency to be recrafted into the distinctive legal form known
as plea bargaining.

Timing of Crisis: Convergence of Forces and Innovation

By locating the beginnings of plea bargaining in the 1830s and 1840s, as we have, we shall see that it arose amidst a perceived crisis of unrest and social instability in the republic. It was also a time of intense partisan contest as the Federalist elite, now under challenge, attempted to reconsolidate their long-standing political power in Boston and to complete the transition to the second party system. This timing was crucial because it occurred just as suffrage was "universally" extended. Together these events evoked new state responses to social conflict.[1] As the already substantial voting public grew, uncertainty ran high as to whether self-governance would prove viable and what path politics might take.[2] At this unique moment, state response to the crisis was needed that would be defensible in a world of popular rule. This created a fertile ground for legal improvization. Amidst a rescripting of legal practices that took place, one innovation, plea bargaining, achieved special prominence. Plasticity of institutions and practices at this dynamic time, when judges were forging law into a modern form, much of which it retains today, facilitated the creation of new legal mechanisms and, once formed, allowed them to achieve a centrality and permanence that would perhaps otherwise not have been possible.

During the 1830s and 1840s, rioting and unrest were widespread. The earliest factories were constructed which changed both forms of production and working conditions. City life brought diverse strangers of unequal rank into contact. These, coupled with new waves of immigrants, created a vibrant and tumultuous urban scene. Officials, already focused on the danger that inequality posed to property, social order, and growth, grew anxious (Horwitz, 1977; Nedelsky, 1990). Perceived crisis was amplified by the fact that religious belief, previously a source of cohesion, and social consensus, which had pervaded small-scale community life, were also eroding (Nelson, 1981; Lockridge, 1981). Constant spatial movement and turnover among residents in city neighborhoods amplified the strains of inequality (Sellers, 1991). Irish immigrants began to coalesce as a major presence too. Amidst these pressures, conflict, unrest and violence, rather than harmony, were the order of the day. Because self rule was still relatively new and local political capacity for responding to conflict was limited, there arose a sense of crisis and of threat to both the social order and the partisan control of the beleaguered Federalist elite that had retained power in Boston long after waning in other cities. Unrest never overtly challenged state authority but it created unease and posed a real electoral challenge to the Federalists and their progeny. It was desire, in this context, to protect order and to reconsolidate the city elite's partisan control that elicited new state responses.

Between 1833 and 1836, spurred on by the election of Andrew Jackson to the Presidency, strikes by the Workingmen's Movement swept the American northeast (Sellers, 1991, p. 338). Their crusade was for a limit of ten hours to the working day. Though this had, by 1836, largely been achieved, their mobilization continued (p. 338). Workingmen challenged that a privileged few flourished at the expense of the many. Resentment simmered. By the 1830s, public concern was widespread about the future of republican self-rule. Workers began to use the language of republicanism in new modestly socialist ways (Forbath, 1991). Social disorder, riots and strikes riveted elected officials who turned for help to the ideology of a "rule of law."

By this point, conflict had gripped the popular imagination. Ethnic diversity and contention soared as did ethnic tensions and a public fear of crime. During the 1830s, a remarkable series of riots and routs occurred. By then, city officials, who were very aware of similar events in England and on the continent, were acutely sensitive to the political potential of such events (Lane, 1971, p. 30). In 1836 and 1837, an economic downturn, followed by financial panic, further fanned fears about the fragility of the new order. Unease created by daily contact among persons of diverse ranks in the city amplified fears as the lives of the poor impinged ever more on the consciousness of the affluent (Lane, 1971).

As labor unrest, ethnic conflict and crime mounted, shockwaves were buffered less than they had traditionally been by the erosion of shared religious values and cultural commonalities (Wiebe, 1966). Thus, during the 1830s, when social conflict grew, amidst weakened cultural consensus, it produced an acute sense of crisis in the new order. Response to this crisis was shaped by its timing which caused state actions to be devised in the context of two other key happenings (Poulantzas, 1975). Extension of the vote meant that any initiative must take a form that would sustain the popular consent crucial to self-rule. There was also emerging a new conscious campaign to promote social policy and the "people's welfare" through law (Horwitz, 1977). The fact that crisis emerged during this "formative era" of American law created a special window of opportunity for cultural change.

With their hold on political power now tenuous and implications of the recently extended franchise fully in mind, the Federalists and, later, National Republicans and Whigs sought new approaches for resolving conflict that were more consonant with the imagery and language of popular rule. This was done not as a movement toward democratization but as a reaction to partisan challenge and attempt to reconsolidate power. The courts emerged as leaders in this project of maintaining order by modulating conflict and seeking to promote greater security of property and the person. Thus, legal innovation began, as Weber (1978) argues it has throughout time, at the initiative of a status group that found an existing legal repertoire insufficient to address its new needs. Much as Tigar and Levy (1977) have shown that the modern legal system arose from the twelfth century onward in response to the needs of merchants as spokesmen for nascent commercial capitalism, my analysis suggests that crucial adaptations were called forth in the lower criminal courts by the shift to popular rule.

Plea bargaining emerged, then, during the first of the country's two great eras of reform and during the very decade when liberalism, in the form of Bentham's ideas, made its entry to the new republic as part of an oppositional discourse. This new legal practice was able to address the dual demands of political stabilization and partisan consolidation and to do so in a language that reinforced the legitimation of both political authority and self-rule. Of particular interest here is how long-standing legal and political traditions in British common law legal culture were reworked and used in new ways as social structure changed and new political groups that were coalescing articulated their interests.

Changing Class Structure and Challenge to Elite Control

During the 1830s and 1840s, Boston grew and experienced major structural changes.[3] The city's population, which more or less doubled in size every twenty years from 1790 to 1850, grew from 43,298 in 1820 to 61,392 in 1830, 101,000 in 1840 and 136,881 in 1850 (*Statistics of the United States*, Seventh U.S. Census Compendium, 1850, Table CCXVI, p. 192). This pace of growth outstripped state-wide growth in Massachusetts where population rose from 610,408 in 1830 to 739,699 in 1840 and 994,514 in 1850 (*Statistics of the United States*, Seventh U.S. Census Compendium, 1850, Table XL, p. 61).[4] About one percent or 9,064 of that population in 1850 of 994,514 consisted of "free coloured" persons (*Statistics of the United States*, Seventh U.S. Census Compendium, 1850, Table XLII, p. 63). Mounting economic inequality, class-based tension and early ethnic conflicts combined to produce increasing public concern about order. As Parsons (1835) saw it, one might "find some . . . analogy . . . between the existing . . . conflicts of the present age, and the universal disturbance of Europe, during the centuries when her nations were assuming the forms which, in the main, they have since retained" (p. 26).[5] Although the class structure and occupational base of Boston primarily reflected the city's roots in commerce, the patterns of its growth and stratification were shaped by the swift industrially based economic development occurring during this period. In Massachusetts, the path that industrialization took represented a sharp break with the Commonwealth's recent past. It also differed from the British experience. In contrast with England, not only was the pace of industrialization more rapid but also, since it occurred during America's "formative era" when her legal traditions were being established and common law heritage adapted, any effects on the legal system were amplified relative to Britain, where legal institutions had been established centuries before.

Industrialization in Massachusetts was distinctive in several ways. Its rise was precipitous and brought about a sharp change in the economy. Although factory construction began with the first modern American production facility in Waltham in 1814 (later than in Britain), the Commonwealth had already surpassed British levels of labor force conversion to factory work by the 1840s (Siracusa, 1979). (Figure 6.1 compares graphically these American and British rates of labor force conversion.) In addition, industrial output was by then so extensive as to rank Massachusetts first among the states in total output throughout the antebellum period and first in per capita output until nearly the end of the nineteenth century. As a result of this productivity, Massachusetts was termed "the most thoroughly industrialized state" (Siracusa). By the 1840s, numbers of factory-based textile workers swelled noticeably. To some extent by the 1830s and increasingly thereafter, this laboring "class" was riven by strong ethnic cleavages as wave after wave of immigrants flooded to the opportunities that New England offered. Ethnic conflict among these diverse groups was by then already evident.

Despite the rapid advance of industrialization in the state as a whole, the city of Boston itself did not boast vast manufacturing establishments. Instead it remained the home of commerce and finance, mercantile activity, craft, and continually expanding masses of unskilled labor (Handlin, 1979, p. 9). The port of Boston grew into a bustling hub of trade and finance, craft workshops, and construction projects (p. 9). As Handlin has noted, "while Boston capital built great industries outside of Boston, it failed to develop them at home" (p. 9). After financial devastation during the War of 1812, prosperity returned and production skyrocketed in the Commonwealth's textile centers at Lowell and Fall River and the mill towns along the Merrimac River. This much-awaited restoration of growth was financed, however, primarily by the great wealth garnered by Boston merchants and shipping companies in the Federal period through the China trade.[6] As textile production brought profits, the proceeds flooded back into that city. Bankers used these new funds to underwrite Bos-

TABLE 6.1. Population of Boston and Its Environs[a]

	1790	1810	1820	1830	1840	1845	1850	1855	1860	1865
Boston (proper)	18,038	32,896	43,298	61,392[§]	85,475	99,036	113,721	126,296	133,563	141,083
Islands	282	519	...	...	277	292	325	530	1,000	1,300
East Boston	...	18	...	...	1,455	5,018	9,526	15,433	18,356	20,572
South Boston[†]	...	354	...	...	6,176	10,020	13,309	16,912	24,921	29,303
Roxbury	2,226	3,669	4,135	5,259	9,089	...	18,364	18,469	25,137	28,426
Dorchester	1,722	2,930	3,684	4,074	4,875	...	7,969	8,340	9,769	10,717
Brighton[‡]	...	608	702	972	1,425	...	2,356	2,895	3,375	3,854
Charlestown	1,583	4,954	6,591	8,783	11,484	...	17,216	21,700	25,065	26,399
Brookline	484	784	900	1,041	1,365	...	2,516	3,737	5,164	5,262
Chelsea	472	594	642	770	2,390	...	6,701	10,151	13,395	14,403
Cambridge	2,115	2,323	3,295	6,073	8,409	...	15,215	20,473	26,060	29,112
West Cambridge[‡]	...	...	1,064	1,230	1,363	...	2,202	2,670	2,681	2,760

[a]Derived from Carroll D. Wright, *Analysis of the Population of the City of Boston as Shown in the ... Census of May, 1885* (Boston, 1885). 8 ff; *Massachusetts House Documents, 1837, no. 19*. pp. 9, 10; United States. Census. *Aggregate Amount of ... Persons ... According to the Census of 1820s* (s.l. n.d. [Washington, 1820]; *Massachusetts House Documents, 1842, no. 48*. pp. 1–6; *Massachusetts House Documents, 1831, no. 10*, pp. 1–6: *Report and Tabular Statement of the Censors ... May 1, 1850, Boston City Documents, no. 42, 59*; Joseph C. G. Kennedy, *Population of the United States in 1860; Compiled from the Original Returns of the Eighth Census* (Washington, 1861), xxxi; Francis DeWitt, *Abstract of the Census of ... Massachusetts ... 1855 ...* (Boston, 1857), 32–50.

† Part of Dorchester until 1804.

‡ Part of Cambridge until 1807.

§ This figure includes Boston proper, and the Islands.

Source: Oscar Handlin (1979)

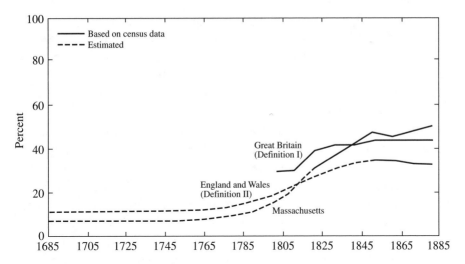

FIGURE 6.1. Labor Force Conversion: Manufacturing Population as Percentage of Whole, Great Britain and Massachusetts, 1685–1885.
Note: In Definition I, manufacturing population includes all those in Great Britain engaged in manufacturing, mining, and construction. In Definition II, it includes all those in England and Wales engaged in manufacturing only.
Source: Siracusa (1979)

ton's sensational rise in finance and banking to eventually rival New York as a financial capital through the antebellum years.[7] What industry existed in Boston proper, though, remained relatively small in scale.[8]

By 1845, the occupational structure of the city had for almost two decades produced growing inequality—primarily amongst the small traders, proprietors, artisans and handicraftsmen, and the "merchant princes" who invested in shipping, trade, finance, and manufacturing (Handlin, 1979, pp. 11–12). Bostonians had clearly envisioned since the early 1800s that their city's future would be linked to the development of its hinterland. Into the city flooded goods from the Merrimac's textile factories and the shoemakers of Lynn bound for distant American cities or ports abroad (p. 7). Though industrial workers were few in Boston, unskilled laborers, often immigrants working either as seamen or in construction of streets, office buildings or wharves, multiplied apace (Handlin and Handlin, 1969).

As prosperity returned, missionary, reform, and benevolent associations poised for "conquest" of its growing middling and laboring classes. A national temperance movement joined in to imbue an ethic of self-disciplined effort at work (Sellers, 1991, p. 237). Entrepreneurs motivated both themselves and their workers by enshrining class as a "[quasi-]moral category" and touting the promise of upward social mobility (p. 237). Disdaining both the "idle rich" and the "dissolute poor," these traders, shopkeepers, and small manufacturers failed to gain entry to a "virtuous middle class" of the industrious (p. 237). In a market-based society that promised reward proportionate to effort, middle-class imagery both motivated and justified prosperity to overcome simmering discontent with inequity (p. 237).

In reality, Boston afforded little chance for mobility unless one possessed the dual advantages of "birth and capital" (Handlin, 1979, p. 12). Young men seeking better prospects recognized this and steadily left that city.[9] Handlin notes that "By 1850, only half the descendants of the Bostonians of 1820 still lived there" (p. 12). Population expanded nonetheless but far more slowly than in other urban centers. Between 1820 and 1840, immigrants arrived, not so much from Europe as from outlying areas of rural New England until the great flood tides of Irish began (p. 12). (Table 6.1 shows the pace of population growth for the city of Boston.) Already by the 1830s, an identifiable Irish immigrant community was beginning to form in Boston. In 1850, 16.6 percent of Massachusetts' population was foreign born with much of it Irish and most living in Boston (Statistics of the United States. Seventh U.S. Census Compendium, 1850, Table CLV, p. 152). From the 1840s onward, Irish migrants worked as unskilled laborers, greatly expanding the ranks of artisanal Boston's lower or "dangerous" classes, and thus contributing to growing class-based tensions.

The financial and mercantile, but nonindustrial, role played by the city generated great increases in wealth—but sharp inequities in its distribution. Nor did this pass unnoticed. Bostonians of the 1820s and 1830s lived through the most precipitous increase in the permanent inequality of conditions in American history (Sellers, 1991, p. 238). The share of wealth held by the richest 10 percent of families rose, primarily after 1820, from 49.6 percent in 1774 to 73 percent in 1860 (p. 238). Wealth concentrated in the cities. Nor were the largest fortunes the fruits of efforts by self-made men, a fact that further strained relationships. Of the 2,000 wealthiest citizens between 1828 and 1848, 94 percent in Boston had been born to rich or eminent families as were 92 percent in Philadelphia and 95 percent in New York (p. 239). Stresses induced by this growing inequality and the atomization of "market society" was exacerbated by constant geographic movement and turnover in communities. Of the families listed in the 1830 Boston census, fewer than half remained by 1840. The Irish immigrant community was forged from those who stayed.

By the late 1820s, the early moral reform societies, as a source of order, had failed. Why this happened says much about the dilemmas of social control in that day. Reverend John Chester noted that, "armed with statutes and followed by officers," moral reformers were viewed as threatening "to abridge the liberties and destroy the rights of the community" (Sellers, 1991, p. 263). Voicing prescient words, Chester concluded that "you can not coerce a free people that are jealous to fastidiousness of their rights" (p. 263). Instead, he exhorted, one must persuade them in order to win their consent.

Harmonious consent would not, however, be readily forthcoming; instead, generalized unrest, social conflict, and violence would. Deference to one's "betters" in politics had faded. Precipitated by the democratic turn in national politics with Jackson's election, a rash of strikes erupted in the cities of the Northeast between 1833 and 1836 (Sellers, 1991, p. 338). Organized by the Workingmen's movement, their quest was for a ten-hour working day, a goal that by 1838 had essentially been achieved (p. 338). Yet their discourse endured. It decried the fact that "capital divided society into two classes, the producing many and the exploiting few, by expropriating the fruits of labor" (p. 338).[10] Workingmen had questioned rampant inequality. Even more ominously, labor unrest began to contest the ethos of unremitting industry for a wage. Public fears grew palpable about potentially explosive tremors in the fragile system of republican self-rule. Workers adapted the language of republicanism in ways that interpreted the pursuit of the holistic interests of the community in a new more politically militant vein (Forbath, 1991). Crime, strikes and rioting preoccupied citizens and elected officials alike. To defuse resentment and reassert control, public officials drew, as we shall see in more detail in a moment, on the imagery of a "rule of law."

Now social conflict powerfully focused public attention. Ethnic tensions and, with them, contentiousness rose as did perceptions of the Irish as causing much disruptive turmoil. (Table 6.2 shows the relative magnitude of the streams of migration by ship from various foreign ports between 1821 and 1865.)[11] Data from the House of Corrections, at first glance, appear to support this view. In 1834, Irish-born persons comprised 35 percent of Boston's inmates and 40 percent in 1837—a far greater share than they yet constituted in the city's population (*City of Boston Documents*, no. 13, 1834, p. 14; no. 23, 1837, p. 19 [*Report of the Inspector of Prisons for the County of Suffolk as to the Gaol, House of Correction, House of Reformation and House of Industry*, December 1837]). By 1871 the chief of police would report figures for the city prison showing that 14,673 out of a total of 23,858 prisoners (or 61.5 percent) in 1870 were Irish-born (*Annual Report of the Chief of Police*, Boston, Massachusetts. 1871). Yet, whether this is due to the fact that they were victims of selective law enforcement or were penalized for drinking in public houses rather than, in Yankee style, at home, it is not possible to know. Records of the House of Industry similarly note that, in 1833, 55 percent of those admitted were foreign-born (*City of Boston Documents*, no. 11, 1834, p. 17; no. 13, 1834, p. 14; no. 23, 1837, p. 19). The *Annual Report* for the same House of

TABLE 6.2. Passengers Entering Boston by Sea, 1821–1865

Place of Origin†	Five-Year Period ‖ Beginning								
	1821	1826	1831	1836	1841	1846	1851	1856	1861
Great Britain and Ireland	...	...	...	6,996	...	...	...	19	...
Great Britain	164	3,030	581	58	7,010	3,603	990	9,654	1,324
England	286	506	1,712	172	4,545	12,513	10,264	748	3,931
Wales	16	...	7	6	24	316	354		23
Scotland	90	55	102	24	389	2,249	2,469	1,870	682
Ireland	827	549	2,361	443	10,157	65,556	63,831	22,681	6,973
British North America	525	648	3,943	3,537	5,654	16,816	21,233	18,240	14,542
Germany	58	311	253	449	301	1,385	2,653	1,198	1,287
France	66	167	57	212	239	381	605	529	362
Italy	14	23	40	42	59	137	186	247	89
Spain and Portugal‡	48	41	48	80	147	176	540	943	1,017
Holland	27	27	80	182	30	484	399	298	292
Switzerland	3	163	137	7	10	45	25	200	63
Scandinavia	9	38	62	244	110	723	4,120	1,317	708
Latin America§	80	83	147	264	172	429	772	300	226
Russia	4	12	23	4	5	66	40	28	28
Asia Minor	7	18	11	21	20	32	58	45	19
Asia and Pacific Islands	1	1	8	9	8	34	17	85	69
Africa	6	1	16	3	13	15	21	112	92
Unknown and Miscellaneous	2	54	31	228	671	18	1,018	1,013	760
United States	1,564	1,727	2,149	3,921	7,177	7,686	7,910	10,396	10,234
Total	3,797	7,454	11,768	16,902	36,741	112,664	117,505	69,923	42,721

† Cf. Dissertation Copy. 424.

‡ Includes Azores.

§ Includes Mexico, West Indies, Central America, South America.

‖ 1832 and 1834 are for nine months only; 1842 includes figures for England and Ireland only.

Source: Handlin (1979)

Industry in 1834 notes that "a considerable change has taken place in the comparative numbers of native and foreign poor . . . The former have diminished while the latter have increased" (*City of Boston Documents*, no. 17, 1834). In this context, real and perceived increases in urban crime, especially violence and social disorder, involving as they did large numbers of foreign-born, were experienced as particularly threatening.

Adding to these tensions was a marked increase in public fear of crime—especially violence.[12] Addressing the Boston City Council on September 18, 1837, Mayor Eliot decried the threat posed by "the incendiary, burglar and the lawlessly violent" that was "increasing at a ratio faster than that of the population" (cited in Lane, 1971, p. 34). Data on overall arrests in Boston are available only for the years 1831 and 1851 so that, if one puts questions of how arrests compare to offenses actually committed aside, only the most limited analysis of arrests over this period is possible. It does appear that Massachusetts, which in 1840 incarcerated 1 in 2,522 of its white citizens, had higher per capita rates of imprisonment than did many other states though states including Connecticut at 1 in 2,414; New York at 1 in 2,056; Maryland at 1 in 1,708 and Louisiana at 1 in 1,115 showed still higher rates (*Statistics of the United States. Seventh U.S. Census Compendium*, 1850, Table CLXXXI, p. 167). However, commitments of those convicted and imprisoned reveal only modest increases for the years 1824 to 1833 and in some instances 1841 for which they are available (see table 6.3). Comparison of five-year averages for 1824–29 and 1829–34 show growth of 1.8 percent for the House of Correction; 2.8 percent for the Jail for crime and debt; and 5 percent for the State Prison. It is the House of Industry and the House of Reformation of Juvenile Offenders, which focus on poverty, disorder and youthful deviance, that show growth of 19.5 percent and 24 percent, respectively (see table 6.4), while the city's total population grew, as we have seen, by between 50 and 60 percent between 1830 and 1840 (Handlin, 1959, p. 239). Thus, the 1830s appear to have posed a threat of continuing the insecurity and violence of the 1820s along with growing fears about disorder, poverty and political instability.

One striking feature of these years is the large proportion of repeat offenders among prisoners (see table 6.5). One challenge facing the court was to distinguish hard working citizens who had made a misstep from more troublesome persistent offenders. Since court caseload grew far less in these years (in fact the five-year caseload average of 2,027 for 1823–28 actually declines slightly to 1,894 for 1829–33), trends in rising imprisonment may have reflected greater use of incarceration—perhaps due to a perception that the crimes were a more serious problem.[13] Probably the best indicator of public apprehension is that the Mayor requested and obtained funds to establish a

TABLE 6.3. Commitments of Those Convicted

	House of Correction	Jail	State Prison
1824–25	588	1784	49
1825–26	592	1689	37
1826–27	572	2130	35
1827–28	505	1889	43
1828–29	523	2002	31
Average 1824–29	$\overline{X} = 556$	$\overline{X} = 1898$	$\overline{X} = 39$
1829–30	569	2249	37
1830–31	586	2144	50
1831–32	474	1442	22
1832–33	676	1716	51
1833–34	526	2197	49
Average 1829–34	$\overline{X} = 566$	$\overline{X} = 1949$	$\overline{X} = 41$
Percent Change	+1.8	+2.6	+5

Source: Pamphlet entitled "Plain Facts addressed to the Inhabitants of Boston on the city expenses for the support of pauperism, vice and crime." Published by the Council of the Massachusetts Temperance Society. Boston: Ford and Damrell, May 1834.

TABLE 6.4. Commitments of Those Convicted

	House of Industry	House of Reformation of Juvenile Offenders
1824–25	866	—
1825–26	677	—
1826–27	630	38
1827–28	643	100
1828–29	640	60
Average 1824–29	$\overline{X} = 691$	$\overline{X} = 66$
1829–30	755	48
1830–31	675	48
1831–32	867	58
1832–33	895	55
1833–34	940	43
Average 1829–34	$\overline{X} = 826$	$\overline{X} = 50$
Percent Change	+19.5	−24

Source: Pamphlet entitled "Plain Facts addressed to the Inhabitants of Boston on the city expenses for the support of pauperism, vice and crime." Published by the Council of the Massachusetts Temperance Society. Boston: Ford and Damrell, May 1834.

TABLE 6.5. Careers of Repeat Offenders among Prisoners (1834, House of Correction)

From the Records. Prisoners more than once committed, remaining in the House of Correction 20th of April, 1834, and for what Crimes and Offences.

Names of Men.	Common Drunkard.	Vagabond.	Wanton & Lascivious.	Night-Walker.	Pilferers.	Larceny.	Theft.	Assault.	Total Commitments.
Samuel D. Joy,	1	1				1			3
Matthew Winneberger,	1					1			2
Robert Clues,	1	4							5
Barnabas Connor,	4	1	2		1				8
John Rodgers,	2	1			1				4
Palmer Scudder,	8	4							12
Martin Barnes,	2				1				3
Wilson Hallet,	4								4
Lewis Whiting,	3								3
Charles Colbourn,	7	2			5		2		16
George Lane,	1		1		1				3
John Hartshorn,	9								9
Solomon Shaw,	3	1			1				5
Charles I. Woodman,	4								4
John Rochford,	2		1						3
Thomas Falvy,	6								6
George Smith,	2	2							4
John Bowman,	4	2							6
Samuel Robinson,	2	1	1						4
Aaron Smith,	2	2							4
Edward Roach,	6	1							7
George Lewis,	2								2
John Ferguson,	3								3
Otis Willis,	3	1							4
Abijah Bemis,	3	6							9
Michael Early,	2								2
Thomas Garrety,	13								13
James Hennessey,	2	2	1						5
Henry Wright,	10								10
James Kearney,	2								2
Ephraim Skerry,	2								2
George Duffy,	6								6
Nathan Cooledge,	5								5
Thirty-three men,	127	31	6		10	2	2		180
									(Continued)

Source: Pamphlet entitled "Plain Facts addressed to the inhabitants of Boston on the city expenses for the support of pauperism, vice and crime." Published by the Council of the Massachusetts Temperence Society. Boston: Ford and Damrell, May 1834.

TABLE 6.5. Continued

Names of Women.	Common Drunkard.	Vagabond.	Wanton & Lascivious.	Night-Walker.	Pilferers.	Larceny.	Theft.	Assault.	Total Commitments.
Cecilia A. Jones,	2								2
Elizabeth Robbins,	2	1	2					1	6
Caroline Lewis,	1		6				1		8
Elizabeth Swaine,	2	2				1	1		6
Mary Ann McCabe,	2								2
Sophia De Wolf,	5	2	6						13
Harriet Harvey,	6	1	4	1	1		1		14
Rosanna Patterson,	4	2	2	2					10
Margaret McCarty,	6	3		4					13
Lucy Carr,	3	2	3	1					9
Catharine Perry,	3		2	1					6
Lucy Richardson,	12	13							25
Ann Gordon,	6	5							11
Mary Belding,	2								2
Maria Clark,	6	3		2					11
Eliza Fletcher,	3								3
Sarah Humphries,	2	1	1	1					5
Rebecca Newcomb,	5	3	1	2	1				12
Eliza Harrington,	1		1						2
Lydia Rainey,	2	2	1	1					6
Phoebe Kelley,	2	2							4
Jane Johnson,	5	2							7
Caroline Smith,	5					1			6
Hannah Gardiner,	2	1	1		1		2	1	8
Harriet Fisher,	2	1	2	1					6
Mary Ann Jones,	3								3
Elizabeth Gray,	4		3						7
Mary Kyer,	2	1	1						4
Sophia Robb,	5	1	3						9
Eliz'th. Perkins or Dodd,	3								3
Mary Ann Duvall,	3		2						5
Catharine Boyle,	5								5
Hannah Lunnon,	4	2	2						8
Catharine Forrestor,	2								2
Roxanna Reed,	3	1	3						7
Betsey Rallion,	2								2
Martha Cliff,	4		3						7
Sarah Payne,	4	3	2	1					10
Thirty-eight Women.	135	54	51	17	3	2	5	2	269

financially much begrudged and long-resisted paid professional police force for the city.[14] Pointing to the "spirit of violence abroad," Eliot argued that appropriate steps had to be taken to protect the city.

Whether disorder and crime actually were rising, continuing at unacceptably high levels, or merely perceived as becoming more threatening, it was clear that violence was pervasive and presented a shocking contrast to expectations of prosperity, harmony, and deference. Witness the remarkable spate of riots and routs that occurred in Boston during the 1830s. Two events, in particular, brought public distress to a fever pitch: the burning of an Ursuline Convent in Charlestown in a flare-up of anti-Irish sentiment in 1834 and the famed Broad Street riot of 1837. Sparked by a clash between a volunteer fire company and an Irish funeral procession, this outburst involved 15,000 persons or one-sixth the population of Boston and took 800 horsemen to quiet (Lane, 1971).[15]

After the "Mount Benedict Outrage," as the convent fire was known, public agitation soared. Concern over violence and disorder intensified markedly as if a danger chord had been struck. It was seen as "a riot with social, even political, implications" (Lane, 1971, p. 30). Further, by the mid-1830s, the city's officials, well aware of events in England and on the Continent, recognized all too clearly the prospects for political riot (p. 30).[16] Such a reminder echoed (as the nation recalled its revolutionary past) "on the fourth of every July" (p. 30). In 1836 and 1837, the strain of these outbreaks was aggravated when a severe economic downturn, followed by a financial panic, further heightened fears about the fragility of the nascent social and economic order. Unease created by encounters at close hand with persons of diverse ranks in daily life enhanced angst as the lifestyles of the poor impinged ever more intimately on the affluent (Lane, 1971).

During the 1830s and 1840s, then, Boston emerged as a city in which a changing class structure combined with heightening ethnic conflicts, concern about crime, and what we will see to be mounting pressure to extend the franchise to produce considerable unease among the city's old political elite. Contrast between the stirring pressures for democratization and the adapted republican sensibility of the Federalists could hardly have been more stark. Yet the power of even vestigial Federalist sway remained great. Justice Henry Orne (1820) of the Boston Police Court, the only antebellum justice to be appointed by a Democratic Governor to that bench, captures that sensibility in his observation that "whatever might be the legal rights of opulence, the deference of mankind . . . [yields] to its influence what it . . . [denies] to its claims" (p. 13). Amidst social and economic tension, then, real or perceived increases in urban crime, especially violence, were experienced as particularly threatening to the social order of the day. Their psychological impact was likely heightened through juxtaposition with remnants of the traditional customary relations of deference linking the privileged with the middling and lower ranks of the society. Not only were configurations of opposing interests beginning to congeal but, as the city grew, the lives of persons of diverse social backgrounds were coming more and more into contact with each other in the course of daily affairs. Urbanites experienced at close hand encounters with strangers—that is, persons whose identities and personal histories were unknown—in contrast to the strict regulation of the movement of transients and visitors in earlier village settings. Thus, increasingly the problems of the poor and the laboring classes affected quality of life in wealthy neighborhoods of the city.

As labor and ethnic conflict mounted, shock waves were amplified due to erosion of both religious values and cultural consensus (Wiebe, 1966). Although the small "island" communities that were a legacy of colonial times waned, the imaginative structure of republicanism with its strong dependence on the legal order remained strong. Weakening of the vital role of religious ideas and institutions in the decades after the American Revolution and a growing separation of church and state were key cultural developments in the United States that diverged from the British experience during this period (Nelson, 1967).[17] Massachusetts had always been a contentious and litigious society, a practice some attribute to its use of legal struggle to define social rules in changing times and to adapt the common law heritage to the American setting (Konig, 1979). Religion had, however, traditionally provided binding elements of commonality. Yet by the 1830s, that changed. Secularization, coupled with industrialization had, by 1840, reduced the role of religion as a substantive grounding of the moral basis of the law—revivalism notwithstanding. Widening disengagement of church and state, culminating with disestablishment in 1833, speeded the spread of secular outlooks. Cultural consensus, rooted in shared norms and bonds of reciprocal obligation, declined. While social and legal historians differ regarding the precise date this process began, all agree that by 1840, there had been a significant weakening (Nelson, 1975; Zuckerman, 1978; Lockridge, 1981).[18] Thus during the 1830s, social conflict, in a setting of diminished cultural consensus, produced a heightened sense of crisis in the new order. Republican political ideology and the paradigmatic social discourse of law were left to shoulder a particularly heavy burden in ideational and cultural terms. The sense at every hand was of change. Yet the imaginative structure of republicanism was nostalgic for a bucolic past and, though being molded by new groups, was fundamentally skeptical of the advance of commerce and capitalism.

Much of the explanation for the nature of political and legal response to this crisis lies, then, as Poulantzas (1975) has argued more generally, in timing that produced a convergence of mounting sense of disorder, cultural dissonance, and weakening political control. It caused state response to be devised during an historical moment when two other key happenings came to pass (Poulantzas). The franchise was extended at precisely this time, making it likely that state response would take forms attuned to sustaining the popular consent crucial to self-rule. There also evolved a new conscious focus on social policy in law for this already heavily regulated society in which judges attuned decision making, including sentencing, to the objectives of the state. Judges assumed a new activism that edged into policy-making as they considered decisions in light of their broader implications beyond the case at hand (Horwitz, 1977). The fact that crisis emerged during a formative period of unique plasticity in American law created a special window of opportunity for cultural encoding of this change. Even as political officials, who were the partisan heirs of the Federalists, moved to begin to act, new currents of change were stirring in the form of movements for social reform. As with any people, the cultural repertoire likely to inform the court's activity was what was known to them and familiar—in this case, the traditions of the common law. However, events would endure and transform significantly beyond what these Federalists had in mind.

Extension of the Franchise and Movements for Social Reform

As social conflict grew rife, contestation of Federalist political power, which had been increasing, gradually became more strenuous too. By the end of Jackson's second presidential term in the mid-1830s, "universal" suffrage was a fact of life and was reconstituting politics. By easing restrictions such as property ownership (though still retaining the poll tax), Massachusetts, like other states, extended voting rights already widely shared among the middling ranks to new segments of the laboring classes though a goodly share of the Commonwealth's citizens had already voted before (Pole, 1957). Artisans and workers now produced more representative legislative assemblies whose statutory enactments more closely reflected the popular will though a lingering tradition of deference meant that the result was not immediate. Elected leaders, in turn, faced new constraints as they shaped state administration and lines of political action. At once, it became far more important that their decisions engender some modicum of broad-based popular consent. This abetted a move, already underway, to challenge the political control of Boston's Federalist elite (Lane, 1971). It also aroused worries about what other forms, particularly with respect to property, contestation might take. According to Mensch (1982), "the universal principle that . . . [received] the most zealous protection was the sanctity of private property" (p. 20). Story opined in those years that the lawyers' most "glorious and not infrequently perilous" responsibility was to protect the "sacred rights of property" from the "rapacity" of the "majority" (Story, 1829; cited in Mensch, 1982). While proprietors, professionals and others of the middling ranks complained that conflict marred quality of life, city leaders worried about even more far reaching consequences of unrest (Lane, 1971).

Intellectuals, such as de Tocqueville (1997), questioned the capacity of the masses to carry out such weighty civic responsibility. Privately, he and others ambivalently speculated whether cultural mediocrity and political initiatives to equalize property and wealth might not be the ominous result of this expansion of the voting public (Parsons, 1835, pp. 13–16; de Tocqueville). Speaking of such potential on the part of popularly elected legislatures, Justice Theophilus Parsons (1835) went so far as to warn:

> Regard it . . . as the first deep murmuring, the warning voice, that the yet distant tempest sends before it. It is not civil war that is coming upon us; for there cannot be resistance enough to make a war . . . The laws and the institutions of the country will be the subjects of attack, and the subjects of change; your halls of legislation will be the battlefields in this combat; and there the war has already begun. (p. 15)

Focusing attention directly on property, Parsons queries

> have you forgotten that the most active among them now declares, that the despot against whom the liberty of America is called to contend, is aggregated property. (p. 15)

One primary consequence of extending the franchise in this context of heightened unrest and weakened cultural consensus was to produce mounting partisan challenge to Boston's old Federalist elite (Lane, 1971).[19] Familiar as they were with the rioting and revolt in Britain and on the European continent during the 1820s and 1830s, Boston's politicians worked feverishly to restore order, reconsolidate their partisan base, and cement popular commitment to the institutions of the republic. They touted the "sanctity of property" and explained that "the redistributive passions of the majority, if ever allowed to overrun . . . the barrier of legal principle, would sweep away the nation's whole social and economic foundation" (Mensch, 1982, p. 20). Nedelsky (1990) has shown that this intent interest in the protection of private property so central to the Federalist agenda was not new and was descended from interests that had powerfully shaped both the contours of the Constitution and the conceptions of civil and political rights on which it was based decades earlier. Because the franchise precluded solutions to disorder and unrest that jeopardized voter support, new responses had to be devised, not only to violence, property crime, and riot but to growing political tensions too.

The courts, which, along with tax collectors, had provided Americans' primary experience of the state before local political parties formed in the 1840s, now assumed a key role (Skowronek, 1982). Beginning in the 1820s, just after the financial panic of 1817, a first wave of court reform had been undertaken to stem perennial criticisms that universality and fairness were lacking. Among other things, it established the Boston Police Court. It was a reform spearheaded by Boston's leading citizens and it aimed to re-establish the lower courts as a respected and well-used forum for resolving conflict (Hindus, 1980; Dimond, 1975).

By the 1830s, Boston's local officials were "no longer so firmly united by ties of class and [state] party [affiliation] as their predecessors [had been] a generation before" (Lane, 1971, p. 46). The city remained a "one-party [Whig] city" temporarily, where "candidates labelled Democrat or [later] Locofoco had [in most years virtually] no chance of local [electoral] success" (p. 47). However, the times and, especially, movements for humanitarian reform were creating intractable dilemmas for these beleaguered Federalist and, later, Whig municipal authorities (p. 47). The arrival of immigrants, Lane notes,

> also helped exasperate a tense political atmosphere. As the Free Soil and Know-Nothing Movements grew and the older parties splintered and regrouped, men's hopes for the material future were balanced by fear for the political. Humanitarian reform in the city, no longer new, was in some ways accepted. In others the movement was discouraged, brought to a peak and then frustrated. (p. 60)

Under pressure, affluent and privileged Bostonians, unwilling to rely on the moral suasion of the mayor and warnings of the aged city marshall to uphold order, turned reluctantly to consider new alternatives.

Strategies to restore order were being conceived, then, at a time that precluded politics as usual. The Whigs feared threats, not only to property per se, but even more to the stability in day-to-day affairs that investment and growth required.[20] While the republic and its markets were felt to be generally robust, uncertainty that introduced unusual risk could be nearly as deleterious to commerce as would be a change of regime. Risk was something these seafaring merchants and financiers well understood. Fearing for the future, leaders worked to nurture order and predictability in public life and to cultivate the consent of citizens to both institutions of self-rule and the stewardship of their party. To this end, they approached social control, not through overtly coercive means, but, as the Reverend John Chester had presciently understood, in ways that underscored the party's claim to serve the will of the people (Sellers, 1991). This meant adopting lines of action that were beyond reproach in the eyes of the voting public.

City officials and elite civic leaders accomplished this by appealing to the pre-eminent social discourse of the day—that of a "rule of law." By common agreement, they argued, social life must proceed according to a body of rules specified in advance and oriented to fairness. Such rules, they contended, apply universally to every citizen and prescribe equal treatment for each accused person in court. Then, in a gesture ripe with political drama, it was argued that, even when such rules depart from popular opinion, they must, unceasingly, be observed. Only through adherence to legal principles and procedures, leaders argued, could the new project of self-rule be sustained. By appealing to the language of the widely revered "rule of law" as a basis for order, they hoped to bolster both social order and the legitimacy and authority of republican institutions. With order restored, they believed they could resecure their hold on power.

The language in which the reforms were introduced reveals something of how officials viewed them. When, in 1822, the Police Court had been established, where trial judges replaced the much maligned system of justices of the peace, Mayor Josiah Quincy unveiled his plan by denouncing the potential for social conflict inherent in the previous system. Quincy (1822), in the course of a charge to the Grand Jury of the Municipal Court of Boston summed up the spirit of that reform thus:

> A new arrangement of the administration of justice, in its lower department, has been obtained for this metropolis, in consequence of a very general and prevailing sense of abuses, which had been the consequence of the system antecedently existing. (p. 4)

Its object, as he saw it, was

> to insure to the poor, in their narrow and humble sphere, an independent and disinterested tribunal for the protection of their rights, the healing of their wrongs and the settling of their controversies. (pp. 4–5)

Emphasizing the corrosive influence of the absence of such a tribunal on the moral qualities and political commitment of citizens, Quincy queried:

> If it be true of all means of carrying down and disseminating moral influences among the mass of mankind, none are to be compared with those which result from the just distribution and wise execution of the principles of justice, can anything be more destructive ... than to permit the mass of the community to know justice chiefly by its administration in the hands of men, whom experience teaches them to consider as on the watch after opportunities for gain, from their vices; as making profit by their passions; and as interested to enhance their losses and miseries, by multiplying or lengthening out their controversies? (p. 6)

Speaking particularly of the lower court, Quincy argued that

> Whenever, ... confidence does not exist in the lower tribunals, there is no justice ... [for] the poor, who cannot afford to carry their causes to the higher. (pp. 7–8)[21]

Such injustice, he proclaimed, corrupts the morality and political commitment of citizens. Quincy referred, among other things to the prior fee structure whereby magistrates had prospered the greater the number of cases heard. Quincy's remarks provide a reminder that perceptions of injustice and infringements on the rights traditionally accorded free-born Englishmen had contributed mightily to the revolution that had so recently terminated America's colonial relation with England. Raised and left open was the question of what consequences similar treatment and indifference to the situation of the laboring classes might bring in the new American republic. Anticipating a point later made by Max Weber (1978), Quincy argued that where political authority is of a rational-legal sort that anchors its legitimation in legal rules and specification of its offices in law, the danger is especially great when that law is perceived as unjust. The risk is that laws, so viewed, may be treated as no law at all, and that the foundation of political authority itself will then be undercut. Given the centrality of law's place in the discourse and cultural webs of meaning of the day, such a loss would have been devastating for the political prospects of the republic. Following quickly upon court reform, other major new institutions including prisons and reformatories, a House of Industry and a professional police force were all set in place.

As Quincy's remarks illustrate, concern to provide a forum to resolve the conflicts of the laboring classes, to uphold the legitimacy of the legal system, and to draw disputes into the court marshalled reluctant support for a sub-

stantial agenda of reform in Boston.[22] Under pressure, elite Bostonians experimented with new options. Far from generous in their readiness to spend
public monies on those bypassed by the economic opportunities of the day,
the city's leaders seized on social order and—not just any order—but social
order as it had been.[23] In a sense, the initiatives for reform, like much of the
ideology of republicanism that guided it, may be understood as stemming at
first from a sort of reaction to the social and political developments of modernity, in general, and of their own day, in particular. Within this context,
reforms that promoted social order and, with it, prevailing arrangements of
power topped the public agenda (Hindus, 1980). Among the reforms proposed
in early nineteenth-century Boston, court, police, and penal improvements
were of highest priority. This responded both to the demands of the propertied
for security and, even more, to the "claims [for a just forum on the part] of a
[lower] class [whom they felt it] unsafe to deny" (Lane, 1971, p. 23). Additional
changes soon followed.

Prior to these reforms, criticisms of the courts and polity were widespread.
Allegations of delay, high costs, and unfairness, especially in responding to
debt, threatened political support and potentially authority itself. In an effort
to strengthen acceptance of the rule of law, reform of the courts and related
institutions was begun. Every effort was made to direct widespread crime and
conflict into institutional channels (Hindus, 1980; Dimond, 1975). Once reform started in the 1820s, extension of the franchise during the 1830s brought
intensified pressure for change. All these projects and choices helped shape
what became the second great reform movement in Boston during this period.
Following quickly on the court, other new institutions and a professional police
force were also formed (Lane, 1971). In 1822, the House of Industry was built,
followed by the House of Correction in 1823. In 1826, the House of Reformation of Juvenile Offenders was established. In addition, in 1822, after almost
two decades of abolition, revival, and reorganization of the lower tier criminal
and civil courts of the city, the Boston Police Court was established. In 1837,
just after the Broad Street riot, Boston also grudgingly accepted the establishment of a professional full-time, paid, day-time police force on the London
model—overcoming, to some extent, fears of its being used as a secret police
for state political purposes along the lines of the French police in Paris (Lane).

Thus, the Federalists' agenda of reform in Boston was not the democratic
order proposed by the movements for social reformation or the Statehouse
where Democratic-Republicans were, between 1823 and 1825, for the first time
ensconced in office but rather social order much as it had been at the height
of their own political influence. To take one step "backward" to reconsolidate
elite power, this city with its tradition of single-party Federalist and, later, Whig

control was forced to rethink the logic of its dominance and to take several small steps forward in the service of consensus building and reform. Yet, these changes so hard won by reformers would paradoxically help to reproduce the very order they challenged. As Boston's leaders crafted new responses to restore social order, a world view that was more oriented to compromise, restitution, and the free play of interests—that of a "market society"—was moving to center stage to challenge the claim of the traditional early republican vision on the minds and hearts of Boston's citizens. But reforms and innovations of this period would not be limited to institution building.

Law and Social Policy in Sentencing

As new institutions moved into motion, judicial decision making and court procedure also changed, although more informally and incrementally. Specifically, judges' decisions during this period of change took on a policy focus (Horwitz, 1977). This was part of a broader sea change that altered the role of the courts and contributed to the development of one distinctive feature of American democratic state formation: the primacy of the judiciary. Judicial preeminence centered on: a separation of powers, independence of judges, the power of judicial review, capacity of the courts to assess the constitutionality of legislative enactments, and the role of the courts in articulating a conception of citizenship and inculcating a sense of its obligations. In the criminal courts, pardons, the nolle prosse, the plea of nolo contendere, and grants of immunity had, as we have seen, already begun to be used in new, more explicitly conditional ways to further specific policy goals. Plea bargaining now made its debut in the courts.

During the "formative era," judges began to reconceptualize American law as an instrument of social policy. This transformation in law, combined with state structure, made it likely that political response to the current crisis would come through the courts. While the courts had long interpreted and upheld the socially "regulated" society of the Commonwealth in pursuit of the "people's welfare," judges began to change the way they envisioned their role. As they did, judges increasingly crafted their decisions with an eye, not just to sound implementation, but to policy implications beyond their case at hand (Horwitz, 1977). In private law, case decisions aimed to facilitate healthy markets and economic growth (Horwitz). What my own work shows is that a policy orientation arose in the criminal courts too. In the criminal courts, judges sought to ensure behavior that would uphold social order and, especially, foster the security and predictability needed for commerce and market development

(Vogel, 1999). It appears to be for this reason that earliest plea bargaining in Boston's Police Court concentrated in offenses against property and the person such as larceny and assault and battery.

According to a weak version of this claim, policy considerations arise only in cases that legally can be decided in more than one way, whereas a strong version construes the influence of policy goals on judicial decision making more broadly in what is potentially almost every case (Barak, 1989; Llewellyn, 1981 and 2000; Horwitz, 1977). Previously it was demonstrated in Chapter 5 that pardons, the nolle prosse, the plea of nolo contendere, and grants of immunity began to be used explicitly in new, more conditional ways to promote desired behavior. Ashael Huntington's well-known case dramatically illustrated official awareness and acceptance of such practices. By the 1830s, however, judges increasingly moved beyond such specific behaviors, and even the oversight of social regulation by the judiciary, to include in their case decisions broad-based considerations of social policy. Horwitz describes this shift in terms of the rise of an "instrumental" conception of law. He sees this procedural change extending beyond remedies, sanctions, and even ambiguous cases to fundamentally shape judicial interpretations and precedents themselves. As mentioned earlier, this argument has been challenged in some quarters for the underlying materialism of its formulation. Other critics who counter that policy concerns predated the formative era are often commingling court administration of well-specified frameworks of social regulation with judicial decision making shaped by what may be more aptly described as a policy climate. This growing social policy awareness in the courts provided a flexibility that made it likely that the state's response to social instability might take a judicial form.

Yet, existing cultural practices of leniency, though being used in new, contractual, and more-structured ways, generated strong public outcry over both the intrusiveness of state oversight into the lives of defendants and the high legal costs of negotiating them, which placed them beyond the reach of many people. In the quest for a response to the violence, unrest, and perceived instability of the day, the existing cultural repertoire of the common law came under fire. It is precisely this situation, of a status group confronted with a situation pertinent to its needs, where existing cultural responses prove lacking that often produces innovation and, particularly, legal innovation (Weber, 1978). Responding to public criticisms regarding the intrusiveness of the prolonged state oversight necessitated by the courts' new uses of leniency, plea bargaining arose out of the cultural repertoire of previous legal forms to constitute a unique innovation in lawyerly practice.

Insight from Weber (1978) illuminates how just such a process of legal change works. Weber contends that new legal norms and practices are usually produced through innovation, or the emergence of new lines of action, when an existing repertoire does not suffice (pp. 753–84). These changes are, Weber contends, often initiated by status groups acting on the basis of their interests. As time goes on, innovations first acquire the power of habit, then of norms and, finally, they are formalized in law. Plea bargaining appears to have developed very much in such a progression.

Did circumstances of that process determine that plea bargaining would take the cultural form that it did and no other? No, almost certainly not. However, the customary practices of episodic leniency from the British common law and the Puritan religious practice of admonition provided strong cultural images on which to draw. They offered a rich symbolic repertoire that made confessional and conciliatory elements more likely components of this new practice. Existing means being insufficient, a new line of action was needed. Although plea bargaining arose during a period of reform, it does not appear ever to have been advanced as a unitary or formal initiative, nor is there any indication that it was the offspring of liberal, or even democratic, impulses. Instead, it emerged as an informal and pragmatic accretion of small changes in the customary practice of the courts that was, only then, culturally codified.[23] By providing leniency, financial accessibility, and, most important, reduced state oversight of those accused, the courts staked a claim to fairness, openness, and modulation in the exercise of state power. This was crucial in helping to bring conflicts before the courts and in maintaining both the legitimation of judicial decisions and popular adherence to the rule of law.

Lawyering in an Era of Popular Politics

Boston lawyers, during the 1830s, were embarked on a struggle, whose roots hark back to the guilds, of a craft to regulate itself. For the elite members of the "law craft," what was new and gave a unique flavor to their quest was the context of industrialization, "market revolution" and nascent popular politics. Challenges were being raised to the common law which was depicted as a colonial residue more familiar to elites than to ordinary people. Judges garbed in black robes and tye wigs still rendered justice in the higher courts in a style similar to that in England (Jones et al., 1993, p. 119). Lawyers, themselves, and their practices were said to highlight the "difference between rich and poor" (p. 25). The role of lawyers and the way they practiced changed. One of the most significant transformations was the rise of plea bargaining. How lawyers organized as a group, the institutional setting where they worked and their strategies for resolving cases all underwent metamorphosis.

The tradition, among Boston lawyers, of corporate fraternity loosely modeled on the guilds was long. One finds John Adams speaking in his diaries of journeying with judges and other lawyers when he argued cases on the Superior Court's circuit. Many were the nights that the road-weary travelers slept at the same inn and dined together in the evening (Adams; cited in Jones et al., 1993, p. 19). Often the talk turned to law or politics.

Although comradely association was well-established, self-regulation as a corporate body proved far harder to come by. Fee structures, for example, were originally regulated by the state and established by statute. We know that Adams' practice involved him in hundreds of cases each year. The hectic pace of his work was due, at least partly, to the limited fee structures of that day which allowed a lawyer to charge six shillings for a case tried in Inferior Court and twelve at the Superior Court (Jones et al., 1993, p. 19). Adams had grumbled, apparently with the fees much in mind, "Let me remember to keep to my Chamber, not run abroad . . . Law and not Poetry is to be the Business of my life" (Adams; cited in Jones et al., p. 19).

At its first meeting in 1763, the Suffolk County bar had drafted a proposal to regulate who could be admitted to practice law before the courts. They sought to exclude "irregular practitioners," who came to be known as "pettifoggers," and to reserve appearance in the Inferior Court for "sworn attorneys" (Jones et al., 1993, p. 19). When James Otis openly opposed the exclusivity of their plan, the court declined to adopt it. Two years later, the bar specified the qualifications for advancement to the status of barrister with members hoping to control both the quality and the numbers of competitors practicing law (p. 20). Adams himself lamented that "Every county . . . swarms with Pupils and students and young Practitioners of Law" (Adams; cited in Jones et al., p. 20). In 1770, at the Bunch of Grapes Tavern, the Suffolk County Bar Association was formally established when twelve barristers and attorneys formally voted it into existence. In this new, more institutionalized guise, the pre-Revolutionary bar sought to set in place "uniform standards," regulate "competition" and reform and simplify trial procedures (Jones et al., p. 21).

As storm clouds of Revolution gathered, lawyers in Boston had found themselves central to the many legal aspects of dissent. Some defended merchants who resisted tariffs imposed by customs officers on imports such as tea while others challenged change in the term of judicial appointments from "good behavior" to "the pleasure of the governor" (Jones et al., 1993, p. 21). As

John Reid has noted, the colonists, as they defied the Crown, demonstrated powerfully their rootedness in the "rule of law" as a guide for grappling with adversity. General Thomas Gage, commander of the British forces in that War, had laid much blame for colonial dissent at the doorstep of lawyers saying, "The Lawyers are the Source from whence the Clamours have flowed" (Jones et al., 1993, p. 21). Yet when colonists closed the Boston courts in 1774 to prevent the enforcement of unpopular laws, almost a third of the city's lawyers had remained loyal to the Crown (p. 21).

In the aftermath of the Revolutionary War, the country, as we have seen, embraced a republicanism which initially depicted a "return of the values of a simple rural society to reverse modernizing tendencies of American life" (Jones et al., 1993, p. 22). It promised a society based on "merit, equality and virtue" (p. 22). Within this vision, lawyers were problematic because of their perceived ties both to privileged elites and to the British common law. When, several decades later, a new urban republicanism emerged that accepted economic competitiveness and property accumulation, lawyers embraced it eagerly (p. 22).

During the 1780s, seven former members of the pre-Revolutionary Suffolk County Bar Association assembled and voted to reinstitute it. Continuing on their prior path, they resumed efforts over the next two to three decades to establish standards, specify the educational requirements for the practice of law and control admission to the bar (Jones et al., 1993, p. 22). They also adopted by vote a higher fee schedule, attempted to regulate business procedures such as soliciting clients, and prepared to assist members or their families in times of need (p. 24). At this point, the bar also began to oppose policies or practices that might hamper their business opportunities.[24]

Almost without exception, the Massachusetts bar, after the War of Independence, consisted of, first, Federalists and, then, Whigs (Warren, 1931, pp. 174, 178). During the early decades of the nineteenth century, they achieved new influence after they recovered from an immediate post-Revolutionary period of disrepute. This political collegiality in the sympathies of the bar, combined with a long tradition of fraternity, practical exchange of ideas and fellow feeling, on the one hand, and, first, Federalist, and, later, Whig control of the Commonwealth's judicial appointments, on the other, to ensure that the courts were presided over by judges in step with the policies of these elite-dominated parties.

Popular Challenge to the Common Law

How and why did a policy orientation on the part of judges come about and what role did lawyers play? Critique of lawyers, largely on grounds of their Federalist views, gradually came during the 1800s to be associated in the public mind with opposition to the common law. The early 1800s had been a "disruptive and potentially radical period" (Mensch, 1982). It was a time when premier American leaders and jurists devoted their energies to "re-establishing [post-independence] political authority" (p. 19). As they did, they came to rely heavily on the courts where the role of judges was changing (Mensch, 1982, p. 19). After the American Revolution, many states had initially adopted much of British common law. Public attitudes toward it had been positive. After 1800, however, things changed (Horwitz, 1977, p. 5).[25] Previously, the common law had been viewed as a fixed, customary standard. Judges envisioned their task as discovery and application of preexisting rules (pp. 8–9). This produced a strict conception of precedent and a popular view of law as, if not always fair, at least known.

In the closing years of the eighteenth century, however, signs of change appeared in this view of (and popular tolerance for) the common law, in both the criminal and civil spheres (Horwitz, 1977). Its roots were two. The first was states rights constitutional theories that depicted law finding based on precedent as a form of "ex post facto" law. The second was new conceptions of the basis of legitimation of political authority which portrayed the customary approach of common law as outdated in light of political forms that now emphasized popular sovereignty. The constitutional challenge argued that when judges imposed criminal penalties without laws being enacted by a legislature in statute, the application of precedent after an act had occurred constituted "ex post facto" law. It was argued that this punished persons left in ignorance of precisely what the law prohibited and, so, breached constitutional limits on state power (pp. 11, 14).

As ideas about the basis of political authority changed, it also meant that the common law with its roots in custom came to be seen as incompatible with a vision of authority that reflected popular sovereignty. Popular support surged for the codification movement, which sought to recognize the primacy of "the people's" elected representatives and to move from case law to statutory enactments.[26] Yet judges, who were overwhelmingly Whig-appointed and political leaders resisted the move to statute precisely because of the power it would have given to legislative bodies dominated by the middling and lower classes (Horwitz, 1977, p. 21). Instead, they, together with what was then the

Federalist and later Whig elite, fought to maintain judicial discretion by preserving reliance on the complex ancient forms of common law (p. 21). Given the strong Federalist associations of most members of the bar, there is every reason to think most judges espoused that view. Thus, citizens challenged the power of received tradition and sought new clarity and representation in enacted law. Political elites countered by fighting to retain discretion and control by protecting the common law focus on precedent and opposing a shift to statute. Although the codification movement ultimately failed, it signalled public interest in reducing the discretion of judges and in simplifying and clarifying the law, before the fact, and communicating knowable legal rules and procedures to the citizenry.

It was the effort to reconcile the tension between judicial discretion and the popular will, mentioned above in the context of the common law, that contributed mightily to what Horwitz (1977) has called the "transformation of American law." Judges increasingly bridged the gap between common law and "the people" by envisioning themselves as agents of "popular sovereignty." Nor was this stance in contradiction with the pervasive regulations of the day, for judges came to view their role as that of activist and innovator functioning amidst the many levers of public power on behalf of the "common good" (p. 30). In the course of this change, judges began to view law as an instrument of social policy.[27] As they did, their mainly Federalist convictions influenced the way they diagnosed social problems and the responses they prescribed. Increasingly, judges articulated decisions with an eye toward the policy implications of a decision beyond the case at hand. Their task became a process, through their decisions, of making, and not just discovering, law. Now judges articulated decisions based on a self-conscious consideration of their consequences for broad-based social policy goals. They began to use law as a tool to shape the path of social change. In Mark DeWolfe Howe's words, "it was [as] clear to laymen as it was to lawyers that the nature of American institutions . . . was largely to be determined by the judges . . . [and that] questions of . . . law were . . . considered as questions of social policy" (Howe, 1947–1950; cited in Horwitz, 1977). Howe's words bespoke a conscious turn by the state to the courts, among other institutions, to promote its policies.[28]

While the policy role of the civil courts has long been acknowledged, we now see that it extended to the criminal sphere as well. In the criminal courts it centered on the structure and mechanics of sentencing. This policy stance was demonstrated both by new conditional uses of leniency explicitly to deter specific undesirable behaviors and by the focus of these efforts on crimes against property and the person. The thrust here was to promote social and economic stability, a move that virtually always redounds to the advantage of political incumbents and economically privileged groups. It also promoted the predictability that had been recognized by economists since Adam Smith to be vital to commerce and economic growth. In the criminal law, this policy sensitivity arose as social conflict and perceptions of political challenge surged during the early 1800s, at a time when there was as yet very little local government infrastructure in place. Because American law was in its formative period, the timing of this crisis prompting state action created unusual openness for innovation in the court's response.

How do we know that plea bargaining, specifically, constituted such a policy instrument? The concentration of plea bargaining on cases of wrongdoing that were of prime state concern—breaches of security of the person and of property—provides one indication. Emergence of this new discretionary cultural practice at precisely the historical moment when virtually all forms of leniency received from the common law were being reworked into more-explicit and formally structured vehicles for ensuring behavior consonant with productivity and growth also suggests a policy focus. As Huntington's very high profile case showed, public knowledge of such approaches to sentencing was widespread, and the practices themselves met with public approval (House Report, Massachusetts Legislature, no. 4, January 1845). It is worth noting that the criminal justice enterprise as a whole was undergoing a shift during these years under the influence of the penal philosophy of Cesare Beccaria (1986). Originating in the Enlightenment, Beccaria's thinking helped focus sentencing in Boston on concepts of deterrence. It is to these ends that new uses of leniency were initially turned.

Judicial discretion, which was strengthened by plea bargaining, was especially adaptable to the nuances of policy. Mayor Josiah Quincy emphasized the existence of such discretion in his address to the Grand Jury of Suffolk County when he observed, "There is, indeed, a discretion invested in judges" (Quincy, 1822, p. 12). That he believed such discretion should be informed by social policy in shaping sentencing, Quincy left no doubt. He proclaimed that "The utility of a concentrated system of penal and criminal law in which punishment shall be graduated by the nature and aggravation of crimes, and *adapted to the actual state of society and public sentiment* [emphasis added], . . . [is] appreciated" (p. 14). Quincy also emphasized that the judges' discretion in the criminal sphere centered on sentencing policy. He noted that a judge's discretion included selecting "time and place [of imprisonment]" as well as other aspects of the severity of sanction (p. 12). Plea bargaining, by enhancing discretion in judicial decision making in criminal cases expanded judges' capacity for policy initiatives.

Concentration of plea bargaining, as we have seen, in crimes against property and the person in Boston provides an indication of how the policy focus of the practice was used because these offenses threatened the security of goods, buildings, and facilities as well as the predictable social order that was crucial for investment and growth. Another signal lies in patterns of plea bargaining over time, specifically in the relation of concessions to social unrest, the financial climate and party coherence. Patterns of offense-specific temporal variation in bargaining in relation to restiveness, economic vitality, and party consolidation suggest possible systematic changes by decade, most strongly during the antebellum years (refer to table 4.16). The evidence is not conclusive on this point and further study would be beneficial. In larceny and, to a lesser extent, assault cases, where early bargaining primarily occurred, both concessions and guilty plea rates oscillated somewhat in the antebellum years. While crime rates are only occasionally available during those years, it is known that those decades were marked by powerful economic cycles of boom and bust. Major economic downturns occurred in the mid-to-late 1830s, 1850s, 1870s, and 1890s. Most severe were those recessions of the late 1830s and 1890s, which reached the depths of major economic depressions.[29] Currently, the best evidence suggests that 19th century social unrest peaked during what appear to have been relatively prosperous years, such as the 1820s to 1830s, the 1850s, the mid-1870s, and the 1880s to 1890s when rising expectations surged (Wilentz, 1984; Sellers, 1991).[30]

Increasingly, it appears that, at least until the American Civil War, the lower criminal courts in Boston moved in their policy efforts to contain conflict, protect property, and dampen the violence and rioting most clearly in the lean years of the early 1840s and 1860s when unrest may have been temporarily less intense than when restiveness was near its peak. While one may query why a response to instability would appear most actively operative in relatively quiescent times, three points might well shed some light on the matter. First, this followed the British tradition, depicted by Brewer and Styles, of modulation in quiescent times. Second, there may have been a process of institutional learning where leniency in restive times was found less productive. Third, it is possible that those pleading not guilty initially received higher sentences than was the norm. This point could usefully be informed by further research.

While more research is needed, this may have provided an opening to, much as had the British before, engage the good will of the citizenry by offering moderation. More active threats, especially to the state, seem to have been dealt with more harshly by invoking the full force of the law. Plea bargaining, which begins on a mass routinized basis in response to guilty pleas quite perceptibly in 1836 in Boston's lower court, appears, then, in just such a window. This cultural practice starts just after the ominous crime, violence and unrest of the

1820s to early 1830s and amidst the economic weakening of the late 1830s and, especially the unique political demands of the election of 1836 which we shall explore in the next chapter. Ability to innovate was relatively unconstrained due to the extraordinary fluidity of legal arrangements at the time.

Contours of the State

To be persuasive, an explanation of plea bargaining must show why it did not appear in other similar societies undergoing similar strains as they adapted to popular rule. Britain, which shared the common law, is especially interesting here. The answer appears to lie in contextuality and the contingency of cultural practices in at least their formative days. Two distinctive features of the American state powerfully shaped Boston's response to this period of crisis. They clarify both why response came from the judiciary and why plea bargaining did not arise in the otherwise seemingly favorable context of England. These characteristics are the relatively weak central state and decentralized administration of the courts in America, on the one hand, and the unusually close linkage of law to local politics, on the other. This was complemented by the work arrangements in the lower court and the success of court officials in preserving judicial discretion during the 1830s and 1840s despite movements afoot to codify law. While these did not cause plea bargaining, we shall see that work place incentives to judges and lawyers and to court officials and staff do help, along with norms of deference, to explain why no strong opposition to plea bargaining materialized as it arose and why institutionalization of the practice occurred so rapidly.

Virtually every previous historical work emphasizes the broad discretion of American prosecutors and judges as a cause of plea bargaining (Alschuler, 1979; Friedman, 1981; Fisher, 2000; Steinberg, 1984). Many forget that, while capacious procedural discretion exists in America, it also exists in Britain, but less so in the more formally rationalized legal systems of the European continent. Weber (1978) suggests that broad judicial discretion in the common law may stem from its substantive orientation to justice (pp. 809–38). Discretion is also enhanced by decentralized administration of the courts, which enables innovative local variation in decisions. Since discretion is a central dimension of plea bargaining, this suggests one reason why plea bargaining did not arise initially on the continent. More puzzling is why it did not appear first in England. It is argued in what follows that the structure of the American state combined with the timing of political crisis in the 1830s and transformation of the American judiciary to move legal innovation along paths not viable in

England. Along with decentralized courts, the uncommonly close linkage of law and politics in the United States played a key role in producing legal compromise in the form of plea bargaining.

Weak Central State and "Local" Administration of the Courts

Essential to the rise of plea bargaining in Massachusetts were the relatively weak American state and the decentralized system of court administration that prevailed. This enabled "localization" in judicial decisions which varied regionally. In contrast to the strong central bureaucratic states of some European nations, the early Madisonian state in antebellum America was, largely one of "courts and parties" (Skowronek, 1982).[31]

Decentralized administration of the courts, which was a tradition in both Britain and America, also left them freer in those countries from national supervision and control. Locally focused judicial activity and spatial variation in justice administration flourished more fully than where courts were centrally coordinated by a strong national state. This decentralized approach tended to produce a "familiar" series of court proceedings where litigants personally knew the magistrate or judge and regional differences in the "justice" meted out could be considerable. Judges had greater latitude to adjust to local circumstances and, it appears, to compromise. In this sense, the American system reveals affinities to the British courts but differs from those on the continent. Since discretion is so significant for plea bargaining, this weak central state and relatively decentralized court administration in the United States suggest two powerful reasons why plea bargaining originated there and not on the European continent.

But why did plea bargaining not emerge first in Britain, which shared a substantial procedural discretion from the common law with the United States? While comparable in some ways to the British system, localization was carried further in America to include state appointment or election of judges as well as state or local funding of the courts.[32] This contrasts with Britain, where, as on the Continent, appointing judges and funding courts are national tasks. Where, as in Massachusetts, both are controlled by the Governor, this exposed the courts to the policy preferences of state officials through appointments and thrust them into budgetary politics. Thus, the American experience diverged sharply from both Britain and the European continent. This was important because Massachusetts, which was highly litigious as early as the colonial period, had an established tradition of using the courts to rescript social rules in times of social change (Konig, 1979). Periodic attempts were made by the state legislature, as they had been at the national level under Jefferson and in other states as well, to limit court autonomy and to expand political control over them—often in the name of accountability, reduced costs or improved administration (Knudson, 1970, p. 248).

The paradoxical result was that court operations grew in scale and their role in conflict resolution expanded even as attempts were made to keep the judiciary relatively weak and to limit its autonomy (Hindus, 1980). Hindus notes that what was distinctive about Massachusetts, in contrast with states such as South Carolina, was a tendency to channel conflicts into the courts rather than resolving them privately or extra-legally. My research suggests that this was the product of concerted political effort. As local awareness grew of the potential for labor unrest and disorder at home similar to the Bristol Riots, Birmingham Bull Ring Riots, Last Labourer's Revolt and the Rebecca Riots in England during the 1830s, Bostonians, under Whig leadership, sought to provide better forums for resolving the grievances of the popular classes—forums that they could control.

Yet officials also feared and sought to curb the power of too independent a judiciary. In this effort, they found support from citizens who deplored excess of state power in any form. Although vigorous state activity was touted in some areas, such as road construction or promoting industrial development, the stance of citizens toward the courts contained powerful contradictions (Siracusa, 1979; Handlin and Handlin, 1969). The Jacksonian Era was a period of growing focus by Democrats on individual rights and of renewed concern over limits on state power.[33] Thus, just as public concern about rising violence spread and efforts got under way to channel disputes to court, some legislators in Massachusetts attempted to reduce the courts' budgets.[34] Citizen resistance to increased taxes and public spending, a legacy of the overwhelming debt of the Revolutionary era, provided a favorable climate for such initiatives. The mayor clearly recognized this tension when he acknowledged that one major obstacle to policing was public resistance to funding it (Lane, 1971, p. 34).

Not only were budget cutbacks attempted when court burdens were rising—a move that might simply have reflected real financial constraints. The full thrust of these proposals is illuminated by the fact that, during the 1830s, the legislature reduced salaries of court officers across the board by as much as one-third—a powerful technique for prompting resignations that enabled Governors to appoint new judges. This occurred in a setting where, as Handlin and Handlin (1969) notes, "miserly salaries kept promising men off the bench" (p. 135). Other battles erupted over attempts to determine judges' salaries individually by legislative appropriation, a move, eventually rebuffed, for political review of the judiciary. Thus, numerous relatively transparent initiatives that, whatever their aim, would have enhanced political control of the courts were ventured. Whatever the outcome, these efforts can hardly have helped but further attune judges to the policy preferences of their leaders.[35] Though most such efforts failed and formal independence of the judiciary was preserved, coercion turned out to be unnecessary because, after years of strong political challenge during the early to mid-1830s, the political fortunes of the Whigs were such as to ensure that the political attitudes of the bench and bar continued to be closely aligned as a matter of course to their own.

Local administration, appointment of judges, and funding of the courts, then, reduced standardized supervision and injected the courts into local political controversy in ways sharply different from countries where courts were run nationally by a central administration. This heightened both exposure of the courts to local political dynamics and fostered greater variety in justice administration in ways that cleared the path for legal innovation.

Politicization of the Courts

Even as the tradition of "localism" in justice administration opened the way for compromise, and local funding infused it with the play of regional interests, uniquely close linkages of the lower courts to politics in the United States intensified pressures to consider policy concerns in case disposition and sentencing. Such linkages with politics also contributed to the turn to bargaining as a cultural solution. Leniency on the part of the courts, in this case the lower one, if it met with popular approval, had the capacity to help strengthen support for both fragile local political institutions and incumbents in office as well. Discretion, which was especially characteristic of bargaining, bolstered the professional autonomy and power of sitting judges and, later, prosecutors alike.

Appointments and court reorganizations provided another key connection between law and politics. The power of the judiciary to aid or obstruct an incumbent party had long been recognized since the Jeffersonian "reorganization" of the Federalist-appointed judiciary between 1802 and 1805. Upon Jefferson's accession to office, no federal court judge in the country had, thus far, been a Republican (Knudson, 1970, p. 55).[36] The Democratic-Republicans moved swiftly to repeal the Federalist Judiciary Act of 1801, one of the last acts of Adams' Presidency, and to name an entirely new federal court bench. Then, beginning with an attempt to impeach Federalist U.S. Supreme Court Justice Samuel Chase, the Jeffersonians worked to weaken the Federalist cast of that court. Vociferous outcry erupted that independence of the judiciary had been violated.

In Massachusetts, political control of appointments played a prominent role at the state level as the Democratic-Republicans, after 1800, began to challenge Federalist domination of public office. Goodman (1964) notes that "realizing the value of political favors in building a permanent majority, the [Democratic-Republican] party experimented until, by 1812, it had refined a theory and policy of patronage"—a central element of which was the allocation of public jobs of every sort (p. 145).[37] By the early 1820s, however, when the Democratic-Republicans at last consolidated their hold on political power at the state level in Massachusetts by electing one of their own as Governor, the role and vigor of this party activity had abated temporarily (Goodman).

At the state level, however, courts were abolished in 1809, 1814 and 1821, each time with new judges appointed. In addition, as we have already seen, the new Police Court was established in 1822. While judicial appointments were formally lifetime ones, "electoral shifts [both within and among parties] frequently led to court reorganizations and the turning out of all sitting judges" (Goodman, 1964). The strength of partisan control of state positions is conveyed by Republican Joseph Story, who, during the Democratic-Republican challenge to the Federalists in 1806, observed only half in jest that state notaries ought to be made federal officials so that "in this way in Massachusetts a [Democratic-] Republican would, at least, hold office" (Story, 1851).

By 1823, with the collapse of the Federalist party at the state level, the Democratic-Republicans elected two governors, William Eustis (1823–1825) and Marcus Morton (1825), and claimed a fleeting hold on political power in the Massachusetts State House. This period sent Justice Henry Orne, the only Police Court judge of the antebellum years to be appointed by a Democratic-Republican governor, to the bench. The Democrats would not hold the State House again until Marcus Morton was re-elected Governor in 1840.

In the city of Boston, Federalist domination persisted much longer and lasted through the 1820s. Party politics at the city level began to emerge in earnest during the mid-to-late 1830s and 1840s, along with a general resurgence of party activity throughout the state (Lane, 1971, pp. 46–47). In 1834–35 Theodore Lyman, Jr. was elected the first Democratic Mayor of Boston. It would be more than a quarter century before that city office would again be occupied by a Democrat. With the exception of Thomas A. Davis' election as the Native American Party candidate in 1845, another Democrat would not be chosen mayor of Boston before the American Civil War. Elections were, however, often fiercely contested. In Boston, with this revitalization of partisanship and the weakening of the class-based unity that had supported the Federalist elite, political appointments again grew more salient (p. 47). In this setting, selection of judges was seen not only as a means of nurturing policy sensitivity in the courts but also of fostering responsiveness to informal petitions for leniency and help for constituents.

Thus, local court administration, gubernatorial appointment of judges and state funding of the courts precluded national standardization and supervision. They exposed the courts to local political forces in ways quite different from societies with strong national administration. Judges increasingly appear to have operated from a policy perspective that was politically situated.

The Micropolitics of Consent

Besides providing advantages to city officials, to Boston's social elite, and to defendants, plea bargaining, once established, held out specific advantages for judges, prosecutors, and defense attorneys. While not presented here as causes of the rise of plea bargaining, these advantages help to explain "bargaining's" acceptance by the court. Plea bargaining reinforced the legitimation of the courts in the public eye through leniency, increased financial accessiblity, ensured reduced state oversight, and promoted improved relations between members of the laboring and upper classes through the leniency it afforded. For judges, the practice provided a rejoinder to criticisms of court discretion and reliance on precedent. While the codification movement, which had sought to reduce judicial discretion by moving to legislative statutes, had failed, the threat posed by its underlying sentiment remained. For judges, plea bargaining offered a new, more conciliatory, customary means of maintaining discretion— yet in a depersonalized, knowable, and relatively predictable market-like form that was more palatable to the masses.

Strong popular outcry over the quality of justice in the lower tribunals of the state during the early decades of the nineteenth century had focused considerable attention on the Police Court when it was created in 1822. Previously criticisms had been launched at the fee system whereby justices of the peace and constables had been paid by the case, the high costs of litigation, and the fact that the costs of appeal for a trial "de novo" in the high court placed it in reach of only the privileged few (Quincy, 1822). While complaints about fees subsided when salaried justices were provided for the Police Court, concern over costs and privilege continued to be sensitive issues. In the higher courts, delay had been an additional constant criticism since the colonial era, although all evidence is that cases moved expeditiously indeed through the lower court.[38] As in our courts today, it is very hard to distinguish how much of the delay was at the behest of one or more lawyers or parties to some cases.

In such a context, the guilty plea bargain provided numerous advantages— some of which would have been provided by another discretionary practice, others of which would not. For judges during the compilation of the Revised Statutes (or basic legal code) and movement for codification, plea bargaining afforded a means of preserving their discretion in handling cases, a feature vital both for professional autonomy and for one's security of tenure and career in this system that had been historically so beset by reorganizations and political pressures. Similarly, later, the discretion of prosecutor and defense attorney were also safeguarded in ways that served their interests.

Justices in the lower courts, whose salaries were annually appropriated, also had reason to believe, rightly or not, that they faced subtle pressure for consonance with the policies of governor and legislature because of initiatives proposed in the legislature to examine the performance of judges individually during the appropriation process—an abortive attempt at political review of the judiciary. Politically motivated court reorganizations, which turned out all sitting Judges and appointed new ones, had, as illustrated above, also historically been common. Since these justices typically each sat only two weeks per month, they were free to continue their legal practices (Goodman, 1964). That they did so is suggested by restrictions noted in the rules of criminal procedure citing kinds of cases they could and could not handle in their private practices. As practicing members of the bar, they were well integrated into it—a circumstance that facilitated cooperation, affinity of outlook, and compromise. To the extent that guilty pleas expedited case flow, it is possible that they may have eased the workload of justices in the lower criminal courts though there does not appear to have been a backlog.[39] However, trials before a judge (since there was no jury in the Police Court) were such expeditious affairs that newspaper vignettes suggest little difference in timing (Gil, 1837). While delay was a long-standing criticism in the higher courts, all signs are, as we have seen, that cases moved quickly through the lower ones—almost always reaching trial before a judge in one day during the first half of the century (Gil, 1837). In this context, plea bargaining, provided a low profile and implicit form of discretion that facilitated sentencing consistent with prevailing policies and purposes of punishment.

In addition to Whig influence through judicial appointments and social policy, there existed by 1840 a tradition of judges, justices of the peace, and district attorneys who had careers that mixed judicial and political life (e.g., Mayor Josiah Quincy). Eventually, after 1858, district attorneys were elected, and prosecutors were linked to politics directly. This heightened the value of discretion that plea bargaining accorded judges and prosecutors in cases that could color their political prospects. This is not to say that judges and prosecutors crafted positions with an eye to political gain. Reliance on plea bargaining, however, did accord them latitude in high-profile situations of consequence. This connection between judges and prosecutors, on the one hand, and elected office, on the other, is not one that existed in England. It is a crucial factor explaining why England developed the pardon but not a direct system of bargaining with its locus in the courthouse itself.

Plea bargaining also had other bureaucratic consequences that served prosecutors and defense attorneys well. Cases in the lower courts were usually handled swiftly by a judge alone with public prosecutors rarely involved before 1850.[40] While district attorneys were salaried and so had no financial interest in case outcomes, the 1830s saw the state legislature first require annual reports detailing court caseloads and dispositions. This appears to have been part of the court reform movement to establish impersonal and regularized justice. Thus, although the plea bargain appeared in the lower court long before the district attorney did, which precludes a causal argument about the high conviction rate that it produces tending to elicit plea bargaining, such rationalized reporting meant that a process, which inherently produced a high conviction rate, grew desirable as the century wore on and public prosecutors handled more lower court cases.[41] This important advantage of plea bargaining was further reinforced in the 1850s, when the office of district attorney became elective. While such required reports contributed to growing emphasis on efficiency and rational criteria of performance, their effect was limited in the lower courts during the 1830s when plea bargaining began because cases were typically handled without attorneys for either defense or prosecution.

Perhaps most salient, bargaining provided a daily power resource for the prosecutor. This was important at a time when rationalization of the law threatened to reduce his discretion and when that office, too, like the judiciary, increasingly became a stepping-stone to a political career. By increasing his control over the real decision making power in a case, plea bargaining gave the prosecutor major access to the granting of leniency and the appreciation that it could win. The guilty plea, then, drew on an old respectable Puritan theme of admonition and yet fit in well with new reporting mechanisms and attempts to rationalize law. It appears to have reinforced eroding norms of deference by providing defendants with strong incentives in the form of concessions to tolerate traditional elements of subordination and dependency in their relationships with employers or community patrons who might intercede in the courts, among other forums, on their behalf.

For defense attorneys, criminal cases were not particularly lucrative, so they stood to lose little in fees as a result of expeditious bargaining. Though attorneys often defended serious criminal cases in the higher court, most lower court cases, before mid-century, were resolved without defense counsel, so that attorneys lost virtually nothing at all. Lack of need for costly legal representation surely enhanced the appeal of the plea bargain to defendants in these minor cases. To the extent that attorneys defended these cases, professionalization of the bar and movement away from a guild model in Massachusetts appears to have promoted a competitive and businesslike ethos and to have removed traditional prescriptions on compromise. When defense attorneys did appear, plea bargaining enhanced their discretion as it did that of the prosecutor. Plea bargaining thus closely safeguarded the prerogatives of judges and to the extent that they gradually came to serve in the lower courts, of prosecutors and defense attorneys as well. Because plea bargaining served each actor well, it was variously embraced or accepted, rather than opposed, within the courthouse.

Finally, from the point of view of the defense, plea bargaining offered the defendant the semblance of choice, helping to explain why those accused did not object more strenuously to a practice that abated court emphasis on exercising their rights against self-incrimination. Regarding costs that often totalled several times the amount of a fine in the lower court, pleading guilty definitely produced savings. The guilty plea bargain also offered the defendant certain technical advantages in light of the emerging structure of work in the court and in legal practice. First, in its early stages, plea bargaining appears to have operated primarily on an implicit, and thus relatively accessible, basis and in marked contrast to the private meetings in which pleas of nolo contendere and also nolle prosequis were reported to be negotiated. Second, they could be entered without the assistance of counsel and so could produce savings in attorneys' fees and could be concluded even by those too poor to afford counsel. Third, the guilty plea, once negotiated, was closed and final, unlike the nolle prosequi, which could be reopened at the discretion of the state or the plea of nolo contendere, which could be negotiated and then left open and continued by the prosecutor. Thus the guilty plea terminated state intervention in the affairs of the defendant and provided no basis for ongoing control, a significant consideration in days of popular concern over the appropriate extent of state power. Fourth, unlike the compromise of cases with complainants for "satisfaction," the guilty plea could be negotiated with state officials having no personal interest in the case and who, to the contrary, faced bureaucratic and political incentives to compromise.

Bargaining thus responded to perennial (but now, amidst crisis, highly salient) public criticisms that the courts eluded the financial reach of the laboring classes and that state practices for oversight of the accused were unduly intrusive. Yet, it closely preserved the prerogatives of judges and court personnel. Strong popular outcry over the quality of justice in the lower tribunals of the state during the eighteenth and early nineteenth centuries had been catapulted to significance, given recent extension of the franchise and amplified popular demands for clarity, fairness, and reductions in cost. Criticisms, which had originally centered on the fee system, on high costs of litigation, and on the unbearable costs of appeal for a trial "de novo" in the high court, began to subside. Complaints about the fee system had waned with the establishment of the Police Court in 1822 and its provision for salaried justices, but costs and privilege remained sensitive issues. Discretion might have been maintained by any of a number of legal practices. However, it is clear that bargaining was consonant with the needs of each actor in the court and so was likely to gain currency.

Whereas a decentralized and relatively weak national state had created pressures for innovation and compromise, and the close linkage of law and politics had thrust the courts into the arena of local politics and created strong pressures for consideration of policy concerns by the courts, bargaining also synchronized with a complicated web of relations as officials acted in ways consonant with prevailing notions of virtue to provide a forum both for complaints and for those accused—a purpose for which this practice with its discretionary application of leniency was particularly well suited.

Plea Bargaining and Popular Consent

What we have seen is that the challenge to social order from Boston's changing class structure and the erosion of traditional bases of normative life produced a political challenge to the city's elite. While the swelling middle class criticized the effects of conflict on their quality of life, the city's patricians who, though beleaguered, still controlled the city, grew wary of extralegal or political efforts to resolve the conflicts of the laboring ranks, transients, and the poor. Well aware of restiveness in Europe through the 1810s, 1820s, 1830s and then as the watershed "year of revolution" in 1848 approached, Boston's leaders worked tirelessly to win popular consent to prevailing political arrangements and to their own partisan control by promoting stability and order in a modulated way.

The courts, which, along with the tax collector, constituted the primary experience that most citizens had of the state until local political parties formed and mobilized in the 1840s, played a key role in this process. In this context, judges drew on old common law traditions of discretion and episodic leniency, reworking them into a new legal practice, plea bargaining, as part of an emergent rule of law that could serve as one basis of a political language and culture of popular consent. Since the scale of urban life was growing apace, a new practice almost inevitably would have to be one that would not slow the court in handling large numbers of cases by placing new burdens on court staff. Plea bargaining emerged in Boston during the late 1830s as one cultural practice that was a basis for transforming legal culture. Consonant, at once, with new Whig uses of legal discretion, older common law traditions of episodic leniency, and Puritan religious thought, plea bargaining, while originating as a move of political reaction by the Whigs to reconsolidate their power, had the poetic quality of symbolic accessibility to all.

Therefore, plea bargaining mediated at the symbolic level the countervailing tensions of the times. It combined acknowledgment of guilt with the symbolic form of the receding religiously based order, yet in a most pragmatic practice as the newly won liberties of the republic came to be traded for concessions from the court in the manner of a quid pro quo. Paradoxically, the plea bargain also provided an incentive to the defendant to acquiesce to the forms of deference by adopting the dependent status of the supplicant—but "voluntarily," as we shall see, as free citizens of the republic.

Plea bargaining can be seen, then, as one facet of a sustained political engagement, sometimes modulated and other times heated, by competing social groups to gain influence over court action and the informal system of social control that it upheld. In this setting, where stabilization focused on the courts, both upper and lower classes worked to carve out some degree of influence by attempting to retain the discretion inherent in American law at the dawn of the nineteenth century—each perceiving it to be in their interest.

7

Reconsolidating Political Power in an Age of Popular Politics

Whig Reform and Social Reproduction

If the structure and language of nineteenth-century Boston provided the terms and patterns of interest in which its citizens interpreted their world, the politics of the city shaped both the dynamics of its creation and the strategy for their response to crisis. By deconstructing these politics, we unearth the micromotives and mechanisms driving this process of legal change. Specifically, we find a small elite, richly aware of its power, that was committed to its identity as the core of Boston's civic-spirited political leadership. Drawn from the city's leading families, it was embarked on a quest for social order and political stability, on the one hand, and, on the other, reconsolidation of its partisan power in the face of Democratic contestation. This elite acted swiftly to transform itself, its institutions, and its culture to counter the rapidly changing economic climate of the day that threatened it with obsolescence. Improvization in law as a means of social ordering was crucial to the social reproduction of elite power.

This urban elite, privately and through the incumbent Whig party, adopted a self-conscious and comprehensive approach in pursuing what it believed to be the holistic interests of the community. It focused the resources of employment, philanthropy, and the city's public institutions on what was seen to be the crisis at hand. Believing that the solution lay in imbuing citizens with character, industriousness, and attention to the consequences of one's acts, the city's leaders enlisted reformers, churchmen, educators, and judges alike in their campaign to nurture order. Since virtually all lawyers in the state were, initially, Federalists and, later, Whigs, most members of the bar shared a commitment to these goals. In Massachusetts, it is also the case that every judge was appointed by the governor. This meant that the elite-sponsored Federalist and, later, Whig parties that occupied the State House almost continuously through the antebellum years controlled all judicial appointments.

In Boston, as nascent industrialization and the rise of market society brought fears of challenge to the social order, this combined with erosion of traditional bonds of community and of normative life to present obstacles for the exercise of political power as it had been. While the middling ranks complained about the consequences of growth and conflict for quality of life, the Federalist and, later, Whig elite eyed with concern the possibility of threats to property and of extralegal or political solutions to the discontents of artisans and laborers. They also believed, rightly it seems, that the stirring democratic spirit of the masses jeopardized their own partisan hold on political power. Well aware of political rioting and restiveness afoot in Europe that had produced, among other things, Britain's Reform Act of 1832, these eminent Bostonians worked tirelessly to cultivate the consent of their city's newly enfranchised citizens to both prevailing political arrangements for self-rule and to the stewardship of their party. They did this by approaching the problems of social control and political stability, not through coercive means, but rather in ways that supported the claim of their city's government to represent and serve the will of its people. This meant adopting lines of action that were unquestionably acceptable to them.

The elite of Boston did so by appealing to the preeminent social discourse of the day—that of a "rule of law." That is, they argued that, by common agreement, social life must proceed according to a set of rules specified in advance and oriented to fairness. Such rules, it was argued, applied universally to all citizens and prescribed equal treatment for all who came before the court. Even where such rules departed from the popular will of the moment, they must, it was argued, be observed. Only through common acceptance of such principles could social order be upheld in a new world of self-rule. By appealing to the widely revered "rule of law" as the basis of a social order over which they presided, city fathers sought to bolster both the legitimacy and authority of the city's political institutions and, consequently, their own hold on power for the time being.[1]

The courts, which provided the main experience that most citizens had of the state until local government institutions were formed and local political parties grew well established in the cities during the 1840s, played a key role in this process. By the 1830s, judges had already begun to incorporate social policy considerations in their decision making. They drew, in the criminal law, on traditional forms of discretionary leniency and were using them in new ways already described. Older forms of leniency were reworked into a new, more-contractarian legal repertoire. Plea bargaining was one key practice that this adaptation of leniency from the common law yielded.

Notions of choice, freedom, and responsibility were also being elaborated in the criminal courts, as they were in labor litigation, which would serve as the basis for an emerging conception of republican political authority and citizenship that were in the making. As we shall see, the outline of a two-sided and contractarian vision of citizenship gradually took on a form that guaranteed citizens various freedoms of choice, even as it specified duties; but that reserved to the courts and to the community the broader ability to structure the options available and the terms on which choices could be made.[2] In the advance it made over previous more hierarchical and patrimonial views, such "freedom" represented an advance and so seems to have won the tolerance and, increasingly, the acceptance of the republic's citizens. But in the discourse of social ordering, the paradigmatic language of law was not alone. In its capacity for power, the imagery of Christianity came during the 1820s and 1830s to rival, even as it complemented in purpose, that of the courts.

Second Great Awakening and Ideological Transition

Plea bargaining arose, as we have now seen, during a time of extremely rapid social transformation that was impelled by the beginnings of industrialization, vast immigration, and the rise of market society (Sellers, 1991; McLoughlin, 1980; Formisano and Burns, 1984). Amidst this change, many leaders worried about the lack of a common ethnicity or culture to serve as a unifying force. One common bond, however, was religion and they turned to it as a source of homogenization. As changes began to pave the road to a new way of life, Americans had sensed anxiety due to the fact that their cultural worldview was no longer adequate to their experience. At the heart of this unease lay questions about what it meant to "be American" in the post-Revolutionary world of republican self-rule (McLoughlin). Out of this angst came a cultural movement known as the Second Great Awakening.[3] This was one of several periods of major ideological reconfiguration through which Americans adapted to massive social, ecological, and economic shifts that were occurring in their midst (p. 8). In the American experience, these Awakenings have been overwhelmingly religious in cultural tone. They have also tended to be periods of faith-based revivalism and reform (p. 8).

More specifically, the Great Awakenings in America may be defined as four historical periods when a people possessed of "an outmoded, dysfunctional worldview" recognized the need to convert their "mindset, . . . behavior and . . . institutions" to more useful ways of understanding and acting (McLoughlin, 1980, p. 8). The Second Great Awakening, like the period of religious revivalism and reform that was such a part of it, centered on defining the nature of the new nation, including its transformation to an industrial and capitalist society, and what it meant to be a citizen. Anxiety of a sort that frequently accompanies cultural change was heightened by the widespread rioting, crime, unrest, and political challenges of the day.

In Boston, the period of the Awakening during the early 1800s, was one during which the city of Boston was formally chartered, vast municipal improvements were made, and the problem of destitution among its inhabitants was discovered. In religious terms, the primary legacy of this period was the consolidation of Unitarianism's position as the religion of choice among Boston's elite (Formisano and Burns, 1984; Sellers, 1991). Reformers, particularly during Josiah Quincy's term as mayor from 1823 to 1828, reorganized municipal assistance, founded the Perkins Institute for the Blind and other benevolent societies, built a House of Industry, and established the Police Court. Later, during the 1830s, the city would build a formidable jailhouse and establish a paid full-time police force that replaced the voluntary night watch.

In accounting for urban ills of poverty, disease, and vice, some contemporary observers turned to strands of ideas that had begun as part of the American Revolutionary ideology of republicanism, which depicted England as "corrupted by commercialization" (Sellers, 1991, p. 35). According to this view, the primary political challenge of the Early National Period was to protect from corruption the civic virtue upon which the new republic was founded (p. 35). Specifically, it was feared that commercialization would undermine virtue by fostering lavish consumption and self-indulgence among the affluent while rendering the poor too dependent and, as a consequence, too vicious to properly assume the duties and privileges of citizenship (McCoy, 1980, pp. 76–104; cited in Sellers, 1991). Planters of Virginia, in particular, took exception to what they perceived to be Federalist plans to cultivate commerce over agriculture. As a result, the tobacco gentry turned in large numbers to the ideology of Republicanism, soon called Democratic-Republicanism, and to Thomas Jefferson and James Madison as its leading representatives (Sellers, p. 35).

The Republican party of Jefferson championed democracy and civic virtue against what it then depicted as the quasi-aristocratic Federalism of Alexander Hamilton. While Hamiltonian Federalists worked to promote the development of trade and industry, the Jeffersonian Republicans proposed to strengthen the republic by preserving the virtuous independence of America's yeoman farmers and mechanics. Appalled by the squalor and vice evident in the commercial cities of Europe, Jefferson believed that it was in "the virtue of ordinary citizens" that the nation would find its best protection against the corrupting influence of the market (Sellers, 1991, p. 35). In part, Jefferson's stance arose from his recognition that the majority of America's citizens then were farmers "who labor the earth" and whom he saw as uniquely virtuous (p. 35). Referring to America's farmers as the "chosen people of God," Jefferson noted that they turned "to their own soil and industry . . . for their subsistence" and, by so doing, avoided the "subservience and venality" of those in commerce, who depended on the vagaries of the market and the "caprice of customers" (Ford, 1899, pp. 268–69; Matthews, 1985; Sellers, p. 35). Believing that political equality must build on a foundation of economic equality, Jefferson proclaimed that "it is not too soon to provide by every possible means that as few as possible shall be without a little portion of land" (Ford, pp. 268–69; Matthews; Sellers, p. 35).

Much of this struggle between commerce and the Jeffersonians unfolded most fiercely at the state and local levels after the commercially-oriented Federalists lost control of the federal government to the Republicans in the election of 1800. Here the contest centered on efforts to define and shape the contours of Republican politics in commercial states (Sellers, 1991, p. 38). Because of Federalist tendency to favor those trading with Britain, merchants who traded elsewhere were particularly prone to espouse Republican positions (p. 38). This tended to produce heterogeneous urban parties that contained "jarring elements of class, interest and culture" (p. 38). In Massachusetts, as in New York, partisan contest in state elections was even more intense than in campaigns for federal office. Political cacophany escalated when many Federalists moved, as their own party collapsed, to embrace the Republican party (Formisano and Burns, 1984). Soon, there emerged in Massachusetts two distinct Republicanisms—Democratic Republicanism, a relatively commercialized variant of the party of Jefferson, and National Republicanism, a party that was nearly indistinguishable from Federalism.

Under the shrewd national leadership of Thomas Jefferson, the Republican party consciously cultivated the support of both "disaffected" and "aspiring" elites and accommodated entrepreneurial elements into their ranks to the extent that he and Madison felt it politically necessary (Sellers, 1991, p. 38).[4] In this way, the anti-Federalist masses, who were seeking democracy and equality, empowered the aspirations of those searching for opportunity and elite power (p. 38). As men from the middling ranks, especially entrepreneurs and mechanics, reaped gains from new avenues for profit, they voiced their discontent with the exclusivity of the Federalist establishment by embracing the Republican party (p. 40). As a consequence of that party's burgeoning effort to attract entrepreneurs, state "aid to enterprise" became a Republican policy as it had been a Federalist one previously in Massachusetts, Pennsylvania, and New York, among other industrializing states (p. 40).

By the mid-1820s, "a general mass of disaffection with government" was rife (Sellers, 1991, p. 201). Ultimately this sentiment would, by the end of the decade, boost the fortunes of the common man through the offices of the Democratic party, which it energized, and usher in Andrew Jackson's presidency. Far-reaching cultural changes also occurred during these years that had roots in the religious realm of the spirit and of feeling (p. 202). Already by the 1820s, the discourse of the Moderate Light of the Great Revival and Second Awakening was sweeping through the "self-making" populace of the urban Northeast by means of pamphlets and, most of all, voluntary associations (p. 263). Through the Awakening, Christianity was being assiduously adapted to the "market revolution" (p. 202).

The Great Revival that ushered in the broader cultural movement of the Awakening introduced new religious outlooks that eased the strains of adaptation to the new productive arrangements and work discipline of capitalism (Sellers, 1991). New ways of seeing the world focused human attention and energy on the value of work, on avoiding vice, and on belief in one's personal goodness amidst the waning of traditional ethics and the rising egoism of the capitalist marketplace. This worldview also provided an ideational framework for repressing impulses contrary to work discipline (Sellers). Of all the new sectarian perspectives, Unitarianism "reshaped Christianity most fully to the market mentality" (Sellers, p. 202). Emerging in New England, and particularly in Boston, with a distinctive blend of "Calvinist calling and arminian effort," the Unitarian view of a "unitary, remote and [especially a] benign creator-God" rapidly gained acceptance from the city's elite families (p. 202). Members of the congregation imagined themselves to possess sufficient rationality, prudence, and morality to realize, if inclined to apply themselves, earthly success in the kingdom of this world as their due (p. 202). Moreover, according to Reverence John T. Kirkland, then president of Harvard, Unitarianism justifies that success. Kirkland argued that the Unitarian God "secures the rich from rapacity, no less than the poor from oppression; the high from envy, no less than the low from contempt" (p. 202). With its worldly appreciation of material success, Unitarianism robed "market cosmology" in "the forms of Puritan tradition" and provided a strong base of conviction to which entrepreneurial elites might turn after rejecting traditional otherworldly forms of piety (p. 203). Whilst assuaging personal angst over abandoning communal norms, traditional ethics, and household authority, "spiritual rebirth [that it fostered] reinforced the disciplined striving for success" (p. 203).

The cool rationality of Unitarianism fostered, however, a degree of liberation from tradition that was not palatable to all. And so another movement known as the "New Light" organized Methodist and Baptist revivalism, which eventually blended with a more market-oriented "Moderate Light" alternative to Unitarianism, that combined arminian effort with antinomian love in a blend that achieved considerable sway in Boston (Sellers, 1991, p. 203). The New Light emerged out of southern New England, where "traditional culture was hardest pressed by market stress" (p. 203). The New Light, in contrast to Unitarianism's liberation, revitalized tradition and vindicated the less-privileged ranks but it also provided a cultural bridge to the self-interested ways of the new order.

In political terms, the power of New Light revivalism made its debut as one thrust of a strong bid by relatively traditional mainline Massachusetts clergy to defeat republicanism, which it held responsible for the excesses of the French Revolution and feared might threaten comparable upheaval in America. In part due to this religious movement, rural Massachusetts maintained a paradoxical affiliation with the Federalist party long after republicanism in its more Jeffersonian forms had won the hearts and minds of agrarian elites in most other parts of the country. Gradually, New Light revivalism was transformed into a variant of "Moderate Light," which purged it of mystical antinomian notions of religious rebirth, and, instead, led its members to seek salvation through earthly good works, which were equated with disciplined labor in the capitalist economy as well as prayer and Bible study (Sellers, 1991, p. 210). Interpreting hard work in market enterprises as a sign of grace, the Moderate Light conversely viewed unskilled day laborers as "shiftless, diseased or vicious" (p. 211). Embracing "entrepreneurial visions of a disciplined capitalist society," the Moderate Light worked to nurture a culture that would create "a Christian capitalist republic" (p. 211).

According to Lyman Beecher, religion was "the central . . . unifying [force of] the dangerously diverse and fragmented new capitalist order" (Sellers, 1991, p. 213). He exhorted that "[t]he integrity of the Union" required "institutions . . . [that would exert a] homogeneous influence" and tend to "produce a sameness of views, and feelings and interests" (p. 213). To this end, Beecher prescribed "a Bible for every family, a school for every district, and a pastor for every thousand souls" (pp. 213–14). The godly community would hold workers to the "straight and narrow," proclaimed the Great Revival, as its leaders anticipated the way that capitalism would dominate the cultural movement of the Second Great Awakening and, later, the Age of Jackson. While the Moderate

Light soothed the consciences of entrepreneurs who were experiencing the anxiety of ethical change, it also provided a cultural means of subordinating the unruly "democratic antinomianism" of the masses (p. 216).

Out of the Awakening came a flurry of projects of civic benevolence as Christian businessmen, in particular, began using their skills to organize charitable societies with humane aims beyond pure and simple evangelizing (Sellers, 1991, p. 216). Appalled by the crowds of destitute persons discovered in Boston in the 1820s, urban evangelicals mobilized voluntary associations to impart literacy and assistance. Nationally, the cause most avidly espoused by the Moderate Light was the American Society for the Promotion of Temperance. Its proposals for total abstinence from alcoholic drink were, however, opposed by Boston's now Cool Light Unitarians, who instead sought moderation of use in this, as in all things. Controversial from the start, the temperance movement responded to the realities of what was by the 1830s both escalating alcohol consumption, generally, and an epidemic of alcoholism, in particular. While both Europeans and Americans traditionally accepted "the good creature [of drink]" as wholesome and a buffer against cold winters in drafty buildings, economic changes had now brought cheaper and stronger spirits into popular use (p. 259). The temperance movement proved so efficacious that alcoholic beverage consumption fell almost 75 percent over the next decade and a half (p. 259). Even wealthy Unitarians, who rejected many moral and social reform initiatives as repressive, eventually joined in to establish the Society for the Suppression of Intemperance in the Commonwealth of the Bay State.

As the residual economic malaise from the War of 1812 and gloom of the 1820s lifted, alarm began to spread over the immensity of the temperance movement pervading the country, "combining hosts [of souls]" and possessed of "revenues such as a king might envy" (Barnes, 1964, pp. 3–28). The Unitarian minister William Ellery Channing voiced intense concern over the "gigantic . . . power [of the movement], systematized, compact in its organization, with a polity and a government entirely its own," which he feared to be "independent of all control" (Barnes, p. 17; Sellers, 1991, p. 217). Ultimately, the movement crescendoed in what evangelist Charles Grandison Finney termed the "burnt-over" district of western New York, where its intensity was fueled by the upheaval attending the construction of the Erie Canal, the residuum of the economic setback from the post-war years, uprooted migrants, and stirring antinomian democratic sentiment. Here "the [relatively traditional] New Light of the lowly [ranks] challenged the Moderate Light of the [more commercially oriented] Presbygational [Presbyterian and Congregational] establishment"

(Sellers, p. 217). Among the main priorities of this New Light revivalism, along with benevolence and feeling, was an intense familism (p. 219). For the traditionalists of the New Light, emphasis on the primacy of family brought a ritualistic reaffirmation of patriarchy at a time when "[t]he manhood of a generation of young fathers was threatened by [economic] inability to meet [customary] family obligations" (p. 225).

By the mid-1820s, the Moderate Light's Yankee clergy saw in Finney's New Light a dangerous strand of unruly and emotive antinomianism, which they viewed, like poverty and illiteracy, as evading the constraints of social roles and threatening social order (Sellers, 1991, p. 229). In the New Light's treatment of all sinners alike, "without respect to age or station in society," the clergy saw the Finneyites promoting "a levelling of all distinctions of society" that boded ill for the social order (Finney, *Memoirs*, 1903; McLoughlin, 1971 and 1980). Opponents of the New Light feared that "Like the mobs of the French Revolution, the 'impudent young men' converted in the western revivals would be poured out as from . . . hives . . . to obliterate civilization and roll back the wheels of time [and contours of rank] to semi-barbarism" (Finney; McLoughlin, 1971, pp. 14–64; Sellers, p. 229). Perhaps most problematic, warned Lyman Beecher of Boston, Finney's New Light would destroy "the [homogenizing force of the] great evangelical [Moderate Light cultural] assimilation which is forming in the United States" (McLoughlin, pp. 14–64; Sellers, p. 229). In 1827, Beecher issued a direct warning to Finney saying, "I know your plan" and that "[y]ou mean to come into Connecticut, and carry a streak of fire to Boston." "But if you attempt it," Beecher continued, "I'll meet you at the State line, and call out all the artillery-men, and fight you every inch of the way to Boston, and I'll fight you there" (Finney; McLoughlin, pp. 14–64; Sellers, p. 229).

Ultimately, the Finneyites would demonstrate to the Moderate Light "how much of the antinomian enthusiasm . . . those moderates would have to appropriate to remain [institutionally] competitive" (Sellers, 1991, p. 229). Finney also showed the Moderate Light "how antinomian enthusiasm could be channelled through benevolence into [the] capitalist discipline" that they propounded (p. 229). The basis for this intersection lay in the fact that, although Finney was instinctively a Methodist, he had been raised and well educated among those who would form the Moderate Light to disdain "ignorant Methodist exhorters" and was closely attuned to "the stresses of rising entrepreneurs" (p. 229). His rapprochement with the hierarchs of the Moderate Light was eventually eased by his success at drawing businessmen (to whom they appealed) to instead embrace the "heroic piety" of the New Light (p. 229).

These included merchants, lawyers, millers, and entrepreneurs. To them, Finney offered both an approach to capitalist discipline and emotional relief from ethical distress (p. 230).

Men and women participating in the religious revivals and the cultural transformation of the Second Great Awakening were seeking answers, then, to the stresses of transformation to a capitalist society. Camp meetings reshaped the Christian mentality to ease the distress caused by the waning of traditional ethics and helped adapt it to the discipline of the new workplace. Amidst the turmoil of the day, first the Moderate Light and then the New Light soothed anxiety over change and eased fears about disorder by showing how religious belief and fellow feeling might be bent to nurturing both capitalist effort and the social order on which it rested.

Market Revolution and Fears of Disorder

On the fourth of July in 1826, Americans celebrated the semicentennial anniversary of their independence. The republic also celebrated a return to prosperity after the economically disastrous years following the Embargo and the War of 1812. This renewed growth sparked a decisive phase of "market revolution" in America, and it did so in both economic and cultural terms. Culturally, a vision of a meritorious middle class fueled industriousness and explained inequalities inherent in the social order of the day.

As prosperity returned, missionary, reform, and benevolent associations prepared for "cultural conquest" of the laboring classes, and a national temperance movement moved "to school a spreading 'middle class' in self-disciplined effort" in the workplace (Sellers, 1991, p. 237). In a market society that promised reward in proportion to effort, their "middle class mythology [like the newly congealing worldviews of the revivals] both fueled and justified success to . . . [overcome] rising anger over the . . . reality of . . . [class inequality]" (p. 237).[5] It was a vision that appealed to "clerks, salesmen and bookkeepers aspiring to bourgeois enterprise" but also to "farmers entering the market, to master mechanics becoming capitalist bosses, and to manual workers [facing] . . . the disgrace of fading respectability" (p. 237). Thus, a middle-class consciousness was actively fostered that was embraced by people of diverse ranks who clamored for greater status and occasionally achieved some modicum of success, though at the cost of embracing the bourgeoisie's "self-repressive norms, competitive consumption, and middle class [ideology]" (p. 237).

Although entrepreneurs proclaimed that unlimited prospects were open to self-made men, the reality was much more at odds with the middle-class myth. Inequality increased most rapidly during those decades of any time in American history (de Tocqueville, 1997; Sellers, 1991, p. 238). The share of wealth held by the richest 10 percent of families rose, primarily after 1820, from 49.6 percent in 1774 to 73 percent in 1860 (p. 238). Wealth centered in the cities. Nor were many of the largest fortunes the fruits of the effort of self-made men, for of the 2,000 wealthiest citizens of three Northeastern cities between 1828 and 1848, 94 percent in Boston were born to rich or eminent families as had been 92 percent in Philadelphia and 95 percent in New York (p. 239). Yet growing inequality joined with an ideology of the certainty of reward for effort to threaten patriarchal families of the middling ranks with a sense of failure for which they alone would be responsible. Still, from pulpit, schoolhouse, and press streamed an unremitting proclamation of the middle-class ethic (Kaestle, 1983). Thus, workers and farmers found themselves impelled to join in the "struggl[e] for middle-class status" in a desperate bid "to salvage patriarchal honor" (Sellers, p. 239). At the hearths of such families, a culture that would mobilize strenuous effort and instill work discipline was forged (p. 239).

Social strain produced by changes arising out of the "market revolution" was heightened by surging tides of migration. The Boston City Directory of 1836 removed 24 percent of the households that were listed just one year before. The cumulative consequence of these demographic flows for the city is vividly illustrated by the fact that fully 3.3 million people resided briefly in Boston and then moved on between 1830 and 1890. However, the swelling flood of migrants produced a net population growth of only 387,000 persons (Thernstrom and Knights, 1970, pp. 7–35).

The combination of the mounting structural inequality of positions and geographic uprootedness meant that many men would probably never achieve what the mythology of the day touted as the "self-made manhood of success." Nonetheless, motivation continued to be drawn from images of middle-class "masculinity" that pushed acquisitive egoism to "extremes of aggression, calculation, self-control and unremitting effort" (Sellers, 1991, p. 246). In a *Student's Manual* published in 1835, John Todd exhorted the young that "SUCCESS fixes the eye" of every True Man, and through his religiosity he is enabled to "call forth the highest efforts" to pursue it (p. 247). Apart from the fervid industry it inspired, this ethic also imbued the lives of its adherents with a pathos that was poignantly noted by de Tocqueville during the 1830s. This ethos, he observed, engenders the "habit [among self-made men] of always considering themselves [to be] standing alone" (p. 251). It "throws . . . [a man] back upon himself . . . , and threatens in the end to confine him entirely within the solitude of his own heart" (p. 251). Paradoxically, by spurring industrious effort and conformity to a homogeneous social order, this ethic, through the isolation it produced, strained already feeble bonds of community. In place of fellowship, it produced atomized and competitive individualism in a market society that was ever less likely to be seen as guided by a benign secular manifestation of the "invisible" hand of divine providence. It was to govern such secular and isolated men and women, that public officials drew on the discourse of a "rule of law." What the rules of God could no longer control, it was thought, must now be contained by the laws of man if order would be had in a world of self-rule.

By the 1820s, the moral reform societies that preceded the temperance movement had largely failed. The causes of their failure, as commented on earlier by Reverend John Chester, provide crucial insight into both popular views of law and the ideas of freedom in that day. From the foreshortened life of these moral reform movements, a vital lesson was learned that even non-coercive forms of social control could be seen as a threat to liberty (Sellers, 1991, p. 263). It became clear that governance must instead persuade in order to win popular consent.

Awareness of this lesson was voiced by Lyman Beecher who, in unveiling his strategy for a new temperance movement in 1825, observed that "[o]ur Fathers could enforce morality by law, but the times are changed and unless we can regulate public sentiment, and secure morality in some other way, WE ARE UNDONE" (Beecher, *Sermons*, 1829; Sellers, 1991, p. 263). Offering Unitarian commitment to moderation in all aspects of life as a possible solution, Beecher urged that efforts be made to create "a correct and efficient [harmonious] public sentiment" (Beecher; Sellers, p. 263).

Even as social control through elite-dominated deferential politics and the efforts of moral reformers were being supplanted, printing presses and voluntary associations were serving as a conduit for a wave of cultural change that fostered a new approach to order through voluntaristic emphasis on the quest for success and the self-making of the work-disciplined "self-made man" (Sellers, 1991, p. 263). It was a discipline built primarily around rewards that elicited anxious desire to attain them rather than harsh and coercive penalties. In its focus on the gains to be had through hard work, this new cultural vision eschewed coercion; it rendered choice free while creating a discourse that could not help but energize all but the most laggardly.

It was as a challenge to these Moderate Light cultural and political influences of capitalist transformation that Jacksonian democracy arose. Andrew Jackson emerged from Baptist/Methodist New Light roots to champion democracy and remake the presidency in its image (Sellers, 1991). Jackson strode onto the national stage in 1829, trumpeting "triumph of the great principle of self government over the intrigues of aristocracy" (Remini, 1963, pp. 199–202). To his adversaries, such as Justice Story, however, it was instead "the [disruptive] reign of King 'Mob' [that] seemed triumphant" (Schlesinger, 1945, p. 6). Jacksonian politics was fueled by popular discontent against aristocratic elites and against banks and state charters that shaped credit, debt, and every manner of economic advantage. Thus, the stirring democratic spirit challenged the newly laid ideological justifications for the machinations and the fruits of capitalist enterprise.

Harmonious consent to politics of any stripe, however, would not be readily forthcoming. Instead, generalized unrest, social conflict, and violence would. Deference to one's "betters" in politics had by now faded. Encouraged by the democratic turn in national politics, a rash of strikes by the Workingmen's movement erupted in northeastern cities during the mid-1830s (Sellers, 1991, p. 338). This wave of labor unrest prompted questions about how growing inequality embedded in the social order of the republic could be justified. Even more ominously, it began to undercut the ethos of regular work for a wage. The focus of the strikes was a ten-hour day, a goal that, by 1836, had been achieved (p. 338). Yet, the legacy of Workingmen's pamphlets and its discourse endured. It decried the division of society along class lines created by capitalists expropriating the produce of labor (p. 338). Taking aim at the mill owners of the Merrimac Valley, worker pamphlets claimed America's "young Nobility" to be more exploitative than even Europe's landed gentry and urged resistance through Workingmen's politics and unions (p. 338). In the words of Boston strike organizers A. H. Wood and Seth Luther, "Capital which can only be made productive by labor is endeavoring to crush labor, the only source of wealth" (Schlesinger, 1945, pp. 166–67). Depicting the strikes as "neither more nor less than a contest between Money and LABOR," Wood acknowledged that mobilization of Workingmen was "arraying the poor against the principles of the rich, and if this be arraying the poor against the rich, I say go on with tenfold fury" (pp. 166–67).

Despite assiduously cultivating the self-control and sustained effort demanded by the emerging middle-class ethos, an ever-greater number of families found themselves, due to growing inequality after 1820, faced with economic failure. Recognizing that a privileged few flourished at the expense of the many, working men challenged growing inequality and democratic resentment simmered. By the 1830s, unease was palpable about potentially explosive tremors in the fragile new system of self-rule. Workers began to adapt the language of republican ideology to reflect more closely their experiences, needs and interests. This atmosphere of challenge brought Jackson to the Presidency as the 1830s dawned. It elicited extension of the franchise in Massachusetts six years later. It was surely no coincidence that these years also saw the extension of the franchise by the Reform Act of 1832 in Great Britain. By the mid-1830s, social disorder, riots, and strikes were rife and were a source of preoccupation to elected state and city officials. To defuse resentment and reassert control, Whig officials in Boston drew, as we shall see in more detail in a moment, on the ideology of a "rule of law."

Market Culture and Victorian Reconstruction of Punishment

In their quest for political consent, the strategy of Boston's leaders for preserving order and property centered, then, not simply on vigorous policing, but also proactively, on building character, creating cultural homogeneity conducive to harmony, and inculcating a sense of the consequences of one's actions. This was attempted, in part, by changes in the courts and punishment. Fears for security stemmed from worries that the rise of markets, with their emphasis on acquisitive self-interest, would free a willful "natural man" of passion and license. Classic constraints of "habit, custom and 'morality' " were, it was feared, losing their sway (MacFarlane, 1987, p. 119; Wiener, 1993; Appleby, 1992). Simultaneously, "technological innovations" and "increased productive power" multiplied the force and consequences of an individual's actions (Wiener, p. 137). Thus, early Victorians, both in England and America, viewed markets ambivalently, seeing on the one hand, a " 'civilizing' force . . . [that] reward[ed] self discipline" but on the other, a phenomenon that "encourage[ed] impulsive, willful behavior" (Tomlins, 1993; Wiener, p. 137; Sellers, 1991). The market did this both by "encouraging the hope of the immediate gratification of desires [which] shift[ed] the psychic balance in individuals in favor of impulse" and by "shifting social power to the young" since child labor enabled "independence [from parental supervision] before their minds were schooled in self government" (Wiener, p. 138).[6] Of rioting in the British Isles around 1840 it was said, "The mobs of Bethnal Green, Bristol and Manchester, which had recently rampaged, were all youthful: the great havoc . . . was committed by mere boys" (Flinn, 1842, pp. 266–67; cited in Wiener, p. 139). Thus "character" and its alternatives, "license" and "passion," emerged as significant concerns in early Victorian discourse, in both England and America (Wiener, p. 139).

To address this situation, reformers shifted attention to "emotions, the will, rather than the mind" (Wiener, 1993, pp. 139–40). Views of the child as inherently "depraved" arose and nudged aside Enlightenment emphasis on reason. This view, widely discussed in England, also appears in the United States despite Americans' generally more-optimistic view of human nature and of the prospects for market society. In contrast with the tendency of much Enlightenment thinking to view instincts as benign and susceptible to the mastery through reason, a leading medical manual observed at mid-century that "there is a latent devil in the heart of the best of men; and when the restraints of religious feeling, of prudence and self-esteem, are weakened or removed by the operation of mental disease, the fiend breaks loose, and the whole character of the man seems to undergo a sudden and complete transformation" (Bucknell and Tuke, 1858, p. 273; cited in Wiener).[7]

Given these incipient fears about human nature and fragility of the social order, it is not surprising that crime and punishment were a prime focus of discourse and public policy (Wiener, 1993, p. 141). That citizens in America saw in the "crime wave" of the early- to mid-nineteenth century a severe moral threat is certain. In England, where crime also rose, "Tories, Whigs and Radicals agreed that the age was witnessing a 'constant and uninterrupted increase in crime' against both property and person" (*Blackwood's Edinburgh Magazine*, 1844, p. 533; Wiener, p. 141). We now know that this perception was probably exaggerated somewhat due to improved recordkeeping, strengthened law enforcement, and changes in law that expanded the range of criminal liability (Wiener, p. 141). Further, most offenses during this period, both in England and America, were "prosaic and undramatic, involving small amounts being stolen, squalid robberies, burglaries and assaults, in which roughness was common, but not fatal violence" (Phillips, 1828, p. 287; cited in Wiener, p. 142). Goods taken were often cloth, money, food, artisanal equipment, or household belongings.

The extent of the threat envisaged by the early Victorians in these "crime waves" is evidenced by the fact that the initial meeting in 1857 of the prestigious British Social Science Association took as its keynote theme "the threat of 'unlicensed appetites, bold, rebellious will, vicious and enthralling habits'" (Turner, 1857, p. 5; Wiener, 1993, p. 142). In England social reformer Henry Mayhew warned in 1862 that, paradoxically, "not only was the material progress of society not being accompanied by a moral progress, but . . . moral disorder was increasing" (Mayhew and Binny, 1862, p. 384; Wiener, p. 143). In London, Mayhew found greater numbers of "habitual criminals . . . than ever before" (Wiener, p. 142). The reformer contended that such habitual criminals were distinguished by "an undisciplined and 'nomadic' character structure . . . [and described them as] persons who feel labor to be more irksome than others, owing to their being not only less capable of continued application to one subject or object, but more fond of immediate pleasure, and, consequently, less willing to devote themselves to those pursuits which yield only [its prospect]"

(Mayhew and Binny, p. 384; Wiener, p. 143). Women's magazines and chil-
drearing manuals in America warned of the dangers of the willful child and
counseled reining in that spirit before it eluded control. Like many social anx-
ieties, this early Victorian fascination with the dangers of "unchained impulses
and self-will" generated a popular literary response during the 1830s and 1840s
(Hughes, 1980, p. 175; Wiener, p. 143).[8]

More deliberate measures than previously taken seemed required (Sellers,
1991). As a consequence, one finds running through early Victorian social
policy in both England and America, along with emphasis on industriousness
and citizenship, "the aim of containing and mastering an impulsiveness [and
willfulness] that the market . . . itself . . . [cultivated rather] than subdued"
(Wiener, 1993, p. 143). In every quarter, the discourse of the state, churches,
schools, voluntary associations, and philanthropists, along with the language
of everyday life, centered on how to develop 'character.' The quest was not so
much for "fixed and external . . . standards of behavior" (p. 144). Instead, a
"psychological state [was sought] in which the passions were . . . mastered by
reflection, the pressures of the present controlled by the perspective of the
future" (p. 144). The philosophical counterpart was Utilitarian "consequential-
ism," popular among reformers on both sides of the Atlantic, which highlighted a focus on the long-term consequences of action. Such a cast of mind,
J. S. Mill argued, would lead one automatically "to defer gratification . . . [and
thereby to] gain mastery over his 'animal nature' " (Wiener, p. 145).

Discourse about the cultivation of character reoriented the nature of punishment and, as a corollary, key aspects of the antislavery debate. Among the
impulses that early Victorians sought to check were not only sexuality and
willfulness but also aggression. Thus, public demonstrations of aggression or
open infliction of physical harm, whether of prisoner or slave, met with strong
disapproval (Wiener, 1993, p. 145). Evangelical Christians joined with secular
Utilitarians to initiate the humanitarian reform movements focused on punishment and the abolition of slavery (p. 145).

Criminal law figured prominently in this struggle to control impulsiveness
and to build character.[9] Law had already been accorded an interventionist role;
now, informed by Enlightenment notions of the capacity for reason and human
perfectibility, it was seen as instrumental in inculcating a capacity for reflection
that would reconnect with God's grace and penitence, bolster self-control, and
deter future misdeeds (Wiener, 1993, p. 146). By compelling acknowledgment
of guilt and attention to the long-run fruits of one's actions, consequentialists
believed law would nurture the capacity to defer gratification and thus build
character that would deter crime.[10] Early Utilitarianism, which was "rule ori-

ented" rather than "act oriented"—that is, it "aimed at instilling principled patterns of behavior," would, it was hoped, nurture a "self-restrained character" (p. 147).

As sweeping social changes eroded the "comparatively stable, loca[l] and personalized structure of social relationships" in which eighteenth-century pre-Revolutionary British criminal justice had been embedded, the "discretionary and particularistic justice . . . [of that period came] to appear both arbitrary and ineffectual" (King, 1984, p. 25; Wiener, 1993, p. 147). The sentiment that pre-Victorian British justice was "a private and negotiable process involving personal confrontation rather than bureaucratic procedure" sums up much popular feeling of the day (King, p. 25; Wiener, p. 147). While particularism was targeted less as a problem in America, incentives embedded in the fee structure there induced public outrage. Reformers protested what they depicted as fluid and arbitrary proceedings for minor crimes, which, they contended, could encourage neither farsightedness nor character. Considerable discretion, uncertainty, and personalism inherent in eighteenth-century British criminal justice had constructed what one reformer termed a "lottery of justice," where penalties for misdeeds were largely a matter of fortune and encouraged "a sort of gambling into vice" that encouraged men "to take a chance, yield to impulse, and think not on the consequences" (1 Parliamentary Debates, Feb. 9, 1810, p. 19 and April 8, 1811, p. 744; cited in Wiener, p. 148). Similarly, Josiah Quincy's critique of Massachusetts' justices of the peace prior to founding the Police Court decried the moral degeneration produced when officials are seen as on the watch for gain through the vices of the poor and fair forums for resolving grievances are lacking.

To counter this tendency, criminal proceedings were rescripted so as to imbue habits of mind that dictated care and attention to consequences. Swiftness and certainty were emphasized. In both criminal and civil law, "the principle of fault, and the notion of intent [were broadened]" (Wiener, 1993, p. 148).[11] By criminalizing intentions and preparations as well as the failure to exercise "reasonable care," the state partook to build character by requiring more "farsightedness" and, thus, fuller consideration of the consequences of one's deeds (p. 149).[12] By mid-century, judges had come to expect greater care, prudence, and self-control (pp. 151–52).[13] As plea bargaining arose, the acknowledgment of culpability and calibrated participatory calculation of penalties for which it provided were ideally suited to this framework. By depersonalizing and demystifying sentencing, plea bargaining communicated a clear, customary menu of payments to be exacted by society for various offenses. It drew the citizenry into an understanding of the penalties to be meted out and collaboration in imposing them. Yet, unlike the proposed and defeated move for clarity through codification, this was achieved without sacrificing judicial discretion.

The campaign to control impulses and nurture character also produced a reconstruction of society's thinking about punishment. Public violence of any sort, even against convicted offenders, came to be seen as "socially dangerous" because it "legitimated the expression of violent passions" (Wiener, 1993, p. 152). Both in Europe and America fear that public flogging or hanging would inflame those viewing the spectacle impelled the increased use of incarceration. Grotesque and pornographic scenes of state-imposed violence such as those described by Foucault in *Discipline and Punish* were believed to "stimulat[e] ... the passions, disorde[r] the minds of spectators and ... [create] just such scenes of saturnalia as would ... [rouse] the fears of ... [these] reformers" (p. 152).[14] In 1852, Charles Dickens observed that "it is bad for a people to be familiarised with such punishments ... [as] the whip is a very contagious kind of thing and difficult to confine within one set of bounds"—an argument taken up by American [anti-slavery] abolitionists ("Lying Awake," Household Words, Oct. 30, 1852 in Collins, 1962, p. 255; cited in Wiener, p. 152). Dickens found himself "haunted ... by the bestiality of the crowd" (Collins, p. 240; cited in Wiener, p. 154). Similar contagion appears to have affected the town of Salem during the famed "witchcraft" trials. In this spirit humanitarian reform of criminal justice was undertaken.

In America, increased use of confinement as an alternative to physical punishment began with the Quaker experiment at the Walnut Street jail in Philadelphia during the late eighteenth century. Inspired by the writings of Beccaria and Bentham, reductions in physical harshness of punishment took place through the antebellum years. In Britain, public whipping was restricted by statutory enactment in 1816 and abolished altogether in 1862. After 1820, physical punishment of any kind was limited to men. In 1868, the use of gallows for the spectacle of public executions was also ended (Radzinowicz, 1968, pp. 343–53; Cooper, 1974; Wiener, 1993, p. 155). By the time of the American Civil War, punishment had for the most part been reconstructed. In place of physical pains and deprivations were placed "new, more measured forms of secluded punishment that would [stimulate reflection and] appeal to the capacity ... [for] calculation rather than [stirring] the passions ..." (Foucault, 1988; Wiener, p. 155). Courts and prisons became closed schools of "moral discipline" that operated by invariant schedule and regime. In them, prisoners were increasingly seen as having responsibility for their own inner rehabilitation (Walker, 1980; Foucault, 1988). To nurture the ability to reflect on consequences, an effort was made to make "the future ... as foreseeable as possible" (p. 156). To this end, rationalization and impersonality were cultivated. As bureaucratic procedures budded, "power . . . [came] to be seen as most legitimate and most effective when [exercised] least personal[ly], most 'humane' when least 'human'" (p. 157). Even prison life was designed, to the extent possible, to impose passive constraints, such as architecture and routine, rather than the discretionary decisions of staff. Attention turned to prison design as a means of control less likely to arouse the passions of inmates. Customary practices such as plea bargaining, with its market-like regularity, were favored by the court partly because of a belief in their capacity for socializing citizens. Yet, paradoxically, though this discretionary practice sought, like a market, to achieve continuity and predictability in the service of reform, its reliance on intercessors preserved a traditional elite perquisite and the power of informal social hierarchies where a patriciate held sway. In this way, the innovative cultural practice of plea bargaining that began as reform ultimately contributed for a time to the social reproduction of elite power.

Reconsolidation of Elite Power and the Whig Ascendancy

As in most coastal cities, the Early National period had brought an "urban patriciate" to prominence in Boston (Jaher, 1984, p. 59). While much akin to those in other Eastern cities, it was "the most notable and long lived of this species" (p. 59). From the 1780s until the early twentieth century, the social circle known as "the Boston Brahmins"[15] exercised vast influence in both the public and private life of the city (p. 59). Unlike other cities where it would be an overstatement, one can say correctly that in Boston, the Brahmins operated consciously as a ruling elite (p. 59). During the antebellum years, the formal political power of this group was wielded first through the Federalist party, later through the National Republican, and then through the Whig parties in Massachusetts. After 1910, these Brahmins largely withdrew from candidacy in electoral politics to exert their influence socially and economically (Blodgett, 1984, p. 106). Especially from 1800 to 1860, however, and to a large extent through the turn of the century, this group, through its dominance of business, politics, culture and education, and philanthropy, functioned as a "ruling elite" (Jaher, p. 59). The ascendant Whig party organization was their political touchstone.

During the period between 1780 and 1820 when this Brahmin enclave of Boston's upper class grew closed as a status group, the approximately forty families cosetted under its social canopy came together from diverse roots (Jaher, 1984, p. 59). Some, such as the Endicotts, Winthrops, and Saltonstalls, represented the pre-Revolutionary "Puritan oligarchy" (p. 59). A second group of families, including the Amorys, Quincys, and Otises, had been prominent in colonial government and merchant life outside of Boston (p. 59). Still a third group of families, such as "the Higginsons of Salem, the Danas of Cambridge and the Jacksons of Newburyport," had risen to the highest rank from leading positions in local elites throughout New England for several generations (p. 60). Their fortunes had typically been made in trade and speculating during the Revolution and in the post-Revolutionary China trade. A final group of families had amassed substantial fortunes and achieved respectability in the last two decades before the Revolution or, in a few cases, in the last decades of the eighteenth century just after the War for Independence. Among the families that gained prominence just before the Revolutionary years were the Lees of Salem and the Tracys and Lowells of Newburyport (p. 60). Self-made men of note who ensconced their families in the Brahmin world after the Revolution included William Sturgis, William Gray, Peter Chardon Brooks, and Samuel Eliot (p. 60). Finally, with the incorporation a generation later of the Appleton and Lawrence brothers, sons of affluent and respectable farmers of New Ipswich and Groton, "the Brahmin enclave, composed eventually of some forty interrelated families, was substantially [formed]" (p. 60).

As in other cities, prominent Massachusetts families often relocated from small towns and farms to the state capital in Boston. The personality that could "cut roots and break with traditions" augured well, it seemed, for pursuit of material success, power, and prestige during times of economic and political transformation (Jaher, 1984, p. 60). As the social identity of the Brahmins congealed, differences in origin were gradually muted by the development of "shared interests, activities and intermarriage" (Jaher, 1984, p. 60).

In large part, the remarkable longevity of the Brahmins' preeminence stemmed from the fact that theirs was not solely a political elite. In their cultural, philanthropic, and, especially, economic ventures, these families established a multifaceted power. Dominance in municipal government was used to enhance prospects in other facets of urban life, which, in turn, reinforced their political position—producing a unified elite with a conscious sense of leadership (Jaher, 1984; p. 60). This multidimensional "hegemony"[16] consolidated the position of the Brahmins as an upper class and distinguished them from more narrowly based elites in the fractionated power structures of other cities (p. 60).

In its early formative years, the economic base of Brahmin power lay in shipping and in great overseas trading enterprises, especially the China trade (Handlin, 1979). Gradually, however, these merchant entrepreneurs turned to "speculative and land development enterprises" to extend their empires (Jaher, 1984, p. 60). For instance, Massachusetts First National Bank of Boston, which until 1815 was New England's largest bank, as well as the other major banks in Boston, and the local branches of the Bank of the United States were all owned or dominated by Brahmin merchant families. From 1800 until the 1860s, a Brahmin commercial elite played an active role in "financ[ing] and direct[ing] . . . the development of Beacon Hill, Back Bay and large parts of South Boston and the waterfront, the city's largest antebellum undertakings" (Morison, 1921; Shurtleff, 1871, pp. 385, 417–22; cited in Jaher, 1984, p. 61). These initiatives began what would become a Brahmin tradition of cultivating "the public good" in ways that also proved to be extremely profitable for them. Thus, under Brahmin stewardship, "[b]anks, bridges, improved wharfage, widened streets, better markets and building construction facilitated transportation and trade, provided employment and upgraded land values" (Jaher, p. 61).[17]

Beyond their economic role, the Brahmins exercised cultural and professional influence as well. As their members assumed leadership positions in virtually every sphere of public life, the families multiplied their wealth, justified their dominance through the shaping of ritual and symbol, and reinforced their position by molding civic values (Jaher, 1984, p. 62). Nowhere was the influence of this circle more evident than in law. At the bench and bar, one finds Harrison Gray Otis and the familial "legal dynasties" of the Lowells, the Danas, and the Paines (p. 62). In medicine, distinguished physicians from Brahmin families established the Massachusetts General Hospital for care of the sickly poor (p. 62). In the realm of ideas and symbols, the "churches and schools [that they established played their traditional role of] cultivat[ing] the conceptions, inspir[ing] the beliefs, and advocat[ing] the arguments that [depict and] legitimize [an existing order]" (p. 62). In antebellum Boston, Unitarianism, Harvard, and the *North American Review* became the cultural voices of the Brahmin-led Federalist establishment (pp. 62–63). Celebrating Boston as a nineteenth-century " 'Athens' of [human] . . . advancement, moral inspiration and intellectual refinement" in America, these financiers, administrators, and philanthropists secured a national reputation for the city which, in turn, enhanced their own status. Cultural attainments of the city were seen as a major advantage in the burgeoning interurban rivalry of the day (pp. 63–64). In this American "Athens," philanthropy played a key role in congealing elite consciousness by "foster[ing] . . . cohesion and . . . [justifying its] leadership" through its "goodworks" on the city's behalf (p. 64).[18] Impelled by dual motives of altruism and self-interest, "the Harvard-Unitarian-business-Federal-Whig establishment dominated organized private charity [as it did virtually every other sphere of social, economic and political life in the city]" in its unrelenting quest, not only to lead the city, but to legitimize its position of influence and to win popular support for its stewardship (p. 64).

Beginning in the 1820s, the Brahmin elite realized with alarm that large numbers of poor families inhabited Boston. They began to doubt the adequacy of traditional forms of charity (Jaher, 1984, p. 64). Destitution was feared as not only morally problematic but also socially dangerous. Poverty, city leaders believed, "led to delinquency and, enflamed by Jacksonian democracy, . . . [im-migration], local riots, and rising rates of [crime] . . . could . . . [ignite] a confla-gration that might consume the propertied" (p. 64). The political order, relying as it now did on popular consent, could, they realized, be repudiated if citizens perceived it to bypass their interests. Along with an economically based desire for order, apprehension about potential class conflict combined with moral angst "to stimulat[e] public and private efforts to reform the [lives of the] poor and improve the quality of relief" (p. 64). In 1821, Mayor Josiah Quincy chaired a General Court Committee on Pauper Laws, which publicized the problem of poverty and reorganized assistance to those in need (p. 64).

With ambition and projects to uplift social life rife, Boston's Brahmins created a comprehensive leadership that guided the city's upper class. In par-ticular, this elite minority sought consciously to restrain the centrifugal forces of "unbounded individualism" and to nurture cohesion and cooperation among Boston's leading families (Jaher, 1984, p. 66). Assuming a proprietary stance toward the city, the Brahmins worked to promote the "people's welfare" and the "common good" in ways felicitous to their own interests (p. 66). Bos-tonians from other backgrounds, even wealthy ones, found the Brahmins ex-clusionary. Views of governance and proposals to redistribute wealth that em-anated from outside the patrician circle were resisted by this elite struggling to preserve its hegemony and the opportunities that it afforded them (p. 66).

It was in politics that the Brahmins consolidated their dominance. In the decades after the American Revolution, Boston had been well known as "the center of New England Federalism and the party directorate, known as the Essex Junto, came mostly from . . . [its] mercantile clans" (Jaher, 1984, p. 66). Progeny of these clans served as governors, senators, congressmen, mayors, city council members, state legislators, and judges (p. 66). From this group alone came two United States Senators (George Cabot and Harrison Gray Otis), six Congressmen (Otis, Francis Dana, Jonathan Jackson, Josiah Quincy, John Lowell, and Stephen Higginson) and two Mayors of Boston (Otis and Quincy) (p. 66). After the state Federalist party collapsed in 1823, Boston's elite turned briefly to Democratic-Republicanism en route to National-Republicanism and, then, to the Whig party though the Federalists, per se, remained strong in the city into the 1830s.

While decidedly Federalist, and later Whig, in their political loyalties, Boston's Brahmin families were not without their internal rifts—both political and generational. This inbuilt elite opposition included Democratic-Republicans Russell Sturgis, John Quincy Adams, William Gray, and especially the Crowninshield clan of Salem, who, despite strong political differences, maintained ties of marriage and commerce with Brahmin Boston (Jaher, 1984, p. 66).[19] What was remarkable about the urban leadership of the Brahmins was the way economic, political, and cultural power were used to reinforce and nourish one another, producing a unified elite with a heightened consciousness of its influence (Jaher). Members of this mercantile upper class worked simultaneously at national, state, and local levels, using their resources and social standing at each level to enhance their position elsewhere.

From the outset, "Junto" members assiduously promoted national policies favorable to maritime enterprise.[20] In Alexander Hamilton, city leaders found an ally who urged decisions favoring mercantile interests, espoused financial strategies that boosted the value of securities that they held, aided banks, and ensured ample access to credit (Jaher, 1984, p. 67). In the words of historian Samuel Eliot Morison, "No section or interest . . . was so favored by Washington's and Adams' administrations as maritime Massachusetts" (Morison, 1921, p. 165; cited in Jaher).

At the state level, the Federalist merchant families of Boston initially prevailed in framing a state constitution in 1780 that was highly protective of commerce. Half a decade later in 1786, Brahmin resources provided much of the finance for the military force that was sent to western Massachusetts to crush post-Revolutionary agrarian debtor uprising known as Shay's Rebellion (Morison, 1921, pp. 36–37; cited in Jaher, 1984, p. 67). Fear of more rioting and debtor discontent led the Brahmins a few years later to support the proposed U.S. Constitution with its protections of propertied interests (Jaher, p. 67). Brahmin success in winning approval for the U.S. Constitution in Massachusetts reaped "considerable national . . . currency" in Washington that enabled them to advance Commonwealth interests nationally (p. 67). This, in turn, heightened their standing at home (p. 67). Finally, in 1821, the Brahmin mercantile and maritime elite served at the forefront of the process of framing Boston's city charter and promptly sought and won many of the top offices that it created (p. 68). In each of these controversies, "maritime interests" bested their perennial adversary, the Democratic-Republican "agrarian enclave," to establish the primacy of the Federalists' power in Boston (p. 67).

Such multilayered politics permeated the world of banking and finance so central to Brahmin fortunes. Bank charters were granted at the discretion of political leaders (Jaher, 1984, p. 68). Should they choose to limit charters, this could restrict entry of competitive newcomers "who . . . [might] divert profits, . . . [upset business relationships,] or [otherwise] challenge the [status quo]; agreeable entrants . . . , conversely, could expand the pool of . . . resources available for . . . [joint] ventures" (p. 68).[21] No little financial advantage accrued to Boston's banks from the fact that its directors and officers were exceedingly well connected politically.

Brahmin political connections redounded to particular advantage in urban real estate development.[22] Administrations headed by members of this mercantile elite also advanced the interests of monied families by advocating low tax rates and assessments (Jaher, 1984, p. 69). Even bridge construction projects required legislative approval (p. 69). Perhaps the clearest evidence of direct financial gain was Mayor Josiah Quincy's decision to actually purchase a city wharf and privately operate warehouses there (p. 69).

Despite its seeming invulnerability, the Boston patriciate had endured an extended economic and political setback that reoriented it and changed the logic of its relationship to those less privileged in the city. It began with Jefferson's Presidency in 1800 and the devastation for overseas traders of his Embargo and, later, the War of 1812. This dark period extended through to the demise of the state Federalists and, while it lasted, the city's "merchant princes" combatted extraordinary losses (Jaher, 1984, p. 69). What enabled the Brahmin mercantile elite to weather this situation was its younger generation's swift turn to manufacturing (p. 70). Moving quickly, they introduced mechanized textile production to outlying areas near Boston. By the 1820s, the economic logic of Brahmin pre-eminence had changed and these families were operating America's first modern factories, along with a railroad, to move goods from mill to port (p. 70). Such transport facilities enabled strict price control and ensured competitiveness in other regions and abroad. Incorporating next the capital and ability of leading entrepreneurs, like mill magnates Amos and Abbott Lawrence, the Brahmins had averted collapse. The laboring ranks of the state became then, no longer simply their servants and builders of their cities, but their paid labor force in whose outlook and living conditions the Brahmins had a direct personal stake. A core group of families, known as the Boston Associates, moved into cotton manufacturing, which constituted the core of a transformed economic base of Brahmin Boston (p. 70).

Initially, this turn created intraelite friction, as "the old patrician merchants reacted to the [new] textile titans with bitterness" (Jaher, 1984, p. 70). Tension mounted between "the mill and the mast" or between "the archaic and progressive wings" of the Boston gentry (p. 70). Eventually, when, after the 1820s, shipping recovered, "the maritime [clans had grown sufficiently persuaded of the merits of industry to continue] invest[ing] in textile mills and . . . partici-pat[ing] in cotton manufacturing and railroad enterprises" (p. 70). Almost im-mediately, however, this beleaguered elite then faced the onslaught of Andrew Jackson's presidential campaign and a surge of crime, rioting, and unrest.

Intraelite tensions between traditionalists and progressives also appeared in politics. As in finance, the wounds healed during the 1820s. First in John Adams' foreign policy and then in Jefferson's election, Boston's urban elite had sensed a weakening of its national influence—fears that were then am-plified with Jackson's presidential candidacy in 1824. Voicing their concern, members of the patriciate had initially responded, though to little avail, by denouncing popular rule (Jaher, 1984, p. 71). They attributed their political displacement to "the insurgence of unrestrained democracy which[, they be-lieved,] . . . could destroy the nation" (p. 71). When they next opposed the War of 1812 in the Hartford Convention, the Federalists also suffered from being depicted as extremists, further weakening their position nationally. Despite these setbacks, the Federalists remained dominant in Massachusetts until 1823 when the state level party effectively collapsed even though it continued to flourish for another decade in Boston.

Yet even the collapse of the state Federalist party did not end Brahmin political dominance. Scions of leading families led the way in politics as in their turn to manufacturing. They briefly embraced the Democratic-Republicans, the leading political party of the early 1820s (Jaher, 1984, p. 71). As they did, older members of the maritime elite again erupted in protests of opportunism. There was no turning back, however, and by the time President James Monroe visited Massachusetts in 1817, he was told with not a little irony that "We are now all Republicans, even the Essex Junto" (H. Lee to P. Remsen and Co., July 8, 1817, Porter, *Jackson and Lees* II, 1257; cited in Jaher, p. 72). Due to the intensity of the outcry, many forget that Democratic-Republicans governed the Commonwealth for only two years, from 1823 to 1825, whereafter the elite-sponsored National-Republicans and then the Whigs presided as gov-ernors, largely uninterrupted, until 1855. Such continuity lent Boston's elite, whose reconsolidating partisan power dominated those parties, enormous im-pact on the policy, generally, and on the courts, in particular, through control of judicial appointments. Since all judges in Massachusetts throughout the nineteenth-century were (and, in fact, still are) appointed by the governor, sub-ject to approval by the Governor's Council, Whig dominance at the state level accorded the Brahmins a direct conduit for helping to craft the policy orien-tation of the courts. Along with the letters, social ties, club memberships, joint financial ventures and political connections, the Whigs, almost continuously, named all judges to every court in the Commonwealth.

As intraelite rifts over the rescripting of old ways healed, the language and imagery of the day reflected this change. Political imagery and rhetoric also reflected the tension between old and new. Initial bitterness and rage over the waning exclusivity of Brahmin influence was gradually replaced by a discourse of popular rule. In 1801, Harrison Gray Otis typified the former when he pronounced that "[t]he follies and confusion, . . . the strife and licentiousness incident to all popular governments . . . [are present in] ours in a most eminent degree" (H. G. Otis to S. F. Otis, Feb. 15, 1801, Morison, *Life and Letters of Harrison Gray Otis* I, p. 208; cited in Jaher, 1984, p. 72). By 1830, as last Federalist Mayor of Boston, the same Otis sounded a very different tone as he celebrated the fact that "[m]any" in the municipal government's "first rank rose from humble beginnings." This "equality," he opined, resulted from the enfranchisement of the "great majority" (H. G. Otis, *An Address to the Members of the City Council on the Removal of the Municipal Government to the Old Statehouse*, p. 72). Similarly, Mayor Josiah Quincy had acceded to defeat in his bid for reelection in 1829 by bowing to "the sound principles of a republican constitution, by which the will of . . . [the] majority . . . [was] expressed" (J. Quincy, "Farewell Address of Josiah Quincy as Mayor of Boston, 1829," *Old South Leaflets* VIII (Boston: Old South Meeting House, n.d.), p. 101; Jaher, p. 72).

Their newfound tolerance can be explained partly by the extensive influence the elite retained through the legislature, the governorship, and, most of all, the judiciary. Despite Federalist defeat nationally by Jefferson in 1800 and the visions of doom that it engendered, the Federalist party had prevailed both in the drafting of a state constitution in 1820–1821 and usually in state elections as well until 1823. Even after 1823, this elite retained considerable influence. Seats in "[t]he state senate remained apportioned according to property . . . [which ensured] an over-representation of Boston in that body, . . . [and] the judiciary retained its [gubernatorially appointed] power [as well]" (Jaher, 1984, pp. 72–73). In their quest to reconsolidate partisan power, Massachusetts Whiggery became the primary instrument of Brahmin leadership even as the middling ranks and labor began to gain growing power in some wards of the city of Boston.

Brahmin power centered in Boston, where its financial interests and property were concentrated and where its men served frequently in city office. Of Boston's first seven mayors, beginning in 1822, five were from this elite status group. When wealthy Brahmin families did not occupy the mayor's office directly, the Federalist, National-Republican and Whig parties in which they were so influential typically did. Of the thirty-nine mayoral terms in Boston between 1822 and 1860, Federalist, National-Republican, or Whig mayors were elected for twenty-nine of them or 74 percent of those terms (see table 7.1). Another three terms were presided over by mayors who were Republicans, the party of choice for the Brahmin elite after the collapse of the Whigs, or who had won the Republican endorsement. This yields a hefty total of 82 percent of the city's mayors who were candidates supported by the patriciate.[23] While mayors of Boston were most often merchants, lawyers were the occupation next most heavily represented. Fully one-third of Boston's mayors were drawn from the bar whose members were strongly represented in the Whig party (Jaher, 1984, p. 73). Consistently, one finds that party leaders and high-ranking public officials were drawn from "among the wealthiest families in Boston. Twenty-four of the seventy-nine (30.4 percent) wealthiest residents of the city in 1835 were common councillors, aldermen, judges, mayors, state legislators, U.S. Congressmen, senators and cabinet members" (pp. 74–75). After the 1830s, the tradition of electing the sons of prominent families to municipal offices other than that of mayor began to wane and Brahmin candidates, when they sought office, ran almost exclusively for mayor (p. 73).

Whig control at the state level, where judicial appointments were made, was, if anything, even stronger. From 1820 to 1850, except for two years, "the Whig Party or its predecessors (including the Democratic-Republicans after

TABLE 7.1. Mayors of the City of Boston

Term	Name	Party Affiliation
1822	John Phillips	Federalist
1823–28	Josiah P. Quincy	Federalist
1829–30	Harrison G. Otis	Federalist
1832–33	Charles B. Wells	National-Republican
1834–35	Theodore Lyman, Jr.	Democrat
1836	Samuel A. Armstrong	Whig
1837–39	Samuel A. Eliot	Whig
1840–42	Jonathan Chapman	Whig
1843–44	Martin Brimmer	Whig
1845	Thomas A. Davis	Native American Party
1846–48	Josiah Quincy, Jr.	Whig
1849–51	John P. Bigelow	Whig
1852–53	Benjamin Seaver	Whig
1854–55	Jerome V. Smith	Native American Party
1856–57	Alexander Rice	Republican (earlier a Whig)
1858–60	Frederic W. Lincoln, Jr.	Citizens Party (won Republican endorsement in 1859)

1823) controlled the governorship, and, except for one year, both houses of the legislature (see table 7.2). Every U.S. Senator and just under 90 percent of the state's Congressmen were Whigs" (Jaher, 1984, p. 75). Of the Whigs, it was said that "The Party dominated Massachusetts and the Brahmins controlled the Party" (p. 76). Ultimately, the Whigs split over slavery with textile families seeking to continue their ties with Southern slaveholding planters, a move that Conscience Whigs (later Free Soilers and eventually Republicans), abolitionists, and Democrats opposed. After the Civil War, Boston's oldest and wealthiest families almost exclusively joined the Republican Party.

The focus of Brahmin rule during this tumultuous period, as articulated by its elected officials, was order. Their program was "to prevent disorder, improve the business district and adjacent exclusive neighborhoods and [to] rationalize public services [in order] to maintain low taxes" (p. 78). "Public policy, therefore, reflected the interests and values of proper Boston—the [small] group [of families] whose members . . . dominated local government" (p. 78). This comes as little surprise since Brahmin families had the most property to lose from rioting, violence, fire, theft, and high taxes and, conversely, the most to gain from improved transportation, strong business infrastructure, well-enforced public safety, and a beautified city (p. 78).

TABLE 7.2. Governors of Massachusetts

Term	Name	Party Affiliation
1816–23	John Brook	Federalist
1823–25	William Eustis	Democratic-Republican
1825	Marcus Morton	Democratic-Republican
1825–34	Levi Lincoln, Jr.	National-Republican
1834–35	John Davis	National-Republican
1835–36	Samuel T. Armstrong	Whig
1836–40	Edward Everett	Whig
1840–41	Marcus Morton	Democrat
1841–43	John Davis	Whig
1843–44	Marcus Morton	Democrat
1844–51	George N. Briggs	Whig
1851–53	George S. Boutwell	Democrat
1853–54	John H. Clifford	Whig
1854–55	Emory Washburn	Whig
1855–58	Henry J. Gardner	American
1858–61	Nathaniel T. Banks	Republican

Sequencing and Convergence of Causal Forces

The timing of this ideological transition to a new market-based world and Whig ascendancy, when plea bargaining arose, was key because of the unique historical context that it provided. It occurred just as the right to vote was extended more broadly to new, less-privileged social groups. It was a time, too, when judges shifted to a more activist stance. This was a formative era in American law and politics, when novel forms of state response to conflict were being introduced. As the voting ranks grew, concern mounted among Boston's wealthiest families, entrepreneurs and professionals alike, about what this would mean for the institution of property and for the very future of the republic. Why, they worried, should a public that was empowered to modify social arrangements with their votes support a system of property that treated them poorly? Concerns such as these spawned far-reaching policy changes that extended into law, penology, and education, among other things. At precisely this time, the Common Schooling movement, under the leadership of Horace Mann, took as its goal to educate children in the habits of mind of productivity and responsible citizenship (Kaestle, 1983).

Amid growing tension, compatibility of the common law, rooted in judicial decisions and precedent, with "popular sovereignty" as voiced through enactments of elected assemblies, came under fire. Attempts to resolve this seeming contradiction had a powerful legacy because it was precisely at this point that institutions were being sculpted into their modern form (Horwitz, 1977). As crime and urban unrest swelled during the 1820s and then 1830s and democratic resentment began to color pamphlets, public meetings, and newspapers, political officials sought to initiate new modes of state response. This spurred a process of gradual legal innovation that created, among other things, plea bargaining. By embedding plea bargaining in the preeminent discourse of the day—that of the "rule of law"—it was hoped to elicit popular tolerance. This canopy of legal discourse incorporated the practice as part of a system of social rules that were universally applied and that ensured formally equal treatment of all defendants coming before the courts.[24] The market-like mechanism of plea bargaining was thought to afford by its very impersonality in the lower courts a modern form of equality in contrast with the more personalistic proceedings of the earlier system of justices of the peace. Plasticity of legal forms at this point of flux provided a window for change that allowed plea bargaining, once it emerged, like the professional police force and lower court public prosecutor after it, to achieve a permanence and centrality not otherwise possible.

As industrialization, immigration, and urbanization converged in Boston during the 1830s and 1840s, they produced growing inequality, culture conflict, and mingling of social ranks in everyday affairs. Rioting, strikes, and unrest were widespread. Divided opinion over slavery and abolition further inflamed public gatherings. Crisis was sensed in a society already preoccupied with the threat posed by an expanded franchise amidst growing inequality (Horwitz, 1977; Nedelsky, 1990). Fears were heightened by the fact that the religious community, previously cohesive in New England, had been eroded by secularism despite evangelism's zealous attempts to revive faith. Because communities had weakened, social consensus and deferential politics that had thrived in the atmosphere of small-scale village life had also eroded (Nelson, 1967; Lockridge, 1981). Since local political institutions and parties were still relatively undeveloped, this perceived problem of order presented city leaders with a dilemma that none of the responses in the existing state repertoire sufficed to solve.

Forms that state response could take were now constrained because broader voting rights meant that such action now had to win popular approval. Growing emphasis on "popular sovereignty" meant that political initiatives increasingly had to generate broad-based public consent. Appearance of, first, republican and then democratic mass politics before a significant local administrative capacity was constructed, meant that no obvious state institutional mechanism existed for responding to the turmoil (Skowronek, 1982).[25] Nor could local officials always rely on informal assistance from the citizenry (Formisano and Burns, 1984). By the 1830s, for example, weakened feelings of communal responsibility led constables to complain that they could no longer rely on passersby for help in apprehending fugitives (Formisano and Burns).

Into this vacuum stepped the courts as agents of the state to shape a response to the disorder and perceived instability of the day. In this "formative era," judges found in the criminal law an "instrument" of social policy and wielded it just as they had in private law. Specifically, judges garbed themselves in the mantle of political "architect" (Horwitz, 1977). Through their handling of cases, judges set in place guidelines and sanctions to shape both individual behavior and, through it, society's institutions too. By proffering leniency, judges sought to resolve and conciliate discord before the tribunals of justice. If cases went to court, those aggrieved were also assured a remedy. Defendants could expect modulation from the state and closure in the case. In its halls, the courts proclaimed, the law would apply to all, no matter how privileged. In words resonant with democratic spirit, judges assured each citizen equal treatment according to the same procedures. Rules would be specified in advance and principles of fairness would be observed. By relying, thus, on the powerful discursive imagery of a "rule of law," the courts marshalled a powerful antidote to the ever more restive and antielite democratic sentiment of laboring Boston. It presaged the approach the nation would take in another facet of the stabilization project, namely, articulating a conception of citizenship.

In the rapidly changing world of republican Boston, Jacksonian voting reforms produced a challenge to the partisan power of Boston's social elite and, among many other changes, a metamorphosis in the city's response to social conflict. No longer was officeholding in Boston the uncontested purview of a privileged elite though candidates of their party continued to dominate elected office in the city through mid-century. Yet politics in Boston was permanently transformed into a popular phenomenon. In this more democratic political context, officials moved to assert their connections to the diverse interests and will of the electorate. Since any resort to coercion by the state tended to undercut the imagery of self-rule and to jeopardize voter support, political officials sought ways of maintaining social order that were consonant with "popular sovereignty." Even as Boston's Brahmins grappled with social conflict under new rules, they found themselves faced with a strong partisan challenge. Their challenge was to reconsolidate their dominance in this newborn world. In this quest, Brahmin leaders turned to the courts and to judges since they, along with tax collectors, were recognized at that time as the primary local agents of the state.

As judges got involved, they justified their efforts in terms of their contribution to political authority, as we shall see in what follows, and as part of the potent notion of a "rule of law." Working as architects of legal change, these judges were also unified by a Whig-inspired canopy of thinking about social policy that equated state interests with security of property and persons, economic growth, and improved quality of urban life. As judges intervened, the courts, which had been criticized for indifference to the plight of debtors and the poor, attempted not only to resolve individual conflicts but also to strengthen the hold of the discourse of a "rule of law" as the basis for a vision of social ordering. As the stirring of democratic sentiment challenged traditional hierarchies, a new web of social niches and cubbyholes had to be imagined lest society be levelled and order undone. For this the courts turned both to the work discipline of capitalism and to citizenship in their search for a language to justify the tense coexistence of political equality and vast material inequity.

Political Stabilization and Consent: Reform and Reproduction

Since Weber (1978) first commented on the key part played by discretion in law, it has become almost commonplace to note that, under virtually every legal system, officials prize practices that preserve their latitude in decision making. Administratively, discretion is one of the prime virtues of plea bargaining. Plea bargaining appears to have been adopted as a cultural practice during a period of Whig leadership partly because its informality and discretion enhanced their control, in a broad sense, over sentencing policy. Such openness provided an opportunity for strong policy stances to be taken by the court. The influence of elites and traditional hierarchies over these policies appears to have operated primarily in two ways: on the one hand, through bargaining's reliance on character references from respectable community members as one criterion for granting leniency and, on the other, through gubernatorial control of judicial appointments. By attempting to draw controversies into court for resolution through its combined message of certainty and mercy, plea bargaining helped assuage fears that democratic/antinomian resentment might flare up into extralegal action or even a politically motivated change of regime. By conserving discretion, plea bargaining and related practices of episodic leniency strengthened judges' abilities to tailor sentences intended to inculcate character.

Defendants before the lower courts, largely day laborers, mariners, spinsters, and, to a lesser extent, artisans, tolerated the practice, albeit grudgingly, because it promised leniency and what appeared to be control over one's own fate through negotiation. At the same time, plea bargaining reduced what had been decried as intrusive state oversight of defendants through the increasingly frequent practice of leaving cases "open" on file. Prior to plea bargaining, this meant that an individual would be kept under surveillance but that no action would be taken in the case unless another complaint were received. Extremely unpopular, this practice left the accused vulnerable to retaliation by disgruntled neighbors or other acquaintances—much as illegal immigrants are today. It encoded with danger any action by such a defendant, no matter how innocent, that might draw state attention to him or her. Thus, it is not entirely surprising that a tradition of malicious prosecution, or false complaint, arose as a form of feud (Steinberg, 1984). Essentially, this was an extension, primarily by the poor, of the traditional practice of vendetta by using the courts to resolve private conflicts (Steinberg). By offering leniency, closure of cases and some control over one's fate, the Whigs hoped to draw conflicts into the courts before they could escalate into other realms—thus providing the stability needed for growth. Confessional qualities of plea bargaining and its reliance on character witnesses of repute, which symbolically reaffirmed imagery of both earlier Puritan community and the tradition of deference, conjured up a fictive "community" in the course of dispute resolution.

Plea bargaining emerged in Boston during the late 1830s. Although the practice arose during a period of reform, it was not advanced as part of a unitary plan or formal initiative. Instead, it emerged as an informal and pragmatic accretion of small changes in the customary practice of the courts that was, only then, culturally codified. The practice afforded one basis for promoting political stabilization and the partisan reconsolidation of elite power. Gradually, it came to play a role, too, in articulating a new political discourse of popular consent. Yet, initiated under the mantle of reform, the practice, through its stabilization of an unequal social order and reliance on traditional hierarchies for character witnesses, paradoxically, contributed to the social reproduction of power arrangements.

The 1830s, when the ideological transformation of the Great Awakening culminated in Boston, were days when the prevailing narrative of republicanism was transmuting due both to growing influence of a commercially oriented elite within the Whig party and to dissent from the widening challenge of the first Democratic-Republican mayor in Boston from 1834 to 1835 (refer to table 7.1).[26] The office of governor, which controlled all judicial appointments in the state, fell briefly from Federalist-National Republican-Whig hands from 1823 to 1825 and again from 1840 to 1843. However, the state government, including the office of governor was securely under Whig control during the tumultuous 1830s. Plea bargaining, then, was a cultural practice that constituted one strand of a political reaction and process of the social reproduction of power on the part of a beleaguered but resourceful elite. It came during a period when the policies of this elite were focused on stabilizing the social order as one thrust of an effort to reconsolidate their own partisan dominance.

In this tumultuous atmosphere, rioting, strikes, and social conflict, coupled with, first, the erosion and, then, the evangelical transformation of traditional Christianity, created an unsettling atmosphere because many of the changes were interpreted as a potential danger to the republic. The republican narrative, which advocated homogeneity as a basis for generating the capacity for the nonself-regarding deliberations and civic virtue that it asked of citizens, was disrupted by pluralism. Pluralism made it nearly impossible to discern any single monolithic "common good" for all members of society. For this reason, it tended to be viewed as a political threat. Bostonians, like other Americans, were generally confident about the robustness of their new market-based society and the ability of political self-rule to survive (Sellers, 1991). However, local leaders were well aware of the rioting and rebellions afoot in Europe during the 1810s, 1820s and 1830s and worked to forestall such mobilization at home.

Thus, Boston's elite welcomed the social policy discretion that accrued from plea bargaining. For these Brahmins, seeking to reinvigorate their influence, the capacity of the practice to contain social conflict in the courts through its twin promises of leniency and case closure was crucial. By establishing a regular and knowable framework for handling cases, however discretionary it might be, plea bargaining bolstered the court legitimacy that had been much criticized for what was felt to be the inscrutability of common law precedent and its arcane forms of pleading. Although plea bargaining operated at the interstices of the law, it was, paradoxically, justified by claims of universality in its application (i.e., it was available to all) and formal equality in its treatment of each defendant (i.e., treatment according to comparable procedures) that are so central to the ideal of a "rule of law."[27] By strengthening court claims to represent both popular will and procedural fairness, plea bargaining constituted an approach to social control that emerged, at once, as one basis for an image of political authority rooted in popular consent and, at the same time, as a practice that fostered the reproduction of the power elite who had turned to plea bargaining as a procedural reform. Suretyship, or the practice of posting bonds to assure fairness, good behavior, and state supervision of cases left "open" was replaced by the private oversight of those who interceded on a defendant's behalf. Character witnesses, who had been solicited by the defendant, now bore informal responsibility for him or her. Besides imbuing a sense of the consequences of one's acts, plea bargaining fostered order by cooperating with society's web of control in everyday life. It emphasized the importance of community ties through the informal and privatized "suretyship" that it revived. Yet, by limiting state powers of scrutiny, plea bargaining, despite this, acknowledges the liberties of the republican citizen relative to the state and bowed to antistatist democratic sentiment seeking clear limits on state power (Mill, 2003). Political officials fervently hoped that these and related practices of leniency would help to reduce any chance that the simmering democratic resentment among those who could count on little prospect of mobility would turn to violence or open revolt.

"Courts and Parties": A Weak Administrative State

If the tradition of episodic leniency from the common law and admonition from Puritanism contributed imagery that shaped the cultural form of plea

bargaining, the context of a unique new state form was the final crucial ingre-
dient that led to the courts, rather than some other administrative entity, step-
ping forward to intervene in response to the perceived crisis of instability.
Facets of the state and its formation that prompted judicial action included: a
relatively weak and decentralized Madisonian state that has led some to term
it a "state of courts and parties" (Skowronek, 1982); a society that created a
state before becoming a nation; and the unusually close linkages between
bench and bar in the United States in that day.

Led by James Madison, the framers of the American Constitution established a federal system of government administered by a limited central state.
Powers not explicitly granted to the national level remained with the states. In
contrast to the strong centralized state administrative apparatus of a country
such as France, one finds in America a much weaker national bureaucracy.
Historically, one consequence of the absence of a strong central state in the
United States was that local government, developing independently from city
to city, formed more slowly. While mayors, city councils, and constabularies
operated, duties such as policing, public health, and education were primarily
accomplished, if at all, either privately or by unpaid and, later, paid volunteers.
Reform movements were active, however, especially during the 1820s. Homes
for the blind, sick, and poor were constructed in one city after another. Reforms
were largely a product of revivalism, the Second Great Awakening and, later,
as it turned from moral to social improvement, of the social policies of the
ascendant Whigs.

Locally, the state presence was experienced primarily through the tax collector and the courts. Tax collectors operated under city jurisdiction in Massachusetts, while judges were, as we have seen, state-level gubernatorial appointees. Under Boston's first charter in 1822, the City Council was
empowered to "lay and assess taxes" and also "to provide for the collection of
such taxes" (Bugbee, 1887). In one particularly significant provision, the council was also authorized to appropriate and spend those city tax revenues (Bugbee). Judges, on the other hand, were "from the highest to the lowest . . . appointed [at the state level] by the Governor and [Governor's] council" (Bugbee;
Goodman, 1964). Judicial salaries and costs of court operations were also
funded by the states. In contrast to the situation in cities and towns, an administrative apparatus for the Commonwealth of Massachusetts was securely
in place by the early nineteenth century (Bugbee; Goodman). Since the dominant political parties at the state level in Massachusetts were, until 1855, primarily National-Republicans and, then, Whigs, who represented a transmuted
and more commercial version of the older Federalist party, gubernatorial appointees tended to reflect the policy preferences of that elite constituency,

which was, successively, the political core of each of those parties. After 1850, as the fortunes of ward-based ethnic politicians prospered, tensions heightened between Boston's elected leaders and the policy stances of elite-sponsored state politicians.

As tumult, rioting, and crime mushroomed and no local bureaucracy existed to implement routine social control beyond the handful of constables, the courts, as we have seen, stepped forward to promote stability. In so doing, they eschewed overt force and worked to justify the project of self-rule. Through their modulated practices for dispensing justice, they began an arduous process of articulating for the public something of what it meant to "be [an] American" citizen. At first glance, it might appear that the courts abdicated their educative role at a crucial moment by moving to a practice, such as plea bargaining, which compromises instead of communicating specific rules and norms that the society holds dear. Earlier I mentioned that impersonal market-like exchange appears to have been seen as fairer than the prior more personalistic dispositions of justices of the peace. If we then look at the practice in terms of the relationships that it created, the courts also cultivated, through bargaining, a connection between the state and society's members. It was one that conveyed assumptions about the limits of state power, the need for political participation, and the nature of the freedom that would constitute a context for an emerging notion of citizenship.

Local officials in Boston who attempted to address rioting and conflict benefited from the new conception of law as a social policy instrument that had recently materialized. Judges increasingly turned in deciding their cases to consider the broader policy implications that they held. During the 1800s, which were a "disruptive" and "potentially radical" period, American judges also "devoted themselves[, in particular,] to re-establishing [post-independence] political authority" (Mensch, 1982). This project, as we shall see, was complicated by growing mass recognition of the primacy of the legislature, which reflected the "people's voice," over the courts in a society committed to self-rule. Popular sentiment was strong in some quarters for replacing common law, which emphasized precedent, with enacted and codified statutes.

The codification movement sought to recognize primacy of "the people's" elected representatives and to move from case law to statutory enactments. Robert Rantoul, who led the charge, argued that "The common law sprang from the Dark Ages . . ." and that it originated out of "folly, barbarism and feudalism" (Jones et al., 1993, p. 34). Rantoul contended that the common law was used by elites to control ignorant and uneducated people, until, in his day, "judges use the common law to override legislative power, the enlightened voice of the majority of the people" (Jones et al., 1993, p. 34). Terming the common law a process of "special legislation" by a judge, Rantoul argued for codification.

Codification eventually failed and the court's interpretive role continued to be strong in many areas important for social policy. Brahmin leaders, however, pressed on to counter mass support for expanded legislative power still further with attempts to reinforce the common law, mainly by demonstrating its compatibility with ideas of "popular sovereignty." Judges, as we have seen, began to depict themselves as reflecting the popular will and as activists working on behalf of the common good (Horwitz, 1977). Acting thus, judges played a central role in shaping "the nature of American institutions" during this formative era (Howe, 1947–1950). Because plea bargaining arose at a time of unique plasticity in law, it provided an unusual opportunity for the practice to achieve permanence.

Bowing to what Sellers (1991) describes as evangelical reformers' "farsightedness," the courts moved in disposition and sentencing to nurture attention to future consequences of present actions by replacing earlier personalized forms of discretionary leniency with a more structured, semicontractual and routinized one. Like the "Invisible Hand" of the market, which transformed the pursuit of self-interest by each into the provisioning and well-offness of all, plea bargaining would mete out swift and impersonal justice in a sort of "market for sentences" according to the terms of trade of the day. By relying on the mechanism of leniency, it provided a device for distinguishing those who were employed, had families, and were community members from others, thus recognizing and creating incentives to enter into those statuses, each of which contributed to constructing a stable and industrious populace. From a Whig viewpoint, this approach was simply one of a number of means chosen by community leaders for promoting the "common good."

While the timing of the crisis of political stability was essential, the state response it occasioned might conceivably have taken other forms. Availability of the cultural repertoire of episodic leniency in the common law and of the imaginative constructions of Puritanism provided a symbolic template with which to work as the courts stepped in to pursue stabilization. The political preferences and attitudes of the bench and bar also exerted a signal influence.

Bench, Bar, and the Legacy of Post-Revolutionary Federalism

Lawyers in Massachusetts during this "formative era" occupied a position of newfound influence after post-Revolutionary years of disrepute. Almost without exception, the Massachusetts bar consisted of, first, Federalists and, then,

Whigs (Warren, 1931, pp. 174, 178). This political cast of the bar, together with Federalist and, later, Whig control of judicial appointments, ensured that the courts were presided over by judges in step with the policies of these elite-dominated parties.

Early in the 1800s, many of the nation's leading Federalists had retreated to their power base in the Massachusetts state house after losing national power with Jefferson's election. They brought with them both the legacy of the Essex Junto in national politics and a relation of vituperation and dislike toward Jefferson's Democratic-Republicans. These Federalists were certain that the only hope of preserving the social order and property itself lay inter-twined with the future of their party. Animus escalated between Massachusetts' Federalists-National Republicans-Whigs, on the one hand, and her Democratic-Republicans and, later, Democrats, on the other. In the quest to preserve order and guard against "Jacobinism," two groups of Federalists initially rose to prominence. The first was the coterie known as the "Essex Junto." The second was the "law craft" and the "pettifoggers," as Nathaniel Ames, a Democratic-Republican, termed the predominantly Federalist legal profession and its lesser aspirants.

In this highly charged political atmosphere, the fact that lawyers in Mas-sachusetts were almost all Federalists assumed particular significance. Inevi-tably their political outlook would color their activities as members of the bar and bench. Even more than in countries such as England, the stance of the bar was significant because, in America, separation of powers dictated that the judiciary had the last word. Any act of the legislature could be overridden by judicial review.

The Junto had been a dominant force in both national and state politics for decades (Warren, 1931, p. 163). Ideologically, the Democratic-Republicans viewed the Junto, its members, and their champion, Alexander Hamilton, as openly hostile to popular rule. The Junto, in turn, saw in their own leadership the only true hope for self-governance. In speeches and letters, the Junto voiced skepticism about the prospects of democracy and fear about what political future it would bring. Although a more tolerant rhetoric eventually developed, this informal political directorate sensed that society's prospects and, perhaps, social order itself hinged on their capacity to devise forward-looking policies and to inculcate both character and consent to their leadership among the masses.

With Jefferson's election at the dawn of the nineteenth century, the Fed-eralists grieved the passing at the national level of a social order that they had cherished. They voiced fear for what was to come politically. The Federalist *Columbian Centinel* lamented the passing of the Adams administration saying:

Yesterday expired
Deeply regretted by millions of Grateful Americans
and by all good men
The Federal Administration
of the
Government of the United States
animated by
a Washington, an Adams, a Hamilton, a Knox, a Pickering, a
Woolcott, McHenry, Marshall, Stoddart and Dexter.
At 12 years.
Its death was occasioned by the
Secret Arts and Open Violence
of Foreign and Domestic Demagogues.
. . . Notwithstanding all . . . [their] services and blessings—
there are found
Many, very many, weak degenerate Sons
Who, lost to virtue, to gratitude
and Patriotism
Openly exult that this Administration
is no more
and that
The 'Sun of Federalism is set forever'
Oh Shame—where is thy blush?

Despite the humorous tone of this *Centinel* article lamenting the passing of one generation of Federalists, the tenor of political criticism in the early nineteenth century was anything but playful. As Henry Cabot Lodge noted in his *Life and Letters of George Cabot,* "[t]he Federalists hated Jefferson [and the Republicans] with no common hatred, but rather with the vindictiveness of men toward a deadly foe, who, as they firmly believed, sought the ruin of all they most prized. They sincerely believed Jefferson to be " . . . the embodiment of French democracy, and advocate and promoter of principles which[, as had been the case in France's Revolution,] menaced with destruction all the rights and customs which alone made life worth living" (Warren, 1931, p. 155).

Jefferson's election evoked fears on the part of Federalists that Jacobin forces might threaten the future of self-rule. Fisher Ames wrote: "All fears now will be for the safety of all the Government has yet erected. Stocks have fallen and rich men have begun to find out that they ought to bestir themselves" (Warren, 1931, p. 159). Ames continued to exhort: "To encourage Mr. Jefferson to act right, and to aid him against his violent Jacobin adherents, we must make it manifest that we act on principle, and that we are deeply alarmed for the public good; that we are identified with the public. We must speak in the name and with the voice of the good and the wise, the lovers of liberty and the owners of property . . . An ardent spirit must be roused in every town to check the incessant proselytizing arts of the Jacobins" (Fisher Ames to Timothy Dwight, March 19, 1801; cited in Warren, p. 160). Yet, Ames feared that "[t]he next thing will be, as in France, anarchy: then Jacobinism . . ." (p. 160).

Fisher Ames, like other Federalists, believed firmly that their party contained the only great [remaining] hope for the country saying: "The only chance of safety lies in the revival of the Federalists who alone will or can preserve liberty, property or Constitution" (Warren, 1931, p. 160). Given the loss of Federalist dominance at the national level, Ames exhorted his partisan brethren to "entrench themselves in the State Governments and endeavor to make State justice and State power a shelter of the wise, and good, and rich, from the wild destroying rage of the Southern Jacobins" (Fisher Ames to Timothy Dwight, April 16, 1802; to Gore, Dec. 13, 1802; to J. Smith, Dec. 14, 1802; cited in Warren, pp. 160–61).

The Essex Junto drew its members from many of the most prosperous and prestigious quarters of New England life, and its style, to some extent, reflected that. Writing of the Junto in his *Life and Times of Stephen Higginson,* Thomas Wentworth Higginson noted that it was led by "two ex-sea-captains and the chief maritime lawyer of his time [Cabot, Higginson and Parsons] . . ." (Higginson, 1907; cited in Warren, 1931, p. 164). Expounding on the implications of this vocational bent on the political style of the Junto, Higginson observed laconically that "[t]he habits of the quarterdeck . . . went all through the Federalist party of Massachusetts . . . The slaveholders themselves did not more firmly believe that they constituted the Nation" (Higginson, 1907).[28] The rare combination of cool, irascible character and consummate ability of the Junto members caused it to become "more cordially detested by its opponents than any other set of politicians in the country" (Warren, p. 164).[29]

Democratic-Republican opponents of the Junto lashed out against its members as enemies of self-rule and even of liberty itself. This view was well summed up by Benjamin Austin who observed: "I believe it can be clearly proved that every embarrassment under which the country labors arises from [the Junto], that all the virulence of parties originated through this pestiferous medium, that all the deception which has been practiced, originated from this artful, aggrandizing faction" (Warren, 1931, p. 165). Austin went on to claim: "This Junto have, from the first . . . watched every opportunity to forward their destructive projects" (p. 164). Referring to the controversial Jay Treaty with England and the initial propaganda campaign in its favor that spawned the

Junto during the 1790s, Anthony Pasquin noted: "From the time that Mr. Jay arrived, after this fatal transaction, we may date a new order of things to have taken place among us [in the rise of the Junto]" (p. 165).[30] Pasquin went on to point out that it was at the time of the Treaty that the Junto was formed with [major] political ramifications . . . [for] the United States (p. 165). Austin contends that, in their quest to influence public opinion toward England, "[t]hese persecutors of human freedom suborned every press that could be corrupted . . . A reign of terror was enforced . . . and every man was threatened . . . who would not abandon his regard for his native land and defend this Tory treaty" (p. 165). Targeting the Federalists, Austin denounced "[t]he Federal Monarchists . . . [who] began that horrid system of proscription, obloquy and violence which has since been properly denominated 'the reign of terror'" (p. 165).

Junto members' defense of their enterprises and their protests of piety and religious commitment roused particular ire. Such indignation led the *Independent Chronicle* to criticize the Junto on the occasion of a dinner held for Rufus King, American Minister to England, saying "a political cabal . . . associate[s] under the name of Bacchus to give publicity and circulation to the most inflammatory, seditious and abominable opinions . . . These voluptuous sneering wretches, these political pharisees . . . who would manifest their piety by toasts and sentiments that would dishonor a pagan in his orgies . . . They are eternally insisting that Religion is in danger . . . If Religion is in danger, it will arise from the hypocrisy, malignity, and wickedness of th[is] Royal Faction who are impiously using the name of Heaven for the furtherance of their own traitorous designs against the Republican Institutions of their country" (*Independent Chronicle*, Oct. 18, 1804; cited in Warren, 1931, p. 166).

Jeffersonian Republicans, in their quest for equality, acknowledged on their part that the "rights of man" had lost sway during the Reign of Terror in France. Nonetheless, Nathaniel Ames, Republican and brother to Fisher Ames, wrote that its successor "Bonaparte [has now been] made Emperor of France without any stipulation for Rights of Citizens . . . The abject condition of the French after such high-toned pretensions to liberty, strikes the world with astonishment" (Warren, 1931, p. 167). Jeffersonians replied that they sought to imbue American republicanism with a greater portion of protection for lasting liberty and criticized the Federalists for their autocratic style.

At an ideological level, the Republicans could hardly have been more at odds with the Junto and its political champion Alexander Hamilton, whom they alleged to hold affinity for "English and monarchical forms of government." We know, Republicans asserted in their publication *Hamiltoniad* that "a [Federalist] confederacy was formed for the abolition of an equality of rights, and he [Hamilton] was at the head of that political association . . . Mr. Hamilton may justly be regarded as the founder of the Royal Faction in this country. He raised it from the dregs and embers of Toryism and placed it for security in the circle of anti-Gallican antipathies" (*Independent Chronicle,* Aug. 23, 1804; cited in Warren, 1931, pp. 170–171). Hamilton's pro-Anglican and elitist views [along with those of the Junto] were further decried saying, "The aristocracy, which he . . . [wished to] for[m] would have been an aristocracy of [mere] wealth, the most repulsive of all, as it would have embraced the pride of distinction without its refinements" (*Independent Chronicle;* cited in Warren, p. 171). Referring to the alleged antidemocratic sentiments of the Junto and of Boston's Brahmin elite, the *Chronicle* noted: "It is an objection, . . . [of] the Royal Faction, particularly in New England, that every citizen may be a legislator [through extension of the franchise]; but we rejoice that . . . [the citizen] has this power, and we hope he will always retain it while his plain but sound intelligence is correspondent with the simplicity of the governing [natural rights of] law" (*Independent Chronicle;* cited in Warren, pp. 171–172).

The vituperation hurled by Republicans at the Junto was not completely unjustified. In their speeches and letters, members of the Junto often voiced what sounded like skepticism about the prospects of democracy and fear for the kind of political future it would bring. In 1803, Fisher Ames of the Junto wrote to Timothy Dwight of his belief that "[o]ur country is too big for union, too sordid for patriotism, too democratic for liberty." He continued to ask: "What is to become of it, [only] He who made it best knows? Its vice will govern it, by practicing upon its folly. This is ordained for democracies" (Ames to Dwight, Oct. 26, 1803; cited in Warren, 1931, p. 172). Ames told Josiah Quincy in 1806, "I have long thought a democracy incapable of liberty" (Ames to Quincy, Feb. 12, 1806; cited in Warren). Referring to Jefferson's accession to the Presidency, Ames further wrote: "Let us . . . be just to this man. Is he not a good chief for us? Would any man, who was free from the lowest passions and prejudices of the lowest mob, manage our affairs with success?" (Ames to Quincy, Dec. 11, 1806; cited in Warren). In a similar vein, George Cabot of the Junto wrote in 1795: "After all, where is the boasted advantage of a representative government over the turbulent mobocracy of Athens?" (Cabot to King, Aug. 14, 1795 in Lodge, 1877; cited in Warren, p. 173). Writing to Timothy Pickering, Cabot observed: "We are democratic altogether, and I hold democracy, in its natural operation, to be the government of the worst . . . If no man in New England could vote for legislators, who was not possessed in his own right of two thousand dollars value in land, we could do something better" (Cabot to Pickering, Feb. 14, 1804 in Lodge; cited in Warren). Thus, the Junto clearly harbored doubts about democracy in the United States—particularly the egalitarian political course charted by Jefferson's Democratic-Republicans.

Even as the Junto and its associates were widely criticized, another group of Federalists provoked, if anything, more bitter contempt from Democratic-Republicans and other Anti-Federalists. This was the "law craft" as the legal profession was termed. Antagonism toward lawyers, arising after the American Revolution, had its wellspring in their role in pressing postwar debt foreclosures. Debt after the war, both public and private, was widespread and burdensome. The courts were filled with suits by creditors for collection and the jails clogged with debtors, many of whose arrears accumulated whilst serving in the war, who were unable to pay. Outraged by foreclosures, litigation, and the burden of fees and court costs, the people "mistook effects for causes and attributed all their evils to the existence of lawyers in the community" (Warren, 1931, p. 174).

Indignation toward lawyers grew to the point that the town of Braintree, home of John Adams, approved the proposal that "there may be such laws compiled as may crush, or at least put a proper check or restraint upon, that order of Gentlemen denominated Lawyers, the completion of whose modern conduct appears to us to tend rather to the destruction than to the preservation of the town" (Warren, 1931, p. 175). Benjamin Austin wrote to the *Independent Chronicle,* urging that "[t]his order of men should be annihilated. No lawyers should be admitted to speak in court, and the order [should] be abolished as not only useless but a dangerous body to the public" (Austin, *Observation on the Pernicious Practice of Law;* cited in Warren, p. 175).

Already by the 1790s the Massachusetts legislature had sought to weaken the position of lawyers by passing laws that enabled parties to plead their own causes or to use "such counsel as they see fit to engage" (Jones et al., 1993, p. 25). After an initial loss, the bar recouped by persuading the courts that the legislature had used the term "counsel" to apply only to trained attorneys. Though the bar controlled admission to its own ranks, legislators, at this point, also moved to fix minimum requirements that attorneys must meet to practice law (p. 25). Artisan leader, Benjamin Austin, pressed the attack on the lawyers by urging that the state use ordinary citizens to settle disputes based, not on common law, but on principles of republicanism (p. 27). His claim was that the law should be comprehensible to all. This quest for comprehensibility and simplification in law pervaded the antebellum years. Lawyers responded by defending their specialized role as "crucial to the maintenance of social order and the preservation of private rights" (p. 27). Nonetheless, in 1790, John Gardiner called for complete abolition of the bar and common law as it was practiced in America.

Republicans had, however, another reason for denouncing the "law craft." This was the political one that "the bar of Massachusetts was almost [entirely]

Federalist" (Warren, 1931, p. 178).[31] This affinity carried on well into the nineteenth century. Joseph Story, one of the very few Democratic members of the Essex County Bar in Massachusetts, wrote: "At the time of my admission [to the bar], I was the only lawyer within its pale who was either openly or secretly a Democrat" (p. 178). Story continues to say that "[a]ll the lawyers and all the Judges in the County of Essex [also home of the Essex Junto] were Federalists and I was not a little discouraged" (p. 178). Similarly, James Sullivan, Republican and Attorney General of Massachusetts, wrote in 1804: "I have in the day of the cockade tyranny, suffered every abuse that Dana, Thacher and Parsons [great Federalist lawyers and jurists all] and the greatest part of the Bar could give . . ." (p. 178).

During the early republican years, the bar was also extremely exclusive. In contrast to today, bar membership was open "only [to] those admitted to practice before the Supreme Judicial Court, a separate process involving previous admission to and years of practice before the Court of Common Pleas" (Jones et al., 1993, p. 31). The size of the group during the early nineteenth century is estimated at between four and five dozen members. Such background enhanced the likelihood of sympathy with Federalist policies. It represented a considerable concentration of power that was heightened further by the bar's practice of electing a standing committee to carry out most of its business to the point that, during some years, the bar in its entirety never met (p. 31). By the 1820s, the members of this committee were widely viewed as "the power behind the Boston legal establishment" (p. 31). In 1822, the quorum for the committee was reduced to one so that any member could, alone, act under the canopy of the group's authority (p. 31). Significantly, this rule change was never questioned.

Requirements for legal education established by the bar reinforced popular images of lawyers as an elite group. By 1808, admission to the bar required a college degree and three years of study with an attorney accepted for practice before the Supreme Judicial Court (Jones et al., 1993, p. 31). Law schools would not be established until 1819 when Harvard opened its doors to students. The cost of this apprenticeship was 150 dollars per year in 1808 and 500 dollars by 1810—putting it out of reach of all but the most affluent (p. 31).

Concern about lawyers' political allegiances was aggravated by the extensive part they were playing in state government. Nathaniel Ames argued that separation of powers was breached as lawyers wrought their influence simultaneously by their votes, their courtroom activities, and their candidacies for elected office (Warren, 1931, p. 179). This fear had some basis because "lawyers constituted the mainstay [and frequently also the candidates for office] of the Federalist party" (p. 179). Denouncing the lawyers' influence in colorful terms,

Nathaniel Ames observed: "The air of a Court [these days] is poisonous and apt to change [even] an honest man into an intriguer" (Anonymous letter to the *Columbian Minerva*, March 30, 1802; cited in Warren). Commenting on the tendency of lawyers to become legislators, Ames voiced worry that they would be temperamentally ill-equipped to represent voters well. He remarked: "However art and cunning may be thought essential to an advocate, [very different traits of] honesty and attention are the greatest attributes of a legislator" (p. 179). Nathaniel Ames went on to point out that "[t]he making [of] lawyers [into] legislators seems to defeat the grand principle of keeping the Legislative Department distinct and separate from the Judiciary—and where these two, or any two of any three departments of Government, are confided to the same hands, tho' the forms under the real sovereignty of the people are still observed to amuse them, the substance is gone" (p. 179). Challenging the rapidly growing influence of these "pettifoggers," Ames wrote: "he that is not now a Lawyer, or tool of a Lawyer, is considered only fit to carry guts to a bear in New England" (Nathaniel Ames, *Columbian Minerva*, Sept. 6, 1803; cited in Warren, p. 180). Noting the affinity of lawyers for the Federalist party, Nathaniel Ames recalled that a recent talk by Thomas Paine had "[set] Federal Tories and lawyers roaring" (p. 180). He continued "[Excluded] under the . . . Jefferson [administration], [now] under the guise of Federalism, the Order of lawyers are barking destruction at all that won't submit to their domination" (p. 180). Despite the preference of most lawyers for the Federalist party, their opposition to Jefferson, personally, was unusually strong. Nathaniel Ames commented that "Jefferson, tho' bred a lawyer, despises the narrow spirit of Pettifoggism, therefore the lawyers hate him" (p. 180).

Throughout the Jefferson administration, "lawyers as a class continued to be largely associated with the Federalist party" (Warren, 1931, p. 181). Jefferson's opposition to Chief Justice Marshall's broad construction of the Constitution and, thereby, the power of the judiciary, articulated especially in *Marbury v. Madison*, only heightened their partisan allegiance.[32] This was especially true in New England. On the support voiced by Federalist lawyers for Marshall's position on the powers of the judiciary, Nathaniel Ames states: "It is alarming to find the Order [of lawyers], the would-be judges, arrogating that veto on the laws for the Judiciary [through judicial review], which the people in their Constitution had so cautiously refused to their Presidents, Governors, etc." (p. 182).

Thus, the "law craft," as a bastion of Federalism, possessed a distinctive ideological stance. As lawyers' status improved after the Revolution and they moved between careers in the bar, the judiciary, and politics, they carried with them the unique political outlook of the Federalist/Whig elite and, with it, a clear commitment to their policies as ones that might best serve the "public good." As criminal courts innovated in their efforts to contain conflict, protect property, and dampen the violence and rioting so destructive to prosperity, first Federalist, and, later, Whig ideas colored the thinking of judges about the need for order and what policies might achieve it.

Courts and Policy: Control through Traditional Hierarchies

How, we may now ask, were the political views of officials and of lawyers translated into a policy orientation on the part of the courts? In their effort to focus public attention on the consequences of action and to build character, it is reasonable to believe that judges drew on their own ideas and that those bore some resemblance to the views of other members of the social and political networks in which they moved. The diaries and papers of leading lawyers and judges of the day are strangely silent about plea bargaining. This may suggest that they saw it as simply an extension of earlier practices such as the ongoing adaptations of grants of episodic leniency, and not entirely new. The name "plea bargaining" may well have been a customary epithet first attached to the practice amidst the heated politics of the elections of 1836 in which not only the terms of the Jackson/Clay rivalry were revived but fierce struggle ensued to woo members of the dissolving Anti-Masonic party to the Democrats or Whigs.

In formal terms, the basic reality that funding came from the state in Massachusetts implied a measure of involvement in budgetary politics to garner the resources for court administration. Given the significance of those funding decisions, it was inevitable that court officials would talk with politicians about their accomplishments and the affairs of the day. If budgetary discussions were one conduit of information, the movement of lawyers between active membership at the bar and the bench was another means by which viewpoints migrated. Court reorganizations were a third mechanism through which new outlooks were introduced.

While the appeal of Federalism to lawyers was well known and debate over social policy was widespread, it is also important to remember that the judiciary battled through the first decades of the nineteenth century to ward off attempts to control it politically. We have seen, for example, that judges defeated efforts by the Massachusetts legislature to individually appropriate and approve the salaries of each sitting judge. Judges saw in this initiative what surely amounted to a legislative effort at review of the judiciary (Hindus, 1980).

While efforts of the legislature to control the judiciary were successfully averted, informal working relations between the judges and elected officials were established. Along with more formal contacts, this was a natural extension of the fellowship developed by judges, as respected members of the bar, with other lawyers and city leaders in the context of Boston society, its cultural and philanthropic activities, and its clubs such as the "Friday Club." It is true that judges in Massachusetts were appointed for life, subject to good behavior. At first, this appears to suggest that judges appointed under one administration would be free from the changing political directions of later ones. This misses, however, the point that, prior to the 1830s, Massachusetts had regularly experienced court reorganizations (Goodman, 1964). When a candidate was voted into office, it was frequently the case between 1800 and the 1830s that an entire sitting bench of judges would be turned out by abolishing the court. A new court would then be established and new judges selected. So, while a judgeship was formally a lifelong appointment, tenure on the bench was traditionally fragile nonetheless. Although court reorganizations abated in the 1830s and did not formally touch the Boston Police Court until 1866, other comparable Courts of Common Pleas continued to be established anew. This tradition created an expectation of connections between the courts and politics.

The content of the social policies nurtured by the Whig elite centered on pursuit of growth, prosperity and stability. Despite the confluence of Whig popularity at the state and city levels until 1850, the slightly faster movement of the commercially oriented Whigs to dominance in state government produced a succession of forward-looking Whig judges who were attuned to Brahmin sensibilities and who could lead the way on issues of economic development in Boston (refer to table 7.2).

Apart from the capacity of its discretions to be used to further policy goals, plea bargaining also presented an impersonal mechanism that was relatively immune from charges of particularism. Plea bargaining inserted a more contractarian and routinized vehicle of leniency. A newspaper vignette from the *Boston Morning Post* of 1837 suggests that plea bargaining may have won a certain tolerance from defendants though its naming, as we shall see, appears to suggest partisan Democratic critique of the practice (Gil, 1837).

For defendants, plea bargaining closed their cases and initially eliminated repugnant ongoing state supervision of their lives though that would return in the late 19th century with probation. These qualities gave plea bargaining some appeal to the masses who were, thus, more likely to accede to resolution of complaints in court. Complainants, seeing the prospect of an outcome, were also more likely to turn to the bench. By establishing a court where judges, unlike the earlier Justices of the Peace, had no financial stake in the outcome,

Boston's mayors sought a return to earlier Puritan use of courts to define new social rules by resolving conflicts before a judge (Konig, 1979).

In human terms, routinized leniency of plea bargaining conveyed a seemingly benign reformist willingness on the court's part to engage the problems of the poor. Modulation by the state in its exercise of power was also assured. Appeal to this moderate but fair, universally impersonal and formally equal means for resolving conflicts and discontents seems to have lent an air of legitimacy to efforts at social control and safeguarded popular consent to the "rule of law." The process of dispensing leniency, which distinguished servants as members of the household of established citizens or laborers as "productive" hands among the laboring masses from the "unproductive" hands of ne'er-do-wells, rewarded those bound by social ties to the domestic authority of the family patriarch, the church, or the work discipline of the employer. The courts retained discretion under this community-based secondary system of social control. Yet, by reducing the state's direct role in suretyship and relying instead on character witnesses or community ties, this effort to stabilize and socially incorporate the "dangerous" classes was rendered more palatable than were previous ones.

Plea bargaining emerged, then, as one facet of a political struggle on the part of competing social classes and, later, on the part of ethnic groups as well, to establish a policy orientation on the part of the courts that fostered a perceived "common good" through discretionary application of the common law vehicles of leniency. The Federalist-Whig elite and the judiciary appointed by them kept considerable discretion but in less personal and more apparently egalitarian forms. Defendants, largely lower class and, increasingly, immigrants, achieved closure of their cases, a sense of participation in their treatment through negotiation, and reductions in state oversight that they experienced as more consistent with their hard-won liberties as citizens.[33] At a time when crime was coming to be viewed as the product of destructive social forces instead of a fall from the path of godliness, acknowledgment of culpability reflected both personal autonomy and recognition of the need to work for improvement. Both were integral to the goal of focusing the attention of offenders and the public on the consequences of action and on cultivating character and reasonable care on their part in daily affairs. Thus, plea negotiation constituted a sort of social "trade" or "bargain" itself among competing social groups, as the time-honored tradition of leniency was depersonalized and incrementally adapted for an age of popular politics.

Social Class and the Elections of 1836: Collapse of the
Anti-Masonic Party

As we look at the rise of plea bargaining, one can pinpoint the year 1836 quite precisely as the point at which the practice takes hold on a basis that will flourish and continue into the twentieth century. What was remarkable about that year was that it saw a presidential election in which Henry Clay, the "Great Compromiser," emerged again as a candidate after an earlier defeat by his rival Andrew Jackson. It was the first national election after the collapse of the extraordinary Anti-Masonic party and a time when both Whigs and Democrats were trying hard to win its members to their ranks.

Freemasonry had grown in America in the decades after the American Revolution. In a time of tumult and change, the Masons provided a brotherhood that offered its members "the eternal and invariable principles of a natural religion" (Felch, 1821, p. 7; cited in Goodman, 1964, p. 10). They were "as old as the laws of harmony and symmetry" and "marked a decisive step in the emergence of civilization from the dark ages" (Goodman, p. 10). Their stated goal was "to promote human happiness by enlightening men about the path to virtue" (p. 10). In practical terms, the Masons were a society whose membership was public but whose rituals and oaths were secret. Denying that the order was a substitute for religion, Masonry was presented as broad-minded and its "handmaid," emphasizing a benevolent deity and commitment to moral behavior. One could, it was believed, approach this benevolent God through charity, tolerance, and fraternalism—the key commandments of Masonry (p. 10).

Amidst a turbulent world, Masonry sought to assuage angry passions. In a secularizing society it offered hierarchy, belonging, respectability, and ritual (Goodman, 1964, p. 10). In times of atomization and competition, Masonry was a chance to re-establish community (p. 12). Historically, it drew members from upper and middle strata though its membership became increasingly middle class as it grew during the nineteenth century. It offered businessmen professional contacts and an assured circle of friends that supported their ventures and lent them civic status (p. 10).

In nineteenth century America, resentment gradually surfaced against the "worldly, aggressive, better-connected" Masons (Goodman, 1964). The Masons, it was argued, had spawned a secret network that rewarded brotherhood over merit in business and politics. This sentiment found its voice in the Anti-Masonic Party. Though relatively short-lived, the party urged opposition to both monied aristocracy and class-based workingmen's movements in favor of their own more communitarian approach. Anti-Masons were "responding to the emergence of industrial society, [secularization, and cultural pluralism] which clashed with the remnants of a pre-industrial order" (Goodman, 1988, p. 36).

Across America, Masonry grew with the development of market society and the middle class (Goodman, 1964, p. 110). The Anti-Masonic Party was the voice of the hinterland protesting changes beyond its control. It flourished during the early 1830s and crested in 1833. In 1830 neither Democrats nor National-Republicans had commanded deep partisan support (p. 152). In the 1828 presidential election, which had sent Andrew Jackson to the White House, turnout of adult male voters was an extremely low 24 percent (p. 152). Weak party attachments allowed Anti-Masons to create an independent political movement that drew its members primarily from disaffected National-Republicans and new voters (p. 152). Their strong showing in 1831 combined with the Democratic vote to hold the National-Republican gubernatorial majority of Levi Lincoln to 54 percent and to convert an essentially one-party state into a competitive three-party one (p. 152). The Anti-Masonic Party was important in arousing voters and by 1832 voter turnout had risen to 41 percent. Citizens, once again, felt their vote mattered. In its peak year of 1833, the Anti-Masons attracted two-thirds of their support from those previously voting National-Republican. By 1834, the Christian Republican Anti-Mason Party began to fade. Temperance and abolitionism replaced the concerns of this party as causes (p. 188). Sobriety had been a major Anti-Masonic concern.

For the most part, Boston's Brahmins who had their own identity and social circle, were not attracted to Masonry (Goodman, 1964, p. 156). Masonry for them was too inclusive and middle class. Among Boston's Masons over two-thirds were merchants, retailers, master mechanics, and manufacturers. Another quarter were doctors, ministers, professionals, and public officials. Among Anti-Masons 84 percent were merchants, retailers, master mechanics, and manufacturers. Thus Masons were more diverse occupationally and also higher in status. Boston's tax rolls show 22 percent of Masons as owning property worth 25 dollars or more but only 10 percent of Anti-Masons (p. 157). Masons were more likely to be merchants and Anti-Masons manufacturers (p. 157). Anti-Masons drew many moralistic, self-made manufacturers who sought through perfectionist reform movements to resolve the tension between ideas of rights, on the one hand, and competitive individualism and class-based stratification, on the other (p. 157).

As the Anti-Masonic Party waned, its state Committee met to decide on a political course. Masonry had been badly damaged and was on the decline. They felt the best course to prevent resurgence of Masonry was an alliance with the Democratic party. In 1834, the Anti-Masons had failed to elect any of their candidates and the Whigs had installed fifteen Masons. In the watershed year of 1836, the Anti-Masons threw in their lot with the Democrats and, together, they elected 18 out of 40 senators (Goodman, 1964, p. 190). Together they also produced the *Report on Secret Societies* for the Senate of the Commonwealth which exposed patterns of influence of "the Circle" (p. 190). Democrats proved welcoming and incorporated Anti-Masons into their party ranks. Then in 1836, these coalitionists successfully endorsed Marcus Morton for Governor. It would be one of the very rare moments when a Democrat would win the Massachusetts State House until the Civil War.

The warning bell had sounded against "secret monopoly of the few at the expense of the many" (Goodman, 1964, p. 190). Anti-Masons found a new home amidst Democratic themes of equal rights and opposition to corporation privilege and bank monopoly (Goodman, 1964, p. 191). The party that resulted emerged as the champion of moral, social, and religious reform. The Anti-Masons had previously opposed anti-republican privilege and supported the pre-eminent importance of equal laws. Publisher Ben Hallett, in 1836, termed the Anti-Masons "the original Jacksonians" (*Boston Advocate,* 1 Feb., 17 Sept. 1836; Hallett, *Oration,* p. 46; cited in Goodman, 1964, p. 191).

Popular Skepticism: A Language of Protest

Despite the readiness of defendants to engage in compromise, popular skepticism toward plea bargaining appears to have abounded. Crucial clues as to the origin of the name "plea bargaining" can be found in the emergence of this practice amidst the politics of the election of 1836.

Foremost among the signs of criticism that met this practice is the very name "plea bargaining" with which the public appear to have dubbed the practice. By situating the name historically, we can see it as one that is replete with pejorative connotation. In choosing this name, ordinary men and women, probably Democratic partisans, turned to language and honed it as a vehicle of critique. Their awareness in doing so belies any sense of veiled consciousness.

In the years leading up to 1848, deference, which had led the laboring and middling ranks to support the political campaigns of their "betters" during the early nineteenth century, contributed mightily to images of popular consciousness as distorted, or false, and conducive to action that ran counter to one's own interests (Marx and Engels, 1848). Yet, in Boston, signs are abundant that the popular classes were, by the 1830s, awash with the democratic spirit and that, as strikes and contestation grew, critical awareness was rife of the inequalities of the day. Few signs of this acute political consciousness are more telling than the name "plea bargain" with which the new practice of leniency was christened.

While my thoughts here are still somewhat speculative, the words "plea bargain" increasingly appear to be a thinly masked public reference of the 1830s to the famed "corrupt bargain" alleged to have transpired between Henry Clay and John Quincy Adams of Massachusetts during the presidential election of 1824 (Schurz, 1887; Eaton, 1957; Baxter, 1995; Remini, 1991; Poage, 1965; Kohl, 1991; and Watson, 1990). As election results were tallied, Adams trailed Jackson in the popular vote but neither had won a clear majority. As a result, the election went to the U.S. House of Representatives, where Clay held a seat, for decision. When the House selected Adams, Jackson's supporters protested that Clay's backing of Adams had significantly influenced the outcome. When Clay was then named Secretary of State, popular outcry erupted that a "corrupt bargain" had been consummated.[34] While such would be of little note today, in 1824, overt ambition was viewed as opportunism and a sign of flawed character. Jackson went on to triumph over Adams and gain the presidency four years later in 1828 and then to beat Clay himself in 1832—four years before early signs of plea bargaining are evident—but bad blood always lingered. In the presidential campaign of 1828, the rallying cry was: "The rights of the people against corruption and bargain" (Schurz, 1887, p. 225). Very much a part of the ideological lore of Jacksonian Democrats, with whom the Anti-Masons had thrown in their lot, the words "corrupt bargain" captured the popular imagination and hampered Clay, a Whig known as the Great Compromiser, throughout his career. He was not to win that presidency.

In dubbing the new form of leniency "plea bargaining," the public or, perhaps more consciously, Jacksonian partisans themselves, seem to have borrowed linguistically the term "bargain" with its intimation of opportunism, flawed character, and corruption. They applied it, partly ironically, to this new Whig-inspired legal practice at once so corrosive of rights and yet so integral to the court project of "character building." It connoted "compromise" in the service of ambition—namely, Whig ambition to preserve privilege and partisan office holding in their "one-party" state in the face of Democratic and Anti-Masonic political mobilization. When plea bargaining arose in the mid-1830s, just after Jackson defeated Clay in 1832, campaign rhetoric protesting the "corrupt bargain" still permeated the air. While Democrats had taken the White House, the Massachusetts state house traditionally remained a bastion of Whig power. By appropriating the imagery of a "bargain," Democratic partisans may have hinted that Whig power was being unfairly controlled through elite (possibly Masonic) dealings that compromised the integrity of public office—

among them, judicial extension of leniency in the form of bargained "compromise."[35] Although no evidence has been found to suggest that plea bargaining mobilized overt mass protest, the language used to signify the process, consciously chosen or not, speaks volumes in itself.

Recrafting the Tradition of Episodic Leniency

Given these motives, how conscious a decision it was to turn to the cultural traditions of the common law in creating plea bargaining as a response to the circumstances of the day is still somewhat unclear (Vogel, 1999). What is clear, however, is that judges looked to the broadening policy role of the courts that had been developing in private law as they crafted policies to deal with social unrest. The court dockets also reveal that the discretionary practice of leniency, which had eased political tension in England, was increasingly invoked by Boston judges (Hay et al., 1975; Vogel, 1999, 2001). Building on new uses of leniency already developed in the United States, legal innovators in Boston abandoned what had previously been a reticence about accepting guilty pleas and began to abate the sentences of some defendants who acknowledged culpability for their acts. With responsibility accepted punishment could be depicted by the state, not as coercive or unjust, but as deserved.

Though leniency operated differently than heretofore in England, it was used, as it had been earlier, to protect social order and promote stability. Plea bargaining sought to draw disputes into court and to dispense justice in ways that were acceptable for a state claiming to represent the popular will. Judicial discretion provided leeway for judges to reflect policy priorities in sentencing.[36] By moving rioters, strikers, and wrangling off the streets, and into the courtroom, plea bargaining, along with other forms of leniency, calmed the fears of citizens about disorder in a way that promoted an image of mastery at the same time it exhibited modulation by the state. It was an image desirable both for quelling criticism of the courts and also for assisting the Federalist-Whig elite to reconsolidate partisan power.

By encouraging social ties with employers and other established persons who could either appear as character witnesses or suretors before the court or even simply attest to the existence of a community or work relationship, plea bargaining underscored the importance of social participation. Since not just one's job but the good will of one's employer was needed to summon his or her intercession, discretionary leniency created incentives to enhance workplace productivity, community involvement, and the settled domesticity of "family life"—each often taken as an indicator of upstanding character. Plea bargaining, thus, helped forge community ties through the informal and privatized suretyship it revived.

Ball Fenner illustrates the reliance on traditional hierarchies of such intercession in his colorful 1851 portrait of the Police Court in Boston titled *Raising the Veil, or Scenes in the Courts*. He observes that "[o]ne of the girls was now called up to the prisoner's stand. She pled guilty to the charges preferred against her. 'I'll bail that young woman for thirty days, your Honor,' cried John Augustus. 'I know her parents, and very respectable people they are, too. If I can't reform her, I'll bring her into court at the expiration of that time, to be disposed of as you will.' [Said the Judge,] 'Mr. Clerk, you may take Mr. Augustus for bail, in the sum of thirty dollars, for the prisoner's appearance here in thirty days'" (Fenner, 1856, p. 33). As John Augustus gradually routinized his participation in the bail decision, he came to be also the originator of the practice of probation.

Episodic leniency had, as we have seen, long operated in England to ease class tensions. Now, with the accused participating through a guilty plea, it imposed warranted and defensible punishment. Crime was now coming to be seen, not as an absence of God's grace, but as a product of corrosive social influences, and choosing freely to acknowledge guilt was seen as a first step on the path of change.[37] In its reliance on intercession from patrons, plea bargaining emphasized the importance of a place in the traditional hierarchical social order that still largely persisted alongside the formal political liberties of the citizen. That hierarchy still structured the options, relationships, and the terms within which a citizen could exercise autonomy and choice.

Forms of leniency had by the 1830s already moved toward explicit conditionality, more formally structured contractual agreements, and negotiation of leniency prior to disposition, but political crisis inspired additional changes. In the plea bargain, judges met acknowledgment of guilt with less-severe sentences while abating state oversight, thus holding out a conciliatory olive branch to those accused. In its response to popular criticisms of state intrusiveness, high costs, and indifference to the grievances of the poor, plea bargaining paradoxically appeared to champion the liberties of those less privileged even as it eroded the right to a presumption of innocence. By evoking the participation of the defendant, it sidestepped any image of coerciveness and joined step with the trucking and bartering of a market for sentences that seems, like its economic cousin, to have been portrayed providentially, as leaving all better off. It was an apt metaphor for the free exchanges of a merchant society but one robed in the nostalgic garb of its Puritan past. Discretion, so much a concern of judges, was preserved and strengthened in the area of sentencing.

While earlier innovations had simply used old forms of leniency in new ways, the "plea bargain" offered a new legal form—one influenced, it appears, by the time-honored practice of Puritan religious admonition. Among the Puritans, forgiveness was, as we have seen, traditionally accorded a sinner only after guilt had been confessed to the congregation assembled and the sinner admonished (Nelson, 1981). In the criminal courts, one change that had already occurred, during the early 1800s, was to use leniency in an explicitly conditional way whereby consideration was extended prior to conviction in exchange for both past and promised good behavior and involvement in the community ties to assure it. In its reliance on such relationships as an indicator, early plea bargaining, in a sense, operated on the basis of a social control/social bond theory of crime. It was as if judges were saying that any of us can err unless embedded in the web of social relationships to restrain us. While introduction of the guilty plea into the scheme of leniency might seem at first glance to be purely a revival of the Puritan confessional motif, the reality is a touch more complicated. This is because the rise of guilty pleas was accompanied by the disappearance of "admonition," which had previously been administered by a judge from the bench. In the new Unitarian world, presided over by a benign creator, admonition took a gentler form than the earlier outcry of disapproval from a congregation. Like earlier Puritan practice, though, it was accompanied by leniency as a basis for reconciliation and acceptance back into the community. The confessional scenario was likely to have conjured up an image of earlier community life as it had evoked an immanent communal image for the Puritans. Judges, for their part, acting prudently to bestow leniency where it was warranted, departed from retribution and exercised moderation to punish no more than was necessary to focus the accused on the distant consequences of present action so as to deter future wrongdoing.

New forms of leniency that were already established provided a precedent for using it to promote policies conducive to the "common good." In its appearance of fairness, universality, and formal equality so vital to the ideology of a "rule of law" and in its responsiveness to public criticism of the courts, plea bargaining imposed social control in a way that avoided any delegitimating use of force or even a hint of coerciveness. Contours of state structure, the cultural repertoire of the common law, and Puritanism in the United States, along with the timing of these events during the formative era of American law, help to explain why plea bargaining did not first appear in England, which shared the common law heritage of the United States.

Transformation of Community and Ambivalent Deference

Despite the language of protest that the practice of plea bargaining elicited, its confessional motif symbolically reaffirmed an image of community as had Puritan admonition before it. What, we may now ask, was the consequence of such an affirmation? By acknowledging a community with which reconciliation was being sought, plea bargaining symbolically reconstructed the practice of deference, directing it now toward the state as a representative of the community rather than toward another private citizen. By introducing the guilty plea into leniency, new forms of deferential politics, now at once acknowledging and protesting traditional social hierarchies, were adapted in a voluntary and more egalitarian way that was consonant with citizenship. It has recently been much asked how long deference persisted in America. What this work suggests is that, although it became unpopular by the 1830s, the reality of the power those hierarchies represented persisted to mid-century. By the late nineteenth century, judges began to move away from this model of community-based control in which they asked whether the relationships existed in a case to inhibit offending. As they did, they began to shift toward the inherently fraught exercise of using science and professional judgment to assess chances for successful rehabilitation and to predict the future dangerousness of offenders.

Plea bargaining conjured up community by holding out the prospect of leniency to defendants in exchange for recognition by a formally free and autonomous defendant of both a community of unequal ranks and the political authority wielded by the Federalist-Whig elite within that orb. In entering a guilty plea, the defendant inherently drew on the image of what was now an imagined secular community to whom the acknowledgment was made. The plea also implied a vision of a state that was tolerated as the representative of the people to receive it. Just as the experience of penitents seeking reconciliation reaffirmed prior religious communities, the defendant's plea revived the image of what was now a "fictive community" in a secular world, where the reality it represented was, despite the revitalization of the Awakening, passing into history (Speziale, 1992).

While many restrictions on voting were ended when the franchise was extended in Boston during the 1830s, it was not the first time that any artisanal and laboring men had been granted access to the vote. The ranks of voters in Boston had traditionally included a goodly number of those of "the middling sort" and even laborers. What was intriguing was that it had been customary in Boston, as in other cities of Europe and America in that era, that such voters would frequently cast ballots in large numbers for their social "betters" (Pole, 1962).[38] Yet, by the 1820s that cooperative spirit had broken down (Formisano and Burns, 1984, p. 35). Just as Boston was established as a city, the strata of the oligarchy just below Boston's "aristocratic" families expressed itself in a movement called "The Middling Interest" (p. 38). This movement, notable more for its symbolic significance than for its consequences, protested that government was for a "common interest" and "not for the profit or interest of 'any one man, family, or class of men'" (p. 38). It is not known with certainty if this movement was a Masonic one but it may have been.

With the rise of the Middling Interest, deference had, in practical terms, been ended. Yet, until the Civil War, the script of social life continued fundamentally to require reading through the dual principles of social rank and religion. The urban elite of Boston struggled to regain its preeminence and to revive old ways, even as many of them adapted successfully to changing economic and political times. Traditionally, in colonial Massachusetts, one of the most significant occasions for acknowledging community had been moments of admonition in the religious congregations where a penitent acknowledged sin to all who were assembled and was reconciled (Speziale, 1992). By his or her acknowledgment, the penitent was invoking a community to whom the confessional expression was addressed. The congregation then acted communally in approving reconciliation (Speziale). The symbolic structure of plea bargaining entails a commensurate invoking of community. While, in actuality, that community had faded, this Whig-inspired practice summoned its form and symbolically revisited the "imagined" community that would be fueled periodically over the ensuing decades by Nativist sentiment and by nationalism.[39] Meanwhile, the mechanism that meted out leniency created an impersonal and humane exchange for sentences that operated on the self-interested actions of each to benefit and provision all, much like the "Invisible Hand" of the economic marketplace.

8

The Transformation
of Plea Bargaining

*Control through Middle Level Institutions
and Social Welfare*

As Bostonians moved beyond the Age of Jackson into mid-century and after, their city, like much of the United States, underwent important changes. While manufacturing establishments continued to be located beyond the city limits,[1] the working people of Boston increasingly were found on their payrolls. Growing employment in industrial manufacture combined with an immigrant population that swelled rapidly until the 1870s to give rise to changes in the class structure of the city. The traditional commercial and artisanal base of the city was composed of a diminishing share of a population that was polarizing into professional and laboring classes.

Equally important was the reconfiguring of local political parties into the third party system along Democratic and Republican lines. The context was one of ethnic identities, nativist outcry and movements for social reform, labor organizing, and a nascent politics of residential taxes and services. In the latter decades of the nineteenth century, the concessions granted through the episodic leniency of plea bargaining, already informed by social policy considerations, remained highly attuned to the developing needs of policing, stabilization, and an harmonious transfer of a minimum of power to Irish hands. The ward-based political system of those years was one that, at once, "provided for" constituents and at the same time sought to sustain their favor through the jobs, services, and help that it dispensed in times of need.

In these years guilty pleas first rose in frequency and then, beginning with the economic crisis of the 1890s, began to decline somewhat in frequency. The exercise of leniency prior to the 1890s involved, as we shall see, shifts in the entire sentencing structure as Yankees attempted to ward off Irish political encroachment. However, the financial depression of the 1890s eventually made unsupportable the vast economic burden of the patronage and social welfare effort this political rearguard action required. By 1900 the transition to power of Boston's strong independent Irish leaders was inexorable. While their political fortunes, like those of others, would ebb and flow, they were established ever after as a permanent force in the dynamics of power in the city.

As the new century dawned, the dispensing of leniency fell increasingly to what Foucault has termed the "disciplines"—the relatively informal institutions of social control that exist alongside and parallel to the formal legal institutions of the state. These institutions, through their work of classification and normalization, promote personal change and shape the life chances of citizens. With the rise of probation, parole, and institutions of juvenile justice, the exercise of leniency by a bench that increasingly included Irish-surnamed judges sometimes involved no formal plea, conviction or formal criminal record at all. At first, in what appeared an extension of social work, three or four continuances—during which period good behavior was observed—might well be followed by dismissal free and clear or, if greater supervision were required, by placing the case open on file. Under this latter practice, the case could be revived in the event that more complaints were received in the future.

In the courts, from the post-Civil War years through the Progressive Era, the expeditious processing of cases that marks much of the nineteenth century is replaced by large numbers of continuances and repeat court appearances by defendants (see table 8.1). In these appearances the courts engage in a process of social classification. Unlike the community-based sorting of earlier years,

TABLE 8.1. Continuances: Boston Municipal Court

	1870	1880	1890	1900	1910	1920
0	87.9%	75.1%	85.4%	61.2%	54.0%	31.6%
1	6.1%	12.1%	10.2%	25.2%	23.3%	25.4%
2	4.0%	4.6%	.7%	7.2%	14.1%	18.4%
3	1.5%	2.9%	2.2%	3.6%	5.5%	10.5%
4	—	—	.7%	2.9%	2.5%	5.3%

Note: Prior to 1866 the Boston Municipal Court was the Boston Police Court.

Source: Random samples of the docket of the Boston Police Court produced for this project. Table shows the percent of cases each year receiving each number of continuances.

this one relies more heavily on the opinions of experts and the records of society's middle level institutions—especially hospitals, schools, and social welfare agencies. In the "disciplines," probation and parole inhabit an informal realm between law's majesty in the court and the humanitarian assistance of the social worker. As city functions come increasingly to be performed by large-scale institutions, professional expertise grows more prominent in decision making.

During this period, the community-based suretyship of the antebellum years is supplanted by state surveillance, assessment and reporting. Typically the interim between court appearances is spent more or less formally on probation where a defendant's behavior is scrutinized and reports are written (see table 8.2). Moments before the judge are spent assessing an individual's progress toward rehabilitation. Personnel are more numerous than in the antebellum courts and specialized services proliferate in the growing world of large urban institutions. Now adaptiveness and malleability become the hallmark of the healthy.

Heightened tension between labor and capital in these years, when social democracy consolidates its position as a force in Europe, raises questions about inequalities in the representation of political interests. From the late 1800s through the Progressive Era, despite middle class strength and talk of reform, patronage ameliorates some of poverty's most severe hardships but the courts take a hard line with labor and attention turns to professionalization of city

TABLE 8.2. Duration in Days of Time to Case Disposition (Boston Municipal Court)

	1870	1880	1890	1900	1910	1920
Duration						
0	68.2	59.5	78.1	60.4	54.0	24.6
1	10.6	9.2	3.6	5.8	3.7	.9
2	5.1	5.8	5.8	5.0	1.2	4.4
3	1.5	4.0	.7	2.2	1.2	2.6
4	0	3.5	1.5	1.4	1.8	1.8
5	.5	.6	.7	2.9	1.2	2.6
6–10	3.0	3.0	1.4	6.4	7.9	9.7
11–20	1.0	1.2	1.4	2.1	3.0	9.8
21–50	4.5	5.4	3.6	1.4	4.2	9.9
51–100	1.5	4.8	0	6.7	1.2	.9
101–150	15.0	.6	2.1	3.5	0	1.8
151–200		1.2	0	1.4	15.1	16.0
201+					6.0	14.4

Source: Random sample of the docket of the Boston Municipal Court (prior to 1866, the Boston Police Court).

police forces along with establishment of specialized national ones such as the Federal Bureau of Investigation. One sees that in Boston reliance on patronage by a coalition of former Whig Yankees turned Democrat and minor Irish ward leaders forestalls, until undone by the Depression of the 1890s, the rise of strong independent ethnic politicians to power. As their hold on power grows, an emergent middle class—in the name of "good government" reform— moves to transfer much of the real power from city to metropolitan government or state.

Within the city, judges in the lower courts, which only slowly come to include some Irish names, begin to wield the power of the disciplines to move toward new forms of leniency and less formal dispositions of cases. This leaves less of a debilitating record to quash future life chances as the mills of society's middle level institutions, through their decisions, grind on.

Social Class and Ethnicity as Bases of Conflict

While manufacturing establishments lay, for the most part, outside the city's boundaries, nineteenth-century Bostonians increasingly turned for jobs to those concerns or to industries such as "clothing, footwear, foundries and [to] sugar refineries [that] employed great numbers of workers" (Vogel, 1980, p. 16). At the same time, the rising number of persons working in manufacturing was coupled with a rapid expansion of the ranks of other unskilled labor. By 1880, fully 33 percent of Boston's populace was employed in manufacturing (see figure 6.1). Eleven percent more were unskilled laborers and still another 18 percent were engaged in domestic or personal service. In addition, some indeterminate fraction of the 27 percent of those working in trade and transport—primarily the thousands of stevedores and teamsters who hauled cargo for the city's active coastal trade—rounded out the ranks of the unskilled in Boston. By the last decades of the nineteenth century, then, a considerable shift was evident in the class structure such that unskilled or semi-skilled positions were most common.

It was to this large mass of laborers that members of Boston's Brahmin elite pointed in their frequent references to Boston's "dangerous classes" (Sellers, 1991). Of special concern to upper- and middle-class Yankees was the massive influx of Irish immigrants to the city (Higham, 1964). To Bostonians, the Irish appeared to combine a lax morality typified by their drinking in public houses with a pro-statist authoritarianism that was repugnant to Yankees who were fearful of state excess in their newly established democratic society. When the Irish resisted assimilation by establishing separate religious schools for their children and, as papists, were seen by many as owing their primary allegiance to a foreign head of state—the Pope in Rome—they were greeted with much unease in Boston (Handlin, 1979). Labor unrest also spread. While protest at mid-nineteenth century had emerged under the leadership of craftsmen (particularly, the spirited shoemakers of Lynn), labor conflicts later in that century assumed the tone of a confrontation of labor and industrial capital.

An Incongruous Democratic Alliance: Pragmatic Patricians and the Irish Working Class

Despite the reservations of Boston's elite, the latter half of the nineteenth and early twentieth centuries brought a transition from Yankee Bostonians to Irish-Americans as the dominant electoral power in Boston. While the popular image of this political metamorphosis tends to be painted in vibrant colors of the displacement of an upper class that was arrogant in its exercise of power, the actual records of the day belie that image of the Yankees. In fact, their letters, diaries, and papers convey a blend of doubt and recurring dour pessimism coupled with boldness. What one does not find on their part is a "single-minded class stance" (Blodgett, 1984, p. 88). Instead, one sees them developing resourceful and increasingly pragmatic approaches to coalition-building amidst ethnic politics that inevitably involved power sharing and a widening of the circle of political control. Politically active members of the Yankee upper class played a crucial role as "mediators" of the "ethno-cultural political strife" of the city and worked initially with compatible minor Irish-American leaders to modulate passions and to maintain a strong Yankee presence in the electoral politics of the city (p. 88).

Unlike their counterparts in New York and Philadelphia, the Boston patriciate maintained an active working involvement in electoral politics through the turn of the century. The key to their longevity lay in the same resourcefulness and forward-looking adaptability that had enabled the Brahmins to weather the challenge of the Democratic-Republicans earlier in the century. While the social and economic elites of other cities had been reduced to "angry, episodic and relatively ineffectual reform protests against 'machine' politics," practical Brahmins forged a fragile and unlikely alliance under the political canopy of the Democratic party with selected, like-minded leaders of the Irish working-class majority (Blodgett, 1984, p. 88). While some see in this incongruous alliance a cooperative stewardship of the transfer of power to the Irish-American constituencies, such altruistic generosity is not evident in the events of the day. Instead, one finds an effort to sustain Yankee political centrality and to further the status of leaders within the Irish-American community, who were too weak to go it alone in the fractionated ward politics of the day and, thus, open—or susceptible, with inducements—to a politics of cooperation. Despite inevitable tensions and the inherent instability of the alliance, "its arbiters managed to define a fund of shared interests which held . . . [it] together as the dominant force in the city's politics over the last quarter of the nineteenth century (p. 88). The result was an interlude of post-Civil War ethnic political "detente" presided over by the Democratic party and shaped by commitments to ethnic tolerance, deference by the Irish to elite Yankee leadership, and "Yankee acknowledgment of the legitimacy of Irish power in the city" (p. 84).

Until the late 1890s, animosity and confrontation emanated neither from the Yankee elite nor from Irish-American political leaders but rather from "middle-class native Protestants and working-class Canadian Protestant immigrants, whose values and interests clashed directly with the mores of the city's Irish-Catholic population" (Blodgett, 1984, pp. 88–89). While Irish immigration had abated somewhat by the 1860s and European migration would not resurge until the east central and southern influx began in the 1880s, the postwar years saw massive migration of rural New Englanders and Canadian Protestants into a city notable for its slow growth rate relative to New York, Philadelphia, and Chicago and for its lack of economic and social mobility. When these simmering antagonisms erupted in the late 1880s, as the mayoralty passed into Irish hands for the first time, it was the progeny of patrician Boston who worked to temper the conflict and to uphold the legitimacy of Irish-American interests and political power. This was the annealing influence that sustained the unlikely Democratic alliance. With Yankee recognition of their power established, several Irish-American leaders turned to patrician circles of leadership over their bitterly fractious brethren in the Irish-dominated wards and created alliances that sustained the pragmatic Yankees in partisan control. As the late 1890s ushered in a major economic depression, the financial burden of maintaining these cooperative arrangements became unsupportable, as we shall see, and they began to come unglued. Despite the energetic efforts of Yankee mayors, the early twentieth century saw a shift by Irish-American leaders to reliance on their own resources and a gradual retreat by Boston's social and economic elite to the margins of the city's electoral politics.

First, however, these shrewd patrician families embarked on a round of ostensibly "nonpartisan" good government reform that stripped the city of many of its powers of the sort plied earlier in New York and Philadelphia. One main component of this reform movement was a project to establish a metropolitan government much like a multi-county one and to shift numerous city functions away from the control of mayor and city council to this new form of governance. Those functions that would remain with the city government would be consolidated, insofar as possible, according to the new City Charter of 1909, in the hands of the mayor, who, because he was elected citywide, was seen as slightly less susceptible to the rapacious patronage wielded by ward-based ethnic politicians. As ethnic politics and reform of ward-based patronage assumed center stage, one crucial arena of contest was the city's institutions. These included the hospitals, the library, and the police. While the courts were presided over by judges appointed by the governor, they nonetheless played a significant role in this crucial period of transition.

Clearly the events shaping plea bargaining's transformation in Boston during these years are specific to that city. They occurred later than in other cities and so cannot be fully generalized. What can be examined in such general terms, however, is the influence of changes in social context on laws and legal practices that had originated earlier in a very different setting and the role that status groups played in such change. In Boston, one sees both the emergence of the disciplines and reliance on social welfare to forestall the political consequences of a crisis of legitimation. One sees too that cultural practices devised for one setting, even as they promote continuity, may sometimes have unintended and even destructive consequences when they operate in new conditions as that initial context changes.

The Faces of Ethnic Status Conflict: Struggle between City and State

As struggle over the city's institutions unfolded, contest between native-born Yankees and foreign born immigrants sparked and colored the relationship between political leaders of the city and the stewards of the Commonwealth (Blodgett, 1984). In Massachusetts, the state, "an anxious watchdog of municipal behavior," overtly "hovered closely over the city" from the State House, "a bastion of Yankee Republicanism," which was a mere ten-minute walk from City Hall (p. 90). As early as the 1860s, and before any Irish-American had gained a place on either the city council or police force, movement had begun in the General Court of the Commonwealth for "imposing state sponsored law and order on the city" (p. 90). Such "reform" focused on removing policing and liquor licensing from control by city politicians and "placing that authority under state-directed metropolitan oversight" (p. 90). Demands for change were fueled by what was perceived to have been lack of police protection for ante-bellum abolitionist meetings, the threat posed by the draft rioting of 1863 that riveted the fearful attention of the city, and long-standing pressure (dating back to the Anti-Masonic party and the early temperance movement) for more stringent control of liquor sales, prostitution, and the operation of public houses (Blodgett, 1984, p. 90). Following the draft riot, a committee of the state legislature proposed "to adopt the metropolitan principle in order to prevent the elements that are destructive of property and laws from keeping practical control of the city, and . . . undermining the prosperity and peace of the commonwealth" (Whitten, 1898; cited in Blodgett, p. 90). In its report, the committee depicted the cities socially as "the common sewers of the state" (Whitten; cited in Blodgett, p. 90).

As the Irish presence among police, council members, and aldermen increased during the 1870s, protest mounted and finally crescendoed in 1884, when Hugh O'Brien was elected the first Irish mayor of Boston. Almost immediately, the General Court of the Commonwealth acted decisively to shift control of the police to a metropolitan commission whose members were selected by the governor (Blodgett, 1984, p. 90). This move was fiercely opposed by Boston's Irish Democrats, who correctly interpreted the step as one that paved the way to use the political sway wielded by Yankees statewide, to control immigrant behavior through policing. Irish-American Democratic leader Patrick Maguire protested that "[t]he venerable hayseed legislators from Podunk and other rural sections, aided by Boston hypocrites and frauds, lay and clerical, [have] deprived Boston of the control of her police for the purpose of making her a moral city" (*The Republic*, June 9, 1894; cited in Blodgett, p. 90).

As tensions heightened after the election of Irish-American Mayor Hugh O'Brien, schooling was added to policing and the licensing of taverns as a crucial issue of political dispute between the city and the state and, within the city, between Irish Catholics and Protestants (Blodgett, 1984, p. 91). One thrust of the schooling initiative was to regulate Catholic schools by means of state-sponsored inspection (p. 91). By 1888, this effort to require routine surveillance of Catholic schools had been supplemented by a drive to bar Catholics from the Boston School Committee (p. 91). The reform movement that articulated these demands consisted primarily of ministers, suffragists, temperance advocates and anti-Catholic Canadian immigrants (p. 91). Schooling ignited passions that proved more volatile than even policing had. It rekindled tensions that had smoldered for many years around the perennial issues of liquor sales and consumption; worries about the political designs of the Catholic hierarchy in America; and the newer issue of women's desire to vote. Protestants, galvanized by the controversies over schooling and policing, responded by defeating Hugh O'Brien's bid for reelection as mayor of Boston in 1888 (p. 91). To many of Boston's Irish-Americans, these events challenged the very legitimacy of their power in a city where they constituted a majority. These debates clearly revealed the depth and fierceness of statewide resistance to the power of the substantial Irish-American community in the city.

While less volatile, metropolitan political integration was still another issue that mobilized intensifying anti-Irish feeling. Metropolitan integration referred to the process of extending the political boundaries and, hence, the tax base of the city through annexation. Initially annexation of nonimmigrant neighborhoods was seen as desirable by Yankees in the State House because it counteracted politically growing Irish-American power in the center city. Between 1860 and 1880, the population of Boston had doubled—half of this growth coming from annexation of Roxbury, Dorchester, Brighton, Charlestown, and West Roxbury in the seven years between 1867 and 1874 (Blodgett, 1984, p. 91). After 1874, this process of political absorption came to an abrupt halt. Annexation as a strategy had rested on the belief of affluent merchants, financiers, and professionals residing in the outlying areas (such as Lexington and Concord) that they could control the politics of the center city so vital to their business interests (p. 91). As Irish-American Democratic power grew and city tax rates to support services (and possibly patronage) skyrocketed, "Yankee voters on the perimeter recoiled" (p. 91). Fears that what they viewed as "the immorality and corruption of city life would encroach on their peaceful towns, where old Yankee families still held sway, . . . [also undercut] hopes of controlling the center from the rim" (p. 91). These fears were reinforced by traditional values of cultural homogeneity, deference to old families, and reliance on the town meeting as the basis of self-government to assure staunch resistance to any further political annexation despite growing economic interdependence between the region and the center city (pp. 91–92). The decades between the Civil War and the turn of the century brought even greater interconnection through public transit and electronic communications (p. 92). In addition, the state then moved unilaterally to create other linkages by integrating water, sewer, and park systems (p. 92). This rich web of interdependencies notwithstanding, the Yankees of Boston's rim towns remained implacable in their resistance to political incorporation.

Stewards of the Transfer of Power: Politics of the Yankee-Irish Democratic Alliance

Precisely because of the depth and intensity of racial tension in Boston, the political alliance between forward-looking Brahmins and the leaders of some of Boston's Irish wards was an exceptional accomplishment. In contrast to other cities, this unlikely alliance controlled the Boston mayoralty for two of the last three decades of the nineteenth century and, with one exception, placed in office "native-born Yankee patricians" (Blodgett, 1984, p. 92). The exception, of course, was, as previously mentioned, Hugh O'Brien. The three mayors who served longest—Frederick O. Prince, Nathan Matthews, and still another Josiah Quincy—were Harvard-educated sons of old and prominent Boston families (p. 92). This sort of upper-class, well-educated Yankee Democrat was little in evidence in Boston politics after the turn of the century.

Ultimately, the primary consequence of this unlikely alliance between the Yankees and Irish-American immigrant community was to preside over and mediate the transition of the Irish to power, both in the city of Boston's electoral politics and in the local Democratic party, by skillful initiatives in coalition politics. In their multiethnic alliance, these resourceful Yankees found partners among Irish-American ward leaders in Patrick Collins, Patrick Maguire, Hugh O'Brien, Thomas Gargan, and Joseph O'Neil (Blodgett, 1984, p. 93).

The fragile Democratic alliance began to coalesce in the 1850s during the period of the dissolution of the second party system. At this point, "Irish and Yankee opponents of anti-slavery agitation in Boston found themselves thrown together in the Democratic party" (Blodgett, 1984, p. 93). The Yankees were primarily former Whigs, mostly merchants, lawyers, and shippers, who shared with Irish Democrats "a mutual aversion to the moral [reformist] agenda of the new Republican party for purifying the social order, whether the object of purification was the Southern slave owner or the urban saloon" (p. 93). Opposition to the use of public authority to promote an agenda of moral reform would remain central to the Democratic party and a key dividing line between Democrats and Republicans into the twentieth century (p. 93). This point of agreement played a vital role in enabling the Democratic party to bridge ethnic, class, and religious differences that otherwise would have obstructed cooperation under the canopy of the party (p. 93). It continues to this day in the Democratic party's strong focus on personal freedoms and separation of church and state.

Between 1860 and 1880, four of Boston's coalition-supported mayors were former Whigs who were elected to office as Democrats (Blodgett, 1984, p. 93). The mayoralty of Frederick O. Prince, a lawyer from an old patrician family, was notable for dramatically incorporating Irish interests and, especially, its reliance upon leaders of the Irish-American community. One key to Prince's political success was his "candid Democratic partisan[ship]" and his acute grasp of how important linkages were with the Democratic party at the state and especially the national level (p. 93). As a platform for acting upon his philosophy, Prince had the advantage, after entering the Democratic party in 1860, of being chosen Secretary of the Democratic National Committee, a post that he held for 28 years. Upon being elected mayor of Boston, Prince repudiated traditional ideas that city politics were independent of national party politics and patronage (p. 93). While dependent on the Irish-American vote for electoral success, Prince drew on his national position to act as "both a patron and a client in his dealings with [them]" (p. 93).

To win election, Prince had to surmount the hurdle of gaining the nomination of the city Democratic committee. In that process, the pivotal figure was Patrick Maguire, an Irish-born printer and investor in real estate, who was a powerful broker in political dealings in Boston. In return, Prince assured Maguire's attendance at Democratic national conventions for the remainder of his political life (Blodgett, 1984, p. 93). This both consolidated Irish support for Prince's bid for re-election as mayor and laid the groundwork for strong local support of Democratic presidential candidates in Boston (p. 94). In his role as mayor, Prince also cultivated Irish support with "patronage, including seats on municipal boards charged with management of police and liquor licensing" (p. 94). While Prince's patronage was later seen as "meager and condescending," he was "a realistic practitioner in the art of patron-client politics, and his response to Irish demands for recognition" was a major step in the transition of the Irish to power (p. 94).

Both Yankee and Irish-American factions of the Democratic alliance received fresh infusions of support during the 1880s. For the Irish, this came from high rates of natural increase. For the Yankees, new recruits arrived as a result of the Mugwump revolt against Blaine in his bid for the presidency and their shift to the Democratic candidate, Grover Cleveland (Blodgett, 1984, p. 94). While the Mugwumps were not sufficiently great in numbers to carry Massachusetts for Grover Cleveland, the wealth and social status of these former Republicans gave them unusual influence in the Democratic party that was far greater than their numbers would suggest with significant consequence for local, state, and national politics (p. 94).

The political impact of the Mugwump presence among the ranks of Democrats was neither sought nor anticipated by these new arrivals nor was it easily accepted by the Irish-Americans within the party (Blodgett, 1984, p. 94). Among Mugwumps, interest in city government was low. Nonetheless, they were drawn into city politics, distasteful as they found it, by their desire to build support within the city for Grover Cleveland's presidency. Some degree of cooperation with Irish ward leaders was thus a must despite palpable distrust on the part of the Yankees as their comments about "saloon Democrats" and the "dynamite [Irish] wing" of the party made clear (Blodgett, 1984, p. 94). The Mugwump vision of citizenship had much in common with the earlier republican one—namely, "the personal autonomy of the free individual citizen" (pp. 94–95). It was a vision of politics that stood in inherent tension with the "ethic of bloc discipline and party regularity" espoused by the Irish-Americans (p. 95). Mugwumps introduced a number of initiatives, such as civil service reform, that were intended to disrupt this political way of life among the Irish. While these reform initiatives combined with religious, educational, and cultural differences would seem to have precluded cooperation, a working alliance at the level of leadership was sustained even though the constituencies mingled little if at all (p. 95). Mugwump involvement in the city began with efforts to mobilize support for Cleveland's presidential candidacy in 1884 and continued into "negotiations . . . to regulate the flow of presidential patronage into the city in ways that satisfied both the hunger of party regulars and the lofty standards of the Mugwumps" (p. 95).

Amidst considerable variation among Mugwumps in their willingness to engage the Irish, Josiah Quincy and John F. Andrews, motivated by local political ambition, took the lead. Soon they were joined by other Yankees, mainly Harvard-educated lawyers from old Boston families that had a tradition of public service, such as William E. Russell, Nathan Matthews, Sherman Hoar, and Charles Hamlin (Blodgett, 1984, p. 95). Given their ambitions for elective office, cooperation with Irish leaders was a necessity. By the 1880s, the demographic and political configuration of the city dictated that coalition tactics were a given for anyone seeking office as a Democrat (p. 95). In political terms, the objective of these men was to imbue municipal and, to the extent possible, state politics with the policies Cleveland was implementing at the national level. Thus, these Yankee reformers were possessed of "a lively sense of group identity and positive purpose," far more so than their earlier Whig predecessors in the Democratic party in Boston (p. 95).

In part, the outlook of these Mugwumps-turned-Democrat was shaped by the new secular sense of public mission being touted at Harvard by President Eliot (Blodgett, 1984, p. 95). During these years, the Harvard President urged a new more meritocratic "national upper middle class style: cosmopolitan, moderate, universalistic, somewhat legalistic, concerned with equity and fair play, aspiring to neutrality between regions, religions and ethnic groups" (Jencks and Riesman, 1968, p. 12; cited in Blodgett, p. 96). To consolidate their leadership role in the tension-fraught city of Boston, these reformist Yankee Democrats sought to softpedal cultural differences as part of their defense of Irish interests and the legitimacy of Irish power (p. 96). Far from being motivated by sheer fellow-feeling, these men realistically recognized that "[o]nly in a public environment that maintained some degree of cultural comity could their upper-class claim to a leadership role prevail" (p. 96). Arriving on the local Democratic political stage in Boston during the mid-1880s, it was also the practical reality that one found the city's first Irish mayor, Hugh O'Brien, ensconced in office. The political pragmatism of the day was reflected in Quincy's words: "The world has entered upon a period of change . . . The problem is to make the results of study and cultivated thought acceptable to the mass of the people; for it is into their hands that the government of all civilized states is now rapidly passing" (p. 96). A series of volatile local issues provided dramatic openings for Yankee Democrats to make good on their promises of cooperation. These included the proposal for parochial school inspection; the controversy over Boston "home rule"; temperance, prohibition and liquor sales; and extension of suffrage to women (Blodgett, 1984, p. 96).

The parochial school inspection initiative was a thinly veiled effort to rein in public schooling by imposing state regulatory control. President Eliot of Harvard, together with his colleague and fellow-Bostonian William James, decisively opposed it, while Nathan Matthews mobilized opposition in the General Court (Blodgett, 1984, p. 97). Although they, like those of their social circle, had no affection for the Catholic Church, they were moved to action by political interests, commitment to private schooling (of all types) of which their families had partaken for generations, and "a strong distaste for Evangelical efforts to impose Protestant cultural uniformity"—be it in public morality or in schooling (p. 97).

What came to be known as the question of "home rule" for Boston involved the potential return of functions such as police from the metropolitan district commission to the city and the lifting of state-imposed constraints on city governance, such as limitations on tax rates or levels of indebtedness that the city could accrue (Blodgett, 1984, p. 97). As descendants of old and wealthy Boston families, Yankee Democrats were no less critical than Republicans about crime and disorder in the city or about soaring city tax rates. After the election of Mayor O'Brien, these Yankees "made no serious effort . . . to return control of Boston police to City Hall or to lift state-imposed ceilings on municipal taxation and indebtedness" (p. 97). Despite lack of action on "home rule," Yankee Democrats drew nonetheless on the rhetoric of the Democratic tradition of "Jeffersonian laissez-faire localism" to exhort tolerance for the customs and behavior of Irish ward-based constituencies in the city (p. 97).

Republican initiatives to impose prohibition provided still another source of common ground. Despite sharp contrasts in styles of social drinking, both Yankee Democrats and Irish shared an abiding opposition to the "dry ethic" (Blodgett, 1984, p. 97). Positions on temperance had long been evident along party lines with Republicans supporting and Democrats opposed to it as part of the general Democratic party resistance to the use of civic authority to establish a public morality or to undertake moral reform. When Republicans attempted to introduce liquor control during the late 1880s, Yankees and Irish rose up in unison over what they saw as an infringement on their personal liberty (Harmond, 1974, pp. 91–93; cited in Blodgett, p. 98).

On the question of suffrage for women, support also mobilized along the same partisan lines. Support for suffrage came mainly from "middle class Protestants of Republican background" (Blodgett, 1984, p. 98). While a number of prominent Yankee Democrats such as Quincy initially called for suffrage for women as well, Boston's Irish Democrats were strongly opposed (p. 98). Among Democrats, opposition to female suffrage deepened by the 1890s and endured for two decades more.

What emerged, then, was a cross-class Democratic "alliance . . . as upper-class Yankee Democrats collaborated with leaders of the [Irish] Catholic working class to contain the eclectic moral impulse of Boston's Protestant middle" (Blodgett, 1984, p. 98). Chagrined by the defeat of O'Brien's bid for re-election in 1888 and another defeat of a different Irish candidate the following year, Patrick Maguire concluded: "Only by reviving the politics of deference could the Irish regain access to . . . City Hall" (p. 99). He, meanwhile, supported the city Democratic committee decision to run an upper-class Yankee Democrat for mayor as they had Prince in years before.

Their choice was Nathan Matthews, architect of the Democratic party renovation since 1884, shrewd campaign organizer, and adept fundraiser (Blodgett, 1984, p. 99). Matthews, who was elected and served from 1891 to 1894, brought to the mayoralty a business-like focus on efficiency that unsettled the Irish by curbing city patronage but could point to many accomplishments in support of urban development by the time he left office (p. 99). He was also the first to seize the new power transferred to the mayor by the city charter reforms of 1885. Power over city expenditures, previously handled by the free-spending city council, was now vested in the mayor who, due to his citywide election, was seen as somewhat more insulated from Irish ward politics. As a realtor, who understood the dynamics of urban development, he acted on early concepts of city planning to construct new parks, to improve the city water supply and utilities, and to begin work on a subway (p. 99). Though the city payroll was pared back under his administration, public improvements meant contracts that translated into jobs, albeit low-paying ones (p. 99). Such "low-wage patronage," while grudgingly accepted, sufficed to "tur[n] out annual majorities to float Matthews' re-elections" (p. 99).

Because of Matthews' inherent fiscal conservatism, patronage under his administration was directly dependent on the construction and roadwork as-

sociated with growth. The national financial collapse of 1893 thoroughly disrupted these arrangements (Blodgett, 1984, p. 99). When plans were suggested
to increase city spending to provide jobs to counteract rising unemployment,
Matthews resisted (p. 99). Railing against what he termed "the insidious encroachment of socialism," Matthews inflamed Irish-American sentiment by
embarking instead on a "politics of retrenchment" (Matthews, 1895, pp. 104–
7, 175, 182; cited in Blodgett, pp. 99–100). The Depression of the 1890s, by
drying up the flow of patronage, caused the citywide Irish organization that
Maguire had orchestrated since the 1870s to crumble. In the absence of any
compensating concerted public relief or supply of jobs from the city or state
governments, hard times brought to prominence the activity of ward bosses in
helping to stave off hunger and poverty (p. 100). In this way, the Depression
of the 1890s brought a new generation of Irish leaders to power, who were far
more independent of spirit and opposed to deference of any sort. With the rise
to power of Martin Lomasney, John Fitzgerald, James Donovan, and Patrick
Kennedy, the old cross-class, multiethnic Democratic alliance had come to an
end.

Eclipse of Yankee Leadership: From Municipal Socialism to Progressive Reform

As the Depression of the 1890s settled in and the capacity of the Democratic
alliance to use municipal expenditures to guarantee a flow of patronage was
lost, a profound transition occurred in social and political life in Boston. As in
many cities, an aspiring middle class came to power. Though such social forces
often ushered in Progressivism, their numbers in Boston included a strong
and newly independent Irish middle class which gave early 20th century politics a unique tone in that city. Social problems came to be recognized as urban
ones and large-scale institutions were constructed to address them. In this
milieu of change, the American courts moved swiftly to limit the capacities of
organized labor for activism. Opposing firmly the use of nationwide strikes
and boycotts that fueled labor unrest during the late nineteenth century, judges
pointed to collective bargaining as acceptable instead. Judicial decisions themselves now expressed more of a laissez-faire stance than in the earlier days of
"well-regulated society." As the contours of a liberal administrative state took
shape, it operated in a society where inequality had gradually grown deeply
structurally embedded. Advancement now would be an individual phenomenon as those moved ahead who flourished amidst a social world increasingly

defined by corporate interests and the middle class. In the courts as well, individualized treatment and personal responsibility for one's own rehabilitation became the hallmark of the day.

Economic depression during the 1890s, which led to the collapse of local patronage arrangements, combined with the declining political fortunes of the Democratic party to weaken the fragile Democratic alliance between Yankees and Irish-Americans that had governed Boston since the 1870s. As Irish ward leaders started to act independently, middle class Progressivism moved to contain them through "good government" attacks on their system of patronage, long so artfully exploited by the Yankees. Despite Progressivism these new independent ward bosses would establish the Irish as an enduring political force in Boston. In the 1890s, deteriorating economic conditions only reinforced the fiscal conservatism of Nathan Matthews. Always slow to spend under the best of conditions, economic downturn in 1893 aroused his alarm about what he termed "the insidious encroachment of socialism" and caused him to embark on more spending cuts rationalized by an ideal of self-help (Blodgett, 1984, p. 99). Brusquely, Matthews rejected all proposals to increase municipal outlays to limit unemployment among the laboring classes. With no significant city or state public relief program, hard times exacerbated "patterns of dependence among the urban poor" and enhanced "the role of ward [leaders as a cushion] . . . against privation" (p. 100). Thus, one primary consequence of the depression was to "radically expan[d] the power of . . . [those] men who ran the wards" (p. 100).

The fragile multiethnic Democratic alliance in Boston—built on the interplay of power in the national, state, and municipal arenas—crumbled after 1894 (Blodgett, 1894, p. 100). What arose in its place was a hotbed of factionalism. Nonetheless, Democrats made one last major effort at cross-class collaboration in the wielding of urban power. In this effort to reestablish community, they chose as mayor Josiah Quincy, who served in that office from 1896 to 1899.

The willingness of the Irish to support Quincy's candidacy reinforced the view of him held by his Yankee brethren as "a Mugwump who had long since lost his virtue" (Blodgett, 1984, p. 101). Yet the same activities that produced political marginality in Yankee eyes strengthened him as a prospective candidate for the foundering Democratic alliance. Quincy had risen to prominence in 1886 with his election to the General Court, as the state legislature was known. His successful campaign, won the same year that O'Brien lost his bid for mayoral reelection, was accomplished with strong support of the relatively militant and activist Knights of Labor (p. 101). In the Republican-dominated legislature, this mayor, Boston's second by the name of Josiah Quincy, rapidly emerged as a leader of the Democratic minority as well as a party manager and power broker of considerable repute (p. 101).

Among Quincy's major legislative accomplishments was a much admired modernization of the state's labor law that was strongly rooted in English precedent—still influential in the commonwealth. His knowledge and views were far from parochial as he had been an avid student of the socialist British Fabian writings and of the philosophy and practice of continental urban governance (Blodgett, 1984, p. 101). Possessed of strong national political connections as well as local ones, Quincy spent much of the year of 1893 in Washington "helping President Cleveland swap patronage for votes during the fight to repeal the Sherman Silver Purchase Act" (p. 101). Building on this potent combination of national prominence, socialist ideas, and a strong constituency amidst the ranks of labor, Quincy embarked on what appeared to many to be "the most far-reaching municipal experiment in America" (p. 101). It would attempt to institutionalize the patronage based system of social insurance initiated by his predecessors. In the eyes of his critics, Quincy's efforts would be villified as a "premature adventure in municipal socialism" (p. 101). Lomasney, one of Boston's most powerful of the new style of independent Irish ward leaders spoke scornfully of Quincy's "visionary ideas on government" and worked assiduously to obstruct them (*Boston Herald*, Dec. 11 and 13, 1925; Silverman, 1977; both cited in Blodgett, p. 103).

In much of Europe, the 1890s were years when working-class militancy was met by the middle class in the conciliatory political compromise that came to be known as social democracy. Closer to home in cities across the United States, this tension between labor and the middle class was met by decisive court action to weaken the power of labor in terms of strike and boycott activity, on the one hand, and the rise of a predominantly middle-class Progressivist reform movement, on the other. In Boston, where the middle class had in growing numbers abandoned the city to ethnic ward leaders and their constituencies for residences in the traditional New England towns that constituted the inner suburbs, labor retained a stronger voice. Politics in Boston veered in a direction aptly characterized as closer to socialism—if only for a limited time.

In the crisis of the 1890s, Quincy saw not an occasion for fiscal conservatism but an opening for movement toward "a more collectivist future" (Blodgett, 1984, p. 102). Fully aware of the heightened historic significance of the impending turn of the century (so extravagantly commemorated in the capitals of Europe and celebrated in the famed Vienna Exposition), Quincy articulated a vision that has been described as "oddly reminiscent of Edward Bellamy's urban utopia" (p. 102). Throughout his administration, Quincy sought "to bring Bostonians together, despite their differences, in a spirit of advancing civic pluralism" to spur action in concert for "a common cause" (Blodgett, 1984, p. 102). Writing in *Arena,* the journal of radical reformers in Boston, Quincy opined: "The people of a city constitute a community in all which that significant term implies; their interests are inextricably bound up together, and everything which promotes the well-being of a large part of the population benefits all" (Quincy, 1897; cited in Blodgett, p. 102).

In his pursuit of this collectivist vision, Quincy instituted an expansive system of "participatory bureaucracy" and radically extended the scope of the city's agencies (Blodgett, 1984, p. 102). In this development of large-scale urban institutions, Quincy was much in step with other American cities that also developed new institutions to promote social order (Wiebe, 1966). However, Quincy diverged in the nature of the institutions he sought to provide. Moving boldly to establish new departments and committees, Quincy sought not just the support but also the active involvement of each of the city's myriad classes and ethnic groups in the enterprise of making the city function. Suburban Republican merchants with business interests in the city were formed into a Merchant's Municipal Committee to advise the mayor on taxation and transportation (p. 102). Reformers and social workers were pressed into service on his plans for public baths, playgrounds, and gymnasiums (p. 102). Patrons of the arts were formed into committees to execute plans for public lectures and for city-sponsored art shows and concerts (p. 102).

Most important, he held out job-oriented initiatives and created incentives for them to take part in city affairs to Boston's trade unions. Specifically, Quincy expanded public works projects, which created jobs (Blodgett, 1984, p. 102). He also attempted to increase the hiring of union labor either along with or even instead of the private nonunion contractors traditionally favored by the city's ethnic ward leaders as a conduit of patronage (p. 102). The use of nonunion labor had been patronage's reply to traditional union exclusion of the Irish. Perhaps Quincy's most dramatic urban reform was an experiment in public ownership of industrial and other production facilities. Working first on a demonstration basis with Boston's famed typographical union, Quincy established a city-owned municipal printing plant as his pilot project. The mayor's desire was that this experiment in collective ownership would be "a showcase of enlightened labor relations, complete with an eight-hour day, paid holidays, and the promise of eventual retirement pensions" (p. 102).

At the same time that Quincy's innovations attracted considerable attention nationwide, they elicited much skepticism at home from a variety of diverse sources. Pointing to the expansive public spending that his innovations involved and the extensive supply of jobs that it produced, some interpreted his enterprises as "an ingenious new version of the Jacksonian spoils system" of political patronage (Blodgett, 1984, p. 102). Despite Quincy's reelection to a second two-year term in 1897, criticism of his ventures continued. Maintenance of deference on the part of the Irish-American constituencies through patronage was one thing, but Quincy's publicly funded social experiments substantially outpaced the beliefs about what constitutes a legitimate use of state authority on the part of Yankee citizens in the Democratic party of his day. Among Boston's social elite, the tendency to reserve judgment on Quincy's ventures was strong. Unease among the Brahmin gentry is typified by George H. Lyman's remark to Henry Cabot Lodge that "[t]he curious thing about it all is that I haven't found one single Democrat of first-class standing who has been willing to tell me personally that he believes in Josiah Quincy" (Letter of George H. Lyman to Henry Cabot Lodge, Dec. 23, 1897, Lodge Papers, Massachusetts Historical Society; cited in Blodgett, p. 103).

Despite this consternation among his peers, Quincy's own concern centered on the Irish ward leaders in whom he saw more of a political threat (Blodgett, 1984, p. 103). His efforts to rechannel contracting of city work that had previously gone to nonunion labor away from them and towards the city's trade unions raised especially thorny issues. This was because contracting of the city's low-wage jobs to nonunion labor (heavily Irish-American who tended to be excluded from union membership) had traditionally been arranged through city aldermen and had constituted a primary source of patronage in the city (p. 103). Others of Quincy's initiatives brought large numbers of "good government" reformers into his administrative orb with what often seemed to be little tangible benefit. Initially, Quincy managed to allay the discontent of ward leaders and to co-opt them by naming them to an advisory city leadership council, which became known as the Board of Strategy. This was similar to a tactic employed by Maguire's Democratic city committee during the 1870s (p. 103). Eventually, however, a welfarist approach to social order grew expensive and came to be seen as an unsupportable financial drain. The tenuous cooperative efforts of this Board collapsed over the issue of city expenditures which Quincy recognized had grown excessive (p. 103). The mayor attempted to disengage expenditure decisions from the influence of ward leaders among the city council members and aldermen by reserving them to experts in scientific management but that change brought cries of elitism (p. 103). This weakened Quincy politically and left him vulnerable to his leading critic among the ward leaders, Lomasney, as well as a rebellious city council and political adversaries in the Republican-dominated state legislature (p. 103). The spending controversy effectively brought to a close Quincy's bold experiment or what some critics termed his "insolvent utopia" (Copeland, *Harpers Weekly,* 44 (June 16, 1900): 549; cited in Blodgett, p. 103). It also brought down the curtain on the fragile Irish-Yankee Democratic coalition.

During the ensuing decade of 1900 to 1910, party unity among Democrats was completely lost (Blodgett, 1984, p. 103). Instead, feuds and bargaining produced transitory coalitions as individual Irish party leaders sought to lend their support to local candidates to enhance their own power and positions (p. 104). In this effort, they were constrained neither by partisan identity nor ethnic fraternity. Lomasney ushered in the new era when he worked to ensure the defeat of Irish Democratic candidate Patrick Collins and then drew strength from the patronage bestowed by an appreciative Republican mayor (p. 104). During the decade of the ascendancy of Irish Democrat John F. Fitzgerald to the mayoralty, "freewheeling maneuvers of the Irish leaders did not always cancel each other out, but they enforced a factionalism among their followers that sometimes verged on ethnic fratricide" (p. 104). Yankee Democrats largely shifted their focus to state politics where, with Quincy's help, unity was successfully restored to the Commonwealth's minority party (p. 104).

Coalition Building and the Rise of Patronage Politics

As Bridges (1984) has shown in her brilliant study of the rise of machine politics in New York, the politicians of the urban Northeast in these years faced a distinctive challenge. Specifically, they needed to forge a majoritarian consensus amidst an electorate that had recently been broadened by the elimination of restrictions on suffrage. Lacking extensive personal wealth or resources on which to draw, politicians from the late 1840s on, Bridges argues, drew on the only resources available to them: jobs, services, and a sort of general assurance of help in times of need.

Careful study of patterns of plea bargaining through mid-nineteenth century suggests, however, that at least one other resource was available to political parties competing for the support of voters, namely, concessions or grants of episodic leniency in cases appearing before the courts. During the Jacksonian era, the tradition of episodic leniency, with its roots in the British common law, was reworked into an emergent process of plea bargaining to promote political stabilization and to help legitimate democratic institutions. Later, during the mid- to late nineteenth century, as political parties jostled for dominance in Boston, plea bargaining underwent a transformation. Still very much a mechanism in the politics of creating consent, concessions on the part of the court increasingly began to be crafted narrowly to appeal to specific groups in a city that, in political terms, grew increasingly fragmented as the twentieth century dawned.

In a political context where electoral shifts that ushered in new incumbents to high office had frequently resulted in court reorganizations as well and the turning out of all currently sitting judges, the ability to deliver leniency before the court emerged as a means of strengthening constituent support. This is not to suggest corruption in individual cases but rather a capacity to ensure that mitigating circumstances were fully considered or to see that certain kinds of cases, notably drunkenness, were not treated with undue harshness. The practice of patronage was a tradition that had been well established at the state level by the early 1800s. What was new in the 1840s was the rise of party politics and, subsequently, of patronage at the city level.

That the practice of patronage was already operating in the legal sphere at the state level in Massachusetts by 1806 is indicated by Republican Joseph Story's recommendation in that year that "state notaries [ought to] be replaced by federal officials who would constitute a small learned, able body of men giving uniformity and technical precision to the authentication of documents." Moreover, he concluded, "in this way in Massachusetts a Republican would at least hold . . . office. You know that we are now systemically excluded" (Story as cited in Goodman, 1964, p. 146).

While Jefferson had urged moderation in patronage efforts to woo wavering federalists, the patronage policies of Republicans, once they gained office briefly at the state level in the Commonwealth in 1806, stood in stark contrast to Jefferson's subtlety. Goodman (1964) notes that "long exclusion from office coupled with Jefferson's gradualism created a large, pent-up demand for rewards" (p. 149). For the first time, Massachusetts saw "rotation in office . . . as Republicans abolished jobs filled by Federalists and staffed new ones with their own followers" (p. 150). The position of state treasurer and notaries who were selected by the General Court "began to change hands as parties alternated in control of the State House" (p. 150). Justices of the peace were a favorite plum (p. 150).

Goodman (1964) points out that "when Jeffersonians captured the governorship, they liberally commissioned new justices of the peace whose numbers increased successively with each switch [of the party] of the executive" (p. 150). When Republicans sought control over higher-level judicial posts and Federalists proved hard to dislodge, "the solution was to alter the structure of the courts, creating new tribunals and new positions" (p. 150). "Office or no office you know is now the question," an observer wrote, "every man wants, each man is best and all must be accommodated" (p. 151). In 1810, for example, abolition of the old court of common pleas eliminated the positions of fifty-four justices and created jobs for eighteen Republicans on the new circuit court—a sweeping example of institutional housecleaning (p. 152).

Thus, the practice of enmeshing the courts in the web of patronage was well established at the state level by the 1820s. When local party politics crystallized in the 1840s, it was a natural step that the courts be incorporated into that system of patronage too. In this context, plea bargaining emerged as an adaptable vehicle for extending patronage beyond the occasional promise of a job as a court official to broader grants of leniency to citizens themselves.

By reducing court costs, the practice of bargaining responded to a leading contemporary criticism of the judiciary and reduced the likelihood of extralegal or politically subversive actions to right perceived wrongs. By creating gratitude and perhaps a feeling of indebtedness through concessions, the court could promote allegiance to existing political authorities and possibly divide the existing party loyalties of the defendants. Since the alternative was the relatively harsh penalty formally prescribed by law, a defendant faced considerable pressures to comply and participate. Interestingly, the fact that Massachusetts had an especially punitive habitual offender law by the early nineteenth century meant that compliance, in the first instance with a plea of guilty that produced a conviction, created cumulatively enhanced pressures to comply should the defendant reappear before the court later on another charge—now as a repeat offender already convicted of a prior offense.

Ethnic Politics and the Socializing Role of Middle-Level Institutions

At the local level, the enmeshing of Boston's public institutions in politics is well demonstrated by the debate over Boston's public hospitals and a parallel debate over control of the police. Public hospitals during the nineteenth century were clearly seen as vehicles of social control, which, as Vogel (1980) notes, "would help cope with the masses of threatening and increasingly alien poor crowding the city" (p. 24). Dr. Francis H. Brown, founder of Boston's Children's Hospital, argued that the institution would "commence the education of the poorer classes" (p. 25). In this way, patients would be brought "under the influence of order, purity and kindness" (p. 24). Here the affinity to Foucault's vision of the socializing influence of society's middle-level institutions is uncanny.

Vogel (1980) points out that, in the view of these hospitals' supporters, "[s]ociety profited not just by saving these workers but also by rekindling in them their faith in the social order" (p. 26). A fund-raising appeal for the New

England Hospital for Women and Children observed that "in no possible manner can the Commonwealth be more directly benefited than in the restoration of its industrious women to their daily work, as their influence is strong for good over the idle and worthless classes" (p. 26).

Underlying this interest in the stewardship of the privileged and the education of the lower classes was a concern for preserving order, both social and political. An article in the *Boston Evening Transcript,* a local newspaper, stated: "The only sure way to reconcile labor to capital is to show the laborer by actual deeds that the rich man regards himself as the Steward of the Master" ("Fireside," *Boston Evening Transcript,* Jan. 22, 1879; cited in Vogel, 1980, p. 27).

Policing also exhibited the subtle influence of patronage and politics. As Wilbur R. Miller (1977) notes in his well-known comparative study of the nineteenth-century police in England and the United States, the style and structure of the American police lent itself to politicization. In England, Sir Robert Peel, the founder of the British police, had insisted forcefully that appointments and promotions be kept free of political patronage (p. 2). In the United States, such a model seemed too authoritarian, intrusive, and susceptible to state manipulation. It was feared that such a professional police would "acquire the habit of looking with indifference upon the public interests . . ." (p. 17).

The Courts, Sentencing Policy, and the Mayoral Elections

In this light, the period of political crossover between the 1860s and 1900s, when the Irish moved from outgroup to a position of political power in Boston, presents a fine laboratory in which to explore for evidence of linkages between politics and the courts. Here I examine changes in the extent and kinds of concessions granted, the types of offenses that met with leniency, and the distribution of concessions among occupational, ethnic, and racial groups.

Analysis of data for the years 1860–1890 show that, for cases of drunkenness, guilty pleas and concessions, which had been relatively infrequent during the earlier part of the century, evidence a sharp rise beginning in 1860. Guilty pleas reach 60 percent of all pleas entered by 1860 and 97 percent in 1880. Data for 1880 show that, in contrast to other years that follow an economic downturn, guilty pleas plummet and concessions shrink for many offenses—except for drunkenness, where the guilty plea rate virtually reaches its nineteenth-century high and concessions grow stronger. Interestingly, this was just four years before O'Brien was elected Boston's first Irish mayor. Insofar as drunkenness cases primarily affected the Irish—either because they drank overtly in public houses or because of discrimination against them in law

TABLE 8.3. Growing Frequency of Probation

1870	0%
1880	1.2%
1890	0%
1900	5.7%
1910	17.7%
1920	31.1%

enforcement—increasing concessions for drunkenness may reflect an effort to win the appreciation and loyalty of Irish voters and to forestall political challenge.

During these years, probation emerges as a formal court practice building on its informal roots in the humanitarian work of John Augustus during the 1840s. Among the cases that I studied, the share of defendants placed on probation rose steadily from none at all in 1870 to 31.1 percent in 1920 (see table 8.3). The courts also began to use continuances as a more informal supervisory mechanism. In my sample, one sees the share of cases continued at least once rise from 12.1 percent in 1870 to 68.4 percent in 1920 (see table 8.1).

Changing Patterns of Concessions and Their Social Incidence

Analysis of changing patterns of concessions and their incidence across persons of various social groups coming before the court that produced findings that prove quite interesting. Examination of the incidence of concessions on a case by case basis focused especially on the 1880s when the ethnic ward bosses mounted their challenge for political control.

Not surprisingly, defendants before this court tended to be drawn from the lower ranks of the city's class structure. They were, for the most part, laborers, small traders, petty artisans, and handicraftsmen. In 1830, fully 24 percent of all defendants in the random sample cases were laborers. Another 24 percent included traders, woodsawyers, bricklayers, truckmen, a plasterer, a milkman, and other comparable trades. Only about 5 percent of the defendants held professional, or what later came to be known as white-collar, occupations. Of the remainder, 21 percent of the defendants were women or minors and a few percent more were mariners. In all, 17 percent of the cases were left blank. Thus, the defendants in 1830 were quite representative of the petty artisanal and commercial base of the city's class structure of the day.

TABLE 8.4. Largest Northern Urban Black
Populations, 1860

City	Black Population	% of Total Population
Philadelphia	22,185	3.9
New York City	12,472	1.5
Brooklyn, New York	4,313	1.6
Cincinnati, Ohio	3,737	2.3
Boston	2,261	1.3

Source: Hollis, Lynch, *The Black Urban Condition* (New York, 1973), p. 4.

Interestingly, complainants were also heavily drawn from those groups in the year 1830 for which data are most complete. As the nineteenth century progressed, laborers, in particular, became more and more numerous among the defendants listed in the docket as they did in the class structure of the city.

In racial terms, the docket also provides interesting findings. Despite the fact that Boston had an extremely small and proportionally declining black population during the early nineteenth century, blacks were overrepresented in the docket. They constitute fully 5 percent of the defendants listed in the docket. (See tables 8.4 and 8.5.) Whether this reflects selective enforcement of the law is difficult to say but blacks clearly are disproportionately represented among the city's defendants. (See table 8.6.) While only suggestive, it is worth noting that Boston was also one of the most racially segregated northern cities of this period. (See table 8.7.)

Gender distinctions are also evident. In 1830, approximately 13 percent of all defendants were women. What is most noticeable is that women are cited far less often than men in the complaints of crimes against property or persons. However, they are greatly over-represented among complaints for crimes against morals.

TABLE 8.5. Black Population of Boston, 1830–1860

Year	Total Population of Boston (thousands)	Black Population	% of Total Population
1830	61.4	1,875	3.1
1840	84.4	1,988	2.4
1850	136.9	1,999	1.5
1860	177.8	2,261	1.3

Source: Peter R. Knights, *Plain People of Boston, 1830–1860* (New York, 1971), p. 29.

TABLE 8.6. Index of Dissimilarity
Showing Residential Segregation of
Blacks and Whites in 1860[a]

Boston	61.3
Chicago	50.0
Cincinnati	47.9
Indianapolis	47.2
Philadelphia	47.1
New York	40.6

Source: Ira Berlin, Slaves without Masters (New York, 1974), p. 257.

[a]Boston's ward six (Beacon Hill area) accounted for more than one-third of the Index of Dissimilarity for that city. A higher index value denotes greater segregation.

Among the most interesting and controversial findings is that persons of Irish or Irish-American ancestry moved from a proportional presence in the docket in 1830 to a clear over-representation by 1880. However, the shift was not as strong as might have been expected. Whereas in 1830, 23 percent of all defendants in the random sample were identifiable as of Irish ancestry or nativity, the proportion had climbed to 34 percent by 1880. However, by 1880, the population of Irish descent had grown too. Irish nativity alone constituted approximately one fourth of the population of Boston—with persons of Irish descent being, obviously, much more numerous.

What is particularly interesting is that those of Irish ancestry, for whatever reason, constitute a far greater share of the drunkenness cases in the docket than they do of the caseload as a whole. In 1880, persons of Irish ancestry constituted 44 percent of the defendants in drunkenness cases. Thus, drunkenness cases involved the Irish very disproportionately and were likely to be highly visible in the Irish wards of the city; leniency in these cases could have had strong symbolic effect.

In terms of concessions from 1870 onwards, leniency was concentrated in three practices—use of fines rather than imprisonment from 1870 to 1890; reliance on formal and informal probation in guilty plea cases from 1900 on; and reduction in amount of fines. Concessions continued to be evident in larceny cases in terms of the probability of receiving a more mild fine or, increasingly, another penalty such as probation rather than a harsher term of imprisonment (see table 8.8). While fines were also frequent in assault cases, this was not more likely where a plea of guilty was entered. After 1900 "other" penalties became more frequent in guilty plea cases. Drunkenness cases,

TABLE 8.7. Paupers and Prisoners: Their Race, Age and Nativity (Massachusetts, 1850)

| | Total | Native | | Foreign | | | Whites | | Free Colored | | | | Age | | |
		In State	Out of State	Ireland	Germany	Other or Unknown	M	F	Black M	Black F	Mulatto M	Mulatto F	<14	≥14 and <24	24+
Whole Number of Criminals Convicted Within Year	7250	3366		3884											
Imprisoned June 1, 1850	1236	653		583											
Total Convicts in Penitentiaries, 1850	431	170	130	74	3	54	389	0	34	0	8	0	0	165	266
Persons in Jails and Houses of Correction	1215	410	222	443	7	133	906	212	69	17	12	8	140	458	617
Paupers in Poor Houses June 1, 1850	3,712	2488	218	803	13	190	1947	1676	32	38	11	8	800	365	2547

Sources: Statistics of the United States, Seventh U.S. Census Compendium, 1850, Tables CLXXIV, CLXXVI, CLXXVII, CLXXVIII, pp. 164–5.

TABLE 8.8. Probabilities of Final Case Dispositions (Stratified Sample)

	Larceny		Assault and Battery		Common Drunkard		Drunkenness		Nightwalking	
	Pleads Guilty	Pleads Not Guilty	Pleads Guilty	Pleads Not Guilty	Pleads Guilty	Pleads Not Guilty	Pleads Guilty	Pleads Not Guilty	Pleads Guilty	Pleads Not Guilty
1870										
Other than Guilty or Not Guilty	.1333	.0000	.0000	.1053	.0556	.0000	.0000	.0000	.0000	.0000
Not Guilty	.0000	.3500	.0000	.2237	.0000	.0000	.0000	.2667	.0000	.3333
Other than fine/imprisonment	.0000	.0499	.0714	.0000	.1111	.0000	.0000	.0000	.5556	.0000
Fine	.6665	.2500	.7144	.6151	.1667	.0000	.9677	.6666	.0000	.0000
Imprisonment	.2001	.3500	.2142	.0000	.1667	1.0000	.0323	.0667	.4444	.6666
1880										
Other than Guilty or Not Guilty	.0770	.1667	.0588	.0385	.0000	.0000	.0000	.0000	.0000	.0909
Not Guilty	.0000	.3332	.0000	.1154	.0000	.0000	.0000	.0000	.1176	.0909
Other than fine/imprisonment	.0769	.0000	.1765	.0769	.0944	.0000	.0000	.0000	.2353	.0908
Fine	.3076	.1666	.5294	.6528	.0000	.0909	1.0000	.6667	.0000	.0000
Imprisonment	.5385	.3333	.2353	.1154	.8500	.9091	.0000	.3333	.6471	.7272
1890										
Other than Guilty or Not Guilty	.0000	.0000	.0909	.0455	.0000	.0000	.0000	.0000	.2000	.0000
Not Guilty	.0000	.2500	.0000	.1364	.0000	.4000	.0000	.1333	.0000	.1333
Other than fine/imprisonment	.0000	.0000	.0000	.0455	.5000	.0000	.0455	.0667	.0000	.0000
Fine	.5454	.2499	.6294	.6362	.0000	.0000	.3181	.2666	.1332	.0666
Imprisonment	.4546	.5000	.2797	.0430	.5000	.6000	.6363	.5333	.6667	.7999

1900									
Other than Guilty or Not Guilty	.0000	.1000	.0000	.1905	.0000	.0000	.0000	.0000	.1429
Not Guilty	.0000	.2500	.0000	.1904	.0000	.0000	.0625	.0000	.1428
Other than fine/imprisonment	.2222	.0500	.1053	.0000	.0000	.1428	.0625	.6667	.0000
Fine	.3337	.1500	.6843	.5238	.0000	.2379	.1874	.0000	.0000
Imprisonment	.4444	.4500	.2104	.0952	1.0000	.6192	.7333	.3333	.7142
1910									
Other than Guilty or Not Guilty	.0000	.1786	.0588	.0741	.0000	.0000	.0000	.0000	.0000
Not Guilty	.0476	.1428	.0000	.1852	.0000	.0000	.0000	.0000	.1667
Other than fine/imprisonment	.4762	.0715	.5294	.1852	.0000	.5789	.3182	.6924	.6666
Fine	.1429	.0714	.2941	.3703	.0000	.0000	.0000	.0000	.0000
Imprisonment	.3333	.5357	.1177	.1852	1.000	.4211	.6818	.3076	.1666
1920									
Other than Guilty or Not Guilty	.0000	.3333	.3001	.3334	No valid cases		Drunkenness moved to separate docket	.5000	.0000
Not Guilty	.0000	.3334	.0000	.1481				.2500	.1765
Other than fine/imprisonment	.0000	.0000	.3500	.2592				.2500	.2353
Fine	1.0000	.0000	.2999	.2222				.0000	.0000
Imprisonment	.0000	.3334	.0500	.0370				.0000	.5881

TABLE 8.9. Effect of Plea on Amount of Fine

	All Cases	Larceny	Assault & Battery	Common Drunkard	Drunkenness	Night Walking
1870						
b	−6.0740***	−16.0666***	+1.9636	All pled	+.0500	No valid
Constant	11.0740	27.1666	9.6363	guilty	3.0000	cases
Significance	.0002	.0070	.4633		.8094	
N	110	16	21	3	70	
1880						
b	−2.5455*	+1.5000	−1.4313	All pled	−.9571*	No valid
Constant	7.0750	7.5000	9.7647	guilty	2.8571	cases
Significance	.0635	.5226	.6430		.0901	
N	74	6	26		34	
1890						
b	−.5559	+1.4444	−1.5294	No	+.3095	No variation
Constant	7.1212	10.0000	8.5294	valid	4.5000	in fine
Significance	.5509	.8227	.2032	cases	.4080	amount
N	79	10	30		33	
1900						
b	−1.9100	−1.5000	−1.2307	No	+.3333	No valid
Constant	10.7500	13.3333	10.0000	valid	6.6666	cases
Significance	.2513	.8047	.5145	cases	.9132	
N	45	9	24		8	
1910						
b	+5.7692	+17.5000	−.5000	No valid	No valid	No valid
Constant	9.2307	12.5000	8.5000	cases	cases	cases
Significance	.3157	.5080	.8595			
N	22	5	15	0	0	0
1920						
b	−1.4285	All	+.8333	No	Drunkenness	No
Constant	11.4285	plead	10.000	valid	moved to	valid
Significance	.7882	guilty	.7342	cases	separate	cases
N	8	1	12		docket	

Legend: *** = ≤ .01, ** = ≤ .05, * = ≤ .10

while initially slightly more likely to receive fines when guilty pleas were entered, grew especially likely to receive other penalties from 1900 onward.

Leniency was also extended for guilty pleas in terms of the amount of a fine for larceny in 1870 and drunkenness in 1880—a time when Yankees sought to maintain order without the help of Irish allies (see tables 8.9 through 8.12). Temporally, leniency was evident with special clarity in use of fines and other penalties in 1900, just after the Depression of the 1890s. It is possible

TABLE 8.10. Effect of Plea on Duration of Sentences

	All Cases	Larceny	Assault & Battery	Common Drunkard	Drunkenness	Night Walking
1870						
b	+.4331	+7.8571	−.3333	+.9583	+.5000	+.7500
Constant	3.7407	7.1428	2.0000	2.6250	2.0000	2.5000
Significance	.7165	.2289	.6667	.1181	6667	.6328
N	50	9	4	28	3	6
1880						
b	−.7443	+1.7500	+1.0000	−3.4888	None	−1.6136
Constant	7.1818	5.2500	3.0000	8.6000	plead	9.2500
Significance	.5431	.7016	.3992	.2296	guilty	.3584
N	65	10	6	19		19
1890						
b	+.7500	−5.0000	No valid	−1.0000	No valid	+1.1333
Constant	4.6666	8.0000	cases	5.0000	cases	4.6666
Significance	.4674	.		.6667		.3779
N	30	2		4		22
1900						
b	−1.4986*	−.6785	−1.7500**	All plead	−1.8230	+3.0000
Constant	4.9629	4.4285	3.500	guilty	4.9000	5.0000
Significance	.0744	.5900	.0225		.2262	.2390
N	55	15	6	1	23	7
1910						
b	+.0500	+.9333	−1.7500	None	−.3571	+1.0000
Constant	3.1000	3.0666	3.7500	plead	2.5000	3.0000
Significance	.9336	.3702	.4445	guilty	.7221	.5720
N	50	22	6	1	15	5
1920						
b	None	No variation	+1.0000	No valid	Drunkenness	All
Constant	plead	in	2.0000	cases	moved to	plead
Significance	guilty	sentence	.		separate	not guilty
N	11	1	2		docket	8

Legend: *** = ≤ .01, ** = ≤ .05, * = ≤ .10

that leniency may have generally been more readily granted under such adverse economic conditions. The data from this study seem to suggest this could be so. As for leniency during the late 1800s, however, the effect of plea on magnitude of sentence is neither universal nor strong as guilty plea bargains begin to decline somewhat. Concessions start to move through other mechanisms of leniency—notably repeated continuances (as an informal sort of probation) followed by dismissal of the case which left no record. Before that change,

TABLE 8.11. Effect of Plea on Amount of Fine Controlling for Career

	All Cases	Larceny	Assault & Battery	Common Drunkard	Drunkenness	Night Walking
1870						
Guilty Plea	−6.0984	−16.0666	1.9636	All plead G	−.0169	No cases
Significance	.7768	.0070***	.4633	—	—	
Career	2.0243	No careers	No careers	No careers	4.01669	
Significance	.7768	—	—	—	.8927	
Constant	11.0740	27.1666	9.6363	—	3.0000	
N	110	16	21	3	70	0
1880						
Guilty Plea	.8801	1.5000	−1.4857	All plead NG	−.9000	No cases
Significance	.7708	.5226	.6391	—	.1269	
Career	−2.8217	No careers	1.0392	No careers	2.2000	
Significance	.0448**	—	.8539	—	.0646*	
Constant	7.3252	7.5000		—	2.8000	
N	72	6	26	1	32	0
1890						
Guilty Plea	−.5502	1.4444	−1.5242	No cases	.3095	All fines constant
Significance	.5577	.8227	.2133	—		
Career	.6743	No careers	−.2839		No careers	
Significance	.8188	—	.9057	.4080	—	
Constant	7.1007	10.0000	8.5461		4.5000	
N	79	10	30	0	33	3
1900						
Guilty Plea	−1.9100	−1.5000	−1.2307	No variance	.3333	No cases
Significance	.2513	.8047	.5145		.9132	
Career	No careers	No careers	No careers		No careers	
Significance	—	—	—		—	
Constant	10.7500	13.3333	10.0000		6.6666	
N	45	9	24	1	8	0
1910						
Guilty Plea	5.7692	17.5000	−.5000	No cases	No cases	No cases
Significance	.3157	.5080	.8595			
Career	No careers	No careers	No careers			
Significance	—	—	—			
Constant	9.2307	12.5000	8.5000			
N	22	5	15	0	0	0
1920						
Guilty Plea	−1.4285	No variance	.0000	No cases	Drunkenness	No cases
Significance	.7882		1.0000		moved to	
Career	No careers		No careers		separate docket	
Significance	—		—			
Constant	11.4285		10.0000			
N	8	1	7	0		0

TABLE 8.12. Effect of Plea on Duration of Sentence

	All Cases	Controlling for Career				
		Larceny	Assault & Battery	Common Drunkard	Drunkenness	Night Walking
1870						
Guilty Plea	.5242	7.8571	−.3333	.9583	.5000	.7500
Significance	(.6638)	(.2289)	(.6667)	(.1181)	(.6667)	(.6328)
Career	−1.8244	No careers	No careers	No careers	All have careers	No careers
Significance	(.4718)	—	—	—	—	—
Constant	3.8083	7.1428	2.0000	2.6250	2.0000	2.5000
N	50	9	4	28	3	6
1880						
Guilty Plea	−1.2818	1.7500	1.0000	−3.4534	All plead NG	−2.3636
Significance	(.3165)	(.7016)	(.3992)	(.2423)	—	(.1842)
Career	−2.5453	No careers	No careers	−3.1925	1.6666	−6.0000
Significance	(.1709)	—	—	(.5002)	(.6667)	(.1307)
Constant	7.7988	5.2500	3.0000	8.9192	1.6666	10.0000
N	65	10	6	19	7	19
1890						
Guilty Plea	.7107	−5.0000		−1.0000	No cases	1.0727
Significance	(.5032)	(.)		(.6667)		(.4243)
Career	−.7058	No careers	No cases	No careers		−.7272
Significance	(.8069)	—		—		(.8193)
Constant	4.7058	8.0000		5.0000		4.7272
N	30	2	0	4	0	22
1900						
Guilty Plea	−1.5000	−.7500	−1.8333	No cases	−1.8230	3.0000
Significance	(.0878)*	(.5838)	(.0486)*		(.2262)	(.2390)
Career	−.5000	No careers	.3333		No careers	No careers
Significance	(.8273)	—	(.6749)		—	—
Constant	5.0000	4.5000	3.5000		4.9000	5.0000
N	54	14	6	0	23	7
1910						
Guilty Plea	.1711	.9397	−1.4000	No variance	−.1666	All plead G
Significance	(.7852)	(.3875)	(.5898)		(.8765)	—
Career	−.2108	−.0421	−1.4000		No careers	No careers
Significance	(.8204)	(.9741)	(.5898)		—	—
Constant	3.1252	3.0722	4.1000		2.5000	—
N	48	22	6	1	14	4
1920						
Guilty Plea	All plead NG	No variance	No variance	No cases	Drunkenness	All plead NG
Significance	—				moved to	—
Career	−1.7500				separate docket	−.6666
Significance	(.2372)					(.3153)
Constant	3.7500					3.1666
N	11	1	1	0		8

however, guilty plea bargains exert, during the 1880s, one very striking and narrowly targeted effect.

During the years just before Hugh O'Brien is elected first Irish Mayor of Boston, one sees strong concessions suddenly offered for guilty pleas in drunkenness cases. In this year, those of Irish ancestry, who were charged with drunkenness, fared slightly better than did other defendants— paying an average fine of $1.25 while others averaged $1.34. More importantly, the average fine for drunkenness fell markedly from $3.36 in 1860 and $3.35 in 1870 to $1.29 in 1880 for cases where a guilty plea had been entered. Thus, while the Irish did fare slightly better than others, the main consequence of leniency was to reduce the magnitude of penalties for all defendants for an offense primarily involving the Irish. While maintaining an appearance of equity, this was a step from which the Irish benefited disproportionately.

The Struggle for Control of Socializing Institutions

The vital role played by public institutions in winning and maintaining the political support of the electorate is underscored by the protracted battle for extensive reorganization of the courts, public hospitals, the public library, and police as the political power of the ethnic ward bosses increased during the late nineteenth century. In each case, the primary purpose of the reorganization was to transfer control over the institution from the city to the state level where urban ethnic power was relatively weak.

In 1880, Dr. David Cheever, president of the medical staff at Boston City Hospital, proposed key changes in the governance of that institution. He argued for "a restructuring of the board of trustees . . . [primarily focused on their] selection by the mayor rather than the [city] council and incorporation of the hospital as a state chartered body" (Vogel, 1980, p. 29). Vogel points out that "[a]pportionment [of trustees] by the mayor rather than by the council was preferred because the former was responsible to a city wide constituency, and thus more respectable than the [ethnic] ward bosses rising to power in the council." Cheever sought to attract as trustees "gentlemen who are perhaps not so extremely occupied by their affairs outside that they cannot devote a great deal of time to the institution" (Cheever, City Document, no. 27, Boston, 1880; cited in Vogel, p. 30). Thus, Cheever sought members of Boston's Brahmin elite who would, he felt, be more beneficial for the hospital and its staff than the "politician-trustees especially noticeable . . . during the last five or six years" (Cheever, City Document, no. 27, Boston, 1880; cited in Vogel, p. 30).

Equally important, Cheever proposed that the hospital be chartered as a state institution. Vogel (1980) notes: "The expressed fear of those favoring incorporation was that Boston City [Hospital] was becoming enmeshed in city politics" (p. 30). It was not just politics, in general, but the turn they saw Boston politics taking, which aroused unease. In response to the ward-based system of ethnic patronage politics, the medical staff viewed state incorporation as a preemptive step aimed at maintaining governance of the hospital by Boston's old moneyed elite. Vogel states:

> In reality, the hospital staff was troubled by the emergence of a new kind of city politics. Boston's new immigrant-based politics—with its professional politicians, ward leaders and patronage system—had already challenged the political hegemony of the native born merchant elite. But only the first ripples of that challenge had reached the city hospital. Two of the council's 1879 appointments to the hospital board had been opposed—Dr. Michael F. Gavin and Councilman Israel Cohen. Their selection apparently set off the campaign for incorporation that began in 1879. Incorporation was preemptive in nature. It was meant to preclude changes that might occur but had not yet occurred. (p. 30)

Thus, proponents of incorporation acted out of fear of the rising political influence of the ethnic wards.[2] Vogel (1980) observes that "the [Massachusetts] state legislature, dominated by rural and small town Protestants, recognized the threat to Boston's Protestant elite and incorporated Boston City Hospital in 1880."

Conflict over incorporation of Boston City Hospital as a state institution was part of a broader controversy being acted out in Boston during the 1870s and 1880s. That conflict centered on the class-based struggle for control of the city's public institutions. Vogel (1980) notes that "Boston's historic ruling class displayed a siege mentality in developing mechanisms to limit the discretionary power of the alien groups that were achieving political power" (p. 31).

Controversy over control of the hospitals paralleled similar struggles for control of the Boston Public Library and the police department. Vogel (1980) notes: "State incorporation duplicated the process and the statute which in 1878 had removed the Boston Public Library from the control of the city council and put it under a blue-ribbon mayoral board" (p. 31). Opponents of state incorporation of the Hospital feared similar results. It was noted that "[i]n the last annual report of the trustees they say there should be two libraries in two places, one where the literary men could frequent it, and one in another place where the masses could go" (Walter Muir Whitehill, *Boston Public Library: A Centennial History*, Cambridge, Mass., 1956, pp. 107–112, 133; cited in Vogel, p. 31).

The politics surrounding control of the Boston Police Department represented still a third struggle for institutional power. Vogel (1980) notes:

> In 1878, the state legislature removed the police from city council authority and vested control in a mayoral board; in 1885, a newly created state authority removed control of the police from Boston altogether. (p. 31)

The watershed year of 1885 was, as we have seen, the year in which Boston elected its first Irish mayor.

In the legal arena, conflict arose somewhat earlier, during the 1860s, and continued until the end of the nineteenth century. Initially, the result was a thoroughgoing reorganization of both higher and lower courts. Over the remainder of the century, original jurisdiction over an increasing number of the more serious offenses in the docket was gradually removed from the Police Court (later called the Municipal Court) to the state-controlled Superior Court. For instance, after 1860, common drunkard cases virtually disappear from the Municipal Court docket and find original jurisdiction in the Superior Court— to which they had frequently been appealed prior to that time anyway. In 1866, the old Boston Police Court, which had served as court of original jurisdiction for most offenses in Suffolk County since 1822, was terminated and a new Boston Municipal Court was established to serve as the equivalent of a county district court for Suffolk County.

Over the course of the mid- to late-nineteenth century, then, we see plea bargaining transformed as it becomes inextricably intertwined with the rise of patronage politics in the city of Boston. Still a mechanism for engaging and cultivating the consent of Bostonians to prevailing political arrangements, plea bargaining shifted gradually and imperceptibly from a vehicle for political stabilization to part of the armamentarium of patronage in the competition for power.

One interesting demonstration of a possible consonance of patterns of bargaining with social unrest during the nineteenth century lies in the relation of concessions to prevailing economic conditions. Concessions appear to have been less readily granted in good years from an economic point of view—not necessarily because of the financial conditions but perhaps because the years were traditionally politically and socially more restive as rising expectations surged.[3] In the British tradition, unrest that threatened state authority was met with the full force of the law (Brewer and Styles, 1980). As has been well documented, the nineteenth century was characterized by a series of approximately twenty-year business cycles of economic boom and bust with major economic downturns occurring in the mid- to late-1830s, 1850s, 1870s, and 1890s. Most severe among these were the downturns of the 1830s and 1890s, which constituted major economic depressions.[4]

Looking back at the tables in chapters 4 and 8 shows that patterns of concessions appear stronger just after the lean years of the late 1830s, 1850s, and 1890s—suggesting that concessions appear to have been granted more regularly during relatively quiescent years, when leniency could be afforded, to win the good will of the populace and bolster consent for democratic governance. Thus, concessions appear strong and multifaceted in 1840, 1860, and 1900 but consistently weaker in 1850, 1870, and 1890. Concessions for the year 1880 appear to assume a distinctive form due to the special political circumstance of that day.[5]

While it is generally unwise to rely too heavily on any data on crime and particularly on arrests, it is worth noting that historical trends in the homicide arrest rate for Boston over the course of the nineteenth century show sharp drops for the years 1860, 1880, and 1900. This suggests that violent crime as well as labor unrest may well have been reduced in those years—thus further opening a window for using bargained leniency as a vehicle of community-based control. By contrast, during years of turbulent unrest and of crime waves, justice may have been of a harsher sort. One major asset of plea bargaining as it operated over the course of the nineteenth century was its flexibility in enabling adaptive response to changing currents in social unrest and political challenge.

9

The Making of Post-Revolutionary Political Authority

In the years after the American Revolution, politicians worked to re-create political authority anew for a self-governing republican society (Mensch, in Kairys, ed., 1982). Central to their project was the challenge of articulating a conception of the political subject (i.e., the political actor) for a new world of self-rule during the early nineteenth century. Owing now no allegiance to Britain, how could postcolonial Americans begin to understand themselves as committed to the rules and commands of another very different sort of regime? In that drama, it turns out that the judiciary played a key and very interesting part. As they did, judges drew, among other things, on the common law tradition of leniency, particularly the practice of plea bargaining, in the American courts.

What I would like to show is that fundamental to the vision of authority and the political subject that was constructed was a very distinctive conception of freedom. It was elaborated in the common law during this period—arising particularly in the area of labor law but gradually appearing in some aspects in the criminal courts as well. This vision of freedom that came to underpin Americans' understanding of themselves as political subjects was foundational to an emerging political identity. It was an identity rooted in an idea of liberty and operationalized in citizenship as a criterion of political membership. The vision was articulated under Whig political leadership and was one that strongly reinforced the existing social order—an order that embodied increasing inequality during this period.

This notion is one with which upstart Jacksonian Democrats took exception. As a result, the story of liberalism from 1830 to 1850, when the Whig party collapsed in the United States, was that of its rise as an oppositional discourse among Democrats and of their effort to reclaim and recraft concepts of liberty and citizenship away from this notion of freedom and toward one rooted in rights that were consonant with their own experiences and interests. What this vision of freedom and the liberal Democratic contestation that it engendered has done is to direct our attention to the role of the common law and the courts as crucial components in the process of forming the new American state during the early to mid-nineteenth century.

Let me lay out briefly, first, the contours of the vision of political authority that took shape, showing how it drew on the ideology of a "rule of law" for legitimation and on the common law for much of its practical machinery. I will show that political authority, thus envisioned, strengthened both social order and hierarchy. Second, I will briefly show how a conception of freedom emerged that was drawn from labor law, embraced by the criminal courts and, finally, used as the basis for a developing concept of citizenship. I will argue that this same conception of freedom pervaded the market transactions of the day. Finally, I comment on how these developments colored the early life of liberalism.

The project of establishing political authority faced the obstacle that it was to be anchored in popular self-rule but to be constructed during the 1830s which was a period when concentration of wealth and economic inequality increased more rapidly than at any other time in the nineteenth century. Recently, historians such as Gordon Wood have shown compellingly how intensely conflicted was the social and political landscape of the early American republic. It has long intrigued scholars why such disparate life chances failed to mobilize a sustained labor-based political party or to produce a class-based political challenge once the franchise was "universally" extended—perhaps even to the institution of property itself. This enigma has long been treated under the rubric of "American exceptionalism" (Katznelson and Zolberg, 1986). Many explanations ranging from prospects for individual economic mobility, ethnic diversity that breached labor solidarity, and the rise of a politics of residence have been proffered by Sombart, Shefter, Bridges, and others to account for it. What has wrongly been downplayed, until now, in accounting for the remarkable continuity in America of popularly elected political leadership, preservation of the institution of property, and limited labor mobilization is the distinctive contribution of the common law that entered into a project of political stabilization, the legitimation of institutions of self-rule and, especially, the construction of political authority in ways that had far-reaching consequences.

Drawing on common law traditions, particularly on widely used practices of discretionary leniency, the courts fostered a new form of political authority that was both rooted in the ideology of a "rule of law" and incorporated traditional social hierarchy. In so doing, political equality was emphasized, whereas the economic inequality, manifest in those hierarchies, was not only soft-pedalled but reinforced. Articulation of a unique conception of citizenship, also profoundly influenced by the common law, further incorporated assumptions that bolstered the prevailing hierarchies of economic power and social rank.

As the franchise was extended during the 1830s and the old traditions of deference, whereby those less-privileged paradoxically elected their social "betters," began to fade, political and social elites gradually retreated from candidacy for electoral office to a less-formal position of power in which their expansive resources nonetheless continued to wield sway. As this electoral shift occurred, the attention of elites, especially in the nation's major hub of legal innovation in Boston, turned to the courts. It is the role of the courts during this crucial period to which I turn.

Reestablishing Authority: A "Rule of Law"

In the new polity, governed no longer by monarchy but rather by self-rule, there was a realization that social order must rest, not on power or coercion, but instead on popular acceptance of sovereign commands and on a sense among the people of a duty to obey. That is to say that a vision of political authority consonant with popular rule was needed. What emerged was, at first appearance, a conception of modern political authority rooted in a "rule of law"—the paradigmatic social discourse of the day. In practice, however, despite the "modernity" of the new republic, the form of authority that they constructed was composed of a unique blend of legal and traditional elements.[1] Laws and rules provided normative guidance while embeddedness in traditional social hierarchies infused that authority with an institutional base.

During the early nineteenth century, there was acute concern among both the urban political elite and other city dwellers alike about widespread crime, rioting, and unrest. At this point, local political institutions were still spare and fragmentary and thus not well equipped to deal with the turmoil. Instead, as civic leaders and city officials worked to nurture order and predictability back into public life and to cultivate the much-needed consent of newly enfranchised citizens to institutions of self-rule, they sought to adopt lines of action that were beyond reproach in the eyes of the public. Initially, they appealed to the preeminent social discourse of the day: that of the "rule of law." Drawing on its imagery, by common agreement, they argued, social life must proceed according to a body of rules specified in advance and oriented to fairness. Such rules, they contended, must apply universally to each citizen and prescribe equal treatment for every accused person before the court. Then, in a gesture ripe with the seeds of political drama, it was argued that, even when such rules depart from the popular political opinion of the moment, they must unceasingly be observed nonetheless, for only in this way could self-rule be sustained. By appealing to the widely revered "rule of law" as a basis for order, the intent was to bolster both social order and the legitimacy of existing institutions of self-rule. Rules that officials made and commands that they uttered would, it was hoped, inspire compliance because of their basis in law. Thus, the United States, like many republics, moved toward a vision of political authority of what we shall see to be a "rational-legal" sort (Weber, 1978, p. 215). Introduction of the guiding principle of a "rule of law" into a political world committed to "popular sovereignty" would produce an inherently conflicted form of authority, yet no more so than in most other modern democratic states and less so than many.

Role of the Judiciary: Implementation of "Law Rule"

In practice, the "rule of law" was established in a very particular way. Faced with social conflict and turmoil, the courts, which, along with tax collectors, were one of the few local public institutions yet in place, stepped forward as agents of the state to promote political stabilization and, ultimately, to help inculcate relations of citizenship. Among other things, judges drew on and reworked a time-honored tradition of episodic leniency (that is, frequent but irregular grants of leniency, so that it could not be counted on) from the British common law and adapted it to an age of mass politics. I have already shown that through changes in their use of the plea of nolo contendere, nol prosse, grants of immunity in exchange for testimony as a state's witness, and, especially, the emergence of plea bargaining, the courts sought to draw conflicts and grievances into the legal arena for resolution lest extralegal or political solutions be sought instead. This effort was initiated by the Federalist/National Republican/Whig elite, which increasingly came under challenge during this period of turbulence, and which sought to reconsolidate self-rule, generally, and, specifically, their own partisan power within it. By mid-nineteenth century, the majority of cases in the criminal courts were resolved not through a jury trial by peers but through these vehicles of leniency.

As we have also seen, various authors, including British historians, E. P. Thompson and Douglas Hay et al., have shown that what was distinctive about these mechanisms of leniency was that they required intercession before the court by one or more respected members of the community for leniency to be granted. Consequences of this were two. First, leniency worked proactively to create strong incentives for formation of cross-class social ties as those who were less privileged forged relations with lawyers, neighbors, and notables who could intercede on their behalf if they ran afoul of the law. The result was a system of justice that produced bonds of loyalty and reciprocity that strength-ened the existing class structure at the same time that it legitimated the political system by conveying, through the impersonal market-like regularity of plea bargaining, a formal message of universality and equality before the law. A second major consequence was a conscious effort to use these discretionary practices to enmesh those accused in the web of social membership, especially those of family and work, that had traditionally been cornerstones of customary authority and social control. This occurred through the use of intercessors and character witnesses, usually kin, neighbors, and, especially, employers in the dispensing of leniency.[2]

Forms of Authority: Rational-Legal and Traditional

The result of this invocation of the "rule of law" and concomitant turn to episodic leniency was a move during the nineteenth century in the United States toward a vision of political authority that is, at first appearance, of a rational-legal sort—that is, authority whose legitimation is based in the enact-ment of rules in law and the specification of offices in law. Introduction of this guiding principle of a "rule of law" into a political world, first republican and, then, democratic, that was committed to popular sovereignty produced an in-herently conflicted form of authority—producing an enduring tension between "law rule" and "self-rule." This tension, in some form, later comes to charac-terize most modern democratic states.

Yet, as judges focused on the problem of creating political authority anew, their reliance on tools of discretionary leniency, in addition to the powerful discourse of a "rule of law," was quite shrewd. Despite the basic post-Enlightenment modernity of the new "republic," they were crafting authority of a unique blend of rational-legal and traditional elements. Prescient leaders recognized, however, that ideology, unsupported by the stabilizing influence of participation in an integrative network of social roles, could prove a fragile basis on which to build social order. The Jacobin excesses in France during the 1790s had been vividly seared into the collective American political imagination. Local politicians sensed that, along with laws, the subjects of political authority that is solely rule-based (and thus devoid of the personal and customary imagery) required the normative guidance that comes from a secure place in the web and routines of social structure.[3] Many believed that, during the excesses of the 1790s following the Revolution in France, mobs took to the streets because they had become detached from their places in the habitual rounds and activities of everyday life (Piven and Cloward, 1979).

Because religion, social consensus, and the deference accorded status were eroding apace, the established view was that hierarchy and a sense of social position had to be sustained lest the masses be turned out as radically unconstrained individuals whose penchant for violence and excess might equal that of the French. If political stability could be had in America, the interconnected networks of social roles that honeycomb society (e.g., family, community, and, especially, work) must, it was believed, play a vital part. New uses of leniency in the courts and the "symbolic suretyship" that I have been describing were well suited to accomplish that embeddedness. In doing so, the plea bargain and other new forms of leniency linked the rule-based authority of the courts with the traditional authority that had historically served as an anchor for the socializing web of communal membership of everyday life. Conscious effort was then made to reintegrate defendants into the networks of relationships, particularly family and work, that traditionally had been a primary mechanism of customary social control.

Thus, the model of authority that emerged was a unique mix of rational-legal and traditional authority—the former basing its legitimation in enactment of rules and offices in law (and empowering a "rule of law") and the latter legitimated through enduring regard for the sacredness of custom that endowed everyday social ties with a formidable capacity for social control. Each social tie, such as householding, kinship, parenting, employment, property ownership, tax payment, borrowing, and voting, afforded society an opportunity to structure the freely made choices offered to its members about how they would behave.

Beyond the open turmoil of crime, riot, and unrest, however, political leadership of the day faced the deeper problem of how to translate the dreams of the Framers of the Constitution, in practical terms, into an enduring social and political order capable of wise political action. As a vision of political authority was articulated, an image of the political subject and of membership in the polity also congealed. In ways consonant with the corporatist approach of some European societies, American republicanism and, later, the Whigs initially conceived of political inclusion in terms of individual autonomy, though in a highly contextualized, relational sense, and in terms of duties as well as privileges (Novak, 1996). Only later, as we shall see, did the language of liberalism and a focus on rights move to center stage in American politics. Central to the vision of a new order was a distinctive concept of freedom or liberty. Its dual emphasis was on the choices of formally free persons, on the one hand, and subtle efforts to rely on constraining social hierarchies of rank and privilege, on the other. This was nowhere more powerfully expressed than in the idea of liberty and the practice of citizenship that, as we will see, took shape as the foundation of an emergent American political identity. Citizenship emerged as a constructed status of political membership that established the parameters of political behavior needed to sustain the liberty the new nation espoused. The role of citizen was a decidedly two-sided affair: rights and social membership were accorded at the same time that acceptance of material inequality—specifically in the milieu where choices would be made—was expected in return. Freedom itself came, as we shall see, to signify formal autonomy of choice that was, at the same time, powerfully constrained informally by the normative and economic structures as well as the elite policy stances of the day. Citizenship, it will become clear, assumed a more corporatist tone in America than has previously been believed, though with an unusual twist.

Traditional social hierarchy, notions of liberty, and the practice of citizenship, then, buttressed the nascent "rule of law" that was being drawn on to contain growing tension over economic inequality (despite political equality) under capitalism (Marshall, 1964). What was seized on as a tool for responding, ultimately, was education in all its many forms to inculcate an outlook that would render citizens homogeneous and their voluntary acts constructive and benign. The habits of mind that could make the new political order viable in the long run must, it was believed, be imparted both formally and informally through society's institutions, including family, schools, cultural institutions and, especially for adults and new immigrants, work and the courts. The courts' use of new mechanisms of leniency proved particularly well suited to this task.

Political Equality and Material Inequality: Threat to Property

Impetus for the making of authority and citizenship came from inequality that was mounting apace. Crime, rioting, and unrest also heightened unease. While industrialization and market development brought economic growth, fortune did not smile equally on all. Concentration of wealth intensified. In 1833, the richest 1 percent of Boston's families held one third of the city's noncorporate wealth. By 1848, their share was 37 percent, and it increased throughout the antebellum years (Pessen, 1967, pp. 1020–31). Schoolmaster George Bancroft denounced "this increasing, unequal distribution of wealth" as cause for "feud between the house of Have and the house of Want" (Schlesinger, *Age of Jackson*, pp. 159, 162–63; cited in Sellers, 1991, p. 340).[4] Rejecting the argument that property-based Lockean liberalism constituted the intellectual foundation of American democracy, Bancroft, under the influence of the German Romantics, turned instead for political inspiration to the Inner Light of Quakerism. Analyzing capitalist transformation from the standpoint of this Inner Light, Bancroft exhorted workers to respond to its spirit and to cast their lot with the Jacksonian democratic opposition to the avarice of privilege (p. 341). In Bancroft's eyes, as in others', far greater danger lay in monopoly and the inequality that it produced than in the combinations of working men (p. 341).

In accounting for the mounting concentration of wealth and for the vast poverty of the many in the cities, sources of that inequality in the capitalist economy were recognized and decried. Social observers increasingly blamed an order that, they argued, encouraged the expropriation of the fruits of the "producing many" by the "exploiting few" (Sellers, 1991, p. 338). Some began to call for change. So widespread did popular resentment become that even Samuel Clesson Allen, a pillar of Federalist orthodoxy, on retiring from Congress in 1830 protested: "All wealth is the product of labor and belongs of right to him who produces it . . . and yet how small a part of the products of its labor falls to the laboring class" (p. 339). Pointing to speculators and industrial capitalists as the source of this inequity, Allen urged resistance to their power. He argued that it must be contested as none would be voluntarily relinquished (p. 339). Applauding the opportunity to rectify inequality through "universal suffrage," Allen proclaimed that "thanks to our free institutions, the people can now do it . . . [i.e., redistribute property] without violence or wrong" (p. 339).

From the viewpoint of Boston's elite families, it was just such a tendency on the part of the masses to use newly won political rights to redress material inequality, perhaps to restructure property relations, that was most feared. Awareness of the centrality of property was strong at all levels of society. Samuel Clesson Allen contended, for example, that any effort at social reform must begin with the economy, which, he argued, shapes society "more than government, more than morals, more than religion" (Sellers, 1991, p. 339).[5] Foreshadowing the class-based discourse that would arise after the Civil War, he lamented that prevailing economic arrangements for production had "divided society into two classes, enabling 'accumulators' to impoverish 'producers' "

(Sellers, 1991, p. 339). Allen's distinction between "productive" and "unproductive hands," which can be found in Adam Smith's *Wealth of Nations* in 1776, honed in on this key social cleavage of the day.

By imputing to the producers of tangible goods a status as society's most worthy members, Allen echoed a popular view that use-value should accrue to its creators, who produced that value through labor. It was not until after the Civil War that this inequality that arose during the antebellum years would ripen in America into class conflict between organized labor and capitalists. According to the popular wisdom of the 1830s, the "mighty instruments of accumulation" and concentration of wealth were "currency, and credit, and the interest of money ... [though] they produced none of the objects of wealth" (Sellers, 1991, p. 339). Through speculation and financial manipulation, great fortunes were amassing "in stocks and bonds and notes and mortgages," while the onerous costs of a paper currency then in use fell on "the productive class and not on the capitalist" (p. 339). Despite the complexity of the new market-based society, Allen declared, "the [basic] truth cannot be concealed, that he who does not raise his own bread, eats the fruits of another man's labor" (p. 339). Depicting "non-producers, who ... [create] no equivalent ... [value] for what they consume," as "a new sort of aristocracy," Allen decried them as "more uncompromising [in] character than the feudal, or any [traditional] landed aristocracy ever [was] ..." (p. 339).

"Americanization" and Homogeneity: Imbuing Industry

As inequality grew, so did discontent, and efforts were made to contain it. Industrialists and reformers responded to unrest by embarking on a campaign to cultivate homogeneity and work discipline. During the Age of Jackson, the democratic ideology that had germinated in a benign Jeffersonian trust in the virtue of the common man assumed a more radical tone. Among the elite, attention focused on enhancing both industrious participation in the workplace and acceptance of the economic order so as to abate any threat to either property or self-rule. Education was seen as holding the key.

While the *New England Artisan* had in 1832 ceded political dominance to "the aristocracy"—Federalists and, later, National Republicans and Whigs— "who now control all the political parties of the day," the Jacksonian spirit had begun to challenge that dominance. This Democratic sensibility was articulated by George Bancroft who touted a "spirit in [every] man ... that places us in connexion with the world of intelligence and decrees of God" (Sellers, 1991,

p. 341). Because of the universality of this spirit, he argued, it was accessible to the common man as well as to the privileged (Sellers, 1991, p. 341). Striking a radically democratic Rousseauean tone, Bancroft drew the logical but, to the elite, unsettling conclusion that "the common judgment in taste, politics and religion is [therefore] the highest authority on earth, and the nearest possible approach to an infallible decision" (p. 341). Among the wealthy New England manufacturers and other Whigs, this sort of radical message put into words their most unspeakable fears about the hazards of extending the franchise.

Their worry, of course, was that the political equality provided by the vote would be seized upon by a populace convinced of its own democratic infalli-bility and used to pursue material equality as well. This concern about the danger lurking in popular desires for equality was vividly expressed by Whig educator Horace Mann.[6] As the first Secretary of the state Board of Education in Massachusetts, he spearheaded the Commonwealth's middle-class-backed campaign to dispel potential unrest by establishing public schooling.[7] Raising the spectre of socialist and communist agendas gaining acceptance in Europe, Mann noted that the nearly "universal" suffrage existing in Boston established "a community of power" and warned that "nothing but mere popular inclina-tion lies between . . . [it] and a community of everything else" (Mary Mann, 1867, pp. 143–88; cited in Sellers, 1991, p. 368). Mann was referring here, of course, to the communal ownership of communism.[8] As an antidote to that spectral vision, Mann proposed to establish common schooling. Mann's appeal to the fears of the propertied elite about the potential excesses of both mass democracy and their own representation in the legislature led Ralph Waldo Emerson to parody the message of the school campaign in the words, "you must educate [the masses] . . . to keep them from our throats" (Atkinson, 1980, pp. 458–59; cited in Sellers, p. 368). Focusing directly on the potential conse-quences of popular suffrage for property, Mann urged taxpayers to support free schools as a "barrier against . . . those [social] propensities [for change] . . . which our institutions foster" (Norton, 1986, p. 82; cited in Sellers, p. 368). Education, Mann argued, was necessary so that "the nobler faculties can be elevated into dominion and supremacy over the appetites and passions" (Nor-ton, p. 82; cited in Sellers, p. 368).[9]

The "common schooling" movement, which emphasized the pacifying ca-pacity of common experience of public schooling, originated in a widespread belief in early post-Revolutionary American society, eloquently expressed in the writings of Ben Franklin, that the only road to harmony lay through ho-mogeneity. Education was felt to be the surest means of fostering this com-monality. During the Jacksonian era, as part of a conscious effort to establish a nation that was, at once, different from Europe and resistent to its inflammatory political influence, elected officials, educators, and ministers sought to build on that homogeneity to establish a "doctrinal [and ideological] uniformity" that could be used to forge a national identity (Carlson, 1975, p. 41).

The essence of that identity was "individual freedom" or liberty (Carlson, 1975, p. 41).[10] It was the lack of common ethnicity and, thus, the need to focus national identity on a distinctive ideational content that made education and socialization so vital. Spread by means of an "Americanization" campaign, it hailed largely from religiously oriented New England and from Protestant Presbyterian stock. Its sponsors set out to found schools that could instill the "homogeneity" to lay the foundation for this common political identity (Carlson, 1975, p. 41). Quite consciously the Americanizers wanted to distinguish the new nation from Europe as "a land of freedom, equality and opportunity" (p. 42). Many thought a common national identity to be essential for reducing the smouldering sectional strife that was evident as the Civil War neared (p. 43). The result was that a "unique" national identity was forged as a country of "liberty" (p. 44). According to this outlook, the main enemies of this liberty were the great monarchies of Europe and the Roman Catholic Church, whose members were thought to be sent to America by the kings and princes of Europe to subvert the new nation (p. 44). It was the unique doctrinal content of this national identity, rooted in a commitment to "liberty," that lent special urgency to the project of educating.

As resentment among "producers" erupted, Jacksonian democratic "insurgency" flared and Irish Catholic immigration flooded the nation, Whig reformers concluded that informal socialization by parents, schools, and local communities was not enough. To instill the self-control and discipline essential to middle-class capitalist society, their efforts would, it seemed, need supplementing by formal public education. As to how important the process of instilling such values and habits of mind was, Mann opined that parents "who refuse to train up children in the way they should go, are training up incendiaries and madmen to destroy property and life, and to invade and pollute the sanctuaries of society" (Norton, 1986, p. 82; cited in Sellers, 1991, p. 368). Immigrant children, in particular, he claimed, "must be gathered up and forced into school and those who resist or impede this plan, whether parents or priests, must be held accountable and punished" (Norton, p. 82; cited in Sellers, p. 368). While schools focused on early childhood education, the courts highlighted social reformation and the cultivation of homogeneity, industry, and self-discipline among adults, especially, immigrants.[11]

Immigrant Diversity and Social Disorder

Immigrants were a major concern. Many believed that immigrants threatened the country's future, not only because they were culturally different and unfamiliar with American political values, but because they were prone to commit crimes. One Know Nothing newspaper in Albany asserted that immigrants were "ten times more likely to be arrested than native-born citizens," and that immigration represented "the chief source of crime in this county" (*Albany State Register*, Oct. 1, 6, 1855; cited in Anbinder, 1992, p. 108).[12] Responding to what was, at least, perceived as a surge of urban crime, the *Harrisburg Herald* claimed that "crime had reached epidemic proportions in all major cities" and that "[the perpetrators] are FOREIGNORS in nine cases out of ten" (p. 107). These sentiments found support in statistics of almost every major city, including Boston, which showed that immigrants "perpetrated [or, more accurately, were arrested for] crimes far out of proportion to their numbers" (p. 107).[13]

According to the press, immigrants were also swelling the rolls of paupers. Statistics from Buffalo showed that "1,436 of 1,558 paupers had been born abroad" (Anbinder, 1992, p. 108). Know Nothings alleged that the character of foreign immigration, especially the Irish, had changed. While earlier immigrants were seen as industrious and frugal, later arrivals appeared to be "simply too lazy to work" (*Cincinnati Dollar Times*, Sept. 14, 1854). Many thought that rising crime and pauperism had been produced by the European practice of "dumping" convicts and the poor in America. "From the 'refuge of the oppressed,' we have come to be the great Botany Bay of the world," lamented the *Youngstown True Observer* (Feb. 21, 1855). Social critics especially decried the large number of Catholics inhabiting the almshouses while "[their] fat sleek priests . . . buil[t] splendid cathedrals and churches" (*Quincy Patriot*, Nov. 11, 1854). Growing evidence suggests that the British government did, in fact, subsidize emigration of some paupers and convicts to America. Of Britain, it is known, for instance, that the state financed migration of 5,000 Irish paupers annually from 1847 onward (Anbinder, p. 108). In Ireland, "landlords sent . . . 50,000 destitute tenants to America" between 1845 and 1855 (p. 108). In Germany, almshouses were cleared by sending occupants to America (p. 108). Yet, the most monumental challenge was the basic one of socializing surging tides of new migrants—many unfamiliar with American ways—for meaningful participation in a new world of self-rule.

Faced with such onslaught, the courts focused on reforming the offender and on restoring him or her to the path of harmony and industry. Judges sought, in particular, to promote assimilation among immigrants. New York Know Nothing Daniel Ullmann voiced their reasoning when he observed that "where races dwell together on the same soil and do not assimilate, they can never form one great people—one great nationality" (Anbinder, 1992, p. 107). If Americans did not manage to forge "one great homogeneous race," the Know Nothings contended, social division would destroy the nation (Ullmann, 1856; *Hartford Courant*, 1856). Simmering sectional conflicts lent added urgency to this belief. Thus, nationhood emerged as the image of the unity that the society sought to foster. Because no ethnic basis for unity existed, due to the diverse origins of America's immigrant citizens, nationhood came to be understood almost entirely in terms of a common culture centered on the idea of liberty. Cultural incorporation of new immigrants into this political culture assumed special importance.

Faction and Disaffiliation: Marginals and Workingmen's Movement

Concern about the potential of popular suffrage to produce political instability or to transform property relations arose from two distinct but interrelated sources: fear of faction, on the one hand, and fear of disaffiliation, on the other. In *The Social Contract*, Jean Jacques Rousseau points out that faction, in which individuals, rather than acting autonomously, collude to promote a narrow interest, undermines and distorts democracy. Where the forces of faction are active, Rousseau contends, the interests of individuals are no longer freely expressed. Instead, they are tainted by the influence and power of others. Thus, truly democratic expression of the views of the populace is lost.

Primary among the factions of concern during the 1830s were the independent workingmen's parties and the unions established as part of the labor movement that reached its first peak of militancy during this period. These union members, comprising 20–33 percent of urban workers, actively challenged the working conditions generating the wealth that percolated so unequally through the society (Sellers, p. 338). During the mid-1830s, a rash of more than 150 strikes swept the cities of the north Atlantic seaboard (p. 338). Centering on demands for a ten-hour day, these strikes were largely successful (Dublin, 1979; Sellers, 1991, p. 338). In a development viewed by the propertied elite as particularly ominous, unions in trades that were striking received financial backing for the first time from nonstriking trades through the General Trades' Union. Stirrings of a sense of an American working-class consciousness were visible (p. 338).

If worker mobilization evoked concern, so too did the unorganized ranks of the transients, marginals, and otherwise disaffiliated afoot in the cities. These constituted society's "non-productive hands." In economic terms, such nonproducers, of which paupers were the most extreme case, were feared both as consuming more than they produced and as lacking the cast of mind for responsible political action. Though strange to us today, financiers and speculators were included in this category because their work yielded no tangible goods. However, it primarily referred to unskilled service workers such as day-laborers and seamen; social marginals such as widows, orphans, and spinsters; and, finally, the unemployed. While financiers and speculators were seen as exploitative, the unskilled and unemployed, in contrast, aroused moral, polit-ical, and social apprehension as persons devoid of the habits of mind that are conducive to social order. Renowned industrialist Abbott Lawrence emphasized the necessity of participation in work and industry in developing an appropriate cast of mind.[14] Then, bridling against the tendency to characterize speculators and financiers with marginals as "non-productive hands," Lawrence stormily defended them and observed: "We are literally all working-men; and the at-tempt to get up a 'Workingmen's party' is a libel upon the whole popula-tion . . ." (Lawrence, 1856, pp. 103–104).

It was as a potential contributor to the political dangers posed by the un-affiliated that the waves of immigrants, who were arriving from Europe, aroused particular concern. Lawrence, like many of his brethren, believed that their arrival was inevitable and queried merely how they should be treated. He observed: "It seems now certain that vast numbers will emigrate here, rich and poor, from the continent and from England. The question for us is," he noted, "How shall we treat them? . . . We have land enough for them, but have not [yet] the needful discipline to make them safe associates in maintaining our system of government" (Lawrence, 1856, p. 258). In a world of autonomous individuals, the question of into what social fabric the newly enfranchised, and, especially, recent migrants, could be integrated and what normative scheme would guide their behavior was hotly debated. Ultimately, these concerns fu-eled the projects of constructing modern political authority rooted in a "rule of law," articulating a conception of the political subject and crafting relations of citizenship.

Theorizing State Power: Authority, Legitimation, and Consent

In thinking about the state, scholars have recently emphasized power and the multiplicity of forms that it takes, solidarity and duties as part of power, state

power as "symbolic violence," and the processes whereby state power is reproduced.[15] Especially since the rise of the new institutionalism, cultural forms of
power and their preservation have been highlighted. As attention has turned
to power, authority and legitimation have been downplayed partly because
these theories accord scant attention to human agency.[16]

Power, according to Weber, is the ability to impose one's will, even over
the opposition of another (Weber, 1978, p. 53). Authority, in contrast, is well
known as "the probability that a command . . . will be [accepted and voluntarily]
obeyed . . ." (p. 53). This is because authority presumes both a right to command by the person issuing it and a duty to comply on the part of the receiver.
Authority is distinguished by the belief of a people in the legitimacy of an order
and, thus, its valid claim to their subjective acceptance of its commands (p. 213).
Under authority, commands are likely to be followed without recourse to force
or coercion. It is for this reason that authority emerges as central to the project
of self-rule.

Weber distinguishes three types of authority, each with a different basis of
legitimation. They are: traditional, charismatic, and rational-legal authority. According to Weber, their bases of legitimation lie respectively in: the sacredness
of custom, the heroic strength or exemplary qualities of a leader, or the enactment of rules and offices in law (Weber, 1978, p. 215).[17] As the groundwork for
the new Republic was set in place, a justificatory framework for state action
was needed. In constructing that schema, political leaders elaborated a vision
of why commands by the state must be obeyed. To comply was one's duty, they
claimed, because the American polity was rooted in a "rule of law." Informally,
however, they gradually began to bolster this vision of authority by reconnecting
it with the customary social hierarchies of traditional authority. These hierarchies were the honeycombed networks of social roles that reinforced the habits
of mind that foster order and harmonious living. To this end, the courts sought
to reembed defendants in that web of social membership.

The Making of Democratic Political Authority

During the turbulent years of the 1830s and 1840s, political leaders and law-
makers focused on reconstructing post-Revolutionary political authority and
on nurturing a sense of duty to obey among the populace. Responding to
disorder, the courts invoked various discretionary practices that enlisted participation of a defendant, freely given, in the disposition of his or her fate. At
the same time, judges honed the ideology of a "rule of law" with its provisions
of fairness, universality (or applicability to all), and formal equality in the treat-

ment afforded all defendants before the court to justify the actions taken to forestall disorder. By so doing, officials sought to sidestep any appearance of either particularism or coercion that the stirring democratic masses might decry as unsuited to the government of a republic.[18]

In the course of the American Revolution, the authority exercised by British colonial rule had been repudiated. In the aftermath, the task of restoring political authority fell to the popularly elected representatives of the new republic. Because the new form of authority being set in place was primarily a rational-legal one, deriving from reliance on a "rule of law," the role of the courts was central. To reassert political authority, recognition of the power of a web of community relationships was believed to be essential as was creation of a mindset to ensure that commands and rules would meet with a sense of duty to obey. With coercion repugnant because it implied that willing obedience was absent and hinted a lack of legitimation, approaches to order that elicited subjective acceptance were sought. Premium was placed on political or legal mechanisms that embodied free choice by citizens. Such processes were both consonant with the personal autonomy touted by republicanism and, yet, implied the subjective consent so essential to democratic politics.

As the courts moved in antebellum Boston to confront social order, discretionary forms of leniency in the courts were especially well suited to play a role in cultivating public acceptance. The paradigm of the modern political subject that emerged in the criminal courts reflected thinking that was more explicitly elaborated in labor law during these years. Many aspects of it also appear in the criminal courts. Importantly, this view of the political subject additionally constituted the basis of a post-Revolutionary conception of citizenship.

Articulating such a political identity as the basis for a "rule of law" and, consequently, modern political authority was, as we have seen, central to the Second Great Awakening (McLoughlin, 1980). How to instill this identity was, however, a matter of great controversy. It fueled vociferous debates over education for, once defined, the cultural basis of this political identity had to be inculcated (Kaestle, 1983, p. 72). Public schools and the courts were counted on.[19] In a republic where "universal" suffrage prevailed, means to reform the wayward were also needed (p. 73). Instead of economic equality, citizenship would substitute political rights—shifting popular attention away from the inequalities inherent in property in the profound hope that this institution would be left intact by the voting public.

"Symbolic Suretyship": Socially Embedded Free Choice

Beyond contributing legitimation to authority through the ideology of a "rule of law," the courts played a key role in constructing authority, practically speaking, by seeking to reembed defendants in traditional social hierarchies. One key practice in this regard was the courts' use of new forms of discretionary leniency. Using such practices, especially plea bargaining, judges increasingly began to grant leniency after hearing the intercession of character witnesses—most often employers. In England, judicial use of leniency had a long tradition of creating proactive incentives to forge ties of reciprocity with employers and notables that stabilized class relations (Hay et al., 1975).

In the American republic, judicial use of new forms of discretionary leniency promoted, first, Federalist, then National Republican and, finally, Whig policy goals of nurturing political stability and the order necessary for market expansion (Vogel, 1999). Using leniency, judges worked to draw conflicts before the courts lest they magnify if left unattended (Hindus, 1980). Legal cases were used as occasions to educate defendants in the new impersonal, nonparticularistic, market-like workings of justice. However, the courts also relied on the worlds of family and work. Rather than turn to massive incarceration as has criminal justice in the late twentieth and early twenty-first centuries, the courts did everything in their power to systematically reembed defendants in the powerful web of informal social control exercised by membership in these institutions of everyday life.

As part of that attempt to reconnect defendants with that institutional web of social membership, a second element, in addition to the intercession of character witnesses, was borrowed from the common law. This was a set of practices for ensuring good behavior known as suretyship—a practice whereby family, employers, or others posted bond to guarantee a defendant's good behavior.[20] This created a financial stake in the defendant's behavior and ensured informal oversight (Simon, 1993). Use of the courts' mechanisms of leniency created a sort of "symbolic suretyship," where witnesses staked their reputations rather than posting bond. By ensuring informal oversight, it linked the rule-based authority of the judiciary with the traditional authority of the informal social hierarchies that were cornerstones of the socializing web of communal relations. Hierarchies drawn on were primarily two: the patriarchal authority of heads of households over their dependents and servants, on the one hand, and the authority of master over laborer in the workplace, on the other (Steinfeld, 1991, p. 66).

During the early decades of the nineteenth century, despite stirrings of change, discourse was still much influenced by colonial ideas of a hierarchical social order. Pressure for change can be seen in labor law where the freedom of the individual, in terms of a worker's autonomy to stay or leave employment, emerged as a key issue before the courts. Out of this legal discourse, a vision of the political subject was taking shape. It drew on debates about the nature of liberty and contributed to the project of articulating a conception of citizenship. Strong parallels can be seen in the way the liberty of the worker, the choices of the criminal defendant, and the participation of the citizen came to be envisioned. As we shall see, each emphasized freedom of choice, at least in formal terms, while allowing broad latitude to restrict the conditions, or terms, on which choices would actually be made.

Judicial use of leniency, by highlighting patrons, intertwined Old World and New in a manner consistent with this view of freedom. It did so by emphasizing freedom of choice that, at the same time, reinforced cross-class ties and lodged defendants in informal hierarchies under the customary power of social control that intercessors wielded (Vogel, 1999, 2001; Hay et al., 1975).[21] The pivotal element of the most widespread new form of leniency, the plea bargain, was its use of "symbolic suretyship," which distinguished defendants who were enmeshed in the web of community relations from those who were not.[22] Servants and women or minors, who were living under the authority of a head of household, as well as laborers, who were under contract and supervised by a master, were favored over peddlers, vagrants, and other "non-producers" among the disaffiliated (Sellers, 1991). The courts, like the society, valued "productive hands," or the creators of tangible value, over service workers (especially mariners). Status as a "producer," especially one under a labor contract, made a patron's endorsement more likely and boosted its value. Such a patron-employer was a resource that the much-disparaged unskilled "day laborer" did not possess. In sum, "symbolic suretyship" helped promote ties of reciprocity across social classes, linked courts with traditional hierarchies of customary authority, and generally stabilized social relations.

By placing value on patrons, the state, acting through the courts, created a legal practice that fostered social connections between laboring ranks, on the one hand, and Boston's aristocratic families and the "middling interest," on the other. Evidence of intervention by patrons is abundant. It appears both in newspaper vignettes and in the form of timeworn handwritten letters of reference to the court attesting to a defendant's character and commitment to work.[23] Less frequently, a patron might appear in person to testify regarding the industriousness or family ties of a defendant. Given the litigiousness of the society, any given patron might well be called on to testify more than once

(Konig, 1979). Thus, workers found it in their interests to be known to those powerful enough to intercede should the occasion arise.

What is striking here is what Novak has called the "constitutive power" exerted by a purely cultural practice in initiating structural change. Once new mechanisms of leniency created a need for patrons, this encouraged laborers to behave in new ways that were constitutive of new social relationships, that is, to forge cross-class affiliations, mainly with employers, as a proactive approach to immunity. Thus, we find a causal consequence of a cultural practice, not in the form of a "tool kit" or set of responses and strategies (Swidler, 1985), an affective basis for behavioral predispositions (Fulbrook, 1983), or a means for defining group boundaries (Fulbrook), but in the form of a cultural practice, the plea bargain, which provided incentives that prompted specific new behaviors. These were the basis for new relationships that were constitutive of change in social structure through the kinds of social ties that they fostered.

Hierarchy Resurgent: Home, Workplace, and Social Control

As the contours of political authority took shape, legal thinkers found themselves playing a key role. Since this was the "formative era" of American law, much of that thought was innovative. Often, it came from legal circles in Boston that strongly espoused a Federalist and, later, Whig perspective.

As Federalism waned nationally during the presidencies of Thomas Jefferson and James Madison, "... [its partisans] blamed its displacement upon the insurgence of unrestrained democracy, which ... [they] thought could destroy the nation" (Jaher, 1984, p. 71). Primary among their concerns were fear for their property and chagrin over an unfavorable business climate (p. 71). While Federalism had collapsed nationally by the 1820s, it flourished in Boston into the 1830s.[24] At that point, elite families moved astutely to switch their party allegiance—first to the Democratic-Republicans, then to the National-Republicans, and, finally, to the Whigs, until the dissolution of the second party system at mid-century (p. 77). Power and prosperity combined to inspire "civic responsibility on the part of the Whigs and ... impressive ... civic accomplishment accompanied ... by indefatigable pursuit of self and class interests" (p. 77). For a quarter century, candidates chosen by the Federalist/Whig elite dominated the city's politics (p. 77). As political officials, members of the urban elite frequently used their sway to channel urban development along lines conducive to their own interests and those of their associates, though this often resulted in progressive policy (p. 77).

Amidst the elite-dominated politics of this hub of legal change, traditional notions of social hierarchy still prevailed as the nineteenth century dawned. The mercantile and financial base of the city's economy, in contrast with the emphasis on "producers" so prevalent elsewhere in industrializing areas, allowed custom greater longevity. Nonetheless, the free markets of the capitalist economy were starting to erode hierarchies of both household and work. These challenges to hierarchy afford important insight into the conception of the political subject that was taking shape in law.

Colonial Americans, like the early modern English, had drawn on two models to conceptualize the social position of the masses of people who labored for others: that of the servant, on the one hand, and that of the wage laborer, on the other (Steinfeld, 1991, p. 55). Together they embodied many of the key ambiguities of the day about the nature of freedom. Although it was common by the nineteenth century to speak of free wage labor, Montgomery (1993), in his book *Citizen-Worker,* reminds us that freedom in this sense was conceptualized primarily in contrast to indentured servants or slaves. In fact, wage workers, whether servants or laborers, toiled under labor contracts that gave masters considerable control over their persons, their comings and goings, and their economic well-being.

The position of servants and laborers was very much a product of the honeycombed hierarchical social landscape of the early nineteenth century. Masters exercised jurisdiction over servants "by virtue of their [own] status as heads of household" (Steinfeld, 1991, p. 55). This authority was specifically limited to indentured servants, hired domestic servants, and apprentices (p. 66). Over laborers, by contrast, masters exercised authority as a "grant of jurisdiction from the community" (p. 55). Workers governed in this way were engaged primarily in nondomestic production, such as factory work, and were generally under contract (p. 66).

Post-Revolutionary Authority: Modern and Traditional Elements

The result of this invocation of the "rule of law" and concomitant reliance on episodic leniency was a move toward a vision of modern political authority that was primarily of a rational-legal sort, that is, authority whose legitimation is based on the enactment of rules in law and the specification of offices in law. Yet as judges focused on the problem of creating political authority anew, their reliance on tools of discretionary leniency was quite deliberate. Despite the modernity of the new republic, they were crafting authority of a unique blend of rational-legal and traditional elements. There was a strong sense that ideology unsupported by the stabilizing influence of participation in an integrated network of social roles could prove a fragile basis on which to build social order. Local politicians sensed that, along with laws, the subjects of political authority that is solely rule based require the normative guidance that comes from a secure place in the relationships and routines of social structure. New uses of leniency in the courts and "symbolic suretyship" were especially well suited to accomplish that. Thus, the model of authority that emerged was a unique mix of rational-legal and traditional authority.

In constructing new forms of authority, privileges and duties had to be articulated anew. American republicanism and, later, liberalism conceived of them as anchored in an imagery of liberty. At the same time, by reemphasizing family and work, the influence of traditional social hierarchies was reasserted in limiting that autonomy and structuring the terms on which choices would, in practice, be made. Each social tie, such as householding, parenting, employment, property ownership, tax payment, borrowing, and voting afforded society an opportunity to influence the behavior of its members. Though these were the years when the penitentiary was established, the courts sought recourse first through the informal web of social control constituted by those citizens, such as a wife, husband, or employer, who had a stake in a defendant's behavior.

This combination in republican ideology of choice by persons who are formally free with reassertion of traditional hierarchies of rank and privilege was the seed bed in which a conception of the political subject and citizen was formed. Citizenship emerged as a negotiated political status in the United States that was inherently dualistic and fraught with tension. This is because citizenship played a crucial role in buttressing the nascent "rule of law" in a nation attempting to harmoniously reconcile political equality and material inequality.

Freedom and the Web of Membership: Facets of Citizenship

Concern about potential public responses to the tension between political liberty, on the one hand, and material equality, on the other, was met, by elaborating a vision of citizenship to strengthen the link between person and polity, where equality could safely be had without threatening the class structure. A conception of the political subject arose, which underlies the notion of citizenship and which was explicated in law over the course of almost a century and a half.[25]

In his classic study, *Class, Citizenship and Social Development*, Marshall (1964) defines citizenship as "a status bestowed on those who are full members of a community . . . [such that] all who possess the status are equal with respect to the rights and duties with which it is endowed" (p. 92). In practice, citizenship was usually endowed during the nineteenth century on the basis of nationality (Soysal, 1995). Citizenship stood in contrast with social class, which was really "a system of inequality" and which operated as a sort of opposing principle within the same societies (Marshall, p. 93).[25]

In reflecting on the apparent contradiction between the equality provided by citizenship and the inequality inherent in social class, Marshall (1964) distinguished two different senses of class. The first implied "a hierarchy of status, and the differenc[e] between one class and another is expressed in terms of [variation in] legal rights and . . . essential customs which [may] have the . . . binding character of law" (Marshall, 1964, p. 93). Marshall contends that citizenship challenges this meaning of class—what we might refer to today as an institutionalized system of status and privilege—and that, as a result, the awareness of a specific status formally ascribed to each social level diminishes. Class, in the second sense articulated by Marshall, is "not an institution in its own right . . . [but rather emerges] as a by-product of [the interplay of] other institutions . . . [such as those] of property and education and the structure of the national economy" (p. 94). Class in this second sense, of real differences in material prosperity as a result of the workings of society's institutions, remains intact and unaffected by citizenship. While many nineteenth century reformers proposed means of improving human welfare and alleviating poverty, concern about human suffering did not lead many of them to question the justice of the widespread material inequality that already marked American society (p. 95). Thus, citizenship provided a cornerstone for an American political identity that emphasized political equality, as granted through the franchise, but which left striking economic inequality unchallenged. In an ethnically diverse society, citizenship offered a relational basis of political membership that, to an important extent, grew to define what it meant to "be American."[26]

Beyond maintaining social order outright, the republic also faced the challenge of secondary social control, that is, of articulating social norms and laws and of imbuing the populace with an understanding of the duties and responsibilities that accrue both to citizens and, equally important, to those segments of society excluded from citizenship. Initially republican in conception, the earliest view of American citizenship was held to imply "participation as an equal in public affairs, [by civic-spirited persons who saw themselves] . . . pursu[ing] a common good [and linked to those less privileged through relations of deference]" (Michelman, 1988, p. 1503). Traditional republicanism presumed a "moral consensus" that allowed for the possibility of a "common good." Thus, politics assumed a "normative character." Ability to discern this common good required a sound political process that protected "the independence of mind and judgment" that each citizen brought to the deliberative process (p. 1504). One consequence of this view of politics was to heighten the importance of the role of law. Because "Republicanism [is] . . . sensitive to . . . the dependence of good politics on social and economic conditions capable of sustaining 'an informed [,independently minded] and active citizenry,'" it accords primacy to law. This is because it was seen as the work of the legal order to ensure those conditions (p. 1505).

This sense that the conditions necessary for sound politics and citizenship are rooted in law continued to prevail even after elite dominance of electoral politics in Boston splintered at mid-century. By that time, however, law had come to serve, not as the enabling condition of civic-spirited decision making, but as the basis of legitimation of modern rational-legal democratic political authority itself. By extending the franchise during the mid-1830s, the Commonwealth changed the circle of those eligible for full citizenship and, thereby, participation in electoral politics.[27] No image so vividly signalled the change as the strange sights and sounds of the neighborhoods of new immigrants who were radically reconstituting the population of the city of Boston.

Eventually, republican discourse, itself consonant with liberalism in its emphasis on rights and free conscience but distinctly continental in its focus on community and civic duty, was superseded as the nineteenth century wore on by a more typically liberal discourse that highlighted individual autonomy rather than communalism. Since a common cultural basis of ethnic heritage was absent, education came to be the essential crucible for forging relations of citizenship by inculcating its cultural commitment to liberty (Soysal, 1995).[28] In this project, the American courts, along with the schools, played a key formative role.

Markets and Hierarchies: Liberty, Political Subject, and Citizenship

In constructing an image of authority and citizenship, Americans historically drew on "a set of ancient . . . conceptions about . . . the domestic household and about the role of . . . [such] household[s] in the wider polity" (Steinfeld, 1991, p. 56).[29] This view was one of the household as a hierarchically arranged micropolity, and it was a vision held in a broad range of cultures over many centuries (Steinfeld, p. 56; Ladurie, 1979; Stone, 1979, pp. 93–104, 109–13). These imaginative constructions were important because they cast the authority of a master over servants as one form of "relationship [that] heads of household bore to dependent[s] . . . [in] their households" (Steinfeld, p. 56). Resident servants were understood to be dependent members of the master's household much like wives and children—a fact that had important legal implications (p. 56).

According to this conception of the servant, an "unrelated person [who was a servant] could become the legal dependent of another . . . because of the nature of the [contractual] agreement between them" (Steinfeld, 1991, p. 56). It was the nature of this authority of the master in social life that induced the courts to rely on this relation between master and worker as one preeminent form of surety to undergird the new mechanisms of leniency. Work, along with family, became one of the two main hierarchies in the web of social membership amidst which the formally free individuals of nineteenth-century New England lived their lives.

Resident servants, then, were "like wives and children because all were members of the household and all were the legal dependents of its head" (Steinfeld, 1991, p. 56). As dependents, such servants were "legally entitled to be maintained by the head of household . . . [and] were subject by law to his authority" (p. 56). As dependents, neither servants nor children nor wives traditionally "bore full legal responsibility for him or herself" (p. 56). Instead, the "responsibility [both material and spiritual] for all of them rested on the head of their household" (p. 56). Thus, a master represented a servant in any legal proceeding.

In light of this relationship, servants were "understood to come under the 'government' of the head of household and[, through the master, under] that of the state" (Steinfeld, 1991, p. 56). Parallels between domestic authority and political authority were common in the parlance of the day, and "the household was understood to be a polity like other[s]," with the master seen as being "like those [leaders] who governed other polities" (p. 57). In the words of Gouge much earlier in 1622, the family was a kind of proving ground for leadership. Gouge tells us that the family "is a little Church, and a little commonwealth, at least a lively representation thereof, whereby trial may be made of such as are fit for any place of authorities, or of subjection in Church or commonwealth . . . it is as a schoole wherein the first principles and grounds of government and subjection are learned: whereby men are fitted to greater matters in Church or commonwealth" (Gouge, 1622; cited in Steinfeld, p. 57).

Images of household government and domestic authority were not simply metaphors. Strong parallels are evident between the structure and relationships of the household polity and the broader one. In early New England, Edmund Morgan had noted that "[t]he [very] essence of the social order lay [in these hierarchical relationships of authority in the different realms of life], in the superiority of husband over wife, parents over children, and master over servants in the family, ministers and elders over congregation in the church, rulers over subjects in the state" (Morgan, *Puritan Family*, p. 19; cited in Steinfeld, 1991, p. 57). In early New England, children studying the catechism written by John Cotton "learned to answer the question, 'who are here meant by Father and Mother?' with the words 'All our Superiors, whether in Family, School, Church and Commonwealth'" (Morgan, p. 19; cited in Steinfeld, p. 57).

In a very direct sense, "family government [was considered] to be one of the foundations of political order" (Steinfeld, 1991, p. 58). The household was a polity and it, like other polities, was governed (p. 58). Apprehensions of political disorder often led officials to turn to domestic authority. In Massachusetts, the legislature responded to reports of unrest in outlying areas by commanding all towns "to take a list of the names of those young persons within the bounds of your Town, who do live from under Family Government, that is who do not serve their Parents or Masters, as Children, Apprentices, hired Servants, or Journeymen ought to do, and usually did in our Native Country, being subject to their commands and discipline" (p. 58). Shortly after, in Plymouth, a similar law was passed with the intention of maintaining public order by requiring all single persons to live under household government (p. 58).

Such was the emphasis on authority rooted in household relations that, in Virginia, as in England, "the murder of a master by a servant was not treated as a homicide but as treason" (Fischer, 1989, p. 280). Entry into domestic service could endow the servant with respectability. Records of the Suffolk County court in Boston depict such a change in status in the case of Abigail Roberts [name fictitious] who was initially "presented [to the court] for excess in her apparrell and living from under Government . . . [Then] [s]everall of the neighborhood appearing and witnessing that she [now] lived in Service . . . The Court admonish't her, ordered her to pay fees of Court and discharged her" (Morison and Chafee, 1933, 2:751; cited in Steinfeld, 1991, p. 58). Having entered into the web of membership through service, she was no longer considered a threat to social order.

Nonresidential Laborers and Community Jurisdiction

While the jurisdiction of masters over resident servants lay in domestic authority, the cultural basis of the authority of masters over wage workers lay in "community jurisdiction over the laboring poor" (Steinfeld, 1991, p. 60).[30] In the social world of early modern England, "labor [of this sort] was viewed as a common resource to which the community had rights, and laborers and artificers had legal obligations to [work] . . . on terms and conditions [that] the community prescribed" (p. 60).

This conception had its origin in laws and practices that had been enacted as early as the fourteenth and sixteenth centuries. In villages of fourteenth-century England, communities "commonly [had] laid claim to the labor of those who lived in the village, prohibiting their departure from the village while their labor was needed" (Steinfeld, 1991, p. 61). In Bedfordshire in 1304, for example, eight men were fined because "they led their neighbors outside the parish to work for strangers" (Ault, 1965, p. 15; cited in Steinfeld, p. 61).[31]

Communities also prescribed other of the terms and conditions of work. When work was plentiful, "many laborers preferred to take work on a casual basis by the day, week or task and not to serve by the term" (Steinfeld, 1991, p. 62). This was done both because it was "more profitable than long term service [and because it gave them] . . . greater autonomy (Kenyon, 1934, pp. 429–51; cited in Steinfeld, p. 62).[32] Responding to this situation and to the need for reliable year-round labor, provisions were incorporated into statute that proscribed casual labor.[33] Laborers were, however, regularly charged with violating these provisions.[34]

This view that labor was a common resource to which a community had rights remained common among elites for centuries in England (Steinfeld, 1991, p. 62). Mobility of labor geographically was perceived as a problem because "it threatened to disrupt [production and, thus,] good order as English elites then defined it" (p. 63). Concern to ensure labor supply had resulted in enactment during the 1560s of the Statute of Artificers, providing that "workers could not legally interrupt or leave their work without first securing their master's approval" (p. 60). Thus masters retained jurisdiction, but of a more-limited and temporary sort than with servants, over laborers and artificers (p. 64).

These insights into the legal position that was traditionally accorded to labor shed important light on their political status. In contrast to servants, who were part of a master's household, laborers supported households of their own. In descriptions of the English polity of the day, no mention of "servants . . . as separate members of the polity [appears] at all . . . [since] they were . . . counted as members of their master's household" (Kussmaul, 1981, pp. 3, 8–9). Laborers and artificers, by contrast, "did have independent political persona; they were listed separately as members of the polity [though] unlike members of the higher orders, . . . laborers and artificers were described as men who are ruled" (Chamberlayne, 1669, p. 449; cited in Steinfeld, 1991, p. 64). In penning *Angliae Notitia* many years earlier, Chamberlayne stated that "The lowest Member, the Feet of the Body Politique, are the Day Labourers" (1669, p. 449; cited in Steinfeld, p. 64).[35] Persons of even the lowest rank had to be incorporated politically, despite their status, because they were not subsumed into another's household. Smith tells us "they be not altogether neglected . . . [because when they] default of yeomen, enquests and Juries are impaneled of such manner of people. And in villages . . . such low and base persons . . . be commonly made Churchwardens, alecunners, and manie times Constables" (Smith, 1583, p. 46; cited in Steinfeld, 1991, p. 65).

By the eighteenth century, change was afoot but also much continuity. Laborers increasingly "were . . . described as 'their own masters'—at least outside of work" (Steinfeld, 1991, p. 65). Yet, in England, "[the restrictive] provisions of the Statute of Artificers . . . remained in effect throughout . . . [much of the eighteenth] century" (p. 66). Further, they were bolstered by new acts that "made it an imprisonable offense for artificers and laborers to breach their [labor] contracts" (20 Geo. II, c. 19 (1747) and 6 Geo. III, c. 25 (1766); cited in Steinfeld, p. 66).[36] Thus, laborers and artificers [in contrast to servants], by the dawn of the nineteenth century, occupied "an ambiguous legal position—not the legal dependents of a master, as servants and apprentices continued to be, but . . . not yet quite fully free . . . citizens either" (Steinfeld, p. 66).

Along with ideas about the traditional status of labor that drew on political imagery to explain the authority of the master over those that he hired, a second set of images highlighted the economic aspect of the relationship. These images depicted a master's authority as "a kind of property that the master held in the worker's labor" (Steinfeld, 1991, p. 66). While unthinkable today, "medieval and early modern English law recognized . . . [that] not only could various aspects of human personality be the subject of property, but varying degrees of property in persons was also possible" (p. 67). The most extreme form of such a relation was villeinage, which, having been initiated by the Normans in 1066, was the only indigenous form of bondage known in England (p. 67).[37] While a villein remains with a lord, the lord is said to have seisin of him (p. 67). Several centuries later, the locus of a lord's property interest in the villein began to shift from "the person of the villein . . . [to his or her] labor . . . services" (p. 68).[38] This tradition whereby a master's authority would "stand . . . [sometimes] for ownership and . . . [sometimes] for lordship" also endured in adapted form into the nineteenth century (p. 67).

Property in the Work of Laborers

The view of labor as involving an unequal relation of both authority and property was consonant with a society that was hierarchically organized by social rank, even after modern political ideologies began to challenge cultural justifications of such rank. Steinfeld points out that "the social and political theory known as 'possessive individualism,' which emerged in England during the seventeenth century, proceeded . . . from a . . . set of premises" that were fundamentally different from those underlying traditional hierarchical ideas of the polity (Steinfeld, 1991, p. 78). At first blush, it would appear that these premises, which formed the intellectual basis for the rise of the celebrated notion of the "rights of freeborn Englishmen," would have immediately produced a direct challenge to the concept of labor as property. However, this was not so.

Possessive individualism started from the idea that the "social order was constituted by numerous separate autonomous, essentially uniform individuals" (Steinfeld, 1991, p. 78).[39] According to this view, natural sovereignty over one's own person is "an expression of the fact that all individuals, to begin with, own themselves" (MacPherson, 1962; cited in Steinfeld, p. 79). Mac-Pherson went so far as to argue that it is this "property in his own person and capacities . . . that makes a man human . . . [—] his freedom from other men" (MacPherson, p. 142; cited in Steinfeld, p. 79). While free and independent persons sustained that natural sovereignty, "[w]age workers were dependent in precisely the sense that they had alienated the legal right to control and dispose of their own capacities" (Steinfeld, p. 79).[40] The alienation, however, was "not an abandonment but a transfer of right to the master . . . [and] [t]he servant's labour [was] thence forth included in the master's labour" (p. 80). What possessive individualism changed was the way this inclusion was conceived of.

Through the discourse of possessive individualism, "[t]he property that masters had enjoyed for centuries in the labor of their servants now began to be reimagined as the product of a voluntary transaction struck between two separate and autonomous individuals, one of whom traded away to the other the property in his own labor for wages or other compensation" (Steinfeld, 1991, p. 80). Upon such a transaction being completed, that labor belonged no longer to the laborer but to his master. This notion that the labor agreement constituted "an alienation by one individual to another of the property in his capacities endured [relatively unchanged] well into the eighteenth century" (p. 81).

Imagery depicting the status of labor eventually succumbed, however, to more broad-gauged change. If possessive individualism left the notion of property in the labor services of the worker untouched, the ideology of the "freeborn Englishman" to which it gave rise did not. Rising to prominence initially in the course of the English Revolution, the "rights of the freeborn" had been established by 1700, due to Leveller activism, as a defining motif of English culture.[41] In legal terms, it implied that all Englishmen were " 'liberi homines,' that no person in England by this time was born a villein or bond slave" (Steinfeld, 1991, p. 95).[42] The importance of this fact was that it implied an element of equality. Coke observed that "Two parts of three have not forty shillings a year, yet are as free born as they who have" (Coke, 1662; cited in Steinfeld, p. 96). Overton drew on this "shared status of all Englishmen to mean that 'the greatest Peers in the land' should not be more respected 'than so many old bellows-menders, broom-men, cobblers, tinkers or chimney-sweepers, who are all equally free born" (Thomas, 1972, p. 75; cited in Steinfeld, p. 96). Viewed in this light, villeinage was a tyrannical and unjustified infringement of liberty. At the same time, Levellers began to "equate 'all infringements of their liberties' with slavery" (Thomas, p. 75; cited in Steinfeld, p. 96).

How then did restrictions in ordinary service persist into the nineteenth century? By the late sixteenth century, some had begun to question whether the restricted status of servants was consonant with the concept of "liberi homines." Sir Thomas Smith emphasized some of the disquieting similarities between servitude and slavery when he observed "[I]f . . . [a servant] be in covenaunt, he may not depart out of his service without his master's license, and he must give his master warning that he will depart one quarter of a yere before the terme of the yere expireth, or else he shall be compelled to serve out another yere" (Smith, 1583, p. 138; cited in Steinfeld, 1991, p. 98). Smith continued to say that "if any young man unmarried be without service, he shall be compelled to get him a master whom he must serve for that yere . . ." (Smith, p. 138; cited in Steinfeld, p. 98). Both servitude and slavery, Smith opined, consumed human labor in ways that contravened freedom.

Thence began, however, an effort to distinguish slavery from ordinary service. It was argued that, in the case of servants, their service was voluntary for "they were 'in other matters [except as regards their service] in libertie as full free men and women' " (Smith, 1583, p. 138; cited in Steinfeld, 1991, p. 98). By the seventeenth century, Chamberlayne argued that apprentices differed from villeins and slaves because "Apprentices are slaves only for a time and by Covenant" (Chamberlayne, 1669, p. 463; cited in Steinfeld, p. 98). In colonial America, awareness was rife of the tension between prohibitions on villeinage and slavery, on the one hand, and the restrictive constraints of ordinary service, on the other. Statutes in New York and Massachusetts stated that "[n]o Christian shall be kept in bondslavery, villeinage or captivity" while ordinary service

314 COERCION TO COMPROMISE

was, however, allowed (Cushing, 1978, p. 122; cited in Steinfeld, p. 99). Indentured servitude was exempt and continued both in Europe and America to be seen as the harshest form of labor service.

By the late eighteenth century, the notion of the "rights of freeborn Englishmen" began to be used to challenge ordinary service. Traditionally an effort had also been made to distinguish ordinary service by arguing that, in addition to being temporary and limited, it "was undertaken voluntarily while, typically, villeinage and slavery were not" (Steinfeld, 1991, p. 100). Such voluntarism was seen as crucial to the continued legitimacy of the labor relation. Steinfeld notes that, in the American political culture of that day, "Consent . . . was becoming basic to the legitimate exercise of authority. The voluntariness with which ordinary service was undertaken was clearly expressive of a consent to be governed by a master . . . [to whom service was] at least consensual and therefor arguably legitimate . . . [and the] opposite of the arbitrary tyranny imposed on slaves and villeins" (p. 100).

This distinction prevailed during the seventeenth and eighteenth centuries. The English also continued to hold that, in contrast to slavery, in ordinary service, property in the labor performed was conveyed temporarily and "that [it] was only one aspect of the property one held in one's person" (Steinfeld, 1991, p. 100). Ordinary service was depicted as "consensual and limited," while slavery was seen as "arbitrary and absolute" (p. 101). But it was a delicate position to sustain. One crucial assumption that enabled this distinction to be drawn for a time was the prevailing idea that "freedom (and unfreedom) were not absolute[s] . . . but matters of degree" (p. 102).

Contractarian Individualism and Republicanism: Autonomous Subjects

The appearance in the seventeenth and, especially, the late eighteenth and early nineteenth centuries of, first, republican and, later, liberal ideas introduced a new conception of freedom and disputed the notion that liberty could be a matter of degree (Steinfeld, 1991, p. 102).[43] The concept of a continuum of freedom began to lose ground. Steinfeld notes that "By the eighteenth century, all . . . legal restriction on a laborer's right to depart from his work seem [formally] to have been eliminated in the colonies" (p. 103). However, in practical fact, the distinction between free and unfree persons remained a continuum ranging from: laborers, to hired servants, to indentured servants, and, finally, to slaves (p. 104). While laborers were now, at least formally, autonomous and free to leave service, hired servants continued to be much more restricted (p. 104).

Although changes began to occur in the formal constraints on workers' ability to leave service, "the traditional attitudes that society and polity were . . . matters of hierarchy, rank and degree . . . [persisted and affected those choices in practical terms]" (Steinfeld, 1991, p. 105). Further, in the process of ideological contest "new philosophies [of republicanism and liberalism] did not invariably point toward the [complete] elimination of traditional [constraints on labor]. On the contrary, those who subscribed to [the] new views . . . [often incorporated] old practices as integral features of a new universe, flowing unproblematically from new first principles" (p. 105). While some "ideological change[s] pointed to an end to the restrictions on personal liberty entailed in labor law, others began to view such labor arrangements as a form of contractual freedom" (p. 106). Labor continued, as a result, to be considered "an alienation of property in labor" albeit a voluntary one (p. 106). Thus, contractarian individualism did not point the way directly to liberalism, which demands that "all people, whatever their circumstances, formally retain [at all times] the wall of rights . . . insulating them from other individuals" (p. 106). The opening for change came with the reconceptualization of labor contracts. The dilemma was that, though all men were formally regarded as free, in exercising their freedom to make contracts, "they were conveying a property in their capacities that enabled others to control them" (p. 107). As long as traditional views of a hierarchical society supported constraining labor practices, these tensions were masked (p. 107). With the gradual weakening of social hierarchy in antebellum America, the conflict began fully to surface.

Dualistic Liberty: Formally Free Labor and Constrained Choice

In 1821, the Indiana Supreme Court, in Mary Clark's case, drew on long-simmering intellectual controversy to punctuate consolidation of a new understanding of what constituted involuntary labor (*The Case of Mary Clark, a Woman of Color*, 1 Blackf. 122, 124–25 (Ind. 1821); cited in Steinfeld, 1991, p. 146).[44] What was definitively established in this case was that "labor became involuntary the moment a laborer decided to depart and was not permitted to do so—whatever previous agreements she may have made" (p. 147).

This case established the principle that, despite entering into the service of another, laborers and servants continued to reserve to themselves a certain mastery of their own lives, including the ability to leave that service. Thus, "the property in their labor was their employer's only so long as they wished it to be" (Steinfeld, 1991, p. 148). According to this view, laborers warranted full juridical equality because they could not alienate irrevocably, even for a period of time, the control of their capacities.

In this new, more voluntarist view of labor law, masters could no longer lay absolute claim to a capacity to rule or to compel workers to fulfill certain tasks. Instead, "they would be limited to 'influencing' the decisions that workers were entitled freely to make . . . [and] to structuring the 'incentives' that workers faced [in deciding whether to stay or go]—a capacity Steinfeld terms "persuasion" (Steinfeld, 1991, p. 148). Though employers could no longer coerce workers physically, they retained capacities under property, contract, and labor law "[that] constituted the basis for economic power through which to [inexorably] continue to influence wage workers" (p. 148).

What was significant about this emerging view of the employer-worker relationship was that it left . . . ultimate decision[s] formally to the laborer" (Steinfeld, 1991, p. 148). By depicting the worker as formally free, a view of the labor relation emerged that was quite compatible . . . [with] the spirit of "republican liberty and equality" (p. 149).[45] Employers, however, continued to determine the terms of trade among which workers chose. Thus, in cases involving complaints of assault and battery that were brought against employers for correcting by physical means the lapses and misdeeds of employees, the courts generally held that employers might not use physical punishment (p. 150). Coercion was barred and the focus of employment came to center on participatory consent.

Yet, until 1850, attempts by workers to recover wages withheld by employers when workers departed before completing their contractual terms were generally unsuccessful (Steinfeld, 1991, p. 149).[46] In formal terms, working men and women would retain mastery, then, of themselves (p. 151). While "[d]irect coercion would not be permitted, . . . legally sanctioned economic compulsion would" (pp. 150–51). Ongoing debate had produced the conclusion that physical compulsion or coercion by force were incompatible with the spirit of the republic. This model accorded laborers control over the formal decision whether to stay or to go" (p. 151). At the same time, it permitted masters, however, to manipulate [unrestrainedly] the considerations [especially economic ones] that workers would weigh in arriving at their own decisions" (p. 151). In this way, workers retained the formal autonomy and freedom essential to citizenship.

Thus, persons were considered free to choose but society's powerful institutions retained the capacity to structure the contours of choice along with the incentives embodied in them. Such thinking was fundamental to burgeon-ing ideas about citizenship. It was no accident that the concept of the citizen participating in politics during the Jacksonian era came to be expressed in the image of what David Montgomery has termed the "citizen-worker." The nature of citizen as political subject was elaborated in labor law (Montgomery, 1993).

Similarities between Laborers and Criminal Defendants

While the law of employment relations, especially its reflections on freedom, provided a basis for theorizing both labor and the political subject, the criminal courts were rarely so explicit on that point. Yet one finds striking parallels with the labor cases in the conceptions of liberty and images of the political subject tacitly taking shape in the criminal cases.

First, as in labor law, criminal actions emphasized the autonomous choice and participation of formally free individuals in shaping their fates. In the case of the laborer, he or she was free to stay or go. For the criminal defendant, there was freedom to plead guilty or not regardless of whether a bargain was being struck. Second, both laborer and defendant, in the case of those invoking new forms of leniency such as the plea bargain, enter a compact or covenant. In the case of the laborer, it is an agreement to serve for a specified amount of time and wage. The defendant acknowledges culpability in hopes of an exchange for leniency. Thus, both entail two-sided agreements (i.e., labor/mas-ter, defendant/judge) entered into to enhance one's position. In each case, the quality of the agreement one can achieve is constrained by the prevailing terms of trade. Third, while the choice is formally free, terms of the agreement are powerfully leveraged by the more resource-rich participant in each case. In the case of the laborer, this is typically the master. For the criminal defendant, it is the state.

The agreements differ, however, in that while the labor contract conforms to the formal legal standards of the day, new uses of leniency such as the plea bargain are informal and customary arrangements.[47] Public skepticism (at least originally at the hub of legal innovation in Boston) about the role of such practices in supporting the Whig-dominated "well-regulated" society of the day is implied, for instance, by the term "[plea] bargain." While the practice of plea bargaining originated with the Whigs, the name "bargain" applied to it appears to have come from the Democrats and to have been pejorative in tone.[48] The term also appears intended as a rhetorical Democratic critique of the ambition, corruption, and commercially oriented gain of the Whigs as antithetical to a democratic spirit.[49]

State before Nation: Ethnicity and National Identity

In articulating a protocol for political participation and a vision of post-Revolutionary authority, the challenge was heightened by the fact that, in the United States, the state formed before a nation had been consolidated.[50] In America, state formation took place very differently than it had in Europe.[51] In the United States, the state was formed, albeit a limited and decentralized one, on the model of Madisonian federalism when massive migration from Europe was occurring. Because this migration produced vast ethnic diversity, a national identity of an unusual sort arose. Nationalism came to stand for commitment to a particular set of ideas articulated by the state and to preservation of the union that it administered. An ideologically based national identity arose. In practice, national identity was also shaped or, more accurately, distorted by the society's systematic exclusions on the basis of race and gender from the full exercise of political rights.

Republicanism placed a value on homogeneity because it sought to pursue the holistic interests of the community. Homogeneity enabled the "people's welfare" to be more readily identified and sought through "well-regulated society" in a single "common good" (Novak, 1996). This view continued even after the franchise was extended "universally" during the 1830s. Even as immigrants began to flood the urban Northeast, republican ideology, in its American form, still had not developed a concept of pluralism. Since the basis of homogeneity, or unity, could not be found in the usual sources of territoriality or common ethnicity, nationhood, which in Europe had served as a basis of common identity and solidarity, developed very differently in America (Gellner, 1975).

In Europe, nationality had historically grown out of common culture, mutual recognition by community members of each other as persons sharing that culture, and, often, ties of consanguinity (Brubaker, 1992; Gellner, 1975). In the United States, an ideological nationality centered on a commitment to "liberty" arose. Though early tentative views of a racially based Anglo-American national identity were strongly contested, racialism and nativist mobilization for ethnic exclusion, nonetheless, survived throughout the nineteenth century (Higham, 1964). Nativism, from its beginnings in anti-French sentiment during the 1790s, tended to ally with nationalism and to grow increasingly exclusionary toward blacks, new immigrants and, later, Asians as the century wore on (Higham).

Citizenship as Modern Status Contract

If ethnic diversity precluded homogeneity as a basis for national identity, another criterion for political membership was needed. For this, the state placed heavy reliance on a conception of liberty and on citizenship as a basis of membership in that free community (de Tocqueville, 1835). It was a vision that highlighted political equality while softpedalling the vast material inequality of the day (Marshall, 1964). In a way that closely paralleled emergent law of the employment contract, the "citizen" entered into an enduring "contractual" relationship of reciprocity with the state. As part of that contract, which, for new immigrants, was accepted with a pledge made to a judge, the citizen claimed privileges and concomitantly embraced certain duties on his/her own part and on that of the state.[52]

Labor contracts, because of their comprehensive implications for the participants, have historically been conceived of as "status contracts" (Weber, 1975, p. 672). Weber notes that "By means of such a contract" entered into, "a person was to be somebody's child, father, wife, brother, master, slave, kin, comrade-in-arms, protector, client, follower, vassal, subject, friend, or quite generally comrade" (p. 672).[53] He goes on to point out that such agreements implicate "the total social status of the individual and . . . integrate [him or her] into an association comprehending [his or her] total personality" (p. 674). In short, such agreements created an "all-inclusive [set of] rights and duties" (p. 674). As was the case in marriage, "the wider community as well as the [individual] parties were understood to have . . . interests in the terms of the relationship and in its survival" (Steinfeld, 1991, p. 59). Status contracts, then, specified a place in the social order and articulated the advantages and responsibilities associated with it. For Americans, citizenship constituted a contract that specified a comprehensive status entered into by agreement and imbued with both privileges and duties.

This conception of citizenship, with its emphasis on voluntarism, was crucial to the "consent" fundamental to newly re-established post-Revolutionary political authority. At the time of the Second Great Awakening, when thinking about nationhood and citizenship was coalescing around what it meant to "become" American, a key popular concern was state abuse of power (Lane, 1971). Noting that "The struggle between Liberty and Authority is the most conspicuous feature in the portions of history . . . [most] familiar [to us]," John Stuart Mill, speaking foremost of England, pointed out that "liberty . . . [originally] meant protection against the tyranny of political rulers . . .

who were conceived [of] ... as in a necessarily antagonistic position to the people whom they ruled" (Mill, 1859, reprinted in 1975, p. 5). In the period of monarchs, oligarchs, and other ruling castes, the purpose of patriots seeking freedom was "to set limits to the power of the ruler ... [and] this limitation was what they meant by liberty" (p. 6).[54]

When sovereignty shifted to a basis of self-rule, many wrongly assumed that "rulers should be identified with the people; that their interest and will should be the interest and will of the nation" (Mill, 1859, p. 7). Under such a system, the people increasingly fell prey to the belief that state power was benign.[55] As popularly elected government became a reality, it was slowly recognized by those less privileged that state authority still must be guarded against and controlled by a people.[56]

Mixed Model of Citizenship: Civic Corporatism

It is generally accepted today that citizenship defines "bounded populations" and endows them with "a specific set of rights and duties" (Soysal, 1994, p. 2). Yet citizenship is organized, and regimes for incorporating new members are structured in very different ways across societies. Differences emanate from variation in both the institutional structure of citizenship and the stance of the state (Soysal).

Scholars, including Soysal, have argued that the models of 19th-century citizenship that these diverse institutional and state structures in Europe and North America produced were primarily three: a corporatist model illustrated by citizenship in Sweden and the Netherlands[57]; a liberal model exemplified by Britain and Switzerland[58]; and a statist model typified by France[59] (Soysal, 1994, p. 37). Each implies certain discourses and "understandings of the relationship between individuals, the state and the polity ... [and of] the organizational structures and practices that maintain this relationship" (p. 36). The models provide a repertoire for states and citizens to build on in devising policy. They also provide a "language, concepts, resources and mechanisms" for handling the incorporation of new members (p. 36). The models vary primarily in terms of where authority is located and to whom ... [it] is directed, on the one hand, and the extent of state centralization, on the other.

The weak Madisonian central state in the United States has long produced a misperception of an unopposed sway of liberalism through much of the early nineteenth century. Much of the support for this interpretation came from various arguments from constitutional law, such as Story's "immediacy" argument, emphasizing the link of the federal government directly to individuals

(Novak, 1996).[60] Equally important to the rise of liberalism, in reality, was the oppositional Democratic critique of the Whig ascendancy.[61]

Increasingly, historical evidence suggests some parallels to a corporatist model of citizenship that are far greater than previously believed, although the fit is far from perfect. Yet numerous authorities and economic combinations that construct a "well-regulated" society and that contribute to state pursuit of a "people's welfare" present some strong similarities. Though no tradition of guilds as a basis for corporate groups existed as it had in Europe, ethnicity, originally Anglo-Saxon and later more varied, emerged as a mechanism of corporate representation (Formisano and Burns, 1975). Later, occupational groupings, such as the Knights of Labor and voluntary associations such as the Masons appear to have performed this role as well. Absent a strong state administrative capacity, labor market participation served as the primary regime of incorporation. Due to this central role of employment, it is not surprising that the model of the political subject who was "becoming" a citizen bore close resemblance to that being articulated by the courts in labor law. Labor law was of close interest to Whig industrialists whose party, in law-crafting Boston, controlled the State House, which appointed all judges who treated immigration, employment relations, and criminal complaints. Absent an ethnic basis for national fellow feeling, this unusual brand of citizenship sought emotional grounding in a sometimes rapacious nationalism (Higham, 1964).

Democratic Skepticism and the Oppositional Discourse of Liberalism

A vision of citizenship was articulated, at precisely a time when Democrats, led by Jackson, highlighted the need of a people to be on the watch after both state abuse of power and the excesses of other citizens. In contrast to the focus of the Whig-dominated "well-regulated society on a single people's welfare," the bastion of Democratic critique was rights. Critical discourse drew on liberal inspiration as the basis for an oppositional discourse and placed rights, rather than privileges, foremost in the minds of the populace.[62] It also prompted an attack on the common law tradition and an ultimately unsuccessful movement for codification in law. While the masses could influence legislatures through the vote, bitter complaints surfaced that elites were "legislating from the bench"—a claim nowhere better supported than in Forbath's (1991) compelling analysis of the courts' response to the American labor movement during the nineteenth century. In this context, citizenship in America acquired a dual nature. In the eyes of capital and elite power, it signified membership and the demands of cultural homogenization to ensure an industrious and temperate people. To some among the "producing" many, citizenship bespoke the potential encroachments of power to be combatted through appeals to rights. The oppositional discourse of liberalism, gaining sway during the late 1830s and especially the 1840s, provided the symbolic cloth from which the Democratic critique was cut.[63]

Returning to our starting point, why, then, did self-rule leave institutions of property unchallenged? If political authority pointed to a rule of law and citizenship provided social roles and normative guidance, neither queried whose interests were furthered by this order.[64] If a regime is obeyed, accepted as valid, and wins popular consent, it is likely to endure. Thus, the ideology of a "rule of law" and relations of citizenship, while highlighting political equality, downplayed economic inequality and ultimately contributed mightily to its tolerance. What we see, then, is one means by which the consent of citizens was won, not only to the existing order, but to the inequalities inherent in it.[65] The unique role of courts in the United States, after the vote was extended "universally," holds a major part of the answer to the puzzle of American "exceptionalism."

Authority and Hegemony

If political authority established a sense of right to command with concomitant duty to obey and citizenship supplied a sense of social location and normative guidelines for action, both were silent as to whose interests this social order served. While the ideology of a "rule of law" supported authority with rules characterized by fairness, universality, and equality, the equally important question of whose interests were favored by existing arrangements lingered unanswered.

To help explain the paradox that material inequality persists in societies that are governed by self-rule, Gramsci introduces the concept of hegemony or ideological control. In referring to hegemony, Gramsci argues that ideologies such as the "rule of law" and citizenship play a powerful role in maintaining the existing social order with all the inequalities embodied in it.

Distinguishing coercion, or control by force, from hegemony or consent, Gramsci argues that ideological control has a power that guns and tanks do not. Hegemony, in his words, refers to the permeation through civil society of the beliefs, attitudes, morality, and values that are supportive in one way or another of the existing social order and, with it, the pattern of inequality that it embodies. Where hegemony holds sway, it assumes a kind of commonsense quality and causes the existing order to appear to be part of the natural order of things. It is this apparent naturalness conveyed by the ideology that leads the populace to consent to the order it depicts. However, in so doing, the irony is that they consent paradoxically to the inequalities inherent in the existing social order and, thus, to their own subordination.

The ideology of a rule of law claims that society is governed by rules that are specified in advance and known to all, and are fair, universally applied so that no one is exempt, and treat all persons who come before the court equally. In this apparently noncoercive way, it elicits popular support for the rules that sustain it and for legitimate political authority. One man's authority is, however, another man's hegemony. If a regime is obeyed, accepted as valid, and wins popular consent, it is likely to endure. With it endure the inequalities embedded in it. The ideology of citizenship, which highlights political equality, downplays economic inequality and ultimately promotes its tolerance.

Conclusion

In this work, the questions of why plea bargaining emerged when and where it did and why the practice took the particular cultural form that it did have been explored. My argument focuses on the struggle of competing classes and ethnic groups for political power during a definitional period in American law. In this context, plea bargaining constituted an extraordinary mediation at the symbolic level of the struggle of competing social groups both for power and for expressive authenticity in using language to describe social life in ways consonant with their interests and experiences. My claim is that plea bargaining emerged in Boston during the 1830s and 1840s as part of a political struggle to stabilize and to legitimate newly established democratic institutions. Reaching back into the cultural traditions of the common law, Bostonians reworked elements of the tradition of episodic leniency into a creative legal practice, known as plea bargaining, that constituted a new legal and political form for an age of popular politics.

The emergence of plea bargaining had three primary implications. First, what emerged was a powerful system of social control through the nonapplication of the law in ways that bore strong parallels to the British system of episodic leniency but with a uniquely American turn. Initially developed as part of a political project of protecting property, securing stability, and establishing popular consent, plea bargaining soon enhanced the discretionary power of both prosecutor and defense attorney and, along with it, the political currency that could accrue to men seeking to mix law with a career in politics. In years when independence of the judiciary had been contested at the federal level, the judiciary at the state level faced the same struggle. By the 1830s, court autonomy had been formally reasserted. Thus, the ascendancy of the judiciary as supreme in America through judicial review and through immunity from repeal and reorganization (though not, in some states, election) had begun. Power in that forum would become a potent resource for the man who combined a career in law with politics.

Second, plea bargaining, in its reliance on the Puritan confessional motif, reasserted a kind of "fictive" secular community—the elite republican order that the Whigs struggled so mightily to sustain. Soon that "fiction" would also pass, but the courts' use of leniency was laying the groundwork for membership of still another kind. Through "compromise" in imposing penalties, the court was creating a simple, "cognoscible" law that nurtured in uneducated people the capacity to consider long-term consequences in a way that was believed necessary for character building. While it is debatable whether the campaign to build character succeeded, it is clear that the court sought to create a relationship between itself, as agent of the state, and the popular classes. In contrast with earlier times, popularized by images of the Boston Tea Party or the British highwayman, when law was seen as an instrument of oppression and overtly resisted, a new model was being created. Unlike the grandeur of the Napoleonic code, it was a model that, as in England before, was crafted gradually and combined common law precedent with customary law. In this model, under the mantle of the "rule of law," elements of cognoscibility and calculability, now coupled with market-like regularity and impersonality, were being set in place. The model was presented as a participatory one. What was taking shape, in a gradualist way, was the formulation of a model of citizenship. In American society, without nationality for social glue, commonality was defined in terms of liberty exercised by virtue of the status of citizenship. The experience of liberty was thought to center on participation, especially the free exercise of rights and the making of public choices. How citizens could learn to act and choose responsibly in this decentralized Madisonian state was problematic. The lower courts, in their use of customary practices, not only promulgated the "rule of law" in palatable form, they also provided a model for learning the free participatory exercise of structured choice so essential to citizenship. The unspoken subtext was that traditional social hierarchies of power still structured the terms on which choice was made.

Third, plea bargaining, through its use of intercessors, created links between the courts and employers that reinforced the workplace as a central element of societal social control in a way that would endure throughout the century. It integrated the courts with the powerful web of social control in everyday life. It is this third implication of plea bargaining that provides clues as to why the practice is so problematic today.

In reflecting back on the rise of plea bargaining, one finds hints as to why plea bargaining is problematic now in the changing contextuality of the practice. For minorities, lacking in trust of police and the courts, there may be an unwillingness to enter a plea of guilty and rely on subsequent leniency (Bowling and Phillips, 2002). From this analysis, we also see that plea bargaining arose in a world where conviction often meant loss of one's job and inevitable stigma. In a world of attachment where most defendants were employed, these involved real costs. Today, plea bargaining operates in a society where vast segments of our urban populations, especially young males of prime crime-producing age, are unemployed and have little prospect of bettering their situations. For such a defendant, there is less in a tangible sense to lose. While the grace of the state was meaningful in a world where conviction bore a social cost, leniency looks very different in the world of today. Where a defendant has little to lose, largesse from the state may tend to be viewed as weakness and to elicit only cynicism. Perhaps one primary lesson to be drawn from this analysis is that common law–based criminal courts, which depend so heavily on mechanisms of leniency, despite crucial changes in context, deter more effectively when those who are accused are employed and immersed in family—that is, when they have something to lose. Given its emphasis on leniency, the unique logic of the common law is such that employment, as much as incarceration, is essential to maintaining order.

Notes

1. Abrams (1982) highlights the interplay of agency and structure in shaping social life—a theme celebrated by William Sewell (1980) in his classic analysis of labor and revolution in France during the nineteenth century. It is precisely the lack of agency in the poststructural analyses of Foucault (1979) that often elicits critique.

2. The primary focus of plea bargaining in the nineteenth century clearly seems to have been what is today called sentence bargaining. Dockets from the lower court of Boston for the nineteenth century occasionally show explicit notations of charge reductions accompanying changes of plea. Hence, some charge bargaining may also have occurred between arrest and appearance in court. However, the records of the Charles Street (Suffolk County) Jail show strong continuity between charge listed at time of arrest and the charge later listed in the court docket. This suggests that charge bargaining grew prominent only after sentence bargaining was established.

3. Despite its rural origins, republicanism, as an ideology, so pervaded Boston during the early nineteenth century that it colored the discourse of Democratic-Republicans and, later, National-Republicans and Whigs alike. After the collapse of the Federalist party nationally by 1817, there existed only one party, the Republicans, though Democrats and Whigs would soon differentiate themselves politically. An artisanal and, later, working class strand of republicanism also arose that can be traced through the nineteenth century to the mobilization of the Knights of Labor (Forbath, 1991).

4. For instance, it was not until 1837 that Boston established a day-time police force on the London model—a move opposed for many years for fear that it would be used as a secret police for state political purposes along the

lines of the French police in Paris (Lane, 1971). The police force replaced a tiny constabulary and a somewhat problematic night watch that had been a rotating responsibility among the citizenry.

5. Lane (1971) notes that local politics in Boston were controlled by an old federalist political elite largely united by ties of social class. Formal local political party organizations got strongly underway only in the late 1840s.

6. This should not be construed as an argument that stabilization is the primary force shaping contemporary plea bargaining for, as we shall see, plea negotiation was transformed during the mid-nineteenth century as it became intertwined with patronage politics. It was again transformed at the turn of the century with the rise of large-scale urban institutions when the practice became dominated by individualized and conditional treatment and by bureaucratic and career politics during the era of Progressive reform.

7. See Mary E. Vogel, "The Negotiated Guilty Plea: A Review of the Empirical Literature," prize winner, American Society of Criminology Student Paper Competition, 1978, for an analysis of this research and an assessment of its strengths and weaknesses.

8. Research on the consequences of plea bargaining explores the propensity of the practice to increase the likelihood of false convictions, induce sentencing leniency, or reduce the possibility that the guilty will be acquitted or dismissed (Finkelstein, 1975; Rhodes, 1976, 1978; Newman, 1966; Church, 1976; Vetri, 1964; Greenwood et al., 1973; Blumberg, 1967; Miller et al., 1977; Alschuler, 1968, 1975, 1976; Jacob, 1978; Eisenstein and Jacob, 1977; Berger, 1976; "The Elimination of Plea Bargaining in Black Hawk County," 1975; Skolnick, 1967; Cole, 1970; Heumann, 1975).

9. This second strand of research is inspired by the empirical fact that bargaining does not occur in every criminal case. These studies probe what factors account for the likelihood that a bargain will be consummated in an individual case. Among the features highlighted by this research are: case strength; seriousness of the crime; personal attributes of the prosecution, the defense, and the accused; strategies employed by the prosecution and the defense; relations between the defense attorney and his/her client; and the attitude of the police and the victim toward the defendant and the case (Lagoy, Senna, and Siegel, 1976; Alschuler, 1968, 1975; Mather, 1974; Nagel and Neef, 1976a, 1976b, 1976c; Landes, 1971; Rhodes, 1976, 1978; Rabin, 1972; Vetri, 1964; Jacob, 1972; Skolnick, 1967; Posner, 1973).

10. This set of studies, which probe why plea bargaining occurs, usually offers one of two explanations. One is that caseload pressures in the courts—that is, a backlog of charged suspects awaiting disposition, necessitates some alternative that is speedier and more efficient than courtroom trial (Posner, 1973; Cole, 1970; Skolnick, 1967; Blumberg, 1967; Heumann, 1975; Vetri, 1964; Church, 1976). The second set of explanations contends that the practice emerged because it serves the interests of both the defendant and all officials of the criminal justice system who are involved—that is, everyone gains by negotiating (Alschuler, 1968, 1975a, and 1975b; Nagel and Neef, 1976a, 1976b, and 1976c; Rhodes, 1976, 1978; Landes, 1971; Feeley, 1973; Jacob, 1978; Eisenstein and Jacob, 1977). Specific models of the emergence of plea bargaining in this family of approaches are functional analyses, rational decision-making,

social conflict, bureaucratic pressures for collaboration, work group models, market metaphors, and analyses of professional incentives. Models of this latter sort sometimes consider alleviation of caseload pressure as one of several in a rich array of relevant interests.

11. In terms of the possible relation of complexity and bargaining, court vignettes published by Thomas Gil of *The Boston Morning Post* indicate that cases in the lower court were rarely complex. Typically, only the judge and defendant faced each other with witnesses occasionally called. Neither the state nor the defendant were usually represented by counsel before the mid-nineteenth century (Friedman, 1993, p. 391). The vignettes reveal the trial proceeding in the lower court in Boston to be summary in nature and relatively devoid of the complexity that increasingly characterizes the higher courts during the late nineteenth and twentieth centuries—a finding quite similar to that of Roger Lane for nineteenth-century Philadelphia (Thomas, 1839; letter from Lane to Albert W. Alschuler dated October 25, 1978 and cited in Alschuler, 1979).

12. This created an incentive to go beyond mere adherence to the basic terms of a labor contract to render "loyal service." Given the great frequency with which citizens appeared before the courts, the availability of a benign employer or patron was a significant asset.

13. If the exercise of power in modern society is not to be a politically expensive show of naked force, then an approach is needed for stabilizing conflict and a rhetoric showing that things are as they should be must be articulated. Law has historically played a key role in accomplishing both of these purposes. Weber (1968) highlights the centrality of legitimation to the persistence of political authority. Antonio Gramsci (1971) has distinguished two bases of political rule in modern society—coercion or rule by force, on the one hand, and hegemony, which refers to the role of ideology in cultivating and sustaining the consent of the governed, on the other. He points to the strength and durability of political regimes that succeed in establishing such acceptance.

14. Alexis de Tocqueville (1970) illustrates such a rhetoric with his concept of the American philosophy of Self-Interest Properly Understood. Gramsci (1971) has emphasized the tendency of such ideologies to depict existing social relationships as the "natural order" of things.

15. As Patterson (1982) has succinctly put it, "All power strives for authority" (p. 35). In Weber's (1968) terms, a regime attempts to inculcate among a populace a sense of its legitimation, that is, a belief in its "right to command" and in their "duty to obey" (p. 943).

16. This holds particularly true for political authority of the rational-legal variety that bases its legitimation in the enactment of its rules and the specification of its public offices in law.

17. In his application of structuring, Abrams builds on C. Wright Mills' (1959) observation in *The Sociological Imagination* of the centrality of the interplay of biography, social structure, and history in sociological analysis; on Bourdieu's concept of social reproduction; and on the work of Norbert Elias (1982) on the civilizing process.

18. Berger and Luckmann, *The Social Construction of Reality;* Roberto Unger, *Social Theory: Its Situation and Task* (Cambridge: Cambridge University Press, 1987); Max Weber " 'Objectivity' in the Social Sciences," *The Methodology of the Social Sciences,* 1949.

19. Tomlins, 1993, p. 20.

20. The author is indebted to Tomlins (1993) for this concept of "law as a modality of rule."

21. This constituted a dramatic departure from the traditional practice in many societies of sentencing schedules that stipulated a graduated series of penalties that varied according to the social rank of both the victim and the accused as well as the social distance, if any, that separated the two. In England, for instance, some of the most severe penalties were reserved for offenses committed by persons of lowly rank against those of high station. Thus, while a cottager caught stealing from the home of another cottager might find himself fined a few pence, a cottager thus entering the home of a bishop might be fined several hundred pounds or, if the home be of a member of royalty, might be hanged.

22. Mill's (1859) treatise *On Liberty* reintroduces skepticism over state use of power in a context of self-rule. According to Mill, under monarchical rule, the authority of kings was viewed as "necessary, but also as highly "dangerous . . . ," and liberty referred to the successful efforts of patriots "to set limits to the power which the ruler should be suffered to exercise over the community . . ." (p. 6). With the rise of self-rule, however, the idea arose that "rulers should be identified with the people; that their interest and will should be identified with the people; that their interest and will should be the interest and will of the nation" (p. 7). Mill (1975) notes that the hazardous corollary of this vision was the notion that "The nation did not need to be protected against its own will" (p. 7).

As democratic republics grew more widespread, however, it gradually became apparent that "the 'people' who exercise the power are not always the same people with those over whom it is exercised" (p. 8). Thus, the need to conserve liberty by maintaining protections for the masses against misuse of state power remained keen.

23. While one might tend to equate the late eighteenth century notion of "police" with the uniformed service that emerged to patrol the streets and ways of towns and cities in the nineteenth century, we shall see that this is not the case. Instead, "police" here refers to the eighteenth-century notion that order and harmony can be achieved through moderation in social life enabled by the free pursuit of safety and happiness in a world of self-rule.

24. As understanding of causation in human affairs according to scientific laws matured, human agency grew problematic and debate over the extent of voluntarism relative to determinism flourished.

25. For an insightful account of this transition and of the qualities of liberalism, see Tomlins (1993). While I will disagree with Tomlins on this point, he argues that the conceptual hallmarks of liberalism were: individualism in the social and economic spheres, emphasis on the protection of private property, a democracy consistently constrained by judicial review, and a limited state (Tomlins, 1993). See also Wood (1991,

p. 323); Joyce Appleby, "The Radical 'Double Entendre' in the Right to Self Government," in Jacob and Jacob, eds., *Origins of Anglo-American Radicalism*, p. 275–83; Horwitz (1987, pp. 57–74).

26. See Nettl (1968, pp. 559–592); Hegel (1956, pp. 84–87); and Kelly (1972, pp. 2–36, cited in Skowronek (1982)).

27. Hegel attributed the lack of such institutions to the geographic isolation of America from external threats to its security and the ability to abate internal sources of conflict through movement to its vast frontier (1956, pp. 84–87).

28. This "organizational view" of the American state is also one advanced by Poggi (1991, pp. 97–98).

29. While the observation about the weakness and decentralization of the state in America seems apt, it may be that in ignoring the decentralized and relatively weak central state in England, Skowronek overemphasizes the uniqueness of the American situation.

30. For an excellent discussion of these theoretical perspectives to which this author is indebted, see Steinmetz (1993).

31. This work starts from a presumption of social transformation as an ongoing historical process in which law plays a crucial role, or as Novak has put it, a "constitutive" role, taking as a central question for study the mechanisms, events, and choices through which such metamorphosis occurs (Thompson, 1963; Katznelson and Zolberg, 1990; Giddens, 1987). The roles of language and contestation in shaping consciousness, human development, and choice are also highlighted (Sewell, 1980; Wittgenstein, 1958).

32. The author is indebted to Louise Tilly for directing her attention to this distinction and to the central place of Hartz's (1953) work in debates over conceptions of the state.

33. While often referred to as a nation state, the state, as such, must be clearly differentiated from the even more elusive notion of the nation. The nation may be thought of, following Ernest Gellner (1983) as a group of persons who "share the same culture" and "recognize certain mutual rights and duties to each other in virtue of their shared membership in it" (p. 7). No less than statebuilding was the forging of a nation in America during the nineteenth century a central political concern.

34. The author appreciatively acknowledges the contribution of Said Arjomand in first bringing this point to her attention.

35. Nativism was a political movement and sentiment centered on opposition to those not American born. While it persisted more or less continuously throughout the nineteenth and early twentieth centuries, when it culminated in immigration restriction, nativism periodically combined with a virulent nationalism to produce strong exclusionary activity in labor and politics. Nativism primarily took three forms: anti-Catholicism; fear of foreign agitators especially among the ranks of labor; and racism.

36. While Brown (1950) has emphasized that relatively large proportions of men in the towns and cities of colonial Massachusetts could vote, he acknowledges that between 20 percent and 33 percent were typically excluded. Immigration after 1800 began to swell the ranks of the laboring and marginal groups most likely to be ex-

cluded, groups for whom extension of "universal suffrage" during the mid-1830s opened the way.

37. For an exceptionally lucid, programmatic introduction to this methodological approach, see Rheinhard Bendix, "Concepts and Generalizations in Comparative Sociological Studies," *American Sociological Review* 28 (4) August 1963, pp. 532–539; Abrams (1982); Skocpol, (1984); and Victoria Bonnell, "The Uses of Theory, Concepts and Comparison in Historical Sociology," *Comparative Studies in History*, 22 (2) 1980, pp. 156–173.

38. Mann's readiness to play on the fears of the propertied elite about the potential excesses both of the restive democratic masses and their representatives in the legislature led Ralph Waldo Emerson to parody the message of the school campaign in the words "you must educate [the masses] . . . to keep them from our throats" (Atkinson, 1980, pp. 458–59, cited in Sellers, 1991, p. 368).

39. Examples of works in this genre of causal analysis include: Theda Skocpol, *States and Social Revolutions: A Comparative Analysis of France, Russia and China*, Cambridge, England: Cambridge University Press, 1979; Charles Tilly, *The Vendee*, Cambridge, Massachusetts: Harvard University Press, 1964; and Moore (1967).

40. The analysis employs Mill's logical method of difference to control variation as contrasts are drawn between the United States, on the one hand, where plea bargaining initially emerged, and Great Britain and the countries of the European continent, on the other hand, where no practice even roughly comparable appears to have emerged until much later. The logic of concomitant variation, an extension of Mill's method of agreement, is applied to analyze variation over time and across types of offenses within the United States.

41. Despite its many paired comparisons, this study focuses primarily on a single society, the United States, and, within it, the city of Boston, where the earliest known practice of plea bargaining began. Much has been written about the practical methodological dilemmas of case studies (Campbell, 1975; Lijphart, 1971; Ragin, 1981; Ragin and Becker, 1992; and Skocpol, 1984). Most can be handled either by specific paired comparisons to other societies or by formulating multiple independent outcomes for study or the case at hand. Both safeguards are used in this study (Campbell, 1975; Skocpol, 1984). Multiple outcomes mean that, although in any one case study, there is a high probability of apparent association between an hypothesized cause and any one outcome simply by chance, the likelihood of this occurring across multiple outcomes contracts exponentially with each new addition.

42. The years 1830–1855 mark the emergence of the practice of plea bargaining in Massachusetts. The second phase, 1855–1900, marks the rise of local patronage politics in Massachusetts along with the massive European immigrations and industrialization with the social conflict that it entailed. The final period, 1900–1920, is essentially that of progressive reform, and it marks the rise of large-scale institutions for the administration of justice.

43. This necessitated finding a locale whose history as a political unit went back to 1800 and where high-quality records had originally been kept and were preserved to this day. Only a few states have historically noted charge, plea, disposition, and sentence systematically in their dockets, even at the Superior Court level. Several of those

areas emerged as political entities after 1800, and many of their social and political histories are relatively undeveloped.

44. The stratified sample was balanced by plea to ensure both a mix of "guilty" and "not guilty" pleas for analysis and sufficient cell sizes for robust and stable estimation. Cases for the stratified sample were drawn by sampling randomly until a total of twenty cases for each offense had been selected—half involving "guilty" pleas and half pleas of "not guilty." A record of all cases drawn was kept although data were collected only for cases involving the five selected offenses. While cases sampled in this way are not representative of the sample as a whole, this technique does not distort the relation between plea and outcome in the cases sampled—but, in fact, ensures enough variation in the plea to enable sound estimation of its effects on the aspects of disposition and sentencing that are of interest.

45. In a standard sampling procedure, targets of twenty cases involving "guilty" pleas (or pleas changed to "guilty") plus twenty with "not guilty" pleas were sought for each type of offense. If, in progressing through the random numbers, our target had been saturated, no further cases of that type were collected although a complete record of what is, in principle, a second random sample was kept.

46. For classic introductions to this powerful historiographical technique, see Thernstrom (1973, Appendices A and B) and Dublin (1979, Appendices).

CHAPTER TWO

1. Far from preoccupied with progress, Miller found that the lofty ambitions of that community produced greater familiarity with "declension" or noble defeat (Appleby, 1992, p. 21).

CHAPTER THREE

1. In attempting to explain what law is and how it changes over time, sociologists today turn primarily to one of three types of theories of law: internal, mechanical, or social. Internal theories focus, as Friedman (1977) puts it, on "rules, processes and structures inside the system itself," tending to disregard forces in the broader social environment of the courts (p. 92). The second, mechanical theories, envision the legal system in terms of a "machine" metaphor in which inputs and rules yielded outputs that were "correct" decisions on legal problems. While popular for a time during the nineteenth century, this view was subsequently set aside by virtually all serious scholars of law.

The social theories focus on social forces "outside the legal system . . . (and) stress the general culture, economic forces or other social causes of law" (Friedman, 1977, pp. 92–93). In recent decades, the social theories have encountered strongly rising popularity, to some extent as a result of efforts to devise responses to proponents of the law and economics perspective and to the critical legal studies movement.

2. British liberalism in social and political thought is commonly held to have its origin in the work of Thomas Hobbes, with his articulation of the emergence and interplay of passionate self-interest and the designation of a sovereign to whom indi-

viduals surrender themselves in the interest of preserving life, property, and some modicum of peace. In Hobbes' view, rights follow from the establishment of a sovereign and the state.

Liberalism culminates in what may be characterized as a utilitarian variant, which received its classic statement in the works of Jeremy Bentham and John Stuart Mill, and a natural rights variant articulated in the works of John Locke. Whereas Locke, drawing on the writings of Althusius and Grotius, sought to define the contours of a representative government that would preserve the rights of citizens rooted in a natural law, Bentham and Mills sought to define rights as guarantees of the state— guarantees that require limitations on the power of the state as it pursued a "common good" or, in Bentham's terms, "the greatest good of the greatest number."

Departing in many ways such as ethical and legal relativism from liberalism, it has become increasingly popular in recent years to distinguish a republican tradition. Though quite distinct, it affiliates most closely with British liberalism. Features that this republican tradition share with liberalism include: its rationalism, emphasis on natural law and natural rights, its orientation to constitutional government, and, ultimately, its focus on the organization of government, specifically, separation of powers, as the key to preserving liberty. This variant has one root in Montesquieu's *Spirit of the Laws* with its emphasis on civic spirit and public virtue. As an importation to France of natural rights theory, this republican variant was subsequently questioned and developed by Helvetius in *De l'Esprit* into a brand of French utilitarianism that was to greatly influence both Bentham and Beccaria (Sabine, 1973, p. 564).

3. The French communitarian tradition has its roots in the social contract theory of Jean Jacques Rousseau. Rousseau, like Hobbes, explicitly rejects the notion of natural law as a basis for rights and argues that rights emerge in the legal context of a sovereign who reflects a General Will and to whom a people surrender through their participation in the social contract itself. As Sabine (1973) has pointed out, nothing in the concept of the General Will required that it be "shared consciously by the whole people" or that it be "expressed only in a popular assembly" (p. 593). Thus, Rousseau's vision of popular sovereignty is often held to legitimate French Jacobinism and the Reign of Terror and, as Gierke has observed, to promulgate principles of revolutionary foment. If the natural-law theories of the Enlightenment sought to liberate humans from the absolutism of sixteenth- and seventeenth-century political life, Rousseau's sentimental and subjectivist collectivism directly challenged that line of thought.

4. The third enormously rich and heterogeneous tradition, which is termed German idealism and dialectical reaction, fit together most uncomfortably in terms of shared substance but form a clear continuity in terms of the intellectual process of their development. This tradition has its origins in the writings of Immanuel Kant who saw a natural antagonism among humans rooted in self-interest and the desire of every human to direct everything according to his own wishes as the condition that promotes both conflict and the development of human capacities and sets man on the road from barbarism to civilization. The challenge to humankind, Kant observed in his *Philosophy of Law*, is the establishment of a civil society that universally administers justice according to law. As Cairns (1949) has shown, for Kant, the highest pur-

pose of Nature, which is the development of all mankind's capabilities, requires a "society which possesses the greatest liberty, and which consequently involves a thorough antagonism of its members—with, however, an exact determination and guarantee of the limits of this liberty in order that there may be mutual freedom for all members" (p. 395). Thus, the optimal society is one that combines liberty under the laws with the irresistible power of a perfectly just civil constitution.

5. Hegel's work constituted a reformation of German idealism to counter what he saw as analytic reductionism in philosophic and scientific thought and the excesses of modern individualism. Much of Hegel's work can be seen as a continuation of prevailing critiques of natural rights theory. While the nature of Hegel's view of the state precluded a discussion of rights per se, his views on freedom and law are clearly articulated in the *Philosophy of Right*. Freedom, for Hegel, rather than being a state or property of the individual, arises through the moral and political development of the community. Freedom, for Hegel, consists in "the adjustment of inclination and individual capacity to the performance of socially significant work" (Sabine, 1973, p. 655). Thus, liberty is realized only in the context of the state in modern society and requires that "desires coincide with some phase of the general good and . . . [be] supported by the general will" (p. 655).

Thus, rights and liberties coincide with the duties imposed by one's status and position in society, and the "destructive and false freedom" of self-interest is replaced with the "true freedom" of citizenship. For Hegel, the activities of humans in the marketplace or civil society were a mere play of irrational desires, while the state was the sole source of moral purposes that, through citizenship, could open the way to genuine freedom. This collectivistic view of freedom, coupled with Hegel's denial in the preface to the *Philosophy of Right* of the citizen's right even to criticize the state, paved the way for the support of state absolutism that ultimately emerges out of Hegel's work.

Yet, while rights are problematic in Hegel's view, law was not. According to Hegel, state power is absolute but not arbitrary lest it be transformed to despotism. Instead, Hegel contended that the regulatory powers of the state must always be exercised according to law, which is an embodiment of reason and a rational institution. Law ensures that officials do not act on personal interest or caprice and ensures predictability and security of property and person.

6. By way of contrast, Marx accepted Hegel's emphasis on the dialectic but rejected his idealism. In an effort to restore the focus of sociological study to the material conditions of life, Marx depicted law, like politics, as part of an ideational superstructure that largely reflects the prevailing relations of power and ruling class interests.

7. Weber, a neo-Kantian, continues in the debate over idealism, rejecting the Hegelian dialectic and accepting a neo-Platonist focus on values as eternal forms toward which humans throughout history strive. Weber's political vision is that of a German liberal and Parliamentary democracy. Weber views law as a command backed up by the enforcement power of the state. Both Kant and Weber may also, alternately, be seen as thinkers in the tradition of German liberalism while Hegel and Marx manifest strong communitarian themes.

8. Social control was made all the more problematic by the fact that, during the late seventeenth century, the establishment of a professional police force on the continental model had been rejected because citizens feared its emergence as a state-controlled secret police.

9. Stone also takes issue with what appear to this author to be two lesser points in Thompson's work. First, he asserts that Thompson and his colleagues overestimate the propensity for criminality inherent in eighteenth-century British society. Stone (1981) states that "intensive investigation of English social history . . . [suggests] that England in the 1720s was no more corrupt, no more swarming with 'great predators' than it had been at any time in the previous 180 years or was to be for the next fifty" (p. 196). He continues with the observation that "Only a historian looking back from the more respectable and bureaucratic period of the Napoleonic wars would see anything especially corrupt about the England of the 1720s . . ." (p. 196). He concludes that "one looking forward from the 1540s or the 1620s would see a positive improvement" (p. 196).

Stone's (1981) second lesser criticism of Thompson's work centers on the distinction Thompson draws between "nefarious crime for personal gain and 'social crime' which conformed to community standards, received widespread protection and support in the locality, and was often used to pressure the authorities to adopt popular concepts of natural justice" (p. 191). He claims that what is, for Thompson, a key distinction "turns out on close inspection to be sometimes hard to draw and not very helpful as an analytical tool" (p. 198). Here Stone cites, as obfuscating marginal cases, highwaymen, who were popularly supported in their activities of robbing the rich, and a group of Yorkshire "coiners" who coined forged money that provided needed resources for the local community at the same time they undermined the national economy.

10. What lends Stone's challenge to Thompson on this score a bit of a paradoxical air is that it is largely due to Thompson's ground-breaking work in his book *The Making of the English Working Class* (1963), that the central role of craftsmen and artisans in these movements has become well known to historical sociologists and social historians alike.

11. Alexis de Tocqueville (1835) illustrates such a rhetoric with his concept of the American Philosophy of Self-Interest Properly Understood. Gramsci (1971) has emphasized the tendency of such ideologies to depict existing social relationships as the "natural order of things."

12. Thompson (1978) has emphasized the development amidst the culture of the working class of a distinct moral economy—that is, a widely shared sense of what constitute fair "terms of trade" in any interaction, public or private. Popular acceptance of the law required its acceptability in terms of that moral economy.

13. This holds particularly true for political authority of the rational-legal variety which bases its legitimation in the enactment of its rules and the specification of its public offices in law.

14. In sketching the contours of successive generations of legal thinking in this section, I am generally indebted to Novak's superb treatment of this subject in *The People's Welfare*, Chicago, Ill.: University of Chicago Press, 1996.

15. Thus, cultural practices—both formal and informal—shape orderly action.

16. Marx and Engels (1967) go so far as to state that "the theory of the communists may be summed up in a single sentence: Abolition of private property" (p. 96).

17. Autonomy, in this account, may arise, for instance, when warring classes achieve a balance in power and the state, as ostensible mediator, achieves a certain immunity from the claims of each group (Cain, 1979).

18. The author is indebted here to analyses of theories of the state presented in Carnoy (1984); Esping-Anderson (1988, 1990, 1996), Skocpol (1975, 1995), Skocpol and Campbell (1994), Steinmetz (1993), Wickham and Hunt (1994), Calhoun (1994 and 1995) and Holub (1992).

19. So fertile and creative was this period that the Atlantic Republican tradition, of which we have already spoken and which drew on Plato's vision of a participatory, virtuous and democratic republic, also emerged from this same cultural and political foment.

20. Focusing first on policies that would create wealth, cameralists saw it as the duty of a ruler to provide for the prosperity of his subjects," who had been created with dignity in the image of God, by "making them more productive" (Spannaus, 2002, p. 2). Moving beyond a country's natural endowment, such as bullion, mineral deposits and a strategic location for trade, which cannot create wealth per se, cameralism focused on craft and manufactures; the quality, especially the education, of a population; and state policy since it is these which any state can, if wisely managed, use to yield almost limitless surplus (Spannaus, 2002, p. 3). Painters and stonemasons, it was argued, benefit from knowledge of science both in happiness and in the quality of their works. Such thinking led Leibniz to propose creating an academy to foster arts and science.

21. While some see cameralism as a particular and non-generalizable approach to state craft or critique it as a reactionary stance of autocratic states, others see a foundation for Christian political economy and, later, a theoretical cornerstone for social democracy (Spannaus and White, 1977).

22. Becher speaks of society as consisting of three parts—soul, mind and body—with the "soul . . . comprised of government and the church, the mind of the scientists and teachers, and the body of the peasants, craftsmen and merchants" (Spannaus, 2002, p. 5). Health of the first two, according to Becher is fully dependent on that of the third group of productive classes (Spannaus, 2002, p. 5). He offers the metaphor of a violin and observes that "[j]ust as when one is to play on a violin, one must first examine and tune each string, so when its sustenance is to be assured to a community, attention must be paid to every sort of human being that there is" (Becher, "Political Discourse," cited in Spannaus, 2002, p. 5).

23. Countering arguments that prosperity might decrease motivation, Leibniz argued that "One might object that artisans today work out of necessity; if all their needs were satisfied, then they would not work at all. I, however, maintain the contrary, that they would be glad to do more than they now do out of necessity. For, first of all, if a man is unsure of his sustenance, he has neither the heart nor the spirit for anything; will only produce as much as he expects to sell . . . ; concerns himself with trivialities; and does not have the heart to undertake anything new and important. He

thus earns little, must often drink to excess merely in order to dull his own sense of desperation and drown his sorrows, and is tormented by the malice of his journeymen" ("Society and Economy," cited in Spannaus, 2002, pp. 6–7).

24. In England, cameralist ideas also received consideration at the highest levels not only through diplomatic contacts and networks of trade but also perhaps the familial of Britain's royal family, first, to Hanover and, later, to Saxe-Coburg-Gotha through Queen Victoria's courtship by and later marriage to the scholarly German Prince Albert in 1840.

25. What is, at times, this indistinguishability between state and civil society in Hegel arises out of the corporative form of association of his day which "grafted . . . [politics] directly on the economy" (Cohen and Arato, 1994). It is a tendency that appears also later to have influenced Gramsci.

26. Though little enoted, Bourdieu veers, at times, toward the terrain of radical subjectivism occupied by Nietsche and the post-modernists—most notably when he argues that the separation of scientist and object of study is often more apparent than real (Lipuma et al., 1993). This leads him to emphasize the possibilities for misrecognition as one element of a vision of human cognition that paves the way for an alternative to the Marxian concept of false consciousness.

27. In this way Bourdieu seeks to resolve Kant's objections to the possibility of knowledge of the world through the senses. In Lukac's terms, Bourdieu seeks to overcome the subject/object distinction and, in so doing, to unify theory and practice.

28. What results is a reciprocity of social structure and agency in which these dispositions to act are both structured, or constituted, and structuring.

29. The habitus, Bourdieu contends, functions unconsciously within a limited range of possibilities.

30. It yields a view of behavior as socially influenced without being either strictly rulebound or structurally determined. Nor does it tend to instrumental rationality as thinkers of the Frankfurt School had foreseen (Held, 1980; Horkheimer, 1974). It enables capability and mastery in practice, ostensibly without inexorable movement to domination (Held, 1974; Lipuma et al., 1993). By inherently privileging the subjective in his challenge to the notion of objectivity, however, Bourdieu may inadvertently usher in domination of a different sort based on the status differentials of holders of equally valid subjectivities.

31. For Bourdieu, capital is the capacity to exercise "control over one's own future and that of others" (Lipuma et al., 1993). Individuals, operating amidst uncertainty and limited rationality, seek, as Bourdieu sees it, to enhance their capital and to maximize benefits given the limits of their relational place within a field.

32. The former centers on relationships, especially connections to important social networks, while the latter involves cultural experiences, including education, and familiarity with arts and letters.

33. Yet Bourdieu then moves to highlight, not crisis tendencies foreseen by Marx, but processes both of the social reproduction of class distinctions and of institutional continuity that are likely to impede critique, mobilization, conflict and change.

34. Each such field is semi-autonomous with its own logic and forms of capital though the value of capital may be transferable across fields (Lipuma et al., 1993).

35. One can see in the habitus some parallels to the self of George Herbert Mead's symbolic interactionism in its reflexivity as it encounters itself as both agent and object in history.

36. What has occurred in the modern age, Habermas argues, is that social control, initially vested in kinship relations, was re-situated in the state during the period of centralization of state authority in the 16th century. Production processes too were detached from kinship and reconstructed as larger scale means of production. Thus, the state appears as a key enabling force in the rise of capitalism but also a crucial basis of class society and struggle.

37. In a sense, Habermas harks back to Aristotle's classical conception of politics as part of the good and just life—separate from techne or science—and involving establishment of a community of meaningful discourse.

38. It was this recognition that led Habermas to his study of discourse and speech acts as ways of reestablishing meaning.

39. This tendency is fostered by several historical dynamics. In the *Structural Transformation of the Public Sphere* Habermas shows that the rise of the modern state is concomitant with the emergence of authentic politicall discourse in the public sphere. While scholars, such as Nancy Fraser, have pointed out that this discourse was more elitist and less inclusive than often thought, the rise of public debate by a reading public was a major shift in politics in the West. Over the course of the nineteenth century, two historical changes weakened public participation and, with it, the legitimation of authority in the West. First, the rise of consumerism supplants participation with a more passive process of culture consumption wherein critique, initiative and judgment decline. Second, the power of legitimating symbolism is eroded and degraded.

40. According to Kant, everyday ideas and beliefs tend to become internalized and a taken for granted part of our outlook that can muddy our vision and inhibit one from hearing clearly one's inner moral voice. In Habermas's hands, the philosophical influence of Dewey, Pierce and pragmatism leads to a focus on ethics.

41. As Renate Holub points out, Lukacs' opposition to modernism is "well known" and has "cost him influence, credibility and theoretical force" (Holub, 1992, p. 7). She continues: "[Lukacs was] . . . attentive to epistemological models that are capable of accounting for all parts in the whole . . . [H]e rejects a vision of the world that finds delight in fragments rather than totality, in gaps rather than relations, in multiplicities of viewpoint rather than objectivity and truth" (p. 7).

42. In Gramsci's emphasis on the "production and control of needs and desires" as well as potential for the "manipulation and domination of the cultural sphere," he shares a set of distinctly modern concerns and, occasionally, hints of the postmodern, with Volosinov, Brecht, Adorno, Horkheimer, and Benjamin. Through correspondence, he became familiar with the fractured realities of early Russian futurism and also with the structural linguistics of Wittgenstein (Holub, 1992, pp. 9–11).

43. While also sharing a commitment to the articulation of a critical perspective on fascism, Gramsci, like the others, was more concerned with elucidating the forces of modernization that had produced that political movement.

44. Illustrations of the ways Gramsci anticipates later modernists of the Frankfurt School include: "the way the young Gramsci critiques, as a cultural and theater critic in Turin the rise of the culture industry around World War I; the way in which he understands the cultural politics of the hegemonic social class, the gradual industrialization of culture, the increasing regulation, manipulation, surveillance and domination of the public and private spheres; his theory of consciousness or of the subject; which points to his awareness of alienation and reification when it comes to the bourgeois subject, but which he apparently rejects when it comes to the proletariat; his theory of the political potentials inscribed in new technologies; his theory of human nature, his ontology, so to speak, where humans always throughout the ages strive for freedom, displaying, thereby, an inherent principle of hope . . ." (Holub, 1992, p. 12).

45. By the 1930s, one finds in Gramsci's work a focus on "the speech act, . . . performance, . . . productive readings of texts, . . . production of meaning, notions of sign and signification . . ." (Holub, 1992, p. 17).

CHAPTER FOUR

1. What appears to have been the reluctance of most courts prior to the early nineteenth century to accept a plea of guilty is expressed in *Commonwealth v. Battis* (1804), where it was held "the court do not receive the plea of guilty to an indictment for a capital offense, except on due advisement to the prisoner of its consequences, nor without satisfactory proof aliunde, of its being made freely and in a sound state of mind" (1 Mass. 95; cited in the American Law Digest). A similar point is made in *Green v. Commonwealth* (94 Mass. (12 Allen) 155).

2. Typically, such notations took the form of a plea of "not guilty" crossed out in the handwritten docket ledger and changed to "guilty" with similar modifications indicating sentence or, occasionally, charge reduction entered for the same case.

3. See cases # 408, 729 and 1159 in the Boston Police Court docket for 1830 and # 805 and 1015 in that docket for 1840.

4. For instance, Alschuler (1979) notes that, while it has been possible since earliest cases in common law for the accused to confess his or her guilt, such confessions were exceedingly rare in the medieval period (Hunnisett, 1961; cited in Alschuler, p. 214). Similarly, he shows that the common law treatises of the seventeenth century were "hesitant" to accept the plea of guilty and [that] the plea of not guilty "receiveth great favor in the law" (Fulton, 1609, p. 184; cited in Alschuler, p. 214). This same "backwardness of the courts in receiving a plea of guilty" is also mentioned in *Blackstone's Commentaries on the Law of England* (1765–69, p. 329; cited in Alschuler, p. 214) and the court's reticence in accepting a guilty plea is explicitly approved by Chitty (1816, p. 429; cited in Alschuler, p. 214).

Speaking of judicial insistence on a presumption of innocence prior to 1830 in the *Rationale of Judicial Evidence*, Bentham declared "it is grown into a sort of fashion when a prisoner has (confessed and pled guilty), for the judge to persuade him to withdraw it . . . The wicked man repenting of his wickedness, the judge . . . bids him repent of his repentence and in place of the truth substitute a barefaced lie" (1827, vol. 2, p. 316; cited in Alschuler, 1975, p. 214).

5. Other practices, such as "love days" and arbitration or civil settlement appeared at various points (Clanchy, 1982; Moglen, 1983). However, while they involved compromise, they did not entail a grant of leniency from the state, so they are structurally quite different. Alschuler (1979) accurately critiques the tendency of some authors to point to practices, such as "benefit of the clergy," that include "neither plea nor bargain" as misguided efforts to show the ancient origins of plea bargaining.

6. To set these developments in historical context, the decades of the 1830s and 1840s that we are discussing were the days of the close of the Age of Jackson and a period of intense social reform. As the waning years of the Federalists in Boston, they ushered in the 1850s, which marked the beginning of the rise of ethnic politics and patronage at the local level, a practice that had played an exceedingly strong role at the state level since 1800.

7. This finding corresponds to Raymond Moley's (1929) observation that by 1839, 15 percent of all felony convictions in Manhattan and Brooklyn were the product of guilty pleas. By 1869, he found that guilty pleas accounted for 75 percent of all convictions. However, the courts are not strictly comparable, in that the Boston Police Court was a lower court whose jurisdiction excluded felonies. Moley does not present data on the extent to which concessions accompanied guilty pleas.

8. Available evidence from several sources reinforces my argument about a clear growth trend in plea bargaining during these years. In *Boston's Lower Criminal Courts, 1814–1850* (table 3.8, "Selected Outcomes in Police Court, 1826–1850"), Theodore Ferdinand provides the following biannual counts of guilty plea rates for the Boston Police Court: 1826 (0.0%); 1828 (9.3%); 1832 (5.2%); 1834 (8.1%); 1836 (15.9%); 1838 (19.0%); 1840 (19.9%); 1842 (25.7%); 1844 (35.1%); 1846 (36.7%); 1848 (37.2%); and 1850 (37.1%). Ferdinand concludes that "guilty pleas displayed a rising tendency during most of this period . . ." (p. 83). These rates are reportedly based on simple counts of various types of pleas in the docket, although some questions are raised by total caseloads cited of 2,177 and 4,377 cases for 1840 and 1850, respectively, while the Police Court docket shows 2,383 and 4,811 cases for those years. Inconsistencies among the overall and offense-specific plea rates cited for 1826 as well as the work's habit of inexplicably using plea rates that combine pleas of nolo contendere with guilty pleas for some tables are also puzzling (Ferdinand, 1992, pp. 32, 90). Data for 1830 are not presented for unknown reasons. The study then relies heavily on those guilty plea rates in making claims about the plea negotiations they might represent while ignoring criminal career and seriousness of crime that may be crucial in determining whether or not an accompanying sentence constitutes a grant of leniency.

The scenario of a surge of guilty pleas in Boston during the 1830s, which then spread, accompanied by concessions as we shall see, through diffusion to other cities and notably to New York, dovetails closely with Raymond Moley's (1929) finding that, as of 1839, 15 percent of all felony *convictions* in Manhattan and Brooklyn were the product of guilty pleas. By 1869, he found that guilty pleas accounted for 75 percent of all convictions. While the courts are not strictly comparable, as shown in note 6 above, Moley's data suggest that the rise of plea bargaining in New York lagged that in Boston, where guilty pleas accounted for 35 percent of all *convictions* by 1840 (and 17 percent of all cases.

9. Docket entries suggest, as we shall see, that this is because, under the rubric of individualized treatment, other more-explicit and personally customized discretionary means of resolving cases were increasingly used. These included probation and a revival of the old practice of continuing cases "open" on file as an informal variant of what was effectively that same practice.

10. In constructing the counts and plea rates for the aggregate of all offenses, cases with multiple defendants and diverse pleas were classified as "other," since no single plea could be isolated. In constructing the offense-specific counts, cases that involved multiple defendants and offenses were set aside, as were those in which diverse pleas were entered for a single offense. Should other such counts be made again, it may make sense to count offenders instead of cases. Comparison of the counts, thus constructed, to the simple random sample suggests that the effect of this decision rule was not significant.

11. As shown in table 4.4, Ferdinand (1992) provides support for many of the findings reported in my study regarding offense-specific guilty plea rates. Ferdinand also concludes that offense-specific guilty plea rates more than doubled between the early 1830s and the close of that decade for larceny, assault and battery, public drunkenness, and prostitution. Exactly what kinds of cases his study includes in each offense category is, however, unclear.

For the years 1840 and 1850, the Ferdinand study suggests a gradual progressive increase for public drunkenness and for prostitution—a pattern that generally supports my own findings on the common drunkard cases. The guilty plea rate presented by Ferdinand for prostitution, however, is challenged by my data. Close scrutiny suggests an answer. Ferdinand cites a guilty plea rate of 27.3% for prostitution in 1840. However, the Police Court docket for 1840 contains a total of only 20 cases of nightwalking and common nightwalking (i.e., prostitution) in all its pages, and only two of those cases show pleas of "guilty" entered. Given these raw numbers, computing "guilty" pleas as a percentage of either total pleas or total cases yields a guilty plea rate of 10.0 percent. These data raise important questions about the guilty plea rate of 27.2 percent for prostitution cited by Ferdinand as do references to the 113 prostitution cases cited by him for that same year. Clearly, whatever boundaries the study is using for this category are highly inclusive and unspecified, providing results quite different from prostitution per se. This is worth noting because Ferdinand claims that plea bargaining begins with "vice" and regulatory cases.

Guilty plea rates from my random sample for larceny and for assault and battery also present some challenges to Ferdinand's figures. As shown in table 4.3 and 4.4, my study shows a high ratio of not guilty-to-guilty pleas for assault and battery in 1840 and a lower one for larceny in 1850. Since it is not clear exactly how Ferdinand is defining offenses, some discrepancy might be expected. However, consistency of Ferdinand's estimates and my own for 1830 and for the drunkenness cases suggests another explanation. The assault and battery category in Ferdinand's study appears to include everything from simple assault and battery (the sole focus of my own analysis) to "assault with a razor" or "with a revolver and intent to kill" or "on an officer with intent to free a prisoner." Some of these more serious cases are clearly heading on appeal for higher court, and choice of plea becomes part of the appeal strategy rather than a real quest for leniency in Police Court. Including them, without distinguishing from simple assault and battery, mixes noncomparables and distorts the plea rate, as guilty pleas are used in serious cases in an effort to avoid transfer to higher Municipal Court.

By apparently constructing guilty plea rates solely as a percentage of "total cases," Ferdinand may allow them to be dominated by factors such as the rates at which different kinds of cases are eventually transferred to Municipal Court. Frequent transfers prior to entry of any plea would artificially dampen and smooth annual guilty plea rates due to a large group of inert cases. For instance, for larceny in 1840, approximately 40 percent of defendants found that, when the complaint was read, they were ordered to post surety to appear in Municipal Court. Computing guilty pleas as a percentage of all pleas, as well as all cases along with use of plea ratios in my study, attempts to adjust for that.

12. This "model" decomposes the bargaining outcome analytically into a series of potential effects of plea on a series of dispositions and sentencing outcomes in each case. For a technical discussion of the properties of this model, see Daniel L. McFadden, "Econometric Analysis of Qualitative Response Models" in Zvi Griliches and Michael D. Intriligator, *Handbook of Econometrics* Vol. II, New York: North-Holland, 1984. Because a linear regression model with a binary outcome and single binary independent variable essentially computes average probabilities, the use of this approach is completely appropriate here. It also provides a convenient descriptive tool that can be expanded on to include effects of criminal careers as well as those of case seriousness and the social characteristics of defendants, for which data are available.

Where outcomes are probabilities and independent variables are several, re-estimation of coefficients using logit can be undertaken to assure accuracy and good form. However, the results of a logit are foregone in presenting key findings here because the results of such an equation using only one independent variable is equivalent to computing an average probability and so is not susceptible to the hazard of one with more-extended functional form. In addition, the meaning of the simple linear probability coefficients is more readily accessible to most readers. Preliminary analysis provided no evidence of any significant difference in the results when logit was used.

13. Plea was entered as a dummy variable that assumed a value of 1 if the plea was "guilty" or 0 if the plea of "not guilty" was entered. Only cases where a sentence had been imposed were included in this analysis.

14. One other explicit concession that was frequently used was suspension of a term of imprisonment for a specified number of hours to allow a defendant to leave town. If the defendant returned during the term of the sentence, an arrest would follow. If the defendant stayed away, no actual time would be served.

15. In a day when the average daily wage for an unskilled laborer was $1.00 and when large numbers of families, particularly families of recent immigrants, lived at

the financial brink without savings, extended committal for nonpayment of a fine could threaten financial disaster.

16. As we shall see shortly, even if high guilty plea rates for vice and for minor breaches of city ordinances existed during the early 1830s, these pleas do not appear to have produced concessions—at least insofar as close analysis of comparable drunkenness and nightwalking cases show. Instead, these cases tended disproportionately to involve women, children, and servants along with a small minority of businessmen, and their treatment appears to have reflected the earlier Puritan fear of threat to social hierarchy as well as practices such as admonition and reconciliation in the Puritan religious courts. While such Puritan practice was part of the symbolic repertoire on which the common law drew, plea bargaining arose only after other elements came into play (Vogel, 1988).

While breach of ordinances in the higher Municipal Court often involved proprietors selling liquor without a license, cases in Police Court were more likely to include "throwing house offal in the street," "leaving a cellar door open," or "humming tunes." Their "perpetrators" were very often wives, minors, and servants who had no independent political identity and came under the governance of the male head of household in which they lived. It was when the accused was of such potential dependent status but not living "Lawfully" under "household governance" that their cases were treated in ways akin to more serious offenses against the common law.

17. In this part of the analysis, only those cases were included where a sentence of some sort (i.e., either a fine or term of imprisonment) had been imposed. Plea was entered as a dummy variable that assumed a value of 1 if the plea was "guilty" or 0 if the plea of "not guilty" was entered.

18. Somewhat surprisingly, data from the stratified sample suggest that, in these cases, it was not primarily those with prior convictions who pled guilty. Recidivists were more likely to plead not guilty. This suggests a problem in a key assumption of other studies such as that of Ferdinand (1992). If "first-time" offenders are more likely to plead guilty, this greatly increases the danger of inferences about the tendency of guilty pleas to generate sentencing reductions without taking criminal careers into account, since their sentences would be lower because of habitual offender laws in any case. The pool of defendants pleading guilty appears in this docket, at least, during the early- to mid-nineteenth century, to be low on habitual offenders.

19. In interpreting table 4.7, the constant term can be read as the average fine or term of imprisonment received by those pleading "not guilty" and the coefficient of the plea as the average effect of pleading guilty on the amount of fine in dollars or duration of imprisonment in months that is received by those pleading guilty. The sum of the constant and the coefficient is the average fine or term of imprisonment received by those pleading "guilty."

20. If two treatments, in this case guilty and not guilty pleas, produce about the same results, the number of plus signs assigned will be about half the total number of signs. If one treatment performs more strongly, the share of plus signs will increasingly differ from half. When it differs enough, one may conclude that one treatment is performing more successfully or effectively than another. To assign probabili-

ties to the pattern of signs, we use the binomial distribution. In doing so, p, which is the probability of a plus sign, is set to .5 to designate chance.

21. Only those years in which the distribution of cases enabled computation of a coefficient were included in this test.

22. Taking the signs of the coefficients for imprisonment in table 4.7, we find two minuses (−) and seven pluses (+). In the sign test, ties (or a finding of no effect of plea) are set aside. We then ask if this 7–2 split matters or differs significantly from what we'd be likely to find by chance.

23. Increased sample size and, in some cases, pooling of data from random and stratified random offense-specific subsamples revealed a stronger pattern in cases of imprisonment and more variability in fines than had been suggested by earlier exploratory analysis (Vogel, 1988).

24. A relatively simple technology, the nested probability model, is essentially nothing more than a series of multiple regression equations combined with a few calculations simple enough to be done by hand. The point is that this approach was chosen because of its ability to structure and provide a concise, yet rich and detailed, description of an otherwise complicated branched process of disposition and sentencing.

25. One can read the intermediate probability on the uppermost right-hand branch of the top tree (.6923) as the probability of a defendant being fined, given that he or she pled guilty, had some finding of either guilty or not guilty, ultimately was found guilty, and was sentenced to a fine or term of imprisonment. One can read the topmost final outcome (.6922) as the probability that a defendant was fined, given that he or she pled guilty.

26. Because the variables used here, plea and a succession of outcomes, are constructed as simple binary variables, the probabilities for each branch could alternately be computed as simple average probabilities of each outcome for those pleading guilty versus not guilty and multiplied out along the sequence of branched paths to produce the ultimate reduced form estimates of the chance of a case ending in one of five end states.

27. In figure 4.2, for example, the leftmost fork of the upper tree represents the probability of the defendant being found guilty or not guilty as opposed to some other finding, given that a plea of guilty was entered. The next fork of that tree as one moves to the right represents the probability of the defendant being found guilty, given a plea of guilty and given that the defendant was found either guilty or not guilty, as opposed to some other finding. Probabilities for the final, or reduced form, outcomes, which are the probabilities of a case reaching each of the various end points of a particular tree, given the plea entered, are computed as the product of the various intermediate probabilities along those branches that a case would traverse to reach that final outcome.

The probability on the uppermost right-hand branch of the top tree (.6923) can be read as the probability of a defendant who had pled guilty being fined, given that a fine or term of imprisonment was imposed. The topmost final outcome (.6922) can be read as the probability that a defendant is fined given that he or she pled guilty.

28. Here we focus, reading from left to right, on the fourth (or rightmost branch) in the branched tree diagram in figure 4.2. We ask, given that a sentence in the form of either fine or imprisonment was imposed, what is the probability that it was a fine and what is the probability that it was a sentence.

29. For instance, what at first appears to be a negative effect of plea on sentencing magnitude for the aggregate of all cases in the sample in 1850 is, in fact, an illusory result of the fact that many offenders with prior records that year were arrested for simple drunkenness. Even after a premium was exacted for a criminal career, the sentences tended to be lower than for common drunkard cases. This gives a false impression in the aggregate that a criminal record reduces one's sentence that year when the cause is really the underlying mix of cases.

30. According to traditional Puritan practice, "admonition" brought leniency in the form of forgiveness and reconciliation but not necessarily an easing of punishment per se. In fact, incarceration was initially intended, it appears, not to resocialize and rehabilitate, but to remove from corrupting influences and through isolated reflection to come to reconnection with God's graces and penitence. Thus, especially, for habitual offenders, an extended period of reflection is consonant with Puritan tradition.

31. According to Barbara Hobson, in her account of nineteenth-century prostitution in *Uneasy Virtue,* those charged with "nightwalking" sometimes closed their cases expeditiously with a guilty plea in the lower court and appealed them for a trial de novo to the Superior Court, which, with its more affluent stance and emphasis primarily on violence and property, treated "vice" more indulgently.

32. It is important to distinguish these defendants from women who might close their case expeditiously with a guilty plea and take it on appeal to the higher court for a trial de novo. That was not the case here. After entering their pleas, these women were ordered to recognize in one or more hundred dollars to appear at a specified date in Municipal Court.

33. Seven dimensions are highlighted, each of which represents one type of concessionary effect of plea. The dimensions are: reductions in term of imprisonment, reductions in amount of fine, reductions in the probability of imprisonment as a sentence, savings in court costs and attorneys' fees, special explicit concessions, reduced probability of recognizance being imposed in addition to a fine, and reduced probability of committal if unable to pay a fine.

34. While the contours of early plea bargaining indicate that the process was institutionalized as the populace grew aware of the availability of concessions and pled guilty, the paper does not claim that a quid pro quo, or terms of trade, was explicitly negotiated in every case under plea bargaining. To the contrary, the plea bargain differed from the more complicated and costly plea of nolo contendere, which did tend on occasion to be negotiated explicitly by lawyers in the higher courts, in that the plea bargain appears to have been typically undertaken informally, implicitly, and on the basis of customary understandings about the potential prospects that defendants generally faced in court, at least until the mid-nineteenth century.

CHAPTER FIVE

1. The legal systems of the European continent have strong roots in the tradition of legal codification developed in ancient Rome, and their legal systems are, in fact, referred to as Roman law systems.

2. The tradition of episodic leniency meant that prosecution of cases was suspended or sentencing was mitigated on a frequent but unpredictable basis. The result was that any individual defendant could never be sure whether such leniency would be available to him or her.

3. The plea of "nolo contendere" essentially means that the defendant declines to contest the state. The "nolle prosequi" refers to a decision by a prosecutor not to pursue prosecution in a case.

4. Hibbert (1963) notes that in England, the "prayer of benefit of the clergy" originally enabled removal of trial of a cleric accused of a felony to the ecclesiastical courts. However, he points out that it evolved over time into a plea to be exempt from capital punishment in any court and, most important, could be assessed not just by clerics but by any educated man. In practice, Hibbert claims, it extended still further, since the test of clerical status, that of reading a few lines of a standard text, could be met by anyone who memorized the lines with the help of a jailer inclined or paid to assist.

While the practice of "benefit of the clergy" was carried over to the colonial law of Massachusetts, its importance waned as secularization advanced. The practice was abolished entirely with the publication of Massachusetts' first Revised Statutes of 1835 (Revised Statutes, pt. IV, ch. 133, sec. 15; enacted 1784, 56 and 69). Thus, this particular form of discretionary leniency no longer existed as an option during the decade that plea bargaining appears to have emerged.

5. While the earlier view of crime had, in Massachusetts, equated it with sin and presumed that the sinner could be restored only by God's grace, the Enlightenment view of punishment, as received in the United States primarily through the works of Jeremy Bentham, emphasized the responsiveness of perfectable humans to deterrence as well as resocialization through incarceration. It also emphasized proportionality in sentencing—that is, sentencing should be the most minimally severe to accomplish penal goals, and in cases where it would have no effect, punishment should not be applied.

6. Some scholars such as Jeffrie Murphy and Jean Hampton (1988) in *Forgiveness and Mercy*, argue that mercy granted before disposition and sentencing entails a sort of forgiveness but may be seen as implicating the prosecutor with responsibility for the offense.

7. Hibbert (1963) points out that in the early centuries of the system, "the far from universal adoption of surnames ensure[d] that these pardons frequently passed from hand to hand . . ." (p. 17).

8. Langbein (1978) cautions the reader, however, that "if the implication to Wright was that the judges could only advise the monarch of facts found by the jury, that was certainly false and therefore misleading" (p. 278).

9. In its focus on good behavior for a period of time, this use of the plea of "nolo contendere" drew on the tradition of recognizance to keep the peace but substituted the prospect of a more severe sentence for surety. In this sense, it was a precursor to the practice of probation that began on an informal basis with the work of humanitarian John Augustus in Massachusetts during the 1870s. Later, Massachusetts became the first state to enact a statute providing for a formal system of probation.

10. See House Report, Massachusetts Legislature, no. 4, Jan. 1845.

11. In this case, the court held that "where an accomplice testifies in good faith in favor of the prosecution, and in so testifying implicates himself, he will be discharged, although the person against whom he testifies is acquitted" (*U.S. v. Lee*, Fed. Case no. 15,588 (4 McLean 103)).

12. In *U.S. v. Ford*, the federal court held that "the district attorney has no authority to contract that a person accused of an offense against the United States shall not be prosecuted, or his property subjected to condemnation therefore, if, when examined as a witness against his accomplices, he discloses fully and fairly his or their guilt. A person so accused cannot plead the contract in bar of proceedings against him or his property . . . but has merely an equitable title to executive mercy, of which the court can take notice only when an application to postpone the case is made in order to give him an opportunity to apply for the pardoning power" (*U.S. v. Ford*, 99 U.S. 594, 25 L. Ed. 399).

13. In *Commonwealth v. Brown*, the court held that "in the absence of any express or implied pledge to the contrary, the Commonwealth is not barred from prosecuting an accomplice who has voluntarily testified against his co-adjutor in an offense, upon an examination not attended by the district attorney" (103 Mass. 422 (1869)).

14. Per the requirement of the Commonwealth of Massachusetts, Criminal Records Systems Board, names of the parties have been changed to protect their privacy.

15. Prior to the 1840s, the practice of continuing cases "open" or leaving them blank—that is, simply incomplete—in the docket was widespread in Massachusetts and in other states as well. Accounting for the disposition of nearly half the complaints in 1830, cases declined markedly during that decade. From all indications, this was largely due to a combination of reformist pressure and to the establishment of a professional day-time police force to locate and apprehend accused offenders. Amidst the reforms of the 1820s and 1830s, this customary form of unbridled, unstructured, and intrusive legal discretion waned in Boston. Since some cases left "blank" never even saw a hearing for probable cause, it is likely that failure to apprehend the defendant or his or her failure to appear in court was sometimes an issue. However, many such cases were continued and left open to allow state supervision of the accused.

16. The author benefited greatly from early conversation with Steve Rytina, who directed her attention to this potentially relevant practice and to William E. Nelson's excellent treatment of it in *Dispute and Conflict Resolution in Plymouth, Massachusetts*.

17. Nelson (1981) indicates that the cases in the Church courts covered a wide range of offenses against religion and morals over which the state courts also had jurisdiction along with a number of other less religiously oriented offenses as well.

18. As required by the Massachusetts Criminal Systems Records Board, the name of both the defendant and her consort have been changed to protect their identities.

19. In *Kelsey v. Hobby*, the court held that "where a party being arrested in a suit at law, and unable to obtain special bail, makes a settlement with the plaintiff in respect merely to the claim sought to be enforced by the suit, the agreement will bind him unless it is evidently unreasonable and exorbitant or he can prove that it was obtained by improper means" (41 U.S. (16 Pet.) 269 L. Ed. 961 (1842)).

20. This provision states that "Whenever an indictment is found against any person for an assault and battery, or other misdemeanor, for which the party injured may have a remedy by civil action, except where the offence was committed by or upon any sheriff, or other officer of justice, or riotously, or with intent to commit a felony, if the party injured shall appear in court where such indictment is pending, and acknowledge satisfaction for the injury sustained, the court may, on payment of the costs accrued, order all further proceedings to be stayed, and discharge the defendant from the indictment, which shall forever bar all remedy for such injury by civil action" (pt. IV, ch. 136, sec. 27).

21. The exceptions, as noted earlier, are the cases of common drunkards and common night walkers (i.e., prostitutes) who sometimes pled guilty in the lower court as a way of expediting movement of their case to the Superior Court on appeal. There, Hobson has shown, they tend, in fact, to be treated more leniently than in the lower court.

22. Compounding a felony is defined by the American Digest of nineteenth century case decisions as including "promising, giving, accepting or agreeing to accept money, property or other consideration on an agreement not to prosecute" ("Compounding a Felony," pp. 933–934).

CHAPTER SIX

1. Nicos Poulantzas emphasizes the importance of timing in the convergence of social forces in *Political Power and Social Classes*, London: New Left Books, 1975. Similarly, Rheinhard Bendix in *Nation Building and Citizenship*, New York: Wiley, 1964, emphasizes the importance of the timing of industrialization and democratization in defining the nature of politics in a society and the nature of the particular political issues that arise. Other works that highlight the effect of historical timing are: Leonard Binder et al., *Crisis and Sequences in Political Development*, Princeton, N.J.: Princeton University Press, 1971; Amy Bridges, *A City in the Republic*, Cambridge: Cambridge University Press, 1984; and Amy Bridges, "Becoming American, The American Working Classes Before the Civil War" in Ira Katznelson and Aristide Zolberg, eds., *Working Class Formation: Nineteenth Century Patterns in Western Europe and the United States*, Cambridge: Cambridge University Press, 1988.

2. This public concern also spawned the movement for "common schooling" in Boston under the leadership of Horace Mann. Educators worked to establish in every municipality schools that were open to all children to attend. Mann sought to advance the intelligence and habits of mind needed to produce informed citizens and industrious workers so as to ensure the future of the republic (Kaestle, 1983). It is notable that Justice Theophilus Parsons served on the Boston School Committee in 1846, during the tenure of Horace Mann, who founded the Common Schooling movement,

as Superintendent of Schools (Parsons, 1846, p. 10). Interestingly, Parsons refers to a division among the members of the School Committee between the religiously motivated "orthodox" republicans and the popular-spirited "democrats" (p. 10).

3. In formal terms, Boston made the transition from "town" to "city" in 1822.

4. As of 1840, only New York, Pennsylvania, Ohio, Virginia, North Carolina, Kentucky, and Tennessee exceeded Massachusetts in size (*Statistics of the United States,* Seventh U.S. Compendium, 1850, Table XL, p. 61).

5. Parsons (1835) goes on with the query, "Is the epoch which is to be characterized by the establishment of governments founded on these new principles [of self-rule], to be preceded again by convulsions?" (p. 27). As of 1840, only New York, Pennsylvania, Ohio, Virginia, North Carolina, Kentucky, and Tennessee exceeded Massachusetts in size.

6. Handlin (1959) notes that "some surplus funds had accrued from land, particularly from real estate within the city limits, and some, from amassment started in the colonial period—though on a rather small scale. But essentially Boston capital blossomed forth in the Federal period in the fortunes of the China trade princes whose risky ventures yielded large profits in lump unsteady sums which could not immediately be reinvested" (p. 8).

7. In the interval between 1780 and 1840, approximately 2,254 corporations were founded in Massachusetts, financed largely by capital raised in Boston (Handlin, 1959, p. 9). Building on a base of four banks established by 1800, six more were incorporated between 1810 and 1820, 18 between 1821 and 1830, and 33 between 1831 and 1837 alone (Handlin, 1959, pp. 8–9). As Handlin points out, "by 1830 Boston was second only to New York in financial strength and resources, and, when the panic of 1837 intervened, was ready to surpass her rival" (1959, p. 9).

8. Handlin (1969) claims that "In 1845, the whole number of industrial workers . . . was less than 10,000 in a population of 165,000.

9. Handlin (1959) notes that "By 1850, only half the descendants of the Bostonians of 1820 still lived there" (p. 12).

10. Taking aim at the mill owners of the Merrimac Valley, workers pamphlets claimed America's "young [industrial] Nobility" to be more exploitative than England's landed gentry and urged resistance through Workingmen's politics and unions (Sellers, 1992, p. 338). In the words of Boston strike organizers A. H. Wood and Seth Luther, "Capital which can only be made productive by labor is endeavoring to crush labor, the only source of wealth" (Schlesinger, 1945, pp. 166–67). Depicting the strikes as "neither more nor less than a contest between Money and LABOR [emphasis in original]," Wood acknowledged that mobilization of Workingmen was "arraying the poor against the principles of the rich, and if this be arraying the poor against the rich, I say go on with tenfold fury" (Schlesinger, 1945, pp. 166–67).

11. While this table provides some indication of the relative magnitude of the influx of immigrants from various destinations, it understates them seriously since the *Annual Report* for the Boston House of Industry in 1834 notes that "few, comparatively, arrive in Boston by water; they come by land, from the British provinces and from New York" (City of Boston Documents, no. 11, 1834, p. 60).

12. Recently Eric Monkkonen (1997) has presented data for New York City

showing that the 1820s experienced, not just heightened fear, but that a very real increase in actual homicide occurred during this period. This was a trend that peaked nationally during the 1850s (Gurr, 1981).

13. Interestingly, this was a period when Enlightenment ideas about the perfectability of human nature prompted a turn to imprisonment as a vehicle for resocialization. Thus, the surging jail population may well have reflected greater incidence of incarceration or shifting venues of confinement but does not appear to have resulted primarily from increased court caseload, which grew far less during this period.

14. The populace of Boston had long resisted the establishment of a professional police force—some argue on grounds that it would be used excessively by the state, as was the French police in Paris, although the mayor indicated he felt the primary objection was monetary (Lane, 1971, p. 34).

15. Not all the riots of the day were anti-Irish in origin. In 1835, a mob attacked William Lloyd Garrison at the offices of the *Liberator* and, far from responding to the personal intervention of the mayor to desist, the mob turned and stormed the mayor's office at City Hall.

16. Terry DeFilippo notes that "The 18th and 19th century are punctuated by riot occasioned by bread prices, turnpikes and tolls, excise, 'rescue,' strikes, new machinery, enclosures, press-gangs and a score of other grievances. Direct action on particular grievances merges on the one hand into the great political risings of the 'mob'— the Wilkes agitation of the 1760s and 1770s, the Gordon Riots (1780), the mobbing of the king in the London streets (1795 and 1820), the Bristol Riots (1831), and the Birmingham Bull Ring Riots (1839). On the other hand it merges with organized forms of sustained illegal action of quasi-insurrection—Luddism (1811–13), the East-Anglian riots (1816), and the 'Last Labourer's Revolt' (1830), the Rebecca Riots (1839 and 1842) and the Plug Riots (1842).

17. Nelson has shown that, in Massachusetts, emergent capitalism, secularization, and religious disenfranchisement (i.e., ceasing of state collection of church tithes) contributed to refocusing the criminal law away from offenses against religion and morals and toward crimes against property.

18. Primary sources of this weakening appear to have included the differentiation of churches that bred intellectual conflict among sects and the increasing diversity of cultural values and styles due to immigration (Nelson, 1975).

19. While the Federalists had succumbed earlier to political challenge in other cities of the Northeast, they remained dominant in Boston in the Age of Jackson.

20. Adam Smith, in *The Wealth of Nations* (1776), cited the task of providing the security and predictability needed for commerce as one of two essential roles of the post-mercantilist state. Insurance companies were working at just the time of this study to rationalize and diminish risk (Steinberg, personal communication with this author, 1997).

21. Quincy's reference was to the prior fee structure whereby magistrates had prospered more the greater the number of cases that they heard.

22. Piven and Cloward (1966) argue that in the face of rising social movements, political authorities have historically made every effort to channel dissent into institutional forums as well as attempting to isolate dissident groups, co-opt their leaders,

and conciliate with agreements that are later withdrawn. Italian theorist Antonio Gramsci has noted that "A crisis occurs, sometimes lasting for decades. This exceptional duration [often] means that incurable structural contradictions have . . . [matured], and that, despite this, the political forces which are struggling to conserve and defend the existing structure itself are making every effort to cure them, within certain limits, and to overcome them. These incessant and persistent efforts (since no social formation will ever admit that it has been superseded) form the terrain for the "conjunctural," and it is upon this terrain that the forces of opposition organize . . . [I]n the period immediately following, . . . [contestation] is developed in a series of ideological, religious, philosophical, political and juridical polemics . . ." (1971, p. 178).

23. In light of the small informal gradual shifts in court practice through which plea bargaining emerged, its origin bears much resemblance to the process of legal innovation that gave rise to the office of the prosecutor as described by Langbein (1973).

24. Their first campaign was to forestall a law raising the value of the cases that could be tried by Justices of the Peace and, thus, more likely without a lawyer (Jones et al., 1993, p. 24).

25. Horwitz (1977) points out that 11 of 13 former colonies initially enacted provisions for the reception of common law along with some British statutes (pp. 4–5).

26. As part of popular demand for clarification of the law, codification movements mobilized—arguing that much common law was simply the highly subjective and variable determination of English judges (Horwitz, 1977, p. 18). The spirit of the day may be best articulated by jurist Robert Rantoul in his plea for codification in 1836 where he asked, "Why is an ex post facto law, passed by the legislature, unjust, unconstitutional and void, while judge-made law, which from its nature must always be ex post facto, is not only to be obeyed but applauded?" (Rantoul, 1854; cited in Horwitz, 1977, p. 18).

27. Horwitz (1977) cites as one of many examples the shift in riparian (or water) rights cases from "first user" to "most efficient user" as the criterion for legal decision making.

28. While it often overstates the case to impute to elites' conscious collaboration in politics, such was not the case in Boston of the 1830s. Recognizing their position of leadership to be in jeopardy, the city's elite worked in a conscious and comprehensive fashion across the economic, political, educational, religious, cultural, and philanthropic spheres to inculcate industriousness and harmony and to reconsolidate their power (Formisano, 1984).

29. For a discussion of this facet of American economic history, see Milton Friedman and A. J. Schwartz, *A Monetary History of the United States, 1867–1960*, Princeton, N.J.: Princeton University Press, 1963.

30. The relation of labor unrest to prevailing economic conditions is treated in some detail in David Montgomery, *Beyond Equality: Labor and the Radical Republicans, 1862–1872*, Urbana, Illinois: University of Illinois Press, 1981; David Montgomery, *Workers' Control in America*, Cambridge, England: Cambridge University Press, 1979; and Sean Wilentz, *Chants Democratic: New York City and the Rise of the*

American Working Class, 1788–1850, London: Oxford University Press, 1984; and Norman J. Ware, *The Labor Movement in the United States, 1867–1960,* New York: Vintage, 1964.

31. The author is indebted to Alessandro Pizzorno, formerly of the European University in Florence, Italy and of Harvard University, for drawing attention to this key point.

32. Decentralized court administration and the close links of the law with politics have long been recognized as hallmarks of the common law system in England. Developed as a series of case decisions, and later precedents, to resolve actions at hand rather than as an abstract codification by legal scholars, the common law has historically had strong ties to politics (see Tigar and Levy, 1965).

33. One evidence of this concern is the reluctance to adopt a professional police force for fear it would be used for political purposes. Mill gives incisive voice to this new concern about the liberty of the individual despite the phenomenon of self-rule in *On Liberty.*

34. In addition to anti-statist ideology, Handlin (1979) notes that one important legacy of the Revolutionary era was "the specter of overwhelming public debt it left," such that any expenditures, including those in support of efforts to industrialize, were feared because they meant massive new taxes (p. 61). While reduced to some extent by the early 19th century, "loans during the war of 1812 restored the deficit" (p. 63).

Handlin (1979) concludes that the existence for four decades of an enormous charge for the payment of interest and principle conditioned the reactions of government in every sphere that involved the expenditure of more money and threatened with new taxes or new debt. Frugality was a fixed principle. He notes that "torn constantly between the desire to act and unwillingness to increase state expenses, political officials occasionally flatly chose between saving or spending . . . Penny-pinching finance and a political balance that made citizens vigilant about the use of privilege left the members of the General Court slight latitude for action (p. 63).

35. While most of the boldest initiatives to establish overt political control of the courts were doomed to failure, Dimond (1975) demonstrates the massive extent of more informal control through the history of court reorganizations during this period. According to Dimond's account, the County Courts of Common Pleas assumed criminal jurisdiction of the courts of sessions in 1804. In 1811, the Courts of Common Pleas were replaced by the Circuit Courts of Common Plea . . ." and then in 1821 replaced again by a single Court of Common Pleas for the entire Commonwealth. In Sessions, the courts received regular justices in 1807 and 1808, were abolished in 1809, were revived in 1811, abolished again in 1814 in all counties but three, reappeared again in 1819, and were abolished again in Suffolk County in 1821 (pp. 20–21). Thus, links between court officials and local politicians operated largely through the appointment process and appear to have been considerable.

36. During the years of Jefferson's Presidency, Joseph Story lamented that notaries, at least, were not federal appointees for in that way, at least, a Republican might hold office in Massachusetts.

37. This view is consonant with Bridges (1984) observation, in her analysis of

the rise of machine politics in New York, that the politicians of the urban machines were faced with a distinctive challenge. They needed to forge a majoritarian consensus without extensive personal wealth or resources on which to draw. Bridges argues that politicians from the 1840s on, drew on the only kinds of resources available to them—jobs, services and a kind of general assurance of help in times of need.

38. Some evidence suggests that delays in the higher court appear historically to have risen from continuances sought by defense attorneys, who were paid for each day in court rather than from a backlog of cases. However, as plea bargaining spread to the high court, it may have provided the appearance, at least, of responding to claims about workload.

39. Easing the workload of the courts is a different argument than claiming that caseload pressure causes bargaining. For instance, Heumann (1981) found in a study of contemporary Chicago that bargaining eased the workload of district attorneys, but that they had to be socialized into bargaining since constraints on their time were not such as to require it.

40. Police officers or, before that, constables, sometimes presented the evidence against a defendant (Gil, 1837).

41. These annual reports reflected a growing emphasis on efficiency with respect to rational criteria of performance though their effect was limited in the lower courts, where cases were handled without attorneys for defense or prosecution.

CHAPTER SEVEN

1. Not only was the imagery of the "rule of law" significant in maintaining social order, it was a major concern in private law and in economic development as well. By 1815, the courts were playing a key role, under the auspices of, first, Federalists and, later, Republicans and Whigs, in accomplishing a "market revolution" and transformation of the society to capitalism (Sellers, 1991, p. 40). Whereas at the time of the American Revolution, virtually all businesses were small-scale ones in keeping with English legal tradition, which saw accumulations of private capital as threatening to state sovereignty, this had clearly changed by 1820. While it still required a state charter to establish a business corporation—a situation that fanned popular criticism of elite monopoly—the seven corporations of the Revolutionary era had mushroomed to more than three hundred by the 1790s. Adaptation of society's economic and political institutions during the early national period was "most important where least visible, [namely] in the intricacies of law" (Sellers, 1992, p. 40).

2. Interestingly, a view of the citizen very similar to that articulated in criminal law and labor law is evident in the views of the leaders of the temperance movement after 1825 (Finney, *Memoirs*).

3. McLoughlin (1978) argues that in addition to the great Puritan Awakening that began in England, there have been four Awakenings on American soil. The first accomplished the forging of the thirteen colonies into a cohesive unit and provided the beginnings of a sense of nationality. The second, during the first half of the nineteenth century, he asserts, defined "what it meant to be 'an American' and what the

manifest destiny of the new nation was" (McLoughlin, 1978, p. 1). The third, after the Civil War, clarified "the meaning of evolutionary science and industrial progress" (McLoughlin, 1978, p. 1). The fourth, he contends, has been underway since the 1960s and centers on interpreting crises attending "our sense of order at home and commitments as a world power abroad" (McLoughlin, 1978, p. 2).

4. Although both Jefferson and Madison sought to preserve republicanism by cultivating the virtue and independence of farmers, Jefferson feared that commercialization would corrupt farm families, whereas the more market-oriented Madison saw those farm families as "incipient small entrepreneurs" (Sellers, 1992, p. 39).

5. "Class," at this point, though used conversationally, denoted something quite different from what it did by the close of the nineteenth century. Signifying something much closer to a status group unified largely by lifestyle, class did not assume the meaning of an oppositional economic category until after the Civil War.

6. There is also some suggestion that early urban markets for labor also fostered impulsiveness by shifting power to women by creating "alternatives to domestic subordination for young women" (Weiner, 1996, p. 138). Hazards to health and safety in the capitalist workplace also foreshortened the adult life span and shifted the balance to the "young, inexperienced, ignorant, credulous, irritable, passionate and dangerous" (M. W. Flinn, 1842, p. 268; Weiner, 1996, p. 139).

7. A final facet of this view can be found in the works of Thomas Malthus. Malthus contended that the instinct of sexuality virtually ensured population growth, which would consume resources and prevent social improvement (Weiner, 1996, p. 140). Malthus argued that "because the sexual drive was strongest in the young, the vitality of youth, not the debility of age, posed the gravest danger to society" (Weiner, 1996, p. 141). This argument pertained more to Europe than to the United States, with the vast untapped resources of its western frontier.

8. The works of Charles Dickens and the widely read Newgate novels are compelling works in this genre.

9. Often it is claimed that British Utilitarianism, with its emphasis on forestalling positive harm, broadened the gap between law and morality (Weiner, 1996, p. 146). Yet such views miss the fact that "[e]arly Victorian law reform had 'evangelical' ... dimensions, while utilitaria[n] ... [reformers] held [much more of a] ... moral agenda ... [than those of the modern day] (Weiner, 1996, p. 146).

10. Early British Utilitarianism, which reached American reformers during the 1830s through the works of Bentham, was also "rule-oriented" rather than "act oriented"—that is, it "aimed at instilling principled patterns of behavior" and so was suited to the effort to produce a "self-restrained character-type" (Weiner, 1996, p. 147).

11. For instance, as Weiner (1996) shows, the definition of unlawful appropriation of property was expanding to include mere attempts to steal, various "sharp practices," and unknowingly receiving stolen goods, among other things.

12. Mill went so far as to argue that, in a case at law, drunkenness should not be seen as a mitigating factor or excuse; instead, it should, he claimed, be seen as an aggravating factor, as its ill effects on behavior might have been foreseen (Weiner, 1996, p. 150).

13. Consequently, accused offenders were more and more expected, for example, to resist taunting language; to inspect tobacco, milk, and other goods for adulteration; and to exercise modulation in their consumption of alcohol if they were to be acquitted.

14. In an essay in 1840, entitled "Going to See a Man Hanged," Thackeray had decried the "hideous debauchery" of a public execution (Works, 23, pp. 106–7 cited in Weiner, 1996, p. 154).

15. The parallel to the uppermost caste in India reflected both the nature of this group as a status community and the absence of opportunities for mobility either in or out once this group of families had been established by the 1820s. Social honor was reinforced by considerable wealth to underscore status with social class and to create a multifunctional upper class that, some argued, effectively constituted a caste.

16. Antonio Gramsci (1971) defines hegemony as the system of beliefs, attitudes, values, and morality that pervades civil society and that justifies, in one way or another, the existing social order and the relations of power that it upholds.

17. Boston's leading families drew the line, however, at rezoning land for commercial uses in their residential enclave on Beacon Hill despite the gains potentially to be reaped. Instead, they improved nearby Boston Common and constructed the beautiful Public Gardens at the base of their Hill. Through no coincidence the Massachusetts Statehouse was soon built on that very same hill in the turf of this prestigious enclave.

18. Charitable associations distributed resources and "use[d] Boston's money and influence to create rewards and . . . [penalties] that would encourage the underprivileged to accept the . . . established order" as a just and virtuous one (Jaher, 1984, p. 64).

19. So strong was the Federalist hold that even Democratic Republican John Quincy Adams did not leave the Federalist party until after Jefferson's election to his second term (Jaher, 1984, p. 69).

20. As advocates at the federal level for shipping and trade in the Commonwealth, they "secured advantageous tariffs, drawbacks on products imported and exported by Massachusetts traders, and tonnage duties which discriminated in favor of Bay State shipping" (Jaher, 1984, p. 67).

21. Gains from political connection could also be had here because financial institutions were also used to store public monies or to serve as fiscal agents for the public sector with the handsome fees that this brought (Jaher, 1984, p. 68).

22. In real estate, "building permits, incorporation charters, location of public improvements, low property assessments, rights of way and purchase of property [from the state on favorable terms]" hung in the balance (Jaher, 1984, p. 69).

23. Of the seventy-nine (30.4 percent) "wealthiest residents of the city in 1835, twenty-four were common councilors, aldermen, judges, mayors, state legislators, U.S. Congressmen, senators . . . [or] cabinet members" (1984, pp. 74–75). After the 1830s, the capacity of the Brahmins to elect the sons of prominent families to municipal offices other than that of mayor began to wane, as ethnic strength in many city ward increased, and Brahmin candidates ran almost exclusively for mayor when they stood for office at all (Jaher, 1984, p. 73).

24. Here the ahistoricism of the democratic ideology of liberalism presented a distinctive drawback. While highlighting the autonomy of the political subject at a given moment, it ignored the contextual reality that differences in the availability of resources realistically restricted the options on which some defendants could draw. For instance, mariners or transients without employment in a city would likely have no patron or friend to whom to turn for intercession before the court.

25. Lane (1971) describes posses summoned informally by the mayor of Boston to ride on horseback into vice-ridden districts of the city to restore order.

26. From 1834 to 1835 Theodore Lyman, the first Democratic-Republican mayor was elected in Boston—a lapse that would not occur again in the city's history. With the exception of two Native American Party (Nativist) mayors in 1845 (Thomas A. Davis) and 1854–1855 (Jerome V. Smith), all mayors of Boston would be Whigs until 1856, when the new Republican party became the party of choice of the Boston patriciate.

During the 1830s the Federalist-National Republican-Whig political establishment retained a strong hold on gubernatorial power in Massachusetts. At only two points the governorship fell into Democratic-Republican or Democratic hands—during the years 1823 to 1825, when first William Eustis and then Marcus Morton served, and then again from 1840 to 1843, when Morton was reelected governor. During the 1830s, the long service of National Republican Levi Lincoln, Jr. (1825–1834) was followed by the more abbreviated tenure of John A. David (1834–1835), also a National Republican. In the following year, Samuel T. Armstrong, a Whig (1835–1836) was elected. He was followed in office by Edward A. Everett, also a Whig, from 1836 to 1840.

27. While all persons appearing before the court were formally treated equally in procedural terms, the reality was that those without patrons to intercede for them tended ultimately to fare less well in the treatment that they received.

28. Higginson (1907) went on to claim that "To the Essex Junto, Jefferson himself seemed but a mutineering first mate, and his 'rights of man' but the black flag of a rebellious crew."

29. Originally the name "Essex Junto" had been applied by John Hancock during the debates over the Constitution to a small group of men from Essex County in Massachusetts: Theophilus Parsons [Chief Justice of the Massachusetts Supreme Court]; John Lowell, Jonathan Jackson of Newburyport, George Cabot [sea captain], and Nathan Dane of Beverly; and Timothy Pickering and Benjamin Goodhue of Salem (Warren, 1931, p. 164).

30. The Jay Treaty, consummated between England and the United States in 1794, established limited trade relations with England for the first time since the Revolutionary War. This was monumentally important for Massachusetts' Federalists, whose wealth was based in maritime activity and trade, because they had longstanding commercial ties with England. Thus, they strongly supported the treaty and campaigned for improved ties with the former colonial power.

31. It was also the case, as the nineteenth century dawned and the market ideas of the Scottish Moralists made their way to America, that lawyers, as providers of a

service rather than a good, were seen as "nonproductive hands." In a world that increasingly valued "productive hands," who were the creators of tangible value, lawyers' status, like that of servants, financiers, and speculators alike, was met with low regard.

32. In *Marbury v. Madison*, the Supreme Court established its right to decide on the constitutionality of Acts of Congress. Jefferson, believing that the sovereignty of the people was articulated in legislation resisted judicial reviews of the people's enactments.

33. For defendants, the issue of indeterminate limits on state oversight, with the enormous power it carries, would be revisited again during the next great wave of penal reform in the 1870s.

34. Emory Washburn notes in his *Sketches of the Judiciary of Massachusetts* that "There have been ever since the establishment of our government, a class of politicians who have decried the independence of the Judiciary [from popular will] as antirepublican in principle and as a feature of our Constitution which ought to be modified" (p. 396).

35. Robert Gordon (1981) notes in *Law and the American Revolution and the Revolution in Law* that by the early nineteenth century, "the criminal was no longer envisioned as a sinner against God but rather as one who preyed on the property of his fellow citizens" (p. 98).

36. Jackson's backers alleged that Clay's support originated in a "corrupt bargain" that he had struck with Adams. Adams ostensibly met with Clay and, in the meeting, intimated that, should Clay support his candidacy, a Cabinet post would be forthcoming. All indications are that Clay had long thought Adams the better man. When Adams took office, Clay was given the portfolio of Secretary of State.

37. The irony that Henry Clay came to be known throughout his career as "the Great Compromiser" assumed a "double entendre" for these ardent Democratic partisans.

38. Formisano (1984) notes that traditionally "Boston town meetings were run by the aristocratic Federalists with cooperation from a broadly based oligarchy reaching well down into the middle classes" (p. 35).

39. The term "imagined community" is used by Benedict Anderson, in his book by that name, to denote the phenomenon of nationalism in Europe after the French Revolution.

CHAPTER EIGHT

1. Even though accounts of the geographical distribution of manufacturing establishments in the Boston area are sparse, a public account of the city's recovery from the great fire of 1873 states: "The manufacturing establishments being located outside the city, orders were readily duplicated and the work of distribution was not seriously delayed." "Report on the Social Statistics of Cities," Census Office, Washington, D.C. 1886, p. 107.

2. The extent of the popular base for a major electoral challenge is evidenced by the fact that the U.S. Census figures for 1880 show that of 267,750 persons residing

in Suffolk County (then coterminous with the city of Boston except for its inclusion of Chelsea and the Boston Harbor islands), fully 44.8 percent, or nearly half the population of the city, were foreign born. Of the foreign-born, 67,030 or 25 percent of the city's total population listed Ireland as their place of birth.

3. The relation of labor unrest to prevailing economic conditions is treated in some-detail in David Montgomery, *Beyond Equality: Labor and the Radical Republicans, 1862–1872,* Urbana, Illinois: University of Illinois Press, 1981; David Montgomery, *Workers' Control in America,* Cambridge, England: Cambridge University Press, 1979; Sean Wilentz, *Chants Democratic: New York City and the rise of the American Working Class, 1788–1850,* London: Oxford University Press, 1984; and Norman J. Ware, *The Labor Movement in the United States, 1860–1890,* New York, Vintage, 1964.

4. For a discussion of this facet of American economic history, see Milton Friedman and A. J. Schwartz, *A Monetary History of the United States, 1867–1960,* Princeton, N.J.: Princeton University Press, 1963.

5. Examination of means, variances, and maxima for the fines and terms of imprisonment for each year tentatively suggests that the guilty plea rates responded far more strongly to means, and somewhat more strongly to maxima, than to the uncertainty (or variance) of the outcome. The range of outcomes may have been a more subtle measure than popular wisdom could accommodate.

CHAPTER NINE

1. Max Weber distinguishes between rational-legal authority, which finds the basis of its legitimation in the enactment of rules in law and the specification of offices in law, and traditional authority, which is based on long-standing respect for customary leaders and folkways.

2. These discretionary practices borrowed a second common law element, known as suretyship, whereby an intercessor historically posted bond to ensure future good behavior. (Now an intercessor usually staked his reputation instead.)

3. This belief in the importance of social rank and the authority of household and workplace, so popular in the early 1800s, finds extensive theoretical and empirical support in Talcott Parsons' work *Politics and Social Structure.* In it, he describes a state he calls anomie in which large numbers of individuals are lacking integration with stable institutions that are necessary for their personal stability. According to Parsons, these institutions, such as family, church, school, and economy, are nothing more than clusters of independent role patterns that prescribe appropriate behavior. Their significance lies in the fact that they "structure value orientations" and "enable the internalization of value systems into the personality." Social roles, thus, provide the basis for an orientation to action and for socialization.

4. Instead society distinguished between producers and consumers or, alternately, between productive and nonproductive hands.

5. For an introduction to the papers of Samuel C. Allen, this author is indebted to Sellers' exceptional treatment in *The Market Revolution,* Berkeley, California: University of California Press, 1992.

362 NOTES TO PAGES 294-99

6. A debt must be acknowledged to Carl Kaestle's *Pillars of the Republic* for pointing out parallels between the activities of the judiciary and the project of common schooling.

7. Pointing to the danger of popular desires for greater equality, Mann voiced his conviction that "democracy gave free rein to 'the powers of doing evil as much as doing good'" (Cremin, 1980, p. 117; cited in Sellers, 1992, pp. 367–88).

8. Remarking on "the use often made of the elective franchise [in pursuing economic equality]," Mann decried "the crude unphilosophical notions [that are] . . . sometimes advanced in our legislative halls on questions of political economy, the erroneous views entertained by portions of the people . . . and the revolutionary ideas of others" (Horace Mann, Tenth Annual Report of the Board of Education, 1846, p. 235; cited in Sellers, 1992, p. 368). He sternly warned that "if the ignorant and vicious get possession of the [state] apparatus, the intelligent and the virtuous must take such shocks as the stupid or profligate . . . may choose to administer" (Horace Mann, Tenth Annual Report of the Board of Education, 1846, p. 235; cited in Sellers, 1992, p. 368).

9. If it is ever to be accomplished, he argued, it "must be mainly done during the docile and teachable years of childhood" (Norton, 1986, p. 82; cited in Sellers, 1992, p. 368).

10. More specifically, it was freedom "[as conceived of by] the Protestant religion, middle class [orientation to] society and a republican form of government" (Carlson, 1975, p. 41).

11. Ultimately it was to a judge that naturalized citizens demonstrated their acculturation and swore their formal oath of allegiance as citizens.

12. Similarly the Charlestown Advertiser in Massachusetts reported that "forty of forty-one persons arrested" in that town in a given week had been "born abroad" (Charlestown Advertiser in Ithaca *American Citizen*, November 21, 1855; cited in Anbinder, 1992, p. 107).

13. Such assertions, of course, neglect entirely to ask whether immigrants were the victims of selective law enforcement and so more likely than others to be arrested— though not necessarily more prone to perpetrate crimes per se.

14. In his Diary and Correspondence Lawrence stated that "We have no violent political animosities [in the United States] . . . There is a general industry and talent in our population that is calculated to produce striking results upon . . . character . . . [N]o man can attain any valuable influence . . . among us, who does not labor with whatever talents he has to increase the sum of human improvement and happiness . . . An idler, who feels that he has no responsibilities, . . . whatever be his fortune, can find no comfort in staying here" (1855, p. 103).

15. For an excellent discussion of these theoretical perspectives to which this author is indebted, see George Steinmetz, *Regulating the Social*, Chicago, Illinois: University of Chicago Press, 1995.

16. Originally advanced as a complement to theories of state autonomy and state culture, to Marxian and class conflict theories, and to theories of the relative autonomy of the state, institutionalist perspectives have had some unintended effects. Primary among them was de-emphasizing: human agency and contestation; human development and consciousness as a shaper of voluntarism; material bases of power;

conflict; and processes of social transformation and change. This work starts from the presumption of social transformation as an ongoing historical process in which law plays a crucial, or as Novak has put it, "constitutive" role, taking as a central question for study the mechanisms, events and choices through which such metamorphosis occurs (Thompson, 1963; Katznelson and Zolberg, 1990; Giddens, 1987). The roles of language and contestation in shaping consciousness, human development, and choice are also highlighted (Sewell, 1980; Wittgenstein, 1958).

17. In the case of traditional authority, legitimacy rests in a belief in the sacredness of the customs or traditions that underpin an order. Where charismatic authority exists, legitimacy rests in the heroic strength or exemplary qualities of a leader. Under rational-legal authority, legitimacy rests in the "legality of enacted rules and the right of those elevated to authority under such rules to issue commands" (1975, p. 215).

18. Thompson (1975) has noted that, even where law serves the interests of the propertied, it cannot be used in ways that are blatantly unfair in the short term lest it be perceived as unjust and lose its claim on the behavior of the populace that lends it its power altogether.

19. The role of schools was to "teach patriotism, encourage participation in civic affairs, and . . . [show] girls how to . . . [convey to] future sons the same lessons" (Kaestle, 1983, p. 72).

20. Historically in England and often in the United States as well, numerous penal actions involved, not formal indictments and trials, but the issuing of a recognizance bond that pledged the accused to keep the peace or observe good behavior (Simon, 1993; and Samaha, 1981). To accomplish that goal, the bond committed a private member of the community to supervise the accused and to pay a penalty if the terms of the bond were breached. Such bonds also served as an early form of bail. Finally, bonds of surety appear to have been used to prevent abuse of the power of prosecution by pledging that complainants and witnesses would appear when a proceeding was scheduled. While "peace bonds," were used to forestall behavior that threatened the peace mainly through acts or threats of personal violence, bonds of "good behavior" were broader and foreswore any breach. In England, such bonds were aimed expressly at "all them that be not of good fame," which included, among others, "former convicted offenders who refused to work for a living and persons who had in the past breached the peace, rioted or barreted" (Samaha, 1981, p. 199; cited in Simon, 1993, p. 22). Surety bonds for "good behavior" were also required oftentimes of persons who appeared to "threaten the moral or economic life of the community: transients who might become burdens to the town, fathers of illegitimate children who might abandon them, accused adulterers who might continue to covet other men's wives" (Simon, 1993). While peace bonds were usually broken by assault and battery, the bonds for good behavior might be broken for acts as slight as "the number of a man's company" (Samaha, 1981, p. 198; cited in Simon, 1993, p. 22).

Essentially suretyship was a flexible device that was "essentially aimed at strangers and the poor in town" (Samaha, 1981, p. 210; cited in Simon, 1993, p. 22). Persons "lacking property or longstanding in the community were required to demonstrate the existence of supporters in the community interested enough to come forward . . . [with the expectation of their] actively supervising [the accused]" (Simon,

1993, p. 22). While similar to plea bargaining in the link it established between court and workplace, suretyship was very different from the plea bargain in that there was no guilty plea, there was not necessarily any conviction (often no act had yet occurred), and as in the practice of leaving cases open on file, the life of the accused remained vulnerable to ongoing state scrutiny and intervention.

21. When a complaint was made, we have seen that established members of the community often wrote to the court or appeared on the accused's behalf—ensuring that the defendant was of fine character, hardworking, and law-abiding. Commonly the intercessor asked that these traits be considered by the judge in handling the case.

22. Established members of the community often wrote to the court or appeared on the accused's behalf—ensuring that the defendant was of fine character, hardworking and law abiding. Commonly the intercessor asked that these traits be considered by the judge in handling the case. Consequently, those defendants who were enmeshed in the web of community relations were distinguished from others.

23. Files of the Superior Court, formerly the Court of Judicature, are replete with letters and notes on fine stationery attesting to the good character and long service of various defendants—often faithful employees of the signatory. Particularly as the courts shifted their emphasis to rehabilitation and to the prevention of crime, one key task facing them was to sort out and identify integrated, productive individuals from transients and vagrants as an indicator of how extensive a need for resocialization existed. For defendants of the lower classes, unlikely to be integrated socially into influential networks, the availability of a patron to intervene and attest on one's behalf was of inestimable value.

24. Referring to that decade, it is sometimes said that "for many years Federalism survived its party existence as a social cult" (Morison, 1913, p. 249). Long thereafter, prominent Federalist leaders and their progeny "long occupied a position in New England corresponding to that of good Confederate families in the South" (p. 249).

25. The author acknowledges a special debt to Michael Walzer, past Director of the Social Science Honors Program at Harvard University and, specifically, to the Sophomore Social Studies Tutorial for directing her attention to the works of T. H. Marshall on this question.

26. Among the scholars exploring rationality in American civic membership, see Amy Bridges, 1988; Jennifer Nedelsky, 1990; and Margaret Somers, 1996.

27. While Robert E. Brown, in his classic *Middle Class Democracy and the Revolution in Massachusetts, 1691–1780* (Ithaca, New York: Cornell, 1950), has emphasized the fact that relatively large proportions of men in the towns and cities of colonial Massachusetts could vote, he acknowledges that between 20 percent and 33 percent were typically excluded. Immigration after 1800 began to swell the ranks of the laboring and marginal groups most likely to be excluded—groups for whom extension of "universal suffrage" during the mid-1830s opened the way.

28. Marshall notes that "It was increasingly recognized, as the nineteenth century wore on, that political . . . [self-rule required] an educated [and self-disciplined] electorate, . . . [even as] scientific manufacture needed educated workers and technicians" (1964, p. 90; see also Soysal, 1994).

29. My work on hierarchy benefits significantly from Robert Steinfeld, *The Invention of Modern Labor*, Cambridge: Cambridge University Press, 1991.

30. As Steinfeld notes, "Servants and apprentices typically were unmarried, resided with their masters, served by the year or for a longer term, and were subject to their master's household government. Laborers and artificers typically were married, had households of their own, served on a casual basis by the day, week or task, and were generally not members of a master's household" (1991, p. 60).

31. Similarly, Taillour and others were charged in Lincolnshire because "as common labourers, [who] when attached by the constables of the town to work for their neighbors according to the statute, broke the attachment in the manner of rebels, and refused to submit to the law of the crown" (Sillem, 1936 and 1937, p. 6; cited in Steinfeld, 1991, p. 61).

32. Those who worked under contract for a term typically were not paid until the term was completed and, if not completed, could lose any claim to their wages.

33. These provisions required that: "1) service be by the year 'or other usual Terms, and not by the day' and 2) those who held less land than 'shall suffice to the continual Occupation of One man,' should [also] serve [another employer] by the year" (Statute of Laborers, 25 Ed. III, stat. 2 (1350–51); cited in Steinfeld, 1991, p. 62 and 23 Hen IV, c. 12 (1444–45); cited in Steinfeld, 1991, p. 62).

34. At Colchester, the records show that "a ploughman refuses to serve except by day" (Putnam, 1908, p. 74; cited in Steinfeld, 1991, p. 62).

35. This conception of labor as men who are ruled was part of a broader hierarchical view of the English polity of the day. As depicted in Sir Thomas Smith's *De Republica Anglorum*, the English polity of Elizabethan times was a hierarchy constituted of four ranks. "In the highest rank stood the 'Nobilitas Major': just below them stood the 'Nobilitas Minor.' The third rank is said to have been composed of 'Citizens, Burgesses and Yeomen.' The lowest rank was composed of laborers and artificers, among others" (Smith, 1583, pp. 29–47; Steinfeld, 1991, p. 65). More specifically, the fourth rank included "day labourers, poore husbandmen, yea merchants or retailers which have no free lande, copiholders, and all artificers, as Taylors, Shoomakers, Carpenters, Brickmakers, Bricklayers, Masons, &c" (Smith, p. 46; cited in Steinfeld, p. 65).

36. In the American colonies up to this time, Steinfeld notes that "indentured servants, apprentices and, less certainly, hired servants [in contrast to laborers and artificers] remained fully subject to their master's government" (1991, p. 66).

37. As Maitland describes it, "the very person of a villein . . . [initially] belonged to his lord; 'he was merely the chattel of his lord to give and sell at his pleasure" (Pollock and Maitland, 1898, p. 414; cited in Steinfeld, 1991, p. 67).

38. During this same period, "a lord . . . [came to be] understood to have seisin not of the person but of the services of his free tenants" (Steinfeld, 1991, p. 69).

39. John Locke, a primary proponent of this perspective explained that "every man is put under a necessity, by his constitution as an intelligent being, to be determined in willing by his own thought and judgment what is best for him to do; else would he not be under the determination of some other than himself, which is want of liberty" (Locke, 1959, I: 346; cited in Steinfeld, 1991, p. 79).

40. Wage workers "had sold off part of their paternity, the right to the exclusive use and possession of their capacities, to their masters in exchange for wages" (Steinfeld, 1991, p. 80).

41. By 1669, Chamberlayne tells us that "Foreign Slaves in England are none . . . A Foreign Slave brought into England, is upon landing ipso facto free from Slavery, but not from ordinary service" (Chamberlayne, 1669, p. 462).

42. By the end of the sixteenth century it had already been said that "England is too pure an air for slaves to dwell in" (Harrison, 1587, p. 118; cited in Steinfeld, 1991, p. 96).

43. Increasingly it was held that "there was no such thing 'as partial liberty' . . . [Instead it was argued that] he who has authority 'to restrain and control my conduct in any instance without my consent hath in all'" (Bailyn, 1967, p. 234; cited in Steinfeld, 1991, p. 103).

44. Mary Clark's case involved an attempt by slaveholders to introduce slavery into free states by means of the vehicle of indentured servitude.

45. As had been the case in colonial Massachusetts, litigation was, once again, being used to define social rules and the contours of the permissible in the post-Revolutionary world" (Konig, 1979; Steinfeld, 1991, p. 149).

46. Laborers, working under contract for a term, typically were paid their full wages upon completing their service.

47. A key difference exists, of course, in that a defendant's freedom to leave "service" is foreclosed once a conviction is achieved.

48. The name appears initially to have been a colloquial one devised by Jacksonian "democrats" in Massachusetts to communicate their disdain for the new process of predispositional compromise arising in the lower criminal courts. Those courts were under the oversight of the Governor of the Commonwealth of Massachusetts and thus were controlled by the Whigs who were seeking to reconsolidate elite political dominance in Boston and its environs. Derived from the sixteenth-century French whence it denoted an object obtained at a favorable price, the term appears to have caricatured the practice of plea bargaining as quasi-jacobin, lacking in procedural clarity and corrupt just as were the culminating years of political excess during the French Revolution.

49. More specifically, the term appears to constitute thinly veiled innuendo with its reference to Henry Clay's well known "corrupt bargain" with then-Presidential candidate John Quincy Adams of Massachusetts. In years when personal ambition for the Presidency was thought to be corrupt, Henry Clay had met with Democratic-Republican John Quincy Adams in January 1825 and promised his support for the New Englander's quest for the Presidency (Watson, 1990, p. 81). When Adams was subsequently elected and Clay was named Secretary of State, Clay was alleged to have consummated a "corrupt bargain" with the President-elect. Democratic-Republicans then appear to have retaliated by associating the new discretionary practice of the Brahmin-run courts with the opportunistic tendencies of the Whigs implying that it must be this that led them to accord consideration to defendants in response to symbolic trucking and bartering in the courts.

50. The author is indebted to discussions with Said Arjomand for clarifying this point.

51. This was due both to the historic absence of an aristocracy, which lent social life in America an egalitarian and democratic cast, and to the ongoing influx of immigration throughout the nineteenth century when the state was being formed and, then, reformed.

52. In France, such rights came from territoriality. Even foreign workers living in France had such rights of citizenship (Brubaker, 1992). In Germany, they came from membership in a bloodline (Brubaker, 1992).

53. It will be argued below that one could become "citizen" as well.

54. Limits on the power of the ruler were primarily of two sorts. The first were "immunities, called political liberties or rights, which it was . . . regarded as a breach of cuty in the ruler to infringe" (Mill, 1859, p. 6). The second was "constitutional checks, by which the consent of the community . . . [or its representatives] was made a necessary condition to some of the more important acts of the governing power (Mill, 1859, p. 6).

55. Many felt that "[t]he nation did not need to be protected against its own will . . . [and that their rulers'] power was but the nation's own power, concentrated, and in a form convenient for exercise" (Mill, 1859, p. 7).

56. The populace "now perceived," Mill noted, "that such phrases as 'self-government,' and 'the power of the people over themselves,' do not express the true state of the case. The 'people' who exercise the power are not always the same people with those over whom it is exercised; and the 'self-government' spoken of is not the government of each by himself, but of each by all the rest . . . and the precautions are as much needed against this as against any other abuse of power" (Mill, 1859, p. 8). Mill's stunning conclusion was that "The limitation, therefore, of the power of government over individuals loses none of its importance when the holders of power are regularly accountable to the community . . ." (p. 8).

57. In the corporatist model, membership, authority, and action are devised around corporate groups defined by common occupational, ethnic, religious, or gender identities. Individuals gain "legitimacy and access to rights by subscribing to . . . [these] collective groups through which they participate in different [social] arenas . . ." (Soysal, 1994, p. 37). Since the state is charged with substantial responsibility for the collective good, governments in corporatist polities "generate clear top-down policies for the incorporation of migrants . . . [and] have formal avenues by which new populations can gain access to decision making mechanisms and pursue their interests" (p. 38).

58. The liberal model highlights the individual as the locus of action and authority. Most political action is accomplished by individuals and private groups (Soysal, 1994, p. 38). Central authority tends to be weak and the state apparatus loosely organized. Decision making is decentralized with local authorities and voluntary associations playing a crucial role (p. 38). Absent a strong state administrative capacity, "the labor market is the main instrument of incorporation and new members pursue their interests through local associations (p. 38).

59. In the statist model, authority and action center on the state bureaucratic administrative apparatus. As the main provider of most services, the state intervenes actively in social life. Decision making is centralized. While statist polities interact with individuals, their approach is top-down and they lack intermediary organizations to link citizens to state. Migrants "are incorporated as individuals, but with much state involvement" (Soysal, 1994, p. 39). Politics is centralized and migrants often pursue their interests by organizing in social movements targeted at the state.

60. In fact, much of the language of individualism in constitutional law is a byproduct of efforts to combat "states' rights" (Novak, 1996).

61. Rogers Smith (1997) has shown the affinity of Jacksonian Democrats for free market ideology as well as other key liberal themes. Throughout the nineteenth century, it was the Republican descdendants of the Whigs who urged use of public power to control morality and to restrict the political participation of women.

62. De Tocqueville (1997) has eloquently described the Philosophy of Self-Interest Properly Understood which, he argued, caused Americans to make constant small sacrifices in the interest of the community in the conviction that the good that redounds to it will ultimately benefit each member as well. Philosophically or legally articulated responsibilities and duties were left to the European continent with its sense that freedom might entail the fulfillment of one's duties to the community (Taylor, 2006).

63. Jackson, early on, saw the potential of the slavery issue to fracture the union and also moved quickly to link the partisan activity of Democrats to preservation of the nation by imbuing democratic ideas with a strong, and occasionally virulent, nationalism (Sellers, 1991, p. 331). Whigs also argued that freeing the slaves would stabilize the union—thus cementing the link between liberty and ideologically based nationalism.

64. While the ideology of a "rule of law" supported authority with rules characterized by fairness, universality and equality, the equally important question of whose interests existing arrangements favored lingered unanswered. To help explain the paradox that material inequality persists in societies that are governed by self-rule, we must consider that ideologies such as the "rule of law" and citizenship that play a powerful role in maintaining an existing social order, at the same time, inherently preserve the inequalities embodied in that order.

65. The ideology of a rule of law claims that society is governed by rules that are specified in advance and known to all, fair, universally applied so that no one is exemply, and treat all persons who come before the court equally. In this apparently non-coercive way, this ideology elicits popular support for the rules that sustain and legitimate political authority.

Bibliography

NEWSPAPERS AND MAGAZINES

Albany State Register, Oct. 1, 6, 1855; cited in Anbinder, 1992, p. 108.

American Citizen, Ithaca, NY, Nov. 21, 1885

Anonymous Letter to the *Columbian Minerva*, March 30, 1802; cited in Warren, 1931.

Arena

Blackwood's *Edinburgh Magazine*

Boston Advocate, 1 Feb., 17 Sept. 1836; cited in Goodman, 1964, p. 191.

Boston Herald, December 11 and 13, 1925; cited in Blodgett in Formisano and Burns, 1984, p. 103.

Charlestown Advertiser, Nov. 21, 1885

Cincinnati Dollar Times, Cincinnati, OH, Sept. 14, 1854, cited in Anbinder, 1992.

Columbian Centinel

Copeland, *Harpers Weekly*, 44 (June 16, 1900): 549; cited in Blodgett in Formisano and Burns, 1984, p. 103.

"Fireside," *Boston Evening Transcript*, Jan. 22, 1879; cited in Vogel, 1980, p. 27.

Harpers Weekly

Hartford Courant

Independent Chronicle, Oct. 18, 1804, and Aug. 23, 1804; cited in Warren, 1931, pp. 166, 171–172.

"Lying Awake," *Household Words*, Oct. 30, 1852; cited in Wiener, 1993, p. 152.

Nathaniel Ames, *Columbian Minerva*, Sept. 6, 1803; cited in Warren, 1993, p. 180.

North American Review
Patriot, Quincy, MA, Nov. 11, 1854
Quincy Observer, Nov. 11, 1854; cited in Anbinder, 1992.
The Republic, June 9, 1894; cited in Blodgett in Formisano and Burns, 1984, p. 90.
State Register, Albany, NY, Oct. 1, 6, 1885
Youngstown True Observer, Feb. 21, 1855; cited in Anbinder, 1992.

BOOKS AND ARTICLES

Abbott, Andrew (1983) "Sequences of Social Events: Concepts and Methods for the Analysis of Order in Social Processes," 16 *Historical Methods* 129–147.

Abrams, Norman (1971) "Internal Policy: Guiding the Exercise of Prosecutorial Discretion," 19 *U.C.L.A. Law Review* 1–58.

——— (1975) "Prosecutorial Charge Decision Systems," 23 *U.C.L.A. Law Review* 1–56.

Abrams, Phillip (1982) *Historical Sociology*. Ithaca, NY: Cornell University Press.

Adamson, Walter L. (1980) *Hegemony and Revolution*. Berkeley: University of California Press.

Alschuler, Albert W. (1975a) "The Defense Attorney's Role in Plea Bargaining," 84 *The Yale Law Journal* 1179.

——— (1979) "Plea Bargaining and Its History," 13 *Law and Society Review* 211–245.

——— (1968) "The Prosecutor's Role in Plea Bargaining," 36 *University of Chicago Law Review* 50.

——— (1975b) "The Supreme Court, the Defense Attorney, and the Guilty Plea," 47 *University of Colorado Law Review* 1.

——— (1976) "The Trial Judge's Role in Plea Bargaining, Part I," 76 *Columbia Law Review* 1059.

The American Friends Service Committee (1971) *Struggle for Justice*. New York: Hill and Wang.

Aminzade, Ronald (1992) "Historical Sociology and Time," 20 *Sociological Methods and Research* (May), 129–147.

Anbinder, Tyler (1992) *Nativism and Slavery: The Northern Know Nothings and the Politics of the 1850s*. New York: Oxford University Press.

Anderson, Benedict (1991) *Imagined Communities*. London: Verso.

Anderson, Perry (1976/77) "The Antinomies of Antonio Gramsci," 100 *New Left Review* (Nov.–Jan.), 5–78.

Andrews, Kenneth T. (1997) "The Impacts of Social Movements on the Political Process: The Civil Rights Movement and Black Electoral Politics in Mississippi," 62 *American Sociological Review* 800–819.

Appleby, Joyce (1992) *Liberalism and Republicanism in the Historical Imagination*. Cambridge, MA: Harvard University Press.

Atkinson, Brooks, ed. (1950) *The Complete Essays and Other Writings of Ralph Waldo Emerson*. [Reprint of 1840 edition.] New York: Modern Library.

Arendt, Hannah (1959) *The Human Condition*. Garden City, NY: Doubleday Anchor.

——— (1958) *The Origins of Totalitarianism*. New York: Meridian Books.

Arrow, Kenneth (1969) "The Organization of Economic Activity: Issues Pertinent to the Choice of Market Versus Nonmarket Allocation," in Joint Economic Committee, 91st Congress, 1st Session, *The Analysis and Evaluation of Public Expenditures: The PPB System* (Comm. Print) 47, 49.

Ault, Warren O. (1965) *Open Field Husbandry and the Village Community: A Study of Agrarian By-Laws in Medieval England*. Philadelphia, PA: American Philosophical Society.

Avinieri, Shlomo (1972) *Hegel's Theory of the Modern State*. Cambridge, England: Cambridge University Press.

———— (1970) *The Social and Political Thought of Karl Marx*. Cambridge, England: Cambridge University Press.

Axtmann, Roland (2001) *Balancing Democracy*. London: Continuum International Publishing Group.

———— (1997) *Liberal Democracy into the Twenty-first Century: Globalization, Integration and the Nation State*. Manchester, England: University of Manchester Press.

Ayers, Edward L. (1984) *Vengeance and Justice: Crime and Punishment in the 19th Century American South*. London: Oxford University Press.

Bailyn, Bernard (1967) *The Ideological Origins of the American Revolution*. Cambridge, MA: Harvard University Press.

Balbus, Isaac (1977) "Commodity Form and Legal Form: An Essay on the 'Relative Autonomy' of the Law," *Law and Society Review* 571–588.

———— (1973) *The Dialectics of Legal Repression: Black Rebels before the American Criminal Courts*. New Brunswick, NJ: Transaction Books.

Baldwin, John, and Michael McConville (1977) *Negotiated Justice*. Bath: Robinson.

Banning, Lance (1974) "Republican Ideology and the Triumph of the Constitution, 1789 to 1793," 31 *William and Mary Quarterly* 167–188.

Barak, Aharon (1989) *Judicial Discretion*. New Haven, CT: Yale University Press.

———— (2005) *Purposive Interpretation*. Princeton, NJ: Princeton University Press.

Barbara, John et al. (1976) "Plea Bargaining: Bargain Justice," *Criminology* 55.

Barnes, G. H. (1964) *The Anti-Slavery Impulse, 1830–1844*. New York: Peter Smith Publisher.

Basch, Norma (1986) "The Emerging Legal History of Women in the United States: Property, Divorce, and the Constitution," 12 *Signs* 97–117.

———— (1982) *In the Eyes of the Law: Women, Marriage, and Property in Nineteenth-Century New York*. Ithaca, NY: Cornell University Press.

Baxter, M. (1995) *Henry Clay and the American System*. Lexington: University of Kentucky Press.

Beccaria, Cesare (1986) *Crimes and Punishments*. New York: Hackett.

Becker, Carl (1960) *The History of Political Parties in the Province of New York, 1760–1776*. Madison: University of Wisconsin Press.

Beecher, Lyman (1829) *Six Sermons on the Nature, Occasions, Signs, Evils and Remedy of Intemperance*. [Reproduction in 2003 of 1829 text.] New York: Kissinger Publishing.

Bell, Daniel (1962) *The End of Ideology: On the Exhaustion of Political Ideas in the Fifties*. New York: Free Press.

Bendix, Rheinhard (1977) *Max Weber: An Intellectual Portrait*. Berkeley: University of California Press.

———— (1964) *Nation Building and Citizenship*. New York: Wiley.

———— (2001) *Work and Authority in Industry: Managerial Ideologies in the Course of Industrialization*. New Brunswick, NJ: Transaction Books.

Benhabib, Seyla (1996) *Democracy and Difference*. Princeton, NJ: Princeton University Press.

———— (1993) "Models of Public Space: Hannah Arendt, the Liberal Tradition and Jurgen Habermas," in Craig Calhoun, ed., *Habermas and the Public Sphere*, 1–48.

Benjamin, Walter (1969) *Illuminations*. New York: Shocken Books.

Bentham, Jeremy (1827) *Rationale of Juridical Evidence*. London: John Bowring.

Berger, Moise (1976) "The Case Against Plea Bargaining," 62 *American Bar Association Journal* 621–624.

Bertani, Mauro, Alessandro Fontana, and Francois Ewald, eds. (2003) *Society Must Be Defended: Lectures at the College de France, 1975–1976*. New York: Picador.

Best, Steven, and Douglas Kellner (1991) *Postmodern Theory*. New York: Guilford Press.

Binder, Lawrence et al. (1971) *Crisis and Sequences in Political Development*. Princeton, NJ: Princeton University Press.

Bishop, Arthur N. (1974) "Guilty Pleas in Missouri," 42 *UMKC Law Review* 304.

———— (1973) "Guilty Pleas in the Pacific West," 51 *Journal of Urban Law* 171.

Black, Avis E. (1975) "Criminal Procedure—Protection of Defendants Against Prosecutorial Vindictiveness," 54 *North Carolina Law Review* 108.

Blackstone, William (1765–69) *Commentaries on the Laws of England*. Oxford: Clarendon Press.

Blau, Peter M. (1968) "Theories of Organization," in E. Shils, ed., *International Encyclopedia of the Social Sciences*, vol. 2. New York: Macmillan/Free Press, 297–305.

Block, Fred (1987) *Revising State Theory*. Philadelphia, PA: Temple University Press.

———— (1977) "The Ruling Class Does Not Rule," 33 *Socialist Revolution* 6–28.

Blodgett, G (1984) "Gentle Reformers" in Formisano and Burns, eds., *Boston, 1700–1980*. Westport, CT: Greenwood.

Bloomfield, Maxwell (1976) *American Lawyers in a Changing Society, 1776–1876*. Cambridge, MA: Harvard University Press.

Blumberg, Abraham S. (1976) *Criminal Justice*. New York: New Viewpoints.

Bocock, Robert (1987) *Hegemony*. London: Tavistock.

Bohman, James (1999) "Practical Reason and Cultural Constraint: Agency in Bourdieu's Theory of Practice," in Richard Shusterman, ed., *Bourdieu: A Critical Reader*. Oxford: Blackwell, 32–44.

Bond, James E. (1975) *Plea Bargaining and Guilty Pleas*. New York: Clark Boardman Co., Ltd.

Bonnell, Victoria (1980) "The Uses of Theory, Concepts and Comparisons in Historical Sociology," 22 *Comparative Studies in History* 156–173.

Borman, Paul D. (1974) "The Chilled Right to Appeal from a Plea Bargain Conviction: A Due Process Cure," 69 *Northwestern University Law Review* 663.

Bourdieu, Pierre (1991) *The Craft of Sociology: Epistemological Preliminaries*. Berlin: Walter de Gruyter.

———— (1984) *Distinction: A Social Critique of the Judgment of Taste*. Cambridge, MA: Harvard University Press.

———— (1993) *The Field of Cultural Production*. New York: Columbia University Press.

———— (1983) "The Field of Cultural Production or the Economic World Reversed," 12 *Poetics* 311–356.

———— (1986) "The Force of Law: Toward a Sociology of the Juridical Field," 38 *Hastings Law Journal* 805–844.

———— (1985) "The Genesis of the Concepts of 'Habitus' and 'Field,'" 2 *Social Criticism* 11.

———— (1989) *La Noblesse d'Etat*. Paris: Editions de Minuit.

———— (1977) *Outline of a Theory of Practice*, translated by R. Nice. Cambridge, England: Cambridge University Press.

———— (1998) *Practical Reason: On the Theory of Action*. Palo Alto, CA: Stanford University Press.

———— (1994) "Rethinking the State: Genesis and Structure of a Bureaucratic Field," 12 *Sociological Theory* 1–18.

———— (1996) *Rules of Art: Genesis and Structure of the Literary Field*. Palo Alto, CA: Stanford University Press.

———— (1991) *Sociology in Question*. London: Sage.

Bourdieu, Pierre, and Loic J. D. Wacquant (1992) *An Invitation to Reflexive Sociology*. Cambridge, MA: Polity Press.

Bowling, Benjamin, and Coretta Phillips (2002) "Racism, Ethnicity, Crime and Criminal Justice," in Maguire et al., *Oxford Handbook of Criminology*, 3rd ed. New York: Oxford University Press.

Braudel, Fernand (1980) *On History*. Chicago, IL: University of Chicago Press.

Bressler, Fenton S. (1975) *Reprieve: A Study of a System*. London: Harrap.

Brewer, John, and John Styles, eds. (1980) *An Ungovernable People: The English and Their Law in the Seventeenth and Eighteenth Centuries*. New Brunswick, NJ: Rutgers University Press.

Brice, Roger T. (1972) "Grand Jury Proceedings: The Prosecutor, the Trial Judge, and Undue Influence," *The University of Chicago Law Review* 761–782.

Bridges, Amy (1984) *A City in the Republic: Antebellum New York and the Origins of Machine Politics*. Cambridge, England: Cambridge University Press.

———— (1988) "Becoming American: The American Working Class before the Civil War" in Katznelson and Zolberg, eds., *Working Class Formation*. Cambridge, England: Cambridge University Press.

Brown, Kathryn A., and Michael H. Shaut (1976) "The Use of Mandamus to Control Prosecutorial Discretion," 13 *The American Criminal Law Review* 563.

Brown, Robert E. (1955) *Middle Class Democracy and the Revolution in Massachusetts, 1691–1780*. Ithaca, NY: Cornell University Press.

Brubaker, Rogers (1992) *Citizenship and Nationhood in France and Germany*. Cambridge, MA: Harvard University Press.

——— (1996) "Rethinking Classical Sociology: The Sociological Vision of Pierre Bourdieu," 14 *Theory and Society* 745–775.

Bugbee, James M. (1887) *The City Government of Boston.* Baltimore, MD: Johns Hopkins University.

Bulbany, Charles P., and Frank F. Skillern (1976) "Taming the Dragon: An Administrative Law for Prosecutorial Decision–Making," 13 *The American Criminal Law Review* 473.

Burrill, Ellen M. (1932) *A Monograph on the Charters and Constitution of Massachusetts.* Lynn, MA: Thomas P. Nichols and Son Co.

Burt, Robert A. (1992) *The Constitution in Conflict.* Cambridge, MA: Belknap Press, an imprint of Harvard University Press.

Butterfield, Herbert (1952) *Liberty in the Modern World.* Toronto: The Ryerson Press.

Cain, Maureen, and Alan Hunt (1979) *Marx and Engels on Law.* New York: Academic Press.

Cairns, Huntington (1949) *Legal Philosophy from Plato to Hegel.* Baltimore, MD: Johns Hopkins University Press.

Calavita, K. (1984) *U.S. Immigration Law and the Control of Labor.* London: Academic Press.

Calhoun, Craig (1995) *Critical Social Theory.* Cambridge, MA: Blackwell.

——— , ed. (1994) *Habermas and the Public Sphere.* Cambridge, MA: MIT Press.

Calley, Margot (1985) *A Day at a Time: The Diary Literature of American Women from 1764 to the Present.* Amherst, MA: Feminist Press.

Campbell, Donald (1975) "'Degrees of Freedom' and the Case Study," 8 *Comparative Political Studies* 178–193.

Carlen, Pat (1976) *The Sociology of Law.* Lanham, MD: Rowman and Littlefield.

Carney, J., and J. Miller (1975) "Study of Plea Bargaining in Murder Cases in Massachusetts," 3 *Suffolk Law Review* 292; cited in Bond, 1975.

Ceriani, Gary J. (1971) "Prosecutorial Discretion in the Duplicative Statutes Setting," 42 *University of Colorado Law Review* 455.

Chamberlayne, Edward (1669) *Anglia Notitia: Or, The Present State of England.* 3rd ed. London: Np.

Chitty, Joseph (1816) *Criminal Law.* Philadelphia, PA: Isaac Riley.

Chitwood, G. P. (1905) *Justice in Colonial Virginia.* Baltimore, MD: Johns Hopkins Press.

Church, Thomas, Jr. (1976) "Plea Bargains, Concessions and the Courts: An Analysis of a Quasi–Experiment," 10 *Law and Society Review* 377.

Clanchy, Michael (1983) "Law and Love in the Middle Ages," in John Bossy, ed., *Disputes and Settlements: Law and Human Relations in the West.* Cambridge, England: Cambridge University Press.

Clark, Charles E., and Harry Shulman (1937) *A Study of Law Administration in Connecticut.* New Haven, CT: Yale University Press.

Clark, J. C. D. (1994) *The Language of Liberty, 1660–1832.* Cambridge, England: Cambridge University Press.

Cockburn, James S. (1975) "Early Modern Assize Records as Historical Evidence," 5 *Journal of the Society of Archivists* 215.

—— (1978) "Trial By the Book? Fact and Theory in the Criminal Process, 1558–1625" in J. H. Baker, ed., *Legal Records and the Historian*. London: Royal Historical Society.

Cohen, Bernard (1976) *Research on Criminal Justice Organizations: The Sentencing Process*. The Rand Corporation, Santa Monica, CA, R–2018–DOJ.

Cohen, Jean, and Andrew Arato (1994) *Civil Society and Political Theory*. Cambridge, MA: MIT Press.

Coke, Sir Edward (1979) *Coke on Magna Carta: Common Law*. Croydon: Gordon Press Publications.

Cole, George F. (1970) "The Decision to Prosecute," 4 *Law and Society Review* 331.

Cooper, L. (1974) *Policing America*. Englewood Cliffs, NJ: Prentice-Hall.

Corwin, Edward S. (1964) *American Constitutional History*. New York: Harper and Row.

—— (1914a) "The Basic Doctrine of American Constitutional Law," 12 *Michigan Law Review* 247–276.

—— (1936) *The Commer Power versus States Rights*. Princeton, NJ: Princeton University Press.

—— (1911) "The Doctrine of Due Process of Law Before the Civil War," 24 *Harvard Law Review* 366–385, 407–479.

—— (1929) "The 'Higher Law' Background of American Constitutional Law," 42 *Harvard Law Review* 365–421.

—— (1921) *John Marshall and the Constitution*. New Haven, CT: Yale University Press.

—— (1948) *Liberty Against Government: The Rise, Flowering and Decline of a Famous Judicial Concept*. Baton Rouge: Louisiana State University.

—— (1914b) "*Marbury v. Madison* and the Doctrine of Judicial Review," 12 *Michigan Law Review* 538–572.

Cotterrell, Roger (1999) *Emile Durkheim: Law in a Moral Domain*. Stanford, CA: Stanford University Press.

—— (1981) "Legality and Political Legitimacy in the Sociology of Max Weber," in David Sugarman, ed., *Legality, Ideology and the State*. New York: Academic Press, 69–94.

Cottu, Charles (1822) *On the Administration of Criminal Justice in England and the Spirit of the English Government*. Boston, MA: Little, Brown & Co.

Cox, Michael P. (1976) "Discretion—A Twentieth Century Mutation," 28 *Oklahoma Law Review* 383.

Cox, Sarah J. (1976) "Prosecutorial Discretion: An Overview," 13 *The American Law Review* 383.

Cremin, Lawrence (1982) *American Education: The National Experience, 1783–1876*. New York: Harper and Row.

Cushing, John D., ed. (1984) *The Earliest Printed Laws of New York, 1665–1693*. Wilmington, DE: Liturgical Press.

—— (1976) *Laws and Liberties of Massachusetts, 1641–1691*. Woodbridge, CT: Scholarly Resources [Reprint].

Dangerfield, George (1965) *The Awakening of American Nationalism, 1815–1828*. New York: Harper and Row.

Danziger, Herbert (1982) "The Use of Newspapers," in Robert B. Smith, ed., *Handbook of Social Science Methods*, Vol. 1. Cambridge, MA: Ballinger.

Darnton, Robert (1986) "The Symbolic Element in History," 58 *Journal of Modern History* 218–234.

Davis, Kenneth Culp (1976) *Discretionary Justice in Europe and America*. Urbana: University of Illinois Press.

Dewey, John (1997a) *Democracy and Education*. New York: Free Press.

——— (1997b) *Experience and Education*. New York: Free Press.

Dezalay, Yves, and Bryant Garth (1997) "Law, Lawyers and Social Capital: 'Rule of Law' versus Relational Capitalism," 6 *Social and Legal Studies: An International Journal* 109–141.

Dibble, Vernon (1963) "Four Types of Inference from Documents to Events," 3 *History and Theory* 203–221.

DiFilippo, T. (1973) "Jeremy Bentham's Codification Proposals and Some Remarks on Their Place in History," 22 *Buffalo Law Review* 239–251.

Dimond, Alan J. (1975) *A Short History of the Massachusetts Courts*. North Andover, MA: National Center for State Courts.

Dobbin, Frank (1994) *Forging Industrial Policy: The U.S., Britain and France in the Railway Age*. New York: Cambridge University Press.

Donzelot, Jacques (1984) *L'Invention du Social: Essai sur le Declin des Passions Politiques*. Paris: Fayard.

——— (1997) *The Policing of Families*. Baltimore, MD: Johns Hopkins University Press.

Dreyfus, Hubert L., and Paul Rabinow (1983) *Michel Foucault: Beyond Structuralism and Hermeneutics*. Chicago, IL: University of Chicago Press.

Dublin, Thomas (1979) *Women at Work*. New York: Columbia University Press.

Durkheim, Emile (1997) *The Division of Labor in Society*. New York: Free Press.

——— (1975) *Emile Durkheim: On Morality and Society*, edited by Robert Bellah. Chicago, IL: University of Chicago Press.

——— (1997) *Suicide*. New York: Free Press.

Dyzenhaus, David (1998) *Law as Politics*. Durham, NC: Duke University Press.

Eastman, Frank M. (1923) *Courts and Lawyers of Pennsylvania: A History, 1623–1923*. New York: The American Historical Society.

Eaton, Clement (1957) *Henry Clay and the Art of American Politics*. Boston, MA: Little, Brown and Co.

Edelman, Lauren B. (1991) *Legal Ambiguity and Symbolic Structures*. Madison: University of Wisconsin, Department of Law.

Eisenstein, James (1973) *Politics and the Legal Process*. New York: Harper and Row Publishers.

Eisenstein, James, and Herbert Jacob (1977) *Felony Justice: An Organizational Analysis of Criminal Courts*. Boston, MA: Little, Brown and Co.

"The Elimination of Plea Bargaining in Black Hawk County: A Case Study" (1970) 60 *Iowa Law Review* 1053–1071.

Ely, John H. (2000) *Democracy and Distrust: A Theory of Judicial Review*. Cambridge, MA: Harvard University Press.

Esping-Anderson, Gosta (1988) *Politics Against Markets: The Social Democratic Road to Power.* Princeton, NJ: Princeton University Press.

Etzioni, Amitai (1960) "Two Approaches to Organizational Analysis: A Critique and a Suggestion," 5 *Administrative Science Quarterly* 257–278.

Ewald, Francois (1986) *L'Etat Providence.* Paris: B. Grasset.

Ewald, Francois, and Frederic Gros, eds. (2005) *The Hermeneutics of the Subject: Lectures at the College de France, 1981–1982.* London: Palgrave.

Feeley, Malcolm M. (1979a) "Foreword," "Perspectives on Plea Bargaining," and "Pleading Guilty in Lower Courts," in 13 *Law and Society Review* 197, 199, and 461.

———— (1982) "Plea Bargaining and the Structure of the Criminal Process," 7 *Justice System Journal* 338–354.

———— (1979b) *The Process Is the Punishment.* New York: Russell Sage Foundation.

———— (1973) "Two Models of the Criminal Justice System: An Organizational Perspective," 7 *Law and Society* 407.

Felkenes, George T. (1976) "Plea Bargaining: Its Pervasiveness on the Judicial System," 4 *Journal of Criminal Justice* 133–145.

Fenner, B. (1856) *Raising the Veil, or Scenes in the Courts.* Boston, MA: J. French. [1973 edition Patterson Smith.]

Ferdinand, Theodore N. (1992) *Boston's Lower Criminal Courts, 1814–1850.* Newark: University of Delaware Press.

———— (1973) "Criminality, the Courts and the Constabulary in Boston, 1703–1967." Unpublished manuscript.

———— (1967) "The Criminal Patterns of Boston Since 1849," 73 *American Journal of Sociology* 84.

Finkelstein, Michael O. (1975) "A Statistical Analysis of Guilty Plea Practices in the Federal Courts," 89 *Harvard Law Review* 293.

Finney, Charles G. (1903) *Memoirs of Reverend Charles G. Finney.* New York: Fleming H. Revell Co.

Fischer, David H. (1989) *Albion's Seed: Four British Folkways in America.* New York: Oxford University Press.

Fisher, George (2000) "Plea Bargaining's Triumph," 109 *Yale Law Journal* 857–920.

Flanagan, William J. (1976) New Federal Rule of Criminal Procedure 11(e): Dangers in Restricting the Judicial Role in Sentencing Agreements," 14 *American Criminal Law Review* 305.

Fogel, Robert (1975) "The Limits of Quantitative Methods in History," 80 *American Historical Review* 329–50.

Forbath, William E. (1991) *Law and the Shaping of the American Labor Movement.* Cambridge, MA: Harvard University Press.

Ford, Paul Leicester (1899) *Janice Meredith: A Story of the American Revolution.* Reprint Services Corporation.

Forgacs, David, ed. (2000) *The Antonio Gramsci Reader: Selected Writings, 1916–1935* (New introduction by Eric Hobsbawm). New York: New York University Press.

Formisano. R., and C. Burns (1984) *Boston: 1700–1980: The Evolution of Urban Politics.* Westport, CT: Greenwood.

Foucault, Michel (1982) *The Archaeology of Knowledge and the Discourse on Language*. New York: Pantheon.

—— (1995) *Discipline and Punish: The Birth of the Prison*. New York: Vintage.

—— (1984) "On Governmentality," in Paul Rabinow, ed., *The Foucault Reader*. New York: Pantheon.

—— (1986) *The History of Sexuality*. New York: Viking.

—— (1988a) *Madness and Civilization*. New York: Vintage.

—— (1994) *The Order of Things*. New York: Vintage.

—— (1988b) *Politics, Philosophy, Culture: Interviews and Other Writings, 1977–1984*. New York: Routledge.

—— (1980) *Power/Knowledge*, edited by Colin Gordon. New York: Pantheon.

—— (1983) *This Is Not a Pipe*. Berkeley: University of California Press.

Frank, Jerome (1957) *Not Guilty*. London: Victor Gollancz Ltd.

Frankel, Marvin (1973) *Criminal Sentences: Law Without Order*. New York: Hill and Wang.

Fraser, Nancy (1992) "Rethinking the Public *Sphere*" in Craig Calhoun, 1994, *Habermas and the Public* Sphere. Cambridge, MA: MIT Press, 109–142.

—— (1987) *Social Movements v. Disciplinary Bureaucracies: The Discourses of Social Needs*. Minneapolis: Center for Humanistic Studies, University of Minnesota.

Freud, Sigmund (1965) *New Introductory Lectures on Psychoanalysis*. New York: Norton.

Friedman, Lawrence, M. (1993) *Crime and Punishment in American History*. New York: Basic Books.

—— (1973) *A History of American Law*. New York: Simon and Schuster.

—— (1981) "History, Social Policy and Criminal Justice," in David Rothman and Stanton Wheeler, *Social History and Social Policy*. New York: Academic Press, 2033–38.

—— (1977) *Law and Society*. Englewood Cliffs, NJ: Prentice Hall.

—— (1979) "Plea Bargaining in Historical Perspective," 13 *Law and Society Review* 247.

Friedman, Lawrence M., and Robert V. Percival (1981) *The Roots of Justice: Crime and Punishment in Alameda County, California, 1870–1910*. Chapel Hill: University of North Carolina Press.

Friedman, Lawrence M., and Harry N. Scheiber (1988) *American Law and the Constitutional Order: Historical Perspectives*. Cambridge, MA: Harvard University Press.

Friedman, Milton, and A. J. Schwartz (1963) *A Monetary History of the United States, 1867-1960*. Princeton, NJ: Princeton University Press.

Fulbrook, Mary (1983) *Piety and Politics*. Cambridge, England: Cambridge University Press.

Gaffney, Edward McGlynn, Jr. (1976) "Prosecutorial Discretion in the United States," Unpublished paper prepared for the Office of Policy and Planning, U.S. Law Enforcement Assistance Administration.

Galligan, Denis (1990) *Discretionary Powers*. London: Oxford University Press.

Garland, David (2002) *Culture of Control*. Chicago, IL: University of Chicago Press.

—— (1990) *Punishment and Modern Society*. Chicago, IL: University of Chicago Press.

Gaskins, R. (1981) "Changes in the Criminal Law of Eighteenth Century Connecticut," 25 *American Journal of Legal History* 309–342.

Gatell, Frank O., and John M. McPaul (1970) *Jacksonian America*. Englewood Cliffs, NJ: Prentice-Hall.

Geertz, Clifford (1973) *The Interpretation of Cultures*. New York: Basic Books.

Gellner, Ernest (1983) *Nations and Nationalism*. New York: Cambridge University Press.

Genovese, Eugene (1976) *Roll, Jordan, Roll*. New York: Vintage.

Gerth, Hans, and C. W. Mills (1946) *From Max Weber: Essays in Sociology*. New York: Oxford University Press.

Giddens, Anthony (1984) *The Constitution of Society: Outline of the Theory of Structuration*. Berkeley: University of California Press.

———— (1987) *The Nation State and Violence*. Berkeley: University of California Press.

Gil, Thomas (1837) *Court Vignettes from the Boston Morning Post*. Cambridge, MA: Widener Library Collection, Harvard University.

Gilboy, J. A. (1976) "Guilty Plea Negotiations and the Exclusionary Rule of Evidence: A Case Study of the Chicago Narcotics Courts," 67 *The Journal of Criminal Law and Criminology* 89.

Gilmore, Grant (1977) *The Ages of American Law*. New Haven, CT: Yale University Press.

Goebel, J. T., and T. R. Naughton (1944) *Law Enforcement in Colonial New York*. New York: The Commonwealth Fund.

Goldstein, Joseph (1975) "For Harold Lasswell: Some Reflections on Human Dignity, Entrapment, Informed Consent, and the Plea Bargain," 84 *The Yale Law Journal* 683.

Goodman, Paul (1964) *The Democratic Republicans of Massachusetts*. Cambridge, MA: Harvard University Press.

Gordon, Robert W. (1981) "Accounting for Change in American Legal History," in H. Hartog, ed., *Law and the American Revolution and the Revolution in the Law*. New York: New York University Press.

———— (1984) "Critical Legal Histories," 36 *Stanford Law Review* 57–124.

Gorelick, Jamie S. (1975) "Pretrial Diversion: The Threat of Expanding Social Control," 10 *Harvard Civil Rights—Civil Liberties Law Review* 180.

Gouge, William (1976) *Of Domesticall Duties*. Amsterdam: W.J. Johnson. [Reprint of London, 1622 edition.]

Gouldner, Alvin W. (1959) "Organizational Analysis" in Robert K. Merton, Leonard Broom, and Leonard S. Cottrell, Jr., eds., *Sociology Today*. New York: Basic Books.

Graham, Hugh D., and Ted R. Gurr (1979) *Violence in America: Historical and Comparative Perspectives*. New York: Sage.

Gramsci, Antonio (1994) *Pre-Prison Writings*, edited and translated by R. Bellamy and Virginia Cox. Cambridge, England: Cambridge University Press.

———— (1991) *Selections from the Cultural Writings*. Cambridge, MA: Harvard University Press.

———— (1971) *Selections from the Prison Notebooks*. New York: International Publishers.

"Grand Jury Proceedings: The Prosecutor, the Trial Judge, and Undue Influence" (1972) 39 *University of Chicago Law Review* 761.

Granovetter, Mark (1985) "Economic Action and Social Structure: The Problem of Embeddedness," 91 *American Journal of Sociology* 481–510.

Gray, Horace, Jr. (1858) "The Power of the Legislature to Create and Abolish Courts of Justice," 21 *Monthly Law Reporter* 65.

Greenberg, D. (1974) *Crime and Law Enforcement in the Colony of New York*. Ithaca, NY: Cornell University Press.

——— (1975) "The Effectiveness of Law Enforcement in Eighteenth Century New York," 19 *American Journal of Legal History* l73–207.

Greene, Jack P. (1969) *The American Colonies in the Eighteenth Century, 1689–1763*. Arlington Heights, IL: AHM.

Greenwood, Peter W. et al. (1973) *Prosecution of Adult Felony Defendants in Los Angeles County: A Policy Perspective*. Santa Monica, CA: The RAND Corporation, R–1127–DOJ.

Greer, Edward (1982) "Antonio Gramsci and 'Legal Hegemony' in David Kairys, *The Politics of Law*, 304–309.

Grinnell, H. (1938) "The History and Scope of the Existing Rule-Making Functions of the Massachusetts Courts," 23 *Massachusetts Law Quarterly* 10.

Griswold, Rufus (1948) *The Republican Court: American Society in the Age of Washington*. New York: D. Appleton.

"Guilty Plea as a Waiver of Rights and as an Admission of Guilt" (1971) 44 *Temple Law Quarterly* 540.

Gurr, T. (1981) "Historical Trends in Violent Crime: A Critical Review of the Evidence," in M. Tonry and N. Morris, eds., *Crime and Justice: An Annual Review of Research* (Vol. 3). Chicago, IL: University of Chicago Press, 295–353.

Habermas, Jurgen (1998) *Between Facts and Norms*. Cambridge, MA: MIT Press.

——— (1991) *Communication and the Evolution of Society*. Oxford: Blackwell.

——— (1968) *Knowledge and Human Interests*. Boston, MA: Beacon Press.

——— (1975) *Legitimation Crisis*. Boston, MA: Beacon Press.

——— (1990) *The Philosophical Discourse of Modernity*. Cambridge, MA: MIT Press.

——— (1994) *Post-Metaphysical Thinking*. Cambridge, MA: MIT Press.

——— (1991) *The Structural Transformation of the Public Sphere*. Cambridge, MA: MIT Press.

——— (1985) *The Theory of Communicative Action*. Boston, MA: Beacon Press.

——— (1988) *Theory and Practice*. Boston, MA: Beacon Press.

Hage, Jerald (1975) "Theoretical Decision Rules for Selecting Research Designs," 4 *Sociológical Methods and Research*, 131–165.

Hall, Kermit (1989) *Magic Mirror: Law in American History*. New York: Oxford University Press.

Haller, Mark H. (1979) "Plea Bargaining: The Nineteenth Century Context," 13 *Law and Society Review* 273.

———. (1970) "Urban Crime and Criminal Justice: The Chicago Case," 57 *Journal of American History* 619.

Hanbury, H. G. (1960) *English Courts of Law*. London: Oxford University Press.

Handlin, Oscar (1979) *Boston's Immigrants.* Cambridge, MA: Harvard University Press.

Handlin, Oscar, and F. Mary (1969) *Commonwealth: A Study of the Role of Government in the American Economy, Massachusetts, 1774–1862.* Cambridge, MA: Belknap Press of Harvard University Press.

———, eds. (1966) *The Popular Sources of Political Authority: Documents on the Massachusetts Constitution of 1780.* Cambridge, MA: Belknap Press of Harvard University Press.

Haney-Lopez, Ian (1999) "The Social Construction of Race," in Stephen Delgado and Jean Stefancic, eds., *Critical Race Theory: The Cutting Edge.* Philadelphia, PA: Temple University Press, 163–176.

Harrison, William, and Georges Edelen (1994) *The Description of England: The Classic Contemporary Account of Tudor Social Life.* New York: Dover.

Hartshorn, Elinor C. (1964) "The General Court and Constitution-Making in Massachusetts," Master's Thesis, Mount Holyoke College, South Hadley, Massachusetts.

Hartz, Louis (1955) *The Liberal Tradition in America.* New York: Harcourt Brace.

Hattam, Victoria (1993) *Labor Visions and State Power.* Princeton, NJ: Princeton University Press.

Hawkins, Keith (2003) *Law as Last Resort: Prosecutorial Decisionmaking in a Regulatory Agency.* London: Oxford University Press.

Hay, Douglas, Peter Linebaugh, John G. Rule, E. P. Thompson, and Cal Winslow (1975) *Albion's Fatal Tree: Crime and Society in Eighteenth Century England.* New York: Random House.

Hegel, Georg W. F. (1956) *The Philosophy of History.* New York: Dover.

——— (1967) *Hegel's Philosophy of Right,* translated with notes by T. M. Knox. (Reprint of 1835 edition.) New York: Oxford University Press.

Held, David (1980) *Introduction to Critical Theory.* Berkeley: University of California Press.

Henry, Louis (1968) "Historical Demography," 93 *Daedalus* 385–396.

Heumann, Milton (1975) "A Note on Plea Bargaining and Case Pressure," 9 *Law and Society Review* 515–528.

——— (1981) *Plea Bargaining: The Experiences of Prosecutors, Judges, and Defense Attorneys.* Chicago, IL: University of Chicago Press.

Higginson, Thomas W. (1907) *The Life and Times of Stephen Higginson.* Antwerp: Reprint Services Corporation.

Higham, John (1964) *Strangers in the Land.* Westport, CT: Greenwood.

Hilliars, F. (1848) *The Elements of Law: Being a Comprehensive Summary of American Jurisprudence.* New York: John Voorhies.

Hindus, Michael S. (1980) *Prison and Plantation: Crime, Justice and Authority in Massachusetts and South Carolina, 1767–1868.* Chapel Hill: University of North Carolina Press.

Hintze, O. (1975) *The Historical Essays of Otto Hintze.* London: Oxford University Press.

Hirschi, T. (1969) *Causes of Delinquency.* Berkeley, CA: University of California Press.

Hobsbawm, Eric J. (1973) *Captain Swing*. Harmondsworth: Penguin.

——— (1981) "The Contribution of History to Social Science," 33 *International Social Science Journal* 424–640.

——— (1972) "Social Criminality," 25 *Bulletin of the Society for the Study of Labour History* 5–6.

Hobson, Barbara (1987) *Uneasy Virtue*. New York: Basic Books.

Hochschild, Arlie (1983) *The Managed Heart: Commercialization of Human Feeling*. Berkeley: University of California Press.

Holub, Renate (1992) *Antonio Gramsci: Beyond Marxism and Post-Modernism*. New York: Routledge.

Horkheimer, Max (1974) The *Eclipse of Reason*. New York: Continuum International Publishing.

Horton, James, O., and E. Horton (2000) *Black Bostonians*. New York: Holmes and Meier.

Horwitz, Morton J. (1987) "Republicanism and Liberalism in American Constitutional Thought," 29 *William and Mary Law Review* 57–82.

——— (1977) *The Transformation of American Law, 1780–1860*. Cambridge, MA: Harvard University Press.

——— (1992) *The Transformation of American Law, 1870–1960*. New York: Oxford University Press.

Howe, Daniel W. (1979) *The Political Culture of the American Whigs*. Chicago, IL: University of Chicago Press.

Howe, John R. (1967) "Republican Thought and the Political Violence of the 1790s, Part I," 19 *American Quarterly* 147–165.

Howe, Mark De Wolfe (1947–1950) "The Creative Period in the Law of Massachusetts," 69 *Proceedings of the Massachusetts Historical Society* 237.

Hughes, M. Vivian (1980) *The Victorian Family*. London: Oxford University Press.

Hull, N. E. H. (1998) *Roscoe Pound and Karl Llewellyn: Searching for an American Jurisprudence*. Chicago, IL: University of Chicago Press.

Hunnisett, R. (1961) *The Medieval Coroner*. Cambridge, England: Cambridge University Press.

Hunt, Alan (1986) "The Theory of Critical Legal Studies," 6 *Oxford Journal of Legal Studies* 1–45.

Hunt, Alan, and Gary Wickham (1994) *Foucault and the Law: Towards a Sociology of Law as Governance*. New York: Pluto Press. .

Hunt, Lynn, ed. (1989) *The New Cultural History*. Berkeley: University of California Press.

Hunt, Lynn, and George Sheridan (1986) "Corporation, Association and the Language of Labor in France, 1750–1850," 58 *Journal of Modern History* 813–844.

Hurst, James W. (2001) *The Growth of American Law: The Law Makers*. Clark, NJ: Lawbook Exchange.

——— (1964) *Law and the Conditions of Freedom in the Nineteenth Century United States*. Madison: University of Wisconsin Press.

——— (1984) *Law and Economic Growth: The Legal History of the Lumber Industry in Wisconsin, 1836–1915*. Madison: University of Wisconsin Press.

———— (1982) *Law and Markets in United States History: Different Modes of Bargaining Among Interests (The Curti Lectures)*. Madison: University of Wisconsin Press.

———— (1977) *Law and Social Order in the United States*. Ithaca, NY: Cornell University Press.

———— (1987) *Law and Social Process in United States History*. Buffalo, NY: William S. Hein.

———— (1960) *The Law in United States History*. Easton, MD: Lancaster Press.

———— (2004) *The Legitimacy of the Business Corporation in the Law of the United States, 1780–1970*. Clark, NJ: Lawbook Exchange.

Hutchinson, Allan C., and Patrick J. Monahan (1987) *The Rule of Law: Ideal or Ideology*. Toronto: Carswell Legal Publications.

Ignatiev, N. (1996) *How the Irish Became White*. New York: Routledge.

Illinois Association for Criminal Justice (1929) *The Illinois Crime Survey*. Chicago: Illinois Association for Criminal Justice.

"Immunity of Petty Criminals from Punishment" (1910) 1 *Journal of the American Institute of Criminal Law and Criminology* 638–639.

"The Influence of the Defendant's Plea on Judicial Determination of Sentence" (1956) 66 *Yale Law Journal* 20; cited in Bond (1975).

Isaac, Larry W., and Larry J. Griffin (1989) "Ahistoricism in Time-series Analysis," 54 *American Sociological Review* 873–890.

Isaac, Rhys (1988) "The Rage of Malice of the Old Serpent Devil," in Merrill D. Peterson and Robert C. Vaughan, eds., *The Virginia Statute for Religious Freedom*. New York: Cambridge University Press, 139–169.

Jacob, Herbert (1978) *Justice in America: Courts, Lawyers, and the Judicial Process*. Boston, MA: Little, Brown & Co.

———— (1967) *Law, Politics, and the Federal Court*. Boston, MA: Little, Brown & Co.

———— (1972) "Politics and Criminal Prosecution in New Orleans" in George F. Cole, ed., *Criminal Justice: Law and Politics*. Boston: Duxbury Press, 156–157; cited in Rhodes (1978).

Jacoby, Joan E. (1975) "Case Evaluation: Quantifying Prosecutorial Policy," 58 *Judicature* 487.

Jacoby, Margaret C. (1991) *The Origins of Anglo-American Radicalism*. Hinesburg, VT: Humanity Press.

Jaher, F. C. (1984) "The Politics of the Boston Brahmins" in R. Formisano and C. Burns, eds., *Boston, 1700–1980*. Westport, CT: Greenwood.

Jencks, Christopher, and David Riesman (1968) *The Academic Revolution*. Unknown Binding.

Jennings, John B. (1971) "The Design and Evaluation of Experimental Court Reforms," Santa Monica, CA: The RAND Corporation, P–4709.

———— (1973) "Evaluating Administrative Court Reforms," Santa Monica, CA: The RAND Corporation, P–5041.

Jessop, Robert (1977) "Recent Theories of the Capitalist State," 1 *Cambridge Journal of Economics* 353–373.

John, Richard (1998) *Spreading the News: The American Postal System from Franklin to Morse*. Cambridge, MA: Harvard University Press.

Johnson, Harry M. (1969) "Ideology and the Social System," in Edward Shils, ed., *International Encyclopedia of the Social Sciences*. New York: Macmillan/ Free Press, 77–85.

Johnson, James N. (1973) "The Influence of Politics Upon the American Prosecutor," 2 *The American Journal of Criminal Law* 187.

Jones, D. L. et al. (1993) *Discovering the Public Interest*. Canoga Park, CA: CCA Publications.

Jowell, J. (1994) *The Changing Constitution*. Oxford: Clarendon.

Kaestle, Carl F. (1983) *Pillars of the Republic: Common Schools and American Society, 1780–1860*. New York: Hill and Wang.

Kairys, David (1982) *The Politics of Law*. New York: Pantheon.

Kant, Immanuel (1959) *Foundations of the Metaphysics of Morals and What Is Enlightenment*. New York: Bobbs-Merrill.

Kaplan, John (1977) "American Merchandising and the Guilty Plea: Replacing the Bazaar with the Department Store," 5 *American Journal of Criminal Law* 215.

Katz, Stanley N. (1987) "The American Constitution: A Revolutionary Interpretation," in Richard Beeman, ed., *Beyond Confederation: Origins of the Constitution and American National Identity*. Chapel Hill: University of North Carolina Press, 23–37.

——— (1978) "Republicanism and the Law of Inheritance in the American Revolutionary Era," 76 *Michigan Law Review* 1–29.

Katzenstein, P. (1998) *Cultural Norms and National Security*. Ithaca, NY: Cornell University Press.

——— (1987) *Small States in World Markets*. Ithaca, NY: Cornell University Press.

Katznelson, Ira, and Aristide Zolberg (1988) *Working Class Formation: Nineteenth Century Patterns in Western Europe and the United States*. Cambridge, England: Cambridge University Press.

Kelly, George A. (1972) "Hegel's America," 2 *Philosophy and Public Affairs* 2–36.

Kelman, Mark (1987) *A Guide to Critical Legal Studies*. Cambridge, MA: Harvard University Press.

Kennedy, Duncan (1979) "The Structure of Blackstone's Commentaries," 5 *Buffalo Law Review* 211.

Kenyon, Cecila M. (1955) "Men of Little Faith: The Anti-Federalists on the Nature of Representative Government," 12 *William and Mary Quarterly* 4.

Kenyon, Nora (1934) "Labour Conditions in Essex in the Reign of Richard II," 4 *The Economic History Review* 429–451.

Kerber, Linda (1970) *Federalists in Dissent: Imagery and Ideology in Jeffersonian America*. Ithaca, NY: Cornell University Press.

——— (1988) "Making Republicanism Useful," 97 *The Yale Law Journal* 1645–1663.

——— (1999) *No Constitutional Right to Be Ladies: Women and the Obligations of Citizenship*. New York: Hill and Wang.

——— (1980) *The Revolutionary Generation: Ideology, Politics and Culture in the Early Republic*. Chapel Hill: University of North Carolina Press.

——— (1997) *Women of the Republic: Intellect and Ideology in Revolutionary America*. Chapel Hill: University of North Carolina Press.

King, Cornelia (1984) *American Education, 1622–1860*. London: Taylor and Francis Group.

King, Peter (2003) *Crime, Justice and Discretion in England, 1740–1820*. London: Oxford University Press.

King, Susan L. (1984) *History and Records of the Charleston Orphan House*. Charleston, SC: Southern Historical Press.

Kiser, Edgar, and Michael Hechter (1991) "The Role of General Theory in Comparative Historical Sociology," 97 *American Journal of Sociology* 1–30.

Klare, Karl (1982) "Critical Theory and Labor Relations" in David Kairys, ed., *The Politics of Law: A Progressive Critique*, rev. ed. New York: Basic, 539–568.

Kloppenberg, James T. (1993) "The Theory and Practice of American Legal History," 106 *Harvard Law Review* 1332–1351.

——— (1986) *Uncertain Victory: Social Democracy and Progressivism in European and American Thought, 1870–1920*. New York: Oxford University Press.

Knights, Peter R. (1973) *Plain People of Boston, 1830–1860*. New York: Oxford University Press.

Knudson, Jerry W. (1970) "The Jeffersonian Assault on the Federalist Judiciary, 1802–1805," 14 *American Journal of Legal History* 55–75.

Kohl, L. F. (1991) *The Politics of Individualism*. New York: Oxford University Press.

Konig, David T. (1979) *Law and Authority in Puritan Massachusetts: Essex County, 1629–1692*. Chapel Hill: University of North Carolina Press.

Krieger, Stefan (1974) "Defense Access to Evidence of Discriminatory Prosecution," *University of Illinois Law Forum* 648.

Kuntz, W. F. (1988) *Criminal Sentencing in Three Nineteenth Century Cities: A Social History of Punishment in New York, Boston and Philadelphia, 1830–1885*. New York: Garland Publishers.

Kussmaul, Ann (1981) *Servants in Husbandry in Early Modern England*. Cambridge, England: Cambridge University Press.

Ladurie, Emmanuel (1979) *Montaillou*. New York: Vintage.

LaFave, Wayne (1970) "The Prosecutor's Discretion in the United States," 18 *American Journal of Comparative Law* 532–548.

Lagoy, Stephen P., Joseph J. Senna, and Larry J. Siegel (1976) "An Empirical Study on Information Usage for Prosecutorial Decision-Making in Plea Negotiations," 13 *The American Criminal Law Review* 435.

Lamont, Michele (1989) "Slipping the World Back In: Bourdieu on Heidegger," 18 *Contemporary Sociology* 781-783.

Landes, William M. (1971) "An Economic Analysis of the Courts," 14 *Journal of Law and Economics* 61.

Lane, Roger (1971) *Policing the City: Boston, 1822–1885*. New York: Atheneum.

Langbein, John H. (1977) *Comparative Criminal Procedure: Germany*. St. Paul, MN: West Publishing.

——— (1978a) "The Criminal Trial before the Lawyers," 45 *The University of Chicago Law Review* 263–316.

——— (1973) "The Origins of Public Prosecution at Common Law," 17 *The American Journal of Legal History* 313–335.

——— (1974) *Prosecuting Crime in the Renaissance: England, Germany, and France.* Cambridge, MA: Harvard University Press.

——— (1977) *Torture and the Law of Proof.* Chicago, IL: University of Chicago Press.

——— (1978b) "Torture and Plea Bargaining," 46 *University of Chicago Law Review* 3–22.

——— (1979) "Understanding the Short History of Plea Bargaining," 13 *Law and Society Review* 261.

Lawrence, Abbott (1856) *Memoir of the Honorable Abbott Lawrence.* Boston: J. H. Eastburn's Press.

Leiby, James (1978) *A History of Social Welfare and Social Work in the United States, 1815–1972.* Berkeley: University of California Press.

Lerner, Max (1937) "The Constitution and Court as Symbols," 46 *Yale Law Journal* 32.

Lijphart, Arend (1971) "Comparative Politics and the Comparative Method," 65 *American Political Science Review* 682–693.

Lindholm, M. (1991) "Swedish Feminism, 1835–1945: A Conservative Revolution," 4 *Journal of Historical Sociology* 121–142.

Lipton, D., R. Martinson, and J. Wilks (1975) *The Effectiveness of Correctional Treatment: A Survey of Treatment Evaluation Studies.* New York: Praeger; cited in Rhodes (1978).

Lipuma, E., M. Postone and C. Calhoun (1993) *Bourdieu: Critical Perspectives.* Chicago, IL: University of Chicago Press.

Llewellyn, Karl (1981) *Bramble Bush.* New York: Oceana Publications.

——— (1996) *Common Law Tradition: Deciding Appeals.* London: Hein.

——— (1982) *Jurisprudence.* Chicago, IL: University of Chicago Press.

——— (2000) *Jurisprudence: Realism in Theory and Practice.* London: Lawbook Exchange Ltd.

Locke, John (1994) *An Essay Concerning Human Understanding.* New York: Prometheus.

Lockridge, Kenneth A. (1981) *Settlement and Unsettlement in Early America: The Crisis of Political Legitimacy Before the Revolution.* Cambridge, England: Cambridge University Press.

Luce, R. Duncan, and Howard Raiffa (1957) *Games and Decisions.* New York: Wiley.

Lukacs, Georg (1971) *History and Class Consciousness.* Cambridge, MA: MIT Press.

Lyotard, Jean-Francois (1979) *The Postmodern Condition.* Minneapolis: University of Minnesota Press.

——— (1993) *The Libidinal Economy.* Bloomington: Indiana University Press.

——— (1988) *Peregrinations: Law, Form, Event.* New York: Columbia University Press.

MacFarlane, A. (1987) *The Culture of Capitalism.* Cambridge, England: Cambridge University Press.

MacKinnon, Catherine (1983) "Feminism, Marxism, Method and the State: Toward Feminist Jurisprudence," 8 *Signs* 635–658.

MacPherson, C. B. (1962) *The Political Theory of Possessive Individualism.* London: Oxford University Press.

Madsen, Michael, and Yves Dezalay (2002) "The Power of the Legal Field" in Reza Banakar and Max Travers, *Introduction to Law and Social Theory.* Oxford: Hart Publishing.

Maier, Charles (1985) "Preconditions for Corporatism," in John H. Goldthorpe, ed.,
   Order and Conflict in Contemporary Capitalism. London: Oxford University Press,
   179–190.
Maitland, F. W. (1885) *Justice and Police*. New York: Russell and Russell.
Mallory, D., ed. (1843) *The Life and Speeches of the Honorable Henry Clay*, Vol. 1. New
   York: Robert P. Bixby and Co.
Mann, Horace (1957) *The Republic and the School: Horace Mann on the Education of
   Free Men*. New York: Columbia University Teachers College.
———— (1846) *Tenth Annual Report of the Board of Education, Together with the Tenth
   Annual Report of the Secretary of the Board*. Boston, MA.
Mann, Mary, ed. (1868) *The Life and Works of Horace Mann*. Cambridge, MA: Fuller.
Mann, Michael (1987) "The Autonomous Power of the State: Its Origins, Mecha-
   nisms and Results," in John A. Hall, ed., *States in History*. Oxford: Blackwell, 109–
   136.
Mariampolski, Hyman, and D. C. Hughes (1978) "The Uses of Personal Documents
   in Historical Sociology," 13 *The American Sociologist* 104–113.
Marshall, T. H. (1964) *Class, Citizenship, and Social Development*. Chicago, IL: University of Chicago Press.
Marx, Karl (1992) *Capital*, Vol. 1. New York: Penguin.
———— (1979) *Contribution to the Critique of Political Economy*. New York: International Publishers.
———— (1975) *Early Writings*. New York: Vintage.
———— (1988) *Economic and Philosophical Manuscripts of 1844*. Amherst, NY: Prometheus.
Marx, Karl, and F. Engels (1848) *The Communist Manifesto*. [Reprinted in 1975.] New
   York: Penguin.
———— (1970) *The German Ideology*. London: Lawrence and Wishart.
———— (1993) *Grundrisse: Foundations of the Critique of Political Economy*. New York:
   Penguin.
Mather, Lynn M. (1979) "Comments on the History of Plea Bargaining," 13 *Law and
   Society Review* 281.
———— (1974) "Some Determinants of the Method of Case Disposition: Decision–
   Making by Public Defenders in Los Angeles," 8 *Law and Society Review* 187.
Matthews, R. C. O (1985) *Economy and Democracy*. New York: Palgrave Macmillan.
Mayhew, H., and J. Binney (1862) *The Criminal Prisons of London*. London: C. Griffin
   and Co.
McBarnet, Doreen (2004) *Crime, Compliance and Control*. London: Ashgate.
McConville, Mike, Jacqueline Hodgson, Lee Bridges, and Anita Pavlovic (1994) *Stand-
   ing Accused*. Oxford: Clarendon Press.
McConville, Mike, and Chester Mirsky (2005) *Jury Trials and Plea Bargaining: A True
   History*. Oxford: Hart.
———— (1999) "The Rise of Guilty Pleas: The Court of General Sessions, New York,
   1800–1865," 22 *Journal of Law and Society* 443–473.
McCoy, Drew (1980) *The Elusive Republic: Political Economy in Jeffersonian America*.
   Chapel Hill: University of North Carolina Press.

McDonald, William F. (1985) *Plea Bargaining: Critical Issues and Common Practices.* Washington, DC: Government Printing Office.

——— (1979) *The Prosecutor.* London: Sage.

——— (1973) "Prosecutorial Decisions and Case Screening," Paper presented at the Annual Meeting of the American Society of Criminology, New York, November 5.

McFadden, Daniel L. (1984) "Econometric Analysis of Qualitative Response Models," in Zvi Griliches and M. D. Intriligator, *Handbook of Econometrics,* Vol. 2. New York: North-Holland.

McLoughlin, William G. (1971) *New England Dissent, 1630–1883: The Baptists and the Separation of Church and State.* Cambridge, MA: Harvard University Press.

——— (1980) *Revivals, Awakening and Reform.* Chicago, IL: University of Chicago Press.

Mead, George H. (1962) *Mind, Self and Society.* Chicago, IL: University of Chicago Press.

Mensch, E. (1982) "The History of Mainstream Legal Thought," in D. Kairys, ed., *The Politics of Law.* New York: Pantheon.

Meyer, John, and Michael Hannan (1979) *National Development and the World System: Education, Economics and Political Change, 1950-1970.* Chicago, IL: University of Chicago Press.

Michelman, Frank I. (1988) "Law's Republic" 97 *Yale Law Journal* 1493–1665.

——— (1987) "Possession vs. Distribution in the Constitutional Idea of Property," 72 *Iowa Law Review* 1319–1350.

Mill, John Stuart (1998) *On Liberty and Other Essays.* London: Oxford University Press.

——— (1975) *Three Essays: On Liberty, Representative Government, and the Subjection of Women.* New York: Oxford.

——— (2003) *Utilitarianism and On Liberty.* Oxford: Blackwell.

Miller, Frank (1969) *Prosecution: The Decision to Charge a Suspect with a Crime.* Boston, MA: Little, Brown & Co.

Miller, Herbert S. et al. (1977) *Plea Bargaining in the United States, Phase I Report.* Prepared by the Institute of Law and Criminal Procedure at the Georgetown University Law Center, Washington, DC, for the Law Enforcement Assistance Administration.

Miller, Perry (1970) *Life of the Mind in America.* New York: Harcourt Brace.

Miller, Wilbur (1977) *Cops and Bobbies: Police Authority in New York and London, 1830-1870.* Chicago, IL: University of Chicago Press.

Milligan, John D. (1979) "The Treatment of an Historical Source," 18 *History and Theory* 177–196.

Mills, C. Wright (1959) *The Sociological Imagination.* London: Oxford University Press.

Mills, James (1969) *The Prosecutor.* New York: Farrar, Straus & Giroux.

Minson, Jeffrey P. (1986) *Genealogies of Morals: Nietzsche, Foucault, Donzelot and the Eccentricity of Ethics.* London: Palgrave.

Missouri Association for Criminal Justice Survey Committee (1926) *The Missouri Crime Survey.* St. Louis: Missouri Association for Criminal Justice.

Moglen, Eben (1983) "Commercial Arbitration: Searching for the Transformation of American Law," 93 *Yale Law Journal* 135.

Moley, Raymond (1929) *Politics and Criminal Prosecution*. New York: Minton, Balch.

Mommsen, Wolfgang J. (1984) *Max Weber and German Politics, 1890–1920*. Chicago, IL: University of Chicago Press.

Monkonnen, Eric (1975) *The Dangerous Class: Crime and Poverty in Columbus, Ohio, 1860–1885*. Cambridge, MA: Harvard University Press.

———— (1994) *Engaging the Past: The Uses of History Across the Social Sciences*. Durham, NC: Duke University Press.

———— (1996) *Police in Urban America, 1860–1920*. New York: Cambridge University Press.

Montgomery, David (1981) *Beyond Equality: Labor and the Radical Republicans, 1862–1872*. Urbana: University of Illinois Press.

———— (1993) *Citizen Worker*. New York: Cambridge University Press.

———— (1979) *Workers' Control in America*. Cambridge, England: Cambridge University Press.

Moore, Barrington, Jr. (1967) *The Social Origins of Dictatorship and Democracy*. Boston, MA: Beacon Press.

Morgan, Edmund (1942) *The Puritan Family: Religion and Domestic Relations in Seventeenth Century New England*. New York: Harper.

Morison, Samuel Eliot (1917) *A History of the Constitution of Massachusetts*. Boston, MA: Wright and Potter.

Morris, Richard Brandon (1946) *Government and Labor in Early America*. New York: Columbia University Press.

Mosteller, Frederick, Stephen E. Fienberg, and Robert E. K. Rourke (1994) *Beginning Statistics with Data Analysis (Revised Edition)*. Reading, MA: Addison-Wesley.

Mouffe, Chantal (1996) "Democracy, Power and the 'Political' in Seyla Benhabib, *Democracy and Difference*. Princeton, NJ: Princeton University Press.

Munger, Frank (1991) *Miners and Lawyers: Law Practice and Class Conflict in Appalachia, 1872–1920*. Buffalo, NY: University of Buffalo (Baldy Center).

Murphy, T., and J. Hampton (1988) *Forgiveness and Mercy*. Cambridge, England: Cambridge University Press.

Murphy, Tim (2004) "Legal Fabrications and the Case of Cultural Property" in Alain Pottage and Martha Mundy, eds., *Law, Anthropology and the Constitution of the Social: Making Persons and Things*. Cambridge, England: Cambridge University Press.

Nagel, Stuart S., and Marian Neef (1976a) "The Impact of Plea Bargaining on the Judicial Process," 60 *American Bar Association Journal* 1020.

———— (1976b) "Plea Bargaining, Decision Theory, and Equilibrium Models: Part I," 52 *Indiana Law Journal* 987.

———— (1967c) "Plea Bargaining, Decision Theory and Equilibrium Models: Part II," 52 *Indiana Bar Journal* 1.

Nash, Gary B. (1984) "Artisans and Politics in Eighteenth Century Philadelphia," in Jacob and Jacob, eds., *Origins of Anglo-American Radicalism*. London: Oxford University Press.

Nedelsky, Jennifer (1990) *Private Property and the Limits of American Constitutionalism: The Madisonian Framework and Its Legacy*. Chicago, IL: University of Chicago Press.

Nelson, Brian R. (1981) *Western Political Thought*. Englewood Cliffs, NJ: Prentice-Hall.

Nelson, William E. (1975) *Americanization of the Common Law: The Impact of Legal Changes on Massachusetts Society, 1760–1830*. Cambridge, MA: Harvard University Press.

————— (1981) *Dispute and Conflict Resolution in Plymouth County, Massachusetts, 1725–1825*. Chapel Hill: University of North Carolina Press.

————— (1967) "Emerging Notions of Criminal Law in the Revolutionary Era: A Historical Perspective," 42 *New York University Law Review* 450.

Nettl, J. P. (1969) "The State as a Conceptual Variable," 20 *World Politics* 559–592.

Newman, Donald J. (1966) *Conviction: The Determination of Guilt or Innocence without Trial*. Boston, MA: Little, Brown & Co.

New York State Crime Commission (1927) *Report to the Commission of the Sub-Committee on Statistics*. New York: New York State Crime Commission.

Nordlinger, Eric A. (1981) *On the Autonomy of the Democratic State*. Cambridge, MA: Harvard University Press.

Norrie, Alan (2001) *Crime, Reason and History*. London: Butterworths.

North, Douglas C. (1979) "A Framework for Analyzing the State in Economic History" 16 *Explorations in Economic History* 249–259.

Norton, Anne (1986) *Alternative America: A Reading of Antebellum Political Culture*. Chicago, IL: University of Chicago Press.

Novak, William (1996) *The People's Welfare*. Chapel Hill: University of North Carolina Press.

Offe, Claus (1984) *Contradictions of the Welfare State*. London: Hutchinson.

————— (1985) *Disorganized Capitalism*. Cambridge, MA: MIT Press.

"Official Inducements to Plead Guilty: Suggested Morals for a Marketplace" (1964) 32 *University of Chicago Law Review* 167; cited in Bond (1975).

Ohlin, Goran (1966) "No Safety in Numbers: Pitfalls of Historical Statistics" in Henry Rosovsky, ed., *Industrialization in Two Systems*. New York: Wiley.

Ollman, Bertel (1976) *Alienation*. New York: Cambridge University Press.

Olson, Mancur, Jr. (1971) *The Logic of Collective Action: Public Goods and the Theory of Groups*. New York: Schocken Books.

Orren, Karen (1991) *Belated Feudalism: Labor, the Law and Liberal Development in the United States*. New York: Cambridge University Press.

Palmer, Robert C. (1987) *Liberty and Community: Constitution and Rights in the Early American Republic*. New York: Oxford University Press.

Parrington, Vernon L. (1954) *The Romantic Revolution in America, 1800–1860*. New York: Harcourt Brace Jovanovich.

Parsons, T. (1861) *Memoirs of Theophilus Parsons. By his son.* (Reprint of 1835 edition.) Boston, MA: Ticknor and Fields.

Pateman, Carole (1975) *Participation in Democratic Theory*. New York: Cambridge University Press.

Patterson, Orlando (1982) *Slavery and Social Death*. Cambridge, MA: Harvard University Press.

Perlman, Joel (1989) *Ethnic Differences: Schooling and Social Structure in an American City, 1880–1935*. New York: Cambridge University Press.

Pessen, E. (1967) *Most Uncommon Jacksonians*. Albany, NY: SUNY Press.

Petersilia, Joan (1976) "An Inquiry into the Relationship Between Thoroughness of Police Investigation and Case Disposition." Paper prepared for the RAND Corporation, Santa Monica, CA, P-5576.

Phillips, Coretta, and Ben Bowling (2002) "Racism, Ethnicity, Crime and Criminal Justice," in Mike Maguire et al., *Oxford Handbook of Criminology*. London: Oxford University Press.

Phillips, Willard (1828) *Manual of Political Economy*. Boston: Hilliard, Gray, Little and Wilkins.

Piven, Frances, and Richard Cloward (1979) *Poor People's Movements*. New York: Vintage.

Plant, Raymond (1991) *Modern Political Thought*. Oxford: Blackwell.

Platt, Jennifer (1981) "Evidence and Proof in Documentary Research" and "Some Specific Problems of Documentary Research" 29 *Sociological Review* 31–66.

"Plea Bargaining and the Transformation of the Criminal Process" (1977) 90 *Harvard Law Review* 564.

"Plea Bargaining Mishaps—The Possibility of Collaterally Attacking the Resultant Plea of Guilty" (1974) 65 *Journal of Criminal Law and Criminology* 170.

"Plea Bargaining in Oregon: An Exploratory Study" (1971) 50 *Oregon Law Review* 114; cited in Bond (1975).

"Plea Bargaining: The Case for Reform" (1972) 6 *University of Richmond Law Review* 325.

"Plea Bargaining: The Judicial Merry–Go–Round" (1971) 10 *Duquesne Law Review* 253; cited in Bond (1975).

Plumb, J. H. (1977) *Growth of Political Stability in England, 1675–1725*. Atlantic Highlands, NJ: Humanities.

Poage, G. R. (1936) *Henry Clay and the Whig Party*. Chapel Hill: University of North Carolina Press.

Pocock, J. G. A. (1980) "Authority and Property: The Question of Liberal Origins" in Barbara C. Malament, ed., *After the Reformation: Essays in Honor of J. H. Hexter*. Philadelphia: University of Pennsylvania Press.

——— (1975) *The Machiavellian Moment: Florentine Political Thought and the Atlantic Republican Tradition*. Princeton, NJ: Princeton University Press.

——— (1979) "The Mobility of Property and the Rise of Eighteenth Century Sociology," in A. Parel and T. Flanagan, eds., *Theories of Property: Aristotle to the Present*. Waterloo, Ontario: Wilfrid Laurier University Press.

——— (1970) "Virtue and Commerce in the Eighteenth Century," 3 *Journal of Interdisciplinary History* 119–134.

——— (1981) "Virtues, Rights and Manners," 9 *Political Theory* 353–368.

Poggi, Gianfranco (1978) *Development of the Modern State*. Palo Alto, CA: Stanford University Press.

——— (1991) *The State: Its Nature, Development and Prospects*. Palo Alto, CA: Stanford University Press.

Pole, J. R. (1972) *Foundations of American Independence, 1763–1815*. New York: Bobbs-Merrill.

—— (1985) *The Gift of Government: Political Responsibility from the English Restoration to American Independence (Richard B. Russell Lectures)*. Athens: University of Georgia Press.

—— (1962) "Historians and the Problem of Early American Democracy," 67 *American Historical Review* 626-646.

—— (1979a) *Paths to the American Past*. London: Oxford University Press.

—— (1979b) *Political Representation in England and the Origins of the American Republic*. Berkeley: University of California Press.

—— (1957) "Suffrage and Representation in Massachusetts: A Statistical Hole," 14 *William and Mary Quarterly* 560–592.

Polinsky, A. Mitchell (1974) "Economic Analysis as a Potentially Defective Product: A Buyer's Guide to Posner's *Economic Analysis of the Law*," 87 *Harvard Law Review* 1655.

Pollock, Sir Frederick, and Frederic William Maitland (1978) *The History of English Law Before the Time of Edward I*. Cambridge, England: Cambridge University Press. Second reprint of 1898 edition.

Posner, Richard (1973) "An Economic Approach to Legal Procedure and Judicial Administration," 2 *The Journal of Legal Studies* 399.

Poulantzas, Nicos (1978) *Classes in Contemporary Capitalism*. New York: Schocken.

—— (1975) *Political Power and Social Classes*. London: New Left Books and Sheed and Ward.

—— (1980) *State, Power and Socialism*. New York: Schocken.

Pound, Roscoe, and Felix Frankfurter (1922) *Criminal Justice in Cleveland*. Cleveland, OH: The Cleveland Foundation.

Powers, Edwin (1966) *Crime and Punishment in Early Massachusetts, 1620–1692*. Boston, MA: Beacon Press.

President's Commission on Law Enforcement and Administration of Justice (1968) *The Challenge of Crime in a Free Society*. New York: Avon Books.

"Profile of a Guilty Plea: A Proposed Trial Court Procedure for Accepting Guilty Pleas" (1971) 17 *Wayne Law Review* 1195.

Pruitt, Dean G., and Melvin J. Kimmel (1977) "Twenty Years of Experimental Gaming: Critique, Synthesis and Suggestions for the Future," 28 *Annual Review of Psychology* 363.

Pulton, Ferdinando (1609) *De Pace Regis et Regni*. [Reprinted in 1978.] New York: Garland. .

Putnam, Bertha Haven (2002) *The Enforcement of the Statutes of Labourers during the First Decade after the Black Death, 1349–1359*. [Reprint of 1908 edition.] Park Forest, IL: University Press of the Pacific.

Rabin, Robert L. (1972) "Agency Criminal Referrals in the Federal System: An Empirical Study of Prosecutorial Discretion," 24 *Stanford Law Review* 1036.

Rabinow, Paul, ed. (1984) *The Foucault Reader*. New York: Pantheon.

Radding, Charles (1985) *A World Made by Men: Cognition and Society, 400–1200*. Chapel Hill: University of North Carolina Press.

Radzinowicz, Leon (1968) *A History of English Criminal Law and Its Administration from 1750: Vol. 4, Grappling for Control*. London: Sweet and Maxwell.

Ragin, Charles (1981) "Comparative Sociology and the Comparative Method," 22 *International Journal of Comparative Sociology* 102–120.

Ragin, Charles, and Howard S. Becker, eds. (1995) *What Is a Case? Exploring the Foundations of Social Inquiry.* Cambridge, England: Cambridge University Press.

Ragin, Charles, and David Zaret (1983) "Theory and Method in Comparative Research: Two Strategies," 61 *Social Forces* 731–754.

"The Ramifications of *United States v. Falk* on Equal Protection from Prosecutorial Discrimination" (1974) 65 *Journal of Criminal Law and Criminology* 62.

Ransome, Paul (1992) *Antonio Gramsci: A New Introduction.* London: Harvester Wheatsheaf.

Rantoul, Robert, Jr. (1854) *The Memoirs, Speeches and Writings of Robert Rantoul, Jr.,* edited by L. B. Hamilton. Boston: John P. Jewitt.

——— (1836) "Oration at Scituate," in Luther Hamilton, ed., *Memoirs, Speeches and Writings of Robert Rantoul, Jr.* Boston: J. P. Jewett, 1854, 278.

Raynaud, Phillipe (1994) "Bourdieu," in Mark Lilla and Mark Little, eds., *New French Thought.* Princeton, NJ: Princeton University Press.

Reckless, Walter C. (1973) *The Crime Problem.* Fifth ed. New York: Appleton-Century-Crofts.

Reckless, W., and S. Dinitz (1967) "Pioneering with Self-Concept as a Vulnerability Factor in Delinquency," 58 *Journal of Criminal Law, Criminology and Political Science* 515–523.

Reid, John P. (1987a) *The Concept of Liberty in the Age of the American Revolution.* Chicago, IL: University of Chicago Press.

——— (1987b) *The Constitutional History of the American Revolution.* Madison: University of Wisconsin Press.

——— (1978) *In a Defiant Stance.* State College: Pennsylvania State University Press.

——— (2004) *Rule of Law: The Jurisprudence of Liberty in the 17th and 18th Centuries.* DeKalb: Northern Illinois University Press.

Reidy, Joseph P. (1995) *From Slavery to Agrarian Capitalism in the Cotton Plantation South.* Chapel Hill: University of North Carolina Press.

Reiss, Albert J., Jr. (1970) "Book Review, *Discretionary Justice: A Preliminary Inquiry,*" 68 *Michigan Law Review* 789.

——— (1975) "Public Prosecutors and Criminal Prosecution in the United States of America," 20 *Juridical Review* 1.

Remini, R. V. (1963) *Henry Clay: Statesman for the Union.* New York: W. W. Norton and Co.

"Restructuring the Plea Bargain" (1972) 82 *Yale Law Journal* 286.

Rhodes, William M. (1976) "The Economics of Criminal Courts: A Theoretical and Empirical Investigation," 5 *Journal of Legal Studies* 311.

——— (1978) "Plea Bargaining: Who Gains? Who Loses?" An unpublished report prepared for the Law Enforcement Assistance Administration under PROMIS Research Project, Institute for Law and Social Research, Washington, DC, February 1978.

"The Role of the Judge in Plea Bargaining" (1972) 15 *Criminal Law Quarterly* 50.

"The Role of Plea Negotiation in Modern Criminal Law" (1969) 46 *Chi–Kent Law Review* 116.

Rosett, Arthur, and Donald R. Cressey (1976) *Justice by Consent: Plea Bargains in the American Courthouse.* New York: J. B. Lippincott Co.

Rothman, David J. (1980) *Conscience and Convenience: The Asylum and Its Alternative in Progressive America.* Boston, MA: Little, Brown.

Rubin, Lillian (1976) *Worlds of Pain: Life in the Working Class Family.* New York: Basic Books.

Rueschemeyer, Dietrich (1973) *Lawyers and Their Society: A Comparative Study of the Legal Profession in Germany and the United States.* Cambridge, MA: Harvard University Press.

Ryan, Mary P. (1981) *The Cradle of the Middle Class.* New York: Cambridge University Press.

Ryerson, E. (1880) *The Loyalists of America and Their Times, 1620–1816.* Toronto: William Briggs.

Sabine, George H. (1973) *History of Political Theory.* New York: Holt, Rhinehart and Winston.

Salkin, B. L. (1975) "Crime in Pennsylvania, 1786–1859: A Legal and Sociological Study," Ph.D. diss., Harvard University, Cambridge, MA.

Sampson, R. J., and J. Laub (1993) *Crime in the Making.* Cambridge, MA: Harvard University Press.

Sarat, Austin, and Thomas Kearns (1996) *Identities, Politics and Rights.* Ann Arbor: University of Michigan Press.

Sassoon, Ann S. (1987) *Gramsci's Politics.* Minneapolis: University of Minnesota Press.

Savage, Edward H. (1865) *A Chronological History of the Boston Watch and Police, From 1631 to 1865.* Boston, published privately by the author.

Scheiber, Harry N. (1987a) *State Law and Industrial Policy in American Development, 1790–1865.* Albany: The Nelson A. Rockefeller Institute of Government, State University of New York.

——— (1987b) *Ohio Canal Era: A Case Study of Government and the Economy, 1820–1861.* Athens: Ohio University Press.

Scheppele, Kim Lane (1990) *Legal Secrets: Equality and Efficiency in the Common Law.* Chicago, IL: University of Chicago Press.

Schlesinger, A. (1945) *The Age of Jackson.* Boston, MA: Little, Brown.

Schurz, C. (1887) *American Statesman: Life of Henry Clay.* Boston, MA: Houghton, Mifflin and Co.

Scott, Henry W. (1909) *The Courts of the State of New York: Their History, Development and Jurisdiction.* New York: Wilson.

Scott, Joan (1982) *The Glassworkers of Carmaux.* Cambridge, MA: Harvard University Press.

Sellers, C. (1991) *The Market Revolution.* New York: Oxford University Press.

Semmes, Raphael (1968) *Crime and Punishment in Early Maryland.* Baltimore, MD: Johns Hopkins Press.

Seron, Carroll, and Frank Munger (1996) "Law and Inequality: Race, Gender . . . and, of Course, Class," 22 *Annual Review of Sociology* 187–212.

Sewell, William H., Jr. (1987) "Ideologies and Social Revolutions: Reflections on the French Case," 57 *Journal of Modern History* 57–85.

——— (1996) "Three Temporalities: Toward an Eventful Sociology" in T. J. McDonald, ed., *The Historic Turn in the Human Sciences*. Ann Arbor: University of Michigan Press, 245–280.

——— (1980) *Work and Revolution in France*. New York: Cambridge University Press.

Shurtleff, Nathaniel B. (1871) *A Topographical and Historical Description of Boston*. Boston, MA: Published by Order of the Common Council.

Shusterman, Richard, ed. (1999) *Bourdieu: A Critical Reader*. Oxford: Blackwell.

Sillem, Rosamund, ed. (1936) *Records of Some Sessions of the Peace in Lincolnshire, 1360–1375*. Hereford: Lincoln Record Society.

Silverman, Robert A. (1981) *Law and Urban Growth: Civil Litigation in the Boston Trial Courts, 1880–1900*. Princeton, NJ: Princeton University Press.

Simmons, Timothy J. (1971) "Criminal Procedure—Voluntariness of Guilty Pleas in Plea Bargaining Context," 49 *North Carolina Law Review* 795.

Simon, Herbert (1957) *Administrative Behavior*. New York: The Free Press.

Simon, Jonathan (1994) "Between Power and Knowledge: Habermas, Foucault and the Future of Legal Studies," 28 *Law and Society Review* (4) 947–961.

——— (1993) *Poor Discipline: Parole and the Social Control of the Underclass, 1890–1990*. Chicago, IL: University of Chicago Press.

——— (1995) *Rise of Risk: Actuarial Power in American Politics and Law*. New York: Taylor and Francis.

Siracusa, Carl (1979) *A Mechanical People: Perceptions of the Industrial Order in Massachusetts, 1815–1880*. Middletown, CT: Wesleyan University Press.

Skocpol, Theda (1987) "Cultural Idioms and Political Ideologies in the Revolutionary Reconstruction of State Power," 57 *Journal of Modern History* (1) 86–96.

——— (1992) *Protecting Soldiers and Mothers*. Cambridge, MA: Harvard University Press.

——— (1979) *States and Social Revolutions*. Cambridge, England: Cambridge University Press.

——— (1984) *Vision and Method in Historical Sociology*. Cambridge, England: Cambridge University Press.

Skocpol, Theda, and Margaret Somers (1980) "The Uses of Comparative History in Macrosocial Inquiry," 22 *Comparative Studies in Society and History* (2) 174–197.

Skolnick, Jerome H. (1966) *Justice Without Trial*. New York: John Wiley.

——— (1967) "Social Control in the Adversary System," 51 *Journal of Conflict Resolution*.

Skowronek, Stephen (1982) *Building a New American State*. Cambridge, England: Cambridge University Press.

Skrentny, John D. (1993) *The Ironies of Affirmative Action*. Chicago, IL: University of Chicago Press.

Slovic, Paul, Baruch Fischoff, and Sarah Lichtenstein (1977) 28 *Annual Review of Psychology* 1.

Small, Albion W. (1909) *The Cameralists*. New York: Franklin.

Smelser, Neil (1976) *Comparative Methods in the Social Sciences*. Englewood Cliffs, NJ: Prentice-Hall.

Smith, A. (1778) *The Wealth of Nations*. Lausanne: Societe Typographique.

Smith, James M., and William P. Dale (1973) "The Legitimation of Plea Bargaining: Remedies for Broken Promises," *The American Criminal Law Review* 771.

Smith, Joseph A., ed. (1961) *Colonial Justice in Western Massachusetts: The Pynchon Court Record*. Cambridge, MA: Harvard University Press.

Smith, Sir Thomas (1906) *De Republica Anglorum: A Discourse on the Commonwealth of England*, edited by L. Alston. Cambridge, England: Cambridge University Press. Reprint of 1583 edition.

Somers, M. R. (1996a) "Where Is Sociology after the Historic Turn?" in T. J. McDonald, ed., *The Historic Turn in Human Science*. Ann Arbor: University of Michigan Press, 53–90.

——— (1996b) Personal written communication from the author at the University of Michigan, Ann Arbor.

Soysal, Yasemin (1995) *The Limits of Citizenship: Migrants and Postnational Membership in Europe*. Chicago, IL: University of Chicago Press.

Spannaus, Nancy, and Christopher White (1996) *The Political Economy of the American Revolution*. Washington, DC: Executive Intelligence Review.

Specter (1967) "Book Review, *Conviction: The Determination of Guilt or Innocence Without Trial*," 76 *Yale Law Journal* 604; cited in Bond (1975).

Speziale, M. (1992) *Puritan Pariah or Citizen of Somewhere Else: Defamation in Massachusetts, 1642–1850*. Ph.D. diss. (restricted access), Harvard University, Cambridge, MA.

Spindel, D. J. (1981) "The Administration of Justice in North Carolina, 1720–1740," 25 *American Journal of Legal History* 141–162.

Stalnaker, Robert C. (1967) "Events, Periods and Institutions in Historians' Language," 6 *History and Theory* 159–179.

Stearns, Carol, and Peter Stearns (1985) "Emotionology: Clarifying the History of Emotions and Emotional Standards," 90 *American Historical Review* 813–836.

——— (1986) *Anger: The Struggle for Emotional Control in American History*. Chicago, IL: University of Chicago Press.

Steinberg, A. (1983) "The Criminal Courts and the Transformation of Criminal Justice in Philadelphia, 1815-1874," Ph.D. diss., Columbia University, New York.

——— (1984) "From Private Concessions to Plea Bargaining: Criminal Prosecution, the District Attorney and American Legal History," 30 *Crime and Delinquency* 568.

——— (1989) *The Transformation of American Criminal Justice*. Chapel Hill: University of North Carolina Press.

Steinfeld, Robert J. (1991) *The Invention of Free Labor: The Employment Relation in English and American Law and Culture*. Chapel Hill: University of North Carolina Press.

Steinmetz, George (1993) *Regulating the Social: The Welfare State and Local Politics in Imperial Germany*. Princeton, NJ: Princeton University Press.

Stinchcombe, Arthur (1978) *Theoretical Methods in the Social Sciences*. New York: Academic Press.

Stone, Lawrence (1979) *Family, Sex and Marriage in England, 1500–1800*. New York: Harper Perennial.

—— (1991) "History and Post Modernism," 131 *Past and Present* 217–219.

—— (1981) *The Past and the Present*. Boston, MA: Routledge and Kegan Paul.

Stoner, James (2003) *Common Law Liberty: Rethinking American Constitutionalism*. Lawrence: University Press of Kansas.

Story, Joseph (1829) "Discourse upon the Inauguration of the Author as Dane Professor of Law," Cornell Law School Library Collection, Ithaca, NY.

Story, W. W. (1851) *Life and Letters of Joseph Story*. Boston, MA: J. Chapman.

Strayer, Joseph R. (1970) *On the Medieval Origins of the Modern State*. Princeton, NJ: Princeton University Press.

Styles, John (1987) "Emergence of the Police—Explaining Police Reform in Eighteenth and Nineteenth Century England," 27 *British Journal of Criminology* 1.

Sugarman, David, and G. R. Rubin (1984) *Law, Economy and Society*. Richmond, VA: Lexis Law Publishing.

—— (1983) *Legality, Ideology and the State*. London and New York: Academic Press.

Sumner, Colin (1983) "Law, Legitimation and the Advanced Capitalist State" in David Sugarman, ed., *Legality, Ideology and the State*. New York: Academic Press.

Sunstein, Cass R. (1988) "Beyond the Republican Revival," 97 *Yale Law Journal*, 1539.

Swartz, David (1998) *Culture and Power: The Sociology of Pierre Bourdieu*. Chicago, IL: University of Chicago Press.

Sweet, William W. (1944) *Revivalism in America*. New York: Charles Scribner and Sons.

Swidler, Ann (1986) "Culture in Action," 51 *American Sociological Review* 273-286.

Taylor, Charles (1985) *The Liberal-Communitarian Debate*. Cambridge, MA: MIT Press.

—— (2004) *Modern Social Imaginaries*. Durham, NC: Duke University Press.

Taylor, Robert J., ed. (1961) *Massachusetts, Colony to Commonwealth: Documents on the Formation of Its Constitution, 1775–1780*. Chapel Hill: University of North Carolina Press.

Teubner, Gunther (1983) "Substantive and Reflexive Elements in Modern Law," 17 *Law and Society Review* (2) 239–286.

Thernstrom, Stephan (1976) *The Other Bostonians*. Cambridge, MA: Harvard University Press.

—— (1981) *Poverty and Progress: Social Mobility in a Nineteenth Century City*. Cambridge, MA: Harvard University Press.

Thernstrom, Stephan, and T. Knights (1970) *Men in Motion*. Los Angeles: University of California Institute of Government and Public Affairs.

Thomas, Charles W., and W. Anthony Fitch (1976) "Prosecutorial Decision–Making," 13 *American Criminal Law Review* 507.

Thomas, George M., John W. Meyer, Francisco O. Ramirez, and John Boli (1987) *Constitutional Structure: Constituting State, Society and the Individual*. Thousand Oaks, CA: Sage.

Thomas, Keith (1974) "The Levellers and the Franchise" in G. E. Aylmer, ed., *The In-terregnum: The Quest for Settlement, 1646–1660*. New York: Macmillan.

Thompson, E. P. (1978a) "Eighteenth Century English Society: Class Struggle With-out Class," 3 *Social History* 133-165.

———— (1963) *The Making of the English Working Class*. New York: Vintage.

———— (1973–74) "Patrician Society, Plebian Culture," 7 *Journal of Social History* 74.

———— (1978b) "The Poverty of Theory," in E. P. Thompson, *The Poverty of Theory and Other Essays*. London: Merlin Press.

———— (1975) *Whigs and Hunters: The Origins of the Black Act*. New York: Pantheon.

Tigar, Michael, and Madeleine R. Levy (1977) *Law and the Rise of Capitalism*. New York: Monthly Review Press.

Tilly, Charles (1981) *As Sociology Meets History*. New York: Academic Press.

———— (1984) *Big Structures, Large Processes, Huge Comparisons*. New York: Russell Sage.

———— (1990) *Coercion, Capital and European States*. Oxford: Basil Blackwell.

———— (1975) *The Formation of the National States in Western Europe*. Princeton, NJ: Princeton University Press.

———— (1976) *The Vendee*. Cambridge, MA: Harvard University Press.

Tocqueville, Alexis de (1997) *Democracy in America*. Garden City, NY: Anchor Double-day. [Reprint of 1835 edition.]

Tomlins, Christopher L. (1993) *Law, Labor and Ideology in the Early American Republic*. Cambridge, England: Cambridge University Press.

———— (1985) *The State and the Unions*. Cambridge, England: Cambridge University Press.

Tonry, Michael (1992) "Mandatory Penalties," in Michael Tonry, ed., *Crime and Jus-tice*, Vol. 16. Chicago, IL: University of Chicago Press, 250–290.

Traugott, Mark (1985) *Armies of the Poor*. Princeton, NJ: Princeton University Press.

Turner, Nat (1857) *The Confessions of Nat Turner*. New York: St. Martin's/Bedford [Re-print of 1857 edition.]

Tushnet, Mark (1981) *The American Law of Slavery*. Princeton, NJ: Princeton Univer-sity Press.

Tversky, Amos (1974) "Assessing Uncertainty," 36 *Journal of the Royal Statistical* Soci-ety 148-159.

Twining, William (1994) *Rethinking Evidence*. Evanston, IL: Northwestern University Press.

———— (1985) *Karl Llewellyn and the Realist Movement*. Norman, OK: University of Oklahoma Press.

Twining, William, and Ian Hampsher-Monk (2003) *Evidence and Inference in History and Law*. Evanston, IL: Northwestern University Press.

"The Unconstitutionality of Plea Bargaining" (1970) 83 *Harvard Law Review* 1387.

United States National Commission on Law Observance and Enforcement (1931) *Re-port on Prosecution*. Washington, DC: Government Printing Office.

"United States v. Falk: Developments in the Defense of Discriminatory Prosecution" (1974) 72 *Michigan Law Review* 1113.

Vetri, Dominick R. (1964) "Guilty Plea Bargaining: Compromises by Prosecutors to Secure Guilty Pleas," 112 *University of Pennsylvania Law Review* 864–909.

Vogel, Mary E. (1988) *Courts of Trade: Social Conflict and the Emergence of Plea Bargaining, 1830–1890.* Ph.D. diss., Harvard University. Ann Arbor, Michigan: University Microfilms.

———— (1999) "The Social Origins of Plea Bargaining: Conflict and the Law in the Process of State Formation, 1830–1860," 33 *Law and Society Review* 161–246.

———— (2001) "Lawyering in an Age of Popular Politics: Plea Bargaining, Legal Practice and the Structure of the Boston Bar, 1800–1860" in Jerry Van Hoy, ed., *Legal Professions: Work, Structure and Organization.* London: Elsevier.

———— (2007) "Embedded Liberty: Imagining Citizenship for a World of Self-Rule. American Courts in the Early National Period," 18 *King's College Law Journal* 23-59.

Vogel, Morris (1980) *The Invention of the Modern Hospital: Boston, 1870–1930.* Chicago, IL: University of Chicago Press.

Von Hirsch, Andrew (1976) *Doing Justice: The Choice of Punishments.* New York: Hill and Wang.

Von Schomberg, Rene, and Kenneth Baines (2002) *Discourse and Democracy: Essays on Habermas' Between Facts and Norms.* Stony Brook, NY: SUNY Press.

Voss, Kim (1994) *The Making of American Exceptionalism.* Ithaca, NY: Cornell University Press.

Walker, Samuel E. (1980) *Popular Justice: A History of the American Criminal Justice.* New York: Oxford University Press.

Walton, Paul (1976) "Max Weber's Sociology of Law: A Critique," in Pat Carlen, *Sociology of Law.* Lanham, MD: Rowman and Littlefield, 7–21.

Waterston, Ann C. L. Q. (1883) *Adelaide Phillipps,* 2nd ed. Boston: Cupples, Upham and Co.

Watson, Harry L. (1990) *Liberty and Power: The Politics of Jacksonian America.* New York: Hill and Wang.

Ware, Norman J. (1964) *The Labor Movement in the United States, 1867–1960.* New York: Vintage.

Warren, Charles (1911) *A History of the American Bar.* Boston: Little, Brown.

———— (1931) *Jacobin and Junto.* Cambridge, MA: Harvard University Press.

Watson, H. L. (1998) *Andrew Jackson v. Henry Clay.* Boston, MA: Bedford/St. Martins Press.

Weber, Max (1978) *Economy and Society,* edited by Guenther Roth and Claus Wittich. Berkeley, CA: University of California Press.

———— (1954) *On Law in Economy and Society.* New York: Simon and Schuster.

———— (1949) *The Methodology of the Social Sciences.* New York: Free Press.

Weir, Margaret, Ann S. Orloff, and Theda Skocpol (1988) *The Politics of Social Policy in the United States.* Princeton, NJ: Princeton University Press.

West, Cornel (1998) "The New Cultural Politics of Difference" in Charles Lemert, ed., *Social Theory: The Multicultural and Classic Readings.* Boulder, CO: Westview, 521-32.

Whelan, Chris, and Doreen McBarnet (1999) *Creative Accounting and the Cross-Eyed Javelin Thrower.* London: Wiley.

White, Dennis J. (1974) "Curbing the Prosecutor's Discretion: United States v. Falk," 9 *Harvard Civil Rights—Civil Liberties Law Review* 372.

Whitehill, Walter M. (1956) *Boston Public Library: A Centennial History.* Cambridge, MA; cited in Vogel, 1980, 31.

Wickham, Gary (2001) *Rethinking Law, Society and Governance: Foucault's Bequest.* Oxford: Hart.

Wickham, G. and Alan Hunt (1994) *Foucault and the Law.* New York: Pluto.

Wiebe, Robert H. (1966) *The Search for Order, 1877–1920.* New York: Hill and Wang.

Wiecek, William M. (1988) "The Reconsolidation of Federal Judicial Power, 1863–1876" in Friedman and Scheiber, eds., *American Law and the Constitutional Order.* Cambridge, MA: Harvard University Press.

Wiener, M. J. (1993) "Market Culture, Reckless Passion and the Victorian Reconstruction of Punishment," in T. L. Haskell and R. F. Teichgraeber III, eds., *The Culture of the Market.* Cambridge, England: Cambridge University Press.

Wildhorn, Sorrel et al. (1976) *Indicators of Justice: Measuring the Performance of Prosecution, Defense, and Court Agencies Involved in Felony Proceedings.* The RAND Corporation, Santa Monica, CA, R–1918–DOJ.

Wilentz, Sean (1984) *Chants Democratic: New York City and the Rise of the American Working Class, 1788–1850.* New York: Vintage.

Williams, Jack K. (1959) *Vogues in Villainy: Crime and Retribution in Antebellum South Carolina.* Columbia: University of South Carolina Press.

Williamson, Oliver E. (1975) *Markets and Hierarchies: Analysis and Antitrust Implications: A Study in the Economics of Internal Organization.* New York: The Free Press.

Wilson, James Q. (1973) *Political Organizations.* New York: Basic Books.

Wilson, William J. (1985) *The Declining Significance of Race.* Chicago, IL: University of Chicago Press.

Wishingrad, Jay (1974) "The Plea Bargain in Historical Perspective," 23 *Buffalo Law Review* 499–527.

Wood, Gordon S. (1969) *The Creation of the American Republic, 1776–1787.* Chapel Hill: University of North Carolina Press.

——— (1988) *The Fundamentalists and the Constitution.* Charlottesville: Virginia Commission on the Bicentennial of the U.S. Constitution, Centre for Public Service, University of Virginia.

——— (1991) *The Radicalism of the American Revolution.* New York: Vintage.

——— (1976) *Social Radicalism and the Idea of Equality in the American Revolution.* St. Thomas, Virgin Islands: University of St. Thomas.

Wootton, B. (1963) *Crime and Criminal Law.* London: Stevens and Sons; cited in Rhodes (1978).

Wright, J. Skelly (1972) "Book Review, *Discretionary Justice: A Preliminary Inquiry,*" 81 *Yale Law Journal* 575.

Zuckerman, Michael (1978) *Peaceable Kingdoms: New England Towns in the Eighteenth Century.* New York: Norton.

STATUTORY AND LEGISLATIVE MATERIALS (CHRONOLOGICAL ORDER)

20 Geo. II, c. 19 (1747) and 6 Geo. III, c. 25 (1766); cited in Steinfeld (1991), p. 66.

Acts and Resolves, Commonwealth of Massachusetts, 1803.

1 Parliamentary Debates, Feb. 9, 1810, p. 19 and April 8, 1811, p. 744; cited in Wiener (1993) p. 148.

Massachusetts Constitutional Convention of 1820 (1970) *Journal of Debates and Proceedings in the Convention of Delegates Chosen to Revise the Constitution of Massachusetts, Begun and Holden at Boston, November 15, 1820, and Continued by Adjournment to January 9, 1821.* New York: Da Capo Press. Consists of news accounts originally published in the *Boston Daily Advertiser* in place of the official record, which was lost.

General Laws, 1823–1832. Boston: Theron Metcalf.

Revised Statutes of 1835, Commonwealth of Massachusetts.

Commonwealth of Massachusetts (1835) *Journal of the Committees on the Revised Statutes.* Boston: Dutton and Wentworth.

Commonwealth of Massachusetts (1835) *Report of the Commissioners Appointed to Revise the General Statutes of the Commonwealth.* Boston: Dutton and Wentworth.

House Report, Massachusetts Legislature, no. 4, Jan. 1845, pp. 7–8.

Massachusetts Constitutional Convention of 1853 (1853) *Journal of the Constitutional Convention of the Commonwealth of Massachusetts Begun and Held in Boston on the Fourth of May, 1853.* Boston: White and Potter.

Commonwealth of Massachusetts (1853) *Official Report of the Debates and Proceedings in the State Convention, Assembled May 4, 1853, To Revise and Amend the Constitution of the Commonwealth of Massachusetts.* 3 Vols. Boston: White and Potter.

Cushing, L. S., C. W. Storey, and Lewis Josslyn (1853) *Reports of Controverted Elections in the House of Representatives of the Commonwealth of Massachusetts, from 1780 to 1852.* Boston: White and Potter.

General Statutes of the Commonwealth of Massachusetts. Enacted in 1859 to apply June 1, 1860. Boston: White, William, 1860. (Second edition published by Wright and Potter, Boston, in 1873, including all legislation passed between 1860 and 1873.)

City of Boston Documents, no. 27, 1880.

Public Statutes of the Commonwealth of Massachusetts. Enacted in November 1881 to take effect 1 February 1882. Boston: Rand, Avery.

Commonwealth of Massachusetts (1881a) *Report of the Commissioners of the Revision of the Statutes.* 4 vols. and suppl. Boston: Rand, Avery.

Commonwealth of Massachusetts (1881b) *Report of the Joint Special Committee of the General Court on the Revision of the Statutes of the Commonwealth.* 2 vols. Boston: Rand, Avery.

DOCUMENTS, DIARIES, AND LETTERS

Address of Mayor Eliot to the Boston City Council on September 18, 1837. Archives of the Commonwealth of Massachusetts State House, Boston, MA.

Ames Letters, Massachusetts Historical Society

Letter of Fisher Ames to Timothy Dwight, April 16, 1802, and Oct. 26, 1803; cited in
    Warren, pp. 160–161.

Ames to Gore, Dec. 13, 1802; cited in Warren (1931), pp. 160–161.

Ames to J. Smith, Dec. 14, 1802; cited in Warren (1931), pp. 160–161.

Ames to Quincy, Feb. 12, 1806, and Dec. 11, 1806; cited in Warren (1931).

Annual Report of the Chief of Police, Boston, Massachusetts, 1871.

Austin, *Observation on the Pernicious Practice of Law*; cited in Warren (1931), p. 175.

Cabot Letters, Massachusetts Historical Society

Letter of Cabot to King, Aug. 14, 1795 in Lodge, 1877; cited in Warren (1931).

Cabot to Pickering, Feb. 14, 1804, in Lodge, 1877; cited in Warren (1931).

Cheever, *City of Boston Documents*, no. 27, 1880; cited in Vogel (1980), p. 30.

City of Boston Documents, 1834, no. 11, p. 17; no. 13, p. 14; and no. 17.

City of Boston Documents, and no. 23, 1837, p. 19. [*Report of the Inspector of Prisons for
    the County of Suffolk as to the Gaol, House of Correction, House of Reformation and
    House of Industry*, December 1837]

Council of the Massachusetts Temperance Society, 1834, *Report*, p. 81.

Hallett, Benjamin Frank. *An Oration Delivered July 4, 1836 at Palmer in Hampden
    County*. Boston: Beals and Greene; cited in Goodman (1964), p. 191.

Hutchinson, Chief Justice (1967) "Charge to the Grand Jury By the Chief Justice,"
    Quincy's Massachusetts Reports 232, 234.

Justice Henry Orne, *Speech*, 1820, p. 13.

Lawrence, Abbott (1835) Diary and Correspondence.

H. Lee to P. Remsen and Co., July 8, 1817, Porter, Jackson and Lees II, 1257; cited in
    Jaher in Formisano and Burns (1984), p. 72.

Lodge Papers, Massachusetts Historical Society

Letter of George H. Lyman to Henry Cabot Lodge, Dec. 23, 1897, Lodge Papers, Mas-
    sachusetts Historical Society; cited in Blodgett in Formisano and Burns (1984),
    p. 103.

Morison, Samuel Eliot, and Zechariah Chafee, eds. (1933) Records of the Suffolk
    County Court, 1671–1680. 2 vols. Boston, MA.

Orne, Justice Henry, Papers, Archives of the Commonwealth of Massachusetts.

Otis, H. G. (1830) "An Address to the Members of the City Council on the Removal
    of the Municipal Government to the Old Statehouse," pp. 14–15; cited in Jaher in
    Formisano and Burns (1984), p. 72.

H. G. Otis to S. F. Otis, Feb. 15, 1801, Morison, *Life and Letters of Harrison Gray Otis*
    I, p. 208; cited in Jaher in Formisano and Burns (1984), p. 72.

Quincy, J. "Farewell Address of Josiah Quincy as Mayor of Boston, 1829, *Old South
    Leaflets* VIII (Boston: Old South Meeting House, n.d.), p. 101, cited in Jaher in
    Formisano and Burns (1984), p. 72.

Statistics of the United States, Seventh U.S. Census Compendium 1850, Tables XL; XLI;
    CCXVI, p. 192; CLV, p. 152; CLXXXI, p. 167.

CASES

"The Case of Mary Clark, a Woman of Color," 1 Blackf. 122, 124–25 (Ind. 1821); cited in Steinfeld (1991), p. 146.

Commonwealth v. Battis, 1 Mass. 95 (1804); cited in *American Law Digest*.

Commonwealth v. Brown, 103 Mass. 422 (1869).

Commonwealth v. Pease (1819).

In re Deming, 10 Johns, 232, 483 (N.Y. 1813).

Ex parte Garland, 71 U.S. (4 Wall) 333, 18 L. Ed. 366 (1866).

Green v. Commonwealth, 94 Mass. (12 Allen) 155) (1860).

Marbury v. Madison.

United States v. Lee, Fed. Case No. 15, 588 (4 McLean 103) (1846).

Whitcomb v. State, 14 Ohio 282 (1846).

Index

Employment, 247
consent and, 316
order and, 327
relations of, 302–4, 308–17, 365nn30–36, 366nn40–47
Engels, Friedrich, 15, 339n16
England. *See* Britain
English Revolution, 313
Enlightenment, 18, 27, 39, 55, 134, 176, 202–4, 289, 336n3, 349n5, 352n12
Episodic leniency, 7, 13–14, 30, 34, 56–57, 62, 65, 132–34, 171, 187–88, 222, 225, 234, 241–43, 266, 288–89, 304, 325
Equality, 214, 229. *See also* Universality
economic, 46, 193, 219, 287, 291–94, 300, 305–6, 319, 322–23
formal, 222, 236, 243, 299, 316
political, 46, 193, 219, 287, 291–94, 300, 305–6, 319, 322–23
Erie Canal, 196
Essex County Bar, 232
Essex County, MA, 137
Essex Junto, 210–13, 226–32, 359nn28–29
Ethics
class and, 154
politics and, 84
Ethnicity, viii, 26, 28, 48, 98, 121, 127, 129, 149
class and, 250–51
conflicts over, 150–51, 161, 253–55
lack of common, 191, 295, 296–97, 307, 319
pluralism and, 318
politics of, 28, 98, 121, 127, 224, 247, 250–59, 268–69
poverty and, 157
Europe, 128, 132
citizenship in, 320
corporatism of, 290
immigrant dumping by, 296
incarceration in, 206
rationalized laws of, 178, 349n1
social democracy in, 249, 263
unrest in, 161, 187, 222
US and, 295–96, 318
Eustis, William, 182
Evangelical revivalism. *See* Revivalism
Ewald, Francois, 80
Ex post facto law, 174
Extended franchise, 25–28

Fabian Society, 263
Faction, 297–98
False complaint. *See* Malicious prosecution
Family. *See* Household
Federal Bureau of Investigation (FBI), 250
Federalism, 6, 18–19, 24, 38, 147–49, 161, 163–65, 168, 173–75, 181–82, 192–95, 207, 209, 211–15, 293, 301, 318, 329n3, 364n24
in Boston, 303, 353n18
lawyers and, 232–33
legacy of, 225–34
state governments and, 228
Federalist Judiciary Act of 1801, 181
Feeley, Malcolm, 8–9, 12
Felonies, compounding of, 9, 11, 143–44, 351n22
Fenner, Ball, 242
Ferdinand, T.N., 96, 343nn8–9
Financial crisis of 1893, 165, 261
Financiers, 298
Fines
amount of, 110–12, 272, 276
for drunkenness, 280
imprisonment instead of, 115, 272
Finney, Charles Grandison, 196–98
Fisher, G., 10–11, 92–93
Fitzgerald, John, 261, 266
Forbath, William, 19, 47, 56, 321
The Formation of the Nation States of Modern Europe (Strayer), 23
formative era, 151, 169, 176, 218, 303
Foucault, M., 61, 70, 78–85, 127–28, 130, 206, 248, 268, 329n1
Founding Fathers, 17
France, 69, 72, 223, 228–29, 290, 320

Franchise, extension of, 163–69, 186, 201–2, 244, 286–87, 294, 307, 318
Frankfurt School, 84, 86–87, 340n30
Franklin, Benjamin, 294
Fraser, Nancy, 76
Free choice, 301–3, 315
Free Soil movement, 165
Freedom, 49–50, 191, 285–86, 291, 295, 304, 317, 337n5. *See also* Liberty
in market, 286
rightsand, 286
of servants, 313
web of membership and, 305–7
Freemasonry, 237–39, 245, 321
French Revolution, 195, 197, 290
Friday Club, 235
Friedman, Lawrence, vii, 8–9, 12, 54, 56, 66, 128

Gage, Thomas, 173
Gardiner, John, 231
Gavin, Michael, 281
Geertz, Clifford, 42
Gellner, Ernest, 333n33
Gender, 76, 116, 271. *See also* Women
General Court Committee on Pauper Laws, 210
General Trades Union, 297
Generative sociology, 89–90
German Idealism, 55, 336nn4–5
Germany, 69, 73, 75, 296
Gil, Thomas, 125, 138, 140, 331n10
Glover, Zebediah, 140
Goodman, P., 182, 267
Gouge, W., 308
Governmentality, 79, 81
Gramsci, A., 61, 70, 78, 82–83, 86–90, 127–28, 130, 322, 331n13, 341nn42–45, 353n22, 358n16
Gray, William, 208, 211
Great Awakening, 221, 244
Green v. Commonwealth, 342n1
Greene, Jack, 41
Growth, 235
of Boston, 124, 150–51, 252, 261
economic, 127, 169, 291
in guilty pleas, 101t
market, 62–63, 116–17, 165, 291, 301
population, 252
security and, 177
stability and, 165
Guilty pleas, 5, 10–11, 103, 110, 123–25, 131, 134, 138, 144
acceptance of, 91, 241, 342n1
case flow and, 184
change to, 92, 342n2
concessions and, 15, 29, 31, 91–94, 98, 112–13, 121, 269
economics and, 269
growth in, 101t
not guilty pleas and, 118, 335n44
offense-specific patterns of, 96, 99–101t
popularization of, 94–101

Habermas, J., 70, 74, 78, 82–90, 127–28, 130, 341nn36–40
Habitual offender statute, 109, 268. *See also* Recidivism
Hall, K., 66
Hallet, Ben, 239
Hamilton, Alexander, 72, 192, 211, 226–27, 229–30
Hamiltoniad, 229
Hamlin, Charles, 258
Handlin, O., 151, 154, 180, 355n34
Harrisburg Herald, 296
Hartford Convention, 213
Hartz, Louis, 24
Harvard University, 209, 258
Hay, D., 14, 56, 59, 61, 133–36, 289
Hegel, George Friedrich, 21, 55, 71, 74, 337n5, 340n25
Hegemony, 88–89, 129–30, 208, 210, 358n16
authority and, 322–23
coercion and, 61, 322, 331n13
consent and, 322–23
Heumann, Milton, 8, 11, 125